# UNIVERSITY OF WARSAW
# UNIVERSITE DE VARSOVIE

## EUROPEAN INSTITUTE FOR REGIONAL AND LOCAL DEVELOPMENT
## INSTITUT EUROPEEN DU DEVELOPPEMENT REGIONAL ET LOCAL

**REGIONAL AND LOCAL STUDIES**

**ETUDES REGIONALES ET LOCALES**

**10**

# REGIONAL QUESTION IN EUROPE
# QUESTION REGIONALE EN EUROPE

Editors:
Sous la direction:
Grzegorz Gorzelak
Bohdan Jałowiecki

Warsaw 1993,
Varsovie 1993

EDITORS OF THE SERIES:
EDITEURS DE SERIE:
REGIONAL AND LOCAL STUDIES
ETUDES REGIONALES ET LOCALES

Antoni Kukliński
Grzegorz Gorzelak
Bohdan Jałowiecki

ISBN 83–85913–00–9

This volume was sponsored by the State Comittee for Scientific Research

Address:   University of Warsaw
European Institute for Regional and Local Development
ul. Krakowskie Przedmieście 30, 00–927 Warszawa
tel/fax: 26–16–54; 20–03–81 ext. 643, 748

# CONTENTS:
# CONTENU:

# FOREWORD

# AVANT-PROPOS

The European geo-political system, constructed by the Jalta agreements, broke down in 1990. The collapse of communism made the unification of Germany possible and enabled the Central and Eastern European countries to enter on the path of deep changes of their economies, societies and politics. At the same time it triggered the emergence of sentiments for autonomy and separatism in multi-ethnic and multi-cultural countries. The regional-national question, which has been latent for several decades, became vivid and visible. It appeared that the consistency of the Eastern and Central European states was secured only by the political status quo and by the military power of the former Soviet Union. The same factors were, at the same time, responsible for the consistency of the West, endangered by the possible expansion of the communist ideology and by the imperial aspirations of the Cremlin.

L'ordre géopolitique européen, établi à Yalta, s'est effondré en 1990. La chute du communisme en Europe Centrale et Orientale permit la réunification de l'Allemagne et le commencement des transformations politiques, économiques et sociales; elle permit également l'apparition des tendances autonomistes et séparatistes dans les pays pluri-ethniques et pluri-culturels. Les questions régionale et nationale, jusqu'alors ensevelies, réapparurent. Il s'est avéré que c'étaient bien le status quo politique en Europe et la puissance militaire de l'ex-Union Soviétique qui garantissaient la cohésion des pays de l'Europe Centrale et Orientale. Cette puissance renforcait à son tour la cohésion du monde occidental, menacé par l'expansion de l'idéologie communiste et les visées impérialistes du Kremlin.

Voici donc une nouvelle situation, non seulement à l'échelle européenne, mais aussi à l'échelle mondiale. Car l'ordre bipolaire des camps politico-

New situation therefore emerged not only on the European, but also on global scale. The bi-polar system of two political and military camps, controlled by two super-powers: the Soviet Union and the United States, secured some kind of balance and reduced the strength of centrifugal tendencies in each of these camps.

New separatist tendencies are not limited to Central and Eastern Europe only. They come into the fore also in Western Europe. In both parts of Europe the nation state has run into a deep crisis, since its democratic structures are weakened by several factors: by the activities of multi-national corporations which constantly grow in their economic power; by international organisations which take over more and more competencies — according to the subsidiarity principle — from the nation states; by some of their regions, whose societies claim more and more autonomy and in several cases even full independence; finally, by inability of the societies to absorb the culturally different groups of immigrants.

Along with a set of "grand regions"[1] which opt for autonomy or even for full independence and which may be considered as "states in statu nanscendi", there exist several regions — in both East and West — which experience deep underdevelopment and severe social and economic problems.

militaires, dirigés par les puissances mondiales, l'Union Soviétique et les Etats-Unis, garantissait un certain équilibre des forces et frenait les tendances centrifuges dans chacun d'eux.

A l'intérieur des différents pays, aussi bien en Europe Centrale et Orientale, qu'en Europe de l'Ouest, les tendances séparatistes naissent, et l'état-nation subit une crise grave. Ses structures démocratiques sont affaiblies par les grandes corporations transnationales dont le pouvoir économique est de plus en plus étendu; par les organisations internationales qui s'attribuent certaines compétences des états-nations; par certaines régions où les sociétés aspirent à une plus grande autonomie, ou même à l'indépendance; enfin, par l'incapacité des sociétés d'absorber dans leur culture d'autres traits culturels représentés par les immigrants.

A côté des „grandes régions"[1], aspirant à une autonomie ou à l'indépendance, et que l'on peut considérer comme états in statu nascendi, il y a plusieures régions, aussi bien à l'Ouest qu'à l'Est, dont le sous-développement engendre de sérieux problèmes économiques et sociaux.

La politique régionale, menée depuis plusieurs années aussi bien à l'intérieur des différents pays qu'au sein de la Communauté Européenne, s'est soldée par un échec. D'énormes fonds qui y ont été consacrés n'ont

---

[1]See Bernard Poche: *Le modèle de la "grande région: un système societal infraétatique autonome*, in this volume.

[1]cf. Bernard Poche: *Le modèle de la „grande région": un système societal infra-étatique autonome.* Texte publié dans ce recueil.

However, the regional policies conducted by the states themselves and by the European Community appeared to be totally unsuccessful. Vast funds engaged in these policies have not resulted in decreasing regional inequalities, but — on the contrary — these differences grew. In spite of the policies aiming at evening the regional levels of development, the strong regions became stronger and the weak ones did not achieve the expected dynamics of development. The old dilemma: efficiency or equality became apparent even more sharply.

The European Institute for Regional and Local Development of the University of Warsaw studies these processes. Since two years we coordinate the research programme *"Restructuring of Polish regions in an European context"*. Analyses of regional differentiation of Polish reforms and of regional potential for transformation are parallel to international comparative regional studies on European scale. Within this project we also organise international seminars devoted to interchange of opinions and experiences between scientists from the West and the East, who deal with regional problems.

In June 1991 EUROREG organised in Mądralin an international seminar "United Europe — the Challenges of the XXI century". The thesis saying that the model of European integration should be reconsidered in the light of collapse of the Soviet Union was the main conclusion of that seminar. The "European" aspirations of the postsocialist states were said to create new

pas conduit à une diminution des disparités régionales; au contraire, elles ont augmenté. Malgré la politique d'égalisation des différences, les régions fortes se renforcaient, alors que les régions faibles ne revenaient pas au dynamisme souhaité. Le vieux dilemme de la politique régionale, celui du choix entre l'égalitarisme et la compétitivité, a revu le jour avec toute son acuité.

Tout ceci montre qu'au seuil du XXIe siècle la „question régionale" n'a plus seulement la dimension européenne, voire globale, mais elle devient aussi un défi aux gouvernements et aux organisations internationales.

Ces processus sont observés et analysés au sein de l'Institut Européen du Développement Régional et Local de l'Université de Varsovie. Un programme de recherche sur „La restructuration des régions en Pologne comme problème de la coopération européenne", réalisé depuis deux ans, englobe les études des différences régionales dans la transformation de système en Pologne, les études sur la capacité de développement de différents régions, et aussi les comparaisons à l'échelle européenne. Les colloques internationaux, organisés à l'occasion de ce programme, permettent un échange d'idées entre ceux qui, à l'Ouest et à l'Est, s'intéressent à la problématique régionale.

En juin 1991 l'EUROREG a organisé, à Mądralin, un colloque internationale „L'Europe unifiée — défi pour le XXIe siècle". Une des plus importantes conclusions, issue des débats, était celle de la nécessité de repenser le modèle d'intégration

challenges for the structures of the European Community[2].

The new manifestation of the regional question led to another international conference organised in 1992 by EUROREG, which aimed at new approaches to regional policies and its dilemmas. The title of this seminar well reflected its subject: Dilemmas of Regional Policies in Eastern and Central Europe under Transition[3].

The present volume contains proceeding from the third international seminar — organised as the other two in Mądralin — which was devoted to the *Regional Question in Europe* with special attention paid to the ethnic and national problems in their regional manifestations. This seminar took place on June 24–26, 1993. It should be noted at this occasion that this volume is the tenth one in the EUROREG series *"Regional and Local Studies — Les etudes regionales et locales"*.

The regional question is the result of "politicisation" of regionalism, i.e. of a socio-cultural movement which aims at valorisation of a given area. It has its own, double dynamics: from autonomy to federalisation and from nationalism to separatism. The roots

européenne, qui n'est plus adéquat à la situation après la chute du communisme et la désintégration de l'URSS. Les aspirations „européennes" des pays postcommunistes constituent un nouveau défi aux structures actuelles de la Communauté Européenne[2].

La question régionale étant reposée, il semblait opportun de discuter de nouveau sur la politique régionale et ses dilemmes; l'EUROREG a donc organisé, toujours à Mądralin, une nouvelle rencontre internationale sur les „Dilemmas of Regional Policies in Eastern and Central Europe"[3].

Voici les actes de la troisième colloque de Mądralin, organisée du 24 au 26 juin 1993 et consacrée cette fois à la *„Question régionale en Europe"*, surtout dans le contexte ethnique et national. Ce recueil est le dixième de la série *„Etudes régionales et locales"*, publiée par l'EUROREG.

La question régionale résulte de la politisation du régionalisme, c'est-à-dire du mouvement socio-culturel visant la valorisation d'un territoire. Elle a une double dynamique: l'une conduit des tendances autonomistes au fédéralisme, l'autre du nationalisme au séparatisme. En règle générale, les particularités ethniques et culturelles constituent le fonds de la question

---

[2]The conference proceedings were published in a volume: *Repenser l'Europe* (ed.: Bohdan Jałowiecki) EUROREG, Université de Varsovie, pp. 240, 1992.
[3]See the volume: *Dilemmas of Regional Policies in Eastern and Central Europe* (eds.: Grzegorz Gorzelak, Antoni Kukliński), EUROREG, University of Warsaw, pp. 512, 1992.

[2]Les actes de ce colloque ont été publiés en 1992 sous le titre *Repenser l'Europe* (ed. Bohdan Jałowiecki), EUROREG, Université de Varsovie, 240 pp.
[3]Les actes de ce colloque ont été publiés en 1992: *Dilemmas of Regional Policies in Eastern and Central Europe* (ed. Grzegorz Gorzelak, Antoni Kukliński), EUROREG, University of Warsaw, 512 pp.

of the regional question usually lie in ethnic or cultural differences. A territorial society may demonstrate some specific cultural feature and/or may use own dialect and, at the same time, may feel deprived, discriminated or undervalued, which may threat its identity. In order to improve this unfavourable situation such a territorial society tries to add new values to its culture and to defend its identity threatened by unification and assimilation with the majority[4].

The regional question may be also triggered by economic differentiations. Two situations are typical here. The region may be economically underdeveloped and in this case the territorial society tries to achieve more even distribution of the national product. In the second case the region may be economically well advanced, but the redistributive policy of the state directs a great part of its regional product to other regions, which is conceived by this particular region as unjust and it tries to change this state policy.

Regionalisation, i.e. changing the territorial organisation of the state in order to alleviate regional differences, is another way of solving the regional problem. The regional policy should primarily take an account of the network of culture and communication centres, preservation of the local cultural heritage, development of educational institutions, also of permanent education.

[4]See M. Bassand, *Culture et régions d'Europe*, Presses Polytechnique et Universitaires Romandes, Laussane, 1990.

régionale. Une collectivité, caractérisée par une culture spécifique et/ou un dialecte peut avoir le sentiment de ne pas être suffisamment valorisée, d'être déprivée et menacée dans son identité. Pour faire face à cette situation, elle entreprend des actions en faveur de la valorisation de sa culture et de la défense de son identité, devant les actions unificatrices et le danger d'assimilation de la part de la majorité.

Les disparités économiques peuvent constituer également le canevas de la question régionale. Dans ce cas, nous avons habituellement affaire à deux situations. Dans la première, la région peut être économiquement sous-développé et alors la collectivité agit pour une meilleure distribution du produit national. Dans la deuxième, la région peut être économiquement le mieux développée, mais à cause de la distribution effectuée par l'état, une grande partie des richesses produites dans cette région est allouée dans d'autres régions du pays; la collectivité trouve alors ceci injuste et cherche à changer cette situation.

La question régionale peut également être résolue par la politique de la régionalisation, c'est-à-dire par des actions gouvernementales qui visent à réorganiser le territoire du pays pour atténuer les disparités et stimuler le développement. La politique régionale doit surtout prendre en compte l'infrastructure de transport dont est dotée la région, les réseaux de distribution de la culture, la protection du patrimoine culturel, le développement des insti-

We can therefore see that the ways of solving the regional question may be both of "bottom-up" and "top-down" types. Regionalisation is the activity of specialists, planners, technocrats, who operate in an abstract space for which they construct different plans and programmes which do not necessarily take into account the everyday problems and aspirations of the population. On the contrary, regionalism is a social movement which is based on the local culture, concrete needs and wants of the inhabitants who claim greater justice.

Usually, regionalism is based on the feeling of identity. The essence of identity relies, on the one hand, on the feeling of affiliation to own social group, and, on the other hand, on the social distance to other groups. This distance does not always have to lead to alienation from a broader social entity. In this case a group — preserving its own identity — has the consciousness of belonging to a greater community. However, there do exist cases when such a distance leads to alienation and then aversion and hostility replace community feelings.

Alienation may be the result of incapability to achieve — in given conditions — the cultural values which are considered by the group as important, or to fulfil its economic interests. A group then undertakes actions which aim at changing this unfavourable situation. These actions, which assume the form of more or less violent social movements, always trigger defensive reactions of other groups and of the state structures, which consider

tutions d'enseignement, dont celle de l'éducation permanente.

Ainsi donc, les tentatives à résoudre la question régionale peuvent venir aussi bien de l'intérieur que de l'extérieur. La régionalisation est l'oeuvre des spécialistes, des planificateurs, des technocrates agissant dans un espace abstrait, pour lequel ils élaborent plans et programmes ne prenant souvent pas en compte les problèmes quotidiens et les aspirations des habitants. Par contre, le régionalisme est un mouvement social encré dans la culture locale, issu des besoins concrets et des aspirations des habitants qui réclament une plus grande justice[4].

En règle générale, le régionalisme est basé sur le sentiment d'identité. L'essence de l'identité résulte d'un côté du sentiment des liens existant au sein du groupe, de l'autre du sentiment d'une plus ou moins grande distinction par rapport aux autres. Cette distinction ne doit pas nécessairement signifier le sentiment d'exclusion d'un ensemble social plus large et alors le groupe, tout en conservant son identité, est conscient d'appartenir à une plus grande collectivité. Mais il y a des cas où cette distinction entraîne l'aliénation et au lieu d'un sentiment d'appartenance à une plus large communauté, se crée celui de l'aversion ou d'hostilité.

L'aliénation peut provenir de l'incapacité de réaliser, dans des condi-

---

[4]cf. Basand M. (1990): *Culture et régions d'Europe*. Presses Polytechniques et Universitaires Romandes, Lausanne.

regionalism as a phenomenon which may jeopardise the state consistency.

The postulates of the autonomists usually are encountered by smaller or greater resistance and are not fulfilled immediately. This leads to radicalisation of the movement and to formulation of targets going further, up to full sovereignty. When a declaration of independence is proclaimed, the conflict ceases to be a domestic one and becomes internationalised. This adds a new dimension to the regional question and the regional problem turns into an international problem. The state experiencing these events has two choices: to concede to the secession or oppose it, using the pretext of defending its own minority. Slovakia is an example of the first situation, Croatia of the second. The regional movement which has based on cultural factors turns into a national movement for independence and violent conflict becomes to be fed by nationalism demonstrated by both sides of this conflict.

"Nationalism — Ernest Gellner writes — is a political principle, according to which political entities should be congruent with national entities"[5]. It should be added that not only a nation — which is rather a vague notion — but also an ethnic, or in some cases a cultural group, may be considered as a national entity. This is because the process of building up the group identity is dynamic and

tions données, les valeurs culturelles importantes pour le groupe, ou leurs intérêts économiques. Là, le groupe agit pour changer cette situation. Ces mouvements sociaux, plus ou moins violents, provoquent toujours une réaction défensive de la part des autres groupes, et aussi de la part des structures nationales existantes qui voient dans le régionalisme la menace de l'intégralité de l'état.

Les revendications des autonomistes rencontrent généralement une plus ou moins grande résistance et habituellement ne sont pas immédiatement réalisées. Cela entraîne une radicalisation du mouvement et l'élévation de l'enjeu sous forme de l'exigence d'une totale souveraineté. Au moment de la proclamation de l'indépendance, le conflit n'est plus intérieur et se trouve internationalisé. Ainsi la question régionale acquiert une double dynamique et devient une question nationale. L'état, où se déroulent ces événements, peut soit se résigner à la sécession, soit s'efforcer à s'y opposer par force, p. ex. sous prétexte de la défense de sa propre minorité. Le cas de la Slovénie illustre la première situation, celui de la Croatie — la deuxième. Le mouvement régional à caractère culturel ou économique se transforme en un mouvement national d'indépendance, et le nationalisme réciproque engendre un conflit violent.

Le nationalisme, écrit Ernest Gellner, est un principe politique selon lequel les unités politiques doivent

---

[5] Gellner E., *Narody i nacjonalizm*, (Nations and Nationalism), PIW, Warszawa 1991.

may develop from the feeling of being ethnically or culturally different to the consciousness of national difference.

The integration processes which have persisted in Europe for last thirty years lose their pace.

**Europe becomes divided.** In several countries, both in the East and in the West, separatist movements gain in weight and new states are being created. Parallel to the splitting up of former Yugoslavia, which gave birth to several new states, also Czechoslovakia ceased to exists. This example added new momentum to the separatist movement in Flanders. In Northern Italy the Lombardy League claims independence. In Corsica the movement for independence has long tradition and reaches out for terrorist methods. Local languages and local culture become more popular in Wales, Scotland and in several Spanish regions. Separatist tendencies emerged in Silesia, which also opts for greater autonomy.

These processes of division are supported by a wave of nationalism which is to substantiate new identity. Nationalism of a minority does not decrease after this minority achieves its goals, i.e. independence. On the contrary, this nationalism growths further. The nationalism of the majority is not less dangerous, since the majority does not want to tolerate the foreign newcomers on its own territory any longer. European societies for several years have been so open and have accommodated the immigrants with such a great hospitality, have taken advantage of their labour which

correspondre aux unités nationales[5]. Remarquons que cette unité nationale ne doit pas être nécessairement constituée d'une nation, dont le concept est assez vague, mais aussi d'un groupe ethnique, et dans certain cas culturel, car le processus de la formation de l' identité du groupe (depuis le sentiment de distinction culturelle et ethnique jusqu'à celui de la distinction nationale) a un caractère dynamique et graduel.

Les processus d'intégration, présents en Europe depuis les trente dernières années, perdent de leur dynamisme.

**L'Europe se divise.** Dans différents pays, aussi bien à l'Ouest qu'à l'Est, les mouvements séparatistes sont de plus en plus forts; de nouveaux états naissent. A part la Yougoslavie, éclatée en quelques états distincts, la Tchécoslovaquie s'est divisée. Cet exemple a donné de la vigueur au mouvement séparatiste en Flandre. En Italie du Nord, la Ligue Lombarde aspire à l'indépendance, en Corse depuis longtemps le mouvement d'indépendance est terroriste. Les langues locales et la culture sont de plus en plus populaires dans le pays de Galles, en Ecosse et dans différentes régions d'Espagne. Les tendances autonomistes sont apparues en Silésie.

Une vague de nationalisme accompagne ces divisions; il veut renforcer les nouvelles identités, en cours de formation. Le nationalisme des mino-

---

[5]cf. E.Gellner (1991): *Narody i nacjonalizm* (Nation et nationalisme), Warszawa

contributed to the achieved level of welfare.

**Europe becomes closed.** There are several causes of this closing up process. The economic stagnation and growing unemployment may be mentioned as some of them. However, the "cultural collision" should be considered as much more important, since it jeopardises the national identity. European values are threatened by islam and this decreases the level of tolerance and triggers almost atavist defensive mechanisms. "Neorasism", which relies on shifting from the notion of "national differences" (which is badly received) to the notion of "cultural differences"[6], grows in both East and West. It manifests itself especially in the ideology of populist movements, but is also present in attitudes of growing social circles and in everyday behaviour.

Emigrants from Africa or Asia have brought with themselves different customs, religions, value systems and life styles. Foreign culture becomes more and more unbearable for the domestic population. Since the assimilation process has to take a long time, the immigrants were not able to amalgamate with the domestic societies. Moreover, due to the principle of "tolerance for diversity" — which is now becoming worn out — they were not assisted in their efforts to assimilate. The emigrants become to be the "scape goat" of

rités qui aspirent à une autonomie ne faiblit pas après l'acquisition de l' indépendance; au contraire, il monte. Le nationalisme des majorités est non moins dangereux, car elles ne veulent plus tolérer des étrangers sur leur sol. Or, les sociétés européennes, ouvertes et hospitalières depuis des années, acceptaient volontiers des immigrants, profitant de leur travail, qui a contribué à la richesse acquise.

**L'Europe se renferme.** Parmi les causes de cette fermeture, on peut évoquer la stagnation de l'économie et l'augmentation du chômage. Mais le „choc culturel", qui menace l'identité nationale, est beaucoup plus important. La mise en péril des valeurs européennes, p.ex. par l'Islam, abaisse le seuil de tolérance et engendre des réactions défensives, presque atavis-ques. Aussi bien à l'Ouest qu'à l'Est se répend le „néorasisme" dans lequel la notion de la „distinction raciale", mal accueillie, est remplacée par celle de la „distinction culturelle"[6]. Il se révèle surtout dans les idéologies des mouvements populistes, mais aussi, de plus en plus fréquemment, dans les attitudes sociaux.

Les immigrants d'Afrique ou d'Asie ont apporté d'autres coutumes, d'autres religions, systèmes de valeurs, styles de vie. Une culture différente devient de plus en plus insupportable pour la population locale. L'intégration des immigrants n'était pas possible car elle exige un temps long; en plus, au

---

[6]See Nicole Boucher, *Racisme et immigration: Vers l'implosion de l'Etat-Nation?*, in this volume.

[6]cf. Nicole Boucher: *Racisme et immigration: vers l'implosion de l'Etat-Nation?* Texte publié dans ce recueil.

the frustrated societies and an easy target for releasing the accumulated aggression. The Germans, for whom attacking foreigners and putting their houses on fire became an element of everyday life, are the leaders in this behaviour. **Europe is frightened.** It is not frightened only of the newcomers from the Third World, but also of those coming from Eastern Europe. Germany and France, which used to be the examples of the most open countries, make their immigration procedures more restrictive. Several countries reintroduce visas for citizens of selected countries. Rich societies of the West persuade Central Europe to seal its frontiers with the East and are ready to provide financial support for it. In a short period of time the Slovak-Czech border will be one of the most safeguarded borders in Europe, which will be the result of the German financial support of 50 mln Czech crowns to cover wiring, radars and electronic sensors. In this way the human insects, moving from the dispersed hives in Eastern Europe and the Balkans, will encounter in the centre of the continent a new barrier which did not exist a year ago. "In Moravia new curtain grew — this time not iron, but electronic", wrote Der Spigel[7]. It is very likely that similar curtain will appear soon on the easter — if not on the western — frontier of Poland.

---

[7]Quoted after weekly "Wprost", no. 27/1993.

nom de la tolérance pour la diversité, qui s'épuise actuellement, personne ne les a aidé. Les immigrants deviennent des boucs émissaires pour les sociétés frustrées et des cibles faciles pour décharger une agression accumulée. L'Allemagne en a la primeur, où les pogroms des étrangers et les incendies de leurs maisons sont devenus monnaie courante.

**L'Europe a peur,** non seulement des immigrants des pays du Tiers Monde, mais aussi de ceux de l'Europe de l'Est. En Allemagne comme en France, deux des pays les plus ouverts, les formalités d'immigration deviennent de plus en plus rigides; plusieurs états exigent à nouveau des visas pour les ressortissants de différents pays. Les pays riches de l'Ouest appellent les pays d'Europe Centrale à rendre hermétique la frontière avec l'Est et sont enclins à les aider financièrement. Bientôt, la frontière slovaco-tchèque sera une des plus gardées en Europe. Les Allemands s'y sont efforcé, en déboursant 50 millions de couronnes pour dresser les barrières et les installations eléctroniques. Ainsi, les insectes humains, venant des fourmilières démolies en Europe de l'Est et dans les Balkans, rencontrent au centre du continent une nouvelle barrière, inexistante encore il y a un an. „En Moravie un nouveau rideau s'est élevé, il n'est seulement pas de fer mais eléctronique" — écrit „Der Spiegel"[7]. Probablement un tel rideau s'élèvera

---

[7]d'après l'hebdomadaire „Wprost", no. 27/1993.

Europe is afraid of quarrels and of military conflicts which it cannot solve; it is afraid of its own inability to bring bloody ethnic conflicts in former Yugoslavia and the Soviet Union to an end; it is afraid of losing its welfare and of growing unemployment. New divisions and new frontiers constitute new European reality at the end of the XX century. Negative attitudes toward strangers, manifesting themselves in several countries, regions and in entire Europe and the complex of the "fortress under siege" do not seem to create promising grounds for European integration. The regional question turns into the national question which seemed to be for long forgotten, and, in turn, into a European question. Europe faces the most serious problem. The way in which it will be solved conditions the future of this continent.

demain à la frontière occidentale ou orientale de la Pologne.

L'Europe de l'Ouest a peur des querelles et des conflits armés, auxquels elle ne sait pas faire face. Elle a peur de son impuissance face aux conflits ethniques sanglants dans l'ex-Yougoslavie et en ex-URSS. Elle a peur de perdre le bien-être acquit et du chômage qui augmente. Des nouvelles divisions et des nouvelles frontières constituent la réalité de la fin du XXe siècle. L'aversion envers les étrangers dans différents pays, dans des régions et dans toute l'Europe, ainsi que le complexe de la forteresse assiégée ne semble pas être une bonne base pour l'unification européenne. La question régionale se transforme en question nationale, depuis longtemps, semblerait-il, oubliée — et en question européenne. L'Europe est face au problème le plus grave; de sa résolution dépend son avenir.

*Grzegorz Gorzelak*
*Bohdan Jałowiecki*

Michel Bassand
Polytechnique Romande
Lausanne

# THE METROPOLISATION
# OF THE WORLD

## 1. Preliminary Remarks[1]

Metropoles are urban agglomerations with more than one million inhabitants. They are the world's nodal centres and will increasingly perform this function.

We believe that these collectivities are of the dominant urban type within contemporary societies. They manifest the urban qualities characteristic of our times; they are the centres of contemporary social systems.

How should one explain this preponderance? What are the main characteristics of these metropoles? In other words, what are the factors affecting the world's metropolisation? Our main thesis stresses the fact that any urban phenomenon comes into being through an interaction with the surrounding society dead; at the same times, it is no longer possible to use the term 'post-industrial society' to refer to a social system whose new structures are clearly here to last. It is this new society that generates

[1]I would like to thank Jean-Claude Bolay, Dominique Joye, Yves Pedrazzini and Pierre Rossel for their comments and critical suggestions.

a metropolisation of metropoles. Our reflection will be based on these observations.

# 2. A New Social System

The social sciences have yet to decide what this new society should be called: Information society? Services society? Some authors still use the term 'post-industrial society' ... As for us, we choose to follow Alain Touraine[2] and to speak of a 'programmed society'. We shall justify this choice further on.

First we would like to stress that it would be extremely wrong to see the programmed society and the metropolis as diabolical phenomena. Although they do imply perverse asspects, they also contain eminently positive elements.

The new social system that we see being born and of which, in one way or another, we are all actors, may be described in terms of at least six dimensions. Of course, it would be possibile to mention further aspects. The concepts we are using have been developed by the social sciences earlier or later in their history. All of them are now considered very relevent, having been submitted to a process of maturation — which does not mean that hey may not be further refined. Finally, although these six concepts are very much interdependent, they remain extremely specific.

## 2.1. Globalisation

Some authors talk of 'mondialisation' or 'interdependence'. These terms share two common denominators. First, man's actions have expanded to the planetary level. This, of course, has not yet happened systematically, nor completely[3]. Still, human action is no longer restricted to the old territories, wheter at the economic, at the political, at the social or at the cultural level. Second, almost simultaneously, markets have become global. Considering the extent they have reached, these two processes have come to shape a fundamentally new dimension. At the economic

---

[2] A. Touraine, *Critique de la modernité*, A. Fayard, Paris, 1992.

[3] R Reich, *L'économie mondialisée*, Dunod, Paris, 1993; Secrétariat d'Etat au Plan, Entrer dans le XXIe siécle, La Découverte, Paris, 1990.

level, global chains of production and distribution have been created, directly linking raw materials to their final consumers. These chains are extremely sophisticated and no longer take — much — account of the contingent problems of national States. The fall of communism in the Soviet Union has amplifeid these processes and has modified their representations. Politically speaking, these changes mean that the State no longer has a monopoly on socio-political regulation. Market laws have taken over. Despite its great deficiencies, the market has been shown to be more efficient than the State.

The globalisation of the social system does not imply a disappearance of the local, regional and infranational struggles, it reinforces these types of community. The global and the local, together with every intermediary level, are joined by a dialectical relationship.

On the other hand, some people perceive globalisation mainly in terms of the wars that are raging everywhere in the world: globalisation becomes a synonym of tanks.

At a global level, despite (or as some say, because of) a generalisation of the market economy, the centre-periphery split continues to develop, albeit not everywhere to the same degree or in the same form[4]. Its consequences in terms of injustice and humiliation are absolutely mind-blowing.

Although it is clear that interdependences have developed between the different centres and peripheries, it is also — and maybe particularly — obvious that the split provokes the exclusion of peripheries. Some peripheral collectivities are forever waiting in a limbo; they do not succeed in developing or they become gradually more peripheral. It is true that some collectivities manage to 'make a start'... But the great majority remains excluded. What should be done in order to establish a global solidarity?

Exlusion phenomena are found in the world's peripheral zones; they are also found in centres: unemployment[5], a part of the elderly population, low-income neighbourhoods[6] and the periphery of metropoles or large agglomerations, rural regions ... All these elements contribute to the creation of structurally peripheral groups or zones. It is interesting to note that, contrary to what happened in the past, the actors involved in struggles provoked by exclusion phenomena no longer attempt to destroy the excluding system, but aim at an integration.

---

[4] A. Touraine, *La Parole et le sang*, Jacob, Paris, 1988.

[5] B. Perret, G. Roustang, *L'économie contre la société*, Seuil, Paris, 1993.

[6] F. Dubet, D. Lapeyronnie, *Les quartiers d'exil*, Seuil, Paris, 1992.

## 2.2. The Scientific and Technical Matrix

By this, we mean that sciences and techniques have become deeply interdependent within a 'technoscience'[7]. Basically, the scientific and technical matrix is the culture of contemporary societies. The system of values and the knowledge this culture generates and diffuses — but also influences through the media — stem directly from this matrix. Technoscience influences every field of social life: work, politics, health, culture, etc. However, societies have lost their unshakable faith in technoscience: its efficiency is occasionally doubted, its truths are no longer seen as absolute. Scientific knowledge does not bring certainties, it brings back basic philosophical questions. Doubts are thrown upon the notion of determinism.

The scientific and technical matrix touches a global level and contributes greatly to the split between centre and periphery.

Sciences and techniques had long remained (almost) separate entities. Industrialisation brought them closer to each other. Nowadays, as we have seen, they cannot be dissociated.

Labour has been revolutionised by the matrix. The changes have brought about the end of taylorism and fordism[8]. The new organisation of labour influences to a large extent globalisation.

On the one hand, the consequent increase in productivity contributes to a tertiarisation of centres. It also encourages the implantation in the peripheries of industrial activities that cannot be automated — or whose automatisation would not be profitable. This evolution brings other changes: a shrinking of the working class, together with a transformation of its social and political organisations. These changes radically alter the structure of centres. It is becoming obvious that some unemployment is brought about by robotisation and globalisation.

On the other hand, the scientific and technical matrix allows the establishment of a telecommunication and transportation network that makes globalisation possible. Without an efficient exchange system, technoscience would achieve far lesse results. The concomitant globalisation and division of labour have also stimulated the creation of this telecommunication network. The global network of production and distribution could not exist, were it not for telecommuniacation.

---

[7] J.-J. Salomon, *Le destin technologique*, Balland, Paris, 1992.
[8] B. Coriat, *L'atelier et le robot*, C. Bourgeois, Paris, 1990.

The amplification of migratory flows from North to South, and from East to West, is one of the direct consequences of the new social structuration brought by technoscience and globalisation.

## 2.3. Ecology

The ecological crisis stands in direct relationship with the two themes discussed above. This cirisis has taken a new turn[9]. For example, it has a global dimension: pollution, the ozone hole, the raise in the temperature of the Earth, etc. The increase in human activity and its consequences for the environment must also be considered from a global level. Thinking globally is no longer enough, we must also act globally. This means that ecological problems must be solved; they interact with the centre-periphery continuum. Any lasting strategy of development must be based on finding solutions to the ecological cirisis.

What is more, the ecological cirisis has given birth to a social movement that has taken extremely varied forms everywhere in the world. Ecology has become one of the protagonists within programmed societies[10].

## 2.4. Individualism and social relationships

The emancipation of individuals from matter and from socio-political traditions is very old. The recent improvements in the division of labour, in mass production, and in market economies[11] have brought a tremendous promotion of individualism. However, this has not meant an elimination of social dimensions such as gender, age groups, social stratification, or the centre-periphery continum. Individualism does not do away with inequalities; many potential changes and conflicts remain: woman's emancipation, aging of the population, growth of the "middle classes", metropolisation, etc.

Once individuals have acquired a much greater autonomy, they start resisting many forms of social life and of rationalisation. They withstand

---

[9] A. King, B. Schneider, *Questions de survie*, Calmann-Lévy, Paris, 1991.

[10] A Touraine, Z. Hegedus, F. Dubet, M. Wievorka, *La prophétie anti-nucléaire*, Seuil, Paris, 1980.

[11] A. Touraine, 1992, op.cit.; B. Perret, op.cit.

the various types of exclusion and of alienation that autonomy has generated. What is more, individualism brings a loss of solidarity. And at
times of crisis, the individual who has become more independent from
traditional community structures falls more easily a victim to anomy, with
all the consequences that this situation implies.

As a result of all these processes, social inequalities are on the increase
at a global level.

Social sciences make a distinction between individualism and individuation. The first term designates the autonomy acquired by the individual,
among other things, thanks to market economy and the division of labour.
Individuation is the process through which individuals affirm their specificity and their social or cultural differences without necessarily gaining
in autonomy. These two processes are of course complementary, but they
are also very distinct.

Individualism brings the death of many traditional forms of sociability
and of groups. Nevertheless, it does not leave the individuals without any
social support; many benefit from a "bureaucratic solidarity" such as social
security and the various forms of collective insurances. What is more, they
often attempt to re-create forms of spontaneous solidarity that are more
or less inspired by those just left behind. As a careful observer, one may
be struck by the recent birth of numerous social networks[12], connecting
both individuals and groups.

## 2.5. New Groups and Organisations

The new society does not destroy only, it also rebuilds; in this sense, a
disorganisation of social and collective life coexists with a reorganisation.
In brief, the development of individualism implies that those groups and
organisations in industrial societies that are disappearing more or less
quickly are replaced by new groups and organisations that are specific to
programmed societies. For example, groups connected in various manners
to the social movement are born, or organisations are created as a reaction
to the ecological crisis ...

To put it more precisely, groups and organisations such as the village,
the parish, the firm, the family, etc., disappear; they are being replaced

---

[12]M. Bassand, P. Rossel, "Métropoles et réseaux", Espace et société, No. 57–58, p. 196–
208; M. Bassand, B. Galland, Cadmos.

by new organisations with sometimes the same name, although in reality they are very new social forms. Let us take a few examples: The village is being replaced by various types of local collectivities that have nothing in common with the old communities[13]. The same is happening in urban neighbourhoods: only their name has remained, while their reality changed completely[14]. The family is no longer just the nuclear family; other types of households have come to play a very significant role: singles, one-parent families, various parental networks, etc. In industrial societies firms had been greatly influenced by the structural conflict opposing the owner of the production means to a generally largely unionized workforce. Nowadays, this conflict has become less virulent and cooperation has been brought to the foreground. Class-warfare is no longer referred to and has been replaced by corporate culture[15]. Concerns have become very important existential environmments and no longer just provide an income. Obviously, the disappearance of certain groups and organisations has left wistful memories, due in particular to the fact that the new collective structures do not always function perfectly. People now spend their daily life within various types of organisations (those already mentioned, but also training centres, cultural, recreational, and health centres, etc.). Each fully respects their identity while making them participate in a collectivity; but this participation obeys completely new rules.

In short, the social and collective life of programmed societies runs within a very different type of social frame. As an existential environment compatible with individualism, this frame is most relevant to an interpretation of the pratices and representations characteristic of the various social actors.

## 2.6. Programmation

The type of society that is emerging more and more forcefully also brings numerous uncertainties. Nevertheless, its actors are still very much willing to rationalize and they do so in terms of programmation. Their rationalisation is directly connected to the scientific and technical matrix

---

[13] Programme observation du changement social, L'espirt des lieux, C.N.R.S., Paris, 1986

[14] See the book quoted above, on the 'spirit of places', and the work by D. Joye, T. Huissound, M. Schuler, T. Busset et al., Le Quartier: une unité politique et sociale, IREC, Lausanne, 1992.

[15] B. Perret, op.cit.

mentioned above. What is needed is no longer just an organizing of social life. Of course, organisation is still required, but programmation takes it one step further and expands it to the whole of society.

To give an example, the most spectacular forms of programmation are found in the global networks of production and distribution. Apart from a market economy, these require the interconnection and the programmation of numerous complex organisations, both private and public, towards objectives much more global than each of them. The extent of programmation within contemporary societies is shown by the networks serving to the production and distribution of cars, refrigerated products, air transportation, medicines, various household equipments, etc. These programmed networks are clearly not all working as they should; but they exist and everything suggests that they will be very important in the future. Other forms of programmation have been tried out in extremely varied domains, where they have produced good or sometimes not so good results: transportation, education, health, etc. When these attempts occasionally fail and generate chaos, the reaction may be one of amusement. Nevertheless, we think that they are characteristic of nascent societies and this is why we use the term 'programmed society'.

On the other hand, programming has its adepts: they are the various professionals who conceive and implement it, i.e., the technocrats. They justify their work in terms of rationalisation and modernisation. Resistance or opposition to programmation and its actors bring great conflicts. They are expressed in a social movement: ecology. This becomes particularly obvious whenever large technical equipments (transportation systems, energy production[16], etc ... ) are being installed. Opponents bring forth other forms of rationalism and modernism and want to implement a strategy of lasting development. These pragrammations may well be considered to have very positive effects, but some people see them as involving a risk for ecology and for individual autonomy; they will thus resist and often oppose them.

Programmed society is also the stage on which reactionery social movements emerge. This happens because the social changes the programmation described above provoke a nostalgia for past societies. Innovation and the concomitant insecurity brought by programmation are frightening and call forth regressive tendencies. Changes bring about numerous migratory flows, with foreigners becoming an omnipresent component of

---

[16] A. Touraine, 1980, op.cit.

societies. This brings insecurity to part of the population and gives rise to xenophobic, racist, authoritarian and anti-democratic pratices. These reactionary movements are always critical of globalisation — of globalism.

As we have seen, programmed society is not just the great, well-oiled and functional machine that its designation may seem to imply. It is a system in which many actors are torn by numerous conflicts, and its programmation is by no means completed.

# 3. The Metropolisation of The World or The Implementation of a Global Network of Metropoles

This network is the most tangible manifestation of programmed society, even though metropoles may not be very successful instances of programmation. Nevertheless, its implementation is an attempt at programmation that is presently at work, among other things, in the transportation and communication field.

Metropoles are the dominant urban type in programmed societies. This idea must be specified:

1. As a type, metropoles are in no way homomorphic. We shall describe this type below, using eight criteria that are more or less equivalent to those we used to describe programmed society. None of these criteria need be applied in a very strict manner. For instance, metropoles are very large agglomerations. We said that they should have at least around one million inhabitants, but everyone knows that some urban metropoles are much large: five, ten, twenty million inhabitants ... The way they came into being can also vary greatly: some metropoles (such as Paris[17], London, New York[18], etc.) developed out of a large city that "expanded like an oil-stain"; others are made of one or several agglomerations of variable sizes, situated close enough to each other, but without touching: they became interconnected and started forming a whole (this is the case for Ranstadt, the Ruhr region, the Marseilles metropolis, etc.) As we note, as far as

[17]P. Benoit, J.-M. Benoit, F. Ballanger, B. Marzoff, *Paris 1995, le grand desserrement*, Romillat, Paris, 1993.

[18]V. Boggs, G. Handel, S. Fava, *The Apple Sliced*, Bergin and Garvey, Mass., 1984; M.D. Danielson, J. W. Doig, New York, Univ. of California Press, Berkeley, 1982.

official statistics go the type of metropolis that came into being through an interconnection process does not exist.

2. Each metropolis is the bridgehead of a network made of urban agglomerations, cities and towns that may be so close to each other as to be considered part of the metropolis. However, sometimes they are so fart apart that one may not be able to see the network. In general, these urban agglomerations, cities and towns are dependent from the metropolis.

3. The centre of our contemporary world is in effect this network of metropoles. It can no longer be argued that any one of these occupies a dominant position.

4. We did agree above that some segments of the emerging world-system can be centres, while others are peripheries. These segments will continue to show for a long time the characteristics inherent to their national States. Nevertheless, being partof a centre or part of a periphery will remain an important characteristic of a given metropolis. The eight criteria we are presenting below define a metropolis as against the surrounding society, this being either a centre or a periphery. On the other hand, it should be clear that the more central the surrounding context, the more programmed the metropolis will be.

5. In most metropoles the organisation of space is directly connected to one or another kind of urban history. In Western countries, we define at least three types: medieval and classical cities, industrial cities, and urban agglomerations. In short, their characteristics are as follows:

Medieval and classical cities are a product of agrarian and feudal societies. Most goods are produced in the surrounding countryside and its villages, and this explains the basic conflict between urban and rural regions. We still have an emmblematical image of this urban type: a system of city walls serving both a military and an economic function, a dense urban texture, a functioning market, neighbourhoods that were structured by corporations and militia, monuments and prestigious spaces.

The rise of industrialisation creates a new urban type, the industrial city. It differs from the medieval and classical one mainly in that the production function becomes part of the city. Industrialisation brings radically new social dynamics and these create an entirely new type of city.

As industrial growth continues, a new type arises: urban agglomerations. These are made up of various types of crowns surrounding a centre, bringing new segregations, centreperiphery dynamics, and a very strong spatial mobility.

Quite often, the metropolis contains more or less effective remains of these historical types. These come to play an important role and they may prevent one from identifying the emergence of a new type, the metropolis.

Let us now look at the eight criteria used to define a metropolis. We said that they are equivalent to those defining programmed society, that they are interdependent while remaining specific, and that our list is not exhaustive.

## 3.1. Size

A metropolis is a fantastic concentration of population, but also of activities and social, cultural, sanitary, transportation, etc., equipments. Therefore, this criterion is also related to the surface occupied by the metropolis: this surface is enormous. If we combine surface, demography and activities, we may calculate density criteria. This is one of the starting points in the analysis of metropoles.

From the beginning specialists have seen urban environments as large size collectivities; this still applies. Size may not be the most important criterion, but it is relatively easy to measure and to apply. This is why we mentioned it first.

We suggest that a metropolis be defined as having at least one million inhabitants. Obviously, the choice of this figure will greatly influence the other criteria.

## 3.2. Global horizon

We should not forget that a network of metropoles forms the world's centre. In this sense, each of them has global connections and is involved in global migratory flows. This generates multiculturalism and cosmopolitism. Almost each organisation and each equipment (firms, universities, airports, etc.) located within the metropolis will reflect this dimension.

### 3.3. Segmentation

Contemporary societies have restructured social and spatial differentiation. Two specific mechanisms structure the metropolis: space and equipments are (a) functionally specialized, and (b) socially segregated. This means that social exclusion is written down in space. Some of the spaces and equipments are connected to the world, while others look like ghettos. In this sense, each metropolis may be seen in terms of centres and peripheries.

A few authors had come the conclusion that local collectivities were destined to die, that neighbourhoods could not survive in metropoles. But this was before metropolitan space started subdividing, showing this prediction to be wrong. It is true that traditional neighbourhooda are dying, but other types of life within territorial micro-collectivities are re-emerging. They may become the basis for a new local type of democracy.

### 3.4. Flux management

Each spatial collectivity must help manage the goods and services located within its territory and coordinate the flux of goods, people, and information that gives it life. In metropoles, flux management gains more importance than any other type of management, this being so because of their size, their global horizon, and their segmentation.

On one hand, these various types of flux are essential; on the other, they tend to become interdependent trough the networks they create. We are thinking of the various networks connected to transportation, communication, the movement of people, the provision and elimination of goods, of refuse, of information, services and capital, etc. We call these technical or territorial networks; they play a very important role both within each metropolis and between metropoles. They are the material of which the metropolis is woven[19]; what is more, they become the stakes of programmation... Obviously, the management of technical and territorial networks has a great influence on the creation and maintenance of social networks. Each type of network is as important as the other. This is a crucial aspect in the dynamics of metropoles: it is directly connected to the cohesion and the integration of their population.

---

[19]G. Dupuy, *L'urbanisme des réseaux*, A. Collin, Paris 1991.

## 3.5. Environment

More than any other type of territory, metropoles are neuralgic segments of the ecoenvironment. They are the greatest source of pollution. Strategies for a lasting development are first implemented within them.

## 3.6. Individualism

Metropoles breed more individualism in their inhabitants than any other urban type. This aspect results directly from their various structures and especially from their segmentation. Specialisation and the segregation of spaces and equipments are so extreme that inhabitants are required to play completely different roles as they move from one space or from one equipment to another. For instance, housing, transportation, work, leisure, etc., concentrate within a given space so many different social, economic, and cultural contens that the roles played within each space must be totally different. Thus, the actor playing all these various roles becomes more individual than elsewhere. This type of social and spatial structure also generates very specific situations that, in turn, are a source of individualism: see, for instance, 'the fatherless society'[20], a phenomenon that has had consequences far beyond the remonte suburbs in whoch it was first observed.

## 3.7. Conflicts

Metropoles constellate all the conflicts inherent to programmed society, although not necessarily simultaneously. This 'conflictuality' is a very significant criterion of metropoles. Struggles and conflicts take place there, of which some of the most important ones may be: those connected to exclusion phenomena, those concerning the ecological crisis, those around the survival of the poorest population segments, those inherent to programmation, and those specific to the poorest population segments, those inherent to programmation, and those specific to the metropolitan structure. We would like to stress that conflicts are not necessarily negative; but one should try at all cost to avoid violence. Conflicts may function as a

---

[20]A. Mitscherlich, *Psychanalyse et urbanisme*, Gallimard, Paris, 1970.

stimulus for the actors involved to express their identity and their projects. Conflicts also bring together descending and ascending social dynamics[21].

## 3.8. Political institutions

Almost all the criteria we have just mentioned seem to indicate that metropoles require specific political institutions. Yet, rare are the metropoles that have them. The political institutions dating from before the metropolis, such as local governments, specialized private or public organisms, various political institutions, etc., have survived and attempt to collaborate in the management of metropoles. The results are not very convincing. Metropolitan governments haven't succeeded in achieving their aims ...

Can it that metropoles cannot be governed? This is clearly a very important question. Research should concentrate on defining the political institutions that may succeed in managing metropoles, that is, in managing hypercomplex mastodons.

# 4. Conclusion

We would like to close our reflection by summarising our two points, after which we shall answer an objection.

1. What we are observing is not just a number of social changes. An entirely new society is emerging under our eyes. Its emergence had been predicted long ago: the post-industrial society. Yet, this new society is now so well established that one can no longer take refuge behind the prefix post ... Programmed society is in full bloom, with all its advantages and disadvantages. Apart from its programmation, its major characteristics are globalisation, the predominance of a scientific and technical matrix, the ecological crisis, individualism, and metropolisation.

2. Spatially, this social structuration is concretised in the shaping of a new dominant urban type: the metropolis, or rather a global network of metropoles. This is what we call the metropolisation of the world. Within this network, each metropolis shows the characteristics of programmed

---

[21] P.-H. Chombart de Lauwe (ed.), *Culture-action des groupes dominés*, L'Harmattan, Paris, 1988.

society and this applies whether it is situated in a central or in a peripheral zone. The most obvious and significant criteria applying to each metropolis are: size, a global horizon, spatial segmentation, flux management or a system of technical, spatial and social networks, more frequent conflicts, and the absence of specific political institutions.

*As we said, we would like to answer a possible objection. Could it be that the new society will eventually eliminate high density demographic zones and therefore metropoles? This may seem logical, considering that this society is implementing a sophisticated communication network, concomitant to an increasing mobility of its components. Could it be, then, that societies will become more and more decentralized and less dense? We do not think so. We feel quite sure that a system in which everything is extremely mobile and fluid requires fixed points. In the world of today, these fixed points. In the world of today, these fixed points are the metropoles.*

# Bibliography

Bassand M., 1982, *Villes, régions et sociétés*, Lausanne, Presses polytechniques romandes.

Bassand M., Joye D., Schuler M., 1988, *Les enjeux de l'urbanisation: Agglomerationsprobleme in der Schweiz*, Berne, P.Lang.

Bassand M., Rossel P., "Métropoles et réseaux", [In:] *Espaces et sociétés*, no 57–58, pp. 196–208.

Benoit P., Benoit J.-M., Ballanger F., Marzoff B., 1993, *Paris 1995: le grand desserrement*, Paris, Romillat.

Boggs V., Handel G., Fava S., 1984, *The Apple Sliced*, Bergin and Garvery.

Brunet R., 1989, *Les villes "européennes"*, Paris: La Documentation francaise.

Van Der Cammen H., (ED), 1988, *Four Metropolises in Western Europe*, Assen/Maastricht, Van Gorcum.

Castells M., 1983, *The City and the Grassroots*, Berkeley, University of California Press.

Chombart De Lauwe P.-H., 1982, *La fin des villes*, Paris, Calmann-Lévy.

Coriat B., 1990, *L'atelier et le robot*, Paris, C.Bourgeois.

Danielson M. D., Doig J. W., 1982, *New York*, Berkeley, University of California Press.

Doggan M., Kasarda J.-D., 1987, *Les cités en question*, Paris, Plan urbain.

Dubet F., Lapeyronnie D., 1992, *Les quartiers d'exil*, Paris, Seuil.

Dupuy G., 1991, *L'urbanisme en réseaux*, Paris, A. Colin.

Fischer C.S., 1982, *To Dwell Among Friends: Personnal Networks in Town and City*, Chicago, The University of Chicago Press.

Friedmann J., Weaver C., 1979, *Territory and Function*, London, E. Arnold.

Galantay E., 1987, *The Metropolis in Transition*, New York, Paragon.

Harvery R., 1985, "The Geopolitics of Capitalism", [In:] Gregory D., Ury J., *Social Relations and Spatial Structures*, New York, St.-Martin's Press.

Joye D., Huissoud T., Schuler M., Busset T., et al., 1992, *Le quartier: une unité politique et sociale?*, Lausanne, IREC.

King A., Schneider B., 1991, *Questions de survie*, Paris, Calmann-Lévy.

Le Goff J., Guieysse L., 1985, *Crise de l'urbain: futur de la ville*, Paris, Economica.

Morel B., Fellmann T., 1989, *Métropolisation et aires métropolitaines*, Marseilles, E.H.E.S.S., Hospice Vielle Charité.

Perret B., Roustang G., 1993, *L'économie contre la société*, Paris, Seuil.

Reich R., 1993, *L'économie mondialisée*, Paris, Dunod.

Salomon J.-J., 1992, *Le destin technologique*, Paris, Balland.

Touraine A., 1988, *La parole et le sang*, Paris, O. Jacob.

Wallerstein I., 1974, *The Modern World System*, New York, Academic Press.

Wellman B., Berkowitz S.D., 1988, *Social Structures: a Network Approach*, Cambridge, Cambridge Press.

Franco Archibugi
Planning Studies Centre
Rome

# EUROPEAN REGIONAL POLICY: A CRITICAL APPRAISAL AND FORESIGHT

## 1. Premise

The "Single European ACT" (1986) and more recently the Maastricht Treaty (1990) introduces — as is well known — amongst the new objectives of the EC, the "strengthening of the economic and social cohesion" of the Community. And, in particular the Community "shall aim at reducing disparities between the various regions and the backwardness of the leastfavoured regions" (art. 130a of the Single Act)[1].

For this purpose, the member states shall "conduct" and "coordinate" their economic policies. And the Community shall "support the achievement of these objectives through the structural funds and other existing financial instruments" (Art. 130b)[2].

---

[1] The Maastricht Treaty modifies this last expressin of the Single Act with the aim to "réduire l'ecart *entre les niveaux de développment* des diverses regions et le retard des regions les moins favorisées, *y compris les zones rurales*" (Art 130a).

[2] A modification of the Maastricht Treaty to this article allows for the possibility of *"specific actions"* outside funding.

In fact, these Acts do no more than ratify, that which the Community had already many years ago started by developing a so-called "regional policy" about which the Treaty of Rome (1957) had been quite laconic[3].

As is well known already in the Paris Summit (1972) (at which the heads of state of four countries belonging to the first "enlargement" participated), the first concrete developments of a regional policy were suggested from which the European Regional Development Fund (ERDF) and the Regional Policy Committee were born some two years later.

And it was not without difficulty that, after long periods of negotiation, it was possible to establish procedures and rules for the utilisation of the European fund, rules which were then always retouched (for example in !979) right up intil the so-called "reform" of 1984.

The European Single Act (February 1986) states quite clearly, and even more precisely than was ever stated by previous offical documents, that *all* the Community policies and consequently all the structural funds and all ther financial instruments available today must be finalised exclusively with the aim of economic and social cohesion in mind.

In redefining more energetically, trough the European Single Act and the Maastrichr Treaty, *the objective of economic and social cohesion,* and thus discussing the ways and means by which to create — in the new context of Economic and Monetary Union (EMU) post-1992 — such a cohesion (and therefore also the further reform of the funds), it is not inopportune to reflect about and ask ourselves if *the lines along which until now the "structural" policies of the Community have moved should not be reviewed, and there should not be some proposal for working substantial changes.*

One question in particular arises: wheter, *regional policy* (together with social and agricultural policy), has achieved its original objectives, and whether a review of the means and methods of its work should not also be performed.

In fact *European Regional Policy* has , until now, moved according to a general line which appears, because of its nature, to have little capability of achieving its own objectives.

---

[3] It was only with the additional "protocol" relating to Italy (in fact to its "Mezzogiorno") that in the Treaty of Rome the matter of the less favoured regions was dealt with.

And it is on these general lines of the European Regional Policy, its deficiencies and its possibilities of renewal that we would like to focus — in this paper — our analysis[4].

## 2. The European Regional Policy: founded on "indirect" expectations

European Regional Policy, in complete conformity with the method and formulation of those already existing in member countries[5], has in

[4] In this paper we will not dwell long on describing the "European Regional Policy", such as it has developed in the course of the evolution of the Community. In fact, on European regional policy there has developed an enormous literature: amongst which we could select for further historical" analysis some informative works such as those of David Pinder (1983), Keating & Jones (1985) and of W. Molle et al. (1980).

We will limit ourselves to summarising some critical evaluations, which, on the other hand, the author has had several opportunities for developing more extensively on various occasions: for an examination which is among the most complete ther reader is referred to a report delivered at a seminar held in Madrid promoted by the "Frederich Ebert Stiftung" and by the "Fundacion IESA" (Archibugi, 1982a).

For a more theoretical evaluation of the different approaches to European regional policy the reader is referred to the acute essay by Stuart Holland on "The Regional Problem", amply dedicated to the relationships between regional policy and the construction of Europe (Holland, 1976). Very interesting is also the collection of essays edited by D. Seers on "Integration and Unequal Development" (1982).

[5] In effect, the regional policy which has most greatly influenced the European one has been — at least until 1973 — the Italian one, in as much as the Mezzogiorno was the only "backward" area which was explicitly dealt with by the Treaty of Rome.

The Italian regional policy has been entirely dominated by the management of an extraordinary fund (the Cassa per il Mezzogiorno"), completely in the hands of State finance, and made available to the territories (and the local authorities involved) of the Mezzogiorno. Italian regional policy has therefore consisted in a mere addi tional management of funds, distributed in favour of a determined territory (roughly a third of the entire Italian territory) in virtue of its "backwardness": this management, has been founded on the concept of "aid" (and sometimes on that of "compensation", what for is not exactly clear ...), without there being ever a plan of the things to be done with the means made available and of the results to be expected from the projects. Every attempt to "reform" the extraordinary intervention in the Mezzogiorno from a mere availability of funds, to a well-programmed allocation of those same funds, has always come up against an anti-planning culture.

The Italian regional policy (or that of the Mezzogiorno) has failed in almost every way, and today one is always more tempted to ask oneself — after decades of emptiness and dogmatic optimism — if such a policy has not brought to the Mezzogiorno more damage than it has benefist, by placing it in an apparently privileged but substantially "spoiled" position. (For the author's longstanding and constant criticism available in English: Archibugi 1977 and 1978).

the past 20 years been founded on supporting investment and promotion initiatives in those areas and regions considered to be "less favoured (or backward)", establishing those areas susceptible of falling into the "less favoured (or backward)" category (with very approximate and not always significant indicators).

In this way, the European Regional Policy has shown it believes that by intensifying economic activity, especially industrial and productive activity, the advancement of these regions to a more favourable and thus more "cohesive" position within the Community could be achieved.

With these financial or functional operations, some very large territories and some entire regions have been privileged, selected in the framework of the Regional Policy of each country[6]. The interventions, more or less demonstrative, have been made by the rationale of the general requisites of the territories to which they were implemented instead of the rationale of the specific objectives to which they were directed.

In the documents stating Community Regional Policy, as in those National Regional Policy documents from which the base of Community Policy was driven, there has prevailed — in respect of "objectives" — a general definition of the "area" and nature of the proposed intervention; so much so that the rationale used to assess single national or regional request projects was: whether such a request enters or not within the "area" and "nature" of the envisaged intervention.

But the possible outcome, along the objective of economic and social cohesion, to which a request might lead was never measured — neither *ex ante* nor *ex post* — because the relationship between various types of intervention and different types of objectives had never been measured.

Structural funds, and the various chapters of Community programmes to which these funds were directed, thus became a sort of "finance counter" from which funds can be drawn for any project that fell areas already predefined). They are not projects which developed from an evaluation of action to be taken in order to achieve *certain determined ob-*

In essence, today's criticisms of European regional policy are founded on the same criteria as those of the Italian regional policy.

[6]Up until 1973, at the time of entry in the Common Market of the three Nordic countries, the privileged area was that of the Italian *Mezzogiorno*; thereafter it was extended to Grenland, Ireland and Northern Ireland (and with proportionally limited interventions also to other assisted areas of France, Great Britain, Germany and Italy). Lastly with the entry of the three new countries of the South among the areas covered by regional plicy were also included those of Greece and Portugal and 70% of the Spanish territory).

*jectives ad hoc*, in one or another territory of the Community, and linked to the general aim of increasing economic and social cohesion in the Community.

# 3. Some attempts to reform the European Regional Policy

Despite the general lines, about which we have spoken, several attempts have been made on successive occasions to give a more defined and direct, content to the European Regional Policy.

## 3.1. Community intervention in the framework of the regional programmes

An attempt to evaluate more satisfactorily the use of funds according to more precise and measured objectives can be seen in the Regional Policy sector where requests for funds had to be presented in the form of "regional programmes" prepared by the regional and national authorities of each individual country. This was a first "reform" of the usage of the ERDF, implemented in 1984.

But this quite large experience of ERDF management shows that, although it led to the creation of regional programmes by states and regions which previously had not done so, it created at the same time a situation wherby it was not the requests for the ERDF that conformed to the evaluated and quantified list of necessary action but rather the which was "made to measure" specifically for the request to ERDF.

Thus the Community, has been very careful not to define its own guidelines for Community intervention, but rather has left it up to the individual national and regional governments, to programme their own territorial interventions.

## 3.2. The 1988 operational "reforms" of Structural Funds

The entire subject was later reorganised in a series of Council acts which came into force in 1988 and which are generally referred to as the "structural fund reforms"[7].

Announced and motivated in the Communication of the Commission "In order to lead the Single Act to success" (and which goes under the name of "the Delors Plan") of February 1987 (EC Commission, 1987a), the Community acts of this reform (the "Framework Regulations" n.2052/88 and the "Cooordination Regulations" n.4253/88 articulated — as is wellknown — the general objective of a greater economic and social cohesion (and therefore also those objectives of reducing the differences between regions and the backwardness of the less-favoured regions), in five general sub-objectives:

1.  promoting the development and structural adjustment of the regions whose development is lagging behind; (this objective concerns seven countries, in whole or in part, and covers something like 21,5% of the population of the Community, without considering the further enlargement extending to the territories of what was the Democratic Republic of Germany);
2.  converting the regions, frontier regions or parts of regions (including employment areas and urban communities), seriously affected by industrial decline; (this objective concerns 60 regions, in whole or in part, and covers roughly 16% of the Community population);
3.  combating long term unemployment;
4.  facilitating the occupational integration of youngpeople;
5.  and, with a view to a reform of the Common Agricultural Policy:

    5a) speeding-up the adjustment of agricultural structures

    5b) promoting the development of rural areas; (this objective concerns 56 regions in whole or in part and some 5% of the population).

The first objective implied — as it always has — the conventional identification of regions "whose development is lagging behind" or, more simply, "bakward regions".

---

[7]As is known, it was a series of "Regulations" of the Council of Ministers dated 1988, and especially that of N.4253/88 and that of N.2052/88 which made provisions for the presentation in the logic of a passage from a project-based approach to a programme-based one — to the Commission on the part of the various member states of "plans", and in particular of "regional plans".

As is well-known, the only indicator used was that of the GNP. The criterion has been to consider as "backward those "regions" (assumed as such only 6those administrative regions traditionally classed as belonging to level II by the "nomenclature of the territorial units for statistics" — NUTS — which have, at least as far as the GNP is concerned, a totally debatable statistical significance which present GNP inferior to or in the vicinity of 75%of the Community average.

It this way, for the purposes of applying the funds destined for the first objective of so-called "reform", the following have been considered "eligible":
— the entire national territories of Greece, Portugal and Ireland;
— the Italian "Mezzogiorno";
— 70% of the Spanish territory;
— Corsica and the French Overseas "DOM" territories and Northern Ireland.
— and lastly, the territory of eastern Germany (ex DDR)

On the basis of these five objectives, it was possible to intensify activity, defined as "planning and programming", which corresponded moreover to one of the three "inspiring principles" of the reform of the funds themselves[8].

And thus were created the following:
— 18 plans for the first objective: one for each country except France which presented one for each of the eligible regions;
— 57 plans for the second objective;
— 9 plans for the third and fourth objectives (excluding those countries already admitted under the first objective);
— 56 plans for objective 5b);

But even if, on the basis of these five objectives, a more satisfactory series of national and regional "plans" was created which led to an inten-

---

[8]8 Such principles were (and still are):
— that of "planning" (on the basis of plans submittes to the Commission by the member states (see art.8 Regulation dufferent institutions at dufferent territorial levels) (see art.8 Regulation 2052/88; art.5 Regulation 4253/88 and art.2 Regulation 4254/88);
— that of "compatibility and coordination" (between the structural policy and the other Community policies and between the Funds) (see art.7 Regulation 2052/88 and the title of Regulation 4253/88).
For further information on the management of the reform of structural funds there are several exhaustive Commission documents: a "Guide to the reform of the Community's structural Funds" (EC, Commission, 1990a), and the "Annual Reports on the Application of the Reform of the Structural Funds" (EC, Commission, 1991a, 1992).

sification of so-called "programming activity", it was difficult to appreciate *ex ante* — i.e. before the actual assigning of financial means — the "expected results" of the various plans proposed, or of the specific actions prescribed by these plans.

Thus it will be even more difficult to evaluate *ex post* the results obtained if they are not in some way measurable against "programme or planning parameters"; that is, if they have not already been hypothesized independently of the actual result achieved and with respect to the plan itself.

It can only be hoped that the procedures introduced by the so-called "structural funds reform", will encourage the Community — and by this the Commission and its offices — to better define *beforehand the terms of reference for the objectives to be reached*, with their application to the chosen territories and in relation to which the governments (national and/or local) have taken or would like to take the initiative of proposing or requesting intervention.

Naturally, the definitions proposed for the terms of reference to be adopted could be laid down througut forms of partnership of the governments concerned, in a manner compatible with the safeguarding of the necessary operational efficiency.

In fact, too much consultation paralyses action; and an excess of negotiation with the relative organs often risks neutralising the initiative and the propositive efficacy of the Community organs. The indispensability of preventive terms of reference — essentially of a cognitive and indicative nature — could lead the Community organs into finding the right trade-off between "decision-sharing" and "decision-making" on a case by case basis.

It is, however, worth underlining that, only through a preventive definition of the terms of reference of the various projects, a definition which would therefore imply *indicative planning and programming* upstream, would it be possible to create a connection between evaluation of the results and analysis of the objectives, and therefore a real *programming*, worthy of the name, would be achieved.

# 4. The technical conditions needed for an improved management of the European Regional Development Fund and other structural funds

These improvements in planning methods can be expected through a gradual and patient improvement in the decision processes, if supported by appropriate study, reflection and the application of Decision Support Systems (DSS).

The use of methods in no way aim at substituting, but rather at "rationalising", both the negotation (national or international), and the decision-making autonomy of the *decision-makers*.

Improvement will not be a natural result of the passing of time, but rather the result of good will and commitment on behalf of politicians, officials and pressure groups working within the system under discussion.

But even from another point of view, improvements could be made in the programming of interventions promoted by structural funds. An improved *ad hoc* assessment of intervention needs, and of the priorities of the various interventions relating to the measured and identified objectives, necessarily leads to an improved qualification of the areas to receive intervention. Such an area can no longer be a generic definition of territory, but rather an area which is inherently and coherently connected with the specific objective to be reached. The territorial, or spatial, character will be expressed by the intervention itself, which will assume the objective of using to advantage resources only when such resources actually exit and only where they are susceptible to being so used; and not because they just happen to be a part of a generic territory considered in "backward" conditions.

Intervention, formulated as a circumstantiated deduction of the objectives to be reached, would lose all the features of a scattered intervention, of one of uncertain effectiveness and of that carried out for the sole reason that it was endowed with the necessary formal "requisites" which have been generically prescribe ("elegibility"). Each proposal for intervention will be evaluated according to "substantial" requisites: not only with a costeffectiveness analysis in general, but with a cost-effectiveness where effectiveness is assessed as achievement of the specific objectives assigned to the programme or project in question.

When cost-effectiveness analysis is linked to a more organic planning process, the coordination and integration of different points of view by which the intervention is to be judtified also becomes easier.

In the case of structural funds, the problem — as has been noted — is not only that of adapting the interventions to one of the five objectives stated in the "overall regulation" of 1988 (already mentioned) but also to "other" objectives and making sure they are consitent with Community policy in general: e.g. di they respect the rules of fair competition? do they follow Community directives on public contract? and, last but not least, do they respect the environmental compatibility of the programmes and projects requested?

In this last case, in particular, respect for environmental compatibility can be ensured if the programmes and projects requested, come from an overall integrated planning, and are an operational deduction of selected programmes; these in fact — at the level of opportune territories — cannot have failed to take into consideration such compatibility.

On the other hand, only in this way can we respect the other fundamental principle which leads to European construction: the principle of *"subsidiarity"*; the Community should intervene with its own instruments only for projects of a European nature that could not be managed nor even conceived if not on a territorial European scale. In other words, projects that have a true European requisite, corresponding only to Community objectives; and projects corresponding to a common interest for the European citizen as a whole (including that of a social and economic cohesion).

Therefore the adoption of methods of programme and project evaluation, in the context of more vast and organic indicative European programming of the interventions, aimed at a greater degree of economic and social cohesion; it constitutes one of the essential components of a new and different way of conceiving this greater communitary "cohesion" in the Framework of the European subsidiarity.

## 5. "Europe 2000": a new approach to European Regional Policy

At the European level, a substantial change in regional policy, such as been here describe and considered desirable, has been brought about as a result of the initiative taken by the Council of Ministers responsible for Regional Policies in giving birth to an evaluation of future territorial dewelopments on a European scale. We refer here to the first meeting held in Nantes in 1989, followed later by that in Turin in 1990 and, recently the one in The Hague, held in November 1991, where it was decided — among other things — to give birth to an "Interministerial Committee for Special Development", which should establish the guidelines for the new course regional policy is to take[9].

In presenting the study prepared by the Commission to the Council at The Hauge — a document entitled precisely "Europe 2000: Outlook for the Development of the Community's Territory"[10] — the Commis-

---

[9]It would not be right to say that, even before Nantes (1989), there did not appear sings of a territorial policy of that type which today is more generally accepted. For example in a Communication of 3 June 1977 containing recommendations to the Council, entitled "Guidelines for a Community Regional Policy", the Commission putting together its objectives affirmed: "Its comprehensive approach now places the Community regional policy in the perspective of Community land use planning. In implementing the policy, the Commission will, particularly by means of the regional development programmes, make an effort to promote a rational use of space, a balanced distribution of activities over the whole Community territory and effective" (see EC, Commission, Community regional policy: New Guidelines, Bulletin of European Communities, Suppl. 2/27, p.7). But despite these wonderful intentions 12 years were necessary before being able to begin discussion (at Nantes) of territorial planning and even today we are still at the stage of very general studies.

It would mereover be very unjust if we failed to remember in this regard the intense and constant action taken in this direction for over twenty years at the heart of the Council of Europe, especially by the "Conference of Ministers responsible for Territorial Planning" (CEMAT). Right from the first CEMAT Conference (Bonn 1970) the "priority objectives" of a "common policy for territorial planning" were defined; and first amongst these was that of "reducing the historical imbalance between the industrial and the urban centre of gravity in north-eastern Europe and the outlying regions, with weaker structures and in a state of economic backwardness". But already in the fourth Conference (Vienna 1978) there was the decision to draw up a "European Map for Territorial Planning" (a decision ehich was definitively approved in the sixth Conference, at Torremolinos, in Spain, in 1983; and in the fifth Conference (London 1980) it was decided to examine the possibility of drawing up a "European Schema for Territorial Planning" (presented at the eighth session of the CEMAT at Lausanne, 1988 — see CEMAT, 1991). In other words, overall, the work carried out by the CEMAT, of which all 12 corresponding Ministers of the EC Council are members, is much more advanced than that of the EC, and it is not clear why in this latter context governmental resistance to a common territorial policy should be greater than in the context of the Council of Europe (since common sense would lead to think the contrary, given the greater integration of the EC with respect to the Council of Europe!).

[10]Commission of the European Communities, Directorate Gemeral for Regional Policy, *Europe 2000: Outlook for the Development of the Community's Territory*, (Communication from the Commission to the Council and the European Parliament), Brussels-Luxembourg, 1991 (EC, Commission 1991b).

sioner Millan declares that *"Europe 2000 breaks new ground in regional planning at the European level..."* And after having reassured the lukewarm (towards Europe) and the diffident (towards planning) that *"This is no masterplan for Europe. ..."* It is clear, however, that there is a need — *as borne out by this report, for more systematic cooperation between regional planners at the Community level and for polocies and plans in fields such as transport or energy to be considered from a regional development point of view. Throughout the Community there is growing interest in the wider European dimension to regional planning. ... Europe 2000 is a first effort to provide planners with some of the information they need in a reference framework which is Community-wide rather than national or regional. ..."*

Therefore, if it is true that "Europe 2000" represents the *first effort* at giving a truly European dimension to regional policy, then it also coincides with our assumption that up until now European regional policy did not have that dimension; and (our assumption) that without this territorial approach on an European scale (this is the thesis which we try to sustain and which the Author has sustained for a long time) the very efficacy itself is indeed very limited.

Europe 2000, therefore, represents an approach to European regional policy, which is correct at last, though still in the state of *in fieri*, and it represents by itself one of the clearer and more explicit forms of implementation of the subsidiarity principle.

The first document presented by the Commission at The Hague is a set of descriptive territorial evaluations, but containas a few "guidelines" on the desirable developments which are pursuable through a territorial policy at the European level. While it is becoming more impellent to create a connection between *this new approach to territorial policy* and the use of existing conventional instruments for regional policy, namely the use of structural funds. Even the reform introduced regarding the use of these funds in 1988 is more based on the old approach rather than on this new one.

Without a further development of the guidelines for the new territorial policy on the European scale (which in the document "Europe 2000" is still largely absent and which it is hoped the newly-formed "Committee on Spatial Developmnet" will follow-up) there are no more precise methods, than those adopted since the reform of the funds in 1988, for evaluating the plans, programmes, and projects capable of being funded by the structural funds.

In the following paragraphs, we will again riemphasize the character of these changes in approach from a regional policy to a new territorial policy, and we will try to give a further contribution towards the orientation to be given to the definition of the new guidelines for territorial policy (on a Community level).

# 6. A "Single" Territory

The change in the general lines of the European Regional Policy, which we have just discussed in the previous paragraphs (with its impact on further improvement in the rationale of the allocation of structural funds) requires a more detailed discussion of its conceptual basis and its actual formulation. And, as before, such a discussion should aim at rendering it less indirect and generic, and more direct and "programme-oriented", and at rendering it in such a way more in line with the subsidiarity principle ("Don't do anything that can be done in a sufficient way by the States members and do only that which can be done in a better way at a Community scale, because of the size and outcome of the considered action").

As far as concerns exchange, flow of goods, money and financial services, the creation of the European Economic and Monetary Union (EMU) will bring European countries more closely together. This will only emphasise still further the need to conceive Community policies in terms of being united and integrated, if economic and social cohesion is to be effective.

What should the guidelines of a reform of the European regional policy of the 90's be, in order to truly achieve the objective of greater economic and social cohesion?

If the Community effectively become a *single market* for goods, finances, capital, investment and currency (with the creation of a single monetary unit), and if progress is made with the so-called "Political Union", there does not seem to be any reason why the Community could not also be conceived as a *"single territory", regulated and controlled by a single legal and regulatory system*, so as to ensure — as well as an effective economic and social cohesion — conditions of equal competition and production.

In such a formulation, the "regional" policies of the different member countries should merge and become the "territorial" policy of the Community as a whole.

This policy — in a unitarian way, and through a process of negotiation with national and regional sovereignty and autonomy — should change in character: rather than defining generic regional requisites of "Backwardness" (from ehiche derive the suitability of financial transfer), it should assing functions, roles, protection, incentives and promotion to the different parts of the territory. All this could not be realized without first identifying a *"system of territorial objectives"*, each of which has been carefully studied, comparatively assessed and selected by all at the Community level, and appropriately negotiated with States and Regions.

At the Community level this "territorial policy" could take same form that it has taken in the European country which has been less inclined to an excess of centralized public power and whose constitution is more "federal" than the pthers: the Federal Republic of Germany. In this countr in 1975 — after some years of negotiation between the federal government and the laender governments — a "programme of territorial order" was deliberated (*raumordnung programme*) which represented (according to the write) historically the most advanced form of State-Regional cooperation for the real management of the territory[11].

This German model constitutes in fact the least legal, least imposing, but the one which is the most coherent and "cognitive" of regulations and of reference of all free interventions on the territory: both as far as concerns the blu-print planning by experts and the "plurality" of decision-making by private and public operators. These latter, are in fact destined to increase rather than diminish, in the progressively free competition and exercise of private and public and semi-public profit or non-profit making enterprise.

*Territorial order* is a guarantee of, rather than a threat to, the efficiency of free enterprise for any economic operator, be it public or private. And territorial order at Community level is also a guarantee of free competition and equality of conditions between economic operators in the member states who operate in a single market.

At the European level, on what should this "territorial-order" based?

---

[11] BRD, Federal Ministry of Regional Planning, Building and Urban Development (1975). A good survey (but today largely outdated) of the policies for territorial ordering in European countries was conducted by the EC (DGXVI) in 1975 (EC, Commission, 1975). It would be recommendable to carry out a new one at the earliest opportunity.

## 7. A single system of concepts and indicators concerning the territory

Above all it should be based on a common *concept* and *language*.

When one talks of urban quality, or "urban effect", or protection of the environment, it is important to refer to common and well-defined concepts; otherwise the relationship between a commonly-elaborated policy, or commonly-applied interventions and the expected results will be interpreted differently because the concept from which they started will have been different.

If one is to define what is the "urban function", and the requisites for a better quality of urban life, it is necessary to ensure that these concepts result from a common effort to define these conventionally.

If one is to intervene to protect an area of natural environmental importance (and even more so if these areas are to be defined areas of "European", rather than just national, regional, or local, interest) thus it is desirable that basic concepts which lead to the individualisation of such areas, should have been defined and agreed by all the states *together*: moreover, it would be wise, not to deviate too radically from analogous conceptual devices, which in some fields have arisen from a combination of scientific and cultural knowledge, on a different geographical scale: eg: Council of Europe, OECD, United Nations, UNESCO and other international agencies for scientific and cultural promotion.

If one is to establish infrastructural "axes" of European interest, then it is essential that the concepts of European "interest" be defined with homogeneous criteria at European level.

The first task of a European Territorial Policy oriented at a greater degree of economic and social cohesion should be therefore that of defining in common a *"system of social indicators related to the territory and its use"*. Such a system would constitute a common language, founded on common parameters (either qualitative or quantitive) based in their turn on common measurements and evaluations.

This system of social indicators[12], relating to the territory and its use, would essentially be structured in the following three categories: urban,

---

[12] The most well-known and general work of establishing a system of social indicators was carried out in more than one attempt during the 1960s and the 1970 s by the OECD, and then deplorably interrupted (OECD, 1973, 1974,1976 and 1980).

environmental and infra-structural which would correspond respectively to the three facets of a single territorial policy and its use.

This common definition of a system of social indicators relating to the territory and its use can only be implemented by the Community itself, and in particular by the Commission.

Obviously, the usual recommendation is that this definition be implemented with the collaboration of experts with a certain awareness of the different national conditions and "cultures"; and that it be ratified by decisional organs which equally represent the different national governments. But all this is organic and structurally present in the EC. (It is therefore unbelievable how often it is reported that in Brussels they fail to take into account the autonomy and the decisional participation of the individual national authorities, when these dominate the scene in a form which is almost hegemonic!).

# 8. A "Territorial Framework" to be used as reference for European Regional Policy

In addition to the system of social indicators relating to the territory, which constitute the basis of a common conceptualisation, its first application to real communitary territory could be perfomed upon all those *territorial* realities and phenomena which are of strong and inequivocal European interest.

In other words, what is intended by a "first application" of the system of indicators mentioned above, applied to the real concrete European territory — at least for some of those phenomena which are particularly evident in respect of their common European interest — is the following.

## 8.1. A network of "Urban Regions or Territorial Functional Systems" used as a reference in measuring the needs of the "City-Effect"

The "urban" indicators — as usually considered — will tell us what are the *minimum requirements* of the urban services, and of the cultural, managerial, recreational and economic opportunities in such a way that it will be possible to say that we are benefitting from a *"city-effect"* which is satisfactory for all European citizens (and this is the very foundation of greater economic and social cohesion). If further it is considered that such a city-effect cannot be achieved but for certain specific conditions or for certain minimum levels of population and users, then nothing discourages and everything indeed suggests that the Community itself (and on its behalf the Commission) should study and propose *how to structure and aggregate today's different urban locations in new "urban functional systems" capable of satisfying these minimum requirements.*

This should be a first base of reference for measuring the level of urban well-being and city-effect between comparable units of urban settlements and population; units which represent the same characteristics and the same functions at the outset. We have already talked of European "urban systems" or "urban regions" in the phase of study and analysis: it would be advisable if one could come to propose that the networks of such systems be in some way concretely mapped in the European Territorial Framework, with a view to programming the interventions, in such a way as to evaluate the deficiency of urban services and the conditions necessary for the cityeffect, as lines on which to direct the policies of intervention, but in territorial units which are significant and comparable[13]. More of this in Archibugi (1985); see also Klaassen (1978), Paelinck, ed. (1978), Drewett et al (1992), European Institute of Urban Affairs (1992), Cheshire et al (1986).

## 8.2. A mapping of the principal land-use aims to be planned

If the principles (and connected indicators) of environmental safeguarding (fixed by the system of common indicators mentioned above) suggest that the territory be used according to criteria which respect the different intended vocations, then everything suggest that the Community itself (and on its behalf the Commission) studies and proposes an approx-

---

[13]For some time the concept of "urban network" at Community scale has become widespread. "Europe 2000" (cited in the previous chapter) has made it the subject of a special chapter in its latest document (EC, Commission 1991b) dedicated precisely to the "development of a Community urban system". And the Dutch government, at the same meeting in The Hague in November 1991, presented a report entitled "Urban Network in Europe" (Netherlands Physical Planning Agency, 1991).

Many other studies have been carried out this subject some of which were carried out on behalf of the Commission of the EC.

imate classification of *the aimed use of the territory*: for example that thedy indicate the areas of particular European interest which should be marked for specific operations of conservation of nature and/or landscape; the areas which in virtue of their properties (or absence of properties) most lend themselves to receiving activities with a great negative impact on the environment (large industrial complexes with pollution, energy plants, etc.); the areas which being the sites of certain resources should be prohibited from certain usages and should instead be made available for others, such as hydro-geological constraints (hydric faultus), fluvial and lake margins, forests, conservation of the soil and of the coasts, geological risks of various types etc.)[14]. More on this in Section 9 and in Archibugi (1982b).

## 8.3.  A network of the principal transport and communication infrastructures of European interest

If one considers that an improvement in the system of transport on a European scale is an essential factor for greater economic and social cohesion, above all in order to offer and supply equal conditions of access to the peripheral regions of the Community, then certainly everything suggests that the Community itself (and on its behalf the Commission) should study, design and propose a *network* of essential transport and

---

[14]It is obviously a question of choosing the level of approximation (and perhaps of scale) with which these indications should be made. Some indications in this direction have been gathered in the works (already pointed out in Para. 5) of the "European Conference of Ministers responsible for Physical Planning" (CEMAT), which are performed in the framework of the Council of Europe. What is here asserted regarding the contents of the desired Territorial Framework of reference, also applies equally well to what has been decided in the heart of the council of Europe concerning a "European Schema for Territorial Planning". Despite the fact that the *guidelines* set down by the CEMAT (Council of Europe) haven been till now far more advanced than the works carried out within the EC, it is about time that in this latter body the works of the CEMAT be "overtaken" in the direction indicated, in as much as the political-institutional context, and the very number of the member countries, should be far more favourable towards an efficacious integration of intent and mutual coordination, within the EC rather than in the Council of Europe.
A very important chance for this "overtaking" was provided by the Maastricht Treaty in as far as it enriched the scope of community competence in the field of environmental policy (Title VII, which became XVI in the new Treaty), giving to the Council the possibility of emanating directives concerning *"les mesures concernant l'aménagement du territoire, l'affectation des sols ... la gestion des ressources hydrauliques"*, (Art. 130S, comma 2). This point is very important and opens new horizons for community territory policy, which it is necessary now to enrich in content.

communications which can function as a guideline to the national and community interventions to be undertaken in the field of transport and communication infrastructures[15].

With all this one would achieve the construction of a "Territorial Framework of reference" for a regional and territorial policy, as well as an "environmental" one, on an European scale, agreed upon by the different countries and constructed in a homogeneous, harmonic and comparable manner.

This so-called "Territorial Framework of reference" which the Italian Minister for the Environment has in recent months been putting together on a national Italian scale[16] — would serve as an instrument for assessing the *conformity* of programmes and regional development projects, as well as of the various economic, productivity and infrasrtuctural investments, with an overall plan for development and use of European environmental and territorial resources. It would also serve to assess the conformity and compatibility of not only community programmes, but also national programmes to general social, economic and environmental objectives on an European scale[17].

## 9. The contents of the territorial framework to be used as a reference

In order to demonstrate what the possible contents of such a "territorial framework" might be, we will now list here the most important phenomena, useful for the policy-orientated guide-lines of the territory and for the determination of territorial policies, which should be "mapped":

---

[15]After many years (more than ten) of requests for the conception of a financial instrument to promote large infrastructure projects of European interest (and after a proposal made by the Commission in 1986 for an ad hoc Fund) finally in 1989 a first 3-Year (1990–1992) Programme of action was put under way — a programme which allowed the Community to financially distribute to infrastructural transportation projects of European interest. But a mapping of the priorities which can favour a greater economic and social cohesion is still not clear. See the Commission's pamphlet *"Transport in Europe"* (EC, COmmission, 1991c).

[16]In this regard the reader is referred to: *Ministero dell'Ambiente e Consiglio Nazionale delle Ricerche* (1990). See also Archibugi (1992).

[17]This is also the orientation of the "Council of Ministers for regional policies and territorial planning", which, in a preliminary document of the Commission on "Europe 2000", affirmed that the approach chosen was that of not proposing a *Master Plan* but a territorial *Framework of Reference* (see EC, Commission, Europe 2000, etc.,p.35, 1991b).

1.  A map of the "urban systems" or "urban regions", on a European scale, on which one is able to compare the different socio-economic and environmental levels of well-being and to recommend adequate policies aimed at bridging the deficiencies and shortcomings with respect to certain minimum Europea standards[18].

2.  A map of urban use of the territory, of its classifications, and of the policies that it is advisable to adopt for each of them, regarding habitative density, traffic, and social and environmental infrastructure[19].

3.  A map of the different "areas of natural interest" and the different types of conservation and management which might be recommendedfor each of them[20].

4.  A map of the territories with a touristic "vocation" due to landscaping and naturalistic factors and which are to be preserved for intensive developments of other productive activities, and which are to be marked for a gradual environmental and historico-cultural recovery.

5.  A map of the usage potentialities of the different coastal areas and seafronts with an indication of the policies and the interventions to be adopted for a desirable management of each of them.

---

[18] In "Europe 2000", this map has been drafted only for what concerns the "actual" situation (see Chapter on: "the development of an Community Urban System"). A praiseworthy effort has certainly been made in defining the same phenomen on an Europea scale using methods capable of guaranteeing homogeneous readings. But this effort is insufficient. The territorial frame work must also indicate the territorial "guidelines" for the future development of the European urban system, not only following the methods which ensure homogeneous readings (which is an essential requisite for any comparability), but also following homogeneous methods for the determination of the terriotorial objectives of growth of the urban systems (obviously not ignoring contraints, tendencies,intrinsic dynamics, etc.).

Some years ago, the Commission of the EC promoted research (EC Commission, 1987b) which went beyond defining European "functional urban regions" (Fur, *Functional Urban Regions*), the lines analog which the map of which we are talking should develop its characteristics of a programming nature.

A praiseworthy, but insufficient attempt to fix the strategic criteria in this regard has been made in the report on the "European Schema for Territorial Planning" recently compiled in the framework of the CEMAT (CEMAT 1991, see page 116 and following).

Among the literature available on this specific theme are found the works of Hall and Hay (1980), and a study conducted by the Commission of the EC by the "Fere Consultants" group (1991) on the "middle-sized cities" in Europe and their role.

[19] On this point there is work of the Corine Programme (EC, 1989, 1990b) which should be followed-up and strengthened.

[20] As an application of a proposal made under the direction of the Council (Com–88–381 final).

6. A map of the different areas of high industrial concentration with an indication of the policies of reconversion and management which it is advaisable to apply to each type.
7. A map of the areas according the different capacity of agricultural land-use of the soil from the point of view of environmental protection.
8. A map of the forest areas indicating their respective function of usage according to criteria of optimisation of the impact on the environment.
9. A map of the different agricultural areas according to their polluting potential with an indication of the desirable policies of reconversion and management for each respective area typology.
10. A map of the territories subject to natural risk, to allow a common classification of such risk, and a common classification of the usage constraints to be applied to such territories.
11. A map of the hydric potentialities and of the different typologies of intervention and safeguards appropriate to each area Defined.
12. A map of the areas according to the different environmental climate characteristic.
13. A map of the functional network of the transport systems of European interest, as they apply to a policy of grater socio-economic cohesion[21].
14. A map of the network of technological infrastructures of "European interest", functional in developing a policy of greater socio-economic cohesion (one thinks of energy-ducts: electricity and hydrocarbons, etc. and structures of communications and telecommunications).

These, and other eventual "maps" which might prove useful, would constitute a "Framework" of reference for evaluating the conformity of numerous projects and programmes of territorial interventions — effected on a European or national scale, or even at a local (regional) level — with a programme of "greater socio-economic cohesion", a conformity which would be guaranteed by an optimal destination of usage of the European territorial resources.

## 10. From the regional policy to a new territorial policy

The system of territorial indicators and the territorial Framework of reference for the interventions are two of the instruments of "evaluation"

---

[21] Some works of the Commission (Dg VII) have gone in this direction.

which concern *the territorial and regional conditions* of a greater economic and social cohesion. In fact they are two instruments which derive essentially from a renewed conception of regional policy, which we have summarily described with the phrase: "from the regional policy to a new territorial policy".

In this renewed conception, the regional policy is no longer considered as a policy of "compensation" for the damages that a greater degree of economic and monetary integration (for example the EMU) might bring to the more backward regions of the Community. Nor is the regional policy any longer considered to be directed *exclusively* to particular regions of the Community (the "eligible" regions)[22]: those regions which represent — in their undifferentiated territory — some particular "indicators of backwardness" (whose measurement is always more problematic, as will be explained in the next paragraph without a consideration of the real nature, of the state and of the destinations of the territories in question).

The regional policy, in its renewed conception, assumes instead the charactre of a "spatial" policy, of a "territorial" policy — as ot is called. And as such it is no longer aimed at particular regions of the Community, but at the *whole territory*, according to its different properties and specifications and according to the priorities that such properties and specifications dictate. Such a policy is therefore aimed, rather than at indistinct regions, at specific areas of the territory in as much as it is — on the whole-articulated according to its different typologies (the abovementioned properties and specifications) of areas: typologies which are naturally to be defined in common, with common criteria, on a Community-wide scale[23].

From all this there follows also a renewal in the conception of the relationships between regional policy (and use of its instruments, for ex-

---

[22] This is still the optic of certain studies promoted by the Commission; for example that performed by "Columbus Associates" on *"Regional Implications of Economic and Monetary Union"* (Columbus Associates, 1991).

[23] This new optic present in many official documents. It has already been that "Europe 2000" tends towards this renewed conception of regional policy. The document which however explains most clearly the contrast between the two concwptions is not the of the European Community, but that of the Council of Europe. In particular, in the already-mentioned report compiled by the the CEMAT, both "approaches" to European territorial planning are amply described: the *"regional"* approach and the *"guiding image"* approach which regards the settlement equilibrium and the functional network of activities which conform to a rational "use of the territory" (see CEMAT, 1991, p.69–172).

ample the ERDF at Community level) and a policy for economic and social cohesion.

Previously, in the *old concept*, in the framework of the old regional policy, economic and social cohesion was seen essetially as the product of the tendency for the generic indicators (the Gnp in practice), of the regions defined as "least favoured", to approach the *European average* for those same indicators.

Now, in the *new concept*, cohesion becomes the product of a complex operation of *"common evaluation"* of the destined usage of the territory and of the tendency for the individual indicators (urban, environmental, social etc.) to approach *European standards* which have been defined for each phenomenon that is considered significant and comparable on a Community basis.

We are therefore talking of a new conception of "cohesion" which is more complex, but also less vague and misleading; and certainly scientifically more correct.

A territorial policy (seen as a renewed version of the "old-style" regional policy) comes to the aid of this more correct assessment of "cohesion",through its conceptual deffinition and practical delimitations (applied to the real Community territory) of those territorial "units" — called "territorial-urban systems" or "urban regions" — of which we have talked in the preceding paragraphs. Units which allow a comparison to be made of the data which concerns them (and which are not just the product of some occasional and casual administrative delimitation which the history of the member countries has handde down to us!).

And, moreover, it is in this very sense that the problem of "accounting" of economic and social cohesion is to be posed.

## 11. "Accounting" of economic and social cohesion

If one wants to *measure* the state of economic and social cohesion (or of non-cohesion) then one must use appropriate "units of measurment" or "indicators". And moreover one must apply them to appropriate statistical units of territorial survey.

Up until now cohesion has been measured on the basis of certaim generic indicators (in practice only on the GNP) and moreover for large

administrative units (countries and regions) of little significance as territorial units for data-collection.

It is more than ever before opportune that the Community (and on
its behalf the Commission) should begin to seriously study and propose a
"system of accounting of economic and social cohesion" founded on:

— appropriate statistical units (the territorial-urban systems mentioned
 above);

— distinct indicators for the different services and phenomena which constitute environmental well-being.

In this way a policy of intervention could be concretely oriented towards the real needs and the real drawbacks of each territorial-urban
system with respect to the corresponding Community standards.

Such a system of accounting, so performed, is an indispensable pre-
requisite for a new regional policy of the type outined here[24].


# 12. Territorial policy and social policy

The outline of a new territorial policy, as a concrete means of management of the traditional objectives of a regional policy, and as a correct
way of conceiving a "greater economic and social cohesion", has a direct
bearing on the objectives of a social Community policy, at least on that
part of those objectives which regard the quality of life (social services,
housing, health and education etc.).

In fact there are some social needs whose most appropriate dimensions
are bound to "residential conditions and therefore to a "territorial-urban
system" of programmatic reference which we have already descibed; it
also constitues one of the most efficient means of measuring the actual
state of economic and social cohesion between the different territories of
the Community.

Other social needs, however, can be measured without an appropriate
statistical territorial unit of reference. They cannot therefore be reduced
to territorial comparisons, or they might concern any unit of comparison (be it family, geographic area, village, town of whatever size, region,
country, continent, etc.).

---

[24]The territorial dimension of the new "European Economic Accounting" is strongly
envisaged in recent works by Stuart Holland (1987 and 1990).

Economic and social "cohesion", in this latter case, thakes on the aspect of coordination and harmonisation of different social policies.

This harmonisation and coordination together give the "cohesion" an "indirect" contribution: and this time it cannot be criticised because it is not possible to do otherwise. In this case, "cohesion" should be intended as *a common mode of operation, rather than in the sense of common level of well-being and of living conditions.* Cohesion — in this case — is to be intended as cohesion in the manner of conceiving the role of the state, of civil society, of the single operators, all of which can be translated into common methods of management and common institutional formulae[25].

It is what we will call "society policy" (and not "social", exactly because we wish to distinguish it from the conventional approach of the latter).

This type of cohesion should be analysed under the profile of the management forms of the following aspects:

— the management of the relationship between the state and non-statal social initiative;

— the management of the operational programmes and projects aimed at cohesion itself and — more generally — those general processes of "management of public decision-making", above all in the fieldsof public expenditure, of destination of the territory, and social regulation.

In both cases we arre talking of cohesion between the manner in which to implement, or intoducw, processes of evaluation and the corresponding social programming.

Economic and social cohesion — in this sense — is no longer a cohesion of material conditions of life, but rather of the ways of conceiving the functioning of society and of social progress itself.

---

[25] Since the "differences" in the manner of conceiving such questions can also be found between groups, classes and parties even within a single country, greater cohesion between the different countries at Community level must take the shape of greater cohesion between the different "majorities" which might be formed in this or that country. It is inevitable that a reflection of all this will be seen in the European Parliament.

# Bibliography

Archibugi F., 1977, *The Mezzogiorno Policy in Italy: A Retrospective Analysis and Evaluation*, Paper submitted to the UNIDO Seminar "On Industrial Oriject Promotion in Backward Regions", Istanbul 4–15 Sept 1977.

Archibugi F., 1978, *Capitalist Planning in Question*, [in:] S. Holland (ed.), *Beyond Capitalist Planning*, Blackwell, Oxford.

Archibugi F., 1982a, *Une nouvelle politique regionale pour l'Europe*, Paper given at a Semoinar of the "Fundacion IESA" and of the "Frederick Ebert Stiftung", Madrid 20–21 July 1982.

Archibugi F., 1982b, *Principi di pianificazione regionale* [Principles of Regional Planning], Angeli, Milan.

Archibugi F., 1985, *La politica dei sistemi urbani* [Urban Systems Policy], Centro di studi e piani economici, Roma.

Archibugi F., 1992, *The Quadroter Project: An Ecosystemic Reading of the Italian Territory*, Paper given at a Conference organised by the Territorial Science Department, Faculty of Architecture, Polytechnic of Milan, on the theme "The Ecological Aspects of Territorial Planning", Milan 12–13 Nov 1992, Planning Studies Centre, Rome.

BRD, Federal Ministry of Regional Planning, Building and Urban Development, 1975, *Regional Planning Programme for the territory of the FRG (Federal Regional Planning Programme)*, Agreed upon by the Conference of Ministers for regional Planning on 14.2.1975 and by the Federal Government on 23.4.1975.

CEMAT, Conferences Europeenne des Ministres responsables de l'amenagement du territoire, 1991, *Schema europeen d'amenagement du territoire*, Conseil de l'Europe, Strasbourg.

Cheshire P. C., D. G. Hay & G. Carbonaro, 1986, *Urban Problems in Western Europe: A. Review and Synthesis of Recent Literature*, EC Commission, Luxembourg.

Columbus Associates, 1991, *Regional Policy Implications of EMU* (prepared for the EC DG XVI), Brussels.

Drewett R., R. Knight, U. Scubert, 1992, *The Future of European Cities, The Role of Science and Technology*, EC FAST Programme.

EC Commission (Commission des CE), 1975, *Les systemes de Planification physique dans le pays de la CEE*, DGXVI, Bruxelles.

EC Commission (Commission des CE), 1987a, *Portare l'Atto unico al successo: una nuova frontiera per l'Europa ("Piano Delors")* [Bringing the Single Act to Success: A New Frontier for Europe ("Delors Plan"), Communicazione della Commissione 19.2.87.

EC Commission (Commission des CE), 1987b, *Urban Problems and Regional Policy in the EC*, Joint Centre for Land Development Studies, University of Reading, Bruxeles.

EC Commission (Commission des CE), 1989, *Corine, Data Base Manual*, June 1989.

EC Commission (Commission des CE), 1990a, *Guide to the Reform of the Community's Structural Funds*, Document XXII — 16–90.

EC Commission (Commission des CE), 1990b, *The European Highspeed Train Network*, DGVII.

EC Commission (Commission des CE), 1991a, *Annual Report on the Implementation of the Reform of the Structural Funds* (1989), Brussels-Luxembourg.

EC Commission (Commission des CE), 1991b, *Europe 2000: Outlook for the Development of Community Territory*, Directorate-General for Regional Policy, Communication from the Commission to the Council and the European Parliament, Brussels-Luxembourg.

EC Commission (Commission des CE), 1991c, *Transport in Europe*, Bruxelles.

EC Commission (Commission des CE), 1992, *Second Annual Report on the Implementation of the Reform of the Structural Funds 1990*, Brussels-Luxembourg.

European Institute of Urban Affairs, 1992, *Urbanisation and the Functions of Cities in the European Community*, A Report to the Commission of the European Communities, Directorate General for Regional Policy (DG XVI).

Fere Consultants, 1991, *The International Development of Intermediary Size Cities in Europe: Strategies and Networks*, Study prepared for the EC Commission, Paris.

Hall P. & D. Hay, 1980, *Growth Centres in the European Urban System*, Heinemann.

Holland S., 1976, *The Regional Problem*, Macmillan, London.

Holland S., 1987, *The Global Economy*, Vol. 2 of *Toward a New Political Economy*, Weidenfield and Nicholson, London.

Holland S., 1990, *Accounting and Accountability — Towards a New Framework for Regional and National Accounts in the European Community* (Report to the European University Institute on "Multidimensional Analysis of EMU in the EC, Florence, 14–16 February 1990).

Keating M. & B. Jones, 1985, *Regions in the European Community*, Clarendon, Oxford.

Klaassen L. H., 1978, *Desurbanisation at Réurbanisation en Europe Occidentale*, [in:] Paelinck J. H. P. (ed.) *La structure urbaine en Europe occidentale*, Takefield, Farnborough.

Ministero dell'Ambiente e Consiglio Nazionale delle Ricerche, 1990, *Quadro territoriale di riferimento per la politica ambientale (Quadroter)* [Territorial Framework of Reference for Environmental Policy — Quadroter], Rome.

Molle W. et al, 1980, *Regional Disparity and Economic Development in the EES*, Saxon House.

Netherlands, The National Physical Planning Agency, 1991, *Union Networks in Europe*, The Hague.

OECD, 1973, *Liste de preoccupations sociales communes à la plus part des pays de l'Ocde*, Paris.

OECD, 1974, *Elements subjectifs du bien-être*, Serie Documents, Paris.

OECD, 1976, *Mesure du bien-être social: progres accomplis dans l'elaboration des indicateurs sociaux*, OECD, Paris.

OECD, 1980, *Les indicateurs sociaux. Resultats jusqu'en avril 1979 et perspectives futures*, OECD, Paris.

Paelinck J. H. P. (ed.), 1978, *Le structure urbaine en Europe occidentale*, Takefield, Farnborough.

Pinder D., 1983, *Regional Economic Development and Policy: Theory and Practice in the European Community*, Allen and Unwin.

Seers D. et al, 1982, *Integration and Unequal Development*, Macmillan.

Antoni Kukliński
European Institute
for Regional and Local Development
Warsaw

# THE CONCEPT OF REGION IN THEORETICAL AND PRAGMATIC PERSPECTIVE

## Introduction

The seminar — Regional Question in Europe — is an intellectual inducement — to have a hard look at the concept of region presented in the elegant paper by Z. Chojnicki i T. Czyż[1].

This is a traditional approach in our field. I do not know yet how to define the concept of region as a tool to analyze the reality of the turn of the XX and XXI century. However, I would like to propose a framework of a discussion which may lead to new theoretical and pragmatic approaches as a background of a revised definition of this concept. It is important to see not only the formal shape of the region but also the contents of the region as a political, social, economic and cultural phenomenon.

---

[1] Z. Chojnicki, T. Czyż, *Region, Regionalisation, Regionalism*, [in:] *Dilemmas of Regional Policies in Eastern and Central Europe*, Editors: A. Kukliński, G. Gorzelak, Series: Regional and Local Studies, no 8, European Institute for Regional and Local Development, University of Warsaw, Warszawa 1992, p. 419–444.

This framework can be seen as a set of following questions:
I. The region and the transition from fordist to post-fordist space.
II. The region and the globalisation of the economy and society —
transnational corporations.
III. The region and the new European space.
IV. The region and the regional question.
V. The region and the renaissance of locality.
VI. The region as a quasi state and as a quasi firm.

# 1. The region and the transition from fordist to post-fordist space

In the sixties and seventies a deep structural change took place in the leading capitalistic countries[2]. This change was described as transition from Fordism to Post Fordism as a system of the organisation not only of production but also of the economy and society at large. One of the fundamental notions analyzing the *modus operandi* of the new system — is flexibility.

In this context we can say:
— primo: that the region of Fordism was operating in a relatively stiff space
— secundo: that the region of Post Fordism is operating in a relatively flexible space.

# 2. The region and the globalisation of the economy and society — transnational corporations

The region is operating now in a global economy and society[3]. The transnational corporation is the most important locomotive of this globalisation processes. In this context — we have to answer the question

---

[2] A.J.M. Roobeek, *The crisis in Fordism and the rise of a new technological paradigm*, [in:] *Globality versus Locality*. Editor: A. Kukliński, University of Warsaw, Faculty of Geography and Regional Studies, Institute of Space Economy, Warsaw 1990, p. 139–166.

[3] J Lambooy, *Local and Global Economy; a New Dilemma?* [in:] *Globality versus Locality*, op.cit., p. 9–29.

related to the placebound or placeless corporation. In a paper published in 1990 I have answered this qestion in the following way[4].

*"The tranational corporation as both placeless and placebound. They are placeless according to the logic of technology and economy which has drastically reduced the friction of space and distance. From this point of view, the corporation has an increasingly nomadic existence, having wide choices among a seemingly innumerable number of places. However, an important qualification must be introduces: the corporation is looking for a place with strictly defined qualities of economic, social, political and natural environment.*

*If this qualities are important for the corporation, then it will be restricted perhaps not to one place, but to a limited number of places of a certain type. In practical terms, the choice of the corporation falls within a spectrum from placeless to placebound.*

*The spatial behaviour of the corporation is not one-way process i.e. the decision of the corporation must receive a positive response of the local and regional community. Many local and regional communities in Europe are highly selective in the acceptance of external inducements for development generated by large corporations and other enterprises and institutions."*

## 3. The region and the new European space

The new European space is created by the deep structural transformation of our continent at the turn of the XX and XXI century[5].

In this framework we can observe the emergence of new approaches to the new perception of region as an European phenomenon related to regional policy designed and implemented by the European Communities and by the Council of Europe.

In this activities we should see not only the institutional dimension but also the new perception of region as an European phenomenon related to

---

[4]A. Kukliński, *Efficiency versus Equality: Old Dilemmas and New Approaches in Regional Policy*, [in:] *Regional and Industrial Policy Research Series*, no 8, European Policies Research Centre, University of Strathclyde, Glasgow 1990, p. 1–18.

[5]A. Kukliński, *Geography of New Europe*, Colloquy: "The Challenges facing European society with the approach of the year 2000: outlook for sustainable development and its implications on regional/spatial planning" Roubaix, October 22–23, 1992.

regional policy designed and implemented by the European Communities and by the Council of Europe.

# 4. The region and the regional question

In the framework of our Seminar this is the most important topic discussed inter alia in the interesting but also controversial paper of B. Jałowiecki[6].

In this context I would like to say — that the regional question is in most cases seen as a situation of conflict motivated by socio-cultural, ethnic, political and religious consideratiwnes. The process of conflict resolution in this case is extremale complicated and difficult — sometimes — almost hopeless (compare the case of former Yugoslavia).

This regional question is now a Pan-European problem — with different features in different parts of Western, Central and Eastern Europe. Our Seminar should be an important contribution to the understanding of these questions.

# 5. The region and the renaissance of locality

In the Post-Fordist space the region is supported by and confronted with the renaissance of locality.

This renaissance is discussed by S. Boisier[7] in the following way:

*"Modern man's renewed sense of »territoriality« or »return to his home turf«has been prompted in part by the collapse of the Welfare State and the major social support structures that characterized it, which now increases the tendency to feel solidarity with **local areas**. In part, too, in this crisis of modern rationality, with its explosion of heterogeneity and diversity, local territory has emerged as the synthesis between alienation and individuality.*

---

[6]B. Jałowiecki, *The Regional Question*, [in:] *Dilemmas of Regional Policies in Eastern and Central Europe*, op. cit., p. 445–464.

[7]S. Boisier, *Regional Management in the new International Order: Quasi-States and Quasi-Firms*, Santiago de Chile, 1992, ILPES.

> *The crisis of the modern age has been interpreted as a conflict between »territory and function« or between the universal »code« and the specific »territorial anticode«."*

## 6. The region as quasi state and as a quasi firm

This is an extremely useful methological and pragmatic observation of S. Boisier — which is an innovative inducement in our field. Let us quote the last part of the summary of the excellent peper of S. Boisier[8].

*"The third section introduces the concepts of »quasi-State« and »quasi-firm« as two basic pillars, one political and other managerial, which establish the parameters of a modern regional vision.*

*The region as **quasi-State** (»quasi« in the sense of shortfall) is the product of the implementation of political and territorial decentralisation policies which make regions into autonomous entities.*

*The region as **quasi-firm** (»quasi« in the sense of excess) is the product of applying strategic corporate planning criteria to the management of regional development, rather than becoming mired in the concepts of traditional public-sector planning of decades past.*

***Identity** and, as a consequence, **culture**, are again surfacing as key elements in this regional thinking."*

## Conclusion

Let us read once more the elegant paper of Z. Chojnicki, T. Czyż in order to see the great change in the perception of the regional problem related to the shift from fordist to post-fordist space. The concept of the region must be analyzed in a broad framework of changing relations — presented *inter alia* in the volume — *Globality versus Locality*[9].

---

[8] S. Boisier, op.cit.

[9] A. Kukliński, *Globality versus Locality*. Editor: A Kukliński, University of Warsaw, Faculty of Geography and Regional Studies, Institute of Space Economy, Warsaw 1990, p. 129–138.

In a more general perspective it is worth while to look into the challenging book of Paul Kennedy[10].

---

[10]P. Kennedy, *Preparing for the XXI Century*, Random House 1993, see The New York Review — February 2 1993; compare *Looking back from 2992 — A World History* — Chapter 13 — *The Disastrous 21st Century*, The Economist — London — December 26, 1992 – January 8, 1993.

Zbyszko Chojnicki
Institute of Socio-Economic Geography
and Spatial Planning
Adam Mickiewicz University
Poznań

# THE REGION IN A PERSPECTIVE OF CHANGE

## Introduction

The aim of this paper is to discuss some issues connected with changes in the character and role of the region that are a part of contemporary socio-economic transformations.

Recently there has been a livening up of the discussion on this subject. In the article opening this conference, Kukliński (1993: 1) writes: *"I do not know yet how to define the concept of region as a tool to analyse the reality of the turn of the XX and XXI century. However, I would like to propose a framework of a discussion which may lead to new theoretical and pragmatic approaches as a background of a revised definition of this concept. It is important to see not only the formal shape of the region, but also the contents of the region as a political, social, economic and cultural phenomenon"*.

Let us therefore consider, first, what changes have been taking place in the forms of socio-economic organisation, or where they lead; and secondly, what transformations spatial and regional structures have been undergoing, and let us try to find out whether these changes justify the formulation of a new concept of a region different from the traditional one. In our discussion we shall rely on the concept of postmodernisation, whose core is the transition from the Fordist to a post-Fordist organisation of production.

# 1. Changes in the forms of socio-economic organisation

The opinion that has been gaining ground recently is that advanced countries have been going through postmodern transformations which begin to shape new forms of socio-economic organisation and structures. It is assumed that these processes tend to change the present, crisis-generating forms of organisation and structures. This assumption follows from the observation that the economies of advanced countries seem to show a number of symptoms of a structural crisis which requires precisely such transformations in the forms of socio-economic organisation to be overcome. Thus, the hypothesis is put forward that these transformations consist in a shift from the Fordist to a post-Fordist organisation, identified with a flexible organisation. Naturally, this is not an exclusive view, because there are others seeking the roots of the slackening or crisis of the economy in excessive state interventionism and a departure from a purely liberal moneyed-market economy on the one hand, and in the global crisis of the capitalist economy as a social formation on the other.

The Fordist forms of organisation are responsible for the loss of development dynamics and several other negative socio-economic phenomena. The shift from the Fordist to a post-Fordist organisation is considered in two approaches: a narrower one, focusing on the abandonment of the Fordist organisation of work and production, and a broader one, regarding the transformation of the whole system of capitalist economy, and especially its Fordist regime of accumulation and regulation. These changes are interpreted in terms of a modern-postmodern turn (cf. Harvey 1990, Chojnicki 1993).

A fundamental question is the definition of the nature of the emerging post-Fordist forms of organisation termed flexible organisation, or flexible accumulation and regulation. According to Harvey (1990: 147), *"Flexible accumulation (...) is marked by a direct confrontation with rigidities of Fordism. It rests on flexibility with respect to labour processes, labour mar-*

*kets, products and patterns of consumption. It is characterized by the emergence of entirely new sectors of production, new ways of providing financial services, new markets, and, above all, greatly intensified rates of commercial, technological, and organisation innovation. It has entrained rapid shifts in the patterning of uneven development, both between sectors and between geographical regions, giving rise, for example, to a vast surge in so-called »service-sector« employment as well as to entirely new industrial ensembles in hitherto underdeveloped regions".*

Apart from the view represented, among others, by Harvey (1990), that the emergence of the new flexible regime of accumulation and regulation is a new form of organisation of the socio-economic system and a successor to Fordism, there is also the opinion, expressed by Amin and Robins (1990), that it is too soon yet to proclaim the appearance of such a form of organisation. Therefore, while the question of whether the ongoing changes will eventually produce a new, mature form of the organisation of the economic system is still open, it might be useful to watch out for the symptoms of such an organisation being formed.

Without going into details of the nature of flexible organisation, let us pass on to the subject of how it takes shape in the sphere of spatial structure.

## 2. Changes in the nature and role of spatial and regional structures

From the point of view that is of interest to us here, a crucial issue is the impact of postmodern processes, especially a flexible organisation of the economy, on spatial and regional structures considered both in terms of a variety of socio-economic, political and cultural activities and in terms of different spatial scales. The discussion on this subject, however, does not yield a homogeneous picture of change, but only partial hypotheses requiring verification and elaboration. Therefore, I shall restrict myself to remarks on only two issues: 1) changes in the regional organisation of production, and 2) changes in the state-region relation.

## 2.1. Changes in the regional organisation of production

The conception of the postmodernisation of the economy holds that postindustrialisation, small business and a flexible manufacturing are the main components, and also factors, of change. The last has the greatest importance. Flexibility is an attribute of three elements of the production process: 1) an adaptable, reprogrammmable technology, 2) a dispersal of organisational authority and responsibility, so that differentiated organisational segments are free to stay in contact with and respond to market developments, and 3) workers with an expanded capacity and freedom to acquire skills and knowledge and to apply them in decisive ways in order to enhance productive capacity (Crook et al. 1992: 181). Thus, the principal components of flexible manufacturing are: flexible technology, flexible organisation, and flexible labour.

Although expressed sporadically, the view that a new regional organisation of production has already been formed in consequence of the operation of flexible manufacturing (cf. Sunlay 1992: 66) is not justified. What has taken shape, though, are new tendencies changing various components of the regional organisation of the economy. The more important among them include:

a) A shift from internal economies (vertical integration) to external economies (vertical disintegration). According to Scott (1988), the search for external economies has been fundamental to flexible accumulation. It has led to the rise of new localisation of high technology and craft industries, often away from older centres of Fordist industry.

b) An increase in the spatial concentration of flexible manufacturing industries resulting from heightened intensity of external linkages and reinforced by labour turnover and the adaptability of local labour markets with a higher level of labour flexibility (Domański 1992).

c) The development of new agglomerations and industrial districts in advanced countries based on localisation economies and urbanisation economies connected with the vertical disintegration of production (Domański 1992).

d) The development of a so-called 'technopolis' within an urban centre which are clusters of research organisations and universities, enterprises, and financial and economic institutions that generate technological innovations initiating the processes of a region's economic growth (Benko 1991).

This, of course, is not an exhaustive list of the new tendencies altering the spatial and regional structure of the economy. The discussion and research on the subject have only just started; this is a stage of posing problems rather than obtaining reliable results.

Closely related to this set of problems is the research on the structure and development of regions with a flexible organisation of production. Its results show that besides new factors brought about by postmodernisation tendencies, a big role is played by both traditional regional or local values and cultural elements, and new postmodernisation ones associated with the culture of entrepreneurship, the setting of fashion and the introduction of consumerism, ecological considerations, etc. They form specific 'regional syndromes', hardly yielding to typology. There are also opinions that these changes are multi-directional and chaotic, and unpredictable as to effects.

## 2.2. Changes in the state-region relations

Apart from changes in the structure of the regional economy, another significant component of postmodernisation is the change in the mutual relations between the state and the region. They determine the position and role of the region.

When considering the state-region relations one should take into account an area which is a unit of the territorial organisation of the state. The territorial organisation of a country is a single- or multi-level system of territorial units into which it is divided, mostly to facilitate administrative performance and regional and local activities.

The postmodernisation conception assumes that the modern corporate state has been undergoing structural change caused by the system's crisis and disfunctionality. Its result is the process of devolution of state power. According to Crook et al. (1992: 80), four main aspects of the change can be distinguished:

1) a horizontal or functional redistribution of powers and responsibilities from central government to autonomous corporate bodies (trade unions, industrial federations, specialised agencies);

2) a vertical redistribution of powers and responsibilities by decentralisation 'downwards' to self-governing bodies, local groups and civic initiatives;

3) the marketisation and privatisation of previously state-run enter-prises, and

4) the globalisation and externalisation of responsibilities and powers by shifting 'upwards' to supra-state bodies.

These processes converge, reinforce one another and become global trends which cut across political divisions and systems. The change they bring is labelled 'rolling back the state' or a change 'towards a minimum state'.

Although decentralisation processes that shift governmental powers from a centre to multiple territorial units are very important in altering the state-region relations, equally influential are the remaining aspects or trends of state devolution. It looks as follows.

(1) A horizontal or functional decentralisation strengthening the role of non-governmental organisations releases regional initiatives and ac-tion suited to local conditions and based on partnership and loose co-ordination.

(2) The role of vertical decentralisation in regional development is very well known. It is worth emphasising, however, that it not only involves the decentralisation of decision-making and implementing them in the conditions of better local information; it also facilitates the formation of regulatory mechanisms effectively rooted in specific regional or local conditions.

(3) The effectiveness of the processes of privatisation and marketisa-tion is determined regionally; it can be the principal process changing a region's economic structure and its actual position in the inter-regional system. However, its effects must be balanced against high social costs. Positive results of privatisation do not change the nature of the state-region relations, but may be the basis for expanded independence of re-gions.

(4) At a regional scale, globalisation, which is usually associated with economic integration and an international division of labour, can result in a change in some aspects of a region's status, namely elevating it, owing to certain relations, to the level of international links and appropriate regulations, as in the case of Euroregions or so-called frontier regions.

Naturally, these problems do not exhaust issues connected with the change in the character and role of the region; I only want to draw atten-tion to the emerging tendencies.

# 3. Conclusion

The analysis of transformations of spatial socio-economic structures that are taking place as part of postmodernisation processes shows that a region is implicitly taken to be a spatial unit or an area which is either (1) a structure (system) or geographical formation determined socially and economically, or (2) an instrument for organising socio-political activity. Paraphrasing Gilbert's (1988: 209) words, one can say that in the first approach a region is a spatial and local response to capitalist processes, and in the other, a spatial medium for socio-political interaction. They correspond to the 'traditional' understanding of a region as (1) a social-territorial object or system, and (2) a tool for action (cf. Chojnicki, Czyż 1992). It should be noted, however, that the two concepts are compatible in a way, and one turns into the other. Their content and scope are subject to change owing to the operation of new socio-economic, political and cultural processes, and are deeply embedded in the fabric of society. The nature and role of these processes alter; for example, recently we can observe a surge in nationalist movements or the activity of groups explicitly engaged in struggle over the definition and extent of regions as political territories associated with those groups (Murphy 1991).

Both these concepts invite criticism because of their excessively high degree of indeterminacy and identity problems. Of course, researchers are free to make any attempts to formulate new concepts of a region, but they usually turn out to be modifications or more concrete restatements of those offered so far. What one should not do, however, is to give a region a purely formal character reducing its function to that of an umbrella for subsuming only spatial grouping aspects or spatial co-ordinates. What seems to be the key to a further development and elucidation of the concept of a region is the explanation of the influence of socio-economic, political and cultural processes on the shaping of a region's character.

# References

Amin A., Robins K., 1990, *The re-emergence of regional economics? The mythical geography of flexible accumulation.* Environment and Planning D: Society and Space 8, 7–34.

Benko G., 1991, *Géographie des technopôles* Paris, Masson.

Chojnicki Z., 1993, *Postmodern changes in the global socio-economic order.* Unpublished, pp. 44.

Chojnicki Z., Czyż T., 1992, *Region, regionalisation, regionalism,* [In:] Kukliński A., Gorzelak G. (eds), *Dilemmas of regional policies in Eastern and Central Europe.* Regional and Local Studies Series, 8, Warsaw, University of Warsaw, 419–444.

Crook S., Pakulski J., Waters M., 1992, *Postmodernisation. Change in advanced society,* London, Sage Publications.

Domański B., 1992, *Postfordowski elastyczny model produkcji a jej przestrzenna organizacja.* [In:] Chojnicki Z. (ed.), *Studia geograficzne przemian społeczno-gospodarczych,* Biuletyn KPZK PAN 159, Warszawa, PWN, 49–73.

Gilbert A., 1988, *The new regional geography in English- and French-speaking countries,* Progress in Human Geography 12, 208–228.

Harvey D., 1990, *The condition of postmodernity,* Cambridge, Black well.

Kukliński A., 1993, *The concept of region in theoretical and pragmatic perspective.* Unpublished, pp. 4.

Murphy A.B., 1991, *Regions as social constructs: the gap between theory and practice,* Progress in Human Geography 15/1, 22–35.

Scott A., 1988, *New industrial spaces,* London, Pion.

Sunley P., 1992, *An uncertain future: a critique of post-Keynesian economic geographies,* Progress in Human Geography 16/1, 58–70.

Guy Loinger
Groupe d'Etude International
Sur les Stratégies Territoriales
et l'Economie Locale
Paris

# PROSPECTIVE ET TERRITOIRES: PENSEE SYSTEMIQUE ET ACTION STRATEGIQUE

## 1. La prospective comme champ

Quelques personnalités ont fortement marqué l'émergence de ce champ de réflexion, sans toutefois que l'on puisse dire qu'il a encore atteint sa maturité. Notons en particulier Gaston Berger, Bertrand et Hugues de Jouvenel[1], Bernard Cazes[2], Michel Godet[3], Pierre Gonod[4], dans l'ensemble des chercheurs et auteurs français. Mais d'autres courants existent, notamment dans les pays anglo-saxons.

Qu'est-ce que la prospective? La prospective consiste en la construction d'un **cadre analytique** permettant simultanément l'étude des **déterminants** propres à un système social, des **degrés de liberté** et des

---

[1] Revue *Futurible*

[2] Bernard Cazes, *Histoire des futurs*, Edition Seghers, 1986.

[3] Michel Godet, *De l'anticipation à l'action. Manuel de prospective et de stratégie*, Edition Dunod, 1991.

[4] Pierre Gonod, „Dynamique de la prospective", *Aditech* no 136, 1990.

**marges de manœuvre** propres à ce système dans une approche tournée vers l'élaboration de **projets à caractère stratégique**, orientés vers le **futur**, susceptibles d'infléchir durablement l'état des choses actuel.

La réflexion prospective est nécessairement **systémique**, c'est-à-dire qu'elle tente d'analyser les éléments qui composent le système et leur inter-relation, elle est **complexe** car elle vise à mettre en évidence les relations, les formes de réticulation multiples qui organisent et structurent le système, elle est **diachronique** car elle étudie les processus propres à chaque sous-système dans la durée, dans une épaisseur temporelle, la „temporalité des processus".

La prospective représente un effort **d'intégration** des éléments propres à rendre compte de la dynamique d'un système, **resitué** dans son contexte propre, et **exprimé dans la durée longue des processus** sous-jacents à l'ensemble du système étudié.

Dans ce contexte, le présent est ce moment particulier qui vise à relier l'analyse des processus hérités du passé, et l'image que les acteurs tournés vers la prise de décision, l'expression de choix stratégiques, se font de l'avenir.

Ainsi, fondamentalement, la prospective entre dans le champ des **sciences de l'action**, dans la mesure où elle vise l'élaboration de stratégies tournées vers la transformation ou l'adaptation du système, objet de l'analyse, mais selon un mode qui repose sur le principe du **détour analytique**, orienté de plus vers l'expression d'une **réflexion-appropriation** du groupe concerné par l'objet de l'étude, à travers différentes techniques, dont la recherche en créativité, l'élaboration de scénarios et d'images propre à faire des essais de représentation d'une situation donnée à travers un cheminement temporel.

La prospective peut s'appliquer à différents objets, tels que la définition d'une politique d'Etat, un projet d'entreprise, l'expression d'un problème de société, le devenir d'un secteur d'activité économique, les perspectives de développement d'une technologie, etc...

La prospective se différencie par rapport à d'autres approches, en apparence assez voisines, en réalité très différentes dans leur esprit et leur mode de fonctionnement.

**La prospective s'oppose à la prévision**, qui repose sur la projection de variables dans le temps, à partir de leurs évolutions dans une période antérieure à celle que l'on étudie. Implicitement, l'analyse prévisionnelle repose sur le principe: toutes choses égales par ailleurs, et sur le principe d'invariance du système étudié. Dans les périodes de fortes turbulences et de mutation accélérée des systèmes, la méthode prévisionnelle perd de son efficacité. Aussi sophistiqués que soient certains modèles économétriques prévisionnels, cette approche, à caractère mécaniste, ne permet pas d'appréhender la complexité des systèmes, ni de s'en servir comme levier d'une réflexion stratégique.

Toutefois, dans l'étude prospective il y a des emprunts à l'analyse prévisionnelle, ou des moments, de passage par l'exercice prévisionnel.

• **La prospective s'oppose à la futurologie**, tout ou moins dans la forme qu'en a donné le futurologue américain Herman Kahn, notamment dans ses travaux de futurologie technologique. Les erreurs parfois „monumentales" que l'on a pu constater entre les annonces et la réalité, résultent d'une tendance au „mécanisme technologique", et de la non-prise en compte des systèmes comme ensembles complexes, au sein desquels la technologie n'est qu'un élément parmi d'autres. Ainsi, dans une approche à la „manière" d'Herman Kahn, il aurait pu paraître „logique" que l'aérotrain de l'ingénieur Bertin, capable de dépasser les 450 km à l'heure dès 1970 sur un rail en béton, mais séparé de celui-ci par un coussinet d'air, se généraliserait avant la fin du siècle. Il n'en a rien été, parce qu'une amélioration du système classique de transport ferroviaire, avec la technologie TGV, a empêché une „innovation radicale" d'émerger et de s'imposer.

Cela étant, la prospective peut parfaitement intégrer des hypothèses sur le devenir des systèmes techniques, en les replaçant dans leur contexte socio-économique et culturel.

• **La prospective s'oppose de façon assez radicale à la divination, à la prophétie**, au sein de visions pré-établies, d'annonces que le prophète dévoile, à la manière d'un medium, ou d'un intercesseur, entre le réel et le surnaturel: les prospectivistes n'ont pas un accès particulier au surnaturel...

• **La prospective s'oppose enfin à l'utopie**, au sens d'une représentation idéalisée d'un système en dehors du temps. Toutefois, les scénarios de prospective normatifs peuvent s'apparenter à l'exercice de conception d'une utopie. A cet égard, Thomas Moore, l'auteur de la célèbre utopie (U-topos: sans lieu), peut être considéré comme un précurseur et un ancêtre de la prospective.

Ainsi, la prospective se différencie clairement d'autres champs et modes de penser, mais l'opposition n'est pas toujours aussi radicale qu'on a bien voulu le dire: des effets de tangente sont possibles et probablement nécessaires.

- **Reprenons quelques définitions de la prospective**
- La prospective est un regard sur l'avenir destiné à éclairer l'action présente.
- „C'est un panorama des futurs possibles d'un système destiné à éclairer les conséquences des stratégies d'action envisageables" (Michel Godet).
- „La prospective consiste à rassembler des éléments d'appréciation concernant l'avenir de façon à prendre des décisions grâce auxquelles l'avenir effectif sera davantage conforme aux attentes que s'il n'y avait pas eu de réflexion prospective" (Bernard Cazes).
- „La prospective est une représentation rationalisée du réel en devenir" (Guy Loinger).
- Ensemble des recherches ayant trait aux directions possibles du monde contemporain (acceptation anglo-saxonne, en terme sciences politiques).
- La prospective est l'exercice consistant à s'appuyer sur les temporalités longues rétrospectives pour étudier la dynamique des processus en cours, susceptibles de déboucher sur l'élaboration d'hypothèses concernant le devenir du système étudié à travers les „logiques de l'anticipation".
- Sur la base des connaissances des tendances lourdes, issues du passé, des phénomènes actuels en émergence certaine, des phénomènes perceptibles en émergence incertaine, de l'analyse des risques et des aléas de contexte, et des enjeux stratégiques auxquels doit faire face l'objet étudié, la prospective s'efforce, sur la base de ces données, et en effectuant une mise en contexte approfondie, de construire des hypothèses que l'on déroule dans le temps, de façon à mettre en évidence les cheminements possibles de l'objet étudié, susceptible de déboucher sur des prises de décision stratégique fondées sur une prise de risque contrôlée, maîtrisée, raisonnée.
- La prospective se caractérise en outre par une méthode destinée à rendre possible une appropriation collective de la réflexion en vue de déboucher sur des actions et des transformations de l'objet étudié.
- La prospective consiste à penser le temps long pour agir avec plus d'efficacité sur les mécanismes de la prise de décision à courte

échéance, sur la base d'une temporalité qui engage durablement l'avenir d'un système.

- **Pourquoi le détour par le long terme?**
— Parce que le long terme représente un effort de mise en perspective, permet ou s'efforce d'éliminer les aspects secondaires, conjoncturels et factuels qui brouillent l'analyse, et qui se traduit par une logique de tri de l'information.

— Parce que le long et le moyen termes visent à mettre en évidence les potentiels et les atouts structurels, et à corriger les faiblesses ou les déficiences récurrentes.

— Sachant qu'à court terme les „jeux sont faits", la prospective, par l'effort de réflexion à moyen et long terme, vise à retrouver des **marges de manœuvre** et des **degrés de liberté** sur les différents champs qui composent le système objet, économique, social, institutionnel...

— La prospective vise à „**comprendre autrement pour agir autrement**".

- **Comprendre autrement**: Quand un système est invariant, son devenir est inscrit dans le prolongement de son identité actuelle: il n'évolue et ne se modifie qu'à la marge. Par contre, quand un système évolue et se modifie en profondeur, que ses bases mêmes sont remises en cause, son devenir ne peut se déduire d'une simple connaissance du passé, ou faire l'objet d'une projection par homothétie. Il convient alors de saisir la nature profonde des processus par une recherche s'effectuant au croisement de plusieurs catégories de phénomènes.

— La connaissance des „**socles**" **socio-économiques**, linguistiques, culturels d'un système, au sens de l'historien Fernand Braudel, la très longue durée.

— Les **grandes mutations à l'œuvre** ou en émergence, clairement analysables ou encore en gestation au sein du système global dans lequel le système-objet s'insère.

— Les **interfaces et les interférences entre le système-objet** produit par l'histoire longue, et le **système contextuel** qui engendre un processus de transformation du système-objet, variable en fonction de la capacité d'assimilation et de réactivité du système face aux mutations structurelles du contexte.

- **Agir autrement**: Dans un système global complexe, très ramifié et réticulé, où toutes les forces sont en interdépendance fortes et actives, un macro-système réseau, dans lequel l'ensemble du tout est dans chacune des parties (Edgar Morin), la question est de savoir comment positionner

le système-objet, comment optimiser sa gestion et réduire le coût du risque décisionnel, alors même que:
— les marges de manœuvre du système-objet sont réduites,
— le système-objet est en lui-même complexe, parce que fait d'un enchevêtrement de sources de pouvoir sans qu'un seul centre de décision n'émerge véritablement, un „polycentrisme" structurel, assez caractéristique des économies et des sociétés libérales,
— chaque sous-système du système-objet est inscrit dans une **double logique: logique** — souvent très forte — de **dépendance** par rapport à un référent externe qui le façonne et le structure de façon durable, et **logique d'articulation fonctionnelle avec d'autres sous-systèmes à l'intérieur du système-objet**, les effets de contraintes externes de chaque sous-système devant néanmoins autoriser un certain degré de compatibilité des sous-systèmes les uns avec les autres au sein du système-objet,
— le système-objet, en tant qu'expression vécue par un groupe social, cherche les voies et moyens d'une orientation stratégique aussi claire et consensuelle que possible, à travers une dynamique de projet, qui peut s'exprimer ainsi: **Dans un monde complexe, incertain, capable d'évolutions rapides et aléatoires, que voulons-nous, que désirons-nous, quelle est notre place et notre situation adéquate?** La prospective „stratégique et participative" est l'un des facteurs possibles d'émergence d'un projet cohérent et consensuel.

• Les sept caractéristiques de la prospective (développement d'une réflexion de Fabrice Hatem) dans un ouvrage à paraître
1) le caractère **global** de la réflexion (le champ large)
2) la démarche **systémique** (l'étude des systèmes et de la complexité)
3) la **rationalité** (nature du projet méthodologique)
4) le couplage de données **qualitatives et quantitatives** (et non pas l'un ou l'autre)
5) la **temporalité longue**, rétrospective et anticipatrice
6) l'aptitude à la **créativité** (l'avenir n'est pas fait, il est ouvert, logique du projet)
7) une réflexion orientée sur **l'action, la décision, la volonté d'agir.**

• **Les scénarios: C'est la combinaison d'hypothèses destinées à analyser les conséquences de la mise en œuvre d'un système donné dans le futur.**

Un scénario comprend le choix d'hypothèses intrinsèques, une situation initiale, un système de contraintes externes, un cheminement temporel, une image de la situation au terme du processus temporel envisagé, l'ensemble se déroulant en fonction d'une „règle du jeu" préalablement posée.

La construction d'un scénario se pose sur différents principes développés par Michel Godet:
— Principe de vraisemblance (le caractère de scénario)
— Principe de cohérence (une logique)
— Principe pertinence (l'intelligence des choses)
— Principe transparence (règle du jeu)

Auxquels Michel Grenon[5] ajoute:
— Le principe de suffisance (des hypothèses en nombre suffisant) et auquel nous ajoutons:
— Le principe de lisibilité des phénomènes (ou compréhension des formes)
— Le principe de créativité (les deux lobes du cerveau fonctionnent)

Un **scénario maîtrisé implique d'appréhender correctement la temporalité des processus à l'œuvre,** qui varient d'un sous-système à l'autre au sein d'un système-objet — toutes choses égales par ailleurs — et qui ont leur propre dynamique temporelle, variable en fonction de leur ressort socio-économique interne, et de la pression du contexte: il n'y a pas de temporalité „en soi", mais uniquement des temporalités „situées" dans un contexte historique déterminé.

La temporalité effective des processus dépend à la fois d'événements aléatoires et d'une logique propre, spécifique de l'objet, en sorte qu'il existe une dialectique entre les „temps externes" et les „temps internes", qui engendre des accélérations ou des ralentissements temporels, et qui manifeste l'élasticité des logiques temporelles, susceptibles d'engendrer des phénomènes aussi divers que l'implosion, l'explosion, les ruptures complètes, les ruptures partielles... (Alain Gras, Pierre Gonod).

Les scénarios mettent en évidence l'impact supposé d'événements externes sur l'objet lui-même. L'intérêt majeur des scénarios est l'étude de la capacité réactive d'un système, du plus passif au plus actif, ce qui permet cette définition:

---

[5] Michel Grenon est Directeur scientifique du Plan Bleu.

„Les scénarios sont des combinaisons cohérentes d'un jeu d'hypothèse destiné à explorer les conséquences des inter-relations entre les champs de forces d'un système, sous la contrainte d'un contexte historique déterminé" (Guy Loinger).

Il est intéressant de construire des scénarios qui permettent d'appréhender différents types d'évolution du système-objet (développement d'une réflexion d'Hugues de Jouvenel).

— **Premier type:** au „fil de l'eau" à contexte plus ou moins stable.
— **Deuxième type:** l'inscription du système dans un système-contexte qui oblige **certains sous-systèmes à évoluer** ou muter ou se métamorphoser plus rapidement et plus intensément que d'autres, ce qui génère une modification partielle du système, et son inflexion plus ou moins importante, sans que sa structure soit modifiée en profondeur.
— **Troisième type:** une **mutation profonde de chacun des sous-systèmes**, en fonction d'un contexte très évolutif, **sans qu'aucun des sous-systèmes puisse évoluer de façon cohérente par rapport aux autres.** Dans cette **logique de la divergence**, il peut y avoir des degrés allant du plus simple au plus radical (rupture partielle ou globale).
— **Quatrième type:** une mutation de chaque sous-système qui **engendre un processus global de convergence** au terme d'un processus d'adaptation, allant d'une cohérence faible à une cohérence forte.
— **Cinquième type:** un **panachage entre plusieurs types précédents.**
  • **Les temps forts des études de prospective.**

Ce point résulte de différentes expériences et n'a pas de validité universelle. Il est composé de dix points:

1) La **définition et la délimitation de la problématique**, qui implique une forte relation avec l'instance commanditaire.
2) **La construction de la base analytique, qui doit être**
   — approfondie            — des tendances lourdes
   — structurée   autour   — des émergences assurées
   — dynamique              — des émergences incertaines
3) Le test et la critique des résultats auprès du groupe de référence.
4) La **construction d'un système cohérent d'hypothèses.**
5) L'élaboration d'un ensemble de directions et de **représentations du devenir** possible du système.
6) La **mise en œuvre de ces systèmes** de représentation dans une temporalité future ou anticipatrice.

7) Le retour devant le groupe de référence pour discussion et appropriation.
8) Un travail d'application autour de dossiers-enjeux.
9) Une **synthèse générale**.
10) Une transformation du produit en vue d'une communication élargie.

## 2. Prospective territoriale

Les territoires, entendus comme étendues terrestres sur lesquelles vivent des groupes humains, structurés par des règles, des lois, qui disposent d'une personnalité morale d'une capacité variable, allant de l'autorité morale simple et limitée (région) à une autorité et une souveraineté étendue et complète (Etat), constituent un cadre de réflexion et d'action intéressant en prospective.

Les territoires régionaux ou nationaux sont soumis aux effets de la globalisation des marchés et la mondialisation des échanges, et plus largement à une mondialisation des systèmes scientifiques et techniques, des techniques de production, des systèmes de financement, des modes d'approvisionnement, des formes d'organisation économique, des modes de consommation, de distribution, des systèmes de normes, des références culturelles, etc...

Par ailleurs, les territoires sont sous contrainte de dynamiques temporelles propres aux acteurs économiques, qui les obligent à avoir un degré de réactivité élevé, et à être capables d'adaptation rapide à différents niveaux: production, conception, innovation, nouveaux marchés...

De plus, les territoires qui, dans leurs structures profondes sont marqués par des évolutions lentes, sont affrontés à l'instabilité conjoncturelle, à des effets de sensibilité à l'évolution des rapports de forces mondiaux, qui les touchent de plus en plus directement, en particulier à l'échelle régionale, sans l'enveloppe protectrice des Etats. Dans ce contexte à risque, la place des territoires régionaux est forcément contingente, dépendante de forces externes, soumise à des processus qui les dépassent.

Néanmoins, dans ce contexte en mutation accélérée, qui engendre un processus de dislocation des structures productives, héritées des systèmes productifs antérieurs, on observe une nouvelle émergence du „local/régional".

En un sens, dans un monde hyper-complexe et extrêmement réticulé, à fort degré d'interaction entre les forces, on perçoit la nécessité d'espaces intermédiaires entre le „tout" et les unités (économiques) qui le composent, qui filtrent les énergies du monde, dans un sens compatible avec les potentiels locaux/régionaux, qui permettent des processus de régulation entre tous les éléments du système socio-économique localisé, qui aident les acteurs à s'affronter au monde dans de bonnes conditions.

Ces „espaces-support", cadres de la vie quotidienne, ne fonctionnent plus de façon pertinente à l'échelle des Etats-Nation traditionnels, parce que les économies nationales ne servent plus de cadre „naturel" au déploiement des forces productives: trop loin du quotidien local, et inadaptés pour assurer la régulation planétaire, les nations, dont l'émergence et la plénitude correspondent à un moment de l'histoire du monde, sont amenées à repenser leurs logiques d'action, comme condition de leur survie même. D'où l'échappée vers le „haut" (la Communauté Européenne) et vers le „bas" (la décentralisation, l'autonomie des acteurs locaux/régionaux), le principe de subsidiarité.

Reprenons sur ce point Denis Maillat (GREMI), **„le système territorial de production est un lieu dans lequel les interfaces et les synergies entre acteurs et entre partenaires sont importants, et déterminent une dynamique dans laquelle les agents et les ressources disposent d'une compétence décisionnelle, autour de cinq caractéristiques**:
— un ensemble spatial homogène
— un collectif d'acteurs actifs
— des forces matérielles conséquentes
— des forces immatérielles type réseau, interaction
— une capacité d'apprentissage

L'ensemble qui dispose d'une capacité d'action collective, doit permettre une certaine compatibilité avec l'environnement, tout en sauvegardant une forte cohésion interne, sa reproduction et son développement.

Toutefois, des obstacles existent, notamment:
— l'asymétrie interne entre entreprises locales due à la variabilité des conditions d'insertion dans l'économie mondiale

— la recomposition des systèmes techniques qui fait éclater les chaînes productives préexistantes

— la contradiction, plus ou moins bien assumée, entre un principe d'identité et un principe d'adaptation

— la tendance à la dégradation de la cohésion sociale et culturelle localisée, et l'existence de milieux non-homogènes, ayant une capacité de réactivité et d'anticipation diverse, parfois liée à des milieux a-territoriaux.

Il n'en demeure pas moins que ces milieux locaux représentent un atout et un levier non négligeable de développement. D'où l'intérêt croissant pour la prospective comme outil stratégique du développement.

**On observe un intérêt croissant pour la démarche prospective en Région. Sur quoi repose cette motivation, qui prend parfois l'allure d'un engouement?**

**Premièrement: un besoin de lisibilité** vis-à-vis des enjeux actuels et en devenir, susceptibles de concerner, de toucher et de traverser les régions, dans un contexte global difficile à saisir, qui apparaît souvent comme une „boîte noire".

Paradoxalement, la fin de „l'ère des blocs" rend l'analyse des lignes de force du monde actuel plus difficile à saisir, l'horizon plus brouillé. De plus, le positivisme technologique, qui a „sévi" pendant ces deux dernières décennies, n'a plus la même capacité d'entraînement psychologique: derrière l'arbre, la forêt réapparaît, et l'on ne sait guère comment l'appréhender.

La conviction que „tout est possible" ou presque, tant que le plan de la génétique, de l'électronique, de la conquête de l'espace, a moins pour effet d'enthousiasmer l'esprit que de faire prendre conscience de la complexité des implications, tant sur le plan éthique, que sur celui de la gestion des éco-systèmes, et sur celui des nouvelles formes de conflictualité qui apparaissent dans le monde.

A une époque de recomposition, marquée par l'émergence de nouveaux champs de force, par l'effacement des anciens systèmes de référence culturelle et idéologique, il apparaît urgent de prendre le temps de réfléchir, notamment à l'échelle des collectivités territoriales locales et régionales, échelle qui correspond grosso modo aux „**territoires de quotidienneté**" à la fin du XXe siècle.

**Deuxièmement: le sentiment qu'il existe un niveau de décision efficace pour assumer les nécessaires régulations sociales**, politiques, économiques, un niveau intermédiaire entre les „macro-systèmes" (Etats...) et les „micro-systèmes" (entreprises, familles, etc...), ce que l'on tend à appeler les „méso-systèmes".

Cette notion d'espace de régulation intermédiaire, vis-à-vis de laquelle les villes et les régions seraient le cadre le plus adéquat, est probablement d'une grande importance, bien que les gouvernements, dans un pays de tradition jacobine comme la France, n'en ont pas encore mesuré toute l'importance.

Bien que les grands régulateurs, comme la Sécurité Sociale, l'appareil de Formation, etc... resteront encore longtemps l'apanage de la Nation, les mécanismes d'adaptation locaux et régionaux semblent devoir se renforcer, ne serait-ce que pour se mettre à parité avec les modes de régulation dominants en Europe, notamment en Allemagne.

Or, la connaissance et la pratique de ces modes de régulation alternatifs ou subsidiaires sont encore très insuffisants, dans la mesure où les **„logiques verticales" restent terriblement prégnantes, même si la reconnaissance du primat des logiques horizontales ou transversales „fait son chemin"**, par exemple dans le couple emploi-formation. Nous ne sommes qu'au début d'un long processus, qui ira peut-être jusqu'à la disparition de la notion de politique nationale, au profit de simples politiques d'encadrement nationales, le régional ou le „grand régional" devenant le cadre véritable d'expression pratique et effectif de ces politiques.

**Troisièmement: le besoin d'identité culturelle**, comme prolongement „logique" des lois sur la décentralisation. Face à une monde dans lequel la temporalité spatiale se contracte incroyablement vite, le besoin „d'être" ressurgit, mais pas là où on s'y attendait (les espaces-plan de Jean-Pierre Lugnier[6].

Etre Catalan, Lombard, Piémontais, Ecossais prend une signification nouvelle, parfois dans des formes dramatiques (la Yougoslavie). Il n'y a pas de raison pour que ce syndrome ne touche pas, à sa manière, „l'hexagone". Mais comment? Mieux vaut anticiper que gérer des situations dans les urgences... **A cet égard, plus de décentralisation ne nous éloigne pas du principe de Nation, mais représente probablement le meilleur moyen d'en préserver les fondements.**

**Quatrièmement: aider les acteurs à se positionner sur l'échiquier international**. La question de la juste place dans une ambiance où tout,

---

[6]Jean-Pierre Lugnier, enseignant à l'Université d'Amiens.

y compris les territoires, devient un objet de compétition. Jusqu'où cette compétitivité régionale est-elle acceptable? Il y a un risque majeur de „divergence" entre les macro-régions européennes, entre les périphéries et le cœur... Il y a là un enjeu double: à l'échelle des nations et à celle de la CEE.

**Cinquièmement:** Les collectivités veulent savoir sur quelles **forces sociales** elles peuvent s'appuyer, ce qui implique une bonne connaissance du jeu des acteurs, de leur capacité d'entreprenariat, de leur aptitude à saisir la chance ou les opportunités, et à réagir face à une situation compétitive. Or cette connaissance reste intuitive, elle n'est pas „pensée", rationalisée.

**Sixièmement:** Les collectivités veulent connaître quel est l'impact des dynamiques extérieures sur le marché régional; elles ont besoin d'évaluer leur degré de **dépendance** face aux logiques extérieures. Or, cette dépendance est souvent très forte, en particulier lorsque les grands groupes dominent l'économie locale.

**Septièmement:** A contrario, elles estiment nécessaire d'évaluer leur „degré de liberté", leur marge de manœuvre, afin d'élaborer des politiques endogènes/internes, les mieux adaptées à la situation réelle des milieux locaux, taillées sur mesure, différentes d'une région à l'autre, d'un bassin d'emploi à l'autre, car chaque territoire exprime une combinatoire de situations héritées du passé, qu'il convient de transformer en logique de projet.

**Huitièmement:** Ce qui implique de comprendre, de l'intérieur, les **interdépendances internes** de manière à fonder les nouveaux maillages, les réseaux, les articulations porteuses d'avenir.

**Neuvièmement:** Elles veulent donner à leurs **citoyens des référants**, des fils conducteurs, donner un sens à l'activité de chacun, ce qui implique de développer des **projets de régions partagés par le plus grand nombre**: les entreprises, par exemple ont besoin d'un cadre stable comme condition préalable aux investissements, de manière à connaître la „règle du jeu" sans risquer de mauvaises surprises vis-à-vis des acteurs locaux et régionaux.

**Dixièmement:** Elles veulent finaliser les réflexions, en hiérarchisant les objectifs, en adaptant les objectifs aux **moyens disponibles** — qui ne dépendent jamais complètement d'elles-mêmes, mais largement d'instances supra-nationales (Etat, communautés) — et en adaptant les objectifs aux **contraintes de société**, que la montée en puissance du

courant écologique a mis clairement en évidence dans un passé récent...
lourd d'implications dans le devenir des territoires, de moins en moins
„objets" et de plus en plus „sujets"...

## 3. Application: „Les territoires au futur"

Prenons un autre exemple, à l'échelle France entière. Il s'agit de
l'ouvrage réalisé dans le cadre de la DATAR, „Les territoires du futur",
par un collectif d'auteurs[7], à la suite de l'ensemble des études dites
de prospective, réalisées en 1991/92 pour la DATAR. Il ne s'agit pas
d'une synthèse des groupes thématiques, mais d'une lecture originale,
transversale, destinée à mettre en évidence, d'une part les lignes de force
de l'évolution du territoire français, et d'autre part, d'une tentative de
réflexion prospective du devenir du territoire national, dans le double
contexte de la „globalisation" et de la „polarisation /métropolisation".

La question se pose de savoir comment un groupe d'experts (dont
nous-même en l'occurrence, mais il s'agit là de mettre une distance vis-à-
vis de ce travail, réalisé de façon conviviale et avec un fort marquage de
réflexion et d'écriture collective) imagine, pense, rêve, anticipe le territoire
français. Est-ce que l'on peut repérer, à travers ce texte, l'émergence d'un
imaginaire, d'une capacité à „inventer" ou ré-inventer la France à travers
l'exercice de prospective; est-ce que la prospective féconde une vision
nouvelle du territoire national?

La question n'est pas sans importance, s'agissant de l'un des seuls
textes globaux de la DATAR sur le devenir du territoire français, sur
l'ensemble de son vaste programme de recherche.

Tout d'abord, notons que dans cet ouvrage, la partie proprement
prospective ne comprend qu'une place modeste, un tiers de l'ensemble
environ, le reste étant consacré à de l'analyse des tendances lourdes et à
divers préconisations.

La structure de la réflexion de prospective: il ne s'agit pas de scénarios
de prospective, mais „d'images", mettant par la même l'accent sur le
caractère modeste de la démarche, qui n'a, de ce fait rien à voir avec

---

[7] „Les territoires du futur", François Ascher, Lucien Brams, Aliette Delamarre, Guy
Loinger, Michel Rochefort, Alain de Romfort, Jacques Theys, Serge Wachter, Edition de
l'Aube, 1993.

l'investissement considérable qui avait été fait en 1968/72 à l'époque des „scénarios de l'inacceptable".

Mais la modestie de l'intention ne signifie pas que le résultat soit de faible portée: plutôt que de s'embarrasser d'un lourd appareil méthodologique, le groupe d'experts a plutôt voulu laisser son imagination s'exprimer, sur la base d'une forte analyse préalable du tendanciel de l'économie et de la société française.

Ce groupe a par ailleurs voulu éviter le mode habituel d'expression, composé du sempiternel scénario rose, noir, gris, qui le plus souvent aboutit à un discours terne, mi-figue mi-raisin; pas très éloigné du tendanciel, et de nature à ne pas trop effrayer les grands décideurs. De plus, reflet de l'esprit du temps, le groupe a considéré qu'il convenait de ne pas jouer sur la corde plus affective que rationnelle qui prend parfois la forme suivante: „nous allons vers le scénario noir, catastrophique, inacceptable, agissez pour éviter le pire..." ", tout simplement parce que, d'une certaine manière, nous sommes dans une société habituée au risque du pire, et parce que le pire n'est pas le moins probable, et peut-être même le plus probable. Situation qui se traduit par exemple par le fait que l'on va allègrement vers 90% de la population sur 10% du territoire. L'inacceptable est là: nous y sommes. Faut-il rester ou faut-il gérer au mieux les conséquences de cet état de fait?

Donc, évitons le piège du rose/noir/gris, pour nous situer plutôt dans les formes territoriales que la société pourrait accepter de développer, eu égard aux prémisses que l'on perçoit actuellement, et qui, en fonction de divers aléas — politiques, internationaux — sont susceptibles de se réaliser effectivement, à l'horizon d'une génération.

Le propos est organisé de la façon suivante: il consiste en un croisement entre deux variables stratégiques: l'une concerne le **mode de localisation** des personnes et des activités, soit une tendance à la **concentration et à la dualisation** de l'espace, soit une tendance à la **dispersion/diffusion** la plus large sur le territoire.

L'autre concerne les **modèles de société** susceptibles de voir le jour: soit le libéralisme — mais pas sous une forme „pure", un libéralisme „majeur", c'est-à-dire débarrassé de ses aspects par trop caricaturaux, disons un libéralisme „avancé" — soit l'interventionnisme — mais pas sous la forme brutale du „tout étatique", disons la régulation collective des processus — avec deux variantes, l'une ouverte, fondée sur une régulation à l'échelle européenne, l'autre fermée sur la France elle-même, la France du „repli".

De plus, une variable intégrée aux différentes „configurations" concerne le type de croissance économique, fort ou faible, de type fordiste ou post-fordiste.

Le croisement entre les deux variables stratégiques de base permet de combiner six images, intitulées:

1. la grande cité de service (libéralisme + concentration);
2. le développement différencié (régulation européenne + concentration);
3. la persistance de la crise (régulation nationale + concentration);
4. fédération des régions européennes (régulation européenne + dispersion);
5. Suburbia (libéralisme + dispersion);
6. territorial, patrimonial (régulation nationale + dispersion).

Sans développer ces six images, on peut se demander quel **est le potentiel d'inventivité** qui se dégage de ces différentes visions, les deux premières étant d'ailleurs, à tort ou à raison, considérées comme les plus probables à court terme.

## 3.1. La grande cité de service

Cette „vision" est fondée sur un concept de métropolisation renforcée dans un contexte de libéralisme dit „avancé". L'Etat joue un rôle, mais seulement correcteur et assistanciel, à fort marquage de logique de subsidiarité, dans un contexte caractérisé par une dynamique économique fortement en prise sur l'économie-monde. Le résultat, c'est le renforcement de logiques d'exclusion, des poches de pauvreté, la marginalisation de certain groupes sociaux, dans un cadre général marqué par le renforcement de la métropolisation, polarisée autour de quelques grandes villes à rayonnement international, ce qui génère des déséquilibres importants sur le territoire, variables selon la force des effets des réseaux de villes, doublés par une tendance à la dualisation au sein des campagnes. Les politiques nationales d'aménagement du territoire sont réduites à la forme „management" du territoire, s'agissant de gérer les risques de dérapage, plus que de formuler de véritables politiques globales d'aménagement.

Cette vision des choses correspond peu ou prou à la situation actuelle, au tendanciel propre au monde français d'organisation du territoire.

## 3.2. Le territoire des développements différenciés

Dans ce cas, caractérisé par un processus de néo-intervention d'Etat, au sens moderne du mot, axé sur une politique volontariste d'intégration à l'Europe communautaire, et une intentionnalité explicite en matière de redistribution des richesses, le pouvoir central agit en coordination étroite avec les pouvoirs régionaux. Dans ce modèle, l'aménagement du territoire, pour actif qu'il soit, ne vise pas à mettre „Paris à la campagne", ou de déménager Paris en province: on assume l'héritage et le particularisme français, mais en le nuançant et en modelant le système territorial de manière à réduire les disparités territoriales et socio-économiques, à renforcer les grands pôles de province, de façon à ce que chacun d'eux puisse „tirer" son propre territoire régional, sous forme d'une „**décentralisation polarisée**" de la croissance industrielle et tertiaire sur une petite dizaine de pôles-relais du pôle parisien, qui demeure le pôle national incontesté, mais débarrassé de ce qui représente la cause de déséconomies d'échelle majeures. Dans cette optique, un gros effort est fait pour améliorer la vie quotidienne au sein des grandes aires métropolitaines, en créant des pôles d'activité périphériques.

La campagne, le monde rural, s'inscrit dans une logique d'ouverture au monde, cesse d'être exclusivement agricole, se diversifie, joue un rôle croissant dans l'équilibre psychologique global de la société (urbaine) par un renforcement de la fonction loisir/tourisme, et par un développement des produits de terrain à haute valeur ajoutée. Le jeu de pouvoir entre le niveau central et les niveaux locaux se fait par le renforcement du rôle décisionnel local, l'Etat central ou délégué jouant un rôle de coordinateur, d'animateur, en relation étroite avec le niveau européen.

Cette vision des choses correspond peu ou prou à une inflexion raisonnée de la politique d'aménagement du territoire à contexte ouvert à l'Europe et au monde, et avec une „compatibilité accrue" de l'aménagement du territoire français vis-à-vis de l'Europe communautaire.

### 3.3. Un territoire à deux vitesses: la France victime de la crise (régulation nationale, concentration territoriale)

Ce „modèle" est fortement marqué par un effet de crise généralisée qui entraîne un repli sur l'hexagone, une perte de confiance vis-à-vis du projet européen. Repli économique, qui pénalise les agglomérations monoproductrices, à forte base industrielle, sans capacité de réaction dans un monde plus dur, plus hostile, avec un poids croissant du pôle parisien. L'Etat gouverne de manière autoritaire, mais faute de moyens de financement, l'impact réel reste faible, plus idéologique que pratique. L'atomisation des institutions locales est à l'origine d'un effet de retour aux comportements clientèlistes, et un renforcement de l'institution départementale, plus adaptée au contrôle du territoire, dans un contexte de repli généralisé.

Ce modèle du „retour à l'autorité de l'Etat" dans un contexte de montée des barrières mentales et psychologiques vis-à-vis de l'étranger a été rédigé avant les récentes élections législatives. Faut-il le dire...

### 3.4. La fédération européenne des régions (régulation à l'échelle européenne et dispersion des activités et de l'habitat)

Ce modèle explore l'une des composantes du „rêve européen", celui d'une disparition des Etats-Nations donnant naissance à une fédération européenne des Régions. Cette image est intéressante dans la mesure où elle est en rupture avec l'image archétypique d'une France hyper-centralisée, structurellement marquée par une vision jacobine du territoire et de la nation.

Ce modèle apparaît comme la conséquence logique d'un processus fort d'intégration économique et culturelle à l'échelle européenne et par un renforcement des institutions européennes au détriment des Etats-Nations. Présenté comme peu probable à court terme, il est davantage que les précédents en rupture sémantique et idéologique, il inaugure une nouvelle page de l'histoire du pays, car c'est en quelque sorte le passage à une nouvelle donne par rapport à 12 ou 14 siècles d'histoire.

Dans ce modèle d'économie-territoire, très ouvert au monde, la référence serait les régions allemandes en général, marquées par un fort pouvoir régional, et son double, au niveau communautaire, l'Etat lui-même s'inspirant du modèle fédéral allemand ou espagnol. A la limite, les régions deviennent des mini-Etats, avec de véritables transferts de compétences dans tous les domaines où la société civile marque son existence dans la vie quotidienne. Les régions fortement représentées dans les instances communautaires, contribuent à la définition des politiques de développement, en s'appuyant sur le parlement européen, qui devient la véritable source du pouvoir.

Trois variantes sont envisagées: un mode marqué par un fédéralisme explicite et achevé, un mode marqué par le fédéralisme implicite et modulé, qui correspond à l'état actuel de la construction européenne, mais avec un élan politique plus fort; et un modèle de fédéralisme conflictuel et dislocateur, avec notamment l'accentuation des logiques de la dualisation, les régions riches refusant de coopérer et de transférer des ressources en faveur des régions les plus en retard de développement, la référence implicite étant bien entendu les processus à l'œuvre actuellement dans des pays comme l'Italie ou la Belgique.

## 3.5. Suburbia (néo-libéral/diffusion territoriale)

Ce modèle, assez fortement inspiré des travaux de l'architecte américain Frank Llyod Wright et sa „broadacre city", et d'une manière générale du modèle américain de développement des suburb au détriment des villes-centres, tente de montrer ce que pourrait produire, dans un pays de vieille culture urbaine comme la France, une poussée d'un modèle de développement fondé sur la périphérisation accrue des fonctions urbaines, dans un contexte marqué par un libéralisme „sauvage".

Ce modèle est fondé sur une double virtualité: au plan économique et technologique, par le renforcement de toutes les formes d'organisation et de production à fort marquage de télé-travail et de télé-organisation, et au plan social, par l'exacerbation du modèle familial auto-centré, source et fin de toute la vie sociale, très ouverte au monde en terme de capacité d'adaptation et d'intégration des innovateurs, mais très traditionnelle sur l'essence de la vie familiale.

Sur le plan technico-économique, la diffusion très intense de tous les systèmes techniques permet de découp leur l'output économique de la logique du rassemblement des „masses", ce qui a pour effet la fin de la grande usine taylorienne, l'avènement et la généralisation de la petite unité de production très automatisée, très flexible, très adaptable, hyper-reliée au reste du monde, à la fois grâce à un réseau de télécommunication sophistiqué (câble optique, banque de données en réseau...), et grâce à un réseau de moyens de transport physique très dense, et de bonne qualité en divers points du territoire, rendant inutiles les hyper-concentrations urbaines, dans une logique du juste-à-temps a-territorialisé.

Si quelques pôles urbains demeurent, ils ne sont pas nécessairement dans les grandes villes, qui ne jouent plus leur rôle historique de constitution de la **société comme sujet actif**: la ville „disparaît" parce qu'elle ne sert plus à rien, parce que la sociabilité fondamentale n'a plus besoin de passer par ce biais. Sur le plan des modes de vie, la séparation ville/campagne se métamorphose en une sorte de monde mixte, à la fois urbanisé et intégrant des éléments de vie de campagne.

Mais tous n'ont pas accès à ce „rêve américain": ceux qui sont les laisser-pour-compte de la haute qualification, et de ce mode de vie délocalisé/branché, demeurent dans les anciennes villes, qui deviennent de plus en plus des sortes de zones de réclusion pour pauvres, marginaux, exclus.

Mais comme l'Etat ne joue pas son rôle régulateur, et que les collectivités locales sont hostiles à des efforts de redistribution entre commune riches et communes pauvres, la qualité des équipements collectifs dans les vieux centres en voie de paupérisation s'en ressent fortement, avec aggravation des phénomènes de conflictualité latente ou ouverte, avec de soudaines flambées de violence, de la violence a-politique, a-idéologique, à la manière des phénomènes que l'on observe régulièrement aux Etats-Unis, type Los Angeles 1992, qui renforcent encore les disparités culturelles entre les communautés „sauvages urbaines" contre „branchées, petit-bourgeoises", la fonction régalienne de l'Etat jouant un rôle de tampon.

**Deux variantes** sont envisageables: une **variante hyper-dispersée**, et une variante plus proche de la réalité virtuelle, d'une **diffusion limitée** autour des grands pôles urbains, à l'origine de la constitution de nébuleuses urbaines concentrées/dilatées, dont le double est la désertification des espaces ruraux, plus ou moins abandonnés parce que mal reliés au reste du monde.

Ce modèle, violent, radical, non pas au sens politique du mot, mais au sens du film *Orange Mécanique*, la violence post-idéologique dans les villes, n'est pas le moins probable de tous, et il donne la mesure de ce que pourrait devenir le territoire dans une logique du tout libéral, à fort marquage technologique, avec un abandon, non seulement du rôle traditionnel de l'Etat régulateur, mais plus encore de l'abandon de la culture urbaine, pourtant profondément ancrée et néanmoins assez fragile.

Ce modèle apparaît à certains égards comme une variante aggravée du modèle „Metropolis", lourd de disparités structurantes accrues, qu'il serait par la suite difficile de corriger...

### 3.6. Le territoire patrimonial (dispersé + régulateur à l'échelle nationale)

Dans ce modèle, la dominante est le renforcement de la variable écologique, qui joue à tout niveau une fonction régulatrice, politique, culturelle. La tendance est à la dispersion, mais pas sous la forme purement marchande, comme dans le mode précédent, mais en fonction d'une logique patrimoniale que l'on respecte et que l'on valorise: la vieille armature urbaine, millénaire, devient le cadre et support de l'organisation sociale, au détriment de la très grande ville, avec un fort respect des éco-systèmes, qui se traduit par une relation équilibrée de la campagne „vivante" et de la ville (plutôt la petite ville) dans une logique conforme aux principes du développement durable.

## Conclusion

En définitive, l'intérêt de la prospective est de donner une lecture non déterministe du devenir de nos sociétés, autour d'un principe de liberté. Nos sociétés sont, malgré tous les avatars, des sociétés de liberté: l'avenir ne découle pas mécaniquement des processus hérités du passé, ni au plan individuel, ni au plan collectif. Ce sont des sociétés de projet: si l'on ne bâtit l'avenir qu'avec le potentiel dont on dispose, lequel est enraciné dans une épaisseur historique, il n'en demeure pas moins vrai que ce potentiel n'est pas une donnée figée: il s'inscrit dans la réalité à travers des choix, des décisions, qui impliquent de la part de chacun une attitude positive, pro-active, une capacité individuelle et collective d'anticipation. Le „temps à venir" comme élément du jeu social est une donnée fondamentale des sociétés modernes. Or, ce qui est vrai pour l'individu l'est aussi pour la collectivité, dans des formes particulières.

Les collectivités territoriales, quant à elles, sont des constructions „finalisées" sur tel ou tel objectif précis et limité, dont les bases fonctionnelles sont nettes, car elles sont inscrites dans les textes de loi et les règlements.

Elles ne peuvent guère prétendre à une quelconque „hégémonie" de pouvoir et de prérogatives sur les personnes, comme sur les collectivités — ou sous-systèmes — qui les composent et qui constituent les éléments de base de la vie sociale, économique, culturelle, locale et régionale. Les territoires locaux et régionaux apparaissent comme autant de faire-valoir, de cadres et de supports de la société et de la sociabilité, dont les bases dépassent l'objet local, du fait des relations/articulations qui existent entre chaque sous-ensemble localisé avec le reste du monde, au plan économique, administratif, technologique...

Mais, si dans nos sociétés d'économie ouverte, la notion de „gouvernement local" ne peut être prise qu'au sens réduit du terme, il n'en demeure pas moins vrai que le local-régional n'est pas qu'un simple cadre dans lequel se dérouleraient des processus qui lui échapperaient complètement. Il existe une réalité régionale qui, même si elle est secondaire, dérivée, n'en est pas moins réelle.

Ainsi la société déborde de tous côtés l'objet local en le dépassant (dans la nation, ou l'Europe, le monde). Mais celui-ci a malgré tout un certain degré d'existence, à la fois dans la conscience collective (on habite telle ville, telle région), dans la pratique administrative, et dans les pratiques sociales (la proximité), et parce que le „local-régional" peut faire l'objet d'une identification-appropriation. Elle peut prendre corps dans un projet collectif, une vision consensuelle des choses, au-delà du discours de la différenciation politique ou idéologique, et peut devenir le cadre d'un projet (régulation vis-à-vis de certains types d'enjeux: problèmes de société, d'aménagement du territoire, de vie culturelle...)

Les fonctions collectives territoriales peuvent devenir le catalyseur de différentes fonctions principales (la citoyenneté, le développement économique), avec une intensité variable d'un point à l'autre du territoire et générer un processus de réalisation effective, susceptible de faire passer du virtuel au réel, ou de rendre possibles des processus socio-économiques qui risqueraient en cas contraire de rester en l'état latent, faute d'expression collective localisée, faute d'intentionnalité opératoire.

Philip Cooke
University of Wales
Cardiff

# REGIONAL INNOVATION CENTRES: RECENT WESTERN EXPERIENCE AND ITS POSSIBLE RELEVANCE FOR CENTRAL AND EASTERN EUROPE

## Introduction

Regional authorities throughout Europe are trying to fashion a **new approach** to regional development. What has triggered this change is the growing recognition that regions can no longer compete simply by offering a crude combination of semiskilled labour on the one hand and finicial incentives for inward investment on the other. This kind of regional policy made littler or no impact on the central problem of old industrial regions, namely, **low innovation potential**, a problem which afflicts both the indigenous small and medium enterprise (SME) sector and the branch-plant sector.

All the most dynamic regions in Europe today are of the view that their local firms need much more than a liberal macro-economic climate if the are to remain on an innovative footing. Strong regions (like Baden-

Würtemberg and Emilia-Romagna) as well as less favoured regions (like Valencia and the Basque Country) are just a few examples of regions which are trying to create a competitive edge for themselves by building a **regional innovation infrastructure** through which local firms have easy and affordable access to a wide array of technical services.

The most important questions to be asked of these regional innovation infrastructures are twofold. First, how do they advantage firms in the region? Second, what lessons can be learned from the more successful regional innovation systems? In answering these questions reference will be made to research on European and US examples.

In the European Commission's Community Support Frameworks and thinking about Regional Technology Strategies (RETAS: see Hingel, 1992) support for **research and development (R&D)** is often identified as a key item. In particular, stress is placed on diffusion and transfer facilites such as Science and Technology Parks, Applied Research Centres, Innovation Centres and various kinds of technology support vehicles for business. While all of these facilities are commendable it is important that a coherent package of initiatives which suits the regional economy is put in place. Thus, rather than attempting a purely "top down" strategy design, this chapter will focus on a mix of responding to expressed "bottom-up" need from business, **Integrating and enhancing existing institutions** of relevance, and adding appropriate ingredients based on successful experience elsewhere in Europe to produce a **coherent and achievable set of innovation objectives** for regional innovation and development.

# 1. Advantages to firms of regional innovation services

The key technological requirement by firms of innovation centres is that services should consist of **appropriate** and **relevant** information and advice without being over general or over-elaborate.

Receptivity of firms to such services is an important factor in determining how well-synchronised supply is with demand. By and large, German, Japanese and to varying degrees, other continental firms seem to have greater receptivity towards support of this kind than those in, for example, the UK and USA.

Amongst the benefits firms in innovation-rich regions perceive from the innovation infrastructure area:

- **Technical Applications:** many firms need basic testing, measurement, calculation and problem-solving support since these are usually too expensive to have in-house. The Basque Technological Centres are adept at providing this to SMEs.
- **Expert Technological Advice:** more advanced demand and supply, often using sophisticated technologies such as CAD-CAM, or across the board applications in, for example, new telecommunication networks, are highly valued.
- **Information Services:** facilities which can scan sources of value-adding information on, for example, patents, exploaitable technologies, technical partners, or possible joint-venture partners, have immediate practical use.
- **Gateway Services:** EC programmes enable SMEs to be brought into partnership with leading edge firms and research institutes. Innovation centres can act as gateway-members to such programmes.
- **Network Services:** innovation centres increasingly animate "competition through collaboration" via schemes which encourage SMEs to form groups in alliance so they may afford services together which individually they would be unable to.

## 2. Networks as the key to regional economic development

In the past, it was thought that decisions about innovation had to be made by central government. The **"technopole"** idea was a good example of this, but now it is no longer the leading innovation concept. In its place is an emergent set of developmental practices which area commonly described as "networking" or "the networg paradigm" (Cooke and Morgan, 1991). The key elements of networking are as follows:

- **Reciprocity** — a willingness to exchange information, know-how, proprietary knowledge and goods (Powell, 1990).
- **Trust** — a willingness to risk placing faith in the reliability of others (Sabel, 1992).
- **Learning** — a recognition that knowledge develops and best-practice should be learnt (Lundvall, 1988).

- **Partnership** — a preparedness to solidify reciprocal relationships preferentially (Sako, 1989).
- **Decentralism** — a realisation that centralised information and decision-processing is inefficient (Aoki, 1986).

Many of these principles have been taken on board by corporations confronted with the starkest of choices as to whether to continue on a downward path by following the old ways (e.g. the General Motors approach) or radically to transform corporate organisation as Xerox did ten years ago, Ford Motor Co did between five and ten years ago and IBM are seeking to do at present (Morgan, Cooke and Price, 1992).

## 3. Networks in innovation

Evidence that this way of thinking underpins EC research and technology development policy comes from the Commission's DG XII report on "Science, Technology and Community Cohesion" (Hingel, 1992). The proposals arising in this document rest on the following research findings on the actual practices of innovation actors and institutions arising from the 28 dossiers on which the report relies:

- in the dozen or so "islands of innovation" in the EC core area there are dense networks of co-operation between innovation actors on local, inter-regional and international scales.
- estabilishing new islands is possible (e.g. Munich — biotechnology; Grenoble — artificial intelligence; Toulouse — aeronautics) but difficult, costly and rare, with major public investment essential.
- co-operation between the "innovation islands" and EC Objective 1 region researchers is higher (25%–35%) for EC programmes than for European cooperation networks in general (5%–8%).
- such co-operations are long-term, personal and university-led. They are based on "comparable competences" in fields where the "periphery" has local sectoral strengths which produce innovative applications of generic technologies.
- diversity thus enhances learning capacities inside and outside the "islands of innovation" (e.g. big corporations learning "flexible specialisation" from peripheral SMEs). Diversity gives a head-start in specific industrial product and process sectors.

- cohesion depends on interactive learning between local research and technology development actors and units, whether inside or outside the leading innovation islands.

In brief this is an optimistic but still realistic perspective on the development process. It recognizes that there is unevenness in the spread of major innovation centres but it opens the prospect of localised innovation built on sectoral specialisation outside of the major centres. It is also worth noting, in passing, that many major innovation centres are outside Europe.

# 4. The competitively advantaged economies

In looking at achieving excellence for regional economies it is wise to focus on what is achievable within practical limits. Thus, regional and small-nation economic comparisons are more appropriate than , say, the Japanese economy with its scale and cultural, financial and governmental assets. For reasons of mix, Denmark (small economy, innovative firms, few large indigenous corporations), Emilia-Romagna (weak regional institutions, many SMEs, no large firms), and Baden-Württemberg (strong Land Government, innovative SMEs, large indigenous corporations) have been selected to illustrate excellence in a relevant context at an appropriate scale. Because the task at hand is to examine the role of Technology, R&D and Technology Transfer in the creation of economic excellence, these elements will receive most attention. Table 1 summarises some basic economic relativities.

## 4.1. Baden Württemberg

This is one of Germany's strongest regional economies with, at its heart, the Mittlerernecker industrial region centred on Stuttgart, where GDP per capita is 34% above the EC average of 100. Key employers are Automotive (237,000), Electronic (266,000) and Mechanical (281,000) Engineering. Leading firms include Daimler-Benz, Porsche and Robert Bosch, all headquartered in the region, Audi, Alcatel-SEL, Sony, IBM and Hawlett-Packard. World-leader machine tool firms like Heidelberg, Trumpf and Traub are also based there.

**Table 1**

**Economic Indicators for Advantaged Economics**

| | Population % (EUR=100) | Industrial Employment % | GDP per Inhabitant 1986–8 (EUR=100) | Unemployment Rate 1990 (EUR=100) |
|---|---|---|---|---|
| Baden-Württemberg | 2.9 | 47.0 | 119.9 | 35.4 |
| Denmark | 1.6 | 27.1 | 112.5 | 79.9 |
| Emilia-Romagna | 1.2 | 36.5 | 127.6 | 55.9 |

Source: European Commission (1991)

The large and small firms (SMEs) of the region interact fruitfully. Many Mercedes, Audi and IBM supplier firms are present in Baden-Württemberg (BW). Helping the SME or Mittelstand sector keep innovative and large firms to acquire basic research institutes (44) an Steinbeis technology transfer centres (120). These, along with the thirteen Chambers of Industry and Commerce, and the trade and industry promotion and financing activities of the Business Associations and the Ministry of Economic Affairs and Technology, are the basis of BW's regional innovation system. To this should be added BW's much vaunted "dual system" of vocational training.

A good example of the way this network operates concerns the impact of "lean production" upon Mittelstand SMEs (see, Morgan, Cooke & Price, 1992):

- Japanese competition causes large firms to demand greater Innovation from SMEs who supply them with components and services.
- Business associations know that **SMEs cannot afford R&D.**
- Ministry of Economics approaches and appoints International consultans to investigate.
- Consultants' report recommends **SME co-operation**, but they fear loss of know-how.
- BW cabinet recommends on Applied Research Institute as third party R&D broker.

In exchange for accepting this solution, with an **Independent intermediary** protecting the innovation knowledge of the SMEs firms will receive government incentives towards the costs of estabilishing R&D functions. By no means all supplier firms — even in the machinery industry where the pressure is severe — will join the initiative, bat many of the non-joiner will become second or third tier suppliers, go under or become Japanese acquisitions.

## 4.2. Denmark

With a population of 5.1 million, approximately half that of Baden-Württemberg, it is not surprising that Denmark has a relative lack of both large, research based firms and a government technology policy. Research bu the European Commission shows that Denmark was slow to introduce microelectronics equipment and that when efforts were made to catch-up in the 1980s there were organisational inadequacies and skills shortages. However, Denmark is the EC's second most prosperous country in terms of GDP per head. Being small, it can generate communication and interaction economies, especiallyin its system of SMEs (Kristensen, 1992).

Of key importance to this system are the support infrastructures for small business, the most important being:
- Chambers of Commerce and Industry
- Local and regional Technical and Special Technical Schools
- Local and regional banks providing long-term loans for local SMEs
- The Danish Technological Institute and its 15 Technology Centers.

**The Danish Technological Institute (DTI)** is a privatized branch of the Ministry of Industry. It employs 1,200 technologists and others in developing, identifying and transferring generic technologies, largely to SMEs. Some 55% of DTI's contract income is from firms employing less than 50 people.

Recognizing that isolation from information and know-how was a handicap to SME's DTI in 1989 estabilished a "Network Programme" which channeled government support to firms willing to co-operate in certain business activities. In one small town in Jutland, the following case-history is instructive:
- seven small furniture makers found local markets shrinking
- they took advantage of the Network Programme
- they created trading company

- they divided up key tasks, so that, for example, design for all firms is done by two designers
- each firm specialises in a particular production phase
- the company now exports high-quality furniture to the EC and beyond.

By 1992, 175 networks existed, in which 42% of firms had increased turnover per year by 4% or more, and one in five by 10% or more since joining. Of key importance to the success of this programme was the appointment by DTI of **"Network Brokers"**. These are local professionals, lawyers, consultants or engineers whose job it is to create networks of firms, colleges, local authorities, enterprise agencies and so on. These networks then bid for grants from technology programmes aimed at product and process innovation, quality improvement, product differentiation, and, very importantly, design, which is seen as key selling point. These pholosophy is that **"The Competitive Advantage of Regions is Achieved through the Competitive Advantage of Firms"**.

## 4.3. Emilia-Romagna

This nothern region of Italy, centred on Bologna, is home to numerous examples of "industrial districts". Bologna itself is a major centre of machineryproduction, Capri specialises in ciothing, Sassuolo in ceramics and Modena in motocycles (Ducati) and luxury cars (Ferrari, Maserati, Lamborghini). Apart from these famous names, Emilia-Romagna (ER) has few large firms but a large number of SMEs (245,000 — 90,000 in manufacturing — employing less than 50 in 1988).

The industrial SMEs tend to cluster in districts which, because of the polycentic urban system of the region, are spread out at the foot of the Apennine mountains. As in other dynamic SME-based economies ER is rich in buisness support infrastructure. The main institutions and their functions are:

- Artisans Associations — accounting, payroll and income tax returns, training, financial advice, technology and premises.
- Local and Regional Banks — small loans, long-term loans, community-based refeeal etc.
- Chambers of Commerce — information, exports, trade fairs, technological and financial advice, marketing.

- Regional Government — regional development agency (ERVET) and local Innovation Centres.

The regional government, the Chambers of Commerce, banks and business associations have shares in **ERVET** (Ente Regionale per la Valorizzazione Economia del Territorio) which in turn runs nine dedicated Innovation Centres. These provide **"real services"** (not financial grants or loans) to SMEs in secific industries. Services include; research, promotion, certification, technological consultancy and training. As an example of the innovative capacity of **CITER** (Centro Informazione Tessile Emilia Romagna) the clothing innovation centre, the following is illustrative:

- Third World firms are increasingly copyig Carpi clothing designs, taking market share
- Artisans Association tells ERVET of loss of Carpi firms' competitive desing advantage
- ERVET asks Italian energy research institute (ENEA) to work with CITER
- ENEA and Citer develop new CAD-CAM desing system
- SMEs access CAD-CAM; time-to-market reduced tenfold
- Market share recovered.

The time to solve this problem was under one year. Let us now look at the approach being taken in less accomplished regional systems.

## 5. The learning economies

If firms in networks make 4% a year more than those outside them, why doesn't everyone join in? There are there reasons:

- firms are protective of their know-how
- firms area fearful of divulging pricing information
- firms, especially SMEs, cannot reap advantage without the existence of a public support infrastructure, at least in the short term.

The first two objections can never ultimately be overcome because know-how and price are two key areas where market transactions eventually triumph over network relations in a competitive arena. The third point has been recognised as a fact even in the home of "rugged individualism", the USA, where learning from European experience has been developing apace, nowhere more so than in Pennsylvania. After looking at this American case, we will return to Europe to explore the three experiences of olderindustrial regions (Nord-Pas de Calais in France, Wales (UK) and the Basque Country in Spain) and the widely-quoted case of Valencia region in Spain, which has successfully applied innovation practices learnt from Denmark, Emilia-Romagna and Baden-Württemberg in its quest for economic excellence.

## 5.1. Pennsylvania

This state lost large numbers of jobs in the 1980s; 50,000 disappeared from the clothing industry, 15,000 from the foundry industry, for example, adding to the strife caused by the closure of Pittsburgh's steel mills in the 1970s and 1980s which cost 100,000 jobs. Typically, in such a context, state and local governments took the lead in seeking economic regeneration, including trying to stimulate innovation in the regional economy.

Pennsylvania's economic strategy moved trough three phases during this period of extended industrial and employment crisis:
- up to 1975 economic development policy was aimed at providing traditional services (information, buisness advice, "signposting") to help individual firms innovate. This was a clear failure.
- 1975–1988 policy changed as the deepened. The strategy became one of helping firms and institutions (trade associations, colleges, unions, local government) in localities to define collectively the services they need. To manage this the state set up the Ben Franklin Partnership (BFP), a development bank to fund joint R&D projects between firms and universities. The assumption was that innovation required finance and technology so the state provided the means to access both. Key to this was BFP's extension service of nine Industrial Resource Centres. These were needed because it quickly became clear that bank-finance and technology were not enough. Firms (mostly SMEs) needed management, marketing, technical and worker training services as well. Above all, SMEs were discovering that innovating in mature industries was more successful than aiming for breakthrough technologies.
- 1988 — the new phase built on this experience. BFP concluded that the most successful element of its work was helping networks of local firms and institutions to help themselves. To support this the Manufacturing Innovation Networks (MAIN) project was set up in 1989. MAIN was learnt from Europe, Denmark in particular. It works by inviting

bids for strategic regeneration projects up to a maximum of $100,000 for one year. Only networks need apply and only four are selected. The first winners were: Pittsburgh foundries, Lehigh Valley clothing; Lake Erie plastic and Philadelphia/Pittsburgh toll-and-die networks. The networks co-operate around any one of four special Technology Centres who protect network-members' know-how, they also have access to specially skilled workers from any of 45 educational centres of excellence.

Although it is early to judge the significance of these efforts, it is worth noting the move up-market by the Pittsburgh foundries. Of 45 in the locality, between a third and a half were selling design, engineering, drafting, welding and machining services as well as, in many cases, just-in-time delivery. Moreover, some were engaging in successful joint-bidding for contracts and co-operating in provision of complementary services. The region was being advertised as a "Foundry Centre", something that had not happened before.

## 5.2. Nord-Pas de Calais

This region of northern France, centred upon Lille, close to the Belgian border has suffered very badly from the loss of its coal industry and severe decline in employment in textiles and steel-making. Table 2 gives relativities in economic indicators for this and three other less-favoured European regions, and should be compared with table 1 above.

The combat, for example, 75,000 textile job-losses in the 1980s, Nord-Pas de Calais (NPC) definitively adopted a regional technology strategy centred upon the Technopole idea at Villeneuve d'Ascq Scientific City. This classically French growth complex is a new town with 60,000 inhabitants, 95,000 students in five universities, eighteen engineering schools and 340 research laboratories employing 4,000 researchers. Major national research institutes, including the Pasteur Institute, CNRS (natural and social science research council) and three others are joined in the region by three CRITTs (Regional Centres of Innovation and Technology Transfer) and numerous incubator centres for high technology start-ups.

However, the judgement is that innovative cross-fertilisation is too weak. Two phases of development in the strategy explain this:

*Philip Cooke*

Table 2

**Economic Indicators for Less-Favoured Regions**

|  | Population % (EUR=100) | Industrial Employment % | GDP per Inhabitant 1986–8 (EUR=100) | Unemployment Rate 1990 (EUR=100) |
|---|---|---|---|---|
| Nord-Pas de Calais | 1.2 | 36.0 | 87.8 | 138.6 |
| Wales | 0.9 | 33.8 | 87.8 | 95.6 |
| Basque Country | 0.7 | 41.6 | 89.0 | 222.6 |
| Valencia Region | 1.2 | 36.3 | 75.3 | 174.3 |

Source: European Commission (1991)

- 1983–89 a strong belief in the natural synergies that flow from geographical clustering was undermined because there wre too many actors, a few privileged firms got the attention, marketing was poor and technology transfer failed.
- 1989–93, a networking strategy was adopted with an animateur agency charged with easing the interactive processes between firms and researchers. The pole in itself recognised as being insufficient to foster innovation.

Firms in the region are more hopeful now but criticise the lack of "people-skills" amongst the engineering community. Marketing has improved but funding criteria are still to rigid and, not surprisingly, many advanced technology start-up SMEs have such specialised technological requirements that the local pole cannot meet them. In essence the strategy was too big, too isolated and inadequately managed. **Networking is perceived as the solution to these problems** (see, especially, Cooke, 1993).

## 5.3. Wales

Wales has experienced significant economic restructuring since 1980. The two main traditional industries of coal and steel have reduced manpower by some 60,000 and while the steel industry is now competitive, the coal industry has virtually disappeared. Wales is fortunate, in the

UK context, in having both a regional department of government, the Welsh Office, and an economic promotion body, the Welsh Development Agency, the main tasks of which have been to modernize the Welsh economy. While there remain pockets of severe unemployment in the former coalfield areas, these organisations have been remarkably successful in helping to introduce new businesses, many from overseas, and to develop innovative business practices amongst indigenous firms. A recent policy development has been to stimulate partnership between regional and local governments, and networking between firms, supported by innovation policies and functions from government bodies.

At present, a number of these initiatives to boost innovation are in place and, though there is not yet a clear Regional Innovation Strategy in place, this may develop with the assistance of the EC RETAS programme. One key survery that has been conducted concerns the identification of the scale of innovative activity within Wales. This shows the following results:

- Gross Expenditure on R&D as a percentage of GDP (1991) in Wales was 1.1%. This is mostly (0.8%) industry expenditure. Wales scores better than, for example, Denmark (0.8%) and Spain (0.6%) but less than half the rate for Germany and Japan (2.9%).
- In Wales, most innovation synergies are between firms more than between firms and universities. Small and medium enterprises are more active than the UK average in winning EC and UK innovation projects.
- There is an increasing demand from both large and smaller firms for intermediary Innovation Centres that can provide services in technology assessment, information and applications.

In response to this situation numerous initiatives have been taken, especially by the Welsh Development Agency (WDA) to assist innovation:

- a great success has been the WDA and Welsh Office foregin direct investment programme which has attracted up to 15% of all the UK Inward Investment since 1980. The total amount of inward investment and reinvestment in 1992 was over L1 billion. Many of these firms are themselves innovative.
- now, in order to balance this success a Suppller Development Programme, which links "clubs" of medium-sized firms vertically to large firms in a supplychain, has been established.
- to help to improve the skills of workers and management in supplier firms, Innovative Training initiatives, aimed at improving the quality of

products and processes, are in place. These are managed in partnership between WDA, Training and Enterprise Councils, Enterprise Agencies and Higher Education Institutes.

- Technology and Innovation Centres where new start-up firms are housed or applied technology services are supplied to firms have been set up in six locations. An EC Relay Centre, enabling firms to exploit EC science and technology programme results, links to these centres.
- WDA manages Eurolink, a programme linking innovative small firms in Wales to firms in partner regions such as Baden-Württemberg, Lombardy, Catalonia, and Rhone-Alpes. These firms exchange technologies and marketing networks.

The next step, soon to be taken, is to link all of these initiatives together in an Innovation Network which enables firms in any location or industry to be put in immediate contact with the precise business support service they require.

## 5.4. The Basque and Valencia Regions

These two represent an interesting contrast because, although they started out with similar kinds of innovation institution, local divergences have resulted in different policy avenues being pursued. The Basque Country has a better GDP per capita but a worse unemployment index than Valencia because it is an older industrial region (steel and shipbuilding) in decline, while Valencia is an up-and-coming consumer industry economy.

In response to its problems of industrial crisis, the Basque regional government devised a technology strategy which established:

- R&D support funding to firms and to 5 Technology Centres
- SPRI, a regional technology transfer agency
- A Technology Park in a rural, campus setting near Bilbao.

While the Technology Park (L100 million public investment) has begun attracting innovative firms, mostly from the region, it is the R&D support, managed by SPRI (Sociedad Para La Promocion y la Reconversion Industrial), that has yielded the most impressive results. In ten years, Basque R&D expenditure moved from 0.1% of GDP to 1,4%, equivalent to Italy by 1989. Five key technological Centres, employing between one and two hundred scientists and support staff, are responsible for this.

They specialise in new materials, factory automation, information technology, machine-tools and energy technologies. Each works with a "club" of associate SMEs to transfer technology on a contract basis. Subsidy to client and supplier is about 30% of the market rate. The centres are well-networked into EC science and technology programmes so that best practice is quickly diffused into local firms. Special attention has been devoted to automative components firms and machine-tool manufacturers. Some of the latter have grown into major competitors to German companies at the cheaper end of the market and, overall, while there are still problems of receptivity towards innovation by many SMEs, leading firms have been able to survive and some to do well in increasingly difficult and competitive international markets.

Like the Basque government that of Valencia region has also adopted a Technology Centres approach to its innovation strategy and agency, IMPIVA, to manage them. Moreover a Science and Technology Park has been built. Industries in Valencia receiving special support are ceramics, footwear, textiles and sciencebased activities. Each of these is located, as in Emilia-Romagna, in industrial districts. Because of this, Valencia formed a partnership with ER to model its strategy on theirs. But more importantly, the Valencians visited Denmark and borrowed the Danish idea of Network Brokerage.

The **Network Brokerage** idea builds on the other elements of the innovation strategy. There are three networks:

- Inner Network: composed of IMPIVA, the Technological Centres, 5 Business Innovation Centres and the Technology Park.
- Outer Network: 4 Regional Universities, Chambers of Commerce, trades unions, design and training agencies.
- Spanish and EC Network.

Network Brokers are drawn from the professions (consultants, engineers etc.) and link networks of firms in particular industries to any or all of these network players. Firms can thus co-operate, as in Denmark, on distribution, sales and promotion, exports, joint purchasing and product and process innovations. Valencian SMEs are, however, over-dependent on support from what is, nevertheless, an expanding public support infrastructure. Even the Emilians are impressed by the excellence of Valencian ceramics but the shoe industry is surviving than booming.

# 6. Mechanisms for realising the innovation network

There are a number of key conditions that have to be present to mobilise the necessary parts of an innovation network. These can be summarised as the "4 Is":

(i) **Identification**
   It is vital that the base upon which an innovation network is to be constructed has a high degree of self-identification, political coherence, policy-commitment and capacity to deliver. Euro-regions with a high degree of administrative (e.g. German Lnder) or politico-cultural basis of identity (e.g. Basque Country) work well in this respect. Wales is also easily identifable, in addition possessing many of the Wales-wide government agencies capable of assisting development within the region.

(ii) **Intelligence**
   In its twin senses of information and learning capacity, this condition is a key source of advantage. "Intelligent regions" such as Emilia-Romagna or Baden-Württemberg have:
   — Good Antennae
   — Quality Information
   — Capacity to Self Monitor and Evaluate
   — Learning Disposition
   — Desire to Implement Lessons Learnt.

(iii) **Institutions**
   An innovation architecture consists of institutions and the people in them. Innovation is an interactive process. The denser the mass of institutions the greater the likelihood that business will gain access to the intelligence for innovation. An element of "redundancy" (i.e. fail-safe "network circuitry") is common in innovative regions. Key institutions are, foe example; strong Chambers of Commerce, Business Associations, Innovation Centres, Training Agencies, Development Agencies, Higher Education Institutions and Firms themselves. In accomplished regions, the public sector institutions tend to be in the background, in weaker ones they are in the foreground.

**(iv) Integration**

The key to a successful innovation architecture is that these institutions form a network not a "jungle". In other words they must organise a division of responsibilities between each other so that a firm or customer approaching any point on the network can be successfully and accurately relayed to the optimum information point in (or beyond) the regional network. The inegration of a network must, for the sake of efficiency, be animated or facilitated by a primus Inter pares such as major businesses or a development agency, chamber of commerce (where it is sufficiently powerful) and so on.

# 7. Steps towards achieving the "4 Is"

Most regionl administations in the EC do not enjoy the "4 I" conditions. They are present to a greater or lesser extent in the country of Denmark and regions such as some German Lnder (e.g. Baden-Württemberg) the French region of Rhone=Alpes, Lombardy and Emilia-Romagna in Italy, Flanders in Belgium and, in limited ways, Catalonia in Spain.

So what is called for to implant such an architecture in the developed regions? There are five steps:

    **1) Stakeholders**
    **2) Strategy**
    **3) Standards**
    **4) Sectors**
    **5) Skills.**

## 7.1. Stakeholders

Stakeholders are the source of Identification. It is not enough to have verbal support to go ahead; there must be real commitment if financial and human resources. Thus the first task of the animateur is to identify and bring together in a network those organisations, institutions and firms which are to be the stakeholders in the innovation architecture. These will include:

Large firms
Small and Medium Enterprises
Higher Education Institutes
Training Organisations
Economic Development Agency
Regional Government
Chambers of Commerce.

These and others will exercies both partership abd guidance of the network. If stakeholding is to be meaningful stakes will be mainly financial (but could be in kind, e.g. equipment, secondments, property).

**The Aim should be to make the innovation Network as close as possible to being self-financing.**

Network centres could be given a 5-year target to achieve this, with public subsidy at the outset tapered to, say 30% by end year 3 and zero at end year 5. Supplementing the subsidy would be shareholdings which the private-sector could take in the Network organisation. Over time, the Network centres would sell services at market rates to cover costs.

## 7.2. Strategy

So what would the Stakeholders have shares in ? To fulfil the "Intelligence" condition, the Innovation Network must be driven by a Regional Technology Strategy. This involves two dimensions:

(i) Regional Technology Audit: a comprehensive review of existing innovation resources. Comparison of levels of Government and Business Expenditure on R&D as % of GDP with targets to be reached in 3, 5, 10... n years etc. Identification of innovative large firms and SMEs; identification of innovative skills-providers, colleges etc. Emergent technologies in firms and universities; linkages with overseas firms in R&D. Involvement in EC R&D schemes; awards of national government innovation incentives etc.

(ii) Lines of Action: creating further advantage on the basis of the audit. Animated by the Stakeholder Network the primary aim would be the building of local capacities for improvement. The fundamental philosophy should be "continuous improvement" towards and beyond benchmarks. Monitoring, evaluation and measurement instruments need to be designed at this stage and consideration given to the all-important factor of innovation delivery mechanisms.

## 7.3. Standards

The Regional Strategy must be suffused with the "continuous improvement of standards" (Japanese: KAIZEN) philosophy. This means:

(i) far-reaching but focused intelligence gathering about best practice in other, appropriate comparator settings,

(ii) estabilishing detailed profiles of research and technologically-related expenditure and — crucially — quality of output from R&D institutions; comparing with best-practice.

(iii) setting targets for improvements in quality-assurance (e.g. IS 90000) amongst domestic and foreign-owned business, support institutions etc.

(iv) raising the number of Preferred Supplier Status or First Tier Supplier firms to foreign and domestic Original Equipment Manufacturers (OEMs).

## 7.4. Sectors

The tried and tested approach to achieving the above is to adopt an industrysector focus. For example, in the Basque case, the dramatic improvement in R&D perfomance was achieved by focusing support principally on the machine-tool and automotive components sectors. A sectoral focus has the following benefits:

(i) simplifies the management of the innovation support architecture

(ii) gives further identification to the strategy

(iii) focuses commitment from the stakeholders

(iv) clarifies the standards of best practice being sought

(v) concentrates the impact of the delivery mechanisms.

A sector focus suggests that, on the key question of delivery mechanisms, a hub-and-spoke system in which, for example, sector-specific innovation-support centres with outreach points can maximise accessibility of centres to firms. Thus, in the Danish case two main DTI centres link to 15 outreach centres, some but not all of which are sector-specific. The Basque Regional Technology Centres are broadly sector specific but have only limited outreach functions. One reason why centres may be inadequate is that they work best in idustrial clusters (e.g. in the Emilia-Romagna context). Most industry is diffused rather than clustered on Italian lines. However, a network arrangement is flexible enough to allow services to be delivered on a more diffused basis.

## 7.5. Skills

There are crucial skill-considerations involved in adopting an Innovation Network Architecture:

(i) **Policy Skills** — an Innovative Network Architecture is neither a State nor a Market institution, at least at the beginning. Thus neither an Administration nor a Competition model of policy implementation is called for, but something in-between. The key elements of networking are outlined in (ii) below; however, questions regarding the identity of:

a) the animateur/facilitator
b) the appointees of the Regional Technology Strategy group
c) those to whom these are accountable
d) those who appoint innovation Centre staff
e) to whom they are accountable

need to be clarified. In general, an entite-mixte with a public-private board would seem most appropriate, but a longer term aim to establish a private firm to manage the Innovation Network, especially Innovation Centres, ahould not be ruled out.

(ii) **Networking Skills** — some people have these, most do not. Generally, those who will work in the innovation Network require training. Networking involves:

a) Reciprocity — an exchange relationship
b) Trust — risking the reliability of others
c) Learning — preparedness to change
d) Partnership — preferential reciprocity
e) Decentralism — very flat hierarchy

**Such practices are unusual in the regions. They must be learned.**

(iii) **Innnovation Skills** — Whichever personnel occupy whatever roles in the Network "hearts" — the innovation Centres — they must:

  a) have the five key networking skills.
  b) be psychologically open, enthusiastic, "Fanatical".
  c) combine technology/business management/and marketing skills.
  d) must be able to convince firms to become members/associates/subscribers/supporters/users of the network, its hubs and spokes.
  e) must themselves be innovative, initiative-taking.
  f) must be well-networked within their country and beyond to innovation centres and systems in EC, Japan and North America.

# 8. The relevance of the model to Poland and other Central and Eastern European economies

New wave thinking about regional innovation comes at a time when the Central and Eastern European economies seem particularly ill-attuned to take advantage of it. This is because of economic problems which have been wellsummarised by Gorzelak and Kukliński (1992) as:

  (i) Obsolete Industrial Structures
  (ii) Technological Backwardness
  (iii) Low Competitiveness
  (iv) Foregin Debt
  (v) Groving Unemployment
  (vi) Deteriorating Consumption.

In some cases — and here the Polish one is clear — radical systemic reforms have been implemented to transform a redundant command economy into a dynamic market economy based on neo-liberal market princicipies. This situation offers both great threats and once-in-a-lifetime opportunities for setting up a new wave regional policy.

In the book of Gorzelak and Kukliński (1992), many of the authors bemoan the lack of appropriate public budgets to allow traditional western regional policies — as practised from the 1930s — to be established. A summary of this position is provided in the words of Boris Fyodorov, the

Russian finance minister as "a very small stick and no carrots" (Cooke, 1993). One way out of this position, also advocated by numerous authors in the quoted book is to localise "regional" policy. That is, to create the conditions where localities can drive each other forwad by competing for economic prosperity. There are two obvious problems with this: first,localities are to weak to compete industrially in a leading and meaningful way; and, second because of this they are prey to receiving the benefits and disbenefits of economic processes operating at a national level. One serious consequence of this is that local and regional disparities will be exacerbated rather than moderated.

What is needed to provide some counterweight to these inevitable tendencies, is a relatively autonomous economic agent sensitive to local conditions but powerful enough to interact meaningfully in economic terms on the national and indeed, international, stage. Such an organisation is the regional economic development agency. As we have seen, to establish a regional innovation strategy there has to be some kind of regional administrative body. This may or may not be democratically controlled at the regional level in the short term, indeed it may be better if democratic control comes later rather than sooner because of the over-riding need, at the beginning, for policy continuity.

Absolutely central to the economic strategy of such organisations, as Kukliński (1992) notes, is Innovation. The agency must be innovative and stimulate innovation. Should there be regional development agencies in all the regions of a particular country? Should there, as Kukliński suggests be ten large Polish regions? Even in Poland, some areas are already innovative, those near the German border will develop faster, those furthest away slowest. On balance, to offset political problems it may be necessary to establish such bodies everywhere but to vary the budgets available — which in any case will be small — according to economic need. In some regions such as Upper Silesia in Poland, the restructuring problem is so great that it must be dealt with — as in the case of the Basque or Wales steel industry restructuring — by national and even international (e.g. EC) policy measures.

To remain with Upper Silesia as an example for a moment, it would be a potentially excellent, though difficult, location in which to seek to establish new wave regional innovation network thinking. This is for three reasons:

(i) it has a strong regional identity

(ii) it has a great need to learn new economic lessons

(iii) it has some of the institutional infrastructure needed.

Also because the region has an elementary heavy industry supply-chain — coal-steel-automotive industry — it has a sensibility (albeit in need of modernisation) of the relativeimportance of inter-industry linkages for economic development. Around automotive engineering (where FIAT can act as tutor), supplier industries presently in place or capable of being attracted from overseas by the regional development agency can be developed. For the smaller or newer indigenous supply firms a Technological institute capable of providing subsidised services which help improve quality, skills, innovation, marketing and financial engineering to automotive firms could be established by the agency as the main stakeholder. In this way, the beginnings of a network can be established. If firms have skills problems, they communicate with the Technological Institute which can mediate with the training infrastructure, or organise training where the infrastructure is underdeveloped. Financial linkages can be developed with international and national banks or loan agencies. Technology transfer through EC or bilateral programmes can be set in place. Perhaps clubs of SME-suppliers could be encouraged to be stakeholders too, later to turn into industry associations and, through contacts with other industry bodies, local or regional Chambers of Commerce and Industry.

These are the lessons of new wave regional innovation in Western Europe, often in areas with a comparable heavy industry tradition to regions of Central and Eastern Europe. It is more difficult to establish such systems in older industrial regions because so much of the "soft infrastructure" is absorbed in or destroyed by the dominating industries of coal, steel and shipbuilding. Nevertheless, the examples of the Basque Country, Pennsylvania, Nord-Pas-de Calais, Wales and, not discussed here but of immense importance, North Rhine-Westphalia (Cooke & Davies, 1993) in Germany, show that progress can be made.

Crucially, the expenditure of very large sums of money — as in the case of the Nord-Pas de Calais technopole — is no necessary guarantee of success. Rather, it is the judicious reorganisation of existing institutional assets and the addition, at relatively low cost, of missing elements such as Business Innovation Centre or Technology Institute, capable of building intelligence through networks, that is the most important ingredient.

# Conclusions

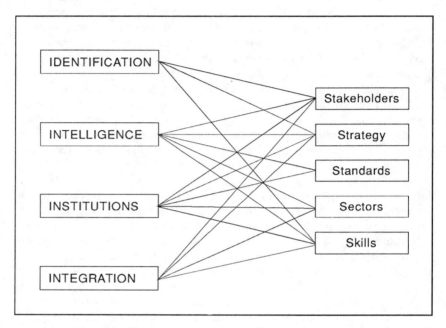

**Fig. 1** Building an Innovation Network Architecture

It is clear from figure 1 that the following are crucial elements of the Innovative Network Architecture.

| Conditions | Steps |
|---|---|
| **INTELLIGENCE** | **Stakeholders** |
| **INSTITUTIONS** | **Strategy** |
| | **Skills.** |

This set of proposals is based on ideas that could, on the experience of selected regions, make a significant contribution to the innovative potential of industry in less advanced regions. The main issue is not whether this should be done, but how soon can it be got underway and what financial resources are needed to set it up. More research is needed into the market demand and technology capability of firms and Higher Education Institutions in development regions. More thinking is needed about the cost of doing this. However, the likelihood is that an innovation Network strategy will not be expensive. The largest Basque technology centres have an annual turnover of ECU 6 million to ECU 8 million. Two Centres at a lesser stage of development than them might warrant an investment of ECU 5 milion each over five years, arranged to boost subsidy at the beginning but on the contractual understanding that subsidy should taper off by the end of the five year start-up and establishment period. Thereafter the Technology Institutes or Innovation Centres, probably one at a time, through a public-private partnership the performance of which can itself be monitored and from which lessons to improve future practice can continue to be learned.

# Biblographical References

Aoki, M., 1986, *Horizontal versus Vertical Information Structure of the Firm*, American Economic Review, 76, 971–983.

Cooke, P., 1993, *Regional Innovation Networks: an Evaluation of Six European Cases*, Topos, 6, 1–30.

Cooke, P., 1993, *A Very Small Stick and No Carrots*, European Planning Studies, 1, 3 (in press).

Cooke, P. & Morgan, K., 1991, *The Intelligent Region: Industrial and Institutional Restructuring in Emilia-Romagna*, Regional Industrial Research Report No.7, University of Wales, Cardiff.

Cooke, P. & Morgan, K., 1992, *Regional Innovation Centres in Europe*, Report to Department of Trade and Industry, London.

Cooke, P. & Davies, S., 1993, *An Economic Profile of North Rhine-Westphalla*, Report to the Welsh Development Agency, Cardiff, RIR.

European Commission, 1991, *The Regions in the 1990s*, Brussels, CEC DGXVI.

Gorzelak, G. & Kukliński, A., 1992, *Introduction* to, *Dilemmas of Regional Policies in Eastern and Central Europe*, Warsaw, EUROREG, 5–7.

Hingel, A., 1992, *Science, Technology and Community Cohesion*, FAST Occasional Paper 300, Brussels, CEC.

Kristensen, P., 1992, *Industrial Districts in West Jutland*, Denmark, [in:] F. Pyke & W. Sengenberger (eds.) *Industrial Districts and Local Economic Regeneration*, Geneva, International Labour Office, 122–174.

Kukliński, A., 1992, *Restructuring of Polish Regions as a Problem of European Cooperation*, [in:] Gorzelak, G. & Kukliński, A., *Dilemmas of Regional Policies in Eastern and Central Europe*, Warsaw, EUROREG, 8–17.

Lundvall, B., 1988, *Innovation as an Interactive Process*, [in:] G. Dosi et al (eds.) *Technical Change and Economic Theory*, London, Pinter, 349–369.

Morgan, K., Cooke, P. & Price, A., 1992, *The Challenge of Lean Production in German Industry*, Regional Industrial Research No. 12, University of Wales, Cardiff.

Powell, W., 1990, *Neither Market Nor Hierarchy: Network Forms of Organisation*, Research in Organisational Behaviour, 12, 295–336.

Sabel, C., 1992, *Studied Trust: Building New Forms of Cooperation in a Volatile Economy*, [in:] F. Pyke & W. Sengenberger (eds.) *Industrial Districts and Local Economic Regeneration*, Geneva, International Labour Office, 215–250.

Sako, M., 1989, *Neither Markets Nor Hierarchies: a Comparative Study of the Printed Circuit Board Industry in Britain and Japan*, paper to Conference on "Comparing Capitalist Economies", London School of Economics.

**Douglas Yuill**
**Kevin Allen**
**University of Strathclyde**
**Glasgow**

# REGIONAL INCENTIVE POLICIES IN THE EIGHTIES: AN OVERVIEW AND ANALYSIS OF POLICY TRENDS IN THE EUROPEAN COMMUNITY COUNTRIES

## 1. Introduction

Looking back to the seventies, most observers interested in regional development issues in the European Community countries would characterise it as a decade where regional policy in general and regional incentive policy in particular were relatively buoyant. Spending on regional development was high and rising, a rich variety of incentive types was on offer and designated problem region coverage was wide-ranging. However, this situation was not to continue. The eighties brought with them a very different environment for regional incentive policy; and this in a number of important respects.

First, as the decade progressed, public expenditure constraints increased in severity in most Community countries. Many policy areas were forced to cut back on expenditure and, in most countries, regional incentive policy was not immune from such developments. Second, in many countries, overall levels of unemployment increased significantly, weakening some of the economic arguments in favour of regional policy at the Member State level. As a result, in a number of countries regional policy declined in priority. This trend was reinforced in some countries by moves towards more free market philosophies and away from direct government intervention. Third, the European Commission's role in influencing regional policy developments grew markedly. On the one hand, the Competition Policy Directorate (DGIV) began to have a constraining influence on certain aspects of regional incentive policy at the Member State level and, in particular, on the types of regional incentive on offer and on area designation systems and coverage. On the other hand, the role of the Regional Policy Directorate (DG XVI) increased in importance as the Structural Funds grew in significance and as the promotion of social and economic cohesion became a key Community objective.

In the light of this changed policy environment it is both interesting and instructive to review the main developments in regional incentive policy in the Community countries since 1980. This is the aim of this paper. It is in six further sections. In the next five sections, a number of the main trends in regional incentive policy are discussed: trends in respect of the **composition** of regional incentive packages (Section 2); trends in regional incentive **administration** (Section 3); trends in incentive**coverage** (Section 4), focusing particularly on change in respect of designated problem regions; trends with regard to maximum **rates of award** (Section 5); and regional incentive **expenditure** trends (Section 6). The final section, Section 7, summarises the main points made and draws together a number of concluding comments.

# 2. The composition of Regional Incentive Packages

The distribution of the main regional incentives in the Community countries by incentive type in 1980 is shown in table 1 (see Annex). It can be seen that the mainstay of most regional incentive packages was the capital grant. Such grants were on offer in all the countries covered and were the key component of the regional incentive package in most. Next in importance were interest-related subsidies, particularly in Belgium and Denmark where they represented the base element of the regional incentives on offer. Fiscal aids were also of significance, being found in over half the countries covered. In contrast, labour-related subsidies were relatively rare and tended to be focused on the service sector or on small firms.

In the course of the eighties there were a number of important changes made to the composition of the regional incentive packages on offer in the Member States. Such changes are highlighted in table 2. Amongst the major schemes to be withdrawn were export sales relief in Ireland (1981), the IDA re-equipment and modernisation programme (1982), the WIR regional allowance in the Netherlands (1983), the company soft loan in Denmark (1985), the British regional development grant and Northern Ireland standard capital grant (1988), the investment allowance in Germany (1989) and the entire Danish regional incentive package (1991). In addition, it has been announced that the special depreciation allowance available in the German Zonal Border Area will be abolished in 1994. On the other side of the coin, major new regional incentive legislation has been enacted in the three countries new to the Community: Greece, Portugal and Spain. Compared to the previous regional incentive regimes in these countries, the new legislation shifted the emphasis from fiscal aids to financial incentives and in particular to capital grants. That having been said, more recent legislation in Greece (1990) has once more moved the focus back towards the fiscal elements of the Greek package. Other new measures introduced since 1980 include training support in both Britain and Germany (though in both countries this was withdrawn towards the end of the eighties), service sector measures in Ireland (1981), regional enterprise grants for small firms in Britain (1988), revamped small firm measures in Ireland (also 1988), two new schemes in France (1991) — the aid to decentralisation and small firm support in rural areas — and the recently-developed business environment policy in the Netherlands.

Overall, a feature of the "withdrawals" in table 2 is that they have tended to be important, large-scale schemes, while — apart from the new Greek, Spanish and Portuguese packages (the significance of which should not be underplayed) — most of the new measures introduced have focused on specific sectors or size groups. Reflecting this, they have tended to be less investment-oriented than most of the large-scale incentives they have replaced.

The current distribution of the main regional incentives in the Community countries by incentive type is shown in table 3. Compared to the 1980 distribution (in table 1), it can be seen that, notwithstanding the reduced emphasis on investment-related measures, capital grants remain central to all the regional incentive packages on offer. Indeed, they have increased in significance during the decade — in part due to the decline in importance of other incentive types (in particular fiscal concessions and interest-related subsidies) and in part because the new regional incentive packages developed in Portugal, Spain and (less so) Greece have a very strong capital grant orientation.

Considering the other incentive types in table 3, interest-related subsidies are now not only relatively rare but are nowhere a key component of the regional incentive package. Over time, budgetary and administrative pressures have caused regional policymakers to favour straightforward and flexible grant support over loan-related finance. As with interest-related subsidies, fiscal concessions have also declined markedly in importance, with the demise of a number of major schemes (export sales relief in Ireland, the WIR regional allowance in the Netherlands and, by 1994, the special depreciation allowance in Germany). Only in Greece, where there have been certain difficulties with the administration of financial incentives, are fiscal concessions a central element of the regional incentive package. Finally, it can be seen from table 3 that the number of labour-related subsidies has grown markedly over the past decade. However, as already mentioned, most of the new schemes introduced have tended to have a specific orientation (towards the service sector or small firms) and have generally involved only limited expenditure. Of the labour-related subsidies listed, only the Mezzogiorno social security concession is important in expenditure terms.

Summing up, the overriding development, since 1980, in respect of the regional incentive types on offer in the Community countries, is that regional incentive packages as a whole have become more straightforward: they are both more grant-oriented than before and, within most packages, offer a more restricted range of regional incentives than was the case in the late seventies/early eighties. These developments reflect the very different incentive environment which now exists, with, as we shall see, reduced overall levels of expenditure (certainly in the northern

Community countries), more European Commission involvement in policy developments and a much greater element of targeting in incentive delivery.

# 3. Trends in regional incentive administration

Turning to consider trends in regional incentive administration, two dominant themes have emerged over the past decade. First, there has been a clear move in a number of Community countries to make regional incentive administration more decentralised; and second, there has been a strong swing of the pendulum away from "automatic" forms of support and towards more discretionary assistance. These twin developments are now considered in turn.

## 3.1. Administrative decentralisation

At the start of the eighties, the administration of regional incentive policy was centralised to a large degree. The main exception to the rule was in the Federal Republic of Germany, where the policy framework was established by the Gemeinschaftsaufgabe, GA, a joint Federal-Land committee, and where individual award decisions were taken primarily at the Land level. However, in the course of the decade, developments took place in a number of countries which increased the degree of administrative decentralisation. These are highlighted in table 4.

Of most significance, in Belgium a Devolution Act was passed in 1980 and extended in 1988 so that, by the end of the decade, the individual Belgian regions (Flanders, Wallonia and Brussels) were entirely responsible for the conduct of industrial (including regional) policy. Elsewhere, too, moves towards more decentralisation occurred, albeit for the most part limited to awards made in respect of small projects and firms. In the Netherlands, for instance, the provincial government level became responsible in 1983 for award administration in respect of projects of up to Fl 1.5 million eligible investment. This limit was then increased to Fl 2 million in 1986 (when fixed annual budgets were also decentralised) before rising to Fl 4 million in 1988 and Fl 10 million at the start of 1993. In France, too, there were moves to decentralise the administration of small and straightforward applications under the regional policy grant, though these had to be abandoned in 1987 in the wake of severe budgetary pressures. On the other hand, the recently-introduced scheme for small firms in rural areas of France (the AIIZR) is to be administered (and co-financed) at the regional level. A further country where there has been administrative decentralisation is Spain. Under 1988 regional incentive legislation, the Autonomous Communities (the Spanish regions) are represented on regional 'working parties' which make award recommendations in respect of smaller projects (awards of up to Pts 1000 million). Finally, table 4 shows that in both Italy and Greece, minor moves towards decentralisation have been introduced in the course of the eighties in respect of very small projects.

All this having been said, and accepting that the trend over the past decade has been almost universally towards more decentralisation in regional incentive administration, it remains the case that, in most countries, the degree of decentralisation is distinctly limited. Only in Germany and Belgium, where the administrative system reflects the federal nature of these countries, is regional incentive administration truly devolved. The lack of any significant administrative decentralisation in most other countries reflects a variety of factors: most notably, the centralist traditions of many of the countries concerned and, in part related, the fear that decentralisation will bring with it wasteful competition between regions for potentially-mobile investment.

## 3.2. Administrative discretion

If the trend towards increased decentralisation of regional incentive administration has generally been limited in its impact, that towards more discretion in regional incentive administration has been far-reaching. At the start of the eighties the picture was straightforward, as table 5 shows. The countries of the Community could be divided into two broad groups. On the one hand, there were those (generally larger) countries which tended to adopt a two-tier approach — a significant automatic base to their regional incentive package (with fixed rates of award and overt award conditions) combined with discretionary "topping up" assistance. On the other hand, the smaller countries, with a relatively low throughput of applications, strongly favoured discretionary support (with rates up to a specified maximum and with administrative discretion in the decision whether or not to make an award).

The current position is very different. As can be seen from table 6, the automatic component of the regional incentives on offer is much reduced. Indeed, only in Italy do large-scale automatic schemes still form the basis of the regional incentive package. Elsewhere, automatic support tends to be restricted to fiscal concessions (most notably in Greece) or else to more narrowly-targeted support — for instance, the ERP regional loan in Germany (aimed at projects, mainly in the service sector, which do not exhibit the primary effect), the SIFIT in Portugal (which focuses on tourism projects) and regional enterprise grants in Britain (limited to small firms). This change in the balance between automatic support and discretionary assistance reflects a variety of developments in the course of the eighties, but in particular the demise of a number of important, automatic schemes — including the WIR regional allowance in the Netherlands, the investment allowance in Germany, the regional development grant in Britain and the capital grant in Northern Ireland.

Although the longer-term trend towards more discretion in regional incentive administration is clear, the point is worth making that there have been some signs in recent years that the swing away from overt, automatic support may be ending. In this context, Law 1892/1990 in Greece not only increased the emphasis on the (automatic) fiscal package in that country, but also introduced fixed and automatic rates of financial incentive award. However, while it is clear from table 6 that overtness in award and simplicity in administration are still highly valued (particularly in the southern Community countries — Greece, Portugal, Italy — but also in the Netherlands and Britain in respect of small projects and in Germany in respect of non-regionally-exporting (mainly service) activities), there remain serious concerns about the budgetary implications of overt, automatic support schemes.

# 4. Trends in regional incentive coverage

Moving on to consider recent developments and longer-term trends in the targeting of regional incentive support, it is obvious that the most important aspect relates to the coverage of the designated problem regions in the Community countries. This is discussed in the next sub-section.

Other elements of regional incentive coverage — specifically industrial eligibility, project-type eligibility and size group eligibility — are considered further in Section 4.2.

## 4.1 Designated problem region coverage

Trends in the population coverage of the designated problem regions in the Community countries are shown in table 7. The table should be read in conjunction with table 8 which provides a narrative of the key changes which have been made to designated problem region coverage since 1980.

From the tables, and in particular from table 7, it is clear that the general trend in designated problem region population coverage has been clearly downwards over the period. Whereas at the start of the eighties just under two-fifths of the Community's population was located in designated regional policy areas, by the early nineties the proportion had dropped to just over one third for the same nine countries (though, interestingly, it was still over the two-fifths mark for the enlarged Community).

However, while there has been an obvious overall decline, it would be wrong to draw the conclusion that all, or even most, countries have cut back on their designated problem regions. Instead, table 7 shows that the countries of the Community divide into two clear groups as far as trends in designated problem region coverage are concerned: those where there has been a significant and steady decline in coverage; and those where coverage is little changed in broad population terms and may even have increased over the course of the decade.

Into the former category, with a significant and steady decline in problem region coverage, come Belgium, Denmark, the west German GA Areas, the Netherlands and the United Kingdom. Over the period, the average percentage population coverage in the designated problem regions in these countries has fallen from just over 35 percent to just over 27 percent, a decline of more than one-fifth. But the cutback in a number of these countries has been even steeper than the table 7 figures would suggest. In Denmark, for instance, regional incentives were abolished at the start of 1991 — in effect reducing, for regional incentive policy purposes, designated problem region coverage to zero. In the Netherlands, the 1990 redesignation exercise has cut back the population coverage of the IPR areas from 19.9 percent to some 10 percent of the national population from the start of 1993 — a decline of almost two-thirds on the figure a decade earlier. And in the United Kingdom, the population coverage of the Development Areas, on which most British regional assistance is focused, has fallen by two-fifths (compared to just one-fifth for the Assisted Areas as a whole).

Overall, then, there have been very significant cutbacks in the five countries mentioned — in part a response to domestic pressures (most obviously, expenditure constraints) but also reflecting the efforts of the Competition Policy Directorate to reduce designated problem region coverage in the more prosperous parts of the Community. One final (and related) point to make in the context of this group of countries where problem region coverage has declined markedly is that, following the decision to withdraw assistance from the so-called "basic areas" in 1991, designated problem region population coverage in Luxembourg has also fallen significantly — to less than four-fifths its 1980 level.

In contrast, the remaining countries in table 7, most of which contain significant Objective 1 regions (ie. those regions which are least developed from a Community perspective), have experienced little or no decline in designated problem region coverage. For instance, in the three newest Member States (Greece, Portugal, Spain) it can be seen that there has been almost uniform stability in the designated areas map since the accession of these countries to the Community. In Ireland, too, designated problem region coverage has changed little over time, perhaps not surprising since the entire country is anyway eligible for regional support. There was, however, a three-year period (1989–91) when extra Irish areas were designated on a temporary basis.

That leaves just two countries to discuss: France and Italy. In the latter, the designation of the Mezzogiorno goes back some forty years. However, while for most of this period the area was treated as a homogeneous mass, significant steps have been taken in recent years to introduce rate discrimination between different parts of the Mezzogiorno. In addition, certain areas of the Mezzogiorno near to Rome have been de-designated while others are under review. Although designated area coverage in Italy has declined only slightly over the period, there are signs that more marked changes will take place in the future.

Turning finally to France, this differs from the other countries in this second group by having no major Objective 1 regions. And yet French problem region population coverage has not declined; on the contrary, it has edged up slightly. In considering the French position, at least two points must be borne in mind. The first is that most of France's designated areas are rural in nature; in the French context this makes de-designation an especially sensitive process (not least given the French view that the Community-wide indicators adopted by the Competition Policy Directorate, with their emphasis on unemployment rates and GDP per head, are not appropriate to the French situation). Second, and perhaps even more important, the wide spatial coverage must be set in the context of very limited levels of regional incentive spending in France. As we shall see, expenditure levels on French regional incentive policy are markedly below those in comparable countries. As a consequence, awards are made on a highly selective basis. As a result, although the designated problem regions in France are widely drawn, only relatively few locations benefit from the award of regional incentive policy support.

Summing up this discussion of spatial coverage trends, it is clear from tables 7 and 8 that there have been a number of major cutbacks over the past decade. Although expenditure constraints have been an important explanatory factor, the role of the European Commission in attempting to reduce problem region coverage in the more prosperous parts of the Community has also been of considerable significance. This having been said, it has to be acknowledged that major spatial cutbacks have been registered in only around half of the Member States — located, for the most part, in the north of the Community. Elsewhere in the Community, and particularly in those countries with major Objective 1 regions, designated problem region coverage has exhibited considerable stability.

## 4.2 Other coverage conditions

The point has already been made that there has been a tendency in recent years for the regional incentives on offer in the Community countries to become more targeted in their application. As has just been noted, this is obviously true of the spatial coverage of assistance, particularly in the northern Member States. However, it also applies to other eligibility criteria — especially those relating to eligible industries, eligible project types and eligible size groups. Key trends in respect of these coverage conditions since 1980 are highlighted in table 9.

In respect of **eligible industries**, an important recent development has been an increasing emphasis on industrial characteristics when making award decisions. Such an approach is found particularly in countries like Portugal, Greece, Italy and Belgium where, as we have seen, there is still a significant automatic component to regional incentive awards. A further industrial focus over the past decade has been on the producer services sector. In the early eighties, new measures introduced in Britain, Germany and Ireland were targeted specifically on this sector. Later in the decade, a wide range of countries took steps to extend their list of eligible activities under the main regional incentive programmes to include specified producer services. Also in the mid-eighties, and to some extent related, there was a trend in a number of Member States to try to improve the attractiveness of regional incentives to innovative activities by widening eligible expenditure to take in intangible factors like the costs of patents and licences. Finally, and again a mid-eighties development, reviews of eligible manufacturing industries were undertaken in some countries (Italy, Portugal, Northern Ireland) with a view to excluding support from sectors where it was felt to be unnecessary or undesirable.

Summing up these developments in industrial coverage, four main themes have been identified in the course of the eighties: within manufacturing, limiting assistance to sectors where it is likely to have an effect (and excluding, in particular, sectors experiencing overcapacity); beyond manufacturing bringing specified business-related services within the scope of policy (initially via service-specific schemes but later by extending the standard list of eligible activities); more generally, encouraging support for innovative activities by providing assistance for "intangibles"; and finally, introducing explicit discrimination within regional incentive packages, based on the industrial characteristics of applicant projects.

In respect of **eligible project types**, it can be seen from table 9 that an important development in the first half of the eighties involved limiting assistance in cases where replacement investment might be aided. In line with this approach, the item-related WIR regional allowance in the Netherlands was withdrawn in 1983 and the previously item-related British regional development grant became project-related in 1984. By and large, the focus came to be placed on job-creating project types (though it is of note that, in nearly all countries, the capability of supporting job-saving projects was retained, albeit often subject to stringent conditions). Within this framework, recent developments in a range of countries (Germany,

Ireland, the Netherlands) have seen significant rate discrimination introduced in favour of setting up projects over extensions. Such moves generally reflect budgetary constraints but, as we have seen, they are also part
of a wider trend to increase levels of rate discrimination within regional
incentive packages.

Turning finally to **eligible size groups**, the point is made in table 9 that
size-related changes have generally been low-key. Just as there are very
few national small firm schemes which have a problem region orientation, so there are few regional incentives with a significant small firm orientation. That having been said, size-related changes have become more
frequent in recent years, though there remains a lack of any major common theme. While in some countries minimum size conditions have been
eased, in others, budgetary constraints have caused smaller projects and
firms to be excluded from eligibility. Against this, a number of countries
do now operate specific small firm measures in the problem regions —
though these generally are only of minor significance, certainly in expenditure terms.

Taking **eligibility criteria** as a whole, the major thrust in recent years
has been towards increasing value-for-money in award. This has involved
a major contraction in eligible problem regions, especially in the northern Member States, and the introduction of more rate discrimination in
award — not only between eligible areas but also involving eligible industries (high-tech sectors being favoured, for instance) and eligible project
types (setting up projects being favoured over extensions). For the most
part, these trends reflect the significantly more restrictive budgetary environment which now applies to most mainstream regional incentive programmes.

# 5. Trends in maximum rates of award

In the course of the past decade the **overall** rate maxima for the regional incentive packages on offer in the Member States of the European
Community have not changed markedly, being determined primarily by
European Commission aid ceilings (see table 10). However, beneath these
ceilings, there have been a number of important developments, as table 11
makes clear.

In the late seventies/early eighties, there was a tendency for rate increases to be registered in response to a deterioration in economic conditions in the problem regions. There then followed a period of relative stability, though it is of note that the new regional incentive package in Greece, following its accession to the Community in 1980, involved increased rate maxima.

Towards the mid-eighties, there was a rise in the frequency of changes in award maxima, with significant cutbacks in respect of specific schemes in countries like the United Kingdom and the Netherlands. However, not all the change was in a downwards direction. New legislation in both Italy and Luxembourg in 1986 resulted in higher rate maxima, while the new regional incentive systems in both Portugal and Spain following their entry into the Community also involved increased award ceilings.

As the eighties progressed, and as budgetary pressures grew in importance, especially in the northern Community countries, both the volume and significance of rate changes increased. Indeed, changes to rates of award were a central characteristic of the policy reviews which took place in many countries in the late eighties. While the resultant rate changes have not all been in a uniform direction, the general tendency has been for lower award ceilings to be introduced for particular policy targets. Thus, as already noted, there were, for instance, significant rate reductions in the Netherlands, Germany and Ireland in respect of extension projects. By the early nineties, rate discrimination had become a feature of many regional incentive packages.

# 6. Trends in regional incentive expenditure

Detailed information on regional incentive expenditure, drawn from national sources in each of the Member States, is contained in the annual publication, **European Regional Incentives**. This information has been brought together in table 12 for the main regional incentives in each of the Community countries. The incentives covered are highlighted in the notes to the table. While a full time-series is available for most Member States, it is worth making the point that no Greek data is available after 1988, while in both Spain and Portugal the statistics relate to the new regional incentives introduced following the entry of these countries into the Community.

In order for expenditure **trends** to be identified it is necessary to bring the data in table 12 on to a constant cost basis. This is done in table 13 which, it will be noted, is in 1990 prices. In considering the trends highlighted, it is useful to deal in turn with each of the countries for which comprehensive time-series information is available.

In **Belgium**, regional incentive spending has been somewhat volatile. An increase in 1981 was followed in most years by decline — but with significant upturns in 1984 and again, very dramatically, in 1988, when expenditure was at its highest level in the period covered. Partly as a consequence of this major increase in expenditure in 1988, both Wallonia and Flanders subsequently took steps to reduce regional incentive spending. Expenditure in 1990 was less than half the 1988 peak, though interestingly it was not very different in real terms from that recorded at the start of the eighties.

In **Denmark**, expenditure has been far less volatile than in Belgium. There has been a steady decline over most of the period covered, with slight upturns in the mid eighties. However, since 1986 decline has once more been significant, with the 1990 figure being less than one half of its 1980 counterpart. Further expenditure reductions can be anticipated as spatial and other policy cutbacks of the late eighties feed through. Indeed, following the abolition of the Danish regional incentive package at the start of 1991, spending in respect of the incentives listed in table 13 is due to end in 1993.

In **France**, too, table 13 shows that the underlying trend has been strongly downwards, particularly in the period after 1984. This decline mirrors the major reductions to the French regional incentive budget in the mid-eighties and the far more selective approach that had to be taken in consequence to regional policy grant (PAT) awards. The increase in 1988 was noteworthy but has since been followed by expenditure figures of one half or less of the 1984 peak. French regional incentive spending remains at relatively low levels viewed from a Community perspective.

In **Germany**, the overall trend up until 1986 was generally more stable than in most other countries. However, there then followed a significant expenditure rise in the late eighties. This is attributable, in large measure, to high levels of spending on the investment allowance over the 1987–89 period, a reflection of the inflow of applications received prior to the withdrawal of the scheme in 1989. With the demise of the investment allowance, the abolition of the special depreciation allowance in 1994 and the recent cutback in GA Area coverage, regional incentive spending in the GA Areas in west Germany seems bound to fall over the next few years, as the focus shifts to the problems of the new east German Laender.

The figures in table 13 in respect of **Greece** are, as already mentioned, less complete than for some other countries, no statistics being available after 1988. The figures in the table focus on the manufacturing sector. They show that expenditure under Law 1262/1982 rose rapidly to a 1983 peak, followed by a gradual decline in the mid-eighties. More recently, that is in 1987 and 1988, expenditure on manufacturing rose again and indeed exceeded the previous (1983) peak. On the other hand, it is of note that expenditure on manufacturing has, over the period, declined significantly as a proportion of total financial aid expenditure in Greece under Law 1262. Indeed, in 1988 it represented less than half the financial aid package total.

In **Ireland**, the broad pattern has been similar to that found in a number of other countries. After a steep rise to a peak in the late seventies/early eighties there was then a significant decline, so much so that the 1983 figure in table 13 is only just over two-fifths the 1981 peak. However, since the mid-eighties expenditure has been more stable, though with a notable peak in 1989 (following on from a low expenditure figure in 1988).

The figures for **Italy** in table 13 must be treated with caution. In the first place the highly-automatic social security concessions (and in particular the historical social security concession) play a dominant role in the figures, accounting for some three-quarters of the Italian expenditure total in the eighties. Second, non-social-security-related expenditure has tended to show considerable swings, particularly in the mid-eighties. It is, moreover, of note that expenditure on the main financial incentives has increased every year following the introduction of revised Mezzogiorno incentive legislation in 1986. The increase in 1990 was especially marked, more than doubling the 1989 figure. This upsurge was attributable to a rush of applications prior to the de-designation of the provinces of Ascoli-Piceno and Roma at the end of 1990. Finally, the point must be made that, different from all the other regional incentive packages in the Community countries, the Mezzogiorno aid package is administered in an almost wholly automatic manner. Rates of award are fixed and conditions of award are overt. Accordingly, the Italian expenditure trends in table 13 do not reflect policy changes to any major extent — rather, they mirror underlying investment and employment creation in the Mezzogiorno.

In **Luxembourg,** no real trend is discernible, expenditure having fluc-
tuated considerably over the period covered. Such fluctuation is inevitable
in a country where one or two major investments can have a massive impact on 'trends'. It is, however, noteworthy that expenditure in the second
half of the eighties (and in 1990) was considerably above that recorded in
the first half of the decade.

In **the Netherlands,** the pattern found in most other countries is re-
peated up until the end of 1984. Investment premium expenditure rose to
a 1978 peak, after which it declined steadily, notwithstanding an upturn in
1982 (apparently attributable to a few, very large projects). However, in
the mid-eighties there was, once more, a notable rise in spending which,
in fact, took expenditure above budget levels. In part, this budget overrun
was due to an upturn in the Dutch economy, but it also reflected the
moves to decentralise decision-making to the Dutch provinces and the
fact that the scheme was under review at the time (encouraging a flood of
applications in the expectation of cutback). In response, there was a considerable tightening of investment premium eligibility conditions which
led to significantly reduced expenditure in 1986 and again in 1987. The
1988 increase once more led to measures to reduce spending. As a result,
a very major fall was recorded in 1989, though there was an upturn again
in 1990. Even so, the 1990 figure is, in real terms, less than half the 1982
peak. Following the introduction of a new Regional Policy Memorandum
for the period 1991–94, investment premium spending seems likely to
continue at these historically low levels.

In **Portugal** and **Spain** consistent time-series information is, as mentioned earlier, limited since the regional incentives in both countries are
of relatively recent origin (dating, in their current form, only from 1988).
A detailed overview of trends is not therefore possible. It is, however, of
note that in both countries levels of expenditure have been generally on an
upward path and have been higher than originally anticipated, leading to
the introduction of measures which are intended to constrain expenditure
in future years.

Finally, in the **United Kingdom,** the picture is one of a significant decline in incentive expenditure for the period covered (and indeed since
1976). While the on-going decline was halted briefly in 1986 with an upturn
in regional development grant expenditure (related to a general improvement in economic conditions and to the transitional provisions associated
with the introduction of a new version of the regional development grant

following the November 1984 White Paper), the fall in British regional incentive expenditure has subsequently been re-established and is likely to continue as the withdrawal of the regional development grant in March 1988 works its way through. As can be seen from table 13, expenditure in 1990 was significantly less than half its counterpart at the start of the eighties.

Bringing these various **expenditure trends** together, it is useful to draw a distinction between the northern and southern Community countries. In the former, there has been a clear decline in regional incentive spending in the course of the decade in most countries. This has been especially true in countries like Denmark, the Netherlands and the United Kingdom where the decline has been more than 50 percent, but it also applies to countries like France and Ireland. In contrast, in Belgium and, to a lesser extent, Luxembourg, there has been no clear trend up or down, while in Germany a tendency for expenditure to fall in the first half of the decade was reversed as spending on the investment allowance increased dramatically prior to its withdrawal in 1989. However, with the demise of the investment allowance and announced withdrawal of the special depreciation allowance in 1994, it is to be expected that regional incentive expenditure in the west German GA Areas will soon return to far lower levels. Indeed, the GA budget for the western Laender is due to fall 30 percent between 1991 and 1994. Overall, then, the underlying expenditure trend in the northern Community countries has been clearly downwards. In contrast, southern countries like Portugal, Spain, Greece and also Italy have seen significant increases in regional incentive spending in recent years, often following the introduction of new legislation in the mid to late eighties. However, here too the signs are that expenditure constraints will become more significant in the nineties.

# 7. Summary and conclusions

The aim of this paper has been to review the main developments in regional incentive policy in the countries of the European Community in the period since 1980.

As far as the **composition of regional incentive packages** is concerned, the past decade has seen the withdrawal of a number of important, large-scale schemes including, in the last few years, the British regional development grant, the Northern Ireland capital grant and the German investment allowance — not to mention the demise of the entire Danish regional incentive system at the start of 1991. While there has also been a significant flow in the opposite direction, with new regional incentive measures being introduced, these have tended to be much smaller scale and to be focused on specific sectors or size groups. Recent examples include the (small-firm-oriented) regional enterprise grants for investment and innovation in Britain, the aid to decentralisation and grant for small firms in rural areas in France and the new business environment policy in the Netherlands. Only in those Member States new to the Community — Portugal, Spain and Greece — have important new capital-grant-based systems been introduced.

Reflecting these various developments, regional incentive packages as a whole have generally become less investment-oriented than was the case in the early eighties. That having been said, capital grants remain central to all the regional incentive packages on offer. Indeed, a comparison of tables 1 and 3 shows that capital grants have, in fact, increased in significance over the past decade — in part due to the decline in importance of other incentive types (in particular, fiscal concessions and interest-related subsidies) and in part because, as already mentioned, the new regional incentive packages developed in Portugal, Spain and (less so) Greece have a very strong capital grant orientation.

Summing up in respect of changes in incentive type, the overriding development since 1980 is that regional incentive packages as a whole have become more straightforward: they are both more grant-oriented than before and, within most packages, offer a more restricted range of regional incentives than was the case in the late seventies/early eighties. These developments reflect a number of important changes in the regional incentive environment and, in particular, as we have seen, reduced overall levels of expenditure (certainly in the northern Community countries), more European Commission involvement in policy developments and a much greater element of targeting in regional incentive delivery.

Moving on to consider trends in **regional incentive administration**, two dominant themes have emerged over the past decade. First there has been a clear move in a number of Community countries to make regional incentive administration more decentralised, as least for small projects and firms. As table 4 shows, there have been very significant developments in this direction in Belgium and important changes, too, in the Netherlands and, to a lesser extent, France and Spain. Even so, it remains the case that, in most Member States, the degree of decentralisation in regional incentive administration is distinctly limited. Only in Germany and Belgium, where the administrative system reflects the federal nature of these countries, is regional incentive administration truly devolved. The lack of significant administrative decentralisation in most other countries reflects a variety of factors: most notably, the centralist traditions of many of the countries concerned and, in part related, the fear that decentralisation will bring with it not only difficulties in ensuring equity in award but also wasteful competition between regions for potentially-mobile investment.

If the trend towards increased decentralisation of regional incentive administration has generally been limited in its impact, the second key administrative trend — that towards more discretion in regional incentive administration — has been far-reaching. Whereas at the start of the eighties automatically-administered incentives played a very important role, especially in the larger Community countries (see table 5), by the end of the decade it was only in Italy that large-scale automatic schemes still formed the basis of the regional incentive package (see table 6). Elsewhere, automatic assistance tends now to be restricted to fiscal concessions (as in Greece) or else to more narrowly-targeted support (as with particular schemes in Germany, Portugal and Britain).

The change in the balance between automatic support (with fixed rates of award and overt award conditions) and discretionary assistance reflects a variety of developments during the eighties, but especially the demise of important large-scale automatic schemes like the WIR regional allowance in the Netherlands, the regional development grant in Britain and the investment allowance in Germany. While it is clear from table 6 that overtness in award and simplicity in administration are still highly valued (particularly in the southern Community countries like Greece, Portugal and Italy but also with regard to more narrowly-targeted support in the Netherlands, Britain and Germany), the serious concerns which exist about the budgetary implications of overt, automatic support schemes mean that there is unlikely to be any major swing back towards such forms of support.

Turning, next, to consider recent developments and longer-term trends in the **targeting of regional incentive support**, the most significant changes to the eligibility criteria attached to the regional incentives on offer have been in respect of the coverage of the designated problem regions in the

Community countries. From table 7 (and the related table 8) it can be seen that the Member States divide into two clear groups as far as trends in designated problem region coverage are concerned.

On the one hand, there is a group of northern Member States (Belgium, Denmark, (west) Germany, the Netherlands, the United Kingdom and also Luxembourg) where there have been very significant declines in problem region population coverage. Whereas at the start of the eighties none of these countries had less than one quarter of its population in designated problem regions and the "norm" lay close to two-fifths of the national population, by the early nineties, most of the group had less than one-third of their population in designated problem regions and in both the Netherlands and (in effect) Denmark the figure was well below 20 percent. In part these cutbacks are a response to domestic pressures (most obviously, expenditure constraints) but they also reflect the efforts of the Competition Policy Directorate to reduce designated problem region coverage in the more prosperous parts of the Community.

On the other hand, the remaining countries in table 7 have experienced little or no decline in designated problem region coverage. Most of these countries contain significant Objective 1 regions, reflecting the fact that they represent the least-developed parts of the Community. Only France does not fall easily into this categorisation. However, in France, the continuing wide spatial and population coverage of the designated problem regions must be set in the context of very limited levels of regional incentive spending and (related) the highly selective nature of regional policy grant (PAT) awards. Although the designated problem regions in France are widely drawn, only relatively few locations benefit from the award of regional incentive support.

Just as there has been a more targeted approach to designated problem regions over the past decade, particularly in the northern Member States, it can be seen from table 9 that other aspects of regional incentive policy have also become more targeted in their application — activity coverage, project-type coverage and size coverage.

Beginning with the first of these, activity coverage, a number of important developments are highlighted in table 9: a tendency within manufacturing to limit assistance to sectors where it is likely to have most effect (excluding, for instance, sectors experiencing overcapacity); a trend to bring specified business-related services within the scope of policy; more generally, a move to encourage support for innovative activities by providing assistance for "intangibles"; and finally the introduction of explicit rate discrimination within a number of regional incentive packages, based on the industrial characteristics of applicant projects. Such an approach is found particularly in countries like Portugal, Greece, Italy and Belgium where there remains a significant automatic (i.e. overt) component to regional incentive awards.

In respect of project-type coverage, a key change in the early eighties involved limiting assistance in cases where replacement investment might be aided (as reflected in changes made to the Dutch WIR regional allowance and British regional development schemes). More recently, explicit rate discrimination has been introduced in favour of setting up projects over extensions in countries like Germany, Ireland and the Netherlands (for details, see table 9). Such moves have generally reflected budgetary constraints but, in addition, are part of a wider trend in recent years to increase levels of rate discrimination within regional incentive packages.

Considering, finally, size group coverage it can be seen from table 9 that size-related changes have tended to be low-key, though they have become more frequent in recent years. On the other hand, there remains a lack of any obvious size-related theme over time. While in some countries minimum size conditions have been eased, in others, budgetary constraints have caused smaller projects and firms to be excluded from eligibility. Against this, a number of countries do now operate specific small firm measures in the problem regions, though these generally are only of minor significance, certainly in expenditure terms.

Taking eligibility criteria as a whole, the main thrust in recent years has been towards increasing value-for-money in award. This has involved a major contraction in eligible problem regions, especially in the northern Member States, and the introduction of more rate discrimination in award — not only between eligible areas but also involving eligible industries (high-tech sectors being favoured, for instance) and eligible project types (setting up projects being favoured over extensions). For the most part, these trends reflect the significantly more restrictive budgetary environment which now applies to most mainstream regional incentive programmes.

With regard to trends in **maximum rates of award**, an important initial point to make is that overall rate maxima for the regional incentive packages on offer in the Member States have not changed markedly, being determined primarily by European Commission aid ceilings (see table 10). That having been said, it should be noted, first, that nominal rate maxima in Greece, Portugal and Spain increased significantly following their entry into the Community and, second, that beneath the ceilings set by the Commission there have been a number of important developments, especially in recent years.

As can be seen from table 11, changes in rate maxima became more frequent and significant towards the end of the eighties, with moves in a number of countries towards lower award ceilings for particular policy targets. Thus, as already mentioned, notable rate reductions were introduced in the Netherlands, Germany and Ireland, particularly in respect of extension projects. By the early nineties, rate discrimination had become a notable feature of many regional incentive packages.

Moving on to deal finally with trends in **regional incentive expenditure**, it is useful, when considering table 13, to draw a distinction between the northern and southern Community countries. In the former, there has been a clear decline in regional incentive spending in the course of the decade in most countries. This has been especially true in countries like Denmark, the Netherlands and the United Kingdom where the decline has been more than 50 percent, but it also applies to countries like France and Ireland. In contrast, in Belgium and, to a lesser extent, Luxembourg, there has been no clear trend up or down, while in Germany a tendency for expenditure to fall in the first half of the decade was reversed as spending on the investment allowance increased dramatically prior to its withdrawal in 1989. However, with the demise of the investment allowance and announced withdrawal of the special depreciation allowance in 1994, it is to be expected that regional incentive expenditure in the west German GA Areas will soon return to far lower levels. Indeed, the GA budget for the western Laender is due to fall 30 percent between 1991 and 1994. Overall, then, the underlying expenditure trend in the northern Community countries has been clearly downwards. In contrast, southern countries like Portugal, Spain, Greece and also Italy have seen significant increases in regional incentive spending in recent years, often following the introduction of new legislation in the mid to late eighties. However, here too the signs are that expenditure constraints will become more significant in the nineties.

# Annex

**Table 1**

**Distribution of Regional Incentives**
**by Country and Incentive Type (1980)**

| COUNTRY | INCENTIVE | CG | IRS | TC | DA | LRS |
|---|---|---|---|---|---|---|
| BELGIUM | interest subsidy | | ✓ | | | |
| | capital grant | ✓ | | | | |
| DENMARK | company soft loan | | ✓ | | | |
| | investment grant | ✓ | | | | |
| | municipality soft loan | | ✓ | | | |
| FRANCE | regional development grant (PDR) | ✓ | | | | |
| | service location grant (PLAT) | | | | | ✓ |
| | local business tax concession | | | ✓ | | |
| GERMANY | investment allowance | ✓ | | | | |
| | investment grant | ✓ | | | | |
| | special depreciation allowance | | | | ✓ | |
| | ERP regional soft loan | | ✓ | | | |
| IRELAND | IDA grant — new | ✓ | | | | |
| | IDA grant — re-equipment | ✓ | | | | |
| | export sales relief | | | ✓ | | |
| ITALY | Cassa grant | ✓ | | | | |
| | national soft loan | | ✓ | | | |
| | social security concession | | | | | ✓ |
| | tax concessions | | | ✓ | | |
| LUXEM-BOURG | capital grant | ✓ | | | | |
| | interest subsidy | | ✓ | | | |
| | tax concession | | | ✓ | | |
| NETHER-LANDS | investment premium | ✓ | | | | |
| | WIR regional allowance | | | ✓² | | |
| UNITED KINGDOM | regional development grant | ✓ | | | | |
| | selective financial assistance | ✓³ | ✓³ | | | |
| | office/service industries | | | | | ✓ |

**Notes**

[1] Incentive type abbreviations: CG=capital grant; IRS=interest-related subsidy; TC=tax concession; DA=depreciation allowance; LRS=labour-related subsidy.

[2] The WIR allowance is taken in the form of a capital grant when no taxable profits are made and in the form of reduced tax payments when there are taxable profits.

[3] Under the Selective Financial Assistance scheme grants or soft loans are available. Most awards take the form of a capital grant.

**Source:** European Regional Incentives, 1980

**Table 2**

### Key Changes in the Composition
### of Regional Incentive Packages 1980–92

**1980** The in-plant training grant scheme was introduced into the British regional selective assistance package (only to be withdrawn in 1988).

**1981** Export sales relief was withdrawn in Ireland (and replaced by a 10 percent rate of corporation tax for manufacturing industry).

New support for service sector development was introduced in Ireland; there was a new special investment grant for high-grade jobs in Germany; and a major new package was introduced in Greece (following that country's accession to the Community).

**1982** New legislation in France saw the regional policy grant (PAT) replace a range of measures (including the PDR, FSAI, PLAT and PLAR). A previously available decentralisation subsidy was withdrawn.

New legislation in Greece emphasised the importance of the financial elements of the Greek package.

The IDA programme for re-equipment and modernisation projects was withdrawn in Ireland.

**1983** A special investment grant for long-term training places was introduced in Germany (withdrawn in 1989).

More importantly the item-related WIR regional allowance was withdrawn in the Netherlands.

**1984** Major new legislation was introduced in Britain. The regional development grant became project-related (having previously been item-related) and also job-related. The office and service industries scheme was incorporated into regional selective assistance.

**1985** The company soft loan was withdrawn in Denmark.

**1986** Important new legislation was passed in both Italy and Luxembourg, but the basic composition of the regional incentive packages remained unchanged.

**1986–8** New regional incentive packages were introduced in Spain and Portugal, based heavily on capital grants.

**1988** Regional development grant was withdrawn in Britain (replaced for small firms by regional enterprise grants); standard capital grant was abolished in Northern Ireland; investment allowance was phased out in Germany; special depreciation allowance was withdrawn in France.

**1990** New legislation in Greece emphasises fiscal rather than financial elements of the package.

**1991** Regional development incentives were abolished in Denmark. Two new schemes were introduced in France — aid to decentralisation (from Paris); and support for small firms in rural areas. New business environment policy was announced in the Netherlands. Also announced was the withdrawal of the special depreciation allowance in Germany in 1994.

**Table 3**

**Distribution of Regional Incentives
by Country and Incentive Type (1992)**

| COUNTRY | INCENTIVE | INCENTIVE TYPE[1] | | | | |
|---|---|---|---|---|---|---|
| | | CG | IRS | TC | DA | LRS |
| BELGIUM | interest subsidy | | ✓ | | | |
| | capital grant | ✓ | | | | |
| DENMARK | no regional incentives[2] | | | | | |
| FRANCE | regional policy grant (PAT) | ✓[3] | | | | ✓[3] |
| | local business tax concession | | | ✓ | | |
| GERMANY[4] | investment grant | ✓[5] | | | | ✓[5] |
| | special depreciation allowance | | | | ✓ | |
| | ERP regional soft loan | | ✓ | | | |
| GREECE | investment grant | ✓ | | | | |
| | interest rate subsidy | | ✓ | | | |
| | increased depreciation allowance | | | | ✓ | |
| | tax allowance | | | ✓[6] | | |
| IRELAND[7] | IDA grant — new | ✓ | | | | |
| | IDA grant — small | ✓ | | | | ✓ |
| | IDA grant — services | ✓ | | | | ✓ |
| ITALY | capital grant | ✓ | | | | |
| | national fund scheme | | ✓ | | | |
| | social security concession | | | | | ✓ |
| | tax concessions | | | ✓ | | |
| LUXEM-BOURG | capital grant/interest subsidy | ✓[8] | | | | |
| | tax concession | | | ✓ | | |
| NETHER-LANDS | investment premium | ✓ | | | | |
| PORTUGAL[9] | SIBR | ✓ | | | | ✓ |
| | SIPE | ✓ | | | | |
| | SIFIT | ✓ | | | | ✓ |
| SPAIN | regional investment grant | ✓ | | | | |
| UNITED KINGDOM | | | | | | |
| (a) GREAT BRITAIN | regional selective assistance | ✓[10] | | | | |
| | regional enterprise grants[11] | ✓ | | | | |
| (b) NORTHERN IRELAND | selective assistance | ✓[12] | ✓[12] | | | ✓[12] |

**Notes**

[1] Incentive-type abbreviations: CG = capital grant; IRS = interest-related subsidy; TC = tax concession; DA = depreciation allowance; LRS = labour-related subsidy.

[2] The regional development grant and municipality soft loan were abolished as from 1 January 1991, together with the rest of the Danish regional incentive package. *Ad hoc* support (by special Act of Parliament) may be available to potential inward investment projects which locate in the former Development Areas. Also, discretionary and temporary support can be given to the industrial development of specific regions where events make this necessary (e.g. large industrial closures).

[3] For manufacturing projects the PAT is generally an amount per job created up to a maximum expressed as a percentage of eligible investment. Given its investment-related ceiling, this component of the PAT scheme has been allocated to the 'CG' column in the table. For eligible non-manufacturing projects (basically research and tertiary activities), the PAT is calculated as an amount per job created. This component of the PAT scheme has been allocated to the 'LRS' column. The new AIIZR for small projects in rural areas takes the form of a capital grant.

[4] A non-regional investment allowance (a capital grant) is available in the new eastern *Laender*. The special depreciation allowance will be terminated by the end of 1994.

[5] The special investment grant for high-grade jobs takes the form of a fixed amount per high-grade job created.

[6] This is in terms of a fixed percentage of investment costs up to a maximum percentage of taxable profits in any given year. As a result of Law 1892/1990, the fiscal component of the Greek package has increased in importance.

[7] Each IDA scheme consists of a package of assistance: new industry programme — includes capital grants, employment grants, R&D grants, management development/training grants, interest relief grants, loan guarantees, rent subsidies; small industries programme — includes employment or training grants, management development grants, capital grants, loan guarantees, rent/interest subsidies, equity participation, R&D grants, with greater emphasis placed recently on repayable support funding mechanisms; international services programme — primarily through employment grants, but including capital grants, rent subsidies, training grants.

[8] The overwhelming majority of awards have been in the form of a capital grant.

[9] The SIBR has three components: grant-related "industrial policy" and "location" components and a job-related "employment" component. The SIFIT has two components: a grant-related "location" component and an award-per-job-created 'employment' component. The SIPE involves grant assistance.

[10] Regional selective assistance normally takes the form of a capital grant but may also involve exchange risk cover for European loans.

[11] These grants divide into investment grants for firms with fewer than 25 employees and innovation grants for firms with fewer than 50 employees.

[12] The main elements of selective assistance are (a) an industrial development grant, (b) an employment grant, (c) interest relief grants or soft loans and (d) marketing grants.

**Source:** European Regional Incentives, 1993

**Table 4**

**Key Changes in Administrative Decentralisation 1980–92**

| COUNTRY | CHANGE |
| --- | --- |
| BELGIUM | A major step towards regional devolution was taken by the Devolution Act of 8 August 1980. Further decentralisation legislation (Law of 8 August 1988 which came into force on 1 January 1989) means that regional governments are now entirely responsible for the conduct of industrial policy. |
| DENMARK | No significant change. However, following the abolition of regional development grants, loans and authorities from 1 January 1991, more emphasis is now being placed on local initiatives to encourage industrial development. |
| FRANCE | The Regional Policy Grant (PAT), which replaced the highly centralised Regional Development Grant (PDR) in 1982, introduced a two-tier system of incentive administration, with small and straightforward cases being dealt with at the regional level. However, budgetary pressures led to the abolition of this regional component of the PAT in 1987. On the other hand, away from the PAT, regional and local authorities in France now have considerably more industrial development powers than at the start of the eighties. Moreover, the new AIIZR, which is aimed at small and medium-sized firms in rural areas, is to be administered (and co-financed) at the regional level. |
| GERMANY | No significant change. |
| GREECE | A degree of decentralisation was introduced into incentive application and decision procedures by Law 1262/1982, albeit only in respect of investment projects of up to Drs 200 mn. This ceiling was subsequently increased to Drs 300 mn in 1985 and Drs 450 mn in 1988. |
| IRELAND | No significant change. |
| ITALY | Applications from artisans *(artigiani)* involving L2 bn less of fixed investment were devolved to the regional level under the 1986 *Mezzogiorno* Law. |
| LUXEMBOURG | No significant change. |

NETHERLANDS
From 1 January 1983 Investment Premium (IPR) administration was decentralised to the provincial government level in respect of projects with eligible investment of up to Fl 1.5 mn. In February 1986, the eligible investment ceiling was raised to Fl 2 mn and, very significantly, fixed annual IPR budgets were introduced to cover decentralised awards made. In June 1988, the eligible investment ceiling for provincial awards was raised again, this time to Fl 4 mn. From 1 January 1993, the ceiling became Fl 10 mn. Decentralisation initiatives have also meant that the new BOB (business environment programme) will be administered via 13 city-regions rather than at the provincial level.

PORTUGAL
No significant change.

SPAIN
In 1984 there was a significant devolution of power to the 17 Autonomous Communities (regions) in Spain. Since then they have played more of a role in regional incentive administration. Under 1988 regional incentive legislation, the Autonomous Communities are represented on "working parties" at the regional level which make award recommendations in respect of smaller projects (awards up to Pts 1000 mn). Within the regional working parties, the Autonomous Communities are responsible for award recommendations for projects involving investment of less than Pts 75 mn. Discussions have taken place to encourage the Autonomous Communities to finance support for projects below Pts 75 mn; since the end of 1990 regional investment grant support has effectively been restricted to larger projects.

UNITED KINGDOM
No significant change.

Table 5

### Degree of Administrative Discretion
### by Country and Incentive Type (1980)

| COUNTRY | INCENTIVE | CG | IRS | TC | DA | LRS |
|---|---|---|---|---|---|---|
| BELGIUM | interest subsidy | | D | | | |
| | capital grant | D | | | | |
| DENMARK | company soft loan | | D | | | |
| | investment grant | D | | | | |
| | municipality soft loan | | D | | | |
| FRANCE | regional development grant (PDR) | A/D | | | | |
| | service location grant (PLAT) | | | | | A/D |
| | local business tax concession | | | A | | |
| GERMANY | investment allowance | A. | | | | |
| | investment grant | D | | | | |
| | special depreciation allowance | | | | A | |
| | ERP regional soft loan | | A | | | |
| IRELAND | IDA grant — new | D | | | | |
| | IDA grant — re-equipment | D | | | | |
| | export sales relief | | | A | | |
| ITALY | Cassa grant | A | | | | |
| | national soft loan | | A | | | |
| | social security concession | | | | | A |
| | tax concessions | | | A | | |
| LUXEM-BOURG | capital grant | D | | | | |
| | interest subsidy | | D | | | |
| | tax concession | | | D | | |
| NETHER-LANDS | investment premium | A/D | | | | |
| | WIR regional allowance | | | A | | |
| UNITED KINGDOM | regional development grant | A | | | | |
| | selective financial assistance | D | D | | | |
| | office/service industries | | | | | D |

**Notes**

[1] Incentive-type abbreviations: CG = capital grant; IRS = interest-related subsidy; TC = tax concession; DA = depreciation allowance; LRS = labour-related subsidy.

[2] D = administrative discretion in award, rates *up* to a maximum
A = little or no administrative discretion in award, rates *fixed*
A/D = basically automatic, but with an element of discretion for large projects and/or cases of special regional importance.

**Source:** European Regional Incentives, 1980.

Table 6

**Degree of Administrative Discretion
by Country and Incentive Type (1992)**

| COUNTRY | INCENTIVE | CG | IRS | TC | DA | LRS |
|---|---|---|---|---|---|---|
| BELGIUM | interest subsidy | | A/D[3] | | | |
| | capital grant | A/D[3] | | | | |
| DENMARK | (regional development grant) | (D)[4] | | | | |
| | (municipality soft loan) | | (D)[4] | | | |
| FRANCE | regional policy grant (PAT) | D | | | | D |
| | local business tax concession | | | | A | |
| GERMANY | investment grant | D | | | | D |
| | special depreciation allowance | | | | A | |
| | ERP regional soft loan | | A | | | |
| GREECE | investment grant | A/D[5] | | | | |
| | interest rate subsidy | | A/D[5] | | | |
| | increased depreciation allowance | | | | A | |
| | tax allowance | | | | A | |
| IRELAND | IDA grant — new | D | | | | |
| | IDA grant — small | D | | | | D |
| | IDA grant — services | D | | | | D |
| ITALY | capital grant | A[6] | | | | |
| | national fund scheme | | A | | | |
| | social security concession | | | | | A |
| | tax concessions | | | A | | |
| LUXEMBOURG | capital grant/interest subsidy | D | | | | |
| | tax concession | | | D | | |
| NETHERLANDS | investment premium | A/D[7] | | | | |
| PORTUGAL | SIBR | A/D[8] | | | | A/D[8] |
| | SIPE | A/D[8] | | | | |
| | SIFIT | A | | | | A |
| SPAIN | regional investment grant | D[9] | | | | |
| UNITED KINGDOM | | | | | | |
| (a) GREAT BRITAIN | regional selective assistance | D | | | | |
| | regional enterprise grants | A | | | | |
| (b) NORTHERN IRELAND | selective assistance | D | D | | | D |

## Notes

[1] Incentive-type abbreviations: CG = capital grant; IRS = interest-related subsidy; TC = tax concession; DA = depreciation allowance; LRS = labour-related subsidy.

[2] D = administrative discretion in award, rates *up* to a maximum.
A = little or no administrative discretion in award, rates fixed.
A/D = incentives with both automatic and discretionary components.

[3] In Wallonia, rates of award are determined by both quantitative criteria (under which awards are automatic, depending on job creation and value added per job) and qualitative criteria (under which awards are discretionary). In Flanders, there is discretion in the award decision (focusing mainly on project viability); thereafter, rates of award are largely predictable, though the (discretionary) "strategic importance" component has recently increased from 3 percent to 6 percent of eligible expenditure.

[4] These schemes were abolished as from 1 January 1991.

[5] Although rates of award are now fixed, there remains discretion in the decision whether or not to make an award.

[6] While the capital grant is basically automatic in character, the first and third implementation plans made provision for so-called "planned bargaining", under which there is discretion to award the maximum possible capital grant (irrespective of project sector or location) to major industrial groups establishing innovative projects in the Mezzogiorno, large individual firms and certain consortia of small and medium-sized firms.

[7] For setting up projects with up to Fl 18 mn of eligible investment (Fl 8 mn for extensions), there is virtually no administrative discretion in the investment premium scheme. Rates of award are fixed and conditions of award are overt. In contrast, for setting up projects with more than Fl 18 mn of eligible investment (Fl 8 mn for extensions), the award relates only to the first Fl 18 mn (Fl 8 mn) of eligible investment. For setting up projects in excess of Fl 18 mn (Fl 30 mn for extensions), awards in the three northern provinces in excess of the automatic maximum are wholly discretionary. In the transitional areas, the equivalent limits are Fl 30 mn for setting up projects and Fl 75 mn for extensions within five years of setting up.

[8] The systems are overt. Applicants should know whether or not they will receive an award and also within what percentage range that award is likely to fall. There is, however, discretion regarding the actual percentage award made (except under the SIFIT).

[9] Although basically discretionary, in certain zones a proportion of the award is determined automatically by employment created.

**Source:** European Regional Incentives, 1993.

Table 7

## Trends in Designated Problem Region Population Coverage 1980–92

As a percentage of the national population

| | | 1980 | 1981 | 1982 | 1983 | 1984 | 1985 | 1986 | 1987 | 1988 | 1989 | 1990 | 1991 | 1992 |
|---|---|---|---|---|---|---|---|---|---|---|---|---|---|---|
| BELGIUM | Development Zones | 39.5 | 39.5 | 36.3 | 36.3 | 34.7 | 33.1 | 33.1 | 33.1 | 33.1 | 33.1 | 33.1 | 33.1 | 33.1 |
| DENMARK | Development Regions | 27 | 27 | 27 | 25 | 24 | 24 | 24 | 24 | 20.7 | 20.7 | 20.7 | 20.7 | (20.7)\(19.9)[1] |
| FRANCE | PDR/PAT Zones | 38.2 | 38.2 | 37 | 37 | 37 | 39 | 39 | 39 | 39 | 39 | 40+ | 40+ | 40+ |
| GERMANY | GA Areas | 36 | 29.8 | 29.8 | 29.8 | 28.4 | 28.4 | 28.9 | 30.9 | 29 | 29 | 29 | 26.9 | 26.9 |
| | GA + Special Areas | 36 | 38 | 40 | 40 | 35 | 35 | 35 | 35 | 32.8 | 34.8 | 34.8 | 27.0[2] | 27.0[2] |
| GREECE | All except Region A[3] | – | 65 | 58 | 58 | 58 | 58 | 58 | 58 | 58 | 58 | 58 | 58 | 58 |
| IRELAND | Designated Areas[4] | 28 | 28 | 28 | 28 | 28 | 28 | 28 | 28 | 28 | 34 | 34 | 34 | 28 |
| ITALY | Mezzogiorno (ie South) | 35.6 | 35.6 | 35.6 | 35.6 | 35.6 | 35.6 | 35.6 | 35.6 | 35.6 | 35.6 | 35.6 | 35.6[5] | 35.6[5] |
| LUXEMBOURG | | 100 | 100 | 100 | 100 | 100 | 100 | 100 | 100 | 100 | 100 | 100 | 100 | 79.7 |
| NETHERLANDS | IPR Areas | 27.4 | 27.4 | 28.7 | 28.7 | 28.7 | 25 | 25 | 25 | 25 | 19.9 | 19.9[6] | 19.9[6] | 19.9[6] |
| PORTUGAL | | – | – | – | – | – | – | 100 | 100 | 100 | 100 | 100 | 100 | 100 |
| SPAIN | | – | – | – | – | – | – | (58.6)[7] | (58.6)[7] | 58.6 | 58.6 | 58.6 | 58.6 | 58.6 |
| UNITED KINGDOM | GB Assisted Areas[8] | 42.7 | 42.7 | 26.7 | 26.7 | 26.7 | 34 | 34 | 34 | 34 | 34 | 34 | 34 | 34 |
| | UK Assisted Areas | 45.5 | 45.5 | 29.5 | 29.5 | 29.5 | 36.8 | 36.8 | 36.8 | 36.8 | 36.8 | 36.8 | 36.8 | 36.8 |
| EC 9 | | 37.9 | 38.4 | 35.1 | 35.0 | 33.8 | 35.5 | 35.5 | 35.5 | 34.9 | 35.2 | 35.4 | 33.6 | 33.4 |
| EC 12 | | – | – | – | – | – | – | 41.0 | 41.0 | 40.6 | 40.7 | 40.8 | 39.3 | 39.1 |

## Table 7 (continued)

[1] Danish regional incentives were abolished at the start of 1991. Nevertheless, a new Development Region map has been agreed with the European Commission for the period 1 January 1992 to 31 December 1996, holding 19.9 percent of the national population.

[2] In March 1991, the GA Areas were cut to 26.9 percent of the west German population, plus 0.1 percent for the special programme area of Aachen-Juelich. These areas encompass 21.7 percent of the total national population. East Germany accounts for a further 20.8 percent of the national population. The entire assisted area population is therefore 42.5 percent of the national total.

[3] Region A is only eligible for support in respect of "special investment".

[4] Although a distinction is made between Designated Areas and Non-Designated Areas, the whole country is eligible for support.

[5] Roma and Ascoli-Piceno lost their designated status at the end of 1980. Information is not available on the population coverage of the areas de-designated.

[6] In 1990 it was announced that those IPR areas outside the north would lose their designated status from the start of 1993, thus reducing population coverage to just over 8 percent. However, following a further review, IPR areas in S. Limburg and Twente will retain their status at least until the end of 1993. Currently, the IPR areas hold some 10 percent of the Dutch population.

[7] Legislation dating from 1985 which introduced new designated problem regions was not operationalised until 1988. Prior to this, the main designated category were the Large Areas of Industrial Expansion, holding some 41 percent of the national population.

[8] Over the same period, the population coverage of the Development Areas, on which most British regional policy support is focused, fell from 24.8 percent to 15.1 percent of the UK total.

**Table 8**

**Designated Problem Region Coverage 1980–92: A Narrative of Change**

| | |
|---|---|
| BELGIUM | New Development Zones came into effect on 22 July 1982, reducing population coverage from 39.5 percent to 36.3 percent. Transitional provisions saw further cuts to 34.7 percent at the end of 1983 and 33.1 percent in July 1985. Development Zones holding 7.3 percent of the national population are subject to three-yearly reviews. |
| DENMARK | An area designation exercise during 1981/2 reduced the Development Region population coverage from 27 percent to 25 percent from the start of 1983 and 24 percent from the start of 1984. A further exercise in 1986 saw population coverage fall to 20.7 percent. This new map came into force at the start of 1988, but with transitional provisions to 1990. Danish regional incentives were abolished at the start of 1991; nevertheless, a new map applies from 1992 to 1996, holding 19.9 percent of the population. |
| FRANCE | In mid 1982 the PAT replaced the PDR. Certain important cities were excluded from the designated problem regions, cutting their population coverage from 38.2 percent to 37 percent. For the remainder of the eighties only minor changes were made, though the ability to make PAT awards outside the designated areas was increasingly constrained. In May 1990, the EC agreed that most of those areas outside the PAT zones where awards could be made should be brought within the permanently designated areas. The European Commission has proposed that a number of the designated PAT areas be de-designated. |
| GERMANY | A redesignation exercise in July 1981 aimed to reduce GA Area population coverage from 36 percent to 29.8 percent, by de-designating areas holding 8 percent and newly designating areas holding 2 percent. New designation took effect from 1 January 1981. However, de-designation was spread — to 31 December 1982 for the investment grant and 31 December 1983 for the investment allowance. Certain special steel location areas |

were designated from 1 January 1982 to 31 December 1985, raising overall (i.e. GA plus special area) coverage to 40 percent in 1982. In 1984, areas holding 1.4 percent of the population were de-designated in response to EC pressures, but Bremen was designated as a special area (1 January 1984 to 31 December 1987) and certain extensions were made to transitional arrangements. Also in 1984 Gelsenkirken was designated a GA Area. A major redesignation was announced in July 1987 (effective 1 January 1987) which was to increase GA Area coverage to 30.9 percent. After lengthy negotiations with the Commission GA Area coverage was reduced to 29 percent (effective 1 January 1988) and special area coverage to 3.8 percent. In addition Land areas were reduced from 10 percent to 5.2 percent. During 1988 a number of mining regions were designated as special areas though Commission pressures led to other areas being de-designated. In March 1991, following a further major designation exercise, the GA Areas were cut to 27 percent of the west German population.

GREECE

Following Greece's entry into the EC, new regional policy legislation was introduced via Law 1116/1981 which restricted eligibility to locations outside Region A. After a change of government, new legislation was introduced in June 1982 (Law 1262/1982) under which Region A was eligible only in respect of "special investment". In February 1987 the coverage of Region D was extended (by 2 percentage points) and that of Region C cut by the same amount in response to earthquakes in the district of Messinia. Special provisions were introduced for Thrace (in Region D) by Law 1882/1990.

IRELAND

Over the entire period the whole of the Republic has been eligible for support. Between 1 January 1989 and 31 December 1991 temporary additions were made to the Designated Areas (the Counties of Louth, Wexford, Wicklow and Offaly plus a small area of Cork), raising overall Designated Area coverage from 28 percent to 34 percent of the national population.

ITALY

The Mezzogiorno has always been the main focus of Italian regional policy. New legislation in 1986 (Law 64) introduced significant rate discrimination between "backward", "intermediate" and "relatively advantaged" areas within the Mezzogiorno. However, the European Commission called into question the designation of a number of Mezzogiorno areas. A compromise agreement in 1988 saw Roma and Ascoli-Piceno lose their designated status from the end of 1990 and Latina and Rieti from the end of 1992. In 1990, Taranto was upgraded from a "relatively advantaged" to an "intermediate" area. In the same year, the rate discrimination in favour of "backward" areas increased. The status of Abruzzo, which has been under discussion with the Commission since the late eighties, will not now be called into question until the end of 1993.

LUXEMBOURG

Throughout the eighties the whole country was eligible for support. In April 1986 the Industrial Framework Law introduced rate discrimination. Six cantons qualified for basic rate awards and the other six for higher awards. Subsequent discussions with the European Commission saw assistance withdrawn from the "basic rate" areas in November 1991. The rest of the country holds 79.7 percent of the national population.

NETHERLANDS

The so-called SIR levy which applied in the west of the country was withdrawn in September 1981, reducing the rate differential between the designated IPR (investment premium) areas and the rest of the country. In part in response, the population coverage of the IPR areas was increased from 27.4 percent to 28.7 percent at the start of 1982. However, European Commission pressures led to downgradings in January 1984, certain de-designations in July 1984 and further de-designations in July 1985 — taking IPR area coverage to less than 25 percent of the national population. A revised map was introduced on 14 April 1988, but with a transition period for de-designated areas until 1 January 1989. Following the 1990 Regional Policy Memorandum, IPR areas outside the north were to lose their designated status from the start of 1993, reducing population coverage to just over 8 percent. However, a 1992 review agreed that S. Limburg and Twente should continue to offer the IPR at least until the end of 1993. Current (1993) IPR area population coverage is some 10 percent of the Dutch total.

PORTUGAL

The entire country is eligible for support.

SPAIN

Following entry into the European Community, new designated areas were introduced. These hold 58.6 percent of the national population. Prior to this, the regional investment grant was available in 5 Large Areas of Industrial Expansion (holding 41 percent of the national population), 34 Areas of Preferential Industrial Location, 3 Zones of Preferential Industrial Location and 1 Development Pole.

UNITED KINGDOM

A phased reduction in the British Assisted Areas took place between 1979 and 1982 which reduced the overall population coverage by over one third. The Assisted Areas map was redrawn in November 1984. Although the overall population coverage increased (from 27.5 percent to 35 percent of the British total) the coverage of the Development Areas was cut from 21.9 percent to 15.5 percent of the British total. The regional development grant (the main regional incentive at the time) was restricted to the Development Areas. RDG was abolished in March 1988. A review of the British Assisted Areas was announced on 9 June 1992. A new map will come into force during 1993.

**Table 9**

**Key Trends in Other Coverage Conditions 1980–92**

## A) Changes in Activity Coverage

1. In the early eighties, a number of new schemes and initiatives were introduced to encourage service sector development: the office and service industries scheme was revamped in Britain; the special investment grant for high-grade jobs was introduced in Germany; and a new package of measures for the international services sector was established in Ireland.

2. In the mid-eighties, there were three main developments of note. First, and affecting a wide range of countries, the list of eligible activities under the main regional incentives on offer was extended to include specified producer services. Such changes were recorded in Britain (where the office and services scheme was withdrawn), Germany, Italy, Luxembourg, Greece, Portugal and Spain. Second, and related, there was a trend in a number of countries to try to improve the attractiveness of regional incentives to innovative activities by widening eligible expenditure to take in intangible factors like the costs of patents and licences. Finally, in some countries (Italy, N. Ireland, Portugal) reviews were undertaken of eligible manufacturing industries with a view to focusing assistance on sectors where it is likely to have most impact.

3. Towards the end of the decade, and into the nineties, industrial characteristics began to play an increasingly important role in award decisions — especially in countries like Portugal, Greece, Italy and Belgium where there is still a significant automatic component to regional incentive awards.

## B) Changes in Project-Type Coverage

1. In the first half of the decade, largely in response to pressures from the European Commission's Competition Directorate, a number of moves were made towards limiting the extent to which replacement investment might be aided. Thus, the item-related WIR regional allowance was withdrawn in the Netherlands, the British regional development grant became project- related, restrictions were placed on support for basic rationalisation and reorganisation projects in Germany and the IDA re-equipment and modernisation grants scheme was withdrawn in Ireland.

2. In the mid-eighties, budgetary pressures caused support in a number of countries (the Netherlands, Germany, France) to be focused on setting up projects rather than extensions — either by restricting the eligibility of extension

projects for regional assistance or else by offering a lower level of grant for extensions. This trend was followed later in the decade in Ireland where the rate maxima for extensions was reduced from 45 percent or 60 percent (depending on location) first to 25 percent and then to 15 percent. Explicit rate discrimination in favour of setting up projects is currently found in Germany, Ireland and the Netherlands; and is part of a wider tendency to increase levels of rate discrimination within regional incentive packages.

## C) Changes in Size Coverage

1. For the most part, size-related changes have tended to be low-key. This was certainly the case in the first half of the decade when no major changes were recorded.
2. In the mid-eighties, perhaps the most significant change was in France where budgetary constraints meant that the main regional incentive on offer came to be focused on larger projects.
3. As the decade progressed, size-related changes became more frequent. In a number of countries, moves were made to ease minimum size conditions (e.g. the Netherlands, Portugal, Italy); in some others, steps were taken to introduce small-firm-specific measures (Ireland, the UK and, later, France); while, in another group, budgetary constraints meant that certain smaller projects came to be excluded from eligibility (Belgium, Greece, Spain). All this having been said, size-related award conditions remain of minor significance in most countries.

Table 10

**Maximum Rates of Capital Grant Award (1992)**

| COUNTRY | DESIGNATED PROBLEM REGION | POPULATION[1] COVERAGE (%) | MAXIMUM CAPITAL[2] GRANT AWARD (%) | MAXIMUM EC[3] AID CEILING (%) |
|---|---|---|---|---|
| BELGIUM | Zone 1 | 22.0 | 20 nge | 20 nge |
| | Zone 2 | 11.1 | 15 nge | 15 nge |
| DENMARK | Priority Regions | 19.9 | 25[5] | 25/20/17 nge |
| FRANCE | Maximum Rate Zone | 40+ | 25 | 25 |
| | Standard Award Zone | | 17 | 17 |
| GERMANY | east German *Laender* | 20.8 | 23/20/15 | 23/20/15 |
| | GA Area | 27.0[6] | 18/15/12/10 | 18/15/12/10 |
| GREECE | Thrace | 12 | 45–55 | 75 nge |
| | Other Region D | | 35–45 | 75 nge |
| | Region C | 32 | 25–40 | 75 nge |
| | Region B | 14 | 15–40 | 75 nge |
| | Region A | 42 | 0–40 | 75 nge |
| IRELAND | Designated Areas | 28 | 60 | 75 nge |
| | Non-Designated Areas | 72 | 45 | 75 nge |
| ITALY | Mezzogiorno-Backward | 8.9 | 56 | 75 nge |
| | -Intermediate | 21.7 | 48 | 75 nge |
| | -Other | 5.0 | 40 | 75 nge[7] |
| LUXEMBOURG | Designated Areas | 79.7 | 25/20/17.5 | 25/20/17.5 |
| NETHERLANDS | IPR Areas | 19.9(10)[8] | 20 | 20net/25/15 |
| PORTUGAL | Zone 3 | | 75 | 75 nge |
| | Zone 2 | 100 | 45 | 75 nge |
| | Zone 1 | | 33 | 75 nge |
| SPAIN | Zones of Industrial Decline[9] | 4.1 | 75/45/30/20 | 75/45/30/20 nge |
| | Zones of Economic Promotion | 54.2 | 50/40/30/0 | 50/40/30/0 nge |
| UK-NORTHERN IRELAND | Whole Province | 100 | 50 | 75 nge |
| UK-GREAT BRITAIN | Development Areas | 15.5 | 30 nge | 30 nge |
| | Intermediate Areas | 19.5 | 20 nge | 20 nge |

**Notes:**

[1] Population coverage of designated problem regions as a percentage of the national population.

[2] Maximum nominal rate of capital grant award. In both Belgium and Britain the rate is expressed in terms of the EC aid ceiling i.e. in net grant equivalent terms, after tax.

[3] Nge = net grant equivalent after tax. The full list of EC ceilings can be found in the Official Journal of 12 August 1988 (OJ No. C 212).

[4] That is, those Ordinary Development Regions which are not designated as Priority Development Regions.

[5] The Danish regional incentive package was abolished as from 1 January 1991. However, the government has reserved the right to offer a maximum 25 percent grant to major inward investment projects locating in the former Development Regions.

[6] The GA Area figure is as a percentage of the west German population. It represents 21.7 percent of the total national population.

[7] From the end of 1990 the nge ceiling for Frosinone fell to 30%. In addition, other parts of the Mezzogiorno lost their designated status at the end of 1990 or are due to lose such status at the end of 1992.

[8] From the start of 1993 the IPR areas were reduced to some 10 percent of the national population.

[9] Although these zones have now been incorporated within the ZPEs, the higher rates of award indicated still apply. European Regional Incentives, 1993.

**Table 11**

**Key Changes in Maximum Rates of Award 1980–92**

1. In 1980 there were increases in maximum award rates in both Ireland (from 50 percent to 60 percent) and the Netherlands (from 25 percent to 35 percent), continuing a trend established in the late seventies. Against this, the British regional development grant was cut from 20 percent to 15 percent in the Development Areas and withdrawn completely from the Intermediate Areas (while remaining at 22 percent in the Special Development Areas).

2. For most of the remainder of the first half of the decade, nominal rate maxima were relatively stable, though it is of note that the new regional incentive package in Greece (following its accession to the EC) involved increased rate maxima.

3. The volume of nominal rate maxima changes picked up significantly around the mid-eighties, with further major cutbacks in the UK (where the RDG maximum was cut from 22 percent to 15 percent and where the Northern Ireland standard capital grant maximum fell from 30 percent to 20 percent) and also in the Netherlands (especially in respect of extension projects). However, not all the change was in a downwards direction. New legislation in both Italy and Luxembourg in 1986 resulted in higher rate maxima while the new regional incentive systems in both Portugal and Spain (following their accession to the Community) also involved increased award ceilings. In Denmark, too, the investment grant maximum increased, albeit by way of (part) compensation for the withdrawal of the company soft loan.

4. Towards the end of the eighties reductions in rate maxima became more frequent (and significant). In the Netherlands, the rate maximum for setting up projects was cut from 25 percent to 20 percent (15 percent for extensions more than five years after setting up); in Germany the investment allowance was withdrawn and the maximum preferential rate ceiling was reduced by 2 percentage points (to 23 percent) for setting up projects and by 5 percentage points for extensions; in Ireland the rate maximum for extensions was reduced first to 25 percent and then to 15 percent; and in the UK both the regional development grant and the Northern Ireland standard capital grant were withdrawn. A feature of most of these rate reductions is that, while cutback has been the order of the day (especially for extension projects), overall rate maxima have tended to remain at levels set by EC aid coordination ceilings. In other words, rate discrimination has grown in importance.

5. Moving into the nineties, it seems as if the trend towards rate reductions may continue (at least in the northern Community countries). In January 1991, regional incentives were abolished in Denmark, while in Germany, following

the ending of the Zonal Border Area preference, maximum rates of award in the west German Laender are now at least 5 percentage points below east German levels. In Northern Ireland, too, a previous 50 percent ceiling under the selective assistance scheme has been replaced by a 30 percent maximum (albeit combined with a potential discretionary award of up to 20 percent).

Table 12

## Regional Incentive Expenditure Trends 1980-90
### (Net Grant Equivalent Expenditure, National Currencies, Current Prices)

EXPENDITURE COMMITTED
(national currency, millions, net grant equivalent)[1]

| COUNTRY | INCENTIVE | 1980 | 1981 | 1982 | 1983 | 1984 | 1985 | 1986 | 1987 | 1988 | 1989 | 1990 |
|---|---|---|---|---|---|---|---|---|---|---|---|---|
| BELGIUM[2] | IS+CG | 4435 | 7814 | (6978) | 6143 | 9795 | 6390 | 6193 | 5414 | 12313 | 8873 | 6761 |
| DENMARK[3] | CSL+RDG+MSL | 83.2 | 88.5 | 105.3 | 95.9 | 105.8 | 116.4 | 127.6 | 129.9 | 121.3 | 71.0 | 62.5 |
| FRANCE[4] | PAT+LBTC | 1439.8 | 1093.6 | 1260.5 | 1589 | 2144 | 1629 | 1335 | 704 | 1476 | 1143 | 1321 |
| GERMANY[5] | IA+IG+SDA | 1217 | 1374 | 1227 | 1380 | 1435 | 1298 | 1463 | 1950 | 2424 | 2460 | 1755 |
| GREECE[6] | IG+IRS | – | – | 1830 | 15168 | 15851 | 16029 | 18665 | 32005 | 36725 | n.a. | n.a. |
| IRELAND[7] | IDA(N)+IDA(ISP) | 155.2 | 194.9 | 155.1 | 100.7 | 143.4 | 134.2 | 170.0 | 158.2 | 127.8 | 226.9 | 163.0 |
| ITALY[8] | CG+NFSL+SSC(N+H) | 2332.8 | 3489.3 | 4780.7 | 5192.1 | 4683 | 5792 | 5416 | 6368 | 7880 | 9087 | 13696 |
| LUXEMBOURG[9] | CG/IS | 678.8 | 299.6 | 963.8 | 313.3 | 463.0 | 349.0 | 1533 | 1495 | 2019 | 1097 | 1243 |
| NETHERLANDS[10] | IPR+WIR(RA) | 448 | 402 | 494 | 339 | 238 | 356 | 279 | 203 | 289 | 146 | 245 |
| PORTUGAL[11] | SIBR | | | | | | | | | | 15100 | 32600 |
| SPAIN[12] | RIG | | | | | | | | | 16321 | 193962 | 92705 |
| UNITED KINGDOM[13] | GB+NI | 694.7 | 804.0 | 758.3 | 666.8 | 691.1 | 692.8 | 794.9 | 602.2 | 647.1 | 564.9 | 555.7 |

## Table 12 (continued)

**Notes:**

[1] The detailed expenditure information is drawn from Yuill et al, European Regional Incentives 1993. The Italian figures in the table are in billion lire.

[2] The Belgian figures cover the interest subsidy and the capital grant. The 1982 figure is an estimate.

[3] The Danish figures cover the company soft loan (abolished in 1985) the regional development grant and the municipality soft loan (both withdrawn from the start of 1991).

[4] The French figures cover the regional policy grant, PAT (and its predecessor schemes) and the local business tax concession.

[5] The German figures cover the investment allowance (withdrawn in 1989), the investment grant and the special depreciation allowance (this last, due to be withdrawn in 1994).

[6] The Greek figures cover the Greek financial incentives (the investment grant and interest rate subsidy). No information is available after 1988.

[7] The Irish figures cover the IDA new industry and international services programmes. Figures for the IDA re-requipment and modernisation programme are included prior to its demise.

[8] The Italian figures cover the capital grant, the national fund soft loan and the Mezzogiorno social security concessions.

[9] The Luxembourg figures cover the capital grant and interest subsidy.

[10] The Dutch figures cover the investment premium and, prior to its demise in 1983, the WIR regional allowance.

[11] The Portuguese figures relate to the SIBR and are only available from 1989.

[12] The Spanish figures relate to the regional investment grant under legislation which came into effect in 1988.

[13] The UK figures relate to the key British incentives (regional development grant — withdrawn in 1988 — regional selective assistance, regional enterprise grant and the office and service industries scheme, which became part of RSA in the mid-eighties) and to the capital grant (abolished in 1988) and selective assistance in Northern Ireland.

**Source:** European Regional Incentives 1993

Table 13

**Regional Incentive Expenditure Trends 1980–90**
**(Net Grant Equivalent Expenditure, National Currencies, 1990 Prices)**

| COUNTRY | INCENTIVE | EXPENDITURE COMMITTED[1] (national currency, millions, nge, 1990 prices) | | | | | | | | | | |
|---|---|---|---|---|---|---|---|---|---|---|---|---|
| | | 1980 | 1981 | 1982 | 1983 | 1984 | 1985 | 1986 | 1987 | 1988 | 1989 | 1990 |
| BELGIUM | IS+CG | 6813 | 11424 | 9655 | 7886 | 11945 | 7439 | 6958 | 5982 | 13398 | 9147 | 6761 |
| DENMARK | CSL+RDG+MSL | 149.1 | 143.9 | 153.7 | 129.8 | 135.3 | 142.8 | 149.2 | 145.6 | 129.6 | 73.0 | 62.5 |
| FRANCE | PAT+LBTC | 2666 | 1811 | 1854 | 2130 | 2680 | 1942 | 1521 | 777 | 1578 | 1175 | 1321 |
| GERMANY | IA+IG+SDA | 1612 | 1750 | 1496 | 1630 | 1664 | 1472 | 1610 | 2102 | 2576 | 2543 | 1755 |
| GREECE | IG+IRS | – | – | 6607 | 45550 | 39727 | 34177 | 33450 | 49774 | 49830 | n.a. | n.a. |
| IRELAND | IDA(N)+IDA(ISP) | 317.4 | 336.6 | 231.2 | 136.1 | 181.8 | 162.5 | 194.7 | 176.9 | 138.8 | 232.2 | 163.0 |
| ITALY | CG+NFSL+SSC(N+H) | 6139 | 7771 | 9037 | 8539 | 6948 | 8011 | 6935 | 7756 | 9057 | 9760 | 13696 |
| LUXEMBOURG | CG/IS | 1077 | 440 | 1289 | 387 | 536 | 403 | 1726 | 1665 | 2166 | 1134 | 1243 |
| NETHERLANDS | IPR+WIR(RA) | 564 | 480 | 556 | 375 | 257 | 380 | 296 | 217 | 304 | 151 | 245 |
| PORTUGAL | SIBR | | | | | | | | | | 17376 | 32600 |
| SPAIN | RIG | | | | | | | | | 18738 | 208337 | 92705 |
| UNITED KINGDOM | GB+NI | 1291 | 1338 | 1174 | 982 | 976 | 925 | 1026 | 740 | 746 | 608 | 556 |

Note: The price index used is that for gross domestic product at market prices.
Source: European Regional Incentives 1993

Antoni Kukliński
European Institute
for Regional and Local Development
Warsaw

# THE CRISIS
# OF SOCIAL DEVELOPMENT
# IN THE 1990s

Notes* for the UNRISD Thirtieth Anniversary Seminar
Geneva, July 7–8, 1993

## Part A. The Diagnosis

The World Summit for Social Development[1] should accept as a starting point a comprehensive diagnosis of the deep crisis of social development not only in the 90s but, practically, in the last quarter of the XX century.

To my mind, there are five causes of this deep crisis:

   I. the crisis of the welfare state
  II. the triumph of the neoconservative ideology
 III. the triadic organisation of the global economy
 IV. the mismanagement of the great historical opportunity of the disintegration of the communistic system
  V. the crisis of the UN system

---

*The responsibility for the content of this paper is related only to the author.
[1]General Assembly Resolution 47/92

## 1. The crisis of the welfare state

The broad diffusion of the idea of the welfare state after World War II has created a favourable climate for the promotion of social development by both the national governments and the international organisations, especially by the UN system. The general crisis and, in some cases, the annihilation of the welfare state have destroyed one of the most important pillars underpinning the theoretical and pragmatic construction of the idea of social development.

## 2. The triumph of the neoconservative ideology

It was relatively easy to promote social development in the framework of the Keynesian doctrines and policies widely accepted after World War II[2]. The doctrine of full emloyment was particularly important in this field.

The end of the suspension of the Keynesian age and the triumph of the neoconservative ideology with neodarwinian overtones - pushed out the idea of social development from the core of the general attention concentrated on the mechanisms of the spontaneous development of the market forces.

## 3. The triadic organisation of the global economy[3]

The trend towards the very strong differentiation of the global economy and the growing gap between the triadic (Western Europe, USA, Japan) center and the remaining periphery is an important phenomenon of the last quarter of the XX century.

The triadic center is more and more "self-sufficient" and inward looking — directing only a very limited attention to the problems of the South and of the post-communist countries where the issues of social development have just dramatic, it not tragic dimensions.

---

[2]Compare: *Keynes here - how can I help you?* Weekend Financial Times April 4/5, 1992 Rip van Winkle's new world order. W. F. Times April 25/26, 1992

[3]R. Petrella, *Les Societés Européennes entre pouissance competitive et nouveau contrat social*. Bruxelles, Avril 1993

## 4. The mismanagement of the great historical opportunity of the disintegration of the communistic system

The Grand Global Establishments are not using well the great historical opportunity of the collapse of the communistic system.

Unfortunately, the idea of the Neo-Marshall Plan for Central and Eastern Europe was rejected. That idea has reappeared on June 29, 1993 in an article by Dimitri Simes on "Get Serious on Russia Aid, or Brace for Disaster", published in **International Herald Tribune**. The Neo-Marshall Plan could introduce a sense of order and direction into the somehow chaotic process of transition from real socialism to real capitalism. In this transition there is a great opportunity to create and apply new ideas in the field of social transformation and development.

I have doubts if this great historical laboratory of social transformation and development is used well both for internal and for external reasoms (compare Annex No. 1).


## 5. The crisis of the UN System

For a few decades after World War II, the UN system was a very strong force introducing innovative approaches in the analyses and sometimes solutions of many global problems, including the problems of social development.

Now we have the impression that this power of innovative approaches has lost its original impetus. We also have to mention that some international organisations, outside the UN Family, like the European Communities and OECD, are acting with particular dynamism, at least in some fields. I would not be astonished if at the beginning of the XXI century UNO will get a new competitor in the form of UCO — United Corporations Organisation. UCO will have a General Assembly composed of the Presidents of 200 biggest transnational corporations.

*<br>*    *

Naturally, these reflections on the five reasons of the deep crisis of social development in the last quarter of the XX century have a very preliminary character. There is no doubt, however, that the World Summit for Social Development should take into account a comprehensive diagnosis of the deep crisis of social development. This diagnosis could follow different academic and political approaches related to different value judgements.

## Part B. The classical model of social development and social policy

The UN Family was deeply involved in the creation of the classical model of social development and social policy. This model was a product of the welfare state.

The essence of social development and social policy was in these conditions - to eliminate, or at least to reduce, the Darwinian dimension of the neo-capitalistic society and economy. Indirectly, the social policy of this type was - in some cases - diminishing the competitive spirit of the society, especially in the field of motivations.

The dilemma efficiency versus equality was, in this context, solved in favour of equality.

The UN Philosophy of Social Development and Social Policy has not yet recognized the far-reaching consequence of the deep crisis of the welfare state.

The future of the classical model is an issue of value judgement. Some countries, persons and institutions would probably argue that the classical model is a permanent model of social development and social policy.

Other countries, persons and institutions would present the opinion that the classical model was a historical phenomenon and it will not enter the XXI century.

## Part C. The new model of social development and social policy

The New Model of Social Development and Social Policy should take into account the new situation created by the preponderance of neo-conservative approaches in the field of economic and social development. These approaches in the field of economic and social development. These approaches, directly or indirectly, stimulate the development of the quasi Darwinian climate. This climate, in the radical version, is changing the social development and social policy into a marginal phenomenon. This marginalisation of social development and social policy could be observed very clearly in some countries.

This is a very dangerous situation in both long- and short-term perspective.

These diagnosis and motivation should generate inducement to outline a new model of social development and social policy.

In the framework of this new model we should try to integrate two functions of social development and social policy:

1) a new function to stimulate the competitive spirit, competitive ability and competitive perfomance of the society,
2) an old function to reduce the Darwinian consequences of economic and political development.

*Prima facie* — these two functions cannot be integrated but this "impossible" task is the challenge of the UN System.

# Part D. Social development — a challenge for the UN System

I strongly believe that the present crisis of the UN System and of the idea and practice of social development are just a temporary phenomenon. The pressing problems of the XXI century[4] will not be solved without the UN System which will regain its original innovative drive. This UN System should develop a new Model of Social Development and Social Policy. This new Model will probably function in an improved global climate — in the conditions of a diminishing role of neo-conservative approaches and more equitable relations between the global centres and global peripheries.

These positive trends could be anticipated for the beginning of the XXI century.

So the World Summit for Social Development may - in the long-term perspective — accept a more optimostic vision of the future. However, in short term, a realistic - perhaps even a pessimistic diagnosis should be prepared and studied with great attention.

Warszawa, July 2, 1993

---

[4]P. Kennedy, *Preparing for the XXI century.* New York 1993.

# ANNEX

# The Barriers for the Development of Social Transformation Policies in Central and Eastern Europe

## Introduction

I am very happy that I have participated[1] in the brainstorming effort which is culminated in the International Experts Meeting — Towards a Competitive Society in Central and Eastern Europe: Social Dimensions, September 20–22, 1992 Kellokoski, Finland.

I fully agree with the Conceptual Outline as designed by Dr. Hannu Uusitalo[2] and with the Proposed Agenda as formulated by Prof. Bernd Marin[3].

The transition in Central and Eastern Europe from real socialism to real capitalism is a phenomenon of great historical importance[4]. This is, at the same time, a unique opportunity to create a really united and integrated Europe — a new Europe as a competitive continent of the XXI century. This grand transformation of the society, economy and the state is a unique historical laboratory of spontaneous and guided structural change.

The transformation processes in Central and Eastern Europe are much more dramatic and difficult than originally anticipated. In this context I would like to discuss the barriers for the development of Social Transformation Policies in Central and Eastern Europe. Without well organised policies of this type the process of the development of the competitive society in Central and Eastern Europe will be extremely long and sometimes very inefficient.

---

[1] See Annex 1.

[2] Hannu Uusitalo, *Towards a Competitive Society — Social Dimension. A Conceptual Outline for a Meeting of Experts*.

[3] Bernd Marin, *Proposed Agenda for the Kellokoski Meeting*, September 1992.

[4] Compare: R. Dahrendorf, *Reflections on the Revolution in Europe*. Times Books 1990. A. Kukliński (Editor), *Poland in the Perspective of Global Change*. Vols I and II. Polish Association for the Club of Rome, Warsaw 1991.

I would like to present the following outline of my paper.

I The ideological barriers
II The psychological barriers
III The material barriers
IV The institutional barriers
V The global barriers

## 1. The ideological barriers

*Grosso modo* all policies in Central and Eastern Europe are very weak. The social transformation policies are just a confirmation of this general observation. The first reason of this situation is an almost total absence of the rigorous rational long-term strategic thinking in Central and Eastern Europe[5].

Short-term problems and short-term solutions are consuming the intellectual capacity and energy of the ruling elites. In this climate it is impossible to design comprehensive social transformation policies which are — *ex definitione* — a long-term phenomenon.

There are two ideologies paralysing the long-term strategic thinking in Central and Eastern Europe.

The first is the ideology of populism which pushes the political decision-makers into the wrong choices related to short-term popularity.

The second is the fascination with the XIX-century laissezfaire approaches.

The power of the invisible hand and automatic blessings of the free market are definitely overestimated in Central and Eastern Europe, especially as an instrument of structural change.

## 2. The psychological barriers

The social transformation processes and policies encounter a strong psychological barrier in human mentality and particularly in the patterns of motivations and behaviours, which were imposed by the communistic rule in Central and Eastern Europe. This is the well known dilemma

---

[5] Compare: A. Kukliński, *The Future of Strategic Planning in Central and Eastern Europe.* Warsaw, July 1992.

— "homo sovieticus" versus "homo democraticus". However the homo sovieticus argument should be used with some analytical caution. When a Polish miner is reacting in a negative way against the idea that his inefficient coal mine should be liquidated — then he is a homo sovieticus. When 25 years ago, the English, German or Belgian miner did exactly the same — this attitude was correctly described as an understandable resistance against the structural change.

We have to note, in this context, that there are two types of social transformation in Central and Eastern Europe — one, a unique transformation related to the transition, the second — a normal European transformation coming to Central and Eastern Europe with a delay of a generation.

## 3. The material barriers

The formulation of long-term social transformation policies in the climate of deep economic crisis is extremely difficult or even impossible if we take as a yardstick the present experience of Central and Eastern Europe.

However this impossibility must be somehow eliminated — taking into account the positive historical experiences in this field. Long-term social transformation policies should be seen as an important vehicle in the broad set of activities which create new inducements for economic growth in Central and Eastern Europe.

## 4. The institutional barriers

The formulation of long-term social transformation policies is possible only within strong and efficient governmental structures. Unfortunately, the governmental structures in Central and Eastern Europe are weak and inefficient. We can hope that the improvement in this field will be very rapid.

The governments of Central and Eastern Europe should absorb the art and wisdom of the Grand Policy Analysis[6].

---

[6]Y. Dror, *Governability, participation and social aspects of planning.* CEPAL Review vol. 31.

## 5. The global barriers

It is difficult to formulate long-term social transformation policies in Central and Eastern Europe in the present global political and economic climate. Unfortunately, the Great Global Establishments were not able as yet to design a grand reaction to the collapse of communism and of the Soviet Empire — comparable to the Marshall Plan after the World War II. Such a plan would provide an international framework for the design and implementation of Social Transformation Policies in Central and Eastern Europe.

## Conclusions

I would like to suggest —
1) to discuss, in the framework of the Kellokoski Meeting, the barriers for the development of social transformation policies in Central and Eastern Europe. These policies are necessary to accelerate the process of the development of competitive society in Central and Eastern Europe. This process must be an efficient integration of spontaneous and guided structural change;
2) to prepare — under the auspices of the United Nations — a White Book on the Development of Social Transformation policies in Central and Eastern Europe. This White Book will stimulate the governments of this Region to develop the art and wisdom of long-term policies;
3) to continue the discussion concerning the idea of a new UN Research Training and Conference Programme — Social Policy in Competitive Societies.

This should be a long-term effort and not only a subject of one conference — even if this conference is just excellent.

Y. Dror, *Grand Policy Analysis. Presidential Address Paper.* Policy Study Association Annual Meeting, Washington D.C., August 1991.

Bohdan Jałowiecki
Institut Européen du Développement
Régional et Local
Varsovie

# ANCIENNE ET NOUVELLES FRONTIERES EUROPEENNES

Citons pour commencer l'expression de Krzysztof Pomian: *seulément une mauvaise géographie qui ne tient pas compte du temps atribue à l'Europe des contours fixes* [Pomian 1990].

Les frontières constituent une notion clé de la géopolitique, aussi bien celles qui existent entre les grandes entités comme l'Etat-Nation, que celles qui divisent les unités ethniques, culturelles, sociales et économiques à l'intérieur de l'Etat, comme régions. Les frontières changent, de nouveaux états émergent, la question régionale apparait.

Au cours du XXéme siècle nous avons pu observer plusieurs bouleverséments géopolitique en Europe et les redéfinitions de la carte de notre continent. La guerre de 1914–1918 a mis en doute l'ordre qui a été introduit par le Congrès de Vienne. Le nouvel ordre a été établi par les puissances victorieuses à Versailles. Le deuxième bouleversément, relativément court, a eu lieu entre 1938 et 1945 quand les Nazi ont essayé de construire l'empire pangermanique. La période suivante d'après Yalta a duré presque 50 ans avec une nouvelle carte européenne. La chute de mur de Berlin a provoqué les nouvelles perturbations et la redéfinition consécutive de la carte de notre continent. Ces processus sont maintenant en cours.

Je voudrai parler des partage, des clivage, des ruptures plutôt que de l'intégration, bien que nous puissions observer ces processus contradictoire à la fois.

## 1. Qu'est-ce que c'est l'Europe?

*L'Europe* — écrit à son tour Edgar Morin — *est une notion géographique dépourvue de frontières avec l'Asie et un concept historique à frontières variables* [E.Morin 1988, p.19].

Il faut aussi remarquer que L'Europe devient de plus en plus une notion subjective. Ce continent aux frontières floues et pas très bien définies n'est pas perçu d'une façon uniforme. Pour un Français ou un Allemand moyen, l'Europe se compose surtout, sinon uniquément, les pays de la Communauté Economique Européenne. Les habitants des pays post-communistes d'Europe centrale et orientale sont enclins à élargir la notion de l'Europe en y englobant leur propre région. Par ailleurs, les habitants de l'ancien l'URSS trouvent qu'eux aussi appartiennent à l'Europe car elle s'étend, comme a d'ailleurs dit le Général de Gaulle, de l'Atlantique jusqu'à l'Oural.

Si l'Europe est une notion mal définie, l'Europe centrale est une notion totalément floue. Un héros de l'une des pièces de Sławomir Mrożek, voulant déterminer la position de la Pologne, dit que ce pays est situé à l'Ouest de l'Est et à l'Est de l'Ouest. Cette expression est juste et montre brièvément toute l'indétermination de la situation, non seulément celle de la Pologne mais aussi celle de l'Europe centrale en général, donc des pays qui se trouvent dans une zone transitoire entre deux mondes culturels distinct, entre deux civilisation. Une de lignes de démarcation entre l'Est et l'Ouest passait toujours à travers l'Etat polonais et était à peu près stable, indépendamment du fait que les frontières polonaise se trouvaient plus à l'Est ou plus à l'Ouest.

Il n'est pas possible de définir ce territoire ni géographiquément, ni d'une manière historique. On peut néanmoins avancer l'hypothèse, que c'est un territoire situé entre deux puissances — l'Allemagne et la Russie. Il constituerait donc un champ entre deux pôles, d'influence qui l'attirent d'un ou de l'autre côté. Ceci est, bien sûr, une définition très générale et s'applique d'une certaine manière à d'autres pays de cette partie de l'Europe. La conception du champ entre les deux pôles peut s'explique sans doute par les événéments du XXéme siècle, en particulier quant à la Pologne. La période de l'entre deux-guerres se caractérise par croissance de l'équilibre entre les pôles, donc par d'une certaine indépendance de ce champ. La IIéme Guerre Mondiale a provoqué le contact des deux pôles, donc la disparition de ce champ, jusqu'en 1989. On traverse actuellément une période d'un considérable affaiblissément d'un des pôles, qui n'est pas capable, au moins pour le moment, d'effectuer une influence efficace. Ceci crée un vide, qui doit provoquer une croissance de l'influence de l'autre pôle. Le territoire polonais se caractérise donc par l'instabilité extrême de ses frontières.

La situation du territoire de l'ex Tchécoslovaquie est meilleure, car la localisation de ce pays par rapport aux d'immémoriaux circuits militaires entre l'Ouest et l'Est lui donne un position de sécurité un peu plus grande. La situation de la Hongrie, petit pays localisé de côté de principaux circuits militaires de l'Europe, mais aussi à l'écart relatif du „bassin balkan" est encore plus favorable . Ces deux pays jouissent aussi d'une situation favorable par le fait qu'ils sont en un certain sens les héritiers de la monarchie des Habsbourgs dont l'appartenance à l'Europe ne peut pas être mise en doute.

Le cas de la Croatie et de la Slovénie et très intéressant. Ces faisaient toujours partie de l'Europe et actuellément, après désintégration de l'artificielle Yougoslavie, veulent revenir à cette entité. La localisation périphérique de la Roumanie et de la Bulgarie avec tout leur passé, les fait appartenir plutôt à l'Europe Orientale.

Tout ce territoire a quand même certains traits communs, ceux de l'appartenance, pendant une période de plus de 40 ans, à l'ancien „camp socialiste". Il reste encore le territoire des pays baltes qui, eux aussi, ont leurs aspirations européennes. L'Europe Centrale est aussi une notion idéologique à caractère très diversifié. Elle englobe les vieux mythes de la mission culturelle et politique de la monarchie des Habsbourgs, plusieurs versions des mythes allemands („Drang nach Osten") depuis la pure colonisation jusqu'à la suprématie culturelle et civilisatrice — et la conception du rempart qui a protégé l'Ouest contre la barbarie bolchevique et qui sépare maintenant l'Occident de l'Orient. Cette façon très subjective de percevoir l'Europe se retrouve en un certain sens dans la réalité — car chaque façon de percevoir l'Europe a une certaine raison d'être.

L'Europe est donc une notion impossible à définir sans ambiguïté. La variabilité de ses frontières résulte des causes politico-militaires, mais indépendamment de celles-ci il existe des frontières entre les civilisations et les cultures

## 2. Les cartes européennes

Le premier grand clivage européen avait lieu eu au VIIéme siècle quand l'Eglise chrétienne se partage entre l'Eglise romaine et l'Eglise byzantine. Cette rupture avait des conséquences très importantes puisque ces deux monde se sont depuis développé séparément et étaient plus au moins hostile l'un au l'autre.

Après la chute de Byzance au XVéme siècle la Russie a hérité de certaines traditions byzantines. Alors L'Europe Centrale et Orientale se divisent en deux parties. Une partie constituée par la Pologne, les pays baltes, l'ex Tchécoslovaquie, la Hongrie, la Slovénie et la Croatie appartient à la civilisation romaine, et l'autre partie englobant la Russie, la Biélorussie, l'Ukraine, la Bulgarie, la Roumanie, la Serbie, la Macédoine et (partiellément la Bosnie) appartient à la civilisation byzantine.

L'histoire européenne est plein des conflits, des guerres des conquêtes et des reconquêtes. Les tourbillons de l'histoire ont tracé et retracé les frontières. Chaque siècle, voire demi-siècle dessinait à nouveau la carte politique de notre continent. Ces changéments n'avaient pas que des conséquences politiques mais aussi ils avaient un impact sur les structures économique, ethniques, culturelles et linguistique.

Mais il ne faut pas en même temps oublier que l'Europe, malgré ces nombreux clivage constitue néanmoins une certaine entité culturelle, avec son architecture, ses universités, sa peinture, sa littérature et sa musique. On peut aussi remarquer, en se référant à Paul Valéry, que les Européens se reconnaissent dans le message gréco-romain et la spiritualité judéo-chrétienne, fondément de la civilisation européenne. Cette unité culturelle est le seul fondément du mythe unificateur de l'Europe.

La carte européenne de XIXéme siècle a été tracée par les puissance victorieuse qui ont combattu l'Empire napoléonien. Cette carte a été ensuite corrigée par l'unification de l'Italie, la guerre entre la France et la Prusse, et par la guerre de Crimée qui a abouti aux changéments de l'image géopolitique des Balkans. Après 50 ans à peine depuis les combats de 1870 avait la Première Guerre mondiale, qui a changé de nouveau les frontières européennes.

L'esquisse du système géopolitique actuel résulte du Traité de Versailles et c'est grâce à ce traité que des pays comme la Lituanie, la Lettonie, l'Estonie, la Pologne, la Tchécoslovaquie, la Hongrie, la Yougoslavie ont pu naître ou renaître. Le processus de la création de l'Etat, qui a commencé au XIXéme siècle et qui ne s'est pas terminé, notamment à cause du manque du cadre formel de l'Etat, se poursuit dans ces pays pendant la période de l'entre-deux-guerres — ainsi que le processus de l'adaptation de la nation en cours de formation au territoire politique dont elle dispose.

L'ordre en Europe après la Deuxième Guerre mondiale, défini par les grandes puissances à Yalta, a provoqué des corrections considérables dans la forme politique de l'Europe Centrale et Orientale. Des pays comme la Lituanie, la Lettonie et l'Estonie ont disparu absorbés par l'URSS, la Pologne a perdu ses territoires de l'Est et a été poussée, au détriment du territoire de l'Allemagne, vers l'Ouest, la Roumanie a perdu la Moldavie.

Les frontières des pays sur le territoire de l'Europe Centrale ont un caractère arbitraire et on peut les comparer en un certain sens à la division de l'Afrique par le Congrès de Berlin. Elles ont été tracées par des puissances victorieuses après la Première et la Deuxième Guerre mondiale au mécontentément de presque tous les pays intéressés.

La frontière entre deux Etat peut devenir, dans certaines circonstances une frontière entre de plus grandes entités. Dans la période de l'entre-deux-guerre, les terres orientales de la Pologne constituaient une frontière de l'Europe, au-delà de laquelle s'étendait l'inquiétant „empire bolchevique". A cette époque l'Etat polonais se penchait vers l'Ouest, et l „Ouest considérait la Pologne comme un „cordon sanitaire" séparant l'Europe de l'Union soviétique.

La victoire de l'Union soviétique sur les Allemands confirmée par les accords de Yalta, déplaça la zone d'influence de cette puissance, avec complaisance des pays occidentaux, vers l'ouest, au delà de la Pologne. En 1945, la frontière politique de l'Europe fut établie sur l'Elbe, et une grande partie de l'Europe centrale tomba dans l'orbite orientale. Pendant les années de la guerre froide, c'était une frontière impénétrable qui, selon Edgar Morin, séparait l'Europe en deux demi-Europes. Le symbole de cette division, beaucoup plus significatif pour l'Ouest que pour l'Est, est le mur de Berlin, élevé en 1961, donc bien après la période stalinienne. Petit à petit des fissures apparaissent dans des barbelés des frontières, permettant non seulément l'existence des relations officielles commerciales et culturelles, mais aussi des contacts entre individus. Lentément, avec bien du mal, beaucoup de portes en Europe sont maintenant ouvertes.

Pendant presque un demi siècle après la Deuxième Guerre mondiale, la ligne qui partagait l'Allemagne était celle du rideau de fer qui séparait le Monde Occidental de l'Empire Soviétique. Cette frontière, beaucoup moins imperméable, mais toujours existante a été récemment repoussée vers l'Est, sur la ligne qu'on peut tracer de Trieste au bord de la Mer Adriatique jusqu'à Szczecin au bord de la Mer Baltique. Une autre frontière qui se confirme actuellément est la frontière orientale de quatre pays de Vichehrad qui craignent l'émigration massive venant des pays de l'ancien Empire Soviétique.

## 3. L'explosion du nationalisme

Le système communiste dans cette partie du continent a arrêté les processus de formation d'Etat non encore terminés. En se servant de la phraséologie internationaliste, il étouffait les aspirations des minorités ethniques et culturelles à avoir, et en particulier à exprimer leurs particularités. Dans cette atmosphère le sentiment d'injustice non dévoilé s'approfondissait, pour éclater avec une grande force en 1990. Les gouvernéments, pour la plupart, ne mettent pas en question ses frontières, mais une partie considérable des populations ne les accepte pas ce qui peut engendrer des conflits ouverts.

Depuis nous avons pu observer l'éclatément de la Yougoslavie et la création de nouveaux états: Croatie, Slovénie, Macédoine, Serbie-Monténégro et Bosnie qui à son tour éclate en trois partie formées par trois groupes ethnico-religieux: serbe, croate et musulmane. Ces groupes mènent entre eux une guerre impitoyable qui a abouti à la purge ethnique et provoquera une nouvelle redéfinition de ce territoire.

Un peu plus au Nord, le partage de la Tchécoslovaquie a été accompli et les deux états commencent à bâtir des nouvelles barrières: barrages sur les routes, postes de douane et de gardes frontières qui sont des symboles de souveraineté toujours fragile.

En dehors de la Pologne on peut observer le processus de la constitution de nouveaux Etats-Nation comme l'Ukraine et la Biélorussie sans parler de la formation de nouveaux états sur l'immense territoire de l'ex Union Soviétique. Au Nord de la Pologne il y a enclave de Königsberg peuplée en grande partie par de centaines des milliers des soldats d'ancienne armée rouge.

Il vaut la peine de se pencher sur les remarques de R.Dahrendorf qui s'exprime ainsi sur l'idée de l'autodétermination nationale:

*Elle est très attractive pour ceux qui se sentent perdu dans le monde contemporain. Elle semble offrir un sentiment d'appartenance et un sens pavoisé de symboles expressifs comme le drapeau et l'hymne, mais aussi le passeport et la constitution. Les hommes, certains du moins, sont prêts à donner leur vie pour l'indépendance de leur peuple. Ce serait une erreur que de sous-estimer une force aussi puissante. Cependant, en tant que principe du droit international, l'autodétermination nationale est une des inventions les moins fortunées. Elle attribue des droits aux peuples alors que le droit devrait toujours concerner les individus. En résultat, on voit apparaître des usurpateurs qui réclament ce droit au nom des peuples, tout en foulant aux pieds le droit des minorités et parfois même les droits civiques des uns et des autres. [1991, p. 127].*

A la fin du XXéme siècle on peut observer l'explosion des nationalismes. L'éparpillément du continent européen et création de plusieurs nouveaux Etat ne peut résoudre aucune question, mais au contraire vont risque d'aggraver les problèmes existant et créer des complications nouvelles, encore plus sensibles. On peut chaque jour voir ce qui se passe à Bosnie-Herzegovine, mais ce n'est ne pas fini. Une importante minorité serbe en Croatie (Krajina) constituera sans doute un facteur destructif de la république indépendante. La minorité albanaise à Kosovo constitue un cas similaire. Il y a encore la Macédoine.

Une situation comparable, mais jusqu'à maintenant moins explosive est à observer en ex-Tchécoslovaquie; en Slovaquie existe une importante minorité hongroise qui craint l'explosion du chauvinisme slovaque toujours possible. Il y a aussi une assez grande minorité polonaise en Lituanie qui doit faire face au nationalisme de cette jeune nation qui parallèment nourrit le nationalisme polonais

Dans différent pays de l'Europe Centrale circulent des nouvelles cartes, qui montrent les revendication territoriales sinon officielles c'est au moins officieuses. En Hongrie on peut trouver une carte de la „Grand

Hongrie" qui englobe de territoires de la Transylvanie, de la partie méridionale de Slovaquie et de la Voïvodine.

En Pologne certains groupes en Haute Silésie colportent la carte de la „Grand Silésie" qui regroupent de territoires polonais et tchèques. La Silésie, selon certaines propositions devrai constituer une région autonome, trilingue, fédérée avec République Fédérale Allemagne.

Tous ces processus signifient que nous assistons à la formation d'un nouvel ordre géopolitique dans cette partie de l'Europe.

## 4. Les frontières intérieures et la question régionale

Il y a bien sûr d'autres exemples des frontières qui partagent l'Europe même à l'intérieur des états existant. Ces frontières ont le caractère ethnolinguistique, économique, religieux. Elles sont très nombreuses. Dans cette communication on ne peut pas en donner que quelques exemples. Pour une analyse plus approfondie l'excellent ouvrage de Jean Labasse „*L'Europe des régions*" est bien sûr à consulter.

Au Royaume Uni nous avons l'Ecosse et le pays de Galles qui affirment de plus en plus leur propre identité. En Espagne il y a le Pays Basque, la Catalogne, la Galicie, l'Andalousie et bien d'autre région où la langue locale devient de plus en plus importante. En Italie, en dehors des enclaves ethnolinguistique (Val d'Aoste, Trentin-Haut Adige, Frioul-Vénetie-Julienne, Sargaigne et Sicile) on peut observer le clivage Nord-Sud qui remonte haut dans la passé. Jean Labasse écrit: „*Dans le Nord, poussé jusqu'en Toscane, la formation des principautés, faisant suite à la féodalité, a suscité la naissance d'une société politique au sein de laquelle la ville exerce sa domination sur la communautés rurales. Rien de tel n'est apparu dans le Sud, voué à un régime retardataire et ballotté entre les deux écueils du micro et du latifundium.*" [1991, p. 59].

En Lombardie donc, on peut observer le mouvément séparatiste qui dans certaines circonstances peuvent menacer l'intégralité de l'Etat italien.

En France nous avons affaire à la fameuse ligne qui partage l'Hexagone du Havre à Marseille, et qui, depuis la première révolution industrielle, oppose traditionnellément les provinces riches du Nord et de l'Est, aux provinces pauvres du Sud et de l'Ouest. S'il y a deux Italie et dans un moindre degré deux Frances il y a en dehors du grande clivage entre l'ex RDA et la RFA, deux Allemagne occidentales de part et d'autre de la Main. La charnière du Main — comme le montre Jean Labasse — est assez évidente. En dehors des données économiques on peut observé que le Sud est largément catholique, le Nord est protestant, le vote du Sud donne depuis longtemps l'avantage aux chrétiens-démocrates, celui du Nord aux socio-démocrates. Les dialectes découlant du bas-allemand règnent au Nord et ceux qui relèvent du haut-allemand, au Sud. (J.Labasse, 1991, p. 64].

Un des exemple intéressants est la cas de la Pologne où l'ont peut observer les clivages qui montent loin dans l'histoire et les frontières bien visibles qui ont été tracées aussi bien par les processus économiques et les impacts culturels, que par les grandes puissances voisines.

Si l'on partage le territoire polonais dans ses frontières actuelles en trois bandes Nord-Sud et en trois bandes Est-Ouest, on constate que la bande Sud comporte au total 39 p. 100 des villes polonaises comptant aujourd'hui plus de 10 000 habitants, mais dont 49 p. 100 existaient déjà au XIIe siècle. Ces chiffres sont respectivément de 31 et 23 p. 100 pour la bande centrale, et de 30 et 29 p. pour la bande septentrionale. A travers une partie de la Pologne passe l'extrémité d'une ligne invisible séparant l'Europe, que Fernand Braudel a tracé de Lyon à Cracovie, en passant par Genève, Bâle, Augsbourg et Vienne.

Les différences sont encore plus grandes lorsqu'on examine les bandes partageant la Pologne dans le sens Nord-Sud. En effet, la bande Ouest regroupe au total 42 p. 100 des villes, mais dont 68 p. 100 existaient déjà au XIIe siècle. Dans la bande centrale, il y a égalément 42 p. 100 des villes en Pologne, dont 31 p. 100 seulément datent de la période ancienne. Enfin, la bande orientale ne comprend que 16 p. 100 des villes, avec moins de 2 p. 100 de villes anciennes. Ainsi donc, du point de vue géographique, le niveau relatif d'urbanisation n'a pas trop évolué depuis Xe siècle, et, comme jadis, les villes sont aujourd'hui concentrées dans les territoires du sud-ouest et partiellément du centre-ouest de la Pologne; comme au XIIe siècle, c'est toujours la Vistule qui délimite la frontière entre les niveaux d'urbanisation. L'Est, l'Ouest, le Nord et le Sud s'interpénètrent et se chevauchent en Pologne. Il en est de même à l'échelle de l'Europe où se constituent — selon Fernand Braudel — quatre „*fuseaux historiques*": l'isthme russe, l'isthme polonais, l'isthme de la Haute Allemagne et l'isthme français [F.Braudel, 1982].

La christianisation de la Pologne par Rome, au Xéme siècle, signifiait l'inclusion de notre pays dans l'orbite occidentale. Par suite de l'union personnelle avec la Lituanie, la Pologne devint un Etat aux multiples minorités ethniques, un creux où se mélangeaient les influences de diverses cultures et civilisations, un lieu où se heurtaient des intérêts politiques variés. En adoptant le christianisme, la Pologne devint une partie intégrante de l'Europe d'alors, mais l'écart séparant l'Est Polonais de la civilisation occidentale était déjà considérable.

En témoignaient non seulement le niveau technique, la valeur artistique des ouvrages d'architecture, mais aussi les donnés caractérisant l'activité économique, tout particulièrement le niveau de la production agricole. Fernand Braudel indique que le rendément des quatre céréales de base était longtemps très faible de 4,1 à 4,7 grains récoltés pour un grain semé. Le rendément n'était pas la même partout, il était le plus élevé en Angleterre où l'indice 4,7 fut atteint le plus tôt, entre 1250 et 1499, puis vint la France avec un rendément de 4,3, qui ne fut enregistré en Allemagne et dans les pays scandinaves que beaucoup plus tard. La situation était la plus mauvaise en Europe centrale et orientale, où l'indice 4,1 ne put être atteint que pendant la période de 1550 à 1820. Or entre 1750 et 1820. l'Angleterre et le Pays-Bas avaient déjà atteint l'indice de productivité 10, alors qu'en Europe centrale et orientale on n'obtenait que 40 p. 100 du rendément des pays les plus avancés. C'était déjà un véritable abîme [F.Braudel, 1967].

Le retard de ces pays de date donc des derniers siècles ni des dernières décennies. Pendant au moins deux siècles, la Pologne fut une puissance européenne (XVéme-XVIéme siècles), mais elle ne fut jamais forte au point de vue économique, ce qui vient à dire qu'elle ne pouvait être ni un pôle de croissance ni un centre d'innovation techniques et de civilisation.

Pendant la période de partages la frontière entre l'Ouest et l'Est, traversant la Pologne s'est consolidée. Les territoires occidentaux, ayant été incorporé à la Prusse, se trouvèrent sous l'influence civilisatrice de l'Occident. Les terres méridionales, intégrées dans la monarchie austro-hongroise, furent également dans la mouvance occidentale, tandis que les parties centrale et orientale de la Pologne, occupés par la Russie, furent soumises pendant presque un siècle et demi non seulément à la russification mais aussi à une orientalisation spécifique. La Russie du XIXéme siècle, quelque peu européanisé, restait cependant profondément ancrée dans son passé asiatique, ce qui se traduisait, aussi bien par la forme de gouvernément et par la structure sociale, que par le niveau de civilisation. Ces éléments asiatiques, par la force de choses, non seulément pénétraient dans les terres polonaises, ce qui avait déjà lieu auparavant, mais étaient sciemment implantés par les occupants.

Pendant l'entre-deux-guerres, la Pologne indépendant continua d'être un pays à deux facettes. Les territoires orientaux, habités — à l'exception des villes — par des populations biélorusses et ukrainiennes, était séparés des terres occidentales, soit de la Grande-Pologne, de la Poméranie et de la Silésie, par un écart dans le niveau de civilisation. Le territoire de la Galicie et les terres occupées par les Russes étaient différenciés. P.ex avant la Deuxième Guerre mondiale dans la voïvodie de Wilno 27,8% des paysans déclaraient le biélorusse comme la langue maternelle, dans la voïvodie de Nowogródek le pourcentage atteignait 42,1%. Par contre dans la voïvodie de Wołyń 75,2% des campagnardes parlaient l'ukrainien. Dans la voïvodie de Stanisławów ce pourcentage était de 53,9%. En revanche, il était beaucoup moins grand dans les voïvodies de Tarnopol (28,1%) et de Lwów (22,2%).

En 1945, les frontières de la Pologne se sont déplacées considérablément vers l'Ouest, ce qui lui donna donc une chance de mieux s'intégrer à l'Europe. Or, la frontière occidentale polonaise fut fixée à la ligne Oder-Neisse, sous la pression de l'Union soviétique, dans sa propre zone d'influence. Ceci empêcha évidemment l'ouverture de la Pologne à l'Ouest et provoqua — le stalinisme aidant — une augmentation du nombre d'éléments asiatique dans de multiples domaines de la vie sociale et une régression du niveau de civilisation.

La Pologne a été donc poussé vers l'Ouest et est devenu un pays ethniquément quasi homogène, mais les frontières anciennes traversent toujours la Pologne, et elles correspondent en gros aux „coutures des anciennes zones d'occupation". De part et d'autre, les terrains diffèrent entre eux au premier coup d'oeil: une autre disposition, un autre système d'aménagément des villes et des villages, des comportéments humains différent, un autre style de vie, des systèmes de valeurs différents Zamość et Przemyśl, villes situées à une centaine de kilomètres l'une de l'autre, diffèrent tellément comme si elles appartenaient à des cercles de civilisation différénts.

## 5. Vers une désintégration européenne?

Il est très symptomatique que depuis la chute du mur de Berlin en Europe Centrale et Orientale on peut observer la processus de désintégration des Etats existant. Ce processus est contagieux parce et il n'est pas exclue ailleurs, par exemple en Belgique où en Italie.

Beaucoup de pays ont essayé de sauver son économie grâce à des différentes mesures protectionnistes. Les agriculteurs et les pêcheurs français détruisent les produits provenant aussi bien de la Communauté que d'autres pays. Les négociations de GATT sur le libre échange piétinent depuis longtemps. La guerre commerciale entre l'Europe de douze les Etats Unis et le Japon se poursuit de façon plus ou moins voilé.

Les nouvelles démocraties de l'Europe Centrale qui constituent le marché important pour l'appareil productif stagnant de l'Europe Occidentale sont enfermés dans le cercle vicieux de frontières économiques. Elles n'ont pas la possibilité d'importé ni les biens de production moderne ni les biens de consommation pour satisfaire les besoins de la population parce qu'elles ne peuvent pas exporter sur le marché européen protégé par les mesures protectionnistes, qui frappent les textiles, l'acier, les produits agricoles et bien d'autres. Le décollage économique est alors très difficile à faire. Tous ces phénomènes ne peuvent que renforcer les frontières.

Au niveau régional la crise renforce des forces centrifuges et pourrait provoqué la désintégration de certains états.

Il n'est pas exclu que toutes ces forces qui jouent aussi bien au niveau régional qu'au niveau national pourront faire éclater la Communauté Economique Européennes alors les nouvelles frontières apparaîtront. La crise rémet en vigueur les disparités régionale un peu oublié pendant la prospérité. Il y a de plus en d'articles et d'ouvrages qui traitent de ces problèmes avec inquiétude. Par contre les différentes études régionales préparées à Bruxelles débordent toujours d'optimisme officiel. Elles se caractérisent par une perspective très technocratique et par une approche macro qui ne tient pas compte ni des problèmes spécifiques, ni des questions sociales, ethnique et politique parfois aiguës, qui peuvent rendre fausses les prévision même le mieux élaborées.

Ces études montrent peut être un phénomène plus profond, celui de l'incapacité de grands centres logistiques et décisionnels, aussi bien internationaux que nationaux, de trouver une solution adéquate à une crise à différents visages c'est-à-dire économique, politique, sociale et culturel. Il y a à craindre que si les institution européennes nationales et transnationales ne trouvent pas une solution valable, l'Europe sera menacé en tant que telle.

## 6. Quel avenir pour l'Europe...pour le Monde?

A la fin du XXéme siècle les phénomènes relativément nouveaux ce sont manifestés, certains n'existants que depuis la chute du mur de Berlin. L'Europe est donc en face de plusieurs processus contradictoires ils peuvent être présenter dans six groupes modèles.

*Mondialisation ou exclusion*

*„Malgré les discours de plus en plus fréquents — écrit Riccardo Petrella — sur la mondialisation de l'économie et de la société, la compréhension et la vision du monde sont de moins en moins universalistes. L'explosion actuelle des nouvelles technologies a engendré une importante distorsion dans la carte du monde telle qu'elle est vue mentalément par les responsables des pays avancés, notamment les Européens de l'Ouest, les Japonais et les Américains. Ils ont l'impression que le monde est de plus en plus petit et unifié autour de leurs propres pôles. Ils pensent que le monde qui compte, sur le plan du développément économique, social, culturel, présent et futur, est constitué par la triade Etats-Unis, Japon, Europe de l'Ouest. Dès lors, le problème majeur des vingt prochaines années est de savoir qui, de ces trois entités acquerra la prédominance mondiale (en Europe de l'Ouest, le problème se dédouble au niveau du leadership européen). Tout le reste n'est que bruit de la périphérie!"* (R.Petrella 1993).

La vague du tiers-mondisme des années 60 et 70, lorsque dans les mass-media et les ouvrages scientifiques ne s'occupait pas surtout de la décolonisation, des relations asymétriques entre le monde développé et sous développé, du centre et de la périphérie, des problèmes économiques et politiques du Tiers Monde et de son intégration au monde développé, est dépassé. On n'en parle plus et ce silence n'est interrompu de temps en temps que par les images sanglants et spectaculaires que la télévision montre pour épater les bourgeois. On parle encore du Monde post-communiste, mais de moins en moins. Aussi bien le Tiers Monde que l'Est est devenu monde à part.

### Intégration ou désintégration européenne

La chute de l'empire soviétique a provoqué le processus de désintégration aussi bien à l'Est qu'a l'Ouest. La cohésion de soi disant „camp socialiste" a été assurée par la force militaire de l'ex URSS. De l'autre côté la cohésion de l'Europe Occidentale a été renforcé par la crainte de cette puissance. Lorsque la menace soviétique a disparu, les forces centrifuges se sont révélées. La crise économique mondiale et surtout européenne est aussi à l'origine de l'apparition de différents particularismes qui se manifestent non seulément au niveau national mais aussi au niveau régional.

### Ouverture ou fermeture

La société ouverte est un de principes de démocratie occidentale, ouvert au sens de Karl Popper et ouvert tout simplément pour les immigrants et pour d'autres étrangers. Or ont peut observer les tendances de fermeture des sociétés européennes sur elles mêmes et quelques autres phénomènes très inquiétant: agressions contre les étrangers en Allemagne, lois contre l'immigration en Allemagne et en France, purges ethnique en ex Yougoslavie, vague de nationalisme et de xénophobie un peu partout.

### L'Europe de nations ou l'Europe des régions

L'Europe de nations est de plus en plus menacée par les forces centrifuges très puissantes: dans la sphère économique par les multinationales, dans la sphère économique et politique par les organisations transnationales (p.ex Commissions des Communautés Européennes) et dans la sphère économique et culturelle par les régions qui veulent avoir plus d'autonomie.

Les disparités entre régions se sont renforcées depuis la fin des années soixante et soixante dix. *„Elles ont été amplifiées par la vague de libéralisation et de privatisation, la priorité donnée au secteur privé et la diminution des dépenses publiques — écrit R.Petrella — Pour renforcer la position des régions, on avait aussi misé sur le technologies de l'information et de la communication, lesquelles auraient dû favoriser la déconcentration et la décentralisation des décisions. Or, c'est l'inverse qui s'est produit, à savoir un renforcément de la centralisation et de la spécialisation des régions"* (Petrella, 1993). On peut se demander de quoi on parle quand on parle de l'Europe de régions. Es ce que de toutes les régions, aussi bien centrales, riches et dynamiques, que les régions pauvres, périphérique et stagnantes, des régions de fameuse banane européenne ou d'autres. régions. Il est très caractéristique que l'idée de l'Europe des régions vient en générale de régions les plus riche, dans les pays riche.

**Pouvoir économique mondiale ou pouvoir politique nationale**

Les décision sur l'allocation des ressources technologiques et financières dans tel ou tel pays ou dans telle ou telle région du monde — donc les décisions qui modifient le présent et modèlent l'avenir — sont prises par les grandes entreprises mondiales. La mondialisation économique signifie la fin du „national" en tant que lieu central de pertinence stratégique, en matière économique et technologique. De ce fait, elle établit des rapports entièrement nouveaux entre l'Etat et les entreprises, entre le pouvoir économique et le pouvoir politique.

**Individualisme ou collectivisme**

L'individualisme est un autre principe de la démocratie occidentale. Le comportément individualiste est opposé au comportément collectiviste qui a caractérisé la société traditionnelle et la société communiste. Après la chute du communisme, paradoxalément, on peut observer la montée du collectivisme tribal. Pour présenter cette opposition je me réfère à la très pertinente diagnose de Ralf Dahrendorf qui met en garde les sociétés européennes contre ce collectivisme nouveau aux racines anciennes.

*„Le modèle d'un Etat différencié du point de vue national s'est trouvé à la croisée des chemins —* écrit Ralf Dahrendorf, un des plus éminents sociologues et politologues d'aujourd'hui-. *Ce genre d'Etat avait été la plus grande conquête de la civilisation politique. C'est dans cet Etat qu'étaient pleinément respectés les droits civiques, l'égalité en droit, indépendamment des appartenances ....Ce qui se passe aujourd'hui en Yougoslavie c'est la vision de ce qui peut apparaître demain dans les parties occidentales et méridionales de l'Union soviétique, peut-être aussi en Tchécoslovaquie ou en Roumanie. C'est un processus étrange et inquiétant qu'il conviendrait de définir comme un retour à la tribu, à l'existence tribale. Les hommes ne veulent pas ou ne peuvent pas supporter de vivre dans des communautés différenciées; ils cherchent les leurs dans la mesure du possible, seulément les leurs....*

*Comme l'écrivait Karl Popper dans «La société ouverte», plus on essaie de revenir à l'époque héroïque des communautés tribales et plus on débarque du côté des inquisitions, de la police secrète et du gangstérisme romancé... Ce n'est pas vrai qu'une moitié du continent se décompose alors que l'autre s'unifie. L'unification occidentale a aussi ses limites. Aujourd'hui elle est souvent et nettément limitée par la revendication de créer l'Europe des régions. Les tribus et la Grande Unité doivent remplacer les pays nationalément différenciés. C'est un mauvais conseil, Franchément, c'est un conseil doublément mauvais... J'ai dit que l'Europe des régions était un conseil doublément mauvais. Il est mauvais d'une part parce qu'il met l'accent sur les tribus contre la communauté différenciée. Il l'est aussi parce qu'il décrit l'Europe comme une sorte d'horizon indéfini où s'estompent tous les contours nets. A quoi bon les capitales puisque nous avons l'Europe? Cette Europe imprécise, rêveuse et en fait utopique ne résoudra aucun problème réel et surement pas les querelles tribales.... Les tribus ne créent pas l'Europe, elles mèneront toujours des guerres entre elles.* (Dahrendorf, 1991b).

# Références

Braudel F., 1967, *Civilisation matérielle et capitalisme*, A. Colin, Paris

Braudel F., 1982, *L'Europe*, Paris

Dahrendorf R., 1991a, *Rozważania nad rewolucją w Europie (Réflexion sur la révolution en Europe)*, Nowa, Warszawa.

Dahrendorf R., 1991b, *Europa regionów*, (*L'Europe des régions*), „Polityka" no. 40.

Labasse J., 1991, *L'Europe des régions*, Flammarion, Paris.

Morin E., 1988: *Myśleć Europa* (Penser l'Europe), Ed. Wola, Warszawa.

Petrella R., 1993, *Recueil d'articles*, Bruxelles

Pomian K., 1990, *L'Europe et ses nations*, Gallimard, Paris.

Bernard Poche
Centre de Recherche sur le Politique
l'Administration et le Territoire
Grenoble

# LE MODELE
# DE LA „GRANDE REGION":
# UN SYSTEME SOCIETAL
# INFRA-ETATIQUE AUTONOME

## 1. Eléments d'approche d'un nouveau type de région

Parmi les éléments du puzzle très compliqué auquel nous avons affaire dans la recomposition générale des territoires en Europe, dans ce qu'on appelle parfois la „nouvelle architecture européenne", une notion que l'on pourrait désigner par le terme de grande région semble émerger, au sein d'une analyse conceptuelle complexe et parfois brouillée, comme un élément intéressant, sinon tout à fait original. Ce texte se propose de l'expliciter et de l'illustrer par quelques exemples. Je me hâte d'ajouter, afin que nulle ambiguïté ne subsiste, que mon propos se situe sensiblement hors des champs disciplinaires de la géographie ou de son avatar contemporain la géo-politique, et également de la science politique (ou administrative). Il est uniquement de me demander quelles sont les logiques sociales (je préfère dire: sociétales) qui sous-tendent telles ou

telles formes en émergence; le terme, que j'utilise ici, de forme, ou „forme
sociale", s'applique à un regroupement caractérisé par trois éléments: son
étendue, l'idiosyncrasie collective — si j'ose risquer ce barbarisme — qui
lui est attribuée, et les limites qui le séparent et le raccordent aux éléments
voisins, sa „frontière". Ce qui peut légitimer, aux yeux du sociologue,
que l'on en parle comme d'une forme sociale, en utilisant le terme au
sens que lui donne Georg Simmel[1], se résumerait en deux éléments: la
grande région est le produit en émergence de la représentation sociale
des groupes concernés; avec les trois aspects de caractérisation que je
lui ai supposés, elle sert de point de référence, de cadrage général, à
la définition (territoriale) du système social (et de l'action sociale). Elle
participe donc, au degré le plus éminent, de ce que l'on appelle auto-
référence[2] ou processus auto-référentiel.

Ceci étant dit, et avant d'aller plus loin dans les caractères que je
prête à la grande région et de donner un certain nombre d'exemples,
effectifs, en voie d'émergence, voire même virtuels, il convient encore de
préciser certains points qui justifient l'attention que l'on peut porter à ce
phénomène. Tout d'abord le niveau institutionnel associé au territoire
en cause peut être de divers ordres. Certains des territoires que je
désigne ainsi peuvent être, ou être devenus, des Etats indépendants.
Certains peuvent être des Etats fédérés, ou des portions d'Etats centralisés
revendiquant une autonomie telle que le processus à terme semble devoir
être plutôt de type confédéral que fédéral. Certains encore peuvent être
des sous-ensembles d'Etats centralisés dans laquelle le processus fédéral
n'est absolument pas à l'ordre du jour (sinon même „tabou"), mais pour
lesquels la singularité qui leur est attribuée par l'auto-représentation des
membres du groupe social correspondant est telle que leur spécificité est,
dans tous les domaines, à peu près incontestable. Le premier cas pourrait
avoir pour exemple archétypique la Slovénie; le second la Flandre belge;
le troisième la Corse ou l'Alsace.

On peut encore aller plus loin, et proposer quelques autres
caractéristiques, soit positives, soit négatives, et quelques autres modes
d'illustration. Il peut arriver qu'une grande région soit de type
transfrontalier, mais le cas est apparemment plutôt rare; en tout cas ne

---

[1] Dans son article célèbre „Comment les formes sociales se maintiennent" republié dans
Sociologie et Epistémologie, Paris, Presses Universitaires de France, 1981.
[2] Cf. D. Bougnoux, *La communication circulaire, enquête sur le paradigme de l'auto-*
*référence, de la littérature aux sciences sociales*, thèse de doctorat de l'Université Stendhal,
Grenoble, 1988.

suffiraient pas, pour la définir ainsi, les ambitions d'hommes politiques ou les stratégies de leaders du monde économique, non plus que la passion de spécialistes des „cultures de contact". On ne peut, selon nous, confondre dans les mêmes catégories les relations, éventuellement étroites et anciennes, qu'entretiennent des populations de part et d'autre d'une frontière, avec l'auto-définition par ses habitants d'un espace unique jouissant d'un pouvoir d'interprétation du monde qui soit unitaire (bien que ceci ne signifie évidemment pas qu'il doive être homogène).

On peut illustrer cette remarque par plusieurs exemples. Le fait que de nombreux citoyens italiens de la bande limitrophe de la Slovénie soient de culture et de langue slovène, au moins pour une part de leur fonctionnement social, et que Trieste soit une ville (qui fut) pluriculturelle, ne justifie pas qu'il doive exister une hyper-région qui regrouperait la Slovénie, l'Istrie (croate), les provinces italiennes de Trieste et de Gorizia, voire le Frioul, thèse qui ne trouverait, dans toute son extension, que bien peu de défenseurs. Le fait que l'influence de Genève s'étende, sous de nombreux rapports, sur le pays de Gex et la partie Nord-Ouest du département français de la Haute-Savoie ne justifie pas que l'appellation (qui semble un peu passée de mode) de Regio Genovensis soit autre chose qu'une métaphore d'assez faible valeur éclairante, chère seulement à certains néo-technocrates du localisme et à quelques esprits romantiques au sein des élites traditionnelles (dont une figure assez emblématique fut en son temps le Neuchâtelois Denis de Rougemont). La même remarque s'appliquerait avec plus de force encore au triangle constitué par les zones du sud de l'Alsace et du pays de Bade, et la région bâloise.

En réalité un des seuls cas, sinon le seul, qui puisse apparaître probant dans la moitié occidentale de l'Europe serait le Tyrol, divisé entre Tyrol du Nord (autrichien) et Tyrol du Sud (italien), mais on voit que les conditions historiques (existence ancienne du comté du Tyrol), politiques (accord De Gasperi-Gruber de 1946) et „culturelles" (existence d'un droit coutumier, et d'une variante dialectale, communs, reconnaissance en Italie des grades délivrés à l'Université d'Innsbrück), sont tout à fait particulières.

En fait, le problème se trouve d'être compliqué par la superposition, aux frontières de l'auto-référence qui sont par essence floues et très perméables jusqu'à une certaine limite (sauf cas particuliers), des frontières culturo-linguistiques et des habitudes de contact qui définissent, autour de chacune de ces grandes régions, un halo de relations préférentielles (dans certains cas sous réserve d'inventaire, ou avec une forte amplification dans l'imaginaire, ou encore avec une dissymétrie marquée des échanges[3]. En fait, il est possible que chaque grande région auto-identificatoire soit entourée, tel le noyau de la vieille théorie atomique par ses électrons, d'une frange en équilibre avec les grandes régions voisines, ce qui justifierait que l'on envisageât deux niveaux de grande région emboîtés l'un dans l'autre — d'autant plus que tous les territoires ne relèvent pas au même degré de cette problématique de la grande région. Mais je n'envisagerai pas davantage cet aspect ici, faisant l'hypothèse que son intérêt se situe, sous l'angle qui m'intéresse, à un stade complémentaire.

Un autre point, plus important, doit être abordé. Les exemples que j'ai pris ont, ainsi que je l'ai posé comme une hypothèse de départ, des statuts institutionnels hétérogènes. Cela ne voudrait-il pas dire que la grande région est un phénomène d'un autre ordre, qui pourrait se définir contre des catégories empiriques en apparence inébranlables, mais qui en fait sont, soit peu explicatives par rapport à la problématique sociétale que j'utilise, soit menacées (ou frappées) d'obsolescence? Tel est bien le cas en effet: la problématique de la grande région s'oppose à la fois, telle que je la propose ici, à la problématique de l'Etat-Nation, à celle de la région administrative obtenue par décentralisation du précédent quels que soient les pouvoirs qui sont dévolus à cette région administrative, et enfin à la problématique de la globalisation.

Cette opposition, telle que je me propose dans ce qui suit de l'étayer et de la développer, ne procède pas d'une polémique entre deux conceptions de la région qui seraient en concurrence (ou plusieurs). Elle vient d'une analyse par niveaux différents. Il peut se trouver qu'une région au sens où je l'entends coïncide de fait avec le produit d'une décentralisation administrative (dans ce cas elle existait le plus souvent au préalable, voir le cas de la Catalogne par exemple). Il peut se trouver qu'elle revêt actuellement la forme d'un Etat (le plus souvent de fraîche date, voir par exemple la Slovénie). Mais ce ne sont jamais ces caractères institutionnels formels qui la définissent, mais le fait qu'elle se présente comme une unité sociale, un quantum élémentaire de société dont la valeur et la pertinence, comme lieu caractéristique de dégagement du sens social, de ce que les ethnométhodologues appellent l'intelligibilité ou encore la „construction

---

[3]On retrouverait facilement ces diverses réserves en examinant de près les cas que nous venons de citer, par exemple le cas des confins triestins.

endogène du sens", est supérieure aux unités de taille inférieure comme à celle des unités de taille supérieure.

A vrai dire, si l'on y réfléchit bien, on voit même que cette position de „maximum de la courbe" est, sur le registre global que nous avons choisi, très accentuée. Bien entendu, la question de la pertinence de Rhône-Alpes ou de Champagne-Ardennes (en France) comme lieux de dégagement de l'intelligibilité du monde ne se pose guère, c'est le moins que l'on puisse dire; mais même en ce qui concerne le concept d'Etat il en va de même. L'Etat n'a pas ce but: il a celui de l'unification politique, non celui de l'expression sociale (sociétale) sui generis; c'est même exactement l'opposé. J'ai développé ailleurs[4] les raisons pour lesquelles l'Etat-Nation tend à développer une société imaginaire, véritable substitut mythique à la société globale dans toute sa complexité en tant qu'elle est plus ou moins artificiellement „découpée" par ses frontières. Cette société fictive, qui a par ailleurs des fonctions d'„interface", est souvent qualifiée de„société civile" ou de „nation au sens moderne"; je n'insisterai pas ici sur ce point. L'Etat fonctionne donc, relativement à cette problématique du sens social, comme une superstructure opératoire.

C'est en fait l'obsolescence souvent notée, voire dans certains cas l'écroulement pur et simple de cette forme sociale caractéristique de la période 1870–1939 qu'a été l'Etat-Nation, qui est à l'origine de la nouvelle problématisation que l'on croit pouvoir observer ici. Il faut en effet remarquer, pour ne plus y revenir, que malgré les apparences et certaines prises de position plus idéologiques que rationnelles, la Tchécoslovaquie ou la Yougoslavie, par exemple (je n'ose dire l'URSS), avaient un discours et un fonctionnement d'Etat-Nation tout aussi clair et tout aussi réducteur des particularismes „nationaux„(les réduisant à un rang bien réel mais relevant de la sphère du privé), que dans les cas de la France, de l'Espagne, de l'Italie, et même de la R„F"A. La lecture de la très fédéraliste Constitution yougoslave de 1974 confirme ce point: la véritable base logique de la „décentralisation auto-gestionnaire" de cet Etat n'était en aucune manière constituée des six Républiques fédérées, non plus que des „nations et nationalités" (narodni i narodnoste), c'est-

[4]B. Poche, *La remise en question de la volonté unificatrice des Etats et la montée du fédéralisme comme forme sociale: l'exemple de la Ligue lombarde/Ligue Nord*, communication au Colloque international Nations et frontières dans la nouvelle architecture européenne, Bruxelles, Université Libre de Bruxelles, 6–8 mai 1993. Actes à paraître par les soins du CERIS, ULB, Bruxelles.

à-dire des éléments constitutifs „ethno-culturels"[5], mais semblait être formée par les éléments de base de la vie civique (la commune yougoslave) et économique (l'entreprise de propriété sociale). Le fait que nous nous trouvions là dans le „monde slave", comme les ambivalences de la théorie (ou plutôt de la pratique) socialiste-marxiste de l'Etat, ne constituent pas, à mon avis, des critères de différenciation formels suffisants.

Si l'on considère en effet cette „usure" de l'Etat-Nation, on voit qu'elle se manifeste aussi bien à l'Ouest qu'à l'Est, et que dans les deux cas les phénomènes qui sont enregistrés sont d'ordre très proches; il s'agit de trouver un élément territorial de visibilisation, on pourrait même presque dire, en utilisant le langage de Bergson[6] et non celui des mouvements d'obédience plus ou moins religieuse, de „conscientisation", d'intériorisation, du lien social, qui ne soit pas d'ordre politique au sens classiquement institutionnel de ce mot. On pourrait donc dire, en reprenant nos trois exemples cités plus haut, que:

— la Slovénie est, au sens où nous l'entendons, une région bien qu'elle soit un Etat, et on pourrait même ajouter qu'elle n'est peut-être devenue un Etat que parce qu'elle n'a pas pu négocier avec la Fédération yougoslave un statut de type explicitement confédéral qui lui aurait reconnu, en tant que partenaire ès-qualités, la gestion interne de tous les éléments sociétaux, culturels et socio-économiques correspondants[7];

---

[5]La Constitution n'établissait d'ailleurs aucun lien direct entre les Républiques et les nations, et multipliait au contraire les clauses stipulant que les droits linguistiques et culturels de chaque citoyen yougoslave étaient les mêmes quelle que soit la république sur le sol de laquelle il se trouvait résider, ce qui tendait, paradoxalement, à faire apparaître la nationalité comme une affaire individuelle.

[6]Tel que A. Schütz lui a donné ses lettres de naturalisation sociologique lorsqu'il écrit: „Un point essentiel de la philosophie de Bergson est sa théorie d'une vie consciente qui se manifeste sur un nombre indéfini de plans différents s'étageant, pour prendre les deux extrêmes, du plan de l'action à celui du rêve. Chacun de ses plans est caractérisé par une tension spécifique de la conscience (...) Pour Bergson, ces différents degrés sont fonction des variations de notre intérêt à la vie. (...) L'attention à la vie est donc le principe régulateur de base de notre vie consciente" (souligné dans le texte), *Sur les réalités multiples* in Le chercheur et le quotidien, Paris, Méridiens Kleincksieck, 1987, pp. 109–110.

[7]Thèse qui est tout à fait clairement avancée par de nombreux intellectuels slovènes. Cf. à ce sujet B. Poche, *Processus d'indépendance des «nouveaux Etats» de l'Est et mise en forme de la symbolique territoriale: l'exemple slovène*, communication au Colloque international La nouvelle Europe centrale et orientale, histoire, culture, économie et politique, Université de Grenoble, 27–29 janvier 1993.

— la Flandre belge est une région, mais l'origine de cette évolution, qui pousse actuellement la Belgique vers un régime fédéral de plus en plus proche d'une confédération, est nettement de type sociétal et non politique, et s'est caractérisé très rapidement par une assimilation presque complète entre les compétences territoriales (la Région Flandre stricto sensu) et les compétences „culturelles" (la Communauté flamande), ce dont il résulte un déséquilibre permanent avec la Wallonie et avec l'entité complexe, sinon artificielle, créée autour de „Bruxelles-Capitale" qui n'ont, ni l'une ni l'autre et pour des raisons différentes, l'intention actuelle et/ou la possibilité de revendiquer ce type de formule[8];

— l'Alsace est une grande région malgré l'inadéquation totale du statut correspondant dans le schéma institutionnel français actuel, c'est-à-dire l'absence totale de reconnaissance opératoire de la gestion du complexe identité/différence; elle l'est en dehors de ce statut, en raison à la fois de phénomènes d'auto-identification qui dépassent largement le monde des Alsaciens „de naissance", et d'une culture ethno-anthropologique qui réussit à survivre au mixte de négation et de folklorisation avec lequel l'Etat français la traite[9].

Nous allons maintenant examiner quelles sont les caractéristiques de ce que nous appelons grande région.

## 2. La logique sociétale de la grande région

Et d'abord, pourquoi cette appellation de „grande région"? Il s'agit pour nous uniquement de ne pas paraître accorder un label automatique à toute région, quelle qu'elle soit, qui revendique une histoire propre; mais bien entendu cette épithète n'est pas à prendre stricto sensu en termes de superficie mesurable. A contrario il est également tout à fait clair que je n'adhère en aucune façon, à travers l'argumentation que

---

[8]Cf. B. Poche, *La Belgique entre les piliers et les «mondes linguistiques»* in Recherches Sociologiques, vol. XXIII no 3, 1992, Louvain la Neuve (Belgique), pp. 43–67.

[9]Le ridicule épisode de la „délocalisation" à Strasbourg de la très parisienne Ecole Nationale d'Administration (ENA), au-delà même des violents remous qu'il a suscités chez les élèves et anciens élèves de cette Ecole, correspond tout à fait à cette tentative d'uniformiser le territoire en disséminant des „objets" porteurs de centralité: il est évident que l'ENA à Strasbourg ne devient nullement „alsacienne", même au sens le moins ethno-culturel de cette qualification.

je présente ici, aux thèses des „fabricateurs" des „régions à l'échelle" européenne (ou autre). Il n'est évidemment pas pertinent, d'un point de vue sociologique, d'attendre d'une technocratie socio-économique (voire macro-urbanistique) ce que la technocratie politico-administrative n'a pu réaliser.

L'expression de grande région est utilisée ici pour faire apparaître que cette structure, bien qu'évidemment „infra-étatique" par ses dimensions aussi bien spatiales que sociétales, se situe, non pas comme une fragmentation de l'Etat (ce qui pourrait s'imaginer, sinon à l'infini, du moins jusqu'à une échelle très restreinte, par scissions successives) mais en „concurrence" avec lui. La concurrence a beau se situer — je vais y revenir — sur un plan quelque peu distinct, ceci n'impose pas moins une „représentation de soi" par la région en question — c'est-à-dire par les groupes sociaux concernés — qui soit à la hauteur de cette exigence. La grande région n'est pas le produit d'une division politique: c'est le résultat d'un réarrangement, d'une recomposition sociale. Elle est donc dans son principe un phénomène typiquement actuel[10], et non pas un mouvement de maintenance culturelle au sens archaïque ou nostalgique de ce mot, ce qui était souvent reproché (à tort ou à raison, je ne tranche pas) aux mouvements régionalistes des années 1960–1980.

On pourrait donc dire, en combinant tout ce qui précède, que la grande région telle qu'on peut en tracer les contours conceptuels à travers des exemples comme que ceux que nous avons proposés (il y en a d'autres, nous les évoquerons dans la troisième partie de ce texte), et non pas — précisons-le — en fonction d'une vision fantasmatique et prophétique de notre part[11], présente trois caractéristiques majeures:
— elle propose, par rapport au modèle politico-administratif, un autre modèle de représentation de la société par elle-même, plus étroitement lié à l'agrégation directe des sensibilités et des volontés personnelles, et moins lié à la médiation par un corps de doctrines (et d'opérateurs publics) se

---

[10]A titre exclusivement de précaution à statut marginal, je précise qu'une autre conception, un temps à la mode, est à l'opposé de notre analyse de la grande région: c'est le tête-à-tête entre la sociabilité micro-locale, qui n'engage que les affects de l'homme privé, et la globalisation de toutes les instances économiques, technologiques et communicationnelles.

[11]Ce type de vision caractérise souvent les „prospectivistes" et autres „futurologues", y compris dans le champ des sciences sociales. Ils ont souvent l'habileté de la masquer sous un imposant appareil technique: l'urbanisme et ses dérivés se prêtent merveilleusement à ce jeu. Pareilles facilités devraient (en principe du moins) être interdites au sociologue.

présentant au nom de l'intérêt général et de la mise en transcendance des valeurs à travers l'„outil politique"[12];

— elle s'appuie sur des phénomènes d'identification collective, c'est-à-dire sur une relation permanente et réciproque entre trois éléments constituants et indissociables: le groupe humain dans sa diversité, le monde matériel au sein duquel et à travers lequel ce groupe acquiert le minimum de cohérence nécessaire au processus d'auto-référence (ce qui ne signifie en rien l'exclusion de l'autre, mais nécessite en revanche le contrôle, et de la socialisation au sein du groupe, et de la cooptation des personnes d'origine allogène), et le „langage" dans lequel s'opèrent les échanges entre les deux premiers;

— elle propose une dualité inaliénable entre représentation sociale (basée sur le double principe d'agrégation des libertés individuelles et de rapport au monde matériel) et représentation politique (basée sur la gestion instrumentale des normes minimales nécessaires au fonctionnement pratique du groupe, et du rapport au monde extérieur). La première détient la clé de l'intelligibilité du monde, de l'expression pratique et sensible des finalités que se propose une société concrète, dans un contexte déterminé, à une certaine période de l'Histoire; la seconde est chargée de constituer, au service de la société en cause, les procédures nécessaires, mais les logiques sont nettement et à jamais séparées, et la relation entre les deux est de l'ordre d'un contrat toujours amendable, le cas échéant renégociable, dénonçable[13].

Ces caractéristiques seraient, si l'on peut dire, à la base d'une „théorie sociologique" nouvelle du fédéralisme. Plus généralement, elles définissent une nouvelle légitimité, qui récupère assez des ressources anciennes de l'identification territoriale (et/ou ethnique, ou ethno-culturelle ou ethno-linguistique) pour avoir un langage propre et ne

---

[12]J'apporte à l'appui de ceci, à travers un article de l'écrivain et journaliste Giorgio Bocca, l'opinion d'une personnalité du monde intellectuel italien (de gauche), Vittorio Foa: „Nous avons vécu une modernisation animée par un ardent individualisme, puis nous nous sommes aperçus qu'au sein de cet individualisme avait mûri une valeur particulière, celle de la personnalité du sujet individuel, sans laquelle les droits et les sujets collectifs demeurent incompréhensibles. A l'abri du néo-libéralisme de droite a mûri la liberté, comme valeur à laquelle les grandes masses populaires ne peuvent renoncer", cité par G. Bocca, *Io ringrazio quei barbari...* in La Republica, 8 juin 1993, p. 14 (traduit par moi).

[13]Situation que certains responsables de la Ligue lombarde traduisent par la formule lapidaire: „ce n'est pas l'Etat qui est mon patron, c'est moi qui suis le patron de l'Etat" (extrait d'interview).

pas dépendre du néo-langage (de la „novlangue", pour citer Orwell)
du consumérisme universel des paysages et des patrimoines, et qui est
assez intégrée aux processus techno-économiques actuels pour ressentir la
nécessité, sinon de les contrôler, du moins d'établir avec eux un interface
de négociation, ce qui n'est évidemment pas possible au niveau des
groupes de proximité. Ces derniers ne peuvent gérer (et encore...) que
les „équipements de voisinage" chers aux urbanistes, et sont, pour tout
le reste, prisonniers de la division internationale du travail (et de ses
„délocalisations" actuelles).

On voit donc que trois circonstances — l'écroulement du mythe de
l'Etat-Nation, les incertitudes dramatiques de la globalisation, la nécessité
impérative de trouver, en regard, une base logique au lien social — ont
fait apparaître ce type de „système sociétal auto-référentiel de fait" que
j'ai appelé la grande région. Elle se situe — c'est évidemment le postulat
de base qui sous-tend plusieurs années de recherches, en particulier sur
les exemples que j'ai évoqués — plus en rupture qu'en continuité avec les
phénomènes régionaux avec lesquels tant chercheurs qu'hommes d'action
ont été habitués à travailler depuis les années 50, la région historico-
culturelle des militants régionalistes, et la région politico-administrative
des „décentralisateurs". La première a eu largement le temps de faire la
preuve presque mathématique de la non-pertinence de la problématique
correspondante, en particulier en s'enlisant dans la question dite „des
minorités"[14]. La seconde est en train de se perdre dans une définition à
la fois fonctionnaliste et subordonnée de ses compétences qui fait que les
régions sont exposées à un double et contradictoire système d'objections
indépassables: elles ne sont jamais assez politiquement légitimes pour
prendre des mesures qui ne soient pas „enclavées" dans la politique
de leur Etat „padro-padrone"; elles ne sont jamais assez sociétalement
légitimes pour que tout essai d'initiative de leurs dirigeants élus soit à
l'abri de l'accusation de vouloir établir des „baronnies féodales"[15]. La

---

[14]Il n'est jamais difficile de définir une minorité. Mais cela conduit à une série quasi-
interminable d'apories, dont celle de la majorité antagoniste, elle-même nettement plus
difficile, voire impossible, à définir. Pour ne prendre qu'un exemple parmi ceux que j'ai
cotoyés, il est très facile de dire que les habitants des vallées occitanes du Piémont
(encastrées dans le versant Est des Alpes occidentales et limitées à la plaine) sont une
minorité. Mais que sont les Piémontais? Et que vaut une théorie de la „différence ethno-
culturelle" qui assimile les seconds au bloc italien, sans doute parce qu'ils ne sont pas assez
minoritaires?

[15]La presse spécialisée française (type Le Monde) bruit en permanence de ce débat
interminable et stérile.

raison de cette double impasse est cependant claire: ni l'un ni l'autre de ces types de région n'ont de rapport avec la problématique de la définition endogène du lien social, fondatrice d'une nouvelle représentation du rapport des groupes sociaux à l'espace.

Mais cette exigence de redéfinition a un revers: les „grandes régions" sont actuellement à la recherche, non de leur principe de légitimité (celui-ci me paraît au contraire assez solidement établi), mais des limites et de la „problématique du contenu" dans lequel il va pouvoir se présenter, „s'incarner", si l'on ose s'exprimer ainsi, de manière fiable, de manière à imposer cette position hautement paradoxale d'un regroupement social à base spatiale dont la rationalité n'est pas et n'a jamais été politico-militaire, et qui doit négocier avec les tenants de cet ordre politico-militaire (ou politico-diplomatique, si l'on préfère) ou avec leurs héritiers[16]. Les deux exemples non virtuels (la Flandre et la Slovénie) que j'ai cités montrent comment, dans des cas assez spécifiques, la chose a été possible. Le cas de l'Italie du Nord, en pleine gestation actuellement, manifeste sinon une incertitude, du moins une difficulté dans ces deux définitions de la limite et du contenu, qui est assez caractéristique.

## 3. L'Italie du Nord; une grande région en gestation?

Il est peut-être inutile de revenir longuement sur les deux premiers cas. Les analyses que nous en avons antérieurement faites semblent bien montrer que ce qui est proposé comme premier, comme finalité véritable, est la création d'un regroupement à caractère consensuel, dans lequel une très forte charge symbolique est appelée en témoignage et en garantie qu'il existe un groupe humain dont le caractère d'auto-définition va au-delà des différences internes. Le problème qui est alors posé — et il n'est pas simple — est double: comment rendre opérant ce processus de reconnaissance? comment caractériser, par des procédures internes de gestion et des processus externes de contact avec le „monde extérieur", avec les autres, cette frontière dont aucun groupement humain, quelle que soit la nature de son „fait générateur", ne saurait se passer?

---

[16]De ce que l'Europe dite de Maastricht figure parmi ces héritiers présomptifs de l'ordre en question, les invocations magiques à „cette Europe qui, si elle avait été unie, aurait pu rétablir la paix en Bosnie" constituent une assez forte présomption.

Bien entendu, on peut toujours prétendre — et certains Slovènes ne s'en font pas faute, dont évidemment les ultra-nationalistes, mais beaucoup d'autres aussi (et ce que je dis ici ne comporte à leur égard nulle attitude de réprobation morale, seulement une différence d'interprétation) — que ce que l'on vise par là est la création d'un nouvel Etat-Nation, sans qu'il soit besoin de chercher plus loin. Formellement, ils ont raison en ce qui les concerne: l'admission à l'ONU et au sein des autres organisations internationales, une Constitution, une armée, des représentations diplomatiques, etc... tous ces signes établissent de manière irréfutable, selon les catégories juridiques, le caractère étatique.

Mais ma démarche est celle du sociologue, non celle du juriste. Si je propose comme démarche d'assimiler des situations entre elles, au risque de heurter certains (pour des raisons dont je ne discute pas la validité, de leur point de vue), c'est qu'elles me paraissent assimilables. J'ai trop souvent en l'occasion de dénoncer, comme plusieurs de mes collègues[17], la difficulté de tenir un discours de théorie sociologique sur ce groupement social particulier qu'est l'Etat, dont on ne parle presque jamais que selon le discours de type positiviste ou à travers des aspects seconds (dont la célèbre „violence légitime" de Max Weber), pour renoncer à analyser dans un contexte de „crise", au sens que William Thomas donne à ce mot, la rupture des habitudes qui entraîne une nouvelle „définition de la situation"[18]. En l'occurrence, les démarches suivies par les Flamands, les Slovènes et — nous allons le voir — les Lombards présentent de troublantes similitudes; il s'agit toujours de récupérer, sur un Etat dont la

---

[17]Renaud Dulong, en particulier, qui dans le premier chapitre, intitulé „Situation d'un discours sociologique sur l'Etat", de son ouvrage Les régions, l'Etat et la société locale (Paris, Presses Universitaires de France, 1978) déclare en préambule que „analyser l'Etat en sociologue n'est point chose simple" avant de déplorer le „nombre dérisoire des travaux consacrés à ce thème".

[18]Je m'appuie ici sur l'analyse que font Meltzer, Petras et Reynolds de la démarche de William Thomas: „Human beings develop habits which persist until something occurs to change the behavior or force a modification of the course it has been taking. Such an event is called a «crisis», and it disrupts habits by re-directing the attention that formerly had been focused by the individual or the group. By meeting the new needs that are defined in terms of the crisis, individuals and groups exert control of the situation" et, plus loin: „This deliberation which takes place prior to any self-determined form of behavior is called the definition of the situation", B.N. Meltzer, J.W. Petras and L.T. Reynolds, *Symbolic Interactionism, Genesis, varieties and criticism*, Boston, Londres, Routledge and Kegan Paul, 1980, pp. 26–27. Les auteurs s'appuient en particulier sur deux ouvrages de W.I. Thomas: *Source Book for Social origines*, University of Chicago, 1909 et *The Unadjusted Girl*, Boston, Little, Brown and Co, 1923.

légitimité est contestée au double niveau de la représentation du groupe et de la gestion efficace des intérêts propres correspondants, le matériau et les compétences symboliques qui sont de ce fait en cause. Mais les signes de la souveraineté absolue ne sont invoqués, lorsqu'ils le sont, qu'au second degré et presque à contre-cour; il est d'ailleurs évident que, dans le cas slovène, une part notable de la démarche est fondée sur la supposition du caractère tout à fait „différent" que devront revêtir dans l'avenir les relations internationales, au moins à l'échelle européenne, par rapport aux époques précédentes[19].

Le cas de la Lombardie, tel qu'il est illustré par le mouvement des Ligues, est peut-être plus significatif encore. Au départ, la sensibilité de son fondateur Umberto Bossi est clairement de type régionaliste-culturaliste dans la façon dont elle s'exprime : récupération des thèmes emblématiques, de la langue locale, etc..., et elle est influencée, sinon même déclenchée, par les deux modèles les plus „présents" en Italie: le Val d'Aoste de l'Union Valdôtaine et le Haut-Adige du Südtiroler Volkspartei[20]. Mais la véritable motivation est autre: il s'agit de „rompre l'étau" de la centralité italienne estimée, par les Lombards, comme néfaste et anachronique — sujet sur lequel tout a été dit[21]. Il est incontestable que, ce faisant, les Lombards (qui sont par ailleurs tout l'opposé d'une minorité culturelle localiste et traditionnaliste) agissent comme un groupe social, ou plutôt déjà comme un macro- ou hyper-groupe; bien que les sensibilités „communales" et par suite la périodisation, ou les phases de progression, de la Ligue soient différentes entre Varese, Brescia, les vallées actives comme la Valcamonica et ses industries métallurgiques et mécaniques, Pavie et enfin Milan, il est manifeste que la réaction est plus commune à la Lombardie qu'elle ne l'est avec les provinces voisines de la plaine du Pô ou de la côte ligure.

---

[19]Attitude que traduit bien cette réflexion d'un chercheur universitaire slovène: „maintenant que nous sommes indépendants, il va nous falloir établir rapidement des relations avec les autres régions de l'Europe" (extrait d'interview, fin 1991, souligné par moi).

[20]Cf. Daniele Vimercati, *I Lombardi alla nuova crociata, il „fenomeno Lega"* dall' *esordio al trionfo*, Milan, Mursia, 1990 et U. Bossi et D. Vimercati, *Vento del Nord, la mia vita, le mie leghe*, Milan, Sperling & Kupfer, 1992.

[21]Cf., à titre d'exemple, B. Poche, *The Lombard League: From Cultural Autonomy to Integral Federalism* in Telos (New-York), no 90, 1991–92, pp. 71–81 et *Identificazione territoriale e crisi della modernità. L'esempio della Lega lombarda* in Iter (Milan-Gênes), no 5–6, 1992, pp. 108–137.

Mais, rapidement, les responsables du mouvement vont se poser la question (de leur point de vue, c'est-à-dire de manière endogène) de savoir si le groupe social le plus pertinent, susceptible de fonder sociologiquement un système régional, ne serait pas de plus vastes dimensions. Ils vont donc en ce sens entreprendre un rapprochement avec des mouvements parfois aussi anciens qu'eux (la Liga Veneta de Franco Rocchetta en Vénétie, l'Union Piemonteisa de Roberto Gremmo[22] ou, ailleurs, susciter des mouvements locaux affiliés (en Ligurie, en Emilie, puis en Toscane) pour élaborer avec eux un ensemble dénommé Ligue Nord (Lega Nord) dont le but est de promouvoir la transformation de l'Italie en un Etat fédéral (en fait, les propositions successives des congrès du mouvement réfèrent clairement à une structure de type confédéral). Au sein de cet Etat transformé, la „République (fédérée) du Nord" agirait typiquement comme une grande région, en particulier dans le domaine de la politique économique et sociale, c'est-à-dire dans ce qui relève de la fusion „sociétale" des intérêts et des dynamiques personnels. Cette „macro-région" constituerait alors elle-même une „fédération", sur le plan culturel (et donc ethno-anthropologique), des régions classiques plus ou moins historiques, et de plus déléguerait aux échelons d'extension plus réduite (régions, communes, plus faiblement provinces) toutes les questions dont il n'est pas indispensable qu'elle décide. On est donc bien dans le „modèle sociétal" avec ses trois caractéristiques évoquées plus haut, modèle qui ici n'est pas univoque, mais présente une certaine „élasticité" en fonction de la nature des problèmes.

Il n'en reste pas moins que, au stade actuel de l'auto-représentation des groupes, seule la „grande région" du Nord possède potentiellement la capacité d'incarner une légitimité dans la négociation contractuelle de la société avec l'Etat, et qu'elle ne peut s'avancer sur cette voie que si l'hyper-groupe social correspondant lui confère cette compétence: ceci n'est pas, ou n'est plus, une question de division en courants idéologico-politiques. Ce dernier aspect est évidemment soit facilité, soit brouillé, selon le point de vue que l'on préfère adopter, par l'âpreté du débat institutionnel dans l'Italie de 1992–1993; mais ce n'est pas solliciter la situation que de dire que ce débat même, c'est-à-dire d'abord l'„usure" du système politique qui le rend nécessaire, sont une manifestation frappante de l'émergence de

---

[22] A la suite de conflits, ce mouvement a été remplacé dans la liste des „associés" par Piemont Autonomista fondé par le chanteur populaire Gipo Farassino, très connu en Piémont. On remarquera dans tous les cas l'usage de la terminologie en „langue régionale" (Liga pour Lega en vénitien).

nouveaux modèles sociétaux, émergence qui est en train de s'opérer au-delà des „péripéties", même spectaculaires, que connaît l'Italie actuelle.

## 4. Application possible du modèle à l'Europe de 1993

Dans cette quatrième partie, assez brève et qui nous servira de conclusion, je n'ai pas l'intention de „proposer" un découpage de l'Europe, même à titre de pure hypothèse de travail; ce serai totalement contraire à l'esprit de notre analyse. Tout au plus voudrais-je sortir de ce que la considération de quelques exemples pourrait avoir de trop restrictif, et de plus „tendre la main" aux autres chercheurs et analystes, à propos de terrains qui sont les leurs ou qu'ils ont étudiés.

La caractéristique en effet de ce que j'ai appelé le modèle de la grande région (modèle bien entendu au sens de paradigme de référence et non au sens idéaliste ou normatif) est qu'il constitue, selon moi, une possible grille de lecture de laquelle on peut rapprocher des situations éventuellement en devenir ou en phase d'incertitude, avec bien évidemment des „variations secondes", peut-être très marquées. Si le cas de la Flandre (belge) et celui de la Slovénie peuvent apparaître, sinon trop simples, du moins un peu simplifiés pour les besoins de l'exposé (cela aurait été alors à l'encontre de mes intentions), celui de l'Italie du Nord fait déjà mieux apparaître le caractère expérimental de cette dérive (je parle de l'expérimentation pratique au sein du monde social, non de l'expérimentation intellectuelle du scientifique). De plus, on se trouve actuellement devant des positions de vulnérabilités très inégales par rapport à la „crise" motrice dont je parlais plus haut. Ces situations différenciées peuvent provenir, soit de niveaux très inégaux de tensions internes aux Etats, soit du caractère plus ou moins occulté de l'auto-représentation des groupes.

Il est probable en effet que ce qui caractérise les Etats centralisés qui semblent actuellement contrôler le phénomène (général, à mon avis) de la menace très proche d'obsolescence du modèle de l'Etat-Nation, c'est la très forte réduction dont souffrent les processus d'identification groupale. Cette réduction historique n'a pas opéré au bénéfice de l'Etat-Nation comme groupe, mais au profit d'une extrême atomisation des comportements en face de l'effet destructeur (des agrégations sociétales) qu'a produit la prétention de ce même Etat-Nation à constituer cette

„société fictive de substitution" que j'ai évoquée au début de ce texte. On notera en effet que, pour des raisons diverses, la Belgique, l'Italie et la Yougoslavie ont toujours été des Etats dont l'emprise sur les phénomènes d'appartenance collective était relativement faible, et qui par conséquent laissaient survivre, nolens volens, des identifications groupales-territoriales marquées. Je ne prétends nullement que la nature de l'ensemble des phénomènes est distincte en France ou en Grande-Bretagne, mais qu'il y a eu une occultation telle que le sentiment d'identification est en grande partie refoulé[23].

Par le fait, dans les Etats centralisés, seuls les sous-ensembles ayant une très forte idiosyncrasie culturelle ou historique peuvent surmonter, et l'effet de laminage des institutions qui vident la „périphérie" de toute capacité à auto-produire un sens du monde[24], et l'effet réducteur de second ordre, mais d'une grande efficacité dans le même sens, qu'a engendré la décentralisation comme processus fonctionnaliste. C'est le cas, probablement et sous réserve d'inventaire, outre l'Alsace déjà citée et la Corse (sans doute les deux seules situations dans l'ensemble français) de la Catalogne et du Pays Basque, ainsi que de l'Ecosse et du Pays de Galles. Ces six configurations, deux en France, deux en Espagne, deux en Grande-Bretagne, pourraient être considérées comme d'autres cas au moins virtuellement possibles de fonctionnement selon le „modèle de la grande région", et ceci bien que:
— en Espagne, le principe des autonomies régionales semble mettre sur un pied d'égalité des régions comme celles que nous avons citées et d'autres (l'Aragon, le pays de Valence...) dans lesquelles les caractéristiques que nous avons évoquées n'existent au mieux qu'à l'état latent;
— en France, l'existence d'une représentation auto-référentielle paraît manifeste dans les deux cas cités, mais l'absence de tout „langage audible et reconnu" lui permettant de se manifester la réduit, soit à un silence plus ou moins „douloureux", soit à

---

[23] Refoulé, mais nullement aboli, ainsi que semble le montrer une recherche réalisée pour le compte du Programme pluriannuel en Sciences humaines Rhône-Alpes qui pourtant, d'après son sous-titre, ne poursuivait pas spécialement ce but: Identité régionale et sentiments d'appartenance — Résultats de l'enquête *Etes-vous Rhônalpin?*, J. Tournon, P. Kukawka, E.F. Callot, P. Lecomte, Universités de Grenoble 2 et de Lyon 3, 1992.

[24] C'est-à-dire amènent les zones correspondantes à se comporter comme une périphérie, précisément, rendue atone par la prééminence du centre, ce qui constitue le phénomène de la „provincialisation".

des manifestations désordonnées qui maintiennent l'affirmation du caractère problématique d'une représentation fictivement homogène, mais dont le risque d'effets pervers est évident.

Si je laisse (volontairement) de côté les mondes germanique et scandinave sur lesquels je ne dispose pas d'éléments d'analyse suffisants, on en arrive à l'Europe centrale et orientale. Je limiterai ici mon analyse à l'ancienne Fédération tchéco-slovaque d'une part, et à l'ancienne Yougoslavie (Slovénie exclue) d'autre part.

Le cas de la Tchécoslovaquie de 1918 est tout à fait éloquent. Il est compréhensible que les Slovaques veuillent faire remonter leur souveraineté à la „Grande Moravie" du IXe siècle et au (légendaire?) „royaume de Samo" (623–658) qui l'aurait précédée[25]. Il n'en reste pas moins que dès le Xe siècle et jusqu'en 1918 la Slovaquie est partie intégrante des territoires d'obédience magyare, autrichienne, austro-hongroise, et devient à cette date partie d'une république unitaire, qui ne sera „fédérale" qu'en 1968 (et, de façon un peu plus effective, qu'après la Révolution de velours). On doit bien considérer (si l'on est français) que cette période de sujétion est beaucoup plus longue que celle qui caractérise l'ancienne Bretagne des ducs ou l'ancien comté de Toulouse (pour ne pas parler, en s'en tenant aux territoires d'une certaine ampleur, de la Franche-Comté, française seulement depuis 1678 après une guerre de conquête de sept ans, ni de la Savoie, française depuis 1860 après un plébiscite qui semblait presque entériner une libre union entre partenaires égaux...).

Si l'on regarde les problèmes que se posait la Slovaquie avant l'indépendance du 1er janvier 1993, il est assez probable que la revendication de la majorité des Slovaques était plutôt de type „grande région", c'est-à-dire une autonomie effective, chose compréhensible dans un pays dont le développement, c'est-à-dire l'industrialisation à outrance à base de production de „demi-produits" sans possibilité réelle de marchés extérieurs propres, avait entièrement été le fait des Tchèques, lesquels tenaient le plus souvent la Slovaquie pour une province arriérée, quelque peu bigote et à jamais marquée par les cinq années du régime pro-nazi de Tiso (la France de Pétain, en quelque sorte). Leur souci de constituer un marché commun avec la République tchèque, leur incertitude sur les

---

[25]Comme en témoigne par exemple une plaquette de type propagandiste intitulée The Unconquerable Slovaks et publiée aux Etats-Unis sous l'égide du Slovak Research Institute of America (Lakewood, Ohio, 1989).

possibilités de „privatisation" de leurs industries lourdes ainsi que sur le sens qu'elle pourrait avoir (si je me réfère à diverses conversations avec des intellectuels de Bratislava en octobre 1992) laissent planer au moins un certain doute. La Slovaquie ne serait-elle pas, comme la Slovénie, devenue un Etat que pouvoir être une „grande région" autonome?

La seule chose qui semble pouvoir être dite, sans prendre le risque d'une présomption démesurée, à propos de zones comme la Croatie ou la Bosnie-Herzégovine, c'est qu'elles pourraient bien constituer une terrible démonstration a contrario de la pertinence de la problématique de disjonction entre société et Etat — démonstration dont il est maintenant à craindre que nul, même bien vivant, ne puisse jamais profiter. Le „découpage" de ces zones en sous-ensembles, nécessairement non homogènes sur le plan ethno-culturel ou linguistique (c'est aussi le cas de la Macédoine), pouvait sans doute se concevoir si l'on séparait très radicalement le principe sociétal (doté, cela va sans dire, de compétences suffisantes d'auto-régulation) du principe politico-étatique, c'est-à-dire si l'on tentait de reconstituer, par exemple en Bosnie-Herzégovine, un système complètement dualiste où „l'Etat" se serait contenté d'accorder une caution, dépourvue de presque tout appareil normatif, à une juxtaposition-imbrication de systèmes sociaux — ce que la Yougoslavie, sous la Constitution de 1974 rédigée par le Slovène Kardelj, aurait peut-être pu envisager d'être, mais avec tant de „si" que cette hypothèse a posteriori n'est guère invocable.

La chose était loin d'être absurde, à condition de renoncer à la „religion de l'Etat". Mais, la proximité de la Serbie y contribuant sans doute pour beaucoup, Croatie et Bosnie ont entrepris de se transformer en Etat-Nation pour le premier, en Etat pluri-national pour le second. Dans un cas comme dans l'autre chaque nationalité (avec l'exception, notable, des Croates pour la Croatie) devenait, de fait, une minorité (et Sarajevo une ville où trois minorités au moins étaient condamnées à coexister), c'est-à-dire un ensemble humain non souverain — et la chose était peut-être pire pour la Bosnie, puisque du même coup la souveraineté, rapatriée de Belgrade donc dangereusement proche, n'en était pas moins mal définie. Des minorités sans majorité, quel tragique paradoxe... Chacune ne pouvait-elle craindre que la souveraineté étatique soit un jour confisquée par l'une des autres?

Le seul moyen, bien théorique, de parer à ce risque, était peut-être de „laïciser l'Etat", en renvoyant la nationalité, c'est-à-dire l'identité, à la sphère non politique, au groupe social. Mais il peut paraître possible d'avancer, là encore, que personne n'était réellement en position d'incarner cette „souveraineté non groupale" à partir du moment où le statut public du „groupe non politique" n'était, semble-t-il, pas défini en regard. N'eut-il pas été possible de distinguer les variables et, sans partager un territoire impartageable, de séparer au contraire les compétences entre celles exercées sur l'espace, les moins nombreuses, et celles exercées sur les personnes à raison de l'affiliation à une communauté, en rendant officielle cette affiliation, c'est-à-dire en rendant „de droit public" ce pouvoir de gestion sur les personnes indépendamment du lieu où elles se trouvaient. „Solution" dont le principe, malgré un contexte bien plus compliqué, fait penser au schéma belge, et qui n'est probablement pas plus absurde ou gratuitement compliquée que le „plan Vance-Owen". Mais le sociologue n'est pas là pour réécrire l'histoire, et ce paragraphe, que j'assume malgré un certain risque de précarité intellectuelle, est seulement destiné à montrer une logique possible, que nul ne semble partager. On peut faire le pari que ce type d'analyse s'appliquerait de façon tout aussi logique aux Républiques dites de l'ancienne URSS, pour certaines dans leur totalité (les pays baltes, la Biélorussie...), pour la Russie par fragments. Ceci dépasse ma compétence pratique. Il m'est encore moins possible de pronostiquer le pouvoir d'incitation de ce modèle. Il ne faut cependant pas oublier que deux choses auront probablement, à l'échéance de peu d'années, vécu: l'idéologie de l'Etat-Nation comme infini limité mais détenteur du pouvoir absolu de dire, dans ses limites, le vrai et le bien; et le partage du pouvoir démocratique en son sein, selon des règles de l'alternance, entre „courants" idéologiques enracinés dans l'Hexagone, dans la Penisola ou dans Britannia. Les réarrangements sont inévitables; ils concerneront, par la force des choses, aussi bien la perception et le jeu du lien social que la définition des territoires pertinents à mettre en regard. On peut, bien sûr, rêver d'un Etat (Nation?) universel. Le modèle de la „grande région" que nous avons ici essayé d'évoquer est peut-être un autre schéma en émergence, pas forcément moins réaliste, peut-être finalement moins dangereux, si l'on tient compte de tous les facteurs. Il semble en tout cas que la nécessité de rendre légitimes des pouvoirs de conception (bien plus encore que de décision) locaux soit maintenant devant nous, sans que le monde européen puisse l'éviter.

Autre paradoxe: alors que certains semblent continuer à raisonner en termes de globalisation (mondiale, donc), plus personne ne semble sérieusement croire à une fusion du continent européen, et encore moins à son „métissage" général (même culturel!) avec ses voisins africain et asiatique. N'est-ce pas en dissociant la régulation sociale (identitaire, et donc à moyen rayon d'action) de la régulation politique (utilitaire et pragmatique, donc faisant intervenir des partenaires plus lourds) que l'on pourrait échapper à ce qui semble bien, dans les termes utilisés actuellement, être une aporie, ultime avatar du vieux problème du tout et des parties?

Nicole Boucher
Université Laval
Quebec

# RACISME ET IMMIGRATION: VERS L'IMPLOSION DE L'ETAT-NATION?

## Introduction

> *«Un jour un vieux rabbin demanda à ses élèves comment on déterminerait l'heure où finit la nuit et où commence le jour. Est-ce quand on peut distinguer de loin un chien d'un mouton? Non, dit le rabbin. Est-ce quand de loin on peut distinguer un dattier d'un figuier? demanda un autre élève. Non, dit le rabbin. Mais alors, quand est-ce? demandèrent les élèves. C'est quand tu peux regarder le visage de n'importe quel humain et que tu vois ta soeur ou ton frère. Jusque-là, c'est encore la nuit.[1]»*

Migrations internationales et racisme sont à l'ordre du jour. La couverture médiatique des nombreux événements à caractère raciste accapare l'actualité dans divers coins du monde occidental et nous laisse

---

[1] Tugendhat, Ernst, *La forteresse européenne et les réfugiés*, «La fin de la nuit», Editions d'en bas, Lausanne, 1985: 58.
Nous tenons à remercier Sylvie Perras, étudiante à la maîtrise en Relations internationales pour sa contribution à cette analyse.

entrevoir une réalité sociale déplaisante et effrayante. Réminiscences d'un passé noir encore trop vivant dans la mémoire collective et craintes de basculer à nouveau dans une folie purificatrice comme celle qui déchire actuellement l'ancienne Yougoslavie, folie dont nul ne se sent vraiment totalement à l'abri, les conséquences du racisme demeurent, dans un tel contexte, quelque peu tabous.

Or, force est de constater que l'évolution des sociétés modernes n'a pas permis d'évacuer les comportements racistes, pas plus que les idéologies. Celles-ci, au contraire, ont survécu mais sous des formes différentes. Sa métamorphose discrète s'est opérée dans la foulée des arguments avancés par les mouvements anti-racistes sans que ceux-ci prennent conscience de l'arme à double tranchant qu'ils avaient ainsi créée.

De plus, la dénonciation scientifique des théories biologiques des races humaines n'a pas eu l'écho escompté dans le corps social. On continue à s'affronter dans un espace limité pour des ressources tout autant limitées. Période de récession et de crise économique oblige, l'intolérance grandit et l'altérité visible de l'Autre est souvent prise à partie. L'étranger dans la cité est souvent le premier à en être expulsé ou à tout le moins exclu, puisqu'il incarne l'usurpateur, celui qui dérange, celui qui n'a pas droit de cité. Ces „étrangers" qui voudront retourner dans leur pays d'origine risquent encore d'être exclus, sinon mal reçus.

Etudier le phénomène du racisme aujourd'hui oblige à une mise en contexte incontournable. A une époque où le système international évolue vers la mondialisation par le biais de l'unification économique, étape ultime du capitalisme, les nouvelles immigrations déstabilisent le jeu sur l'échiquier international. Conséquences de l'asymétrie démographique que les économies du Sud sont incapables d'absorber et du déséquilibre entre le Nord et le Sud, l'Est et l'Ouest quant à la répartition des richesses mondiales, les migrations sont à la fois problèmes (sources de déséquilibre, d'incertitude) et solutions.

Les nouvelles immigrations opèrent également une modification en profondeur du paysage urbain habituel des sociétés d'accueil. Elles se posent de plus en plus en enjeu majeur de société parce qu'elles laissent supposer une subversion des modèles nationaux à la base même de l'identité collective de ces sociétés. Le pluralisme qui découle de l'arrivée de nombreux migrants, de plus en plus distants culturellement des nationaux, constitue un défi de taille. Avec Schecter, nous sommes en droit de nous questionner sur l'avenir dans un tel contexte modifié:

„Sommes-nous en train de réaliser enfin les promesses libérales de la société moderne de faire preuve d'une capacité de différenciation et d'inclusion que l'on croyait inhérente à la modernité? Le pluralisme de fait des grandes métropoles découlera-t-il sur un pluralisme politique: concrétisation de l'accomplissement de la modernité où Auschwitz et Hiroshima n'auront été que des accidents de parcours? Ou le pluralisme contemporain et le racisme qui forme son substrat représentent-ils plutôt une nouvelle étape dans ce qu'Auschwitz et Hiroshima ont déjà signalé comme constitutif de la société moderne, son versant meurtrier une fois qu'elle s'est débarrassée des contraintes libérales qui ont présidé à sa naissance?"[2]

Alors que les comportements racistes sont souvent présentés comme un exécutoire aux problèmes économiques, nous croyons que le racisme contemporain correspond davantage à une résistance protectionniste des nations face à l'unification.

Dans un contexte modelé par des revendications identitaires multiples, la résurgence du racisme s'expliquerait comme une réaction à un pluralisme ethnique et culturel qui s'oppose de plus en plus à la totalité de la *Nation* et de la *Culture*. Une réflexion s'impose donc, dans le cadre de la question régionale, sur le problème du racisme dans les sociétés contemporaines, à l'Est comme à l'Ouest.

Notre hypothèse est la suivante: Dans un contexte social et politique de plus en plus dominé par l'idéologie du relativisme culturel et les questions régionales, les migrations, par le pluralisme qu'elles engendrent, contribuent à fragiliser la structure fondamentale de l'Etat-nation. Nous tenterons de démontrer, à travers l'évolution du racisme dans nos sociétés occidentales modernes, comment les migrations s'imposent comme enjeu régional, national et international.

Dans un premier temps, nous nous attarderons à la genèse du concept de racisme pour en arriver à cerner avec le plus d'acuité possible sa signification et ses formes actuelles. Ensuite, nous confronterons différentes logiques d'Etat pour gérer l'immigration et parallèlement le racisme. Finalement, nous tenterons d'évaluer l'impact des migrations dans un monde de plus en plus interdépendant et d'esquisser des solutions régionales au problème du racisme dans des sociétés résolument de plus en plus pluralistes.

---

[2]Schecter, C. *Revue internationale d'action communautaire*, „De l'autre: réflexions sur la différence contemporaine", 21/61, 1989.

# 1. Le concept de racisme

L'application fréquente, plus ou moins appropriée, du terme „racisme" à différentes situations a permis la dissolution progressive de la valeur du concept et de ce fait a créé une ambiguïté persistante quant à la véritable nature du racisme. L'incompréhension du phénomène qui en découle rend d'autant plus difficile une lutte ordonnée et efficace. L'inflation de l'utilisation du mot, soit son emploi polémique hors des limites préconstituées par l'anthropologie raciale, semble moins correspondre à la réalité d'une race qu'à l'intolérance à l'étranger[3]. Il apparaît d'ores et déjà que le racisme fait référence à un phénomène plus complexe que ne laissent croire les explications figées des mouvements antiracistes traditionnels[4]. Il convient donc, dès le départ, de clarifier le concept autour duquel s'articule notre réflexion.

Il importe avant tout de bien marquer la distinction entre le racisme-préjugé, le racisme-comportement et le racisme-idéologie. Le premier réfère à la sphère des opinions et des croyances qui attribuent à la victime une vision partielle, déformée et incomplète et qui se concrétisent par des attitudes de mépris et d'hostilité. Le deuxième, vise des pratiques de discrimination et de persécution pouvant même aller jusqu'à l'extermination. Finalement, le racisme-idéologie, celui qui retient prioritairement notre attention, fait référence à un ensemble organisé de représentations et de croyances.

Inutile de rappeler qu'à l'origine, la doctrine des races prend sa source dans la théorie de la race élaborée par le comte de Gobineau dans son *Essai sur l'inégalité des races humaines* (1853–1855). Cette théorie utilise l'anthropologie raciale pour expliquer et justifier les rapports de domination alors que l'esclavagisme est à son apogée et que le colonialisme et l'impérialisme sont des systèmes d'enrichissement économique et de domination politique autorisés. Elle se présente comme un modèle explicatif de l'évolution historique sur la base d'un déterminisme racial[5].

---

[3] Taguieff, Pierre-André. *La force du préjugé. Essai sur la racisme et ses doubles.* Éditions La Découverte, Paris, 1987: 57.

[4] Taguieff, Pierre-André. *Face au racisme. Théories et hypothèses, Tome II.* „Les métamorphoses du racisme et la crise de l'anti-racisme", Éditions La Découverte, Paris, 1991.

[5] Taguieff, Pierre-André. *La force du préjugé.* Éditions La Découverte, Paris, 1987: 138.

Dès les années 1922, la notion de racisme se confondra avec l'antisémitisme des nationalistes allemands. Poussée dans sa logique extrême, la théorie gobinienne des races alliée à une interprétation du „darwinisme social" accréditant la supposée supériorité aryenne donnera lieu dans l'Allemagne nazie à la démence génocidaire bien connue.

Cette débâcle honteuse pour l'Occident et l'humanité en général amènera la communauté scientifique à nier tout fondement scientifique à la doctrine biologique de l'inégalité naturelle des races. Ce déni d'existence est confirmé dans la Déclaration sur la race et les préjugés raciaux de 1978 de l'Unesco qui condamne „toute théorie faisant état de la supériorité ou de l'infériorité intrinsèque de groupes raciaux ou ethniques qui donnerait aux uns le droit de dominer ou d'éliminer les autres, inférieurs présumés, ou fondant des jugements de valeur sur une différence raciale." Ainsi déboutée, on aurait pu croire en la disparition du racisme comme idéologie. Pourtant, il semble bien, qu'au contraire, le phénomène ait survécu grâce à sa capacité de métamorphose.

A cause de ces antécédents historiques, deux interprétations du racisme font problème. D'une part, on associe le racisme à toute forme de haine ou de mépris. Dans ce sens, le racisme devient l'intolérance proprement dite et non plus un aspect seulement de cette dernière. L'intolérance, qui se voulait auparavant circonscrite à la condamnation d'un comportement ou d'une attitude, s'est maintenant étendue à toute forme de refus, incluant celui d'une façon d'être, soit l'identité même. L'oppression, dont le racisme en est une expression, s'appuie sur les paramètres de l'identité en tenant compte des caractéristiques générales (biologiques et sociologiques), — l'appartenance à un groupe socio-économique (classe sociale) ou socio-culturel avec (dans le cas de la race) ou sans (dans le cas de l'ethnie) des traits physiques particuliers — et des caractéristiques individuelles dont la transmission est souvent aléatoire[6].

D'autre part, la définition du racisme continue de faire référence presque exclusivement, du moins dans l'imaginaire collectif, à l'extermination de masse telle que préconisée et appliquée par l'idéologie raciste nazie et ce faisant occulte toute la zone d'ombre dans laquelle le racisme contemporain déploie ses nouveaux visages.

De plus, le phénomène du racisme a souvent été présenté à travers la lunette d'une analyse d'inspiration marxiste qui, sans être totalement dépourvue de fondement, ne permet pas de mettre à jour tout l'éventail

---

[6]Noël, Lise. *L'intolérance: une problématique générale.* Éditions Boréal, 1989: 11.

de facteurs pertinents à une compréhension plus complète. Une deuxième analyse réductionniste consiste à expliquer le racisme par la version du „bouc émissaire" qui omet, elle aussi, plusieurs aspects pertinents à l'étude du racisme dans nos sociétés modernes.

## 1.1. Le racisme comme construction idéologique

Le racisme se veut donc un système de valeurs et de normes permettant d'appréhender les relations sociales par le biais de l'anthropologie raciale. Colette Guillaumin caractérise la particularité du racisme comme une: „biologisation de la pensée sociale qui tente par ce biais de poser en absolu toute différence constatée ou supposée"[7].

Nous nous attarderons à la perception du phénomène tel que définit par les mouvements antiracistes traditionnels puisque c'est sur eux que repose actuellement toute l'orientation de la lutte contre le racisme. La vulgate antiraciste s'appuie sur une métadéfinition du racisme qui se divise en quatorze traits principaux[8]. Cette définition figée ne nous permet cependant pas de saisir le racisme dans sa dimension contemporaine.

Le racisme est une croyance qui existe sous une forme conceptuelle. Construction dogmatique à base de rationalisation, le racisme se voit en même temps stigmatisé par les antiracistes comme une maladie de l'esprit (donc irrationnel); perversion de l'ethnocentrisme ou corruption du nationalisme.

L'existence de groupes humains séparables par des traits distinctifs relève de la croyance. L'assertion de la différence est plus souvent présupposée par celle d'une hiérarchie. De plus, le racisme affirme que ces différences sont inséparablement physiques, morales et intellectuelles. Le signe de la différence, „la race" devient ainsi le signe de la permanence.

La perception raciste, en s'attardant à déchiffrer les indices, remplit une fonction de catégorisation sociale. La transmission héréditaire des différences est postulée, et de ce fait, l'hérédité devient reproductrice de l'ordre somatique humain. Le racisme est foncièrement anti-individualiste en ce qu'il propose une uniformité illusoire. „La racisation consiste à

---

[7] Guillaumin, Colette. *L'idéologie raciste, génèse et langage actuel*, Paris, Lahaye, 1972: 4.

[8] Taguieff, Pierre-André. *La force du préjugé*. Essai sur le racisme et ses doubles. Éditions La découverte, Paris, 1987, chapitre 4.

prendre l'être pour le faire, la généralité de l'appartenance pour la singularité de la personne"[9].

Le racisme se pose en déterminisme et en réductionnisme à la fois, puisqu'il se veut un syncrétisme du biologique, du psychologique et du social. Le support commun biologique étant le déterminant de l'ordre racial dont dépend l'ordre social. La relation entre la race et la société est donc causale, ce qui nous ramène à la socio-biologie et à la pensée bio/antropologique du début du XIXe siècle. Les différences sont ensuite projetées sur une échelle hiérarchique.

La composante théorique du racisme implique une représentation de la pratique qu'elle fonde et donc tend vers un monisme bioculturel ou sociozoologique qui permet au racisme de légitimer le droit de conquête et l'impérialisme.

## 1.2. Logiques de racisation

Pour une compréhension adéquate de l'évolution contemporaine du phénomène du racisme, il nous semble important de bien discerner les deux logiques de racisation. Elles se fondent sur les deux mêmes facteurs soit l'inégalité et la différence, mais elles divergent quant à la façon de valoriser cette dernière et de ce fait, présentent une différence fonctionnelle importante.

L'autoracisation affirme l'identité raciale propre et sa supériorité. Elle se concrétise par une relation d'exclusion-extermination de l'instance Autre et donc l'abolition de la relation différentielle.

Dans ce cas, la différence est mise au premier plan, le „nous" s'isolant dans son essence particulière. Ce processus peut dégénérer en logique d'extermination lorsque l'Autre se révèle inclassable dans une échelle hiérarchique donnée. Le génocide se présente alors comme une issue logique, un droit, voire un devoir: „Il est la conséquence logique d'un certain mode de construction de l'altérité, dont le Juif démonisé de Hitler demeure le paradigme..."[10].

D'autre part, l'hétéroracisation affirme la différence raciale en prenant appui soit sur un axiome d'infériorité (l'autre est racisé en tant qu'inférieur), soit sur un axiome d'universalité (les dominants incarnent

[9] Taguieff, Pierre-André. *La force du préjugé*. Éditions La Découverte, Paris, 1987: 157.
[10] Taguieff, Pierre-André. *La force du préjugé*. Éditions La Découverte, Paris, 1987: 167.

l'humanité; ils sont donc „la référence"). On peut penser que l'idéologie inégalitaire de la colonisation et de l'esclavagisme moderne relève de ce processus.

Taguieff identifie donc deux racismes idéaltypiques soit l'individuo-universaliste basé sur un axiome inégalité/universalité et une deuxième traditio-communautariste qui s'appuie sur un axiome différence/commu-nauté.

## 2. Le néo-racisme

Dans les années 70, la focalisation des arguments antiracistes sur la thèse scientifique du racisme et le consensus apparent a apaisé les débats idéologiques autour de la question. Ce relatif relâchement de la vigilance a empêché l'anticipation de formes „inédites" de racisme. Pourtant, dès le milieu des années 70, le détournement au profit de la nouvelle droite de l'idéologie différentialiste prônée par les antiracistes aurait dû sonner l'alarme. Ce que l'on a pris pour une simple version modifiée du racisme inégalitaire fondé sur un scientisme biologique (donc inoffensif parce que démenti scientifiquement) était plutôt l'ébauche d'un nouveau racisme différentialiste sur des bases culturalistes.

De plus, la transposition dans le champ politique de l'idéologie identitariste par le Front National en France dès 1983 aurait dû susciter une prise de conscience quant à la réalité mouvante du racisme contemporain[11].

Depuis la décennie 70, trois grands déplacements des concepts de base, attitudes et arguments de l'idéologie racisante se sont opérés.

Premièrement, le concept de „race" a glissé vers celui de „eth-nie/culture", érigeant ainsi les fondements d'un racisme différentialiste sur bases culturalistes.

Deuxièmement, le concept d'inégalité a cédé la place à celui de différence, permettant du même coup la formation d'une idéologie identitariste que le national populisme du Front national utilise comme cheval de bataille pour la défense du droit à l'identité du peuple français.

Finalement, le passage d'une idéologie hétérophobe à une autre hétérophile qui justifie le „droit à la différence".

---

[11] Taguieff, Pierre-André. *La force du préjugé.* Éditions La Découverte, Paris, 1987:13–14.

Ainsi, le remplacement de la notion zoologique de „race" par celle de „culture" permet-elle un racisme plus discret parce que camouflé derrières des mots et des idées nouvelles, mais du même coup implique une recontextualisation de la problématique et une r 3 4re aux mouvements anti-racistes traditionnels.

## 2.1. L'argument différentialiste dans le discours néo-raciste

Ironiquement, avant d'être récupéré dans le discours néo-raciste, le relativisme culturel a d'abord été élaboré vers la fin du XIXe siècle en réaction au déterminisme biologique et à l'ethnocentrisme porteur des germes de l'idéologie raciste et a présidé à la naissance de la tradition antiraciste. Celle-ci s'est appuyée sur trois principes: l'autonomie des phénomènes culturels, le déterminisme culturel comme élément dominant des structures mentales et des formes de vie et l'égalité en valeur de toutes les cultures. Par la suite, toujours dans la perspective offerte par le relativisme culturel, l'anti-racisme s'est attaché à stigmatiser toute action porteuse de ségrégation, qu'elle soit raciale ou sociale, naturalisée par des différences considérées légitimes. La conséquence de cette emphase sur la culture s'est concrétisée par une explosion de revendications identitaires, valorisant, parfois à l'extrême, la différence. La discrimination que cette dernière a pu induire par le passé est invoquée, encore aujourd'hui, pour justifier les demandes de reconnaissance et les réparations pour les torts passés. La force du mouvement américain actuel de la „political correctness" incarne bien l'éloge de la différence dans tous ses excès. Or, la revendication des différences, d'un „droit à la différence" peut accentuer les antagonismes parce qu'elle conduit à une ethnicisation des relations sociales[12].

Le néo-racisme s'est donc articulé autour de deux axes principaux empruntés aux anti-racistes et au mouvement des droits de la personne soit la défense des identités culturelles et l'éloge de la différence par le biais du „droit à la différence".

Le discours raciste contemporain a su récupérer le vocabulaire de la différence en le détournant de son sens premier. L'affirmation exclusive des différences est utilisée en réponse à la hantise du métissage

---

[12]Costa-Lascoux, Jacqueline. *Face au racisme. Théories et hypothèses, Tome II.* „Des lois contre le racisme". Éditions La Découverte, Paris, 1991: 107.

„culturel". La différence s'érige en norme de préservation des entités communautaires. L'écart à cette norme fait ressurgir l'angoisse de la dissolution finale des identités collectives dans un universalisme abstrait. Le néo-racisme exploite ainsi à fond la réalité différentielle immédiate (couleur de peau, accent, langue, origine) pour promouvoir sa défense des identités culturelles supposément menacées et ce faisant s'apparente à un anti-racisme authentique.

L'idéologie de la différence se situe dans un cadre double soit, premièrement les formes contemporaines hégémoniques d'individualisme et deuxièmement, les réactions ethnistes douces (régionalismes) ou violentes (terrorisme-indépendantisme). Le néo-racisme, quant à lui, utilise concurremment l'éloge de la différence (hétérophile) ou le rejet de la différence (hétérophobie). Ses deux arguments fétiches consistent dans l'existence d'un seuil de tolérance et dans l'inassimibilité supposée de certaines catégories de migrants, les non-blancs, ceux de l'autre hémisphère, étant le plus souvent visés.

L'idée du seuil cherche à conforter une majorité par l'érection d'une frontière artificielle qui établit la distance entre les deux univers disparates, le sien et celui de l'Autre. La notion de tolérance devient paradoxale en ce qu'elle n'incite plus au respect de la liberté de penser et d'agir d'autrui, mais prétend éviter l'intolérance en supprimant ou en diminuant son objet. La perception quasi biologique de la réaction d'intolérance accorde à cette dernière une crédibilité et une justification naturelle. L'intolérance devient normale puisque sa victime en est la cause. „La notion de tolérance est paradoxale en ce qu'elle autorise le racisme en l'assimilant à un phénomène inévitable et elle l'interdit en le contenant par une borne inférieure en deça de laquelle il convient de supporter les immigrés."[13]

D'autre part, l'absolutisation de la différence s'accompagne d'un postulat d'inassimibilité. La différence reconnue comme inconvertible ne peut qu'entraîner la volonté d'un rejet de l'Autre, son effacement, son anéantissement imaginaire ou effectif. De nouveaux modes de racisation par la culture ou par l'ethnie procèdent à la mise à distance de l'Autre et ce, tant par le langage hétérophile (éloge de la différence) que par

---

[13]De Pudler, Véronique. *Face au racisme. Théories et hypothèses, Tome II.* „Seuil de tolérance et cohabitation pluriethnique". Éditions La Découverte, Paris, 1991: 162.

le langage hétérophobe pouvant entraîner de ce fait une corruption idéologique[14].

Ainsi, par un paradoxal mimétisme des discours, les racistes et les anti-racistes se rejoignent. Les débats sont recentrés sur le croisement des questions des identités collectives et leur défense, les droits des peuples, le mélange et/ou les croisements des cultures, sur l'interculturel et le transculturel[15]. Le racisme que l'on avait cru pour un temps anéanti survit toujours. Aux côtés d'un racisme d'exploitation (esclavagisme, colonialisme) et d'un racisme d'extermination (nazisme), un racisme mutant (différentialiste, culturaliste) a pris forme et il s'avère d'autant plus efficace qu'il est plus difficile à reconnaître et à cerner.

Il nous semble que ce néo-racisme joue autant à l'Ouest qu'à l'Est présentement. A l'Est, le passage d'une uniformité de pensée, liée à une uniformité institutionnelle de la ligne politique et des sciences sociales, à la libre-expression et à la pluralité d'opinions, semble propice à la propagation de l'idéologie du „droit à la différence" et aux mouvements de défense des identités culturelles. Ainsi, à travers des cheminements différents, l'Est et l'Ouest sont maintenant touchés par les mêmes maux. Paradoxalement, le mouvement différentialiste s'internationalise et s'uniformise[16].

## 3. Les nouvelles immigrations

Dans l'imaginaire collectif occidental, européen à tout le moins, la peur de l'invasion par les migrants du Sud et de l'Est est quasi viscérale. Ce mythe alimente des réflexes de peur et de repli sur soi qui conduisent à la xénophobie et au racisme. L'orientation prise par les différents gouvernements des Etats-nations fait écho à ces réactions sociales face aux changements visibles des populations autrefois homogènes. Qu'en est-il vraiment de l'immigration dans le contexte contemporain?

---

[14] Taguieff, Pierre-André. *Face au racisme. Théories et hypothèses, Tome II.* „Les métamorphoses du racisme et la crise de l'anti-racisme". Éditions La Découverte, Paris, 1991: 41.

[15] Taguieff, Pierre-André. *La force du préjugé.* Éditions La Dé/ouverte, Paris 1987: 17.

[16] Guenov, Nikolaï. *Revue internationale des sciences sociales.* „La transition vers la démocratie en Europe de l'Est: Tendances et paradoxes de la rationalisation sociale". ERES, UNESCO, Paris, no 128, mai 1991: 353–364.

Il importe au départ de discerner différents types d'immigration, motivés par les intérêts particuliers des sociétés d'accueil. L'option privilégiée par chacun constitue la pierre angulaire sur laquelle se sont élaborées les politiques d'immigration propres. Ainsi, l'Amérique a-t-elle été fortement marquée par une immigration de peuplement et, en ce qui concerne particulièrement les Etats-Unis ainsi que certains pays de l'hémisphère sud, une immigration forcée motivée par l'exploitation économique.

Plusieurs pays d'Europe ont pratiqué une immigration économique dictée par la nécessité de main-d'oeuvre dans une Europe nouvellement industrialisée et, par la suite, par les besoins imposés par la reconstruction de l'après-guerre. La politique d'immigration était, dans bien des cas, assimilée à une politique de main-d'oeuvre et n'impliquait pas automatiquement l'installation permanente des étrangers.

Dans le contexte européen, il importe également de mentionner l'importance des liens culturels et politiques créés par la période de la colonisation. La période de l'esclavagisme pour les Etats-Unis tout autant que celle de la colonisation pour l'Europe sont des réalités incontournables pour bien appréhender la problématique de l'immigration dans toute sa dimension, incluant celle de la définition des identités collectives et de l'attribution de la nationalité et de la citoyenneté.

Le début des années 70 marque une étape charnière dans l'histoire des migrations internationales. Le phénomène migratoire qui se voulait à l'origine conjoncturel afin de répondre aux besoins en main-d'oeuvre des pays demandeurs s'est transformé avec le temps en donnée structurelle des sociétés et des relations économiques et politiques internationales[17]. La crise de l'énergie et la forte récession qui l'accompagne mettent à jour les failles du système international. L'interruption momentanée de la croissance économique des pays du Nord révèle la vulnérabilité de leurs économies et l'interdépendance inévitable dans une économie-monde qui s'accommodé mal des souverainetés nationales des Etats-nations.

Les nouvelles immigrations s'inscrivent dans un contexte complexe: la répartition inéquitable des richesses mondiales entre le Nord et le Sud, la déstructuration des économies des pays en voie de développement (PVD) qui ne permet pas d'entrevoir une possibilité d'absorber l'essor

---

[17]Bolzmann, C.; Jacques, A.; Jacques, G.; Menetrey, A. *La forteresse européenne et les réfugiés*, „Asile et immigration". Éditions d'en bas, Lausanne, 1985: 68.

démographique qui les caractérise, les économies du Nord sont en pleine restructuration, ce qui ne va pas sans provoquer des difficultés d'ajustement social interne, l'Etat-providence est en crise alors que la mondialisation de l'économie se poursuit à un rythme effréné, laissant dans son sillage des communautés politiques et sociales qui n'arrivent plus à marquer le pas. On est en droit de supposer avec Jean Leca que la difficulté d'intégration des nouvelles immigrations aux sociétés d'accueil est rendue plus ardue premièrement pour des raisons structurelles qui sapent la cohésion sociale nécessaire à cet accueil. *„Or, il est plausible que les bases sociales de cette nécessaire propension à la solidarité viennent à s'affaiblir pour des raisons structurelles tenant à la division du travail, la fragmentation des classes, les différenciations culturelles et l'organisation et la représentation politiques. Il n'est pas sans intérêt de les détailler car ce n'est que dans ce cadre général que l'on peut prendre la mesure du problème des nouvelles immigrations trop souvent vues comme une déstabilisation externe de sociétés elles-mêmes stables. C'est en réalité presque le contraire: ces immigrations constituent un problème au moment où (et peut-être parce que) les sociétés européennes font face à des crises de régulation qui les privent des ressources nécessaires pour les traiter."*[18]

Donc, à partir des années 1973–74, les pays européens décrètent une fermeture de leurs frontières à l'immigration de main-d'oeuvre, laissant cependant la porte ouverte à la réunification des familles, à l'entrée de travailleurs qualifiés et à l'accueil des réfugiés politiques. Cette décision équivaut à abolir la politique de main-d'oeuvre et à la remplacer par une politique d'immigration sélective. La conséquence première et imprévue de cette décision fut la sédentarisation de travailleurs étrangers que l'on forçait auparavant à une mobilité rassurante pour la société d'accueil. La deuxième conséquence néfaste de cette décision réside dans la perception populaire d'une utilisation abusive du système d'accueil des réfugiés politiques au profit de candidats à l'immigration qui tenteraient par cette filière leur dernière chance „légale". Finalement, une troisième conséquence s'est manifestée par une augmentation de l'immigration clandestine.

Le problème du racisme dans les sociétés altérées par les nouvelles immigrations se confond avec celui de l'intégration dans des sociétés récemment devenues multiculturelles et multiraciales. Ce sont les

---

[18] Leca, Jean. *Logiques d'États et immigrations*. „Nationalité et citoyenneté dans l'Europe des immigrations". Éditions Kimé, Paris, 1992: 40.

paysages urbains des grandes métropole du monde industrialisé qui se transforment, questionnant par leur nouveau visage le sens profond de l'identité collective nationale. Les conflits qui surgissent sont de nationalité et de citoyenneté et s'expriment au travers des décalages de droits sociaux et politiques, des pratiques discriminatoires ou d'exclusion qui se jouent dans le cadre d'un Etat national affaibli dans sa centralité même[19].

Dans nos Etats de droit fondés sur l'idéologie républicaine qui érige en paradigme des droits individuels la rationalité et la liberté, la culture et l'histoire perdent leur importance significative dans la définition du lien collectif au profit de l'universalité de certaines qualités humaines. Dans un tel contexte, la nationalité et la citoyenneté se superposent au point de devenir des concepts interchangeables. Concepts de „clôture sociale" alliant les localisations dans les structures sociales et la division du travail et les clivages culturels (linguistiques, religieux, couleurs de peau), ils permettent la création de sentiments communautaires d'appartenance et définissent par là-même l'Autre. Les formes de stratifications sociales qui en découlent ne s'appuient pas sur la nature biologique ou sur des arguments génétiques, mais sur les modes d'accès au territoire, le droit de résidence voire le droit de cité[20].

Le pluralisme culturel représente un modèle de construction des identités politiques sur des bas sub ou transnationales: ethnie, langue, région, couleur de peau. La société compartimentée en solidarités ainsi définies se doit d'assurer une distribution égale des richesses nationales à chaque segment culturel. Le processus de modernisation et de capitalisation qui a accompagné la formation de l'Etat-nation avait éliminé en bonne partie ce pluralisme grâce à une citoyenneté qui en permettait le nivellement. Le pluralisme actuel est post-national en ce qu'il multiplie les communautés politiques et donc les niveaux de citoyennetés au sein d'un même espace national: une série de groupes d'appartenance plus immédiats et plus concrets se forme au détriment d'une société plus globale dont la souplesse autorise la viabilité de la société.

---

[19]Gallisot, René. *Revue internationale d'action communautaire.* „Au-delà du multiculturel: nationaux, étrangers et citoyens. Urbanisation généralisée et transnationalisation." 21/61, 1989.

[20]Leca, Jean. *Logiques d'États et immigrations*, „Nationalité et citoyenneté dans l'Europe des immigrations". Éditions Kimé, Paris, 1992.

# 4. Logiques d'états

Depuis la fermeture des frontières européennes des années 70, on peut déceler une certaine convergence des politiques de flux au niveau des Etats du Nord: tous accordent une garantie de séjour durable aux étrangers possédant des titres de résident régulier, tous tentent d'empêcher l'entrée de travailleurs non-qualifiés en provenance des PVD, tous accordent une attention particulière à la réunification des familles et à l'accueil des réfugiés politiques, et finalement, tous pratiquent à un degré ou un autre le „brain-drain"[21]. Ces consensus sont le reflet de contraintes de valeurs, de contraintes politiques et de l'évolution des fonctions économiques de l'immigration[22].

Malgré cette convergence, le particularisme de chaque Etat apparaît dans les mécanismes déployés pour faire face à la situation. La logique qui sous-tend la politique d'immigration de chaque pays relève de l'adaptation à des contextes nationaux propres qui doit tenir compte autant du passé historique que de la perception de la nation et de l'application du droit dans l'attribution de la citoyenneté.

## La France

La France a entretenu une politique de main-d'oeuvre jointe à une politique de famille dès 1945 justifiée par des préoccupations économiques et démographiques. Le passé colonial de la France a imprégné l'immigration et déterminé le modèle de relation à l'Autre; les rapports ne sont jamais directs, mais médiatisés par le phantasme de l'Autre. Ainsi, la France a pratiqué pendant longtemps une politique de main-d'oeuvre auprès de populations dont la nationalité était ambiguë. Entre 1917 et 1962, les Algériens étaient considérés comme des nationaux français (bien que de seconde catégorie) et la fluidité de la main-d'oeuvre d'une rive à l'autre de la Méditerranée était déterminante économiquement tant pour le pays d'origine que pour celui d'accueil. C'est pourquoi, après l'indépendance de l'Algérie en 1962, les deux

---

[21]Weil, Patrick. *Logiques d'États et immigrations.* „Convergences et divergences des flux". Éditions Kimé, Paris, 1992.

[22]Verhaeren, Raphaël-Emmanuel. *Partir? Une théorie économique des migrations internationales.* Presses universitaires de Grenoble, Grenoble, 1990: 221–268.

pays ont cru bon de maintenir ce lien en ratifiant les Accords d'Evian. Ces derniers permettaient la sauvegarde du bénéfice en accordant un nouveau statut aux travailleurs algériens. Les Algériens constituent un cas particulier en France à cause des incertitudes entourant la nationalité héritée de l'époque coloniale; ainsi on peut retrouver au sein d'une même famille une multiplicité de statuts juridiques. Les Algériens qui étaient sur le territoire français au moment de l'indépendance ont pu choisir leur nationalité. Leurs enfants, ou ceux de travailleurs algériens réguliers, nés en France ont obtenu la nationalité française grâce à l'application du *Jus soli*. La politique française depuis 1945 encourageait une immigration de famille motivée pour des raisons économiques et démographiques encadrée par les règles de l'accès à la nationalité.

Paradoxalement, les Beurs, bien que Français, demeurent stigmatisés par leur appartenance à un groupe visible et sont encore souvent désignés par le vocable d'immigrés. Ceci nous ramène à la prétendue inassimibilité de certains immigrés. Or, il faut voir dans la difficulté d'intégration de ces groupes d'immigrés non pas une conséquence de leur différence intrinsèque, mais le résultat de l'application de règles strictes découlant des politiques d'immigration et de la main-d'oeuvre. Ainsi, le contrôle de la mobilité géographique et sociale par des limitations de temps et par l'attribution de cartes de travail circonscrites à certaines régions et/ou professions a permis l'élaboration d'un système complexe et arbitraire qui laissent aux travailleurs étrangers peu de latitude pour l'élaboration de projets d'avenir et contribue de ce fait à leur marginalisation sociale[23].

Les récentes poussées de racisme qu'a connu la France mettent à jour l'influence d'une logique différentialiste d'autant plus puissante depuis sa transposition dans le champ du politique par l'entrée en jeu du Front National de Jean-Marie Le Pen. Il s'ensuit un décalage latent entre la citoyenneté et la nationalité. Les principes de l'État de droit français sont confrontés aux explosions d'un environnement socio-politique profondément xénophobe. Bien que la France se soit formée à partir d'un amalgame de diverses ethnies, la conception de l'État comme un organisme vivant arrivé à maturité, permet de concevoir l'immigration comme un assaut de corps étrangers. L'argument biologique joint au critère de généalogie, légitimise l'appartenance nationale et vient

---

[23] Marie, Claude-Valentin. *Face au racisme. Théories et hypothèses, Tome II.* „L'Europe: de l'empire aux colonies intérieures". Éditions La Découverte, Paris, 1991.

contredire les valeurs universalistes qui président à la conception de la citoyenneté/nationalité prônée par l'État de droit.

Le racisme populaire plonge ses racines dans un vide social issu de l'éclatement des solidarités traditionnelles (dissolution de la famille, désintégration de la force syndicale, etc.) entraîné par les mutations de la société industrielle et urbaine. Cette perte des lieux de sens est exacerbée par la perception erronée que l'immigration s'accompagne d'une capacité de l'Autre à s'organiser et d'une forte identité, notamment religieuse (l'islam). Dans un tel contexte, la montée du Front national et son entrée dans le champ politique laisse craindre une expansion du racisme parce que ce parti canalise et institutionnalise le phénomène issu de processus sociaux éclatés[24].

L'existence de liens culturels et politiques de même qu'une proximité géographique incontournable ont joué dans la composition de l'immigration étrangère en France et dans l'instauration d'une dynamique sociale inégalitaire. Ceux-là mêmes qui ont été victimes de cette logique colonialiste dans le passé, demeurent les plus stigmatisés et ostracisés dans la société contemporaine.

## Le Royaume-Uni[25]

Tout comme la France, le problème de l'immigration au Royaume-Uni est imprégné des séquelles de son passé colonial, mais cela s'est traduit de façon tout à fait particulière dans le cas britannique. L'imbrication des politiques d'immigration et des politiques relatives aux relations raciales a permis la marginalisation progressive de l'enjeu de l'immigration au profit de celui des relations raciales. Il en résulta la sédentarisation des immigrants et de ce fait leur passage à un rôle de minorités ethniques grâce à la réglementation de leur situation juridique plus tôt que dans les reste de l'Europe.

D'ailleurs, l'expérience britannique a différé à bien des égards de celle de plusieurs états européens du continent. Premièrement, l'immigration y est le fait essentiellement de ressortissants des anciennes colonies,

---

[24]Wieviorka, Michel. *Face au racisme. Théories et hypothèses, Tome II.* „L'expansion du racisme populaire". Éditions La Découverte, Paris, 1991: 76–77.

[25]Crowley, John. *Logiques d'États et immigrations.* „Consensus et conflits dans la politique de l'immigration et des relations raciales au Royaume-Uni". Éditions Kimé, Paris, 1992: 73–116.

dont la majorité provenait du monde en développement, de même qu'une bonne proportion d'Irlandais. Deuxièmement, le Royaume-Uni n'a jamais pratiqué ouvertement une politique de main-d'oeuvre. Même la politique d'immigration a été pendant longtemps occultée. Hérité du droit coutumier, le *subjecthood* était en effet l'élément déterminant le statut des personnes à l'intérieur du Royaume-Uni. L'accès à la libre circulation vers le Royaume-Uni et l'accès à la citoyenneté sans formalité juridique étaient ainsi possibles. Le maintien de ce droit coutumier après la création du nouveau Commonwealth équivalait à un choix implicite en faveur de l'immigration, à une époque où la main-d'oeuvre faisait défaut pour la reconstruction. Cependant, la libre circulation des personnes se justifiait principalement par des motivations reliées à la politique étrangère: les élites politiques désiraient préserver la vitalité du nouveau Commonwealth et la place future du Royaume-Uni dans l'échiquier international. Le consensus politique de 1948 favorisait des considérations de politiques étrangères tout autant qu'économiques et était bien le fait des élites. Celles-ci ont ignoré l'impact possible de l'immigration sur le tissu social et ce, même si des événements alarmants avaient déjà eu lieu (deux vagues d'antisémitisme en 1900 avec l'arrivée de flux d'Europe orientale et en 1930 sous l'influence des mouvements fascistes britanniques, puis, en 1919, des émeutes raciales qui démontraient un rejet de la population noire). Paradoxalement, le refus d'adopter une politique d'immigration volontariste s'inscrivait dans une période marquée par la hausse de l'immigration en provenance du nouveau Commonwealth.

Les premières restrictions des flux migratoires apparaissent dès le début des années 60, au moment même où l'immigration de main-d'oeuvre bat son plein sur le continent. L'abandon de la conception impérialiste de l'ouverture des frontières découle de la prise de conscience et de la crainte du potentiel conflictuel de l'immigration. Les émeutes de Notting Hill en 1958 fomentées par l'extrême-droite contre les populations immigrées servirent de catalyseur à cet éveil. Les objectifs implicites des nouvelles lois consistaient en la restriction de l'immigration du nouveau Commonwealth, sans nécessairement fermer la porte aux populations blanches anglophones.

La crainte de la politisation de l'enjeu mènera à un nouveau consensus d'élite plutôt que sociétal, dont la pierre angulaire réside dans l'adoption du *Race Regulations Act* en 1968. Cette décision révèle le paradigme des flux migratoires tel que perçu par les Britanniques: la restriction de l'immigration est indissociable d'une lutte à la discrimination. A partir de ce moment, la situation va évoluer de façon à substituer à l'enjeu de l'immigration celui des relations raciales. La consolidation de la lutte à la discrimination raciale par le *Race Relations Act* de 1976 correspond au passage de la conception des relations raciales comme problème à gérer à une vision des minorités ethniques comme groupes sociaux ayant des revendications spécifiques.

Ainsi, la mutation des populations immigrées en minorités ethniques s'est imposée comme nouvel enjeu politique, laissant l'immigration émerger de temps en temps à la faveur d'événements ponctuels (les ressortissants de Hong Kong, les problèmes relevant du droit d'asile, par exemple). Cependant, ce nouvel enjeu ne va pas sans risque. La reconnaissance politique des minorités ethniques s'est accompagnée d'une augmentation des revendications identitaires collectives. Celles-ci ont été fortement attisées par les mouvements anti-racistes qui s'appuient sur la sociologie radicale britannique. Cette dernière voit dans les préjugés, la discrimination et le racisme les manifestations individuelles d'une structure sociale raciste héritée de l'époque coloniale. La lutte anti-raciste s'est donc attachée à relever tous les éléments de la culture britannique porteurs de stéréotypes racistes implicites. Utilisant un langage familier des tenants américains de la „political correctness", sans pour autant être aussi extrême, les anti-racistes ont amorcé la déconstruction de ce qu'une majorité de Britanniques considèrent normal et ont préconisé l'instauration d'un racisme institutionnel positif. L'action positive soulève pourtant des dissensions au sein même de la classe politique. Les Conservateurs y voient une lutte transitoire à la discrimination de façon à atténuer les clivages raciaux menaçant l'ordre social. Les Travaillistes ont, quant à eux, intégré la politique de discrimination positive dans le programme de leur parti depuis 1979. Ils prétendent que le contexte social britannique, marqué par une forte stratification, est propice à la crispation des différences socio-économiques au détriment des populations noires marginalisées et de ce fait, une action politique est indispensable à la rectification de ce déséquilibre.

Dans un tel cadre, on comprend que la subordination des enjeux de l'immigration à ceux des relations raciales est durable. L'originalité de la conception britannique de la lutte à la discrimination repose sur la légitimation et l'institutionnalisation du concept de communauté ou de minorité ethnique et celui de race. La lutte à la discrimination entérinée par les politiciens peut cependant s'avérer polémique, selon que l'on y voit un élément d'une politique d'assimilation capable de rétablir des droits individuels bafoués ou selon qu'elle entraîne un rejet de l'assimilation par une exaltation de la différence au nom du relativisme culturel. Une ethnicisation ou une racialisation des relations sociales et des cultures devient ainsi possible et lourde de conséquences. „*Les valeurs identitaires britanniques qui unissent éclatent aujourd'hui sous la pression d'une segmentation socio-économique et culturelle de la société multiethnique*"[26].

## L'Allemagne

Les attaques racistes récentes contre des foyers de réfugiés dans différents coins de l'Allemagne s'inscrivent dans le contexte de la réunification et des remous économiques et sociaux qu'elle suscite. Cependant, ces problèmes émergent surtout de la conception de la Nation, du peuple et de la communauté particulière à l'Allemagne dans un contexte de graves restrictions économiques. L'idéologie allemande considère la communauté comme d'abord ethnique avant d'être celle de citoyens d'un Etat démocratique. Il en résulte une construction idéologique bien particulière de l'étranger qui préside à la classification des immigrants selon leur appartenance ou non au peuple allemand.

L'Allemagne refuse encore aujourd'hui de se considérer comme un pays d'immigration. Par le passé, elle a pratiqué comme d'autres pays européens une politique de main-d'oeuvre soutenue jusqu'à la crise économique du début de la décennie 70. Avant la fermeture des frontières, les travailleurs étrangers (une forte proportion de Turcs) étaient forcés à une mobilité perpétuelle entre leur pays d'origine et leur pays d'accueil, celui-ci ne permettant pas la stabilisation de ces „invités", ni le séjour de leurs familles en territoire allemand. L'arrêt officiel de l'immigration de main-d'oeuvre étrangère provoqua comme effet imprévu la sédentarisation de la population étrangère en RFA. L'incitation au retour grâce à l'octroi de primes financières ne reçu qu'un succès relatif.

Cette population étrangère sédentarisée et l'arrivée de nouveaux immigrants obligèrent l'Allemagne à réformer son droit de séjour des

---

[26] Costa-Lascoux, Jacqueline. *Face au racisme. Théories et hypothèses, Tome II.* „Des lois contre le racisme". Éditions La Découverte, Paris, 1991: 123.

étrangers. Une nouvelle loi élaborée en 1990 et entrée en vigueur le premier janvier 1991 consacre la stabilisation d'une large partie de la population étrangère en leur accordant un droit de séjour, mais laisse toutefois intacte la conception nationale de l'Etat allemand comme communauté ethnico-culturelle. De nombreuses catégories d'étrangers sont ainsi instituées, dont celle d'une population durablement installée en Allemagne. *„Ce terme (Auslander) qui qualifie normalement des personnes vivant sur un autre territoire national, donc la population mondiale en dehors des ressortissants d'un Etat-nation bien déterminé, prend une signification autre dans le contexte fédéral: ce sont les ressortissants de l'Allemagne ne disposant pas des droits des nationaux allemands, des Auslanders d'Allemagne"*[27]. Il est ainsi créé un régime de titres diversifiés réparti entre deux pôles, les *Auslanders* d'Allemagne et les étrangers pouvant séjourner provisoirement sur le territoire national. D'autre part, le non-refoulement, sans être un titre de séjour, permet aux revendicateurs du Statut de réfugié de demeurer en Allemagne pour une période de temps fixée par les autorités.

Les *Auslanders* d'Allemagne peuvent consolider leur statut juridique moyennant leur capacité à démontrer qu'ils méritent cette consolidation. L'obtention d'un statut stable est inséparable d'une intégration réussie. L'étranger doit obligatoirement passer par un système gradué d'autorisation de séjour avant de pouvoir se prévaloir d'un titre de résidence après huit ans de séjour, titre qui dépend également de diverses conditions comme celle de ne pas être au chômage, d'avoir cotisé à une caisse de retraite pendant au moins 60 mois, etc.

Par contre, l'acquisition de la nationalité allemande est encore régie par une loi de 1913 et se base sur le *Jus sanguini*. Deux formes de naturalisation sont également possible, soit la naturalisation de droit pour les personnes qui sont allemandes en vertu de l'article 16 de la Loi fondamentale et la naturalisation par décision discrétionnaire de l'Etat. Cette dernière est donc possible après les délais requis, soit 10 ans de séjour pour les étrangers, 7 ans pour les réfugiés et 5 ans pour les conjoints étrangers d'Allemands, et en autant que le candidat, après réception de la promesse de naturalisation, demande une libération de sa nationalité d'origine. L'existence de la première forme de naturalisation explique comment des ressortissants de pays de l'Est

---

[27]Collet, Beate. *Logiques d'États et immigrations.* „La construction politique de l'Auslander: le modèle allemand en question". Éditions Kimé, Paris, 1992: 142.

se prévalant d'ancêtres allemands peuvent se voir octroyer la nationalité allemande automatiquement.

La réunification rapide des deux Allemagne s'est effectuée au prix de la déstructuration économique de la partie orientale accompagnée d'un impact social important. *„Le choc est énorme: près de la moitié des 10 millions d'actifs de l'ex-RDA se retrouvent sans emploi, au moins 1,4 million sont au chômage, 400,000 en travaux d'intérêts publics, 900,000 en stage, 750,000 en préretraite..."*[28]. C'est dans ce contexte que les nouveaux Allemands arrivés par milliers viennent concurrencer les demandeurs d'asile en attente de statut sur un marché du travail très limité. De plus, les demandeurs d'asile sont des cibles aisées parce que la loi allemande les affecte à des habitations collectives réservées[29]. La logique ethnico-culturelle exclusionnaire fonctionne également pour les demandeurs d'asile qui se retrouvent au bas d'une échelle de statuts juridiques.

Il y a donc déplacement des problèmes de l'immigration vers le débat politique entourant les demandeurs d'asile au détriment de ces derniers. Les mesures de plus en plus restrictives de la procédure d'asile politique ainsi que la représentation négative véhiculée par les politiciens et les médias marginalisent politiquement et socialement les demandeurs d'asile. Les comportements xénophobes à leur endroit sont la conséquence première de cette marginalisation. De plus, l'augmentation du nombre de demandeurs interprétée comme une usurpation du droit d'asile permet de disculper aux yeux de la population ces agressions contre des étrangers non-invités.

La logique ethnico-nationaliste se situe donc au coeur même de la problématique de l'immigration dans une Allemagne qui se nie en tant que pays d'immigration. Cette conception du peuple permet une institutionnalisation de pratiques discriminatoires qui, ailleurs seraient réprimées. *„Ainsi, le pouvoir législatif et exécutif continuent à construire l'identité allemande par l'exclusion de ceux qui ethniquement ne sont pas Allemands et produit „au passage" des formes de discriminations institutionnalisées qui, dans d'autres pays, sont réprimées par la loi."*[30]

---

[28] Carroué, Laurent. *Le monde diplomatique.* „Le coût de l'unification à marche forcée". oct. 1992: 6–7.

[29] Weil, Patrick. *Le monde diplomatique.* „Travail et droit d'asile". oct. 1992: 6–7.

[30] Collet, Beate. *Logiques d'États et immigrations.* „La construction politique de l'Auslander: le modèle allemand en question". Éditions Kimé, Paris, 1992: 172.

## L'Europe de 1993

Ce bref aperçu de positions nationales très différentes laisse entrevoir la difficulté d'atteindre l'harmonisation souhaitée quant au Statut de l'étranger dans une Europe communautaire. Ce statut harmonisé risque de se caractériser par un nivellement vers le bas au détriment des individus, particulièrement des réfugiés politiques. La double ambition de l'espace occidental apparaît ici dans toute son ambiguïté; pendant que l'Acte unique encourage une augmentation des échanges économiques, plus de dialogue et de liberté, les Accords de Schengen, en garantissant la libre circulation sur le territoire européen des seuls Européens, procèdent à un resserrement du contrôle à l'entrée et de la sélection des populations étrangères. *„Un nouvel ordre social et juridique se profile, qui élargit les espaces de promotion et de libertés, mais sous condition, c'est-à-dire en renforçant les mécanismes de ségrégation"*[31]. Dans un espace européen protégé par une frontière commune, le risque du contrôle au faciès devient plausible, malgré l'instauration d'un Conseil européen des minorités pour favoriser la concertation et le respect des droits[32].

Le phantasme de l'invasion impose ici des mesures de plus en plus restrictives. Déjà la perception populaire des mouvements de populations du Sud vers le Nord, tant pour les réfugiés que pour les clientèles non-occidentales habituelles de travailleurs étrangers, s'articule autour du thème du clandestin. La logique différentialiste basée sur l'inassimibilité de certains migrants relève d'un choix politique justifiant un racisme politique qui se traduit par une hiérarchisation des nations exercée à l'intérieur d'un territoire national. Le nouveau rôle de protection du territoire communautaire attribué à l'Espagne dans cette Europe nouvelle en est l'exemple parfait. Ce pays autrefois d'émigration participe désormais sans broncher à l'érection d'un mur invisible autour de la forteresse des Douze. *„Aux humiliations et expulsions subies dans les aéroports et postes frontaliers par les candidats à l'émigration originaires d'Asie, d'Afrique et d'Amérique latine, il faut désormais ajouter la tragique récolte de la „traversée de la mort", le passage du détroit sur la zone côtière*

---

[31] Marie, Claude-Valentin. *Face au racisme. Théories et hypothèses, Tome II.* „L'Europe: de l'empire aux colonies intérieures". Éditions La Découverte, Paris, 1991.

[32] Rousso-Lenoir, Fabienne. „Pour un Conseil européen des minorités", dans Telo, Mario — *Vers une nouvelle Europe?.* Institut d'Études européennes, Bruxelles, 1992: 345–351.

*andalouse voisine du Maroc"*[33]. Dans un tel contexte, le cheminement vers un nouvel ordre mondial semble s'effectuer sur la base d'une rupture Nord/Sud de plus en plus consacrée. Pourtant, même si l'Etat-nation est en dissolution, *„La „forteresse Europe" ne devrait pas être conçue comme un château-fort „blanc" assailli par les pauvres „Noirs": la réalité est beaucoup plus complexe"* comme le démontre Robert Miles[34].

## Les Etats-Unis

L'immigration initiale en Amérique du Nord diffère fondamentalement de celle qui s'est déployée en Europe. Sur le continent américain, elle était davantage le fait d'une volonté et d'un besoin de peuplement (tout de même sous-tendu par des préoccupations d'ordre économiques). Par ailleurs, l'esclavagisme, que l'on peut considérer comme une forme d'immigration obligée, a modifié durablement la composition des populations aux Etats-Unis, mais également dans plusieurs autres pays du continent.

Tout comme la France, les Etats-Unis ont été désignés comme modèle démocratique étant donné leur héritage révolutionnaire. Ici aussi, l'idéologie républicaine sous-tend la logique étatique. La particularité américaine réside dans la question raciale incontournable puisque les Amérindiens et les Noirs forment des entités constitutives de l'identité nationale[35]. La société américaine reflète un racisme structurel que le temps et la volonté ont bien de la difficulté à faire disparaître. De plus, la position privilégiée des Etats-Unis dans le monde, mais encore plus dans la région qui lui est propre, ne peut être ignorée. Tout un jeu de politique étrangère dicté par des liens culturels et politiques doit être considéré lorsque l'on tente de comprendre les motivations qui ont présidées à certains choix. C'est dans ce cadre général que s'insèrent les politiques d'immigration et que doivent se comprendre les effets contemporains provoqués par l'immigration plus récente.

---

[33] Goylisolo, Juan. *Le monde diplomatique.* „Les boucs émissaires de l'Espagne européenne". oct. 1992: 12.

[34] Miles, Robert. *Sociologie et Sociétés.* „L'Europe de 1993, l'État, l'immigration et la restructuration de l'exclusion". P.U.M., Montréal, vol. XXIV, no 2, automne 1992: 45–57.

[35] Beaud, Stéphane; Noiriel, Gérard. *Face au racisme. Théories et hypothèses, Tome II.* „Penser l'intégration des immigrés". Éditions La Découverte, Paris, 1991.

Les Etats-Unis sont une terre d'immigration et la diversité culturelle correspondante y a privilégié une forme d'organisation de type communautaire des populations différentes installées sur le territoire national. Cette structure communautaire, souvent appuyée sur des bases religieuses, permet l'atténuation du lien avec le pays d'origine dès la deuxième génération puisqu'elle se substitue à celui-ci et devient son équivalent métaphorique. C'est également grâce à la médiation communautaire, qui devient une instance autant culturelle qu'idéologique, que le modèle d'assimilation américain du „melting pot" est rendu possible. Ceci explique d'ailleurs pourquoi le creuset constitue le fondement même de l'identité de la société américaine[36].

Au début, mis à part les Afro-américains et les Amérindiens, la population était en majorité sinon en totalité d'origine européenne. Dès le lendemain de la Première Guerre Mondiale, les mesures afin de réformer les politiques d'immigration furent envisagées dans le but avoué de réduire l'hétérogénéité de la population et de renforcer les valeurs que l'on considérait à la base de la société américaine. A ce mouvement xénophobe s'ajoutait la pression des syndicats qui allait dans le même sens mais était motivée par le désir de protéger le marché du travail national d'une concurrence jugée déloyale. L'établissement de quotas par nationalité permit de limiter l'immigration en provenance du Sud et de l'Est de l'Europe. Parallèlement, l'immigration asiatique était complètement interdite alors que les populations du Canada ou d'Amérique latine n'étaient soumises qu'à des restrictions „qualitatives". Les Asiatiques qui étaient déjà sur le territoire américain, attirés là par la ruée vers l'or de 1850, s'étaient vite retrouvés en situation de quasi-servage, assimilés de par leur race aux Noirs et aux Indigènes indiens. La naturalisat8/n leur était refusée sous prétexte de leur inassimibilité due à leurs caractéristiques raciales. De plus, tout comme les esclaves noirs, ces travailleurs n'entraient pas dans la catégorie d'immigrants mais dans celle d'importation telle que stipulé dans la Constitution du pays. „*Même après l'abolition du commerce des esclaves, puis plus tard celui de l'esclavage lui-même, la catégorie d'importation a perduré. Ceux qui y étaient rattachés continuaient d'être considérés non comme des personnes à part entière, mais comme travailleurs, amenés dans un but économique spécifique et dont on*

---

[36] Oriol, Michel. *Revue internationale d'action communautaire.* „Modèles idéologiques et modèles culturels dans la reproduction des identités collectives", 21/61, 1989.

*pouvait se débarrasser facilement quand leur utilité aurait disparu — à l'instar des Gastarbeiter contemporains*"[37].

Paradoxalement, ces restrictions imposées à l'immigration n'empêchaient aucunement la tolérance de la porosité de la frontière sud. Ce laisser-faire se comprend par les besoins de main-d'oeuvre agricole des états du sud. De cette façon fut institutionnalisée la „porte de service" de l'immigration américaine. Un mouvement de va et vient de ces travailleurs agricoles fut ainsi institué, dicté par les affrontements conjoncturels entre intérêts économiques et intérêts politiques. C'est dans ce contexte que s'inscrivent les pressions périodiques visant à restreindre l'entrée des *wetback*, mais toutes les tentatives, même récentes, pour limiter leur accès par la „porte de service" se sont butées à un fort lobby des agriculteurs du sud.

Après la Deuxième Guerre Mondiale, la politique d'immigration a été à nouveau réformée cette fois dans le but de l'alléger de ses aspects discriminatoires d'une part et d'autre part, de prendre en compte la situation particulière des réfugiés. Ceci mena à une politique d'asile plus généreuse, distincte du processus de gestion des flux migratoires. Cette ouverture faite aux réfugiés (qui s'inscrit indéniablement dans le contexte de la Guerre froide) participa à la modification des populations dans plusieurs grandes villes américaines. L'accueil des naufragés de la mer et celui des dissidents du régime castriste constituent les sources les plus importantes de ces nouveaux Américains.

Cependant, le problème de l'immigration aux Etats-Unis demeure concentré vers le sud du pays. L'adoption d'une nouvelle loi en 1986 qui visait à réformer la „porte de service" se concrétisa par une sorte de compromis qui avait l'avantage de ménager les lobbys agricoles tout en satisfaisant les lobbys syndicaux désirant protéger un marché du travail national. Dans le même temps, la loi cherchait à rassurer face à la peur de l'hispanisation. Cette loi adoptée au milieu de discussions controversées révèle bien la difficulté propre à un type de migration internationale qui implique la localisation de travailleurs du tiers-monde dans les démocraties capitalistes développées. Selon Aristide Zolberg, ces migrations particulières relèvent d'une inégalité structurelle trop souvent ignorée entre deux pays. *„Bien que cette étude ait eu pour objet exclusif les Etats-Unis, le problème est très répandu, et des histoires similaires*

---

[37]Zolberg, Aristide. *Logiques d'États et immigrations*. „Reforming the back door". Éditions Kimé, Paris, 1992: 223.

*peuvent être racontées avec des collectivités différentes présentant elles aussi des caractères de domination: Français et Algériens, Allemands et Turcs, Belges et Marocains, ou si nous faisons un retour dans le passé: Anglais et Irlandais, Allemands et Polonais. Dans tous ces cas, le flux était encouragé par une relation d'inégalité structurelle entre deux pays formant les secteurs complémentaires d'un système économique transnational au sein duquel le pays dépendant constitue, avant toutes autres choses, une réserve de main-d'oeuvre."*[38]

La société américaine reste donc empreinte d'un racisme que le problème de l'urbanisation et la marginalisation des populations pauvres ne permet pas d'éradiquer. Les nouvelles immigrations se retrouvent souvent en position d'affrontement avec ces populations dans un marché du travail où les ressources sont limitées.

Il importe également de mentionner tout le mouvement des revendications identitaires amorcé par la génération des années 60 et inséré dans un droit des minorités. L'ampleur de ce phénomène appuyé sur un relativisme culturel intransigeant a atteint des sommets inégalés comparativement à l'Europe. La force de la philosophie de la „political correctness" (PC) dans les campus américains et sa percée de plus en plus évidente dans la société en général pourrait remettre en cause les assises mêmes de l'identité collective américaine. *„La culture américaine devient ainsi une auberge espagnole où chaque communauté apporte son héritage, le plus souvent idéalisé. Cette atomisation est pour certains de nature à menacer l'identité culturelle du pays. Car adopter la logique PC, c'est nier l'universalité du vrai, du discours rationnel."*[39]

La particularité américaine réside ici dans le fait que la promotion des minorités raciales, sociales et sexuelles encouragée par le mouvement PC englobe l'essentiel de la société américaine à l'exception des hommes blancs hétérosexuels. Il résulte de cet amalgame une critique de l'universalité de la démocratie américaine au nom d'une lutte pour la „vraie égalité", économique, sociale, politique et culturelle.

---

[38] Zolberg, Aristide. *Logiques d'États et immigrations.* „Reforming the back door". Éditions Kimé, Paris, 1992: 247é

[39] Nora, Dominique. *Le nouvel observateur.* „Les nouveaux maîtres censeurs". 29 août 1991: 50.

## Le Canada

Terre d'accueil depuis ses origines, le Canada a été façonné par l'immigration. Malgré cela, le pays n'a eu aucune politique d'immigration cohérente pendant longtemps. Le racisme d'une société au départ assez homogène, associé au conservatisme des dirigeants politiques avait permis la mise en place d'une politique discriminatoire de préservation d'un Canada blanc, situation qui allait perdurer jusqu'à la fin de la Deuxième Guerre Mondiale. L'apparition d'une volonté politique de concertation au niveau international associée à l'émergence de nouveaux pays dans la fièvre de la décolonisation devait modifier l'ordre établi. Sur une scène internationale de plus en plus variée et dans un Commonwealth de plus en plus multiracial, la „White Canada Policy" contrastait dangereusement avec la nouvelle image internationale positive que le Canada tentait d'acquérir.

La politique d'immigration canadienne s'articulera donc, à partir de la Seconde Guerre Mondiale autour des principes suivants: la réunification des familles, les préoccupations relatives aux réfugiés, la non-discrimination et la promotion des objectifs démographiques, économiques, sociaux et culturels du Canada. L'influence de la logique britannique transparaît au travers du lien accepté entre immigration et lutte à la discrimination. Il nous est ainsi possible de tracer un parallèle entre la décision canadienne d'institutionnaliser le multiculturalisme et les politiques britanniques de lutte à la discrimination. Mais de quelle discrimination s'agit-il aujourd'hui? Selon une étude récente du Conseil économique du Canada: *„il n'y a aucune preuve de la discrimination salariale importante fondée sur la couleur de la peau des immigrants"*[40]. L'accès inégal à l'emploi est souvent dénoncé sans qu'il ait été démontré. Alors pourquoi institué la lutte contre la discrimination?

La promotion des minorités ethniques par le biais de leur institutionnalisation au travers du multiculturalisme prouve que le Canada n'a pas échappé à la tentation d'utiliser le relativisme culturel pour enrayer la discrimination. Or, la notion de mosaïque telle que définie par la doctrine du bilinguisme et du multiculturalisme porte les germes d'une menace d'éclatement. La vulnérabilité de l'identité canadienne, écartelée entre deux langues et deux cultures, est mise à jour par la dissolution des

---

[40] De Silva, Arnold. *Les gains des immigrants, une analyse comparative.* Conseil économique du Canada, Ottawa, 1992: 19 et 35.

valeurs communes au profit d'une tolérance souhaitable, mais qui ne peut à elle seule offrir la cohésion indispensable à l'unité de la collectivité[41]. Ici comme ailleurs, la discrimination positive doit être manipulée avec précaution afin d'éviter les détournements idéologiques possibles.

A la diversité culturelle politiquement reconnue s'ajoute la brûlante question autochtone dont la résurgence au sein de l'actualité dévoile l'existence d'un racisme structurel proprement canadien que l'on tend trop souvent à oublier. Bien que ce problème diffère de celui que soulève les nouvelles immigrations, tous deux remettent en cause la représentation populaire de l'identité canadienne dans l'imaginaire collectif. De plus, les nouvelles immigrations dérangent parce qu'elles modifient profondément le paysage humain des villes. La reconnaissance de la pluralité ethnique, en effritant le consensus autour des valeurs communes, fragilise la société d'accueil. De plus, les difficultés qui en découlent laisse percevoir l'immigration de plus en plus comme un difficile problème de gestion sociale qui ne fait qu'amplifier la peur de l'Autre.

Tout comme les autres Etats du Nord industrialisés, le Canada s'ajuste sur les règles communes qui orientent les politiques d'immigration. Malgré sa réputation d'accueil et de tolérance, les frontières se ressèrent. Ici comme ailleurs, le clivage s'accentue entre un Nord anxieux de protéger ses richesses et un Sud qui se cherche des moyens pour survivre.

## 5. L'impact des migrations: implosion des états-nations

Le processus migratoire Est/Ouest, Sud/Nord semble inévitable du fait des déséquilibres structurels qui affligent le système international. Au cours des âges, différentes formes de domination (esclavagisme, colonialisme, impérialisme) ont permis aux pays industrialisés du Nord de recourir à des bassins de main-d'oeuvre que leurs économies exigeaient. A partir de la crise des années 70, la diminution des facteurs d'attraction dans les pays d'accueil et l'augmentation des facteurs motivant le départ dans les pays du Sud ont contribué à une perte partielle de contrôle du processus migratoire. *„Les systèmes administratifs et juridiques nationaux et internationaux demeurent trop ancrés dans les concepts de*

---

[41]Bissonnette, Lise. *L'intégration des immigrants au Québec: entre la peur et l'angélisme.* Allocution d'ouverture, Colloque des professeurs du MCCI, Montréal, 19 sept. 1991.

*territorialité, révélant une mésadaptation à la réalité d'une plus grande mobilité internationale stimulée par la mondialisation de l'économie et par l'adaptation de l'émigration aux nouveaux modèles de développement*"[42].

Les conséquences sur les migrants et par ricochet sur les pays d'accueil semblent elles aussi incontournables. Ces cultures dérangées par le processus migratoire, arrachées de leur élément naturel, une fois transplantées, deviennent des cultures du dérangement dont la coexistence s'avère souvent complexe, mouvante, parfois brutale[43]. Nous avons tenté d'illustrer par différents cas comment les sociétés nationales ont été formées dans le passé par des politiques propres à chaque Etat, mais qui correspondaient également à la structure inégalitaire du système international. Souvent le racisme structurel présent au sein d'une société n'est que la contre-partie „normale" d'un racisme politique qui a présidé à la hiérarchisation des nations au niveau international. Actuellement, ces mêmes Etats accusent une certaine perte de contrôle tant au niveau externe qu'interne. Nous prétendons que les nouvelles immigrations posent problème parce qu'elles s'insèrent dans des sociétés nationales déjà affaiblies par le mouvement des revendications identitaires qui effrite progressivement la cohésion sociale de la majorité dominante. La reconnaissance des différentes identités se fait au détriment d'une identité nationale qui s'érige en norme de référence.

Les nouvelles immigrations, de par leur composition même, transcendent les frontières des Etats-nations. Elles sont plus politisées et plus citadinisées, on y retrouve moins de paysans et plus de réfugiés, moins de migrants économiques et plus de victimes de l'histoire. Les conflits sont de nationalité et de citoyenneté dans un contexte où la présence même de ces nouvelles populations installées dans les grandes métropoles transcontinentalise les débats en leur donnant de nouvelles dimensions. Avec René Gallissot, nous sommes porté à croire que le multiculturel n'est peut-être qu'un simple feu follet courant sur une transformation de base: l'urbanisation généralisée et la généralisation des cultures urbaines avec comme corollaire le grossissement des relations interethniques. Ainsi s'opère un amalgame des cultures qui appelle une distinction de plus en plus marquée entre citoyenneté et nationalité, obligeant à penser

---

[42] Bolzmann, C.; Jacques, A.; Jacques, G.; Menetrey, A. *La forteresse européenne et les réfugiés.* „Asile et immigration". Éditions d'en bas, Lausanne, 1985: 68.

[43] Médam, Alain. *Revue internationale d'action communautaire.* „Ethnos et poli. A propos du cosmopolitisme montréalais". 21/61, 1989.

une nouvelle citoyenneté plurielle. „Mais n'est-ce pas que l'importance des diasporas, les recoupements des ensembles que sont ces nouveaux espaces d'échanges d'échelle continentale, méditerranéenne ou même transocéanique, qui se nouent ou se condensent dans la polarisation urbaine et dans la coexistence des signes indemnitaire, comme le procès de la transnationalisation culturelle pousse en avant une conception nouvelle de la citoyenneté? La citoyenneté échappe à la nationalité"[44].

L'Etat-nation qui érige la nationalité, la sienne, en universalisme se retrouve contesté par des mouvements minoritaires qui lui oppose l'absolutisation de leurs différences comme arme première. Entre ces deux extrêmes, les principes républicains d'universalité disparaissent au profit d'une conception insulaire de l'identité collective.

Le découplage citoyenneté/nationalité provoqué par les migrations internationales menace l'intégrité de l'Etat-nation, tout comme la perte de souveraineté au profit des grands ensembles, des multinationales et des organisations financières internationales qui contrôlent les leviers économiques et la loi du marché au niveau international.

Pourtant, l'Etat-nation demeure le lieu de la construction des identités collectives. La résurgence du racisme dans nos sociétés contemporaines pourrait très bien correspondre aux manifestations externes d'un difficile ajustement aux mutations sociales et politiques. Les conséquences du processus migratoire obligeront tôt ou tard les Etats du Nord à associer la gestion de l'immigration à l'élaboration d'un nouvel équilibre à l'échelle planétaire qui requiert de nouvelles formes de coopération. Le maintien de leur position défensive à l'égard du Sud ne saura les protéger davantage d'un mal qui les ronge désormais de l'intérieur et de l'extérieur.

## 6. Solutions régionales

Dans un contexte dominé de plus en plus par l'idéologie du relativisme culturel, comment doit-on penser la lutte contre le racisme? D'une part, nous croyons que le difficile cheminement vers une plus grande démocratisation se poursuit et que chacun, en tant qu'individu, mais aussi entant que membre d'une collectivité donnée, doit participer à

---

[44] Gallissot, René. *Revue internationale d'action communautaire*. „Au-delà du multiculturel: nationaux, étrangers et citoyens. Urbanisation généralisée et transnationalisation". 21/61, 1989.

l'universalisation des Droits de l'homme par delà les différences de croyances, de couleurs de peau, de cultures. Il importe de privilégier un type de communauté médiatrice d'universalité au détriment d'une communauté relevant d'un idéal protoraciste, auto-suffisante et dans laquelle l'individu disparaît dans l'élément du corps national. Afin de réhabiliter l'idée républicaine dans les démocraties culturelles, il importe de désabsolutiser le principe de la différence, afin de l'intégrer comme facteur de relativisation dans un humanisme non ethnocentriste. *„L'idée d'une communauté humaine est celle de la démocratie achevée, et non plus enclose dans les frontières d'un peuple-sujet, celles que requiert l'Etat-nation"*[45].

D'autre part, il faut reconnaître que l'exploitation politique des différences de cultures, de religions, de langue, de couleurs de peau, d'origine ou simplement des populations migrantes ou de souches par certains leaders „régionaux" est très dangereuse. En période d'instabilité politique et économique, il semble facile de provoquer des conflits sur la base de simples représentations symboliques. Il faut dénoncer ces processus d'association intempestive du politique et du culturel, du politique et du religieux, etc.

En fait, la région peut être un lieu par excellence d'opérationnalisation politique de ces processus différentialistes culturels. La région peut aussi être le lieu idéal d'émergence des solidarités internationales et interculturelles à condition que l'identité régionale soit construite sur une base égalitaire entre tous ses habitants. Malgré les conflits d'intérêts économiques et les divergences d'opinion politique, la région devrait donc être conçue essentiellement comme un lieu de convivialité entre les citoyens partageant un même territoire, sans distinction ou hiérarchie institutionnalisée politiquement ou juridiquement. Si la région peut être tout autant le lieu de légitimisation des conflits à caractère raciste et un lieu de protection contre toutes les formes de racisme, la vigilance s'impose donc.

Malheureusement, compte tenu de la complexité ethnique de l'ex-URSS, suite aux mouvements de population (volontaires ou non) très importants sous l'ancien régime, ce sont plutôt les tensions ethniques qui font surface. Selon Henri Dorion, géographe, directeur de la recherche au Musée de la Civilisation à Québec, ces tensions s'expliquent par les fortes pressions accumulées au cours des dernières décennies.

---

[45] Taguieff, Pierre-André. *La force du préjugé.* Éditions La Découverte, Paris, 1987: 490.

L'institutionnalisation d'une inégalité entre les peuples, la domination politique et économique par des diasporas et la négation des libertés religieuses seraient à la source de l'éclatement de ces tensions à l'Est. Le fait est qu'il y a toujours de bonnes raisons qui peuvent être invoquées. Le conflit politique-symbolique est naïvement (ou non) entretenu par certains leaders chez vous, comme chez nous. Micheline Labelle, sociologue, professeur à l'Université du Québec à Montréal, démontre que la question du racisme et de l'ethnicité est centrale dans le discours de leaders d'associations ethniques de la région de Montréal parce que c'est politiquement rentable. Comment s'en sortir?

Sur le territoire de l'ex-URSS, l'importance des mouvements migratoires internes et externes, l'ouverture des frontières par Gorbatchev en 1987 et la montée des nationalismes nous laissent croire que le relativisme culturel peut être également politiquement rentable. Comment s'en sortir?

Comment s'en sortir? Cesser de cultiver la haine et la peur de l'Autre, renverser les extrémistes et reconstruire les solidarités régionales et inter-régionales sont un premier pas. Ensuite, il suffit de se rappeler que nous sommes tous de plus en plus liés à des identités multiples, plus ou moins contradictoires, mais aussi interdépendantes. Parmi ces „nous" auxquels nous appartenons chacun, nous n'avons pas à choisir. Ils sont au contraire notre richesse personnelle et collective. Si l'homogénéité culturelle et la pureté de la race territoriale ne sont que mythiques[46], l'avenir ne peut prétendre être construit sur un retour émotif à un équilibre passé. Prendre en compte cette complexité avec courage et lucidité, prendre en compte la force des inconscients collectifs, nous permet au contraire d'envisager l'avenir avec espoir. „*Car il n'est de libération plus grande et plus hardie que celle où l'on parvient progressivement à se dégager de l'emprise de la culture inconsciente*"[47].

Heureusement, selon Jean Rodvanyi[48], on assiste actuellement en Russie (et la situation polonaise est probablement semblable) à une redistribution des cartes entre les anciens leaders économiques et politiques qui sont pour la plupart favorables à des réformes profondes.

---

[46] Guillaumin, Colette. *Sociologie et Sociétés*. „Une société en ordre. De quelques-unes des formes de l'idéologie raciste". P.U.M., Montréal, vol. XXIV, no 2, automne 1989: 13–23.

[47] Hall, E.T. *Au-delà de la culture*. Éditions du Seuil, Paris, 1979: 234.

[48] Rodvanyi, Jean. *Le monde diplomatique*. „Vers l'émergence de „cinquante ou soixante principautés"? Dans une Russie affaiblie, la tentation régionaliste". Paris, no 470, mai 1993: 24.

Des réseaux régionaux forts, très liés aux habitants, peuvent maintenant assurer une certaine stabilité de vie. Ainsi, le renforcement du champ d'action des élites régionales devrait être bénéfique dans la plupart des cas. En assurant directement la régulation sociale avec les habitants, dans la convivialité, les régions servent de rempart au racisme.

En somme, l'implosion de l'Etat-nation peut être une occasion unique de renforcer les solidarités régionales, nationales, internationales.

Hubert Rossel
Suisse

# LA RESURGENCE DES GROUPES ETHNIQUES ET CULTURELS EN EUROPE ORIENTALE SUITE Á L'IMPLOSION DES RÉGIMES COMMUNISTES

## Introduction:
## „Le développement ou l'identité nationale?" Une fausse alternative

L'année passée, en ce même endroit, ce même Institut Européen du Développement Régional et Local a consacré une réflexion intéressante sur les dilemmes et les politiques régionales en Europe centre-orientale, l'accent étant plutôt mis sur la dimension économique. Parmi les différents cas cités d'expériences occidentales dans le domaine des politiques régionales, il est bon de rappeler la contribution de Juan J. Palacios, „Redistribution under neoliberalism in Mexico and East-Central Europe: the demise of regional policy?" (Gorzelak & Kukliński, 1992, 366–392), car il met en évidence, — et en parallèle — des conditions économiques sensiblement pareilles à celles que connaissent les pays d'Europe centre-orientale, mais avec quelques années/décennies d'avance sur eux. La valeur éducative des succès et des erreurs peut donc servir à plein. Mais il semble que l'on ne fasse pas suffisamment la différence entre la „croissance" et le „développement" d'une région ou d'un pays. Les deux concepts ne sont pourtant pas du tout synonymes, contrairement à ce que sous-entendent bon nombre d'économistes. La redistribution néolibérale n'a pas tant pour but la recherche de l'équité de la société que celui de la croissance des régions les plus efficaces, les plus performantes, selon la logique de la politique keynesienne. Pourquoi s'étonner, dès lors, de l'augmentation des disparités régionales — tant sociales qu'économiques — puisqu'on ne poursuit qu'une simple logique de croissance, liée à l'économie marchande, et non pas une logique de développement? Est-ce, dès lors, un modèle pertinent à proposer et à suivre aveuglément? Ne faudrait-il pas davantage tenir compte du concept de „concentration" dans l'analyse des inégalités frappantes, que cette concentration soit géographique au niveau de la localisation, économique, financière ou sociale? Lorsqu'on envisage une politique de restructuration, il ne faut pas confondre les deux, en oubliant la dimension humaine, encore moins en voulant la nier!

L'approche régionale de ces dilemmes était essentiellement économique, laissant un peu au second plan les problèmes identitaires, qui ne peuvent pourtant être évacués ou sous-estimés. De ce point de vue, la contribution de Leonidas Donskis, „Lithuania's dilemma — development or national identity" (Gorzelak & Kukliński, 1992, 109–119), apparaît fondamentale. Quelle priorité: le développement ou l'identité nationale? La question est bien posée, en relation avec les aspirations contemporaines (et lesquelles?) des populations. Mais est-ce une vraie alternative? Est-ce une question pertinente sous cette formulation précise? Cette approche plus philosophique et ethnologique est fondamentale pour autant qu'elle ne soit pas ethnocentrique, sinon gare aux dérives hypernationalistes! L'auteur reconnaît lui-même que c'est une fausse question, parce qu'il n'y a pas de réelle alternative. D'ailleurs, le „développement" vrai (qui n'est donc pas une simple „croissance") englobe d'office les critères qualitatifs des sociétés envisagées. Sa conclusion sert de point de départ pour la réflexion sur les critères identitaires conduisant à la résurgence des groupes ethniques et culturels de l'Europe orientale, étant conscient qu'on ne peut s'ouvrir au monde sans avoir une bonne connaissance de l'analyse de sa propre culture, philosophique et sociologique.

# 1. La notion d'identité

## 1.1. L'identité ethnique

La notion d'identité ethnique est difficile à cerner, parce qu'il ne s'agit pas un concept naturel, une catégorie naturelle bien définie, bien délimitée, une chose toute faite, statique. De plus, outre le fait qu'elle n'est pas vécue de la même façon par tous, elle n'est pas non plus nécessairement perçue de la même façon par tout le monde. L'identité se construit en permanence et évolue constamment; elle se modifie et s'adapte en fonction de l'environnement extérieur. Elle s'inscrit donc dans un processus d'évolution historique constant. L'identité se définit d'abord par rapport à son propre tissus social et culturel; l'identité de soi pour soi. Mais, très fréquemment, la conscience de soi rencontre celle de l'autre, qu'elle se définisse par rapport à elle ou non. Elle est envisagée comme distincte par le jeu des interactions avec autrui, en liaison avec les différents comportements spécifiques de chacun (Gil F., Tap P. & Sindzingre N., 1984).

Le „groupe ethnique" est donc formé par l'ensemble des personnes qui se définissent comme une entité particulière, une unité propre par rapport aux autres, en fonction de leur identité distincte et du choix d'un certain nombre de caractères pertinents. Les membres d'un groupe ethnique présentent un projet particulier, spécifique, différent de celui des groupes voisins, qui s'inscrit dans un contexte historique donné, un passé qui leur est commun ou qu'ils considèrent comme leur étant commun. Ils ont donc conscience d'appartenir à une ethnie donnée ou, plus exactement, ont une face consciente de leur identité ethnique. L'importance de l'aspect inconscient, ou subconscient, n'est pas à négliger, car c'est souvent celui-là qui est le plus attisé, lors de l'utilisation extrémiste des identités ethniques élargies, — ou réduites, suivant les points de vue — aux identités nationales, aux nationalismes pacifiques ou agressifs. En effet, le simple bon sens fait prendre conscience que l'identité collective ne consiste pas en la simple somme des identités individuelles! La psychologie des groupes montre déjà, à un niveau plus élémentaire, qu'un groupe constitué n'est pas la simple addition des individualités de chacun, le petit „quelque chose" en plus provenant de l'interaction produite à l'intérieur du groupe par les membres présents.

## 1.2. Les signes de l'identité

Chaque groupe ethnique se définit aussi par un ensemble de traits significatifs, sans valeur en soi mais rendus signifiants par les gens eux-mêmes. Ces emblèmes ou ces étiquettes — des ethnonymes — ne reposent donc pas des critères absolus ou objectifs, mais plutôt sur une perception subjective, par soi-même ou par autrui, suffisamment explicite pour chacun. Le trèfle symbolise l'Irlande, au même titre que le chardon représente l'Ecosse; le lion noir sur fond jaune identifie la Flandre, alors que le coq rouge sur fond jaune regroupe les Wallons. Si ces ethnonymes sont incontestés, d'autres ne le sont pas: si l'aigle à deux têtes provoque le ralliement des Albanais, cet aigle bicéphale se retrouve bien ailleurs dans l'aire d'extension de l'Europe centre-orientale. Le soleil de Philippe II de Macédoine est repris par les Macédoniens actuels, — qui n'ont plus rien à voir avec les Macédoniens de l'Antiquité — alors que le terme même de Macédoine est contesté par les Grecs aux Slaves, sans parler de l'emblème ethnique proprement-dit.

La recherche de traits significatifs comme base commune pertinente de l'identité ethnique, malgré une diversité des contrastes, peut montrer l'intercomplémentarité des „étiquettes" que l'on va coller sur certaines situations, suivant le contexte dans lequel on va vouloir les remettre. Le problème jurassien, en Suisse, est pratiquement toujours présenté comme un problème linguistique, alors qu'il correspond à un clivage religieux antérieur. En Belgique, les relations entre Flamands et Wallons sont aussi présentées habituellement sous l'angle d'un problème linguistique, alors qu'il s'agit maintenant d'un problème essentiellement économique! L'apport important des recherches sur le concept des groupes ethniques est d'avoir mis en évidence la diversité des contrastes et d'en montrer leur inter complémentarité (Vreeland H, 1958). Tout se passe comme si l'identité avait un aspect objectif et subjectif, selon les choix des critères pertinents. Les contextes tactiques dans lesquels les problèmes identitaires sont situés ne correspondent pas toujours à la réalité de ce qui est perçu

— voire présenté — à l'extérieur. Peut-on réduire l'identité bosniaque à une simple référence ethnique (en contradiction avec la réalité composite de la population), ou linguistique (ce sont des parlers locaux d'une même langue de base), religieuse (la Bosnie était un exemple de tolérance et de convivialité)? *L'espace perçu* est décidément bien différent de *l'espace vécu*. Les différents niveaux d'identification ne sont donc pas les mêmes pour tout le monde et l'identité ethnique n'est qu'un des aspects de l'identité culturelle.

Les différents essais de typologie des groupes ethniques se sont tous révélés insuffisants dès que l'on a voulu procéder de façon comparative, en les localisant sur des territoires spécifiques (Naroll R., 1964). En effet, à part le fait qu'ils sont souvent minoritaires dans leurs différents pays de résidence, il ne peut y avoir de recouvrement absolu des différents critères. Les points de vue linguistique, politique, économique, religieux, territorial n'ont pas des caractères qui permettent un recoupement absolu de toutes ces notions. Il ne peut donc en résulter que des approches imprécises, équivoques, contestables. De plus, les groupes ethniques ne peuvent pas être réduits à de simples combinaisons de caractères. Ils ont aussi des projets de valeur, la projection historique d'une volonté commune, liée à des pratiques sociales, à une logique de reproduction sociale, l' „habitus" du sociologue P. Bourdieu (Bourdieu P., 1977: 87–109).

Si une typologie n'apporte pas en précision ce qu'on attendait d'elle en critères de comparaison, à cause de l'ambiguïté ou de la diversité de la perception, la réalité des groupes ethniques minoritaires au sein des Etats n'en est pas supprimée pour autant! Or, comme nous le verrons plus loin, des „groupes ethniques" qui ont conscience du processus de leur intégration dans un développement historique spécifique forment une „nation", qu'ils soient sans Etat (les Bretons en France), minoritaires dans un Etat pluraliste (les différentes nations dans l'ex-Yougoslavie), minoritaires dans un Etat unitaire (les Grecs en Albanie, les Hongrois en Roumanie), minoritaires dans plusieurs Etats contigus (les Basques, les Kurdes).

## 1.3. Les différents niveaux d'identification

L'absence de critères extérieurs ou leur non-perception ne signifie pas l'absence de „signifié", bien au contraire. Il peut, par contre, y avoir une réponse qui recouvre plusieurs réalités, qui doit se lire à différents niveaux de perception et d'appartenance. Les Hongrois de la période communiste étaient passés maîtres en la matière, — et étaient en tous cas perçus comme tels — déjà au niveau du simple langage courant qui pouvait être interprété au deuxième ou troisième degré de compréhension. Une lecture multiple de la même réalité est possible, ainsi qu'une perception différente suivant le niveau de perception.

Des emblèmes peuvent être destinés à l'usage externe; c'est la dimension *etic* des ethnologues. En soi, ils n'ont rien de remarquable, mais ce sont des analyseurs ou des révélateurs pertinents d'une réalité. La lisibilité en sera toujours diversifiée, puisqu'elle sera perçue par des gens qui la remettront dans un contexte culturel différent. Ces emblèmes sont pratiquement toujours reçus comme des „signes iconiques": ils sont perçus comme arbitraires, même si l'emblème est important ou capital. Les Tyroliens du Sud, communauté germanophone dans le nord de l'Italie, ont toujours été perçus comme les „culottes de cuir" par le gouvernement régional italien du Haut-Adige. L'„étoile jaune" imposée aux Juifs par les Nazi procède de la même logique: le pouvoir et l'ethnie dominante imposent un signe iconique pour repérer directement l'ethnie que l'on veut mettre au banc de la société.

En Occident, on assiste à une disparition apparente des signes iconiques, surtout en milieu urbain. Le libéralisme a apporté une certaine forme d'égalitarisme, lui-même porteur d'une certaine uniformisation, qui a engendré, à son tour, la banalisation des emblèmes extérieurs. En même temps, et paradoxalement, une surproduction de signes a conduit à une telle accumulation que le nivellement les rend moins visibles et/ou moins expressifs. La publicité est, en partie responsable de cet état de fait; les „voitures-sandwiches" aussi... Un BZH (Breizh = Bretagne) ou un CHTI (Chtimi, prononciation locale en Flandre de „je te...", devenant „ch'ti") sur une voiture, en France, est la marque indiscutable d'opinions pro-autonomistes. Même chose pour les VDA qui ont fleuri sur les voitures en Italie, à une certaine époque, pour bien affirmer l'identité de la Région autonome du Val d'Aoste. Les VL (Vlaanderen = Flandre, en flamand), BXL (Bruxelles) et WAL (Wallonie) étaient bien antérieurs sur les voitures à la communautarisation et à la régionalisation de la Belgique! C'est la même logique qui a prévalu en Roumanie, quand les signes distinctifs des voitures sont passés de R à RO après la Révolution de 1989, pour marquer la rupture d'avec l'ancien régime.

En Europe orientale plus qu'en Europe centrale, les emblèmes à usage externe sont restés beaucoup plus marqués: le calot en feutre blanc des Albanais; les costumes traditionnels des populations de Hongrie et de Roumanie où pas une couleur, pas un motif graphique n'ait sa signification symbolique, comprise de tous ceux qui sont initiés; les types de construction ou même les stèles funéraires permettent de savoir qui est qui.

Les signes iconiques et les emblèmes *etic* sont souvent devenus la base de revendications historiques, ethniques, religieuses, culturelles, et même territoriales (pouvant conduire au séparatisme), qui veulent affirmer une altérité totale. Dans les sociétés unitaires, où l'homogénéité est le principe de base, l'altérité est plus ou moins fortement niée en fonction de la structure même de la société. Il n'y a pas d'expression possible par les canaux traditionnels (partis, classes, médias). Et les réactions seront d'autant plus violentes que la différence est cachée ou ignorée officiellement. Dans les sociétés plus pluralistes de l'Europe centrale et orientale, c'était plutôt l'altérité qui était le principe de base. Les grands Empires pluri-ethniques et multinationaux de l'Autriche-Hongrie ou l'Empire ottoman étaient, par la force des choses, des Etats décentralisés. Les populations d'origines ethniques, linguistiques, religieuses et culturelles différentes ont donc appris à vivre ensemble, sinon toujours en bonne harmonie. Etat décentralisé n'était pas nécessairement synonyme d'absence de force centrifuge, d'acceptation de l'autre tel qu'il est ou de respect du droit à la différence et à son expression. La Transylvanie, — tour à tour romaine, autrichienne, hongroise, indépendante, ottomane, roumaine — sera un bon exemple de cette dure réalité au niveau de l'*espace vécu* des populations concernées.

L'autre niveau d'identification fait référence aux stéréotypes destinés à l'usage interne; c'est l'aspect *emic*. Ces stéréotypes sont moins importants pour l'affirmation de l'identité des groupes ethniques; ils sont, par contre, très révélateurs de l'idée que l'on se fait des autres. Il s'agit souvent d'idées préconçues sur autrui, de vues véhiculées entre soi, à l'intérieur d'un groupe ethnique (ou social) concerné, de classifications élémentaires pour maintenir la différence: nous et les autres. Les „cols bleus" pour les ouvriers, les „cols blancs" pour les fonctionnaires, les „gueules noires" pour les mineurs; et, par extension, les „rouges" pour les communistes, les „minériades" pour les descentes destructrices des mineurs roumains, les „hodjistes" pour les Albanais communistes, les „Musulmans" pour les

Bosniaques... Ces cristallisations sont souvent des simplifications abusives, inévitablement réductrices quand elles sont employées dans ce contexte.

Certains de ces stéréotypes (point de vue *emic*) sont parfois repris comme emblèmes (point de vue *etic*), surtout pour défendre des caractéristiques culturelles propres. Ainsi quand on utilise le terme de „tsigane", non pour qualifier un groupe ethnique, mais des activités et des modes de vie spécifiques: certains types d'artisanat (coutellerie, aiguisage, vannerie) ou la vie itinérante de ceux dont on parle. On les utilise aussi parfois comme „images de marque à exporter"; ainsi ces Dalmates rencontrés qui se présentaient comme un peuple hospitalier, accueillant, souriant, ouvert, „par opposition à ces slaves de l'intérieur (sic), beaucoup plus renfermés et introvertis", pour mettre en évidence le potentiel touristique de la région.

## 1.4. De l'„identité ethnique" à l'„identité culturelle"

Un groupe humain passe insensiblement de l'„identité ethnique" à l'„identité culturelle" par la prise de conscience de son identité propre dans un contexte géographique et historique précis, ainsi que des moyens qui lui permettent de maintenir, voire de renforcer, ses valeurs spécifiques. On passe ainsi brusquement de l'histoire, et de la conscience temporelle de soi et de son passé, à la géographie, et à son insertion spatiale sur un territoire déterminé. Et c'est bien là que les problèmes apparaissent souvent, à cause de la revendication exclusive de certains espaces territoriaux par des populations différentes qui se qualifient de „peuples" ou de „nations", — à juste titre ou non, là n'est pas la question pour l'instant —, parce que, à telle ou telle période du passé, elles ont occupé tout ou partie du territoire revendiqué de façon unilatérale. Chacun peut ainsi remonter dans le passé — il suffit de remonter suffisamment loin! — et justifier de son bon droit. Mais est-ce un droit? Et est-ce une raison pour exclure *manu militari* tous ceux qui ne sont pas de l'ethnie dominante, surtout quand on est minoritaire numériquement parlant, mais qu'on a la force armée de son côté? (Castellan G., 1992; Heraud G., 1993; Jouve E., 1992; Kirschbaum S.J., 1993)

L'occupation d'un espace passé suffit-il à justifier son droit de propriété actuel, plusieurs siècles ou millénaires plus tard, en faisant fi de toutes les évolutions socio-politiques et socio-économiques intermédiaires? La Roumanie peut-elle identifier *roumanité* et *romanité* pour justifier d'une occupation permanente de territoires dont l'Histoire nous apprend que les limites de l'une et de l'autre ne correspondent que très approximativement? C'est la base de la thèse de la continuité daco-roumaine pour justifier de l'appartenance roumaine de la Transylvanie (Dami A., 1945 & 1946).

La Grèce peut-elle revendiquer l'appartenance territoriale d'une région qui a été, il y a deux millénaires et demi, dans sa sphère d'influence? Peut-elle refuser aux populations de cette même région jusqu'à leur nom, parce qu'ils sont dans d'autres Etats? Elle revendique la paternité culturelle d'une région qui, comme telle, n'existe plus, est scindée en plusieurs Etats, n'est plus formée des mêmes populations, qui ne parlent plus la même langue (même si elle en porte le même nom!), ne pratiquent plus la même religion; une région qui, de plus, — si on relit l'histoire d'un point de vue *etic* —, n'a pas été colonisée par la Grèce, mais a colonisé la Grèce!... Nous sommes au cœur de la question macédonienne. (Papakstantinou M., 1992; Sivignon M., 1991)

Les Serbes peuvent-ils imposer aux peuples des nouveaux Etats de l'ex-Yougoslavie, dans lesquels ils sont minoritaires, une logique d'exclusive et de „nettoyage ethnique" pour imposer leur ordre et leur *diktat*, alors même qu'ils refusent de laisser appliquer la même logique à l'intérieur même de leur propre territoire? Les Républiques auto proclamées des Serbes de Krajina et de Slavonie orientale, en Croatie, de Bosanska Krajina, Bosanska Posavina, Semberija, Romanija, Hercegovina, en Bosnie, ont-elles plus de justification légale que la République de Kosove, auto-proclamée par les Albanais de l'ancienne Région autonome du Kosovo, et occupée de façon très autoritaire par les Serbes?

Les Croates ont-ils plus de raisons d'occuper militairement la République autoproclamée d'Herceg-Bosna, en Bosnie, en utilisant finalement les mêmes méthodes que les Serbes, eux qui se plaignent d'avoir pratiquement le tiers de leur territoire occupé de façon illégale par les mêmes Serbes?

Ces quelques exemples, rapidement esquissés, montrent que l'ethnogéographie est loin d'avoir épuisé les questions fondamentales qui se posent si l'on veut envisager les choses sous l'angle du droit et de la géopolitique. Mais quel droit, au juste (Cohen-Jonathan G., 1990; Combacau J., 1980; Quadri R., 1980; Smouts M.-C., 1991)? Celui du plus fort (Pizzorusso A., 1993)? Celui des peuples (Jouve E., 1992; Uribe A.,

1976)? Celui des nations (Bœro G., 1993)? Et quelle géopolitique? Celle des Etats (Lafont R., 1993)? Celle des nations (Perrochon D., 1991)? Celle des Etats-nations? Voilà des termes au contenu sémantique fort imprécis et fort contesté. Les points de vue *etic* et *emic* s'entrechoquent à souhait sur ces concepts forts ambigus, que tout le monde utilise, mais que chacun met dans un contexte référentiel différent. Les conférences internationales en sont souvent une triste illustration, tant au niveau des décisions qui sont prises — ou imposées — que des applications — souvent non respectées — qui en découlent...

## 2. La dimension territoriale de concepts ambigus

### 2.1. Ambiguïté et évolution des concepts d',,Etat" et de ,,nation"

Le principal organisme mondial où les *Etats* peuvent s'exprimer s'appelle: Organisation des *nations* unies (ONU). Est-ce à dire qu'il y a identité entre ,,Etat" et ,,nation"? Que les premiers sont l'expression des seconds? L'approche de ces concepts révèle quelques surprises, quand on se rend compte que les uns sont définis *par* les autres et que l'on hésite pas à utiliser une terminologie médiane dont le contenu sémantique se rapporte à la fois aux uns *et* aux autres. Ainsi, sans entrer dans des nuances plus spécifiques ou plus subjectives, liées à des approches plus dogmatiques, le concept d',,Etat" peut se rapporter à:
— une ,,forme de gouvernement, un régime politique et social" (démocratie, monarchie, dictature, tyrannie...);
— une ,,autorité souveraine s'exerçant sur l'ensemble d'un peuple et d'un territoire déterminés". Le concept de ,,peuple" n'est pas univoque, mais il sert de support pour définir celui de l'Etat;
— l',,ensemble des services généraux d'une Nation" (Etat centralisé ou décentralisé, le gouvernement, l'aspect politique des relations entre les différents domaines du pouvoir; en fait la nature du régime). Même remarque quant à l'ambiguïté avec, en plus, l'identification implicite des concepts de ,,nation" et de ,,peuple";
— un ,,groupement humain fixé sur un territoire déterminé, soumis à une même autorité et pouvant être considéré comme une personne

morale". On se réfère implicitement aux concepts de „nation", de „pays", de „puissance".

La même approche générale pour le concept de „nation" révèle la même ambiguïté et la même démarche d'explication de l'un par l'autre. En fait, une nation est:

— un „groupement d'hommes auxquels on suppose une origine commune". On implique donc la notion de race, de groupe ethnique; on songe aussi à la génétique des populations qui permet maintenant de les déterminer de façon génotypique et plus seulement phénotypique comme auparavant;

— un „groupe humain, généralement assez vaste, qui se caractérise par la conscience de son unité et la volonté de vivre en commun". Il s'agit donc d'un groupe ethnique et/ou culturel identifié à ce que l'on appelle couramment un peuple;

— un „groupe humain constituant une communauté politique, établie sur un territoire défini ou un ensemble de territoires définis, et personnifiée par une autorité souveraine". Le peuple est cette fois-ci inscrit dans un espace territorial, il forme donc un pays, une puissance, un Etat;

— l'„ensemble des individus qui composent ce groupe". Est-ce à dire qu'il n'y a qu'un peuple, une nation par Etat? La Déclaration des droits de l'homme ne dit-elle pas que „Le principe de toute souveraineté réside essentiellement dans la Nation"? Le préambule de la Charte des Nations unies confirme en précisant: „Nous, peuples des Nations unies, résolus à..." (Prelot M., 1980).

En fait, il y a une interpénétration des notions de „Nation", „peuple", „Etat", voire même une identification de ces notions, alors que les concepts ne sont pas identiques... Sur cette base déjà non univoque, — et permettant donc toutes les interprétations (honnêtes ou non) lors des tractations internationales! —, viennent se greffer les dimensions politiques et socio-culturelles spécifiques de chacun, liées aux choix de société, acceptés démocratiquement ou imposés selon les cas, ainsi que les dimensions économiques (les marxistes diraient les „dominations" économiques) plus ou moins déguisées menant au pouvoir politique (Bihr A., 1992; Burdeau G., 1980b; Chesneaux J., 1981; Chesneaux J., 1982; De Rougemont D., 1974; Leca J., 1991; Rodinson M., 1980; Sicard E., 1980; Timbal P.-C. & Burdeau G., 1980). La base équivoque, complétée d'éléments complexes et hétérogènes, ne pouvait que conduire à des *relations* internationales qui se sont vite muées en *tensions* internationales (Guillemain B., 1984; Labaki G.T., 1991).

## 2.2. „Etats-nations" ou „Etats légitimes"?

Depuis la Révolution française, il y a eu une identification des concepts de „nation" et de „peuple", doublée d'un glissement progressif de la notion historique de „nation" à celle plus ou moins scientifique de „race". L'historien français J. de Bainville (fin XIXe-début XXe siècle) ne disait-il pas: „Le *peuple* français est mieux qu'une *race*, c'est une *nation*"? Cette identification entre „nation" et „peuple" a pu se faire grâce à l'établissement d'un pouvoir central qui s'est „imposé" „légalement" par la force à l'ensemble d'un territoire considéré comme „légitime". Ce mouvement centrifuge du centre vers la périphérie est caractéristique des nationalismes qui se sont développés tout au cours du XIXe siècle en Europe occidentale, centrale et orientale („Le fait national en questions" [dossier], 1991).

Les interprétations des principes philosophiques de le Révolution française se sont rapidement révélées divergentes dès qu'on a voulu les appliquer aux souverainetés nationales (Akoun A., 1993; Burdeau G., 1980a; Ferry L. & Pisier Kouchner E., 1984; Jacques A., 1981; Lavau G., 1988; Lavigne P., 1980). Car, en fait, quelles sont les normes et les critères de la légalité d'un pouvoir établi, — surtout s'il l'est par la force — , et de la légitimisation d'un territoire administré:

a) le droit des peuples à disposer d'eux-mêmes, selon le principe de la libre détermination des peuples, et donc le respect de la volonté des Nations?

b) le droit des Etats(-nations?) à annexer des régions présentant avec eux des affinités ethniques, linguistiques, religieuses...?

Le second principe a été plus largement utilisé que le premier quand on analyse la politique expansionniste du monde occidental, tant au niveau mondial qu'au niveau européen. Les impérialismes en Europe (Autriche-Hongrie et Empire ottoman, pour ne prendre que les derniers en date ayant conduit à la situation actuelle) ou dans le monde (les politiques coloniales et néocolonialistes) sont très éloquents de ce point de vue. Un simple coup d'œil sur la carte des tracés frontaliers est parfois plus porteur d'informations qu'une longue analyse justificative qui se perd dans des arguties et des argumentations parfois fort spécieuses.

En ramenant la focale au niveau européen, on voit clairement que:

a) la plupart des „Etats" actuels ne sont plus — ou n'ont jamais étédes Etats-nations au sens où l'entendaient les philosophes, car le principe de la libre détermination des „Nations" n'a pratiquement jamais été respecté dans les faits;

b) de nombreux „Etats" sont multinationaux — de droit ou de fait — et de nombreuses „nations" n'ont, par conséquent, pas de souveraineté politique sur le plan international. Ces „nations sans Etat" peuvent se retrouver dans des Etats centralisés ou non, unitaires ou fédérés. Ce seront autant de situations spécifiques, importantes du point de vue *emic* de ces minorités culturelles, qui permettront de comprendre les motivations des agissements de ces populations qui, de toute façon, sont marginalisées par l'Etat qui représente le pouvoir politique et/ou économique (Badie B., 1993; Chaliand G., 1986; Girardet R., 1980). Tout est question de nuances et de degrés dans les droits accordés aux „minorités", ou de celles qui sont considérées comme telles.

Les Albanais de Macédoine sont minoritaires dans la République du même nom, mais les Albanais du Kosovo sont-ils minoritaires? Par rapport à quoi? A la Serbie à laquelle on les a rattachés de force maintenant ou au Kosovo auquel on avait accordé une large autonomie précédemment? Peut-on considérer comme minoritaires, — et les traiter comme des allogènes —, des populations qui sont sur leurs territoires d'origine? Au point de ne leur accorder aucun droit, pas même celui de pouvoir bénéficier d'un enseignement dans sa langue maternelle, pour ne rien dire des aspects socio-politiques et socio-économiques...

Jusqu'à quel point faut-il tenir compte des identités „ethnico-culturalo-nationales" dans la création des Etats? Est-ce une simple question numérique? Dans ce cas comment expliquer l'existence de pays comme Monaco, Andorre, Saint-Marin, Malte, le Liechtenstein ou le Luxembourg? Pourquoi Malte et pas la Corse ou la Sardaigne?

Est-ce une question de grandeur de territoire, de superficie? On pourrait reprendre les mêmes exemples! Mais on est quand-même parvenu à laisser scinder l'île de Chypre en deux Etats, dont l'un n'est théoriquement toujours pas reconnu (sauf par la Turquie, à laquelle il est fédéré). La „République cypriote turque" existe *de facto* depuis février 1975 et la ligne de démarcation, matérialisée sur le terrain par des clôtures électrifiées et un mur coupant la ville de Nicosie en deux secteurs, la ligne verte ou ligne Attila est surveillée depuis pratiquement vingt ans par les troupes de l'ONU! Est-ce l'exemple de ce que l'on veut pour régler les problèmes de l'ex-Yougoslavie?

Est-ce une question de continuité territoriale? Et nous voilà revenus au concept-clef de territoire! Car la notion de territoire n'est pas simplement juridique, sociale ou culturelle; elle implique quasi toujours une dimension affective, une appropriation de l'espace pour en faire une appartenance collective. En fait, il ne peut pas y avoir de nation sans territoire. Mais que reconnaît-on au niveau international? Des Etats, donc des espaces territoriaux, qui sont censés être l'expression des nations. Chaque nation devrait donc pouvoir bénéficier d'un territoire pour être reconnue, ou pouvoir s'exprimer par l'Etat dans lequel elle se trouve.

## 2.3. Pertinence de la notion de „territoire"

La réalité est bien différente... et de nombreuses „nations sans Etat" ne peuvent passer par le canal des représentants officiels de leur Etat. La création de l'„Organisation des peuples et des nations non représentés" (UNPO), en 1991, n'est pas étrangère à cette situation internationale ambiguë qui favorise le *statu quo* des „Etats" qui agissent au détriment des „nations" qui les constituent (Chartier C., 1991 & 1993). Cette organisation se présente comme une ONU alternative; elle est construite selon le même modèle, pour permettre aux différentes minorités marginalisées (régions, enclaves, ethnies, minorités culturelles) de faire entendre leurs voix et leurs besoins auprès des Etats. Cette institution légitime veut réduire les tentations de recourir à la violence chaque fois qu'il y a des doléances à exprimer par ces minorités, mais qu'il n'y a, en fait, pas d'endroit pour les exprimer officiellement...

De plus, vu cette réalité ambiguë et ambivalente, dans quelle mesure la notion de „territoire", délimité par des frontières, — juridiquement reconnues ou pas sur le plan international —, est-elle pertinente comme expression d'une nation ou d'un groupe ethnique et culturel déterminé? Il n'y a pas toujours un territoire donné par groupe; les territoires ne sont pas nécessairement d'un seul tenant; il existe même des cas extrêmes où des groupes ethniques n'ont pas de territoire du tout!

## 2.3.1. Un territoire donné par groupe?

Tous les groupes ethniques et culturels (donc aussi les nations) n'occupent pas nécessairement un territoire donné. Il peut y avoir exploitation diversifiée et spécifique des mêmes niches écologiques, — à plus forte raison de niches écologiques différentes sur le même territoire — , par des groupes ethniques et/ou culturels différents. Cette notion d'„ajustement écologique", mise en évidence par certains anthropologues culturels (Barth F., 1969), souligne des cas de superposition, de recouvrement total ou partiel, de territoires exploités par des groupes différents. La plupart des études ont porté sur des cas de régions non occidentales, mettant en présence des peuples aux habitudes culturelles et culturales différentes, tels des petits éleveurs ou des pasteurs nomades exploitant des régions de montagne d'altitudes différentes, alors que le fond des plaines étaient valorisés par des agriculteurs. La référence classique (Barth F., 1956) fait état des Kohistani, des Gujjars et des Pathans (= Pashtuns) au Pakistan septentrional.

Le cas de la Transylvanie est tout à fait semblable. Lorsque les populations magyares sont arrivées dans un pays qui leur paraissait vide (nous n'entrons pas ici dans le débat de l'antériorité ou non de l'occupation de ces terres par les Roumains, la question est secondaire dans ce contexte-ci), elles ont d'abord occupé les bassins alluvionnaires de ces hauts plateaux, laissant les zones des collines et des montagnes aux éleveurs transhumants, à l'ancienne populat on romanisée. Les Slaves de la péninsule balkanique appelaient ces populations les „Vlahs", soit les Valaques. Ce terme est resté collé à la peau de ce peuple migrateur, — dont les origines précises sont fortement discutées (les descendants des Daco-romains?) mais là n'est pas le problème —, prenant le sens de „barbare" [], c'est-à-dire d'étranger, celui qui n'est pas comme nous, avec toute la connotation négative qui peut parfois être mise dans ce concept. Le terme de „rumani" n'était pas utilisé à l'époque pour qualifier un peuple, mais bien un statut social de serf (Ruegg F., 1991: 38). A partir de ce moment, — et quoi qu'il se soit passé avant —, on assiste bien à une occupation diversifiée d'un même territoire, au même moment, mais à des endroits différents, par des populations d'origines différentes (Köpeczi B. (éd.), 1989: 172, cf. carte no 1). La localisation spécifique de cette zone tampon va la confiner dans une fonction de marche frontière, tour à tour sous l'influence des Hongrois et/ou des Autrichiens, suivant les périodes

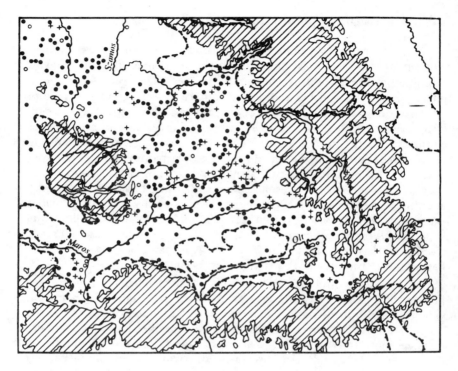

**Carte 1.** *Localités hongroises en Transylvanie au milieu du XIIIe siècle d'après les noms de lieu,* in: Köpeczi B. (èd.), 1989

envisagées, ou des Turcs ottomans, avant de passer sous la juridiction des Roumains. A chaque période, l'ensemble de la population transylvaine va chaque fois se retrouver dans une situation „sociale" de minoritaire et de marginalisée par rapport au pouvoir en place; seule une minorité „sociale" de privilégiés va bénéficier du système du moment, qu'elle soit roumaine ou hongroise. C'est pourquoi il est utopique d'imaginer pouvoir résoudre la question de Transylvanie de façon dichotomique et centralisatrice. Du fait qu'il n'y a pas „un" territoire donné par groupe, il se posera toujours la question d'une minorité „ethnique", — différente par la langue, la religion, la culture — qui se sentira, à tort ou à raison, marginalisée par rapport au pouvoir et brimée dans ses droits les plus fondamentaux, tant que ces droits ne seront pas garantis par une forme d'autonomie à préciser de commun accord, tant au point de vue du contenu que du degré.

## 2.3.2. Un territoire d'un seul tenant?

La question de la pertinence de la notion de „territoire" comme expression d'un peuple ou d'une nation se pose aussi quand les tracés frontaliers attribués à un Etat le subdivisent en un certain nombre d'enclaves, c'est-à-dire de territoires non contigus dépendant d'une région centrale. Sans entrer dans le jeu des territoires insulaires, incorporés ou dépendants d'une zone centrale, qui relèvent plus d'une situation coloniale *de facto*, sinon *de jure*, il n'y a que 14 Etats au monde qui ont des territoires enclavés dans d'autres pays (On n'envisage pas ici les subdivisions administratives au niveau infranational). L'Histoire permet, bien sûr, de mettre les causes en évidence dans chaque cas. Et si ces héritages historiques relèvent parfois plus de survivances „folkloriques" qui font partie du paysage, sans porter à conséquence, — si ce n'est sous l'angle économique et touristique —, pour d'autres, au contraire, ils sont source de bon nombre de difficultés. En Europe, rappelons pour mémoire l'enclave allemande de Büsingen en Suisse (le cas de Berlin, enclave ouest-allemande en République démocratique allemande était plus connu avant la réunification!), ou l'enclave italienne de Campione en Suisse toujours; l'enclave espagnole de Llivia en France; les enclaves belges de Baarle-Hertog aux Pays-Bas et, réciproquement, des enclaves inhabitées néerlandaises en territoire belge. Si les précédentes ne posent pas de problème, par contre, l'enclave britannique de Gibraltar en Espagne, ou les enclaves espagnoles de Ceuta et Mellilla au Maroc, ou l'enclave angolaise de Cabinda entre le Zaïre et le Congo, ou encore l'enclave sud-africaine de Waalvis Baai (Walfish Bay) en Namibie posent problèmes parfois assez complexes.

Ces quelques exemples ont tous en commun de trouver leurs causes dans le passé. Mais que dire d'une logique qui préconiserait une compartimentation enclavée pour former de nouveaux territoires, pour être à la base de nouveaux Etats? Est-ce crédible? Est-ce honnête? Est-ce tout simplement viable? En République d'Afrique du Sud, c'est la base théorique qui a prévalu pour la création des 10 Bantoustans à l'époque de la politique de l'apartheid (cf. carte no 2). Les chiffres officiels de

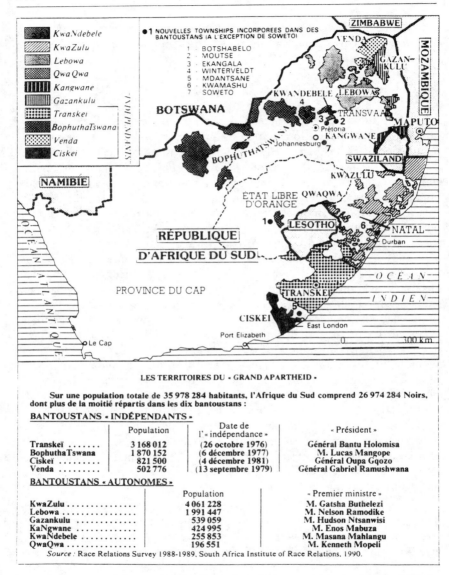

**LES TERRITOIRES DU « GRAND APARTHEID »**

Sur une population totale de 35 978 284 habitants, l'Afrique du Sud comprend 26 974 284 Noirs, dont plus de la moitié répartis dans les dix bantoustans :

**BANTOUSTANS « INDÉPENDANTS »**

|              | Population  | Date de l'« indépendance » | « Président »              |
| ------------ | ----------- | -------------------------- | -------------------------- |
| Transkeï     | 3 168 012   | (26 octobre 1976)          | Général Bantu Holomisa     |
| BophuthaTswana | 1 870 152 | (6 décembre 1977)          | M. Lucas Mangope           |
| Ciskeï       | 821 500     | (4 décembre 1981)          | Général Oupa Gqozo         |
| Venda        | 502 776     | (13 septembre 1979)        | Général Gabriel Ramushwana |

**BANTOUSTANS « AUTONOMES »**

|             | Population | « Premier ministre »   |
| ----------- | --------- | ---------------------- |
| KwaZulu     | 4 061 228 | M. Gatsha Buthelezi    |
| Lebowa      | 1 991 447 | M. Nelson Ramodike     |
| Gazankulu   | 539 059   | M. Hudson Ntsanwisi    |
| KaNgwane    | 424 995   | M. Enos Mabuza         |
| KwaNdebele  | 255 853   | M. Masana Mahlangu     |
| QwaQwa      | 196 551   | M. Kenneth Mopeli      |

*Source :* Race Relations Survey 1988-1989, South Africa Institute of Race Relations, 1990.

**Carte 2.** *Un modèle en voie de dispartion: la compartimentation territoriale en enclaves non contiguës* dans: Le Monde diplomatique, septembre 1990

l'Etat prévoyaient la création de 10 „Homelands", formés de 113 enclaves non contiguës, couvrant 13% du territoire de la RSA. La politique de „consolidation" finale aurait dû permettre d'arriver à 39 enclaves, alors qu'il y en avait 276 en 1970! Mais cette même politique enlevait aux populations africaines les enclaves utiles au point de vue économique pour leur en attribuer d'autres, complètement stériles au point de vue géologique! La carte du Bophuthatswana („Bophuthatswana", 1977: 6–7) montre le „jeu" des échanges de terres enclavées avant d'accorder l'indépendance au futur Homeland, dès qu'on la compare à une carte géologique détaillée de la région. Pourtant ce bantoustan a obtenu son „indépendance" sur une base ethnique, le 6 décembre 1977: plus de 40.000 km$^2$ divisés en six enclaves, l'ensemble du nouveau pays étant entièrement enclavé en Afrique du Sud. Ce pays, comme les quelques Homelands qui ont accepté l'indépendance, n'a été reconnu par personne sur le plan international, sauf par l'Afrique du Sud! Certains Bantoustans ont même refusé d'accéder à l'indépendance, — comme le Kwandebele —, se rendant bien compte de l'inviabilité du nouvel „Etat" proposé (Bole-Richard M., 1986).

Cette politique qui a été condamnée par tout le monde sur plan international, qui n'est même plus appliquée en Afrique du Sud depuis le début du démantèlement de la politique de l'apartheid, cette politique-là est celle que la communauté internationale veut imposer à la Bosnie-Herzégovine depuis plus d'un an! Qu'est-ce que le plan Vance-Owen, sinon une compartimentation en zones ethniques séparées et enclavées les unes dans les autres, d'une région qui était habitée par des populations, — faut-il dire des „peuples" ou des „nations"? — , qui ont vécu ensemble depuis plusieurs siècles (*La Libre Belgique*, Bruxelles, 19–25 janvier 1993; Roux M., 1991: 29, cf. carte no 3)? Leur cohabitation a développé une logique d'interrelations culturelles et religieuses spécifiques qui faisait la fierté de cette région de tolérance, et particulièrement de la capitale Sarajevo. Les différences ne pouvaient être que religieuses puisque, contrairement à ce que disent actuellement les hyper-nationalistes de tout poil, qu'ils soient Serbes ou Croates, ces gens ont la même origine ethnique, ils parlent tous la même langue de base dans des formes dialectales (Garde P., 1980; Garde P., 1992: 30, cf. carte no 4). Leur rattachement, sous des formes diverses, aux grands Empires multinationaux des siècles passés ont fait que les Croates sont essentiellement catholiques (influence autrichienne et surtout hongroise),

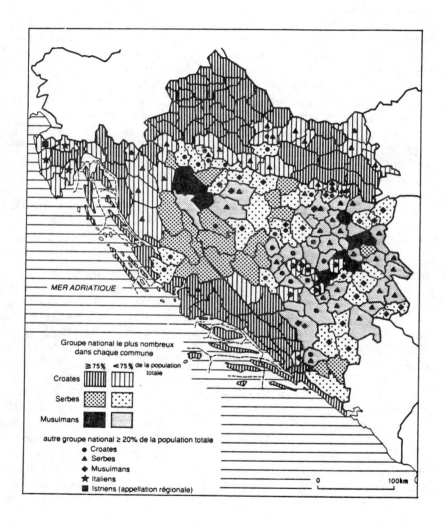

**Carte 3.** *Diversité de la composition ethnique de la Bosnie-Herzégovine et de la Croatie,* dans: Roux M., 1991

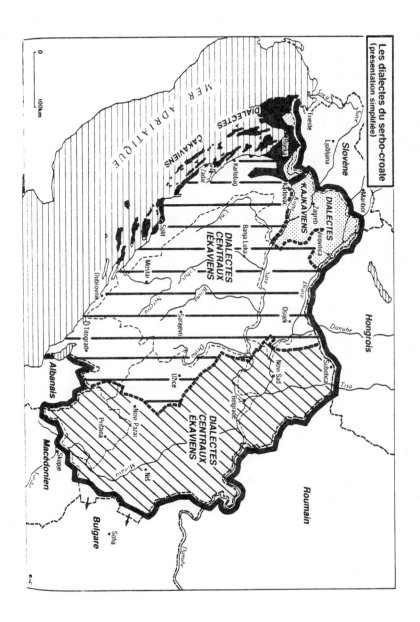

**Carte 4.** *Le fond linguistique commun de la Bosnie-Herzégovine et de la Croatie, dans: Roux M., 1991*

que les Serbes sont plutôt orthodoxes (ils sont parvenus à négocier leur spécificité religieuse, même lorsqu'ils étaient sous l'influence ottomane), alors que les Bosniaques (en dehors des zones d'influence des grands voisins et moins structurés) ont davantage subi la pression des Turcs et se sont progressivement convertis à l'islam par obligation, par réflexe de survie (Garde P., 1992: 30, cf. carte No 5). Avant le développement des nationalismes exacerbés, attisés pour des raisons politiciennes, les populations de Bosnie-Herzégovine étaient parvenues à tisser une vie de relations, basée sur la tolérance et le respect des autres. Le nombre élevé de mariages „mixtes" est suffisamment révélateur de cet esprit d'ouverture. Et c'est pour ce même esprit que se battent encore, côte à côte, des Serbes, des Croates et des Musulmans (avec un M majuscule, pour représenter la „nationalité") à Sarajevo, pour tenter vainement de préserver cet acquis et cette richesse. Vu le degré de compréhension (?) et d'engagement (?) de la communauté internationale, il risque fort d'arriver prochainement à la ville ouverte de Sarajevo (et par le fait même à toute la Bosnie-Herzégovine) ce qui s'est produit à Tolède en 1453: la suppression par la force d'une tolérance et d'une ouverture d'esprit qui dérange tous les partisans de régimes forts, de régimes „purs", quels que soient les motivations qui les animent...

Le plan Vance-Owen, même s'il est accepté (imposé) un jour, — dans les faits et non sur le papier —, ne permettra jamais de résoudre les problèmes parce qu'on veut créer des régions, qui deviendront/deviendraient des „Etats", probablement rattachés à des ensembles extérieurs plus grands; mais on veut les créer sur des bases dites „ethniques". On renforce donc la différence des uns et des autres, en créant tous les problèmes humains auxquels on assiste actuellement, en acceptant l'innommable dans le domaine de tous les excès et en ne faisant rien de façon active pour les faire cesser, mais en obligeant les gens à être interdépendants les uns des autres par la simple disposition des territoires enclavés. Et la communauté internationale ose proposer cela comme un „plan de paix"? Reposons les questions de tout-à-l'heure: Est-ce sérieux? Est-ce honnête? Est-ce viable?

La relecture du plan donnait encore davantage de satisfaction aux artisans de la politique du fait accompli et davantage de raisons d'espérer aux partisans de la légalisation de la politique de la violence. La notion même de „couloirs démilitarisés" n'est pas viable au niveau de la sécurité et ne sera par conséquent pas acceptée par ceux qui ont les moyens de

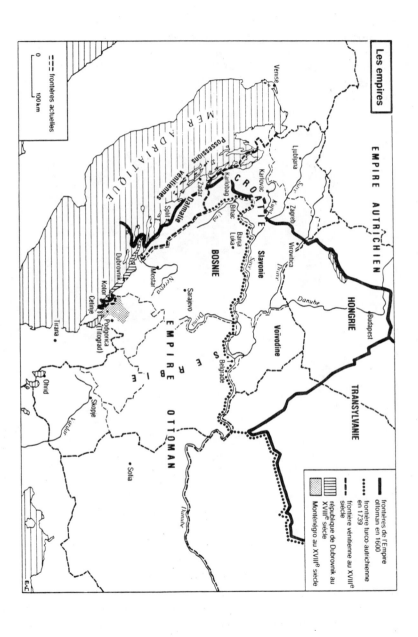

**Carte 5.** *Les limites des grands Empires passés,* dans: Garde P., 1992

les élargir pour en faire de véritables corridors de jonction... au détriment des autres, et particulièrement des Bosniaques (c'est-à-dire ceux qui ne se sont pas ralliés aux Républiques serbes ou croates auto proclamées) qui ne peuvent pas se défendre, puisque la même communauté internationale leur a imposé un embargo sur les armes (Dizdarevic S., 1993).

**Carte 6.** *Les „zones de sécurité" déclarées telles par l'ONU,* dans: Le Monde, Paris, 25 mai 1993

De discussion en discussion, de conférence en conférence, d'attentisme en attentisme, on en est arrivé à une situation telle que les Bosniaques ne contrôlent plus que quelques enclaves, dont le nombre et la grandeur diminuent de jour en jour puisqu'elles sont toujours sous le feu nourri des milices serbes. Les troupes de l'ONU assistent, dénombrent mais n'interviennent pas puisqu'elles ne sont pas mandatées pour le faire.

Alors qu'on articule toujours comme but ultime la mise en pratique du plan Vance-Owen, — auquel plus personne ne croit, ni les „spectateurs", ni les acteurs —, les Serbes et les Croates progressent sur le terrain, en pratiquant toujours la même logique de „purification ethnique", alors que les Bosniaques en sont réduits à quitter les régions dans lesquelles ils vivaient et à être confinés dans ce qu'on a appelé des „zones de sécurité" (*Le Monde*, Paris, 25 mai 1993, carte no 6). Elles ont été fixées au nombre de six (Tuzla, Srebrenica, Zepa, Gorazde, Sarajevo et Bihac) et elles ne sont même pas défendues puisque les Serbes, contrairement à leurs engagements, n'en permettent pas l'accès aux convois humanitaires et continuent à les assiéger pour en chasser leurs habitants. Le monde humanitaire a dû pallier le manque de clairvoyance et d'engagement du monde politique: l'humanitaire comme cible, comme bouc émissaire, comme alibi!... Les Bosniaques qui formaient le groupe humain majoritaire, 44% de la population de leur „Etat", avant le début des hostilités ont dû émigrer en masse et ne contrôlent plus que 10 à 15 % de la Bosnie-Herzégovine. Les Serbes qui formaient 31% de la population sont devenus le groupe majoritaire, vu les méthodes utilisées, et contrôlent effectivement 65 à 70% du pays. Autant dire qu'il y a peu de chances pour qu'ils restituent les territoires qu'ils occupent illégalement selon le plan Vance-Owen et qu'ils sont censés rendre (toute la partie occidentale de la province „musulmane" No 1 de Bihac, la province „croato-musulmane" No 3, la quasi totalité de la province „musulmane" No 5 de Tuzla et pratiquement la moitié de la province „musulmane" No 9 de Zenica). Quant aux Croates de Bosnie, ils formaient 17% de la population; en ayant appliqué, finalement, la même politique que les Serbes, mais de façon plus discrète au début, ils se sont aussi forgé un territoire homogène couvrant 20 à 25% de la superficie de la Bosnie-Herzégovine. Les conflits avec les Serbes et les Bosniaques leur ont pratiquement fait perdre la province „croato-musulmane" No 3, par contre ils ont pratiquement chassé les „Musulmans" de la province No 10 qui leur avait été conjointement attribuée par le même plan Vance-Owen.

Attendons encore un peu et le problème des enclaves ne se posera plus! Les Serbes et les Croates se seront partagés la Bosnie-Herzégovine et auront créé des camps de réfugiés „palestiniens" pour les populations bosniaques, musulmanes. Et la communauté internationale s'étonnera d'avoir créé un nouveau foyer de tensions permanentes, non seulement sur base ethnique mais coloré d'intégrisme religieux... Où est le sérieux?

Où est l'honnêteté? L'inviabilité des territoires morcelés aura été prouvée, une nouvelle fois, avec la caution internationale.

### 2.3.3. Pas de territoire du tout?

Et que dire de la pertinence de la notion de „territoire" quand il n'y a pas de territoire du tout? Il existe certains groupes ethniques et culturels qui n'ont pas de territoire du tout, au sens juridique. Est-ce la raison pour laquelle on leur refuse même l'appellation de „nation" et qu'on les traite avec toute la condescendance et le mépris voulus, liés à la distanciation maximum de l'altérité? Le cas les plus frappant de populations ayant une conscience interne très forte de leur identité propre est probablement celui qui est vécu par les „nomades de la mer". Ils subissent tous une discrimination raciale très forte dans les pays auxquels ils sont rattachés. Cette dernière expression est d'ailleurs à prendre au sens propre, puisqu'ils n'ont, en fait, pas accès à la partie continentale de ces Etats. Ils vivent sur des habitats lacustres au large des côtes ou sur leurs embarcations, voyageant constamment entre des centaines d'îles éparpillées sur leurs „territoires" marins, c'est-à-dire les zones qu'ils sillonnent régulièrement à la bonne saison. Les Moken nomadisent au large de l'archipel des Mergui, au sud-ouest de la Birmanie; les Bagiaos ou Bajau, dans l'archipel des Sulu, au sud-ouest des Philippines; les Vezo, entre les îles coralliennes, au sud-ouest des côtes de Madagascar.

En Europe centrale et orientale, la même situation de nomadisme généralisé affecte les communautés tsiganes, qui ne sont pourtant ni pasteurs, ni conquérants Liegeois J.-P., 1987). On retrouve la même situation d'éparpillement sur des territoires dont ils sont régulièrement chassés ou sur lesquels ils sont régulièrement confrontés à des situations conflictuelles avec les populations indigènes. La même situation d'une conscience *emic* très forte de leur identité propre, — à un point tel qu'ils se considèrent comme un peuple, les „Rom" par opposition aux „Gadje" —, identité renforcée par la distanciation maximum dans laquelle on les maintient partout. Que l'on songe simplement aux appellations *etic* qui leur sont données: un des dialectes *vlach* (venant de Valachie, en Roumanie), le *romani*, a donné Romanichel, qui devient „manouche", avec connotation péjorative en français, alors qu'il s'agit du nom d'un des dialectes non *vlach*, fortement influencé par l'allemand (De Vaux De Foletier F., 1980).

Ces populations nomades dérangent, déjà par le simple fait de leurs déplacements constants (auxquels ils sont d'ailleurs contraints dans la plupart des cas), parce qu'ils ont un mode de vie différent de celui des sédentaires qui les contrôlent ou qui tentent de le faire (Rinderknecht K., 1973). Des tentatives d'intégration ont parfois été entreprises mais, généralement, ils sont l'objet de tous les mépris, de tous les rejets et de toutes les exploitations, y compris par les autorités officielles des pays dans lesquels ils séjournent. C'est en Europe centre-orientale qu'ils sont les plus nombreux, même si leur nombre ne peut pas être évalué avec précision: quelque 150.000 en Bulgarie, 180.000 en ex-Yougoslavie, plus de 300.000 en Tchéco-Slovaquie ainsi qu'en Hongrie, probablement 1.000.000 en Roumanie (surtout en Valachie). Ils forment des minorités importantes qui occasionnent beaucoup de problèmes aux autorités hongroises et roumaines qui, en essayant de les sédentariser, ont accru un prolétariat misérable, lui-même à la base d'un phénomène de „bidonvillisation" accentuée dans ces pays. Les bouleversements récents de l'ex-Europe de l'Est, — ayant amené une ouverture des frontières à l'Est parallèlement à une „fermeture" renforcée des frontières à l'Ouest — , ont mis en évidence le fait de les voir apparaître de plus en plus comme boucs émissaires, tant à l'Est qu'à l'Ouest, dès que des difficultés économiques ou politiques deviennent critiques pour les gouvernements en place. N'ayant pas de territoire, ils n'ont donc pas d'Etat. Ils se considèrent comme une „nation" (point de vue *emic*); mais une „nation sans Etat" n'a aucune reconnaissance juridique. Dans un nouvel *Atlas des Peuples d'Europe centrale*, on ne leur accorde même pas le statut de „peuple", mais celui de „minorité" (point de vue *etic*) (Sellier A. & J:, 1991:48). Les Tsiganes sont donc ballottés à travers l'Europe (Reyniers A., 1993), expulsés par centaines ou par milliers des pays de l'Ouest (Auffray A., 1993), en arrivent même à demander l'asile... en Roumanie (Gauriat V., 1993). Ils tentent surtout de s'organiser en demandant un „Programme européen sur les Rom" pour éliminer les préjugés existant à leur encontre et tenter de limiter les manifestations de violence, d'extrémisme et de xénophobie auxquelles ils doivent faire face quotidiennement, en plus des mauvaises conditions de vie „habituelles" dont ils sont l'objet: analphabétisme, niveau d'éducation insuffisant, chômage et marginalisation systématique.

## 2.4. Ambiguïté de la représentation cartographique

La pertinence de la notion de „territoire" comme base de l'expression et de la reconnaissance des „Etats-nations" montre toute l'ambiguïté de la représentation cartographique. A la confusion des notions s'ajoute leur utilisation infondée et/ou indifférente par les interlocuteurs. Il ne s'agit pas de faire des jeux de mots mais, si les concepts de „groupe ethnique", „groupe culturel", „nation", „peuple" ne sont pas synonymes, ceux de „milieu", „espace", „territoire", „pays", „région", „Etat" ne le sont pas davantage. Des confusions sémantiques graves, — parfois entretenues de façon intentionnelle —, empêchent tout dialogue vrai et constructif par l'utilisation abusive et volontairement restrictive de ces mêmes termes aux contours maintenus ambigus. Que dire alors de leur traduction cartographique, je ferais mieux de dire de leur transposition cartographique!...

Un ouvrage au titre provocateur a eu un retentissement célèbre il y a quelques années: *La géographie, ça sert, d'abord, à faire la guerre* (Lacoste Y., 1976). Il voulait montrer que, derrière une certaine myopie et un somnambulisme certain, la géographie académique et scolaire était coupée de la réalité pratique. Les carences épistémologiques de la géographie universitaire et l'absence de polémique entre géographes cachaient les potentialités de cette discipline qui porte en elle les armes redoutables de la prise de conscience de la réalité spatiale. Savoir penser l'espace pour savoir s'y organiser engendre inévitablement la confrontation des rapports de force, de points de vues différents, des intérêts divergents qui doivent trouver un terrain d'entente. La géographie, vue sous cet angle — et indépendamment de tout contexte philosophique qui peut se surajouter —, peut se révéler une force puissante, car elle saisit dans le paysage l'impact de l'homme sur son milieu: elle observe, décrit et analyse son action. Et la représentation de cette réalité par la cartographie, son „arme" principale, apporte le point d'orgue à ce processus d'„objectivation", par la fixation et la visualisation de cette même réalité spatiale.

Le danger ne tient pas en la carte elle-même (sauf s'il s'agit de véritable manipulation) mais dans le fait qu'on ne prend pas toujours conscience de la finalité poursuivie par le cartographe, ou qu'on n'a pas les éléments de contexte pour y arriver. Une carte n'est jamais neutre, innocente en ce sens qu'elle s'inscrit toujours dans un contexte, qu'il faut connaître pour pouvoir décoder les informations fournies par le document. L'échelle est aussi importante: à un changement d'échelle peut correspondre un changement de point de vue, lié la quantité d'informations objectives, permises par le procédé de la généralisation. Une place plus restreinte obligera à sélectionner les informations. En fonction de quels critères? Qui va sélectionner? Pour s'adresser à qui? Dans quel(s) but(s)?

## 2.4.1. Homogénéité ou hétérogénéité d'un territoire?

Une homogénéité factice peut très bien cacher une réelle hétérogénéité. Dans les atlas courants, une carte d'ensemble de l'ex-Yougoslavie ne révèle pas *ipso facto* sa structure fédérale; pas plus que la mise en évidence de ses frontières administratives limitées aux six Républiques. L'apparition des deux Régions autonomes de la Voivodine et du Kosovo (aujourd'hui supprimées), à l'intérieur de la Serbie, ne permettent pas de savoir les raisons de ces particularismes, même si on se doute qu'il doit s'agir de la reconnaissance de certaines minorités (carte: *Le Monde*, Paris, 11 juillet 1991). Mais la même carte administrative ne laisse pas supposer que d'autres minorités existent, qui ne sont pas reconnues (des Roumains en Voivodine), ou que ces mêmes minorités se trouvent aussi dans d'autres Républiques sans avoir une reconnaissance régionale (des Albanais en Macédoine ou au Montenegro). Quels sont les atlas, avant les conflits actuels, qui signalaient qu'il y a d'importantes minorités serbes en Croatie, que la Bosnie-Herzégovine n'est pas une région de peuplement homogène musulmane, mais comporte d'importantes minorités croates et serbes? Une carte présentant les diverses composantes ethniques, religieuses, linguistiques était rarissime ou était tellement globalisante que la plupart des nuances disparaissaient par généralisation ou simplification abusive. Quelle connaissance, dans ces conditions, la population occidentale pouvait-elle avoir de ces réalités et de ces problèmes en puissance? Comment s'étonner, dès lors, de la force d'inertie extraordinaire de la communauté internationale pour entrer en matière pour dépasser l'événementiel de l'horreur quotidienne dans ce pays?

Il aura fallu attendre que le conflit soit déjà bien engagé pour voir apparaître des articles qui présentent ces cartes tant attendues,

(*chiffre de recensement de 1981*).

**Carte 7.** *La mosaïque des nationalités en ex-Yougoslavie,* dans: Le Monde, Paris, 20 mars 1991

dans des journaux (*Le Monde, Le Monde diplomatique, Le Nouveau Quotidien*: cf. bibliographie), dans des revues („Balkans et balkanisation" [Dossier], 1991, „La question serbe" [Dossier], 1992) ou dans des encyclopédies (*L'Etat du Monde, Encyclopœdia Universalis-Universalia*: cf. bibliographie), ainsi que dans certains ouvrages plus spécialisés (Garde P., 1992). Ces cartes n'étaient même pas trouvables dans les atlas nationaux des Républiques respectives, qu'ils soient géographiques (Dugacki Z. & Prelcec Z., 1975, Andelic M., Kurtovic P. & Bjeletic M., 1981 ou Mastilovic M. & Zivkovic M., 1981) ou historiques (Lucic J. & Dugacki Z., 1980 ou

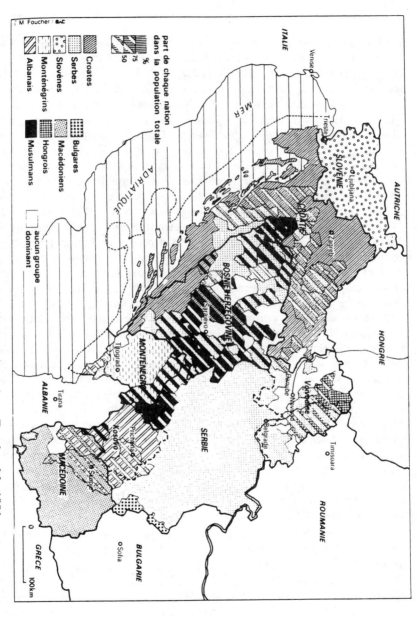

**Carte 8.** *La mosaïque des multinationale yougoslave,* dans: Foucher M., 1991

Légende:

part de chaque nation
dans la population totale
%
75
50

Croates
Serbes
Slovènes
Monténégrins
Albanais
Bulgares
Macédoniens
Hongrois
Musulmans

aucun groupe dominant

ITALIE
AUTRICHE
HONGRIE
ROUMANIE
BULGARIE
GRÈCE
ALBANIE

MER ADRIATIQUE

Venise
Trieste
Ljubljana
SLOVÉNIE
Zagreb
CROATIE
BOSNIE HERZEGOVINE
Sarajevo
MONTÉNÉGRO
Titograd
Kosovo
Priština
Skopje
MACÉDOINE
SERBIE
Belgrade
Vojvodine
Novi Sad
Danube
Timisoara
Sofia
Tirana

0        100km

Izdanje D., 1981), les renseignements humains d'ordre ethnique étant prudemment passés sous silence. Une carte (cf. carte no 7) telle que celle qui a paru dans *Le Monde* (20 mars 1991), représentant les douze nationalités principales du pays, aurait dû figurer dans tout ouvrage un tant soit peu sérieux parlant de l'ex-Yougoslavie, même si elle reste très générale (Elle avait déjà paru dans le même journal le 8 octobre 1987, bien avant tous les événements récents). Elle est beaucoup plus parlante que celles qui ont paru peu après dans *Le Monde* (11 septembre 1991, en noir et blanc) ou dans *Le Monde Diplomatique* (septembre 1991, en couleurs), même si ces dernières sont plus complètes et actualisées au niveau des informations chiffrées fournies. Pour comparaison, la carte de „la mosaïque multi-nationale yougoslave" de Foucher (Foucher M., 1991: 66, cf. carte no 8) présente peut-être une nationalité de moins (les Turcs en Macédoine), mais fournit par contre, par une nuance graphique complémentaire, la part de chaque nation dans la population du pays.

Des cartes montrant l'origine historique des limites des républiques et des ex-provinces autonomes (Roux M., 1991: 19), ou les frontières des anciens empires et des confins militaires (Garde P., 1992: 30, 179), permettent de mieux comprendre (ce qui ne veut pas dire cautionner) les raisons de l'occupation de certaines régions, ainsi que le contexte des revendications de certaines composantes de la population. Une carte de la composition nationale de la population pour chaque commune de la Croatie et de la Bosnie (Roux M., 1991: 29) ou une étude „anatomique" abondamment cartographiée de la Bosnie, débouchant sur les propositions de cantonisation faites par les Serbes, les Croates et les Musulmans (Bougarel X., 1992: 145, 146), mettent en évidence les bases complexes et les intérêts contradictoires dont il faut tenir compte pour un essai de solution acceptable pour toutes les parties. Fallait-il en arriver à un découpage de la Bosnie-Herzégovine en dix régions, basée sur une carte ethnique simplifiée, ne correspondant pas à la carte militaire sur le terrain (les trois cartes in: *La Libre Belgique*, sélection hebdomadaire du 19 au 25 janvier 1993)?

Ne revenons pas sur la question de la pertinence territoriale du plan „de paix" Vance-Owen. Mais du point de vue de l'hétérogénéité réelle, progressivement supprimée par le procédé de la globalisation et de la simplification, il est intéressant de voir ce qu'il en est advenu dans la présentation que la presse en a faite dans les jours qui ont suivi l'annonce de la première mouture de ce plan. La carte parue dans *Le Nouveau*

**Carte 9.** *Deux représentations cartographiques différentes du plan Vance-Owen pour la Bosnie-Herzégovine,* dans: Le Nouveau Quotidien, Lousanne, 3 janvier 1993

*Quotidien* (Lausanne, 3 janvier 1993, cf. carte no 9) parle de provinces à „nette majorité" de telle ou telle tendance, reprenant la situation de ces entités avant la guerre; celle parue dans *Le Monde* (Paris, 5 janvier 1993, cf. carte no 10) fait état de „provinces contrôlées" par les uns et par les autres; la carte de *La Libre Belgique* (Bruxelles, sélection hebdomadaire du 12 au 18 janvier 1993, cf. carte no 11) mentionne des „provinces à dominante" musulmane, serbe ou croate. Les provinces No 1, 5, 9 (musulmanes) et 2, 4, 6 (serbes) apparaissent de façon identique sur chacune des cartes, la carte du *Monde* précisant — hors carte — que la province serbe No 4 comporte une minorité musulmane. Mais

**Carte 10.** *Deux représentations cartographiques différentes du plan Vance-Owen pour la Bosnie-Herzégovine,* dans: Le Monde, Paris, 5 janvier 1993

toutes les provinces dans lesquelles se trouvent des populations croates apparaissent de façon différenciée sur chacune des cartes: la province No 3 est croate pour *Le Monde* et *La Libre Belgique*, alors qu'elle est „croato-musulmane" pour *Le Nouveau Quotidien* , qui précise — hors carte — que des combats ont toujours lieu à ce moment-là entre Serbes et Croates. La province no 8 est croate pour *Le Monde* et *Le Nouveau Quotidien*; par contre elle est „dessinée" comme étant à double dominante dans *La Libre Belgique*: musulmane au nord-est, croate à l'ouest et au sud. La province no 10 est croate pour *Le Monde*, légendée „croato-musulmane" mais dessinée de façon homogène dans *Le Nouveau*

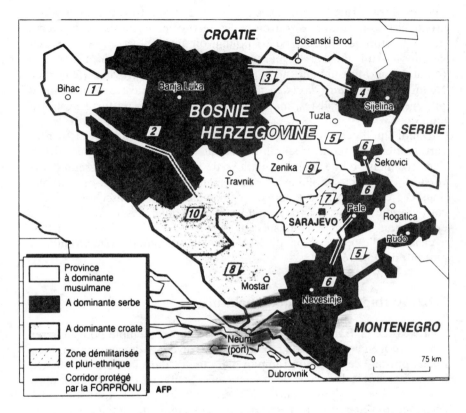

**Carte 11.** *La représentation carographique la moins simplifiée et donc la plus exacte du même project de découpage de la Bosnie-Herzégovine,* dans: La Libre Belgique, Bruxelles, sélection hebdomadaire du 12 au 18 janvier 1993

*Quotidien,* alors qu'elle dessinée à double dominante dans *La Libre Belgique*: musulmane au nord, croate au sud. De plus, la carte de *La Libre Belgique* est la seule à dessiner les corridors, devant être protégés par la FORPRONU (la Force de protection de l'ONU). Ces passages protégés doivent permettre la jonction entre les différentes provinces „ethniques" enclavées (les provinces musulmanes no 1 et 10, à travers une province serbe; les provinces serbes no 2 et 4, à travers une province croate/croato-musulmane) ou entre les territoires enclavés de la même province ethnique (serbe, no 6) pour avoir un contact entre elles et - de plus — un accès à la mer à travers une autre province ethnique (croate/croato-musulmane, no 8) et „dans" cette autre province (le port de Neum)! *Le Nouveau Quotidien* n'a pas dessiné sur la carte ces „passages protégés", bien irréalistes, mais il les mentionne dans un texte explicatif annexé.

Quoi qu'il en soit, tous ces supports graphiques sont censés cartographier la même réalité! Ils masquent tous, à des degrés divers, l'hétérogénéité d'une réalité complexe de départ pour en présenter une version fortement simplifiée et diversement interprétée. Est-ce crédible, dans ces conditions, de la présenter comme base de discussion si elle cartographie de façon approximative et équivoque des paramètres qui, eux-mêmes, sont déjà contestés au départ par les différentes parties, à cause de l'interprétation divergente de leur contenu sémantique et, partant, de leur réalité?

### 2.4.2. Ambiguïté de la nomenclature

Le cas de la Transylvanie pourrait aussi servir d'exemple pour illustrer cette homogénéité de façade recouvrant une diversité de peuplement bien réelle, puisque cette région tampon a été tantôt dans la zone d'influence hongroise, tantôt dans celle de la Roumanie. Seules les cartes linguistiques des atlas géographiques mentionnent ces nuances; elles le font souvent à l'échelle continentale, sans entrer dans beaucoup de détails. Les atlas historiques en font mention quand on aborde des périodes charnières de l'évolution d'une région (Chier W., 1982: 81, pour la monarchie des Habsbourg, et 108/II, pour l'Europe centre-orientale en 1980) ou d'un continent (Putzger [f.w.], 1981: 99, pour la répartition des langues en Europe centre-orientale vers 1910).

Les atlas géographiques nationaux des deux pays concernés sont très discrets sur cette approche: une simple carte européenne des langues pour les Hongrois (Radó S. (éd.), 1979: 24/III ou Radó S. (éd.), 1980: 15/II); pas une seule carte humaine à ce propos dans les atlas roumains, ni dans celui qui présente la géographie mondiale (Peaha M., 1983), ni dans celui qui traite de façon très détaillée les différentes régions du pays (Cucu

V., 1978). Sans consulter les ouvrages spécifiques sur ces régions, il n'y a que ceux qui analysent la mobilité frontalière des Etats et des groupes humains sous un angle géopolitique (Foucher M., 1991: 67, 68) ou ceux qui présentent la nouvelle réalité des peuples de l'Europe centrale et orientale (Sellier A. & J., 1991: 131) qui en fassent mention, même si la représentation cartographique en reste très générale. A cela s'ajoutent des études faisant le point sur les problèmes des minorités ethniques et nationales en Europe centre-orientale (Lomme R., 1988: 113; Chiclet C., 1992b: 203) ou des approches plus ciblées sur les minorités hongroises de Transylvanie (Laselv P., 1988: 308), pour en avoir une représentation plus précise.

Une des rares cartes à en avoir présenté une étude plus fouillée de la localisation des différents ensembles de la population de la Transylvanie, est la „Carte ethnographique de Hongrie basée sur les densités de populations", dressée par le comte Paul Teleki, selon le recensement de 1910. Bien qu'à une échelle assez petite (1:1.000.000), chaque millimètre carré (mm$^2$) représente 100 habitants, on distingue très nettement les emplacements spécifiques occupés par les populations de langue hongroise (Hongrois et Székely), par les Roumains, les Saxons et les autres minorités moins importantes, ainsi que de vastes régions inhabitées ou présentées comme pratiquement vides. Le dernier recensement de la population de Roumanie, le 1er janvier 1992, a rendu possible la publication d'une carte montrant l'importance relative des populations par département, mais pas leur localisation sur le terrain („26 «Ethnic Groups»", 1992: 28).

La représentation cartographique de la Transylvanie est donc révélatrice de l'ambiguïté liée à la nomenclature. Ces villes et ces localités construites et/ou habitées par des Magyars, des Székely, des Saxons ou des Roumains vont porter des noms à la fois hongrois, allemands et roumains. Un choix s'impose pour la cartographie de la région: quels noms faut-il utiliser? Ceux de la langue dans laquelle est rédigée la carte? Ceux de la langue du pays dans lequel se trouve la région? Ceux de la langue de la population résidant dans la région? Qui cartographie quoi, pour qui? Faut-il utiliser un point de vue *emic* strict, à usage interne? Un point de vue *etic*, à destination des „autres"? S'agit-il d'une approche synchronique, faisant référence à une situation actuelle (carte géographique)? D'une approche diachronique, mettant en évidence ces régions qui ont été tour à tour habitées/occupées/conquises par des populations et/ou des peuples différents? La réponse n'est pas aussi simple qu'il n'y paraît au premier abord, pour deux raisons au moins:

a) du point de vue de la rédaction, aucun choix n'est innocent, surtout dans une situation conflictuelle, — et c'est bien le cas entre la Hongrie et la Roumanie à propos de la Transylvanie. Ce choix sera donc inévitablement analysé et interprété, de façon pertinente ou non;

b) du point de vue de l'utilisation de la carte: il n'est pas évident de faire la relation entre „Kézdivásárhely-Tîrgu Secuiesc-Szekler Neumarkt" ou „Nagyvárad-Oradea-Groß wardein", par exemple, et de savoir qu'il s'agit de la même ville dans chaque cas...

Les atlas historiques hongrois utilisent exclusivement les noms hongrois pour parler de la Transylvanie jusqu'à la Première Guerre mondiale, — dissolution de la Double Monarchie austro-hongroise — (Radó S. (éd.), 1981) et sur les cartes de la Deuxième Guerre mondiale pendant laquelle le nord de la Transylvanie était sous juridiction hongroise, — restitué à la Roumanie en février 1947. Sur la carte de l'entre-deux guerres (Csatáry M., Györffy G. & Pamlényi E., 1981: 27/II) les noms de villes de Cluj, Timisoara et Brasov apparaissent uniquement en roumain, alors que sur les cartes antérieures ils avaient toujours figuré sous leur forme hongroise de Kolozsvár, Temesvár et Brassó. Par contre, — à défaut d'avoir pu consulter des atlas —, un ouvrage officiel présentant la Roumanie au public francophone (Alberti A. (éd.), 1979: 57, 62–63, 73) n'utilise que des noms latins ou roumains pour les cartes historiques de la Transylvanie. Le livre d'Histoire roumaine qui vient d'être édité sur la base du programme scolaire de transition n'utilise, lui aussi, que les noms roumains pour tout ce qui touche à la Transylvanie; dès la première carte médiévale, montrant la structure politique du IXe au XIIIe siècles, apparaissent le nom des villes de Cluj, Tg. Mures et Timisoara (Manea M, Pascu A. & Teodorescu B., 1992: 179, 207, 219...).

L'usage hongrois dans les atlas géographiques se rallie à la pratique internationale habituelle: l'utilisation des noms dans la langue du pays, avec une adaptation éventuelle de l'orthographe pour garder les mêmes phonèmes, ou du nom pour les villes de portée internationale. Ainsi (Radó S., 1980: 20–21) Bucarest donne „Bukarest", le nom „Bucuresti" figurant en-dessous entre parenthèses; même principe pour „Brüsszel (Bruxelles)", „Varsó (Warszawa)". Pour les noms des villes ayant fait partie de la zone d'influence hongroise jusqu'au début de ce siècle, — dont la Transylvanie —, on utilise le nom hongrois avec le nom vernaculaire entre parenthèses:

„Kolozsvár (Cluj-Napoca)", „Temesvár (Timisoara)", „Újvidék (Novi Sad)", mais „Belgrád (Beograd)" et non „Nándorfehérvár", qui en est le nom hongrois et qu'on verrait figurer sur les cartes historiques Csatáry M., Györffy G. & Pamlényi E., 1981: 12–13). Sur des atlas géographiques plus détaillés Radó S., 1979: 54–55), on utilise le même procédé sur la carte d'ensemble de la Roumanie(1:2.500.000). Une carte à échelle un plus grande (1:1.250.000) détaille davantage les hauts-plateaux du sud-est de la Transylvanie, celle où la concentration hongroise est la plus importante; les grandes villes y apparaissent en hongrois avec le nom roumain entre parenthèses — par exemple: „Marosvásárhely (Tîrgu Mures)" —, alors que les petites villes et les villages sont en roumain avec, éventuellement, le nom hongrois entre parenthèses — par exemple: „Covasna (Kovászna)" ou „Bretcu (Bereck)". Dans un cas comme dans l'autre, les noms roumains apparaissent toujours sur les atlas géographiques hongrois. La logique est respectée puisque la Transylvanie est maintenant rattachée à la Roumanie; elle n'était cependant pas évidente en soi, vu les liens affectifs qui lient cette région à la Hongrie. Aucun des atlas géographiques roumains cités (Peaha M., 1983 et Cucu V., 1978) ne mentionne quelque nom hongrois que ce soit pour la Transylvanie. Contrairement à ce qui se passe dans les cartes de leur ouvrage d'histoire, la logique est aussi respectée, cette fois, puisque la région fait maintenant partie intégrante de l'Etat roumain.

Les utilisateurs étrangers non spécialistes de cette région, — et ils sont légion! —, sont les plus empruntés face à cette ambiguïté de la nomenclature. Les ouvrages internationaux, en effet, utilisent généralement les noms roumains, même s'ils ne sont que peu ou pas utilisés par les populations locales à majorité magyarophone (*The Times Atlas of the World*, 1974: 82; *National Geographic Atlas of the World*, 1981: 161; *Atlas Universalis*, 1982: 38). Par contre, le *Grand atlas mondial* (Paris, Solar, 1987: 64) donne les noms hongrois, à côté des noms roumains, pour les principaux centres. L'encyclopédie de tous les pays du monde *Le Million* (Paris-Genève-Bruxelles, 1977, IV: 206–207, 234–235 et 160–161, 223) n'utilise que les noms roumains dans ses cartes géographiques; par contre, dans ses cartes historiques, elle utilise indifféremment toutes les possibilités onomastiques, — hongroise, roumaine, allemande —, suivant les périodes envisagées. Sur la même carte du Royaume de Hongrie et ses Etats vassaux, à la fin du XIVe siècle, on voit Nagyvárád et Kolozsvár côtoyer Alba Julia; sur celle de la Principauté de Transylvanie après l'invasion turque (1526), Brasov se trouve à côté de Nagyszeben et de Kolozsvár. Les atlas historiques allemands parleront toujours de Großwardein, Klausenburg, Hermannstadt et Kronstadt (Putzger, 1981: 79, 84, 89, 111...) et ne citeront jamais les noms hongrois ou roumains. La Transylvanie elle-même sera toujours appelée de son nom allemand „Siebenbürgen", du temps des sept villes royales ayant des sièges de la juridiction autonome dont bénéficiaient les Saxons. Même les atlas géographiques allemands (*Atlantis Weltatlas*, Harms/List, 1984: 154) mentionnent encore toutes les villes de la Transylvanie de leurs noms allemands, avec le nom roumain entre parenthèses; celui de la Transylvanie est double: „Siebenbürgen (Transsilvanien)".

Il n'y qu'une possibilité pour s'y retrouver entre les différents noms de cette région qui s'appelle *Transylvanie* en français, *Erdély* en hongrois, *Siebenbürgen* en allemand, *Ardeal* et *Transilvania* en roumain: avoir à disposition les 190 pages de l'index multilingue qui présente tous les noms topographiques de la région dans toutes les langues possibles ayant été utilisées. L'index accompagne une réédition de la carte de Transylvanie dressée au début du XIXe siècle par János Lipszky (Herner J., 1987: 1–190).

## 2.4.3. Les cartes mentales

Les cartes peuvent aussi être utilisées pour faire passer des idées, pour exprimer des évolutions, des développements, des projections. A côté de la représentation (qui se veut) objective des réalités bi-ou tridimensionnelles, les cartes peuvent aussi se révéler un puissant moyen pour représenter non ces réalités elles-mêmes, mais la perception qu'on en a, l'„image mentale" que l'on se fait de cet „espace psychologique". Il n'est, dès lors, pas étonnant que la perception , fatalement subjective, de l'espace dans lequel on vit, — ou dans lequel on voudrait vivre —, soit fort différente de la réalité apportée par les atlas habituels. De nombreuses études (par ex. Downs R. & Stea D., 1974) et de bonnes synthèses (par ex. Gould R. & White P., 1974) ont montré l'importance de l'*espace relatif* dans le monde actuel et la réalité vivante de l'espace mental à côté de l'*espace absolu*. On ne représente plus la réalité de l'„espace vrai", mais *sa* réalité de l'„espace perçu", le sien ou celui que l'on prête aux autres...

Vue sous cet angle, la carte mentale n'est plus une simple caricature, — comme pouvaient l'être certaines cartes satiriques à propos de l'Europe au XIXe siècle —, elle peut, au contraire, se révéler être une puissante arme de propagande et de combat! Il suffit de dire, ou de faire dire aux „autres" (les adversaires), un certain nombre de choses, — vraies ou fausses —, et de les cartographier, pour déclencher des réflexes parfois difficilement contrôlables. Si, de plus, on joue sur la corde nationaliste, tous les dérapages sont possibles.

Un atlas de ce type vient d'être publié sur la Yougoslavie (*Maps of our Dividings / Karte Nasih Podela*, 1991). Cet atlas historico-géographique est bilingue, serbe/anglais; à côté du but auto légitimation à usage interne (point de vue *emic*), il vise donc aussi une large diffusion (point de vue *etic*). Il précise dans son avant-propos qu'il s'agit d'un „manuel pour les étudiants, les touristes et les soldats" (sic). Le commentaire qui accompagne cet ensemble de 28 cartes est engagé; il reflète le point de vue serbe sur la question des territoires disputés par les différentes composantes ethniques de l'ex-Yougoslavie, quelle que soit l'origine des cartes présentées. Il montre, par exemple, que le projet serbe de „Grand Serbie" n'est pas nouveau. Le projet d'une „Serbie homogène" de Stevan Moljevic (carte no 9 de l'atlas), présenté à Niksic en 1941, n'hésite pas à anticiper certaines expansions de la Serbie surtout, mais aussi de la Croatie et de la Slovénie, au-delà des frontières nationales, au détriment de tous les pays voisins: l'Italie, la Hongrie, la Roumanie, la Bulgarie et l'Albanie. Des cartes de „Grande Hongrie", „Grande Bulgarie", „Grande Albanie" de l'atlas serbe) montrent les „rêves" des „sécessionnistes". Après des cartes d'autres projets serbes d'unité et d'homogénéité, ceux de Vojislav Seselj , Vuk Draskovic (cartes No 20, 21), l'atlas dénonce les velléités d'*expansionnisme* des „Grande Croatie"), „Grande Macédoine", „Grande Slovénie" (cartes No 17, 24, 25) en des termes faisant toujours référence au „chauvinisme", „séparatisme" et autre „sécessionnisme" de leurs promoteurs, la Serbie elle-même étant „amputée" (carte No 26). Par contre, la carte de la „République autonome serbe de Krajina" de Milan Babic (carte No 27) y figure déjà, comme si elle était déjà reconnue par la communauté internationale. Le commentaire précise d'ailleurs que les contacts pris par les observateurs de la Communauté Européenne avec les représentants du peuple serbe de Croatie „sont un premier pas vers la reconnaissance international de la légitimité serbe sur ce territoire"... Les espaces psychologiques sont décidément très relatifs.

Sans avoir nécessairement des visées expansionnistes, — surtout si elles se font au détriment des autres par la force armée, dans les conditions

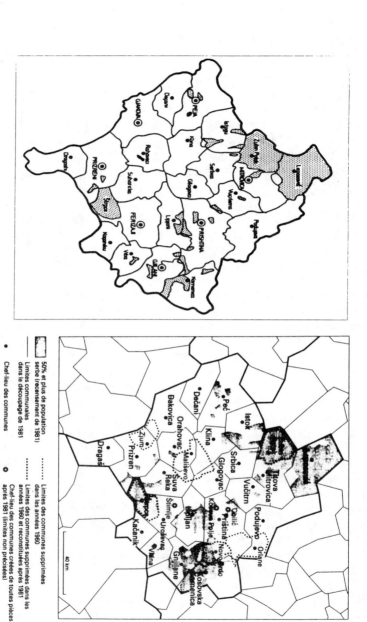

**Carte 12.** *Les enclaves serbes au Kosovo et les modifications du maillage communal au Kosovo, région de très forte majorité albanaise,* dans: Ministère de l'Information de la République de Kosove, 1991 & Roux M., 1992a

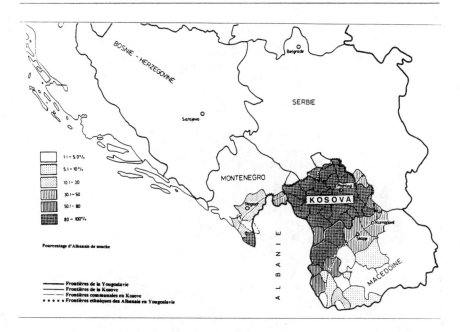

**Carte 13.** *Carte mentale des Albanais de l'ex-Yougoslavie relative à leur eextension ethnique,* dans: Ministère de l'Information de la République de Kosove, 1991

que l'on sait dans l'ex-Yougoslavie! —, les cartes mentales jouent un rôle important, au point de vue *emic*, pour le renforcement de l'identité culturelle des minorités. Cette perception est un moteur puissant de leur action ou de la simple justification de leur existence, surtout quand elle est niée par les autres. Le cas des Albanais du Kosovo est révélateur de cet état d'esprit, comme nous le verrons dans le point suivant, mais la comparaison de la carte des enclaves serbes au Kosovo (Ministère de l'Information de la République de Kosove, 1991: 30) avec celle des modifications du maillage communal au Kosovo (Roux M., 1992a: 400) montre déjà la politique anti-albanaise des autorités serbes (**cf. carte No 14**). Un certain nombre de communes avaient été supprimées dans les années 1960; les seules à avoir été reconstituées après 1981 sont celles qui comportent des majorités serbes. De nouvelles communes ont même

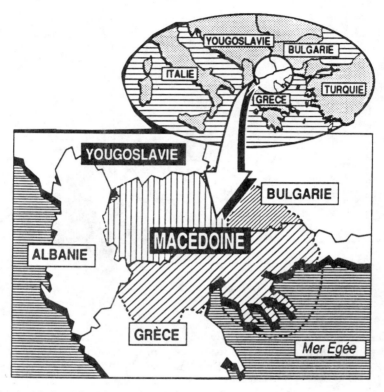

**Carte 14.** *La Macédoine, une région répartie entre trois Etats,* dans: Le Nouveau Quotidien, Lausanne, 14 janvier 1992

été créées de toutes pièces dans deux petites régions du Kosovo à majorité serbe; on peut ainsi venir en aide, officiellement, à des populations (serbes) qui se présentent comme majoritaires, dans une République qui nie la réalité de la majorité démographique (albanaise) d'une population que l'on veut marginaliser dans une région périphérique, sans statut particulier au point de vue politico-culturel. Alors que la carte mentale des Albanais de l'ex-Yougoslavie ne fait état que de la zone d'extension territoriale effective des Albanais de souche dans les Républiques dans lesquelles ils se trouvent en fortes concentrations, — au Kosovo surtout, mais aussi en Macédoine et, dans une moindre mesure, au Montenegro

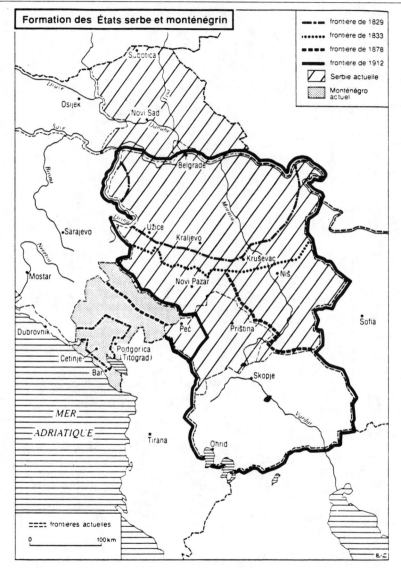

**Carte 15.** *La Macédoine dans l'Etat serbe au début du XXe siècle,* dans:
Garde P., 1992

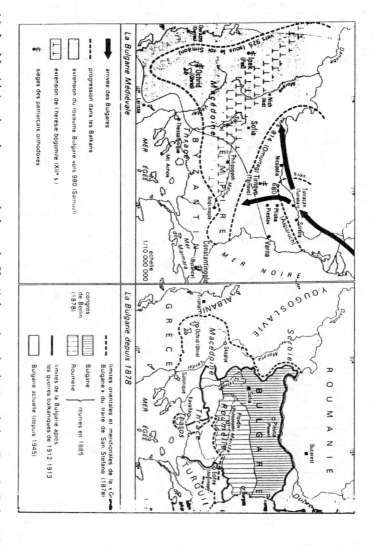

Carte 16. *La Macédoine dans le royaume bulgare du Xe siècle et dans les limites de la „Grande Bulgarie" à la fin du XIXe siècle,* dans: Philippot R., 1980

### La Bulgarie Médiévale

➡ arrivée des Bulgares

┈┈ progression dans les Balkans

▭ extension du royaume Bulgare vers 980 (Samuel)

▭▯ extension de l'hérésie bogomile (XII° s)

✠ sièges des patriarcats orthodoxes

échelle 1/10 000 000

**Carte: La Bulgarie Médiévale**

Danube · Morava · Nish (Niš) · pek (Peč) · Ochrid (Ohrid) · Durazzo (Dyrr) · Larissa · Macédoine · vers 925 (sous le roi Simeon) · 814 (Omurtag) · Sofia · THRACE · BYZANTINE · MER EGEE · Mt Athos · Thessalonique · M E M P I R E · Philippoli Maritza (Tcherno) · Adrianople · Constantinople · Mer de Marmara (dt) (Brátsko) · vers 680 · Nicopolis · Turnovo (Térnovo) · Turtucan (Turtukaï) · Silistra · Presiav (Aspurach) · Pliska · Varna · MER NOIRE

### La Bulgarie depuis 1878

┈┈ limites orientales et méridionales de la « Gr...
Bulgarie » du traité de San Stefano (1878)

▨ Bulgarie ⎫
▩ Roumélie ⎬ réunies en 1885
─── ⎭

─── limites de la Bulgarie après les guerres balkaniques de 1912-1913

▭ Bulgarie actuelle (depuis 1945)

congrès de Berlin (1878)

**Carte: La Bulgarie depuis 1878**

YOUGOSLAVIE · Danube · ALBANIE · Tirana · Ochrid (Ohrid) · Skopie · Macédoine · Vardar · GRECE · Salonique · Kavalla · Pagos · MER EGEE · Morava · Serbie · BULGARIE · Sofia · Plevna · Philippopoli Maritza · Plovdiv · ROUMELIE · Thrace · Edirne (Andrinople) · Burgas · TURQUIE · ROUMANIE · Bucarest · Danube

— (Ministère de l'Information de la République de Kosove, 1991: 31, cf. carte No 13), la carte mentale qui leur est prêtée par les Serbes montre une revendication albanaise sur toute la partie orientale du Montenegro, sur la partie méridionale de la Serbie, — allant bien audelà des zones de l'albanité exprimées par les Albanais eux-mêmes —, et sur toute la moitié occidentale de la Macédoine! De plus, cette revendication n'est pas présentée comme étant celle des Albanais de l'ex-Yougoslavie (ce qui n'est déjà pas exact), mais bien comme celle de l'Albanie voisine...

Le cas de la „Macédoine" est encore plus complexe puisque la région portant ce nom est actuellement partagée entre trois Etats qui, chacun, ont des visées territoriales et/ou culturelles sur les Macédoniens (*Le Nouveau Quotidien*, Lausanne, 14 janvier 1992, cf. carte No 14). L'identité macédonienne est d'autant plus difficile à faire reconnaître par les „autres" (point de vue *etic*) que chacun y place un contenu sémantique différent (Deslondes O., 1992; Lory B., 1992; Béhar P., 1992; Chiclet C., 1989, 1992a, 1993a & 1993b; Lutard C., 1991).

Les Serbes considèrent que cette région forme la Serbie méridionale de l'ensemble yougoslave, en se référant entre autres aux frontières de 1912 (Djuric V., 1980; Garde P., 1992: 40, cf. carte No 15), qui sont déjà une compression de celles de l'extension maximale du Royaume de Serbie du XIVe siècle, avant ses défaites successives et son incorporation dans l'Empire ottoman (*Encyclopœdia Universalis*, 1980, volume 14: 893; Dvornik F., 1970: 1175). Ce que les Serbes ne veulent plus voir est la coupure des Serbes de Serbie et de ceux du Montenegro (ce qui prive la Serbie d'un accès à la mer), par la région du Sanjak qui, comme la Macédoine, était encore sous occupation turque jusqu'à la veille de la Première Guerre mondiale (Yelen A., 1989: 81). Une carte serbe faisant le décompte des Serbes tués pendant la Deuxième Guerre mondiale (Yelen A., 1989: 124) présente encore cette région comme étant la „Serbie du Sud".

Les Bulgares contrôlent la „Macédoine · Pirin" depuis le traité de Bucarest, 1913, qui a mis fin aux deux guerres balkaniques par le partage de la région macédonienne entre la Serbie, la Grèce et la Bulgarie. Les deux conflits mondiaux ultérieurs n'ont pratiquement pas affecté les dispositions du partage. Si la Bulgarie n'a aucune revendication territoriale officielle sur la Macédoine, elle n'en reconnaît pas pour autant la notion de „peuple macédonien". Pour elle, en effet, la population originelle de la Macédoine n'existe plus depuis bien longtemps, et

## MACÉDOINE
(Telle que divisée aujourd'hui entre les États voisins)

POUR LA MACEDOINE
LIBRE ET INDEPENDANTE
V. M. R. O.

This part of Macedonia fell under Serbian occupation (Jugoslavia) in 1913. In 1944 the Macedonian Republic created it's Macedonian fighters that enjoys certain freedoms, but falls short from being totally independent.

This part of Macedonia is under the Greek terror of occupation since 1913.

This part of Macedonia is occupied by Bulgaria.

ALBANIA

JUGOSLAVIA

BULGARIA

GREECE

MACEDONIA

AEGEAN SEA

Οι χάρτες της "Μεγάλης Μακεδονίας" κυκλοφορούν σ' ολόκληρο τον κόσμο και περιλαμβάνουν μεγάλο κομμάτι της Δυτικής και Κεντρικής Μακεδονίας όπως και τη Θεσσαλονίκη.

Carte 17. *Carte mentale des Macédoniens*, dans: Papakonstantinou M, 1992

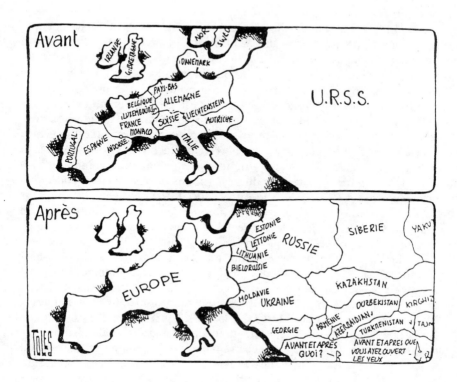

**Carte 18.** *Carte mentale de l'Europe, montrant l'évolution actuelle —
caricaturée — de son unification et/ou de son morcellement,* dans: Le
Nouveau Quotidien, Lausanne, 12 décembre 1991

certainement depuis le peuplement slave puis bulgare de cette région, à
partir des IXe–Xe siècles (Dvornik F., 1970: 1166 & 1171). La langue
macédonienne actuelle n'a plus rien de commun avec le macédonien
antique, ce qui prouve bien le changement de peuplement de la région. De
plus, le traité de San Stefano, à la fin du XIXe siècle (1878), confirmant les
limites occidentales et méridionales de la „Grande Bulgarie", englobait
encore la quasi totalité des Macédoines actuelles dans l'espace bulgare
(Solaroff K., 1919; Philippot R., 1980a, carte: 682, cf. carte No 16). La

position curieuse des autorités bulgares actuelles fait qu'ils reconnaissent l'Etat de la „République de Macédoine", mais pas le nom de „peuple macédonien" à ses ressortissants. La Bulgarie en arrive donc à reconnaître un „Etat" mais pas la „nation" qui le constitue; ce pays constitue pourtant un „Etat-nation", dans le sens juridique international du terme.

La Grèce est celui des trois pays concernés qui a la position la plus nette et la plus tranchée: la Macédoine est grecque et ne saurait être autre chose que grecque. La politique de nationalisme à outrance dans le pays prouve que ce problème de l'identité macédonienne, identifiée à la l'identité grecque, est *perçu* et *vécu* de façon très forte au niveau politique. Cette réalité socio-politique présentée/imposée comme telle, à l'intérieur comme à l'extérieur du pays (points de vues *emic* et *etic* ), est-elle conforme à la réalité socio-historique? Les Grecs actuels, partisans de l'appropriation, semblent perdre de vue que c'est la Macédoine de Philippe II et de son fils Alexandre III le Grand qui a dominé et conquis la Grèce, à l'époque classique (IVe siècle avant J.-C.), et non la Grèce qui a dominé la Macédoine! S'il était tant soit peu pertinent de remonter à cette période du passé, comme le font les Grecs contemporains pour justifier une appartenance ou une dépendance, il serait plus judicieux et plus exact de dire que la Grèce était macédonienne et non que la Macédoine était grecque (Mosse C. , 1980: 222–227; carte: 223). Lorsqu'au IIe siècle avant J.-C., le monde grec de la période hellénistique (et non hellénique) devient province romaine, la Macédoine et le reste de la Grèce forment toujours des régions différentes: la Macédoine sera réduite en province romaine en 148, le reste de la Grèce deux ans plus tard. L'Epire et la Thessalie resteront toujours des régions différentes de la Macédoine pendant la période romaine et, au VIe siècle après J.-C., le découpage provincial du Bas-Empire aura toujours gardé les „Macédoine I et Macédoine II" séparées de l'Epire, de la Thessalie et des autres provinces plus méridionales de la Grèce (Dvornik F., 1970: 1164). L'arrivée ultérieure des Slaves et des Bulgares dans la région ne les a, bien sûr, pas rapprochées davantage.

La Macédoine est-elle grecque? Les „cartes mentales" grecques le montrent, en tous cas, en se référant encore à la Macédoine de la fin du siècle dernier, lorsqu'elle était encore dans le cadre de l'Empire ottoman (Papakntantinou M., 1992: 50). Pour les Grecs, la Macédoine ne peut exister sous ce nom que dans le monde hellénique. Il est donc impensable qu'une région extérieure à la „Macédoine Egée", — la partie contrôlée par la Grèce actuellement —, puisse porter ce nom qui, pour eux, fait partie du patrimoine grec.

Et les Macédoniens eux-mêmes? Les partisans d'une Macédoine libre et indépendante n'ont plus que des cartes pour rêver... Qui sontils et combien sont-ils d'ailleurs dans chacune des trois parties de la Macédoine historique? Aucun recensement neutre n'ayant été fait, les approches sont très différentes suivant les points de vue. La comparaison des statistiques faites au début du siècle (Yerasimos S., 1991: 89), en 1918 (Raufer X. & Haut F., 1992: 134) et en 1926 (Papakntantinou M., 1992: 23) montre clairement que chacun y trouve ceux qu'il veut bien et dénombre les communautés ethniques et culturelles en fonction de ses intérêts (cf. tableau No 1). Les nationalistes macédoniens se montrent les mains enchaînées, séparés les uns des autres et concentrés comme dans des camps d'internement (Papakntantinou M., 1992: 111 & 112, cf. carte no 17). C'était au début du siècle, juste après les guerres balkaniques; la situation actuelle n'a pas vraiment changé.

La représentation cartographique est donc essentielle comme moyen d'expression des problèmes identitaires. L'importance en a déjà été signalée, l'année passée, par Grzegorz Gorzelak dans „Polish regionalism and regionalisation" (Gorzelak G. & Kuklinski A., (ed.), 1992: 470–471 et 481), comme justification de la simple existence des minorités culturelles, surtout quand elle est niée par les autres. Les exemples cités plus haut en montrent aussi toutes les ambiguïtés. En élargissant le débat, on pourrait facilement montrer en quoi la mauvaise perception des réalités socio-culturelles de l'Europe centrale et surtout de l'Europe orientale (ainsi que les „cartes mentales" qui en découlent) est souvent responsable des mauvaises réponses qui sont souvent apportées aux besoins réels de ces pays, qu'ils soient d'ordre humain ou économique. La mauvaise perception peut aussi se doubler d'une réelle méconnaissance des facteurs historiques et culturels de ces populations et peuples de l'Europe centre-orientale, qui ont souvent été perçus de façon très superficielle et globalisante. A l'Ouest, il aura même fallu attendre le déclin progressif et la chute des régimes communistes de la fin de la décennie 1980 pour voir apparaître une explosion d'ouvrages présentant ces contextes historico-culturels de façon plus nuancée (Bárdos-Féltoronyi N. & Sutton M. (éd.), 1991; Béhar P., 1991; Bogdan H., 1991; Castellan G., 1991; Rupnik J., 1993...). Une „carte mentale" présente cette situation sous la forme d'une caricature (*Le Nouveau Quotidien*, Lausanne, 12 décembre 1991): la

**Tableau 1**

**Les statistiques démographiques de la Macédoine au début du XXe siècle,
très variables selon les sources consultées**

| Ethnies | Statistiques bulgares (1900) | Statistiques grecques* (1904) | Statistiques serbes (1889) | Statistiques allemandes (1905) | Recensement turc (1906) |
|---|---|---|---|---|---|
| Turcs | 499 200 | 634 000 | 231 000 | 250 000 | 1 145 000*** |
| Albanais | 128 700 | — | 165 000 | 300 000 | |
| Bulgares | 1 181 000 | 332 000 | 57 600 | 2 000 000** | 626 000 |
| Serbes | 700 | — | 2 048 000 | | |
| Grecs | 228 700 | 652 700 | 201 100 | 200 000 | 623 000 |
| Valaques | 80 700 | 25 100 | 69 600 | 100 000 | |
| Juifs | 67 800 | 53 100 | 64 600 | | |
| Tsiganes | 54 500 | 8 900 | 28 700 | | |
| Divers | 16 500 | 18 600 | 3 500 | | |
| TOTAL | 2 258 000 | 1 724 000 | 2 870 000 | | |

\* Moins le Kosovo.
\*\* Qualifiés de Macédo-Slaves.
\*\*\* Musulmans.

| POPULATIONS | Chiffre le plus bas | Chiffre le plus élevé |
|---|---|---|
| Slavo Macédoniens | 120 000 | 1 200 000 |
| Serbes | 210 000 | 900 000 |
| Grecs | 50 000 | 1 000 000 |
| Valaques | 24 000 | 1 200 000 |
| **POP. totale de la Macédonie** | 404 000 | 4 300 000 |

division de l'Europe occidentale s'estompe progressivement par la volonté
de l'union économique et politique, alors que ce qui paraissait être un
semblant d'unité, de cohésion et d'entraide dans le monde socialiste — ou
qui était présenté comme tel au monde extérieur —, se morcelle et éclate
en une multitude de micro-régions, souvent animées par les mouvements
de revendication nationale des différents groupes ethniques et culturels.

# 3. Les causes et les effets
# en Europe centre-orientale

## 3.1. Le cas paradoxal de l'ex-monde socialiste

L'ex-Union soviétique est une illustration exemplaire des paradoxes et des contradictions qui peuvent exister entre la théorie et la pratique d'une réflexion portant sur les possibilités d'expressions des différentes nations ou nationalités se trouvant dans le pays. Il est exemplaire, non seulement parce qu'il permet de comprendre la recrudescence des identités nationales à l'intérieur du pays, suite à son implosion, mais aussi parce qu'il s'agit de la même logique appliquée à l'ensemble de l'ex-monde socialiste. Le même processus de mystification a été reproduit dans l'ex-COMECON, lié à la tutelle économique de Moscou, présenté comme un renforcement des spécificités de chaque pays dans la *grande solidarité* des *pays frères*. La „division socialiste du travail" a habilement mélangé les domaines économiques et culturels des pays qui étaient „unis" par l'„oléoduc de l'*amitié*".

## 3.1.1. La construction théorique

Il revient à l'un des plus importants ethnologues soviétiques actuels, Bromley (Bromley Y., 1974: 55–72), d'avoir mis en évidence le concept des „communautés ethnosociales" de base dans la vision soviétique de l'ethnologie. Des „nations" ayant une certaine organisation politique, sociale et économique sont regroupées sur des territoires différenciés. En suivant le principe de l'évolutionnisme linéaire de Morgan, ces communautés sont en évolution constante. Elles passent par les différents stades de l'évolution historique: de communautés „primitives" (bandes-tribus), elles passent ou sont passées par l'esclavagisme (tribus-ethnies), par le féodalisme (ethnies-nationalités), par le capitalisme (nationalités-nations bourgeoises) pour arriver au socialisme (nation socialiste-peuple soviétique). Ce processus d'évolution en cours s'inscrit donc dans une finalité précise: la constitution du peuple soviétique, ce que Bromley appelle l'*ethnikos* au sens étroit. Il doit être rendu possible par le regroupement de nombreux individus, originaires des différentes ethnies de l'union (il y en a plus de 100!). Cela ne doit théoriquement pas poser de problèmes puisque, dans leur progression vers l'idéal commun, tous sont imprégnés de l'internationalisme (= le multinationalisme) de fait du pays, du bilinguisme indispensable (sa langue plus le russe), de l'a-religiosité érigée en principe de base et de la richesse culturelle soviétique.

Pour y arriver, on avait recours à trois processus „unificateurs":
1. a *consolidation* devait permettre la fusion des groupes ethniques proches par la langue et la culture;
2. l'*assimilation* devait favoriser la dissolution des groupes restreints dans d'autres ethnies plus importantes numériquement parlant;
3. l'*intégration* devait conduire à des rapprochements inter-ethniques et supra-ethniques (les Baltes, les Caucasiens...).

En fait, ces trois processus dits „unificateurs" ne pouvaient qu'engendrer un morcellement territorial et administratif (Radvanyi J., 1982). Les „communautés ethniques" allaient se retrouver dans une cascade de dépendances administratives qui les isoleraient les unes des autres, tout en leur donnant l'impression d'être solidaires d'un grand ensemble.

## 3.1.2. La pratique de la théorie

La *consolidation*, l'*assimilation* et l'*intégration* sont des processus représentatifs d'une politique volontairement double et contradictoire. Avec le recul, on voit mieux le grand jeu de la mystification qui ne doit pas heurter les „orthodoxes" du régime, — d'où cette centralisation totale et absolue imposée par Lénine —, mais qui ne doit pas heurter non plus les „nationaux", — d'où la reconnaissance des droits ethniques, proposée par Staline, lui-même géorgien.

L'affirmation du respect des identités ethniques allait conduire à la construction d'une superstructure administrative *ad hoc* : un Etat fédéral, des cultures nationales, des Instituts du folklore... Les 180 groupes ethniques parlant plus de 120 langues différentes allaient se retrouver dans:
— 15 RSS (Républiques socialistes soviétiques), républiques „indépendantes", fédérées, aux frontières internationales;
— 20 RSSA (Républiques socialistes soviétiques autonomes), républiques autonomes, dont 16 en RSFSR (République socialiste fédérative soviétique de Russie);

— 8 RA (Régions autonomes), appelés *oblast*, disposant d'une autonomie administrative, toutes en RSFR;

— 10 AN (Arrondissements nationaux), appelés *okrug*, formés de groupes ethniques non urbains, disposant aussi d'une autonomie administrative, et tous en RSFR également;

— ± 50 Minorités nationales, sans territoire, représentant 1% de la population.

Mais, parallèlement, on participait à la déstructuration volontaire des identités ethniques pour trois raisons principales:

1. par le morcellement territorial et la division des mêmes groupes ethniques qui se retrouvaient dans des entités différentes, à des échelons administratifs différents, comme les Ossètes, les Bouriates, les Komis ou les Nenetz;

2. par la déstructuration des structures qui existaient précédemment et, notamment, des réseaux de relations tels que la loi islamique, le mode de vie nomade, le mariage local...;

3. par la russification et la soviétisation systématiques: imposition de l'alphabet latin puis cyrillique en Asie centrale, imposition du russe comme première langue (à un point tel que les langues maternelles étaient en déclin et/ou n'étaient plus enseignées dans les écoles)...

Ces „nationalités", créées artificiellement par Staline, sont devenues progressivement des cadres dans lesquels les revendications de soi-même contre le gouvernement central se sont manifestées. La recrudescence des identités nationales passa par le retour à ses propres racines, à son passé culturel, à son héritage social et, même, à une idéalisation de sa culture basée sur le culte des héros. On assista progressivement à la naissance d'une élite locale, lettrée, porteuse de tout le passé socio-culturel autochtone; les traditions orales et/ou écrites servaient de références et de supports à la valorisation culturelle. Une opposition de plus en plus nette se manifesta entre cette identité ethnique et culturelle et l'intelligentsia porteuse de la culture russe et soviétique: les fonctionnaires du gouvernement central moscovite, qui représentaient le pouvoir, mais étaient minoritaires.

Avant l'implosion de l'ex-Union soviétique, les recrudescences identitaires étaient déjà très actives et les revendications de plus en plus précises et pressantes. La diversité culturelle existait déjà, même si elle était peu connue à l'extérieur et si le pouvoir en place faisait tout pour la nier. C'est la négation même de cette diversité ethnique et culturelle *de facto* qui renforça l'accentuation des différences. Dès que le couvercle de la marmite à vapeur allait se soulever un peu, la pression accumulée ne pouvait que s'échapper. Les conflits identitaires qui ont éclaté un peu partout dans le pays en sont la preuve manifeste (Carrere d'Encausse H., 1978; Urjewicz C., 1990).

## 3.2. Le contexte historique

La même logique de pression et d'étouffement soviétique a agi sur les identités périphériques du monde socialiste d'Europe centrale et orientale, provoquant les mêmes oppositions, les mêmes blocages, les mêmes refus...(Fejtö F. & Mink G., 1978; Rupnik J., 1984) et les mêmes réactions parfois brutales, dès que des velléités sécessionnistes se sont manifestées dans le domaine idéologique: Budapest en 1956, Prague en 1968, Varsovie en 1981. Un pouvoir central fort, autoritaire, n'accepte pas la différence, la diversité, l'expression d'une identité autre que la sienne, surtout si cette identité est basée sur une logique autre que la sienne.

### 3.2.1. Opposition de deux „logiques" différentes

Nous avons rappelé précédemment que les nationalismes et les impérialismes ont favorisé, en Europe, une centralisation au niveau politique, administratif, économique et culturel. Cela a conduit au concept d'Etat-nation par la légitimisation d'un pouvoir établi qui s'est progressivement imposé sur des territoires donnés . La même logique d'expansionnisme a d'ailleurs conduit à la domination du monde par l'Occident lors de la phase coloniale. Comment se fait-il que l'affrontement entre un pouvoir central et des organisations sociales périphériques se solde quasi toujours, — dans un premier temps en tous cas —, par la „victoire" du premier sur les seconds? Est-ce uniquement une question de rapports de force et de puissance? L'anthropologie économique s'est penchée sur cette question au niveau des structures et des organisations sociales, ainsi que des relations mondiales entre le Nord et le Sud. Sans entrer dans les arcanes de leurs développements théoriques et sans accepter d'ailleurs la totalité de leurs raisonnements, on peut valablement en tirer des informations pour analyser *mutatis mutandis* les différences entre l'Est et l'Ouest.

Indépendamment de la différence sociologique entre la logique individuelle et la logique sociale (Daval R., 1984), le monde actuel est construit sur l'opposition de deux logiques sociales et culturelles: la „logique marchande" et la „logique communautaire" (Berthoud G. & Sabelli F., 1979: 745–752, cf. tableau No 2). Le tableau simplifié ci-dessous montre que la première est basée sur la pré-dominance de l'univers économique, visant une croissance quantitative pure et la maximisation des profits. On est dans une logique de production et de croissance. Qu'il s'agisse du libéralisme économique plus pur, le *capitalisme*, ou d'un capitalisme d'Etat, le *socialisme*, tout est „marchandisé": c'est la dynamique du capital qui vise à la rentabilisation, — avec des résultats et des succès très divers, faut-il le dire!

**Tableau 2**

**L'opposition de deux logiques sociales et culturelles
construit d'aprés: Bethoud G. & Sabellif F., 1979**

| „Logique marchande" | „Logique communautaire" |
|---|---|
| **Composantes:** production et croissance | **Composantes:** reproduction et transformation |
| Univers économique prédominant | Univers social prédominant |
| **Objectif:** capital → productivité | **Objectif:** richesse → relations sociales |
| **Pouvoir:** puissance *f* conquête, force | **Pouvoir:** prestige *f* confiance, consensus |

La logique „communautaire" est caractéristique des communautés plus restreintes, plus solidaires, celles qui ont davantage conscience de leur spécificité, de leur identité, et qui la vivent. Tout le monde se connaît, ou pratiquement: c'est le règne de la primauté du social sur l'économique. La terre elle-même n'est pas une „marchandise", un outil de production, mais le support matériel de la reproduction sociale. On vise avant tout une croissance qualitative dans une situation d'autosuffisance. La richesse n'est pas celle de la productivité (puisqu'on ne cherche qu'à répondre à ses besoins) mais celle des relations sociales, qui se vivent dans un univers souvent codifié par une série de pratiques sociales spécifiques à certains moments forts. Le support matériel lui-même n'est pas une richesse en soi car il n'a aucun équivalent, il n'est pas interchangeable. L'„arbre-richesse", par exemple, fait partie du patrimoine car il est à la base des activités sociales, alors que l'„arbre-capital" ne vise que des rendements industriels; c'est du bois en puissance, sans plus.

Le „pouvoir" de la logique marchande est fait de puissance; il ne s'exprime bien souvent que par la force et les conquêtes, qu'elles soient territoriales ou économiques. Cette forme de pouvoir passe par l'appareil d'Etat. Dans le cas des Etats-nations, on assiste à un double mouvement: centrifuge au niveau des conquêtes; centripète au niveau de la concentration du pouvoir légal. La logique communautaire des groupes ethniques et/ou culturels a encore la possibilité de se référer davantage à un pouvoir basé sur le prestige des individus. Il est fait de confiance et de consensus et passe par l'organisation sociale traditionnelle. La tradition joue un rôle moteur, qu'elle soit écrite ou orale, car elle est la mémoire de la communauté; la transmission de la tradition est l'actualisation du passé historique et culturel de la communauté.

### 3.2.2. Accentuation des différences

Si on analyse le processus propre à chacune de ses „logiques", tout se passe, en Europe centrale et orientale, comme s'il y avait eu une coexistence des deux à des niveaux différents, non pas dans des pays différents mais à l'intérieur des pays eux-mêmes. Tout comme pendant la colonisation il y avait eu un semblant de cohésion, parce qu'il y avait un groupe dominant (la métropole) qui imposait sa logique, durant la période de l'„occupation" soviétique, — par socialisme interposé —, il y a eu un semblant d'unicité au point de vue étatique, politique, économique. De nombreuses analyses ont été faites (Entz G., 1993; Karadi V. 1993; Liebich A., 1993; Rezsöházy R., 1991; Bouretz P. & Pisier E., 1990; Foucher M. 1990; Gresh A., 1990; Lagani I., 1989; Lavigne M., 1986; Lomme R., 1989 & 1992; Mink G., 1984, 1988, 1990 & 1991; Mink G. & Szurek J.-C., 1992; Rupnik J., 1990; Sapir J., 1981), montrant que si les Etats de l'ex-Europe de l'Est restaient virtuellement indépendants, ils étaient soumis à un moule idéologique dans les domaines politique, social et économique. L'Etat imposait sa logique qui n'est autre qu'une „logique marchande", à une population qui la subissait et qui réagissait, pour pouvoir survivre, en fonction d'une autre logique, plus concrète, qui s'apparente à la „logique communautaire". La diversité ethnique et culturelle continuait donc d'exister, y compris dans les domaines sociétaux et religieux, mais ne pouvait pas s'exprimer. Elle n'a pas disparu pour autant, bien au contraire; elle s'est renforcée et ne demandait qu'à s'exprimer à la première occasion. En fait, au niveau des processus, il n'y a pas de différence entre la *Pax britannica* dans l'Empire des Indes (qui a donné naissance à 4 Etats: Inde, Sri Lanka, Pakistan et Bangla Desh) et la *Pax sovietica* qui s'est imposée en Europe centrale pendant plusieurs décennies.

Le réveil des minorités nationales est la conséquence d'une situation d'oppression qui se libère. Il s'explique pour des tas de raisons spécifiques à chacune des nations. Mais il est surtout la preuve de l'échec de la conception des Etats-nations. On assiste à un réveil des identités régionales, et souvent des ethnicités, contre un Etat centralisateur (ou perçu comme tel): qu'il s'agisse des Kurdes et des Arméniens en Turquie, des Palestiniens en Israël, des Corses, des Alsaciens ou des Bretons en France, des Flamands et des Wallons en Belgique, ou des Tchèques et des Slovaques dans l'ex-Tchécoslovaquie, des Slovènes, des Croates, des Serbes, des Bosniaques et des Macédoniens dans l'ex-Yougoslavie, pour ne pas parler des Albanais du Kosovo ou de la Macédoine, des minorités magyarophones dans tous les pays riverains de la Hongrie...

Si on est honnête au niveau du raisonnement, il faut constater que c'est aussi l'échec de la conception nationaliste des nouveaux Etats indépendants, — souvent des anciennes colonies —, qui ont été construits sur le principe d'une ethnie dominante qui s'est imposée aux autres ou qui s'est présentée comme la totalité de l'incarnation de la nation. Les cas de pays comme le Zaïre, l'Afghanistan, l'Irak sont suffisamment clairs que pour ne pas devoir être développés ici. Ils s'apparentent à celui de l'ex-Union soviétique avec l'idéalisation du „soviétique" et l'imposition des „Russes".

L'accentuation des différences est la conséquence de la recherche de „collectivités concrètes", où l'on se sent membre d'un groupe à part entière et où on peut s'exprimer comme tel en s'épanouissant. Il s'exprime inévitablement par un retour à ses racines, à ses sources, dans des mouvements d'identité nationale, souvent à l'échelon régional. Mais ces collectivités concrètes sont aussi souvent marginalisées par la société légale, voire réprimées suivant les cas. Le mouvement destructeur de la force (les Serbes au Kosovo) ou du pouvoir (l'Etat roumain contre les minorités de Transylvanie), ou de la force qui s'érige en pouvoir (les Républiques auto-proclamées de Bosnie et de Croatie) n'hésite pas à utiliser tous les moyens à disposition, constitutionnels, légaux ou armés, pour en arriver à des politiques de destruction de la différence ethnique et culturelle. Le processus peut prendre différentes formes: de la simple oppression (opposants politiques en Serbie et en Croatie) à l'ethnocide en douceur (Transylvanie), en passant par le génocide pur et simple (les deux derniers se vérifient actuellement en Bosnie-Herzégovine). Mais il est inquiétant de voir le renforcement de l'acharnement ethnocidaire des Etats-nations actuels (Berthoud G., 1978: 47–59).

### 3.3. Les nationalismes endogènes

Le nationalisme endogène procède d'une forte conscience de soi et de son groupe ethnique et culturel. Il consiste en un mouvement volontaire du groupe pour exprimer ses valeurs, son échelle de valeurs, liées à une logique sociale et à une pratique sociale spécifiques. Le nationalisme endogène peut donc exister indépendamment de tout contact avec autrui, „a pu" et „a dû" exister dans ces conditions...

Les Albanais sont très représentatifs de cette situation: des non-slaves se trouvant à la charnière d'un monde orthodoxe et catholique. Leur langue, un rameau isolé de la famille indo-européenne, les rattache à une origine thraco-illyrienne, antérieure au latin et au roumain (Dami A., 1945: 68–73). Les idiomes „guègue" et „tosque" permettent de distinguer les populations du nord et du sud de l'albanité. Ce sont donc les habitants les plus anciens de la région, et ils y sont bien antérieurs à l'arrivée des Slaves (Dvornik F., 1970: 1159, 1160–1162), qui les ont repoussés, même si cette version des faits est contestée actuellement par toute l'idéologie des Serbes. Certains serbophiles n'hésitent même pas à dire que les Albanais ont été en grande partie implantés là où ils sont maintenant par les conquérants turcs, avant de proliférer (Yelen A., 1989: 18–19)! La vérité serait plutôt de reconnaître que les Turcs ont eu deux conséquences importantes sur le développement futur des Albanais:

1. ils ont apporté un coup final aux structures antérieures, politiques et sociales, des Albanais comme à celle des autres peuples de la fin de l'Empire romain d'Orient (dont les Slaves, d'ailleurs), et les ont obligés à émigrer en vagues successives, d'abord vers les côtes adriatiques, puis, pour certains d'entre eux, vers l'Italie, depuis Venise jusqu'à la Sicile (Ducellier A. & al., 1992);

2. ils les ont obligés à se convertir à l'islam pour ne pas être massacrés, surtout ceux qui habitaient sur les axes de passage privilégiés, tels la côte et les vallées alluviales; auparavant, les Guègues étaient catholiques et les Tosques étaient orthodoxes.

Ils sont restés musulmans pour la plupart, même si ce n'est pas une caractéristique impérative de leur albanité, puisque l'on trouve, encore maintenant, après des décennies de persécution communiste dans le domaine religieux, — surtout en Albanie! —, des Albanais de confession chrétienne, plus en Albanie qu'au Kosovo. Leur évolution historique ultérieure n'a fait que renforcer leur identité albanaise, même si leur situation de minoritaires en Serbie, — bien que majoritaires au Kosovo — , leur a donné une vision parfois légèrement différente en ex-Yougoslavie et en Albanie proprement dite. (Cubrilovic B., 1992; Ducellier A., 1993; Draskovic V., 1989; Kadare I., 1989a & 1989b; Roux. M., 1992a).

Les minorités de Transylvanie ont connu une situation fort semblable, qu'ils soient Székely, Hongrois proprement dits, Saxons ou Roumains. Tous ont connu, — ou connaissent encore —, les conditions particulières, et souvent marginalisantes, que l'on fait aux groupes minoritaires: les Roumains au temps des Habsbourg, de la maison d'Autriche, du Royaume de Hongrie, de la Double Monarchie austro-hongroise; les Hongrois proprement dits, qui sont venus dans le pays avec les maisons régnantes et qui ne sont pas toujours restés après le départ de celles-ci, depuis que la Transylvanie a été rattachée à la Roumanie au début de ce siècle (Budai-Deleanu I, 1991: I, 225–268, II, 344–414, 507–514); les Saxons et les Székely sous les deux „occupations". Les „Saxons", — qui sont d'ailleurs essentiellement originaires de Rhénanie, de Wallonie et du Brabant —, ont colonisé les vallées de la région de l'Olt depuis le milieu du XIIe siècle (Budai-Deleanu I, 1991: I, 275–304, II, 418–424, 515–519). Ils ont apporté avec eux leurs habitudes sociales et culturelles, transplantant en quelque sorte leurs logique et leur pratique sociales dans un nouvel environnement (Nägler Th., 1992). Une grande partie d'entre eux sont d'ailleurs retournés en Allemagne depuis l'ouverture des frontières qui a suivi la chute du régime de Ceausescu en 1989. Le dernier recensement de la population en Roumanie, en janvier 1992, les dénombre à un peu plus d'une centaine de milliers de personnes („26 «Ethnic Groups»", 1992: 27).

Mais le groupe ethnique et culturel de Transylvanie le plus représentatif de ce phénomène du nationalisme endogène est formé par les Székely. Ils parlent le hongrois, — un hongrois qualifié d'archaïque par les Hongrois de Hongrie —, mais ils ne sont pas Hongrois, selon toute vraisemblance. Leur origine reste obscure et fort controversée: certains historiens les présentent comme des vieux Magyars, contemporains de l'arrivée des Petchénègues (XIe s.); d'autres les rendent contemporains des Avars (VIe–VIIe s.), voire des Huns eux-mêmes (IVe–Ve s.); dans ces deux derniers cas, ils seraient antérieurs à l'arrivée des Hongrois eux-mêmes. D'autres encore les considèrent comme des turco-magyars, des Kazars magyarisés, établis comme paysans-soldats dans les postes avancés des confins militaires, ces marches frontières créées par les Autrichiens pour se protéger de l'envahisseur ottoman (Budai-Deleanu I, 1991: I, 269–276; II, 414–418, 514–515; Köpeczi B. (éd.), 1989: 158–194; Dami A., 1946: 47–48). Une charte de 1092 fait apparaître leur nom pour la première fois sous la forme „Sciul, Scichul", en liaison avec des transports de sel, de Transylvanie en Hongrie (Köpeczi B. (éd.), 1992: 155). Ce nom donnera „Sicule", qui deviendra „Szekler" pour les Saxons. Quoi qu'il en soit, les Székely gardèrent pendant très longtemps leur organisation militaire fondée sur une paysannerie libre, pratiquement jusqu'au XVe siècle, en résistant longtemps à la féodalisation imposée par les Hongrois dès leur arrivée en Transylvanie (Castellan G., 1984: 4). S'ils adoptèrent le hongrois, ils durent le faire fort tôt, car ils se sont longtemps considérés comme membres de la nation hongroise, même si la vivacité et la virulence de leurs traditions et de leurs signes identitaires ne les fit pas accepter comme tels par les Hongrois. La force endogène de leur structure sociale parvint cependant à les faire reconnaître, dès le XVe siècle, comme l'une des trois „nations" de Transylvanie: à côté des nobles d'origine hongroise et des Saxons (Köpeczi B. (éd.), 1989: 195–214).

Longtemps marginalisés par les Hongrois au point de vue culturel, — mais intégrés aux structures sociales et économiques de la Transylvanie (contrairement aux Roumains qui ne purent jamais obtenir le statut de 4e „nation", alors qu'ils étaient les plus nombreux en Transylvanie depuis le XVe siècle) —, marginalisés maintenant par les Roumains au point de vue culturel et, dans une certaine mesure, politique, les Székely ont toujours renforcé leur identité propre et ils cherchent toujours à le faire par l'emploi de leur langue et par leur expression musicale particulière. En 1952, une décentralisation administrative permit la création d'une „Région autonome hongroise", — supprimée depuis lors —, où 500.000 Magyars et Székely se sont retrouvés autour de Tîrgu Mures/Marosvásárhely comme capitale. Si la lente agonie de la Roumanie de la fin de l'ère Ceausescu alla jusqu'à provoquer la destruction du centre de Bucarest, la politique de „systémisation" entreprise par le *Conducator* vers la fin de la décennie 80 visait aussi essentiellement des villages de Transylvanie et tout particulièrement les minorités hongroises (Grecu V., 1984; Eliade M., 1992; Iancu G., 1992; Manea M., Pascu A. & Teodorescu B., 1992; Sándor K. & Szacvay I, s.d.; Suciu D., 1992; Bailby E., 1990; Durandin C., 1990; Laselv P., 1988; Le Gloannec A.-M., 1980a; Macovescu G., 1973; Philippot R., 1980b; Planche A., 1985 & 1988; Prunier G., 1990; Tiraspolsky A., 1980; Verrier D., 1990). Le dernier recensement démographique du pays (janvier 1992) fait état de 1.619.368 „Hongrois", soit 7,1% de la population totale du pays, regroupant sous cette appellation l'ensemble des Hongrois d'origine et des Székely. Ils forment près du quart de la population générale en Transylvanie (23,9%), avec des concentrations de 41,3% dans le département de Mures, de 75,2% dans celui de Covasna et de 84,6% dans celui de Harghita („26 «Ethnic Groups»", 1992: 27–29).

Les Slovènes et les Croates peuvent aussi, dans une certaine mesure, montrer à quel point le nationalisme endogène peut renforcer les identités culturelles: les Slovènes, en effet, sont les Slaves du monde autrichien, alors que les Croates sont ceux du monde hongrois. Le problème des Slovènes est fort semblable à celui des Polonais ou des Tchèques du milieu du VIIIe siècle: leur défense contre les Germains. Ils n'eurent pas le temps de se constituer en Etat et furent intégrés à l'Empire de Charlemagne, dont ils formèrent la marche de Carinthie. Toujours dans l'orbite germanique, bien plus tard, le compromis austro-hongrois de 1867 rattacha la Cisleithanie, — dont la Carniole —, à l'Autriche jusqu'à la dissolution de cet Empire au début de ce siècle. Les Slovènes furent donc progressivement germanisés au point de vue culturel, mais ils parvinrent à maintenir leur langue et quelques traditions, la Carniole ayant été moins dominée que les autres régions germaniques, parce que plus méridionale.

Les Croates ont eu l'avantage sur les Slovènes de pouvoir former une nation indépendante qui, dès le Xe siècle, était parvenue a créer un royaume indépendant englobant déjà les régions de la Slavonie et de la Dalmatie actuelles. Ils avaient opté, au IXe siècle déjà, pour le catholicisme romain et, pour ne pas tomber sous une influence germanique, — comme leurs voisins slovènes —, ils reconnurent, au début du XIIe siècle, la souveraineté du roi de Hongrie. Cette union des Croates à la Hongrie était librement consentie: elle stipulait l'autonomie des deux pays et se fondait sur l'égalité de leurs droits. Cette remarque est capitale pour comprendre l'attitude ultérieure que la Croatie a toujours eue vis-à-vis de la Hongrie. Le compromis austro-hongrois de 1867 la fit passer dans la Transleithanie, appartenant à la Hongrie, dans des circonstances tellement défavorables pour les Slaves qu'un autre compromis „hungaro-croate" aménagea le premier l'année suivante (Béhar P., 1991: 16–18, 118). Les Croates sont parvenus à ménager leur identité culturelle de slavophone, à la charnière du monde occidental (catholique) et oriental (orthodoxe) au point de vue religieux, sous l'aile „protectrice" des (Austro-) Hongrois. Des confins militaires furent créés en Croatie, comme en Transylvanie, où des populations d'origines différentes, — dont des Serbes —, furent progressivement invitées à jouer le rôle de „bouclier protecteur" contre les incursions ottomanes. La politique populationniste de l'*Aufklärung* visait essentiellement à peupler les régions nouvellement libérées des Turcs. L'origine des Serbes en Croatie remonte à cette période (Ruegg F., 1991: 85–116). Mais, à l'époque, il n'y avait pas de nationalisme exacerbé et exclusif comme moteur d'action. On se trouvait, au contraire, dans des ensembles pluri-nationaux et les critères identitaires n'étaient pas la seule référence, comme ce sera le cas pour la constitution des Etats-nations. Dans ces circonstances, les Croates se sont accommodés de ces directives qui leur venaient du nord, tant qu'ils pouvaient préserver ce qui leur apparaissait comme essentiel au niveau de leur logique sociale spécifique. Pourtant, ce dernier cas montre déjà le renforcement et la „réactivation" des logiques sociales et culturelles endogènes par une confrontation de plus en plus forte liée à l'expansionnisme exogène des voisins.

## 3.4. Les expansionnismes exogènes

Vu sous l'angle interne des différentes communautés ethniques et culturelles, l'expansionnisme exogène se manifeste sous la forme d'un mouvement d'oppression venant du gouvernement central qui veut imposer son point de vue aux minorités se trouvant dans le pays. Celles-ci sont finalement marginalisées, de façon directe ou indirecte, selon le schéma expliqué plus haut:

| „Neutralisation" → „Normalisation" → [la différence=„anormale"] → „Marginalisation" |

l'impersonnalisation de populations, dans les villes surtout, conduit à la „neutralisation", des villes d'abord puis de l'ensemble du pays parfois, dans un second temps; cette neutralisation de l'identité est présentée comme étant la norme de référence. La „normalisation" de la population en arrive à faire passer l'idée que la différence est „a-normale" et, par conséquent anormale!

### 3.4.1. Marginalisation d'une minorité

La „marginalisation" de la minorité ethnique et/ou culturelle est donc un fait qui va de soi dans cette logique du „rouleau compresseur" vers l'uniformisation. Il n'y a pas de place pour la différence; il n'y a donc aucun respect pour cette différence et encore moins pour les gens qui la représentent! On assiste à un phénomène de maximalisation de la distance inter-ethnique par l'accentuation de la différence. Tous les stéréotypes possibles liés à cette situation de „minoritaires" sont utilisés pour permettre les brimades contre les „autres", les anormaux, — ceux qui ne „font" pas comme nous, ceux qui ne „sont" pas comme nous —, pour permettre leur liquidation culturelle (= un ethnocide) ou leur liquidation physique (= un génocide). Tout le monde connaît les cas „classiques" des Chinois en Océanie française, des Pakistanais en Afrique de l'Est, des Amérindiens dans la plupart des Etats d'Amérique latine, — surtout des Indiens des plaines en Amérique du Nord où les méthodes ont été très expéditives et des Indiens de la forêt amazonienne où les méthodes sont encore pour le moins expéditives, pour ne pas parler des populations aborigènes en Australie ou négro-africaines en Afrique du Sud.

La situation est-elle différente en Bosnie-Herzégovine, où les Musulmans, majoritaires dans leur République, sont en train de se faire „marginaliser", — et de quelle façon! —, par les Serbes et les Croates? Faut-il rappeler les méthodes utilisées: le règne de la terreur pour provoquer les départs et les transferts de populations, les viols systématiques et programmés pour humilier avant de tuer, dans certains cas extrêmes, l'internement dans des camps et l'exécution sommaire de populations civiles?... Toute cette panoplie de techniques dites de „purification ethnique" ou de „nettoyage ethnique", n'est-ce pas de l'impérialisme teinté de racisme, dans la tradition la plus pure de tout système nationaliste poussé aux abois? Quelle différence avec le nazisme, pourtant si décrié, que personne ne voulait voir revenir? Quelle différence avec l'apartheid, officiellement en voie de dissolution, mais qui ne s'est jamais autant renforcé dans les partis extrémistes des *Boers afrikaners* ? Quelle différence avec le stalinisme de triste mémoire aussi, dont les pays d'Europe centrale sortent à peine, qui n'avait rien à envier non plus aux autres grands de la „purification" ou du „nettoyage" de leurs pays? Fallait-il vraiment que le national-communisme d'un Milosevic prenne la relève de cette triste série et soutienne, par contamination, l'attitude quasi paranoïaque d'un Karadzic (De La Gorce P.-M., 1992a, 1992b, 1993a, 1993b)?

Pour infâme et infamante qu'elle soit, cette technique de „systématisation" n'est pas seulement l'apanage des Serbes, comme on le lit bien souvent dans les médias (Roux M., 1992; Lutard C., 1992b & 1992d) ou dans des ouvrages qui paraissent à un rythme assez soutenu ces derniers temps (par exemple: Grmek M. & al., 1993). Les Croates ne sont pas en reste et, s'ils ont été plus discrets — mais non moins actifs — au début, ils dévoilent leur jeu actuellement, aussi, en Bosnie centrale. Leur retournement d'alliance contre les Musulmans et les accords passés récemment avec les Serbes contre leurs anciens alliés, pour se partager la Bosnie-Herzégovine sur le dos des Musulmans, en disent long sur leur attitude, leurs intentions et la franchise de leurs propos. Dans le domaine du terrorisme et de la lâcheté, les Serbes et les Croates n'ont pas de leçons de moralité à se donner car, pour reprendre leurs moyens d'argumentation et de contamination mentale se référant à la Deuxième Guerre mondiale (endoctrinement au point de vue *emic*, propagande au point de vue *etic*), les „Tchetniks", — francs-tireurs serbes —, n'avaient vraiment rien à envier aux „Oustachis", — séparatistes croates —, quoi qu'en disent les uns et les autres!

L'expansionnisme serbe, — à la base de toute cette série de dérapages actuels —, était prévisible depuis 1988 déjà, lorsque le populisme serbe du nouveau président de la Ligue des communistes de Serbie menaça l'équilibre de la Yougoslavie d'alors. Slobodan Milosevic profita d'une crise économique sans précédent dans le pays et des mouvements de revendication nationale qui s'en sont suivis, après plusieurs mois d'agitation ethnique et sociale — entre autres et surtout au Kosovo —, pour identifier la Serbie à ses vues radicales et centralisatrices. Il fallait juguler les „séparatistes" albanais du Kosovo et revoir la Constitution de 1974 qui empêchait le gouvernement de Serbie d'exercer son autorité sur la totalité de son territoire. Il s'était déjà montré intraitable au niveau fédéral, exprimant clairement qu'il ne ferait aucune concession, fût-ce au prix „*des cassures et des affrontements les plus graves*". Si la Serbie n'était pas entendue, elle ne pourrait pas recouvrer sa stabilité intérieure avec tout ce que cela comporte de danger pour l'unité de la Fédération (Yankovitch P., 1988b). Pouvait-on ne pas savoir?

Si, comme on le voit ici, les tensions ethniques entre les différentes composantes de la population sont, de plus, canalisées ou manipulées par l'Etat, tous les excès sont permis puisqu'ils sont „légalisés", c'est-à-dire impunissables *de facto* à défaut de l'être *de jure*. On parvient ainsi à faire passer un malaise „population-Etat" en un malaise „population-minorités". Chacun sait que la situation instable des Philippines du président Marcos n'était pas dû à l'inégalité socio-économique du pays, mais bien aux rebelles musulmans du Sud! De même, chacun sait que la situation précaire de la Serbie des années 1980, n'était pas due à l'inégalité socio-économique des populations de la République, mais bien aux séparatistes musulmans du Sud! Les Albanais de la „Province autonome du Kosovo", selon la Constitution de 1974, perdirent leur statut d'autonomie en 1989 par la force des armes, la police et l'armée ayant encerclé le parlement pour lui en imposer la suppression. La nouvelle loi du 26 juin 1990 sur „les relations de travail dans les circonstances d'exception" imposa le licenciement de tous les responsables albanais dans les domaines de la vie sociale, politique et économique et leur remplacement par des Serbes (Ministère de l'Information de la République de Kosove, 1991: 22–23). Cette politique de licenciements et de serbisation provoqua la déstabilisation totale du tissu socio-économique du Kosovo... dont les Albanais furent rendus responsables! Politique d'intimidation, expulsions, répression dans l'enseignement, perquisitions, brutalités policières, incidents armés et distributions d'armes, acharnement judiciaire, purification ethnique..., autant de pratiques banalisées dans la vie de tous les jours à l'encontre de la „minorité" albanaise (plus de 90% dans le Kosovo), pratiques dénoncées par certains organismes internationaux (*Licenciements et Purification ethnique au Kosovo (octobre 1992)* ) et répertoriées par d'autres (*Yugoslavia: Human Rights Abuses in Kosovo 1990–1992*, 1992), en violation constante des droits de l'homme les plus élémentaires.

En fait, les Serbes ne se battent pas pour les „droits de l'homme", mais bien pour les „droits de l'âme"! Si les Albanais sont les boucs émissaires marginalisés de la société serbe, ce n'est pas tant parce qu'ils sont Albanais que parce qu'ils sont musulmans... Il faut donc „purifier" dans ce domaine là aussi. Des ouvrages l'explicitent de façon on ne peut plus claire (Yelen A., 1989), n'hésitant pas à manipuler le passé historico-culturel des populations pour le faire entrer dans le moule de sa propre vision des choses. Et l'on comprend mieux, dès lors, le transfert rapide qui s'est fait entre les Albanais du Kosovo et les Bosniaques musulmans de la Bosnie-Herzégovine. Le recours à l'identité religieuse n'est pas nouveau pour maximiser la distance interculturelle („Eglises et démocratie en Europe de l'Est", [dossier] 1990; Auge M., 1984; Blanquart P., 1987; Bourricaud F., 1984; Davy M.-M., 1980; Fesquet H., 1980; Gouillard J., 1980; Jomier J., 1980; Lespoir P., 1987; Lhommel E., 1990; Mantran R., 1980a; Michel P., 1990a, 1990b & 1990c; Milcent E., 1982; Roussel B., 1980), mais quand on en arrive à des caricatures telles que celles qui sont parfoisprésentées, on peut se demander ce qui reste de crédible au niveau rationnel: on se perd dans des explications complexes et ambiguës pour prouver le fondement métaphysique de l'âme orthodoxe et de son message de paix, alors qu'une lecture „primaire" du Coran ne présente l'islam que comme une machine de combat, ne prônant que l'intolérance tant au point de vue religieux que socio-politique et économique (Yelen A., 1989: 27–84).

Une confusion est volontairement entretenue entre „islamisation" et „albanisation" pour la question du Kosovo. Par l'identification de l'un à l'autre, on en arrive à rendre les Albanais responsables de la politique turque dans les Balkans pour tenter de justifier la politique serbe actuelle! De la même façon, aujourd'hui, on veut faire passer les Musulmans de Bosnie-Herzégovine pour des terroristes musulmans qui ne se nourrissent qu'à la source de l'intégrisme islamiste. Ce type d'amalgames et de simplifications abusives ne peuvent que prouver la méconnaissance réelle des problèmes par ceux qui les utilisent ou leur désir de manipulation à des fins d'auto-justification. Dans un cas comme dans l'autre la démarche est dangereuse, car elle ne fait que renforcer la marginalisation des „minoritaires", — ou de ceux qui sont présentés comme tels —, en les poussant dans une logique de résistance... dont on les accusera vraisemblablement, après coup, d'être les protagonistes!

En fait, le problème n'est pas tant religieux que démographique, comme le prouvent les analyses comparatives entre l'évolution des principaux groupes nationaux et confessionnels de la Bosnie-Herzégovine

Tableau 3

**Évolution des principaux groupes confessionnels
en Bosnie-Herzégovine (1879–1953)**

|  | 1879 | 1895 | 1910 | 1921 | 1931 | 1953 |
|---|---|---|---|---|---|---|
| Musulmans | 448 613 | 548 632 | 612 137 | 588 247 | 717 562 | 917 720 |
|  | (38,7%) | (35,0%) | (32,2%) | (31,1%) | (30,9%) | (32,2%) |
| Orthodoxes | 496 761 | 673 246 | 825 918 | 829 612 | 1 028 723 | 1 002 737 |
|  | (42,9%) | (42,9%) | (43,5%) | (43,9%) | (44,3%) | (35,2%) |
| Catholiques | 209 391 | 334 142 | 434 061 | 443 914 | 557 836 | 601 489 |
|  | (18,1%) | (21,3%) | (22,9%) | (23,5%) | (24,0%) | (21,1%) |
| Autres* | 3 675 | 12 060 | 26 428 | 28 156 | 19 445 | 325 844 |
|  | (0,3%) | (0,8%) | (1,4%) | (1,5%) | (0,8%) | (11,5%) |
| Total | 1 158 440 | 1 568 080 | 1 898 544 | 1 889 929 | 2 323 566 | 2 847 790 |

* Dont 11 248 juifs en 1931; dont 377 juifs et 310 469 „sans confession" en 1953

**Évolution des principaux groupes nationaux
en Bosnie-Herzégovine (1948–1991)**

|  | 1948 | 1953 | 1961 | 1971 | 1981 | 1991 |
|---|---|---|---|---|---|---|
| Musulmans | 788 403 | 891 798 | 842 248 | 1 482 430 | 1 629 924 | 1 905 829 |
|  | (30,7%) | (31,3%) | (25,7%) | (39,6%) | (39,5%) | (43,7%) |
| Serbes | 1 136 116 | 1 261 405 | 1 406 057 | 1 393 148 | 1 320 644 | 1 369 258 |
|  | (44,3%) | (44,3%) | (42,9%) | (37,2%) | (32,0%) | (31,4%) |
| Croates | 614 123 | 654 227 | 711 665 | 772 491 | 758 136 | 755 895 |
|  | (24,0%) | (23,0%) | (21,7%) | (20,6%) | (18,4%) | (17,3%) |
| Yougoslaves | — | — | 275 883 | 43 796 | 326 280 | 239 845 |
|  |  |  | (8,4%) | (1,2%) | (7,9%) | (5,5%) |
| Autres | 26 635 | 40 029 | 42 095 | 54 246 | 89 024 | 93 747 |
|  | (1,0%) | (1,4%) | (1,3%) | (1,4%) | (2,2%) | (2,1%) |
| Total | 2 565 277 | 2 847 459 | 3 277 948 | 3 746 111 | 4 124 008 | 4 364 574 |

(Bougarel X., 1992: 89, cf. tableau No 3). La comparaison des taux de natalité, de mortalité et d'accroissement naturel des Serbes, des Croates, des Musulmans (au sens de nation constitutive de la Bosnie-Herzégovine) et des Albanais, ramenés à l'échelle de l'ensemble de l'ex-Yougoslavie pendant les décennies 1950–1980 (Bougarel X., 1992: 95, cf. tableau No 4), montre clairement que la démographie travaille dans le sens des Musulmans et des Albanais. Alors que le taux d'accroissement naturel des Serbes est passé de 16,8‰ à 4,3‰ et celui des Croates de 13,1% à 4,1 %, celui des Musulmans est descendu de 26,1‰ à 15,4‰ et celui des Albanais est monté de 22,3% à 25,4% (un taux de 25% correspond à un doublement de la population en 28 ans!). Les Serbes et les Croates étaient donc en voie de minorisation démographique, situation qu'il aurait été difficile de justifier à terme, alors qu'ils détenaient l'essentiel du pouvoir dans l'ancienne structure fédérative de la Yougoslavie. Bien qu'ayant une politique plus nataliste en Bosnie-Herzégovine, les Serbes (7,7‰) et les Croates (8,9‰) avaient cependant un rythme d'accroissement pratiquement deux fois inférieur à celui de Musulmans (14,8‰). Même dans les cinq principales villes de cette République, les Serbes et les Croates étaient en régression ou en stabilité, non pas par rapport à la population des Musulmans — qui connaissaient la même évolution qu'eux! —, mais au regard des autres composantes de la population yougoslave (Bougarel X., 1992: 107, cf. tableau No 5). Les seuls cas d'exception remarquables sont formées par les villes de Sarajevo et de Banja Luka. Dans la capitale bosniaque, les Musulmans étaient passés de 34,6% à 41,5% de la population, alors que les Serbes et les Croates avaient „chuté" respectivement de 36,0% à 27,3% et de 23,3% à 8,9 %. Par contre, à Banja Luka, ce sont les Serbes qui sont passés de 34,8 % à 41,8% de la population, alors que les Croates en brusquement baissé de 27,7% à 13,2% et les Musulmans de 31,9% à 16,9%. On a vu la réaction d'agressivité des Serbes contre Sarajevo, où ils devenaient de plus en plus minoritaires, et celle de triomphalisme conquérant à Banja Luka, dont ils ont fait la capitale de l'Etat serbe auto-proclamé de „Bosanska Krajina", en imposant leur logique de pouvoir, basée sur la force des armes. Les réactions ne sont décidément pas les mêmes lorsqu'on se sent minorisé, selon que l'on a la force du pouvoir légal ou imposé par la violence, ou que l'on réagit selon une logique de „minorité" déjà marginalisée.

### 3.4.2. Réaction de „résistance" des minorités

Les minorités marginalisées réagissent différemment selon leur „logique" sociale et culturelle. Au départ, elles tirent leur force, non pas de la violence ou de la puissance, mais bien de leur cohésion plus grande, liée à la „communautarisation" de leur société. Elles résistent au pouvoir en place en allant puiser dans leur patrimoine culturel ce qui renforce leur identité et les valorise à leurs yeux. Les pratiques rituelles, vues sous cet angle, ne sont pas des survivances du passé mais des manifestations sociologiques de résistance à la pénétration d'une logique étrangère envahissante. Le rite devient un moment de vérité, de conscientisation,

**Tableau 4**

Taux d'accroissement naturel
des nations constitutives de la Bosnie-Herzégovine (1953–1981)

| | 1953 | 1961 | 1971 | 1981 |
|---|---|---|---|---|
| Musulmans (Youg.) | 26,1 | 28,2 | 16,7 | 15,4 |
| Musulmans (B.-H.) | 27,4 | 29,5 | 18,6 | 14,8 |
| Serbes (Youg.) | 16,8 | 11,1 | 6,4 | 4,3 |
| Serbes (B.-H.) | 20,1 | 19,6 | 11,3 | 7,7 |
| Croates (Youg.) | 13,1 | 11,9 | 5,8 | 4,1 |
| Croates (B.-H.) | 21,1 | 24,8 | 14,7 | 8,9 |
| Albanais (Youg.) | 22,3 | 31,3 | 29,0 | 25,4 |
| Population yougoslave | 16,4 | 13,8 | 8,8 | 7,5 |
| * Les taux concernant les Albanais sont donnés à titre de comparaison | | | | |

d'analyse de la société „communautaire" face à la logique centralisatrice de l'Etat qui s'est superposée à son système de valeurs. En ex-Yougoslavie, le recours à l'identité religieuse des populations musulmanes, minoritaires dans un monde chrétien — catholique ou orthodoxe —, a même été utilisée pour l'utiliser contre eux, les „dominateurs" ayant renforcé cette identité religieuse en la présentant de façon uniquement négative: les Albanais ne seraient que de dangereux séparatistes nourris au fanatisme musulman et les Musulmans (de Bosnie-Herzégovine) que des activistes intégristes... En fait, ils ne sont même pas „chiites", — ceux qui sont à la base de l'islamisme —, mais Sunnites, tant les Albanais du Kosovo que les Musulmans (pour ceux qui sont encore pratiquants).

C'est par ces pratiques rituelles que les sociétés communautaires renouvellent leur histoire en la réactualisant à chaque occasion. Chaque décès, chaque mariage est l'occasion d'un partage social rituel et symbolique du patrimoine commun, par la reproduction du savoir que l'on tient dans anciens. C'est particulièrement vrai dans les sociétés de tradition orale du Tiers Monde, mais cette réalité est encore bien présente dans les milieux ruraux de nos sociétés traditionnelles européennes, surtout en Europe centrale et orientale où les traditions sont restées plus vivantes. Le fait d'en avoir interdit, ou très strictement codifié, l'expression durant la période socialiste n'a fait que renforcer ces pratiques en un courant sous-jacent. Le recours à la vie traditionnelle (qui n'est pas synonyme de „folklore") et aux pratiques sociales identitaires (qui ne

Tableau 5

**Composition nationale des cinq principales villes
de Bosnie-Herzégovine (1948–1981)**

| | | Musulmans | Serbes | Croates | Yougoslaves | Autres | Total |
|---|---|---|---|---|---|---|---|
| Sarajevo | 1948 | 39 328 | 40 914 | 26 482 | — | 7 045 | 113 769 |
| | | (34,6%) | (36,0%) | (23,3%) | | (6,1%) | (100,0%) |
| | 1981 | 157 505 | 103 718 | 33 756 | 71 042 | 13 587 | 379 608 |
| | | (41,5%) | (27,3%) | (8,6%) | (18,7%) | (3,6%) | (100,0%) |
| Banja Luka | 1948 | 9 951 | 10 861 | 8 662 | — | 1 749 | 31 223 |
| | | (31,9%) | (34,8%) | (27,7%) | | (5,6%) | (100,0%) |
| | 1981 | 20 916 | 51 829 | 16 314 | 30 318 | 4 550 | 123 937 |
| | | (16,9%) | (41,8%) | (13,2%) | (24,5%) | (3,6%) | (100,0%) |
| Tuzla | 1948 | 13 944 | 4 869 | 7 866 | — | 715 | 27 394 |
| | | (50,9%) | (17,8%) | (28,7%) | | (2,6%) | (100,0%) |
| | 1981 | 30 448 | 11 278 | 5 383 | 16 301 | 1 681 | 65 091 |
| | | (46,8%) | (17,3%) | (8,3%) | (25,0%) | (2,6%) | (100,0%) |
| Mostar | 1948 | 9 981 | 5 039 | 6 062 | — | 524 | 21 606 |
| | | (46,2%) | (23,3%) | (28,1%) | | (2,4%) | (100,0%) |
| | 1981 | 18 414 | 11 353 | 17 621 | 14 732 | 1 307 | 63 427 |
| | | (29,0%) | (17,9%) | (27,8%) | (23,2%) | (2,1%) | (100,0%) |
| Zenica | 1948 | 6 400 | 3 269 | 5 040 | — | 841 | 15 550 |
| | | (41,2%) | (21,0%) | (32,4%) | | (5,4%) | (100,0%) |
| | 1981 | 22 146 | 12 728 | 11 716 | 14 437 | 2 542 | 63 569 |
| | | (34,8%) | (20,0%) | (18,5%) | (22,7%) | (4,0%) | (100,0%) |

sont pas synonymes de „passéisme") renforcent les liens de solidarité des
sociétés minoritaires et/ou marginalisées. Mais il est certain que le savoir
tiré de la valorisation du passé et du „prestige" des ancêtres ne peut que
s'opposer à la logique marchande, nationaliste de l'appareil d'Etat, basé
sur la „puissance", l'expansionnisme centrifuge, qui sera toujours perçu
comme un totalitarisme par le groupe minoritaire.

Les deux formes ultimes de résistances, liées à l'opposition „pouvoir-
prestige / pouvoir puissance", déboucheront toujours sur la même
alternative: soit la résistance passive, soit les conflits armés. La „résistance
passive" d'un peuple marginalisé, vue sous son angle *emic*, est la seule
réponse qui permette de ne pas entrer en conflit ouvert avec le groupe
majoritaire qui dispose de la force légale ou imposée. On fait le dos
rond tant que les excès des „agresseurs" ne vont pas trop loin ou tant
qu'on peut encore les supporter, même s'ils dépassent les limites d'une
situation ordinaire, normale. Mais quels sont les fondements de la norme
et les limites de la „normalité"? Vue sous l'angle *etic*, cette résistance
sera interprétée par le pouvoir en place comme un „conservatisme" qui
ne peut conduire qu'au „séparatisme". Le cas des Albanais du Kosovo est
exemplaire de ce point de vue, malgré toutes les provocations et les actes

de terrorisme légal(isé) dont ils ont déjà été l'objet, en l'absence de toute possibilité légale d'action ou de réaction contre le pouvoir central(isateur) (Allain M.-F. & Galmiche X., 1992b; Chossudovsky E., 1993; Feron B., 1969; Garapon A., 1989; Jacob A., 1986; Lutard C., 1992e).

La situation des Hongrois et des Székely de Transylvanie est fort semblable, même si les conditions actuelles de leur possibilités d'expression ne sont pas tout à fait comparables. La situation politique non plus n'est pas la même puisque, sur le plan constitutionnel tout au moins, tous les citoyens roumains sont égaux devant la loi et les autorités publiques (article 16 de la nouvelle Constitution du 8 décembre 1991). Les minorités ethniques ont le droit d'exprimer leur identité ethnique, tant sur les plans culturel, linguistique que religieux, pour autant que ce ne soit pas de façon discriminatoire vis-à-vis des autres citoyens roumains (art. 6); ils ont le droit d'être éduqués dans leur langue maternelle, mais dans les formes déterminées par la loi (art.32). De plus, le pays étant un Etat unitaire et indivisible, sans distinction de quelque sorte que ce soit (art. 4), il est interdit d'avoir des propos diffamatoires, qu'ils soient nationalistes, raciaux, religieux, incitant à la discrimination ou à la sécession territoriale (art. 30) („26 «Ethnic Groups»", 1992: 27). La pratique de cette théorie est cependant une toute autre chose: l'emploi de sa langue maternelle n'est pas possible avec les instances officielles (même si elles sont magyarophones) puisque le roumain est la seule langue officielle; le maintien des écoles de langue hongroise est rendu très difficile pour différentes raisons et plusieurs d'entre elles ont été fermées pour des raisons dites „de salubrité publique et d'hygiène"; la nomination de préfets magyarophones dans les deux départements de forte concentration székely (Harghita et Covasna) a été aménagée puis supprimée, — provoquant d'ailleurs des manifestations d'opposition dans les zones concernées —, malgré le fait que l'Union Démocratique des Magyars de Roumanie (UDMR) soit un parti reconnu officiellement... (Decornoy J., 1992; „Roumanie. Manifestations de la minorité hongroise", 1993; „Les Hongrois de Roumanie manifestent contre un préfet", 1993). On en est pas encore au point de ne pas pouvoir s'exprimer du tout, comme c'est le cas pour les Albanais du Kosovo, mais les Magyars de Roumanie ont une possibilité d'expression officielle, sinon *de jure* du moins *de facto*, très restreinte. Les articles constitutionnels, parfois ambigus quand on les confronte les uns aux autres, ne sont pas interprétés de la même façon selon que l'on se trouve du côté du pouvoir en place ou de la minorité marginalisée de fait.

On voit donc que ces références à l'identité culturelle, qui sont un facteur si puissant de cohésion au niveau *emic*, sont souvent récupérées et utilisées comme facteur de divisions au niveau *etic* par le pouvoir centralisateur. A côté des exemples cités précédemment, le cas de la Transylvanie est aussi révélateur de l'approche nationaliste que l'on peut faire d'une situation donnée, en niant les spécificités culturelles et régionales, ou en les remettant dans un autre contexte, pour les faire entrer dans un moule unitaire. Les différents conflits sociaux et les révoltes paysannes de ceux qui ne purent jamais devenir la « Nation", — à l'époque où la Transylvanie était dans le giron magyar —, étaient-elles des „luttes sociales" contre leurs oppresseurs, — les nobles et les puissants dont ils dépendaient —, luttes liées à la misère et à la pauvreté des populations de cette époque, ou des „luttes nationales" contre les autorités politiques du moment, donc hongroises (Karnoouh C., 1990: 117, n. 30)? Pour l'historiographie roumaine, la question n'a même pas le mérite d'être posée! Mais y a-t-il vraiment une différence entre la Grande révolte de Horea, Closca et Crisan en 1784, en Transylvanie, et la révolte paysanne de 1907, en Roumanie cette fois, dirigée contre la propre oligarchie du Royaume de l'époque? Vraie ou fausse, la récupération nationaliste *a posteriori* est toujours facile et sert toujours le pouvoir en place du moment.

La richesse culturelle et variée de la tradition populaire du monde rural peut aussi être découpée de façon arbitraire par le pouvoir, — en isolant les éléments de leur contexte d'ensemble —, en vue d'une justification de l'ancienneté des traditions comme vérité (métaphysique) première. La volonté unificatrice de la nation a conduit à ce genre de pratiques où l'on veut présenter une culture nationale de masse comprise comme l'essence des valeurs de l'Etat-ethnie-nation. Souvent même, la relecture du passé des minorités nationales par le pouvoir central conduit à une manipulation de l'histoire, pour faire entrer cet héritage culturel divers et fractionné (celui des ethnies) dans les vues centripètes du pouvoir en place (celui de l'Etat-nation) en vue d'une autojustification. Le linguiste roumain Ovidiu Densusianu, au début du XXe siècle, dénonçait déjà la même pratique imposée par le pouvoir à propos de l'interprétation de l'histoire de la langue roumaine elle-même, — qui n'est pas si unitaire qu'il n'y paraît à première vue —, et des coutumes populaires de son pays. On ne devait défendre „que les thèses qui concordent avec les idées dominantes sur le passé du peuple roumain" (Karnoouh C., 1990: 132 & 165).

A côté de la résistance passive des peuples et nations minoritaires, l'autre branche de l'alternative des formes ultimes de résistances, liées à l'opposition „pouvoir-prestige / pouvoir puissance", est celle des conflits armés, des mouvements d'opposition armée, voire de libération nationale. L'éclatement de l'ex-Yougoslavie et la sortie de chacune des Républiques constitutives de l'ancienne fédération en est l'illustration la plus manifeste. Le malaise était déjà latent, toutefois, et les résistances devenaient de plus en plus fortes (Canapa M.-P., 1977, 1980 & 1981; Elorriaga J.F., 1988 & 1990; Fejtö F., 1971 & 1972; Fralon J.-A., 1987; Lund F., 1992; Roux M., 1990; Valladao A., 1982 & 1984; „La Yougoslavie, banc d'essai pour la nouvelle Europe?" [Dossier], 1990). La Slovénie et la Croatie proclament leur indépendance fin juin 1991, ce qui provoque l'intervention de l'armée fédérale qui s'oppose au dépeçage du pays et au changement de ses frontières (Schreiber Th., 1987). Cette armée se révélera très vite être une armée serbo-fédérale au service de la défense du dogmatisme d'un leadership serbe, tout autant communiste que nationaliste. La „guerre civile" avait commencé. La Macédoine et la Bosnie-Herzégovine proclament leur „souveraineté" respectivement le 8 septembre et le 15 octobre 1991. La guerre fait déjà de nombreuses victimes et redouble de violence et de barbarie à mesure que les reconnaissances internationales commencent à se concrétiser. On est passé d'un „projet d'union libre à l'étouffement des différences" Samary C., 1991a, 1991b, 1991c, 1992a, 1992b, 1992c, 1992d & 1993).

La nouvelle République fédérale de Yougoslavie est réduite à l'union de la Serbie et du Montenegro, le 7 juillet 1991. La Serbie garde toujours la haute main sur la Voivodine et sur le Kosovo (qui ont perdu leur statut de Région autonome depuis 1989). Le fait que la Voivodine représente 80% des terres agricoles de l'ex-Yougoslavie, qu'elle en était le premier fournisseur de produits agricoles, qu'elle concentre toutes les capacités de raffinage de la Serbie, et que le Kosovo détient 60% des richesses minérales de l'ex-Yougoslavie, dont 50% des ressources de lignite, (Jestin-Fleury N., 1992) explique peut être pourquoi la Serbie ne tient pas tant à laisser s'échapper des régions importantes au point de vue économique. Les raisons identitaires sont-elles aussi des alibis pour cacher une réalité plus prosaïque? Et la „fédération" avec le

Montenegro n'estelle plus simplement le débouché indispensable dont
la Serbie à besoin sur l'Adriatique pour ne pas être enclavée? Il y a des
liens indubitables et incontournables entre l'économique, le national et
l'identitaire...

## Conclusion:
## „Vouloir savoir" pour „savoir vouloir"?

Le sujet est loin d'être clos! Une question est-elle jamais résolue
d'ailleurs, puisque le contexte dans lequel elle se situe évolue en
permanence... Cette approche sur la résurgence des groupes ethniques et
culturels en Europe centrale et orientale, suite à l'implosion des régimes
communistes, ne se voulait pas tant une approche historique du problème
qu'une réflexion à propos du problème identitaire. Le regard croisé, —
à la jonction de l'histoire, de la géographie, de l'anthropologie culturelle
et économique, de la sociologie, de la géopolitique..., voulait mettre en
évidence la complexité des questions soulevées, ainsi que le relief différent
que les situations peuvent prendre, suivant le regard que l'on porte sur
les réalités envisagées. L'objectivité scientifique est impossible lorsqu'on
aborde des questions humaines et sociales, les points de vue de chacun
étant trop personnalisés par les prismes déformants des sociétés que l'on
étudie (aspect *etic*), ainsi que ceux de son propre milieu culturel (aspect
*emic*). Reste l'honnêteté du chercheur face à la démarche entreprise...

Il faut „vouloir savoir". Cette première démarche n'est déjà pas
évidente, car elle dérange souvent notre confort et remet en question
notre échelle de valeurs, dès que l'on se pose des questions fondamentales
au niveau de l'approche métaphysique et philosophique des communautés
humaines. Si, de plus, elle doit passer par des intermédiaires, — ce
qui est souvent le cas —, elle risque d'être influencée ou déformée par
ces filtres sociétaux, conscients ou inconscients, entre nous et la Réalité
(Amrani S., 1991; Chauvier J.-M., 1990; Mattelard A., 1981 & 1992; Mond
G., 1987; Roman J., 1992; Vallauzd P. & Fouche E., 1990). Dans notre
société du visuel, nous risquons fort de tomber dans le superficiel et/ou
le voyeurisme. L'aspect répétitif d'une certaine réalité, fût-elle tragique,
a tendance à la banaliser: la guerre-spectacle la guerre désincarnée de la
télévision... Mais les libertés publiques de nos sociétés libérales, parfois
nouvellement acquises, ne nous mettent pas à l'abri de la désinformation

(Balle F., 1984; Chevallier J., 1984; Sanguinetti A., 1993). Les faux charniers de Timisoara, présentés par la télévision roumaine, fin 1989, ou la Guerre du Golfe filtrée par la chaîne américaine CNN, qui en avait l'exclusivité, sont encore dans toutes les mémoires. Si, de plus, des gouvernements partent en croisade pour le rétablissement de la „vérité", c'est-à-dire de „leur" vérité (Hartmann F., 1993), on n'est plus très loin du Ministère de la Vérité de George Orwell! Les informations provenant de Serbie ou de Croatie, ou se rapportant à l'ex-yougoslavie, se rapprochent parfois plus de l'endoctrinement que de l'information vraie (Garde P., 1992 et la réaction de Ivic P., Sarmadzic N., Yelen A., Maurer P. & Despot S., 1992, ou Yelen A., 1989)! Comment interpréter la „disparition" volontaire des Musulmans bosniaques sur une nouvelle carte de la Bosnie-Herzégovine, parue dans un récent manuel scolaire français d'histoire-géographie (Dumay J.-M., 1993b)?

Mais il faut ensuite „savoir vouloir". Que va-t-on faire de cette somme d'informations? Des rapports qui vont s'empiler dans des tiroirs? Quelle suite concrète a-t-on donné aux différents rapports de Tadeusz Mazowiecki, l'envoyé spécial de la commission des droits de l'homme de l'ONU en ex-Yougoslavie, autre que des condamnations verbales? Il s'agissait pourtant d'un chapelet peu courant sur la poursuite des atrocités commises contre des minorités, surtout des civils désarmés: vieillards, femmes et enfants, soit par des civils et des militaires serbes (4e Rapport), soit par des Croates (5e Rapport). Quel écho a eu le „coup de gueule" de M. Skubiszewski, le chef de la diplomatie de Varsovie, lorsqu'il dénonça l'étroitesse de vue de la Communauté Economique Européenne (CEE) dans sa gestion du problème Yougoslave, „l'échec de l'Europe" (Kaufmann S., 1993)? Comment expliquer l'attentisme de l'ONU et notre non intervention active malgré les atrocités qui étaient et qui sont toujours commises? La honte de notre participation „passive" à la „purification ethnique", tant serbe que croate, en cautionnant la politique du fait accompli...

D'un „plan de paix" irréaliste auquel la communauté internationale s'est raccrochée pendant des mois, en le présentant comme la seule alternative possible, avant de l'enterrer à la mi-mai 1993, on est passé à la politique dite des „zones de sécurité", où on ne protège toujours pas de façon active les minorités musulmanes dans ce qui s'avère, de plus en plus, être des „réserves"! On ne protège pas les minorités ethniques et culturelles marginalisées et agressées sur leur propre territoire, — et on ne leur permet même pas de se défendre, puisqu'il y a toujours un embargo sur les armes pour la Bosnie-Herzégovine —, alors qu'on ne fait rien pour s'opposer à la logique de progression de ceux qui ont la force armée, donc le pouvoir réel bien en main. Ce ne sont pas les condamnations verbales qui arrêteront les Serbes de Serbie, de Bosnie et de Croatie sur la voie de la création de la „Grande Serbie". Tous leurs responsables le disent et le reconnaissent maintenant sans ambiguïté; ce n'est qu'une question de temps... Ni ces mêmes condamnations qui arrêteront les Croates dans leur progression en Herzégovine. Les Serbes et les Croates de Bosnie-Herzégovine en sont même arrivés à s'entendre sur le partage de l'ancienne République unitaire, — qui, en fait, n'a jamais vécu —, sur le dos des Musulmans, en signant un accord entre eux qui vaut reconnaissance mutuelle de leurs „Etats". A la carence du pouvoir politique qui pourrait travailler sur les causes, se substitue l'humanitaire qui ne peut que colmater les conséquences de l'absence du politique... L'humanitaire comme révélateur (Poirot-Delpech B., 1993), mais l'humanitaire comme cible aussi! L'humanitaire perçu par certains comme une „gesticulation pacificatrice", dénotant l'impuissance ou la volonté d'une non action stratégique (Joxe A., 1993).

Une partie de la réponse tient peut-être aussi au fait que l'Europe de l'Ouest a aussi des problèmes identitaires et ses propres minorités. Les mouvements de revendication basque ou corse n'utilisent pas toujours la méthode non violente! Ne parlons pas de la question de l'Irlande du Nord qui est suffisamment explicite de par elle-même. Les nationalistes flamands n'ont, jusqu'à présent, jamais utilisé la violence physique pour faire valoir leurs droits; ils n'en revendiquent cependant pas moins une partition de fait de la Flandre, le système fédéral belge actuel n'étant, pour eux, qu'une étape transitoire vers une indépendance totale. L'exemple de la partition des Tchèques et des Slovaques est suivie de très près par tous ceux qui ont des revendications nationalistes en Europe occidentale. Alors, pourquoi l'Europe accorderait-elle à l'Est ce qu'elle n'est pas prête à accorder à ses propres minorités? Comment pourrait-elle le justifier? Une autre idée de l'Europe (Julien C., 1989)? En a-t-on vraiment une et la désire-t-on vraiment? L'Europe des Régions? De quelles régions parle-t-on d'abord (Mollstedt B., 1993)? Ensuite, d'accord, mais sur le plan économique uniquement, quitte à favoriser les „eurorégions", du fait qu'elles sont transfrontalières et parce qu'elles sont transfrontalières, mais sans bouger aux frontières *étatiques*, à défaut d'être *nationales*...

La question de Transylvanie est aussi révélatrice de l'ambiguïté du passage entre le „vouloir savoir" et le „savoir vouloir". L'histoire du „différend" hungaro-roumain du XVIIIe au XXe siècles (Borsi-Kálmán B., 1991) ne risque pas d'apporter des progrès décisifs, si les *frustrations passées des Roumains de Transylvanie* (Borsi-Kálmán B., 1993) se muent en frustrations actuelles des Hongrois de Transylvanie, à cause de la politique des autorités roumaines à leur égard. Lorsque des historiens (?) roumains affirment aujourd'hui, — reprenant la thèse immigrationniste —, que les Hongrois prétendent encore être arrivés sur des terres désertes en Transylvanie (quel historien hongrois défend encore cette thèse?) ou que la Hongrie a disparu comme Etat entre 1526 et 1918, — parce qu'elle était sous la domination des Habsbourg ou des Turcs —, tout en continuant à s'imposer aux Roumains qui étaient sur leurs terres, sans discontinuité depuis à peu près trois millénaires... (Sarambei N., 1992: 34), on ne s'étonnera pas des tensions identitaires, fondées sur une logique d'exclusion! On continue à „arranger" le passé historique et culturel des uns et des autres pour le faire entrer dans des moules idéologiques, par la marginalisation ou la négation, — partielle ou totale —, des „autres". On favorise de ce fait la valorisation totale de sa propre communauté culturelle qui, de plus, est légalisée par l'Etat nouveau dans lequel on se trouve. Si les magyarophones de Transylvanie font partie de l'*Etat* roumain, ils n'en constituent pas pour autant la *nation* roumaine!

Quand des historiens roumains actuels critiquent la politique hongroise du XIXe siècle à propos du traitement des minorités ethniques, prenant l'exemple d'un député roumain qui a provoqué des réactions de mécontentement pour s'être exprimé dans la langue roumaine au Parlement hongrois (Suciu D., 1992: 89), ne feraient ils pas bien de se rappeler que, — un siècle plus tard —, la langue hongroise ne peut toujours pas être utilisée dans les enceintes officielles, non pas au Parlement roumain, mais simplement dans les départements où les magyarophones sont effectivement majoritaires? La négation de l'altérité n'en induit pas pour autant sa disparition, surtout pas si elle repose sur une politique d'exclusion, effective à défaut d'être légale...

„Le développement ou l'identité nationale?" Une fausse alternative, disions nous en commençant. Le développement *et* l'identité nationale. Car chacun sait bien que c'est le développement des économies qui est un des facteurs principaux de stabilisation politique vers la démocratisation et le développement humain. Dans cette perspective, l'Europe occidentale a un rôle certain à jouer, mais lequel et de quelle façon? La CEE, par exemple, ne peut pas se contenter de continuer son intégration com munautaire comme si de rien n'était. Mais faut-il pour autant passer d'une fédération à douze à une confédération à trente? La CEE est-elle l'avenir de l'Est? Faut-il envisager un „plan Marshall" pour les pays de l'Est pour éviter la généralisation d'un chaos plus grand encore (Cassen B., 1989, 1990a, 1990b, 1991, 1992; Lavigne M., 1990, 1993a & 1993b; Turcq D.F., 1991)?

Le développement *et* l'identité nationale. Mais une identité qui ne comporte pas une idée d'exclusion, comme c'est trop souvent le cas dans les „Etats-nations" actuels. Une identité qui respecte celle des autres et qui, à cause de ce respect de la différence, puisse comporter une idée de rassemblement. Une Europe sans nations est un artifice dangereux (Gallo M., 1989), autant qu'une Europe morcelée en nations (Faye J.-P., 1991). On peut faire un plaidoyer pour les minorités, en montrant la richesse de la mosaïque ethnique de l'Europe centrale et orientale (Kiss C.G., 1992), mais il faut aussi attirer l'attention sur le piège que peut comporter le droit des minorités (Meyer-Bisch P., 1993), lorsque l'Etat de droit ne prend pas suffisamment en compte les identités culturelles de chacun. L'égoïsme identitaire procède souvent d'un désordre politique et économique (Attali J., 1993), mais il ne peut engendrer qu'un nouveau désordre politique et économique, au niveau local comme au niveau planétaire. La légitimation du droit des peuples, au-delà des droits de l'homme et des Etats (Uribe A., 1976), n'est pas un droit absolu lorsqu'il se fait au détriment d'un autre peuple ou d'une autre minorité. La grande perversion de l'approche identitaire est de croire que le droit des peuples à disposer de leurs minorités vaut mieux que le droit des Etats à disposer de leurs peuples (Maalouf A., 1993a et 1993b)... L'Europe est-elle prête au dépassement de l'Etat-nation (Morin E. & Kern A.-B., 1991), à l'Est comme à l'Ouest, et veut-elle se donner les moyens de sa politique ou de ses ambitions?

# References

Akoun A., 1993, „Société — Droits de l'homme, droits de l'individu", in: *Encyclopœdia Universalis — Universalia 1993* , Paris, 293–295.

Allain M.-F. & Galmiche X., 1992a, „Une renaissance en loques. Sortie d'enfer pour la culture albanaise", *Le Monde diplomatique,* Paris, janvier 1992: 8.

Allain M.-F. & Galmiche X., 1992b, „La tenace résistance d'un „peuple interdit". Guerre sans armes au Kosovo", *Le Monde diplomatique*, Paris, mai 1992: 6.

Amrani S., 1991, „URSS et Europe de l'Est — La transformation du système des mass media", in: *Encyclopœdia Universalis — Universalia 1991*, Paris, 354–360.

Attali J., 1993, „Démocratie sans frontières", *L'autre journal* , Paris, janvier 1993:14–19.

Auffray A., 1993, „L'Allemagne expulse les Tsiganes par milliers", *Le Nouveau Quotidien*, Lausanne, 29.4.1993.

Auge M., 1984, „Le retour du religieux?", in: *Encyclopœdia Universalis — Supplément II, Les enjeux*, Paris, 46–51.

Badie B., 1993, „Réveil identitaire et crise de l'Etat-nation", in: *Encyclopœdia Universalis — Universalia 1993*, Paris, 112–116.

Bailby E., 1990, „La démocratie roumaine à l'aune des nationalismes", *Le Monde diplomatique*, Paris, février 1990: 12–13.

Balle F., 1984, „Information et «désinformation»", in: *Encyclopœdia Universalis — Supplément II, Les enjeux*, Paris, 747–753.

Barth F., 1956, „Ecologic Relationships of Ethnic Groups in Swat, North Pakistan", in: *American Anthropologist*, 58: 1059–1089.

Behar P., 1992, „Le retour de la question macédonienne", *Le Monde diplomatique*, Paris, mai 1992: 6.

Berthoud G., 1978, „Etat-nation et ethno-résistance", in: *Pluriel*, Paris, 15: 47–59.

Berthoud G. & Sabelli F., 1979, „Our Obsolete Production Mentality: The Heresy of the Communal Formation", in: *Current Anthropology*, Vol. 20, No 4, 745–760.

Bihr A., 1992, „Mondialisation du marché, nécessaire décentralisation. Malaise dans l'Etat-nation", *Le Monde diplomatique*, Paris, février 1992: 7.

Blanquart P., 1987, „Le religieux: un nouvel enjeu stratégique", in: *L'état des Religions dans le monde*, Paris, Ed. La Découverte/Le Cerf, 13–21.

Bole-Richard M., 1986, „Afrique du Sud: la politique des Bantoustans. La longue lutte du Kwandebele... contre l'indépendance", *Le Monde*, Paris, 12 août 1986.

Bouretz P. & Pisier E., 1990, „Révisionnisme — La «révision»" du marxisme", in: *Encyclopœdia Universalis — Supplément **, Le savoir*, Paris, 1665–1667.

Bourricaud F., 1984, „La laïcité: paradoxes et ambiguïtés", in: *Encyclopœdia Universalis — Supplément II, Les enjeux*, Paris, 777–780.

Bromley Y., 1974, „The term „Ethnos" and its definition", in: BROMLEY Y. (ed.), *Soviet Ethnology and Anthropology Today* , Paris-La Haye, Mouton, 55–72.

Burdeau G., 1980a, „Droits de l'homme", in: *Encyclopœdia Universalis*, Paris, vol. 5: 814.

Burdeau G., 1980b, „Etat", in: *Encyclopœdia Universalis* , Paris, vol. 6: 582–585.

Canapa M.-P., 1977, „Trente ans de Titisme... et après?", in: *Encyclopœdia Universalis — Universalia 1977*, Paris, 353–357.

Canapa M.-P., 1980, „Yougoslavie", in: *Encyclopœdia Universalis*, Paris, vol. 18: 846–848.

Canapa M.-P., 1981, „Tito, 1892–1980", in: *Encyclopœdia Universalis — Universalia 1981*, Paris, 602–603.

Cassen B., 1989, „Au secours des économies de l'Est. La Communauté européenne sous le choc", *Le Monde diplomatique,* Paris, septembre 1899: 1, 9.

Cassen B., 1990a, „Une Europe dépassée par sa géographie. Fédération à douze ou confédération à trente?", *Le Monde diplomatique,* Paris, février 1990: 8.

Cassen B., 1990b, „L'autre Europe, simple spectatrice de l'intégration communautaire? La citadelle des Douze", *Le Monde diplomatique,* Paris, juin 1990: 9.

Cassen B., 1991, „Impuissance devant la crise yougoslave. L'Europe à hue et à dia", *Le Monde diplomatique,* Paris, octobre 1991: 1, 11.

Cassen B., 1992, „L'aide ou le chaos. Un plan Marshall pour les pays de l'Est?", *Le Monde diplomatique,* Paris, février 1992: 4.

Chaliand G., 1986, „Les peuples sans Etat", in: *L'état du monde 1986,* Paris, Ed. La Découverte, 463–464.

Chartier C., 1991, „Les peuples et nations «non représentés dans la communauté internationale» se dotent d'une tribune", *Le Monde,* Paris, 12 février 1991.

Chartier C., 1993, „L'Organisation des peuples et nations non représentés se veut une «ONU alternative»", *Le Monde,* Paris, 26 janvier 1993.

Chauvier J.-M., 1990, „A l'Est, la mémoire retrouvée. Une guerre de symboles", *Le Monde diplomatique,* Paris, août 1990: 25.

Chesneaux J., 1981, „Dissidences régionales et crise de l'Etat-nation en Europe occidentale", *Le Monde diplomatique,* Paris, avril 1981: 22–23.

Chesneaux J., 1982, „La crise de la logique d'Etat", in: *L'état du monde 1982,* Paris, Maspero, 66–71.

Chevallier J., 1984, „L'audiovisuel et les pouvoirs politiques", in: *Encyclopœdia Universalis — Supplément II, Les enjeux,* Paris, 741–746.

Chiclet C., 1989, „Condition de la stabilité régionale. Le rapprochement gréco-turc, «à tous petits pas»", *Le Monde diplomatique,* Paris, janvier 1989: 27.

Chiclet C., 1992a, „Blocus serbe, entêtement grec. La Macédoine menacée d'étouffement", *Le Monde diplomatique,* Paris, septembre 1992: 6.

Chiclet C., 1992b, „Balkans — Le retour des nationalités", in: *Encyclopœdia Universalis — Universalia 1992,* Paris, 201–204.

Chiclet C., 1993a, „Balkans — Le retour de la question macédonienne", in: *Encyclopœdia Universalis — Universalia 1993 ,* Paris, 188–191.

Chiclet C., 1993 b, „Grecs et Turcs à nouveau face à face", *Le Monde diplo-matique,* Paris, juin 1993: 8–9.

Chossudovsky E., 1993, „Pour un règlement pacifique au Kosovo", *Le Monde diplomatique,* Paris, juin 1993: 8.

Cohen-Jonathan G., 1990, „Droits de l'homme — Protection internationale", in: *Encyclopœdia Universalis — Supplément *, Les enjeux — Le savoir,* Paris, 726–732.

Combacau J., 1980, „Droit international public", in: *Encyclopœdia Universalis,* Paris, vol. 18: 60–62.

DAVAL R., 1984, „Logique individuelle et logique sociale", in: *Encyclopœdia Universalis — Supplément II, Les enjeux,* Paris, 648–651.

Davy M.-M., 1980, „Bogomiles", in: *Encyclopœdia Universalis*, Paris, vol. 3: 387–388.

De La Gorce P.-M., 1992b, „Dans une inextricable mêlée des ethnies. Les irréparables dégâts de la guerre populaire en Bosnie-Herzégovine", *Le Monde diplomatique*, Paris, septembre 1992: 4–5.

De La Gorce P.-M., 1993a, „Après l'échec des solutions humanitaires. Les risques d'extension du conflit en Bosnie", *Le Monde diplomatique*, Paris, janvier 1993: 8–9.

De La Gorce P.-M., 1993b, „Tragique impuissance internationale. La force et les haines en Bosnie", *Le Monde diplomatique*, Paris, mai 1993: 1, 11.

De Rougemont D., 1974, „La révolte des régions. L'Etat-nation contre l'Europe", *Le Monde diplomatique*, Paris, mars 1974: 30.

De Vaux De Foletier F., 1980, „Tsiganes", in: *Encyclopœdia Universalis*, Paris, vol. 16:355–358.

Decornoy J., 1992, „L'ultranationalisme roumain recrée le spectre d'un «danger hongrois»", *Le Monde diplomatique*, Paris, novembre 1992: 24–25.

Dizdarevic S., 1993, „Découpage ethnique en Bosnie-Herzégovine. Les irrecevables postulats du plan Owen-Vance", *Le Monde diplomatique*, Paris, mars 1993: 3.

Djuric V., 1980, „Slaves du Sud (Art des) — Macédoine et Serbie", in: *Encyclopœdia Universalis*, Paris, vol. 14: 1083–1086.

Draskovic V., 1989, „Les relations serbo-albanaises. Confrontation avec la vérité", *Le Monde diplomatique*, Paris, avril 1989: 8.

Dumay J.-M., 1993a, „Le paradoxe des cultures régionales", *Le Monde*, Paris, 21 janvier 1993.

Dumay J.-M., 1993b, „Les Musulmans bosniaques rayés de la carte", *Le Monde*, Paris, 3 juin 1993: 3.

Durandin C., 1990, „Roumanie — La systémisation", in: *Encyclopœdia Universalis* — *Universalia 1990*, Paris, 332–334.

Elorriaga J.F., 1988, „Tensions interethniques, effondrement économique. La Yougoslavie en proie aux démons du nationalisme", *Le Monde diplomatique*, Paris, décembre 1988: 8–9.

Elorriaga J.F., 1990, „Crise économique et désirs de sécession. La fédération yougoslave est menacée d'éclatement", *Le Monde diplomatique*, Paris, février 1990: 5.

Faye J.-P., 1991, „Europe délivre-nous des nations!", *Le Monde*, Paris, 20 septembre 1991.

Fejtö F., 1971, „La résurgence du nationalisme en Yougoslavie. L'action des forces centrifuges menace-t-elle l'existence de la Fédération?", *Le Monde diplomatique*, Paris, juin 1971:6–7.

Fejtö F., 1972, „La Yougoslavie au tournant. Une fin de règne difficile", *Le Monde diplomatique*, Paris, décembre 1972: 28.

Fejtö Fr. & MINK G., 1978, „La nouvelle contestation en URSS et dans les pays de l'Europe de l'Est", in: *Encyclopœdia Universalis* — *Universalia 1978*, Paris, 111–117.

Feron B., 1969, „Les manifestations au Kosmet. La minorité albanaise souhaiterait obtenir le statut de république fédérée pour sa région", *Le Monde diplomatique*, Paris, janvier 1969: 5.

Ferry L. & Pisier Kouchner E., 1984, „Les fondements des droits de l'homme", in: *Encyclopœdia Universalis — Supplément II, Les enjeux*, Paris, 52–57.

Fesquet H., 1980, „Les religions en Yougoslavie. I. Quand un Etat athée invente la nationalité musulmane; II. L'Eglise orthodoxe: peu de souci pour le régime; III. L'Eglise catholique à la pointe de la contestation et de la collaboration", *Le Monde*, Paris, 19, 20 & 21 février 1980.

Foucher M., 1990, „L'Europe après la «pax sovietica»: de nouvelles sources de tensions?, in: *L'état du monde 1991*, Paris, Ed. La Découverte, 29–33.

Fralon J.-A., 1987, „Economie à la dérive, désagrégation régionale... Crises yougoslaves", *Le Monde*, Paris, 15 avril 1987.

Gallo M., 1989, „L'Europe sans nations, cet artifice, ce mirage dangereux...", *Le Monde diplomatique*, Paris, mars 1989: 8–9.

Garapon A., 1989, „Graves atteintes aux droits de l'homme en Yougoslavie. «Différenciés», les Albanais du Kosovo", *Le Monde diplomatique*, Paris, novembre 1989: 5.

Garde P., 1980, „Slaves — Langues", in: *Encyclopœdia Universalis*, Paris, vol. 14: 1075–1079.

Gauriat V., 1993, „Venus de partout, ils [les Tsiganes] demandent l'asile... en Roumanie", *Le Nouveau Quotidien*, Lausanne, 29.4.1993.

Gil F., Tap P. & Sindzingre N., 1984, „Identité", in: *Encyclopœdia Universalis — Supplément I, Le savoir*, Paris, 652–657.

Girardet R., 1980, „Nation — Le nationalisme", in: *Encyclopœdia Universalis*, Paris, vol. 11: 575–577.

Gouillard J., 1980, „Orthodoxe (Eglise) — Histoire de l'orthodoxie", in: *Encyclopœdia Universalis*, Paris, vol. 12: 254–261.

Gorzelak G. & Kukliński A. (ed.), 1992, *Dilemmas of Regional Policies in Eastern and Central Europe*, University of Warsaw, European Institute for Regional and Local Development, Warsaw.

Gresh A., 1990, „Six nations de l'Est à la recherche d'une politique nouvelle. Les sentiers escarpés du passage à la démocratie", *Le Monde diplomatique*, Paris, février 1990: 14–15.

Guillemain B., 1984, „L'Etat et la violence", in: *Encyclopœdia Universalis — Supplément II, Les enjeux*, Paris, 657–662.

Guillemain B., 1990, „Tolérance (Idée de)", in: *Encyclopœdia Universalis — Supplément **, Le savoir*, Paris, 1875–1878.

Hartmann F., 1993, „Croisade en Serbie pour le rétablissement de la «vérité»", *Le Monde*, Paris, 21 avril 1993: 4.

Jacob A., 1986, „La bombe à retardement du Kosovo", *Le Monde*, Paris, 10 mai 1986.

Jacques A., 1981, „Droits de l'homme et droit des peuples", in: *L'état du monde 1981*, Paris, Maspero, 398–399.

Jestin-Fleury N., 1992, „Dossier. L'économie yougoslave", *Le Monde*, Paris, 3 mars 1992: 32

Jomier J., 1980, „Islam — La religion", in: *Encyclopœdia Universalis*, Paris, vol. 9: 127–136.

Joxe A., 1993, „Quand la gesticulation pacificatrice masque de réels enjeux stratégiques. Humanitarisme et empires", *Le Monde diplomatique*, Paris, janvier 1993: 6–7.

Julien C., 1989, „Une autre idée de l'Europe", *Le Monde diplomatique,* Paris, mai 1989: 1, 12–13.

Kadare I., 1989a, „Pour un apaisement dans les Balkans. Que cessent les vents chauvins", *Le Monde diplomatique,* Paris, février 1989: 6.

Kadare I., 1989b, „L'origine des Albanais", *Le Monde diplomatique,* Paris, octobre 1989: 2.

Kaufmann S., 1993, „Pologne: le «coup de gueule» de M. Skubiszewski", *Le Monde,* Paris, 23 janvier 1993: 3.

Kiss C.G., 1992, „Plaidoyer pour les minorités", *Le Nouveau Quotidien,* Lausanne, 3 mars 1992.

Labaki G.T., 1991, „Les conflits communautaires et ethniques dans le monde contemporain", in: *Encyclopœdia Universalis — Universalia 1991,* Paris, 111–116.

Lagani I., 1989, „Six pays en quête d'une communauté de destin", *Le Monde diplomatique,* Paris, janvier 1989: 24–25.

Lamoureux J.-C. & Shkullaku A., 1993, „L'Epire partagé", *Le Monde diplomatique,* Paris, juin 1993: 10.

Laselv P., 1988, „Roumanie — La minorité hongroise de Transylvanie", in: *Encyclopœdia Universalis — Universalia 1988,* Paris, 307–310.

Lavau G., 1988, „L'héritage des Déclarations de 1789 et de 1793", in: *L'état du monde 1988–1989,* Paris, Ed. La Découverte, 558–562.

Lavigne M., 1986, „Europe de l'Est. L'effet Gorbatchev", in: *L'état du monde 1986,* Paris, Ed. La Découverte, 42–47.

Lavigne M., 1990, „Europe de l'Est — Les économies des pays communistes", in: *Encyclopœdia Universalis — Supplément *, Les enjeux — Le savoir,* Paris, 802–810.

Lavigne M., 1993a, „Discours libéral, pratiques frileuses. Comment aider la révolution sans utopie à l'Est?", *Le Monde diplomatique,* Paris, février 1993: 12.

Lavigne M., 1993b, „Une coopération économique limitée. La CEE est-elle l'avenir de l'Est?", *Le Monde diplomatique,* Paris, avril 1993: 13.

Lavigne P., 1980, „Droits de l'homme — Droits politiques et sociaux", in: *Encyclopœdia Universalis,* Paris, vol. 5: 818–821.

Leca J., 1991, „Citoyenneté, nationalité, nation, nationalisme, Etat-nation, minorités...", in: *L'état du monde 1992,* Paris, Ed. La Découverte, 579–581.

Lespoir P., 1987, „Les religions en Europe centrale: Tchécoslovaquie, Pologne, Hongrie", in: *L'état des Religions dans le monde,* Paris, Ed. La Découverte/Le Cerf, 354–357.

Lhommel E., 1990, „[L'Eglise orthodoxe de Roumanie] Après la compromission, séduire à nouveau", *Le Monde diplomatique,* Paris, mars 1990: 15.

Liegeois J.-P., 1987, „Les peuples sans Etat. Les Tsiganes", in: *L'état du monde 1987–1988,* Paris, Ed. La Découverte, 454–456.

Lomme R., 1988, „Europe centrale: le problème des minorités ethniques et nationales", in: *Encyclopœdia Universalis — Universalia 1988,* Paris, 112–118.

Lomme R., 1989, „Pays de l'Est. Rôle et fonctions des élections", in: *Encyclopœdia Universalis — Universalia 1989,* Paris, 331–333.

Lomme R., 1992, „La recomposition de l'espace stratégique soviétique", in: *Encyclopœdia Universalis — Universalia 1992* , Paris, 139–145.

Lund F., 1992, „Yougoslavie — La dislocation dans l'affrontement", in: *Encyclopœdia Universalis — Universalia 1992* , Paris, 336–338.

Lutard C., 1991, „Convoitises sur la Macédoine", *Le Monde diplomatique*, Paris, juillet 1991: 4.

Lutard C., 1992d, „La Serbie en plein désarroi", *Le Monde diplomatique*, Paris, juillet 1992: 7.

Lutard C., 1992e, „Vojvodine, Sandjak, Kosovo. Le feu sous la cendre en Yougoslavie", *Le Monde diplomatique*, Paris, novembre 1992: 23.

Maalouf A., 1993a, „La grande perversion", *Le Monde* , Paris, 20 janvier 1993.

Maalouf A., 1993b, „Non, les peuples n'ont pas de droit absolu à disposer d'eux-mêmes", *Le Nouveau Quotidien*, Lausanne, 13 mars 1993.

Macovescu G., 1973, „Pour Bucarest, toute discussion devrait respecter l'égalité des droits et la liberté de chaque Etat", *Le Monde diplomatique*, Paris, janvier 1973: 4.

Mantran R., 1980a, „Islam — L'expansion", in: *Encyclopœdia Universalis*, Paris, vol. 9: 136–147.

Mattelard A., 1981, „Culture nationale et interdépendance", in: *Encyclopœdia Universalis —Universalia 1981* , Paris, 131–137.

Mattelard A., 1992, „Information, désinformation, censure: logiques militaires, logiques économiques", in: *Encyclopœdia Universalis — Universalia 1992*, Paris, 103–108.

Meyer-Bisch P., 1993, „Identité. Le piège du droit des minorités", *Le Monde*, Paris, 18 février 1993.

Michel P., 1990a, „De la résistance religieuse à l'utopie nationale", *Le Monde diplomatique*, Paris, mars 1990: 12–13.

Michel P., 1990b, „Les eaux mêlées de la religion et du nationalisme", *Le Monde diplomatique*, Paris, mars 1990: 14.

Michel P., 1990c, „Les Eglises dans la transition en Europe de l'Est", in: *L'état du monde 1991*, Paris, Ed. La Découverte, 527–528.

Milcent E., 1982, „Eglises et vie religieuse dans l'Europe de l'Est", in: *Encyclopœdia Universalis — Universalia 1982* , Paris, 132–138.

Mink G. & Szurek J.-C., 1992, „Post-communisme: «à qui perd gagne»?", in: *L'état du monde — Edition 1993*, Paris, Ed. La Découverte, 550–551.

Mink G., 1984, „L'URSS et l'Europe de l'Est: rapports de domination et forces centrifuges", in: *Encyclopœdia Universalis — Supplément II, Les enjeux*, Paris, 883–893.

Mink G., 1988, „Europe de l'Est: la diffusion de l'«effet Gorbatchev»", in: *Encyclopœdia Universalis — Universalia 1988*, Paris, 105–111.

Mink G., 1990, „L'émergence d'une opinion publique en Europe de l'Est", in: *L'état du monde 1991*, Paris, Ed. La Découverte, 506–508.

Mink G., 1991, „La fin de la satellisation de l'Europe de l'Est?", in: *Encyclopœdia Universalis — Universalia 1991* , Paris, 129–135.

Mollstedt B., 1993, „Tout le monde souhaite l'Europe des régions. Mais de quelles régions parle-t-on?", *Le Nouveau Quotidien* , Lausanne, 5 mars 1993.

Mond G., 1987, „L'information en Union soviétique et dans les autres pays socialistes", in: *Encyclopœdia Universalis — Universalia 1987*, Paris, 147–152.

Morin E. & Kern A.-B., 1991, „Vivre l'Europe en confédération", *Le Monde diplomatique,* Paris, novembre 1991: 13.

Mosse C., 1980, „Macédoine antique", in: *Encyclopœdia Universalis*, Paris, vol. 10: 222–227.

Philippot R., 1980a, „Bulgarie — De la Bulgarie avant les Bulgares à la République populaire", in: *Encyclopœdia Universalis*, Paris, vol. 3: 683–685.

Philippot R., 1980b, „Roumanie — Histoire", in: *Encyclopœdia Universalis*, Paris, vol. 14: 453–456.

Planche A., 1985, „La destruction du centre de Bucarest", in: *L'état du monde 1985*, Paris, Ed. La Découverte, 530–532.

Planche A., 1988, „Roumanie. Un pays à l'agonie", in: *L'état du monde 1988–1989*, Paris, Ed. La Découverte, 216–221.

Poirot-Delpech B., 1993, „L'humanitaire comme révélateur", *Le Monde diplomatique*, Paris, 6 mai 1993: 4.

Prelot M., 1980, „Droits de l'homme — Déclaration des droits", in: *Encyclopœdia Universalis*, Paris, vol. 5: 815–818.

Prunier G., 1990, „Frictions entre la Hongrie et la Roumanie", in: *L'état du monde 1989– 1990*, Paris, Ed. La Découverte, 503–504.

Quadri R., 1980, „Droit international public", in: *Encyclopœdia Universalis*, Paris, vol. 9: 14–17.

Reyniers A., 1993, „Les Tsiganes ballottés à travers l'Europe", *Le Monde diplomatique*, Paris, mars 1993: 6–7.

Rodinson M., 1980, „Nation — Nation et idéologie", in: *Encyclopœdia Universalis*, Paris, vol. 11: 571–575.

Roman J., 1992, „Ethique et journalisme: vers un «civisme» de l'information?", in: *Encyclopœdia Universalis — Universalia 1992*, Paris, 97–102.

Rouland N., 1993, „Au-delà de l'aide humanitaire, conforter les droits des peuples autochtones. Le développement devrait-il tuer la culture?", *Le Monde diplomatique*, Paris, juin 1993: 16–17.

Roussel B., 1980, „Unitarisme", in: *Encyclopœdia Universalis* , Paris, vol. 16: 471–472.

Roux M., 1990, „Le problème des nationalités en Yougoslavie", in: *L'état du monde 1991*, Paris, Ed. La Découverte, 490–492.

Rupnik J., 1984, „Europe de l'Est — Pacifisme et dissidence", in: *Encyclopœdia Universalis —Universalia 1984* , Paris, 238–241.

Rupnik J., 1990, „L'Europe de l'Est en transition vers quoi?", in: *L'état du monde 1989–1990*, Paris, Ed. La Découverte, 32–37.

Samary C., 1991a, „Le marché contre l'autogestion. La Yougoslavie à l'épreuve du libéralisme «réellement existant»", *Le Monde diplomatique*, Paris, juillet 1991: 4–5.

Samary C., 1991b, „La communauté internationale face à la guerre civile en Yougoslavie", *Le Monde diplomatique,* Paris, septembre 1991: 6–7.

Samary C., 1991c, „Fronts et frontières en Yougoslavie. La Serbie dans le bourbier de la guerre", *Le Monde diplomatique,* Paris, novembre 1991: 19.

Samary C., 1992a, „Yougoslavie. Du projet d'union libre à l'étouffement des différences", *Le Monde diplomatique,* Paris, juillet 1992: 8–9.

Samary C., 1992b, „Au nom de l'effort de guerre et de la cause nationale. La dérive d'une Croatie «ethniquement pure»", *Le Monde diplomatique,* Paris, août 1992: 3.

Samary C., 1992c, „Impasse politique, poursuite des combats. L'impérieuse nécessité de penser la paix en Bosnie", *Le Monde diplomatique,* Paris, octobre 1992: 3.

Samary C., 1992d, „Entre la Communauté européenne et les Balkans. La Slovénie saisie par les réalités de l'indépendance", *Le Monde diplomatique,* Paris, décembre 1992: 12.

Samary C., 1993, „Contre tout projet de partition. Des Bosniaques favorables à l'Etat multi-ethnique", *Le Monde diplomatique,* Paris, février 1993: 13.

Sanguinetti A., 1993, „Yougoslavie. Un dossier militaire qui frise l'«intox»", *Le Monde diplomatique,* Paris, janvier 1993: 8.

Sapir J., 1981, „Europe de l'Est: vers la rupture?", in: *L'état du monde 1981,* Paris, Maspero, 27–33.

Sarambei N., 1992, „Ancientness, Continuity, Unity", *Romanian Panorama,* Bucharest, 9–10, 1992: 34–35.

Schreiber Th., 1983, „Yougoslavie. L'armée pour défendre l'héritage", in: *L'état du monde 1983,* Paris, La Découverte/Maspero, 198–202.

Sicard E., 1980, „Nation — La construction nationale", in: *EncyclopŒdia Universalis,* Paris, vol. 11: 568–571.

Smouts M.-C., 1991, „Le droit international en débat", in: *L'état du monde 1992,* Paris, Ed. La Découverte, 40–42.

Timbal P.-C. & Burdeau G., 1980, „Nation — L'idée de nation", in: *EncyclopŒdia Universalis,* Paris, vol. 11: 566–568.

Tiraspolsky A., 1980, „Roumanie — La Roumanie socialiste", in: *EncyclopŒdia Universalis,* Paris, vol. 14: 459–463.

Turcq D.F., 1991, „Europe de l'Est — De nouveaux défis pour le management des entreprises", in: *EncyclopŒdia Universalis — Universalia 1991,* Paris, 263–264.

Uribe A., 1976, „Au-delà des droits de l'homme et des Etats. Légitimer le droit des peuples", *Le Monde diplomatique,* Paris, septembre 1976: 1, 8.

Urjewicz C., 1990, „L'«Etat multinational [en ex-URSS]», un mythe qui cachait un désastre", in: *L'état du monde 1991,* Paris, Ed. La Découverte, 582–587.

Valladao A., 1982, „Yougoslavie. La montée des nationalismes", in: *L'état du monde 1982,* Paris, Maspero, 212–215.

Valladao A., 1984, „Le renouveau des nationalismes en Europe", in: *L'état du monde 1984,* Paris, Ed. La Découverte, 21–27.

Vallauzd P. & Fouche E., 1990, „Hommes, échanges et frontières au coeur de l'Europe", *Le Monde diplomatique*, Paris, février 1990: 16–17. (Erreurs grossières + excuses du journal in: *Le Monde diplomatique*, Paris, mars 1990: 14)

Yankovitch P., 1988a, „La révolte des Monténégrins", *Le Monde*, Paris, 11 octobre 1988.

Yankovitch P., 1988b, „Le populisme serbe menace l'équilibre de la Yougoslavie. Slobodan Milosevic: l'homme fort de la Serbie", *Le Monde*, Paris, 18 octobre 1988.

„26 «Ethnic Groups»", 1992, *Romanian Panorama*, Bucharest, 9–10, 1992: 27–29.

„Bophuthatswana. 6 décembre 1977: indépendance du Bophuthatswana", 1977, *La Revue Sud-Africaine Panorama* , Berne, Ambassade d'Afrique du Sud, 76, septembre 1977: 2–9.

„Droits de l'homme et démocratie" (Dossier), 1988, in: *L'état du monde 1988–1989*, Paris, Ed. La Découverte, 553–582.

„Eglises et démocratie en Europe de l'Est" (Dossier) 1990, *Le Monde diplomatique*, Paris, mars 1990: 12–15.

„La poussée régionaliste en Europe occidentale. L'Etat-nation en question?" (Dossier), 1971, *Le Monde diplomatique*, Paris, avril 1971: 7–12.

„La Yougoslavie, banc d'essai pour la nouvelle Europe?" (Dossier), 1992, *Le Monde diplomatique*, Paris, juillet 1992: 6–9.

„Le fait national en questions" (Dossier), 1991, in: *L'état du monde 1992*, Paris, Ed. La Découverte, 577–596.

„Les Balkans, vibrante et fragile mosaïque" (Dossier), 1989, *Le Monde diplomatique*, Paris, janvier 1989: 24–27.

„Les Hongrois de Roumanie manifestent contre un préfet", 1993, communiqué de l'AFP, *Le Nouveau Quotidien*, Lausanne, 3 avril 1993.

„Nationalismes: la tragédie yougoslave", 1993, *Le Monde diplomatique*, Paris, Manière de voir No 17, février 1993.

„Roumanie. Manifestations de la minorité hongroise", 1993, communiqué de l'AFP, *Le Monde*, Paris, 3 avril 1993.

Roman Szul
European Institute
for Regional and Local Development
Warsaw

# SOME PROBLEMS OF REGIONALISMS IN CONTEMPORARY EUROPE WITH SPECIAL REFERENCE TO EASTERN EUROPE

## 1. Introductory remarks

In the present time we are witnessing in Europe a growing role of such important interrelated phenomena as nationalisms, regionalisms, search for (and change of) ethnic identities, etc. The ethnic wars in former Yugoslavia, implosion of this country and emergence of new nation-states on its territory, the "velvet" dissolution of the Czecho-Slovak federation, the liquidation of the Soviet Union with the consecutive emergence of a number of new nation-states with sometimes difficult ethnic conflicts and strong centrifugal regional tendencies, are only the most spectacular evidences of this situation.

These examples should not suggest that the analyzed phenomena are limited to the Eastern Europe only. It is enough to mention the considerable demand for more economic, cultural (including attempts for revitalisation or revalorisation of local languages) and political autonomy of some regions of Spain, first of all of the Bask Country and Catalonia, the growing popularity of the North League in Italy with its idea of the economic (and political and cultural) autonomy (if not total independence) of Northern Italy, the federalisation of Belgium under pressure of the ethnic factor in this country as well as a number of other examples from the West of Europe to see that the question of nationalism, regionalism and the ethnic factor concerns the whole continent.

What is equally important is that individual cases of nationalisms/regionalisms are quite often not limited to a restricted territory of one country but, directly or indirectly, imply more countries. Transfrontier ethnic or regional communities are only the most visible evidence of it. It should also be added that the very idea of nationalism/ regionalism in one place or country can influence and stimulate regionalistic/nationalistic movements in another place or country without a direct linkage.

In such a situation there is a growing need for studying the above mention processes in order to learn their nature, dynamics, to foresee them and find means to influence them in order to avoid the most negative consequences of them without neglecting the natural and legitimate right of people to feel being member of a community (national, regional, local, ethnic, etc).

The aim of this paper is twofold; first, it is to propose a way of understanding (of analyzing, defining, classifying) of regionalism, and second, to present some (recent) problems of the regional question in some Eastern European countries.

## 2. Regionalisms, regions and the related questions — an Attempt of Definitions

By the term **"regionalism"** it is understood here *a conscious collective movement aiming at preserving or promoting a region's autonomy or specificity in one or more of the following fields: politics (including administration, migration rules, international relations, etc), economy (including ecology), culture (including religion, symbols of cultural specificity, etc), language.* Regionalism can be weak or strong, shallow or deep, one-sided or many-sided depending on the strength of the support behind it, e.i. depending on the number or people engaged, their determination to pursue ideas of a given regionalism, their objective interests and economic, political and cultural power.

In other words, the strength and nature of regionalism depends on the strength and nature or **"regional identity"**. Regionalism can not exist without regional identity, although the vice versa is possible. Regional identity, in its turn, *is an emotional attitude of people towards a given region (as a whole or towards some elements, like people, institutions, landscape, symbols. etc), feeling of emotional belonging to it, identification with interests of people or institutions of this region.*

It must be stressed, that regional identity is only one form of a broader phenomenon of **"territorial identity"**. Territorial identity *is identification of people with a given territory, regardless of its size and location.* As the people usually identify themselves with various territories (a neighbourhood, town, province or another administrative unit, geographical region, country, etc), there exist various kinds of territorial identity. Two of them are very common and almost universal (at least in the European civilisation), namely local identity and national identity. Regional identity stands between the local and the national identity. All those three levels of territorial identity form a structure, and the relative importance of elements of the structure can change in time and space (and be different for various social groups living in the same time and space). The most important changes in this structure concern the relations between the regional and the national identity: e.g. extinction of the national identity in a given region in the condition of a strong regional identity is a signal of the forthcoming movement for independence of this region; emergence of a supralocal subnational identity means emergence of a new regional identity and, possibly, of a new regionalism; extinction (or substantial reduction) of regional (or local) identity of politically leading group in a country (or a regions) usually causes attempts of the authorities to eradicate regional (or local) identities and specificities as "anachronistic" or dangerous.

In this context, the regional identity plays a very important role. Probability of emergence of a regional identity, and its strength and nature, depend, in turn, on characteristic of a given region.

From the point of view of "regional identity creation" the following typology of regions seems to be of relevance:

1. **Geographical regions (GR)** — regions with a pronounced geographical specificity, usually forming a compact territory isolated from the rest
of the national territory. This type of regions creates conditions for emergence among the population of sense of "being different" than the rest
of the country, especially if the geographical isolation is strengthened by
differences in climate, landscape, geographically determined living conditions, etc. If the "sense of being different" than the rest of the country
is complimented by the "sense of being similar to each other" within the
region, then conditions for a regional identity and, consequently, for a
regionalism, are ready.

2. **Economic regions (ER)** — regions with a specific economic situation, usually in an extreme economic conditions — prosperous regions
or regions in deep economic crisis, backwardness or ecological problems.
This type of regions promotes emergence of community of economic interests of (the relevant part of) a region's population as opposed to the
interests of the rest of the country or other regions. This may give rise to
regional identity and regionalism based on economic interest. The prosperous regions tend to preserve their good situation by avoiding, as much
as possible, financing of the less developed or declining regions. To this
end they insist in reducing the redistributive role of the central government, or in receiving greater regional economic autonomy. People in poor
or declining regions quite often blame the central government and/or the
rich regions for their economic problems, so that a desire for more protection from the mistakes or bad will of the central government or from the
exploitation by the rich regions may emerge with consequent tendencies
towards greater regional economic autonomy.

3. **Ethno-cultural and linguistic regions (EthCLR)** — regions populated by peoples differing from the rest of the country by their ethnic
characteristics, culture, traditions, folklore, religion, mentality, language
or dialect, alphabet etc. (Of course, any of these factors may act independently). If the objective ethno-cultural and linguistic specificity of a
territory is perceived by its population (at the beginning by its leaders),
this will be a good soil for a regional, or even national (ethnic), identity. In
fact, this was and is the most frequent way of creation of nationalisms in
the 19th and 20th century Europe. Demands of regionalisms/nationalisms
based on the ethno-cultural and linguistic specificity may vary from preserving of purely symbolic values (e.g. conservation of architectural monuments, demands for "recognition" of a region's own regional identity by

the others, etc), through the promotion in the public life of languages of the region's population (or revitalisation of extinct languages regarded as symbols of the ethnic identity

of the population), to the demands for total political independence.

4.**Administrative regions (AR)** — present or past supralocal territorial administrative units. With their well defined territory, borders, administrative centres and, quite often, symbols, they offer a good reference point for territorial (regional) identity. The longer is the time of existence of a administrative region, the greater are intraregional linkages and the stronger is the regional identity. What is very important is that administrative regions create, by their very nature, regional groups of interest composed by the regional authorities, administration, politicians, some businesses, intellectuals, etc. creating a network of "regional loyalties". The size and strength of such regional groups of interest depend on the political and economic system and on the current political situation. Usually such regional groups of interest are incorporated into a smoothly working national political and economic mechanism, but in some circumstances they may turn into advocates and leaders of movements for autonomy or even independence of their regions. It is important to note that they can act successfully even without a strong popular support.

5. **Historical regions (HR)** — regions which due their specificity to their history. As examples of important regionalisms in Europe (and elsewhere) show, almost all of their respective regions were created by the history. As the histories of regions may be very different, so may be the strength and nature of regional identities and regionalisms. Therefore historical regions need a more detailed scrutiny.

5.1. **(HR1)** — former independent states which became main centres of new bigger nation-states. Regional identity of such regions is usually very week, because the territorial identity of their populations is strongly linked to the nation-state as a whole. Such regions are usually sources of politicians, intellectuals, military commanders and soldiers, etc. acting on the all-national level, defending the territorial unity of the nation-state or fighting for enlargement of its territory. Meaningful regional centrifugal movements in such regions can emerge only in special circumstances as response to successes of regional movements in other regions of the country.

5.2. **(HR2)** — former independent states which became voluntarily or in a distant past parts of new bigger nation-states dominated by other regions. The history gives such regions some very important factors of regional (or ethnic) identity: the memory of being once independent state with its material symbols like the capital city, royal castle or other historical monuments, emblem, etc. The regional identity must compete, however, with the all-national identity. Proportions between the two identities depend on many factors and can change over time. Economic prosperity, great political influence, high cultural prestige, etc. of the country as a whole favour the growth of the all-national identity, while the vice versa reduces this identity so that the regional identity becomes the highest identity with consequent transformation of regionalism into nationalism and independence movement.

5.3. **(HR3)** — former independent states which where (in historically not distant time) forcibly included into bigger states. As in the former case (HR2), the history gives such regions memory, symbols and evidences of the lost independence plus the memory of the injustice and. quite often, personal sufferings. In such regions there is no all-national identity (unless among ethnic minorities or immigrant population), so that they can be kept only by force — military or economic. Regionalisms in such regions are, in fact, nationalisms.

5.4. **(HR4)** — former autonomous regions. The memory and traces of the past autonomy may act as a factor of regional identity and regaining of the autonomy may be the aim catalysing the regional movement.

5.5. **(HR5)** — regions — results of changing national borders and of foreign domination. Specificity (economic, socio-cultural, linguistic, ethnic, etc) of a region stems from changes of national borders, e.i. from belonging of this region to various countries in various time periods. Each period left its traces and the present specificity of the region is a combination of those traces. Such a specificity can be very strong, but not necessarily must be a basis for regional identity and regionalism. It depends on the attitude towards the past. If the past is perceived negatively — as a time of foreign domination, indignity, exploitation, etc. — traces of this past can hardly be source of pride and regional (ethnic, national) identity. Even more — there will be a desire to reduce or eliminate such a specificity, or at lest to ignore it. If, to the contrary, the attitude towards the past is neutral or positive, such a specificity may give rise to regional (or even national) identity. It should be noted that the attitude towards the past can change over time, so can change the attitude towards its traces and what once was a source of shame can become source of pride.

Of course, the same territory can form many or all of the above analyzed regions, for instance it can be at the same time a geographical region, an economic region, an ethno-cultural or linguistic region, an administrative region and a historical region of type RH2. The more elements of specificity a region possesses, the stronger can be its regional identity and its regionalism.

Differences in strength and nature of regional identities result in differences in intensity, forms and aims of regionalisms. One can distinguish the following intensities, forms and aims of regionalisms:

— weak intensity **(WI)** — the regionalistic movement is meaningless even in the region concerned; vast majority of inhabitants of the region is not aware of existence of such a movement,

— medium intensity **(MI)** — the regionalistic movement is meaningful in the region concerned but meaningless in the national scale; regionalistic parties or organisations influence regional authorities,

— strong intensity **(SI)** — the regionalistic movement is the leading force in its respective region and a considerable force in the national scale;

— popular movement **(PoM)** — representatives of all socio-professional groups are engaged in the movement; it is combined with the strong or medium intensity of the movement,

— elitarian movement **(EM)** — only representatives of some groups, usually intellectuals and/of "political extravagants", are present in the movement; it is usually a weak movement, but in favourable conditions it can get popularity and strength,

— professionals' movement **(PrM)** — mostly representatives of small but influential professional groups, especially of public administration, entrepreneurs, etc. are engaged; the movement can be strong despite the lack of popular support;

— political demands (aims) **(PD)** — the aim of the movement is to gain, defend or strengthen political-administrative autonomy,

— economic demands **(ED)** — the aim of the movement is to gain, defend or strengthen economic autonomy or obtain some economic (and ecologic) concessions from the central government for firms or population of the region,

— linguistic demands **(LD)** — the aim of the movement is to introduce or retain a regional language into the public life of the region (together with or instead of the national language) or revitalize once extinct

language(s) of the region or to raise prestige of the local language(s) or dialect(s), usually implying their "purification",
— cultural demands **(CD)** — the aim of the movement is to cultivate, protect and promote material and spiritual cultural values of the region, often combined with linguistic demands,
— "recognition demands" **(RD)** — the main aim of the participants of the movement is to persuade themselves and others (especially outside the region) that the region exists and has its own specificity.

# 3. Regions and regionalisms in Eastern Europe

## 3.1. General remarks

The whole area of Central and Eastern Europe is characterized by growing political and economic role of the regional question (emergence or strengthening of regionalisms) and by changing political and economic "regional setting", although intensity and nature of these tendencies remain highly differentiated from country to country.

The growing role of the regional question in Central and Eastern Europe is due to several factors (not all of them are present in each country):
— democratisation of the political system, freedom of speech and association which made it possible for regional and ethnic communities to express and promote their once "frozen" sentiments and interests, eventually to gain independence (in the case of republics of the federal states of the Soviet Union, Czechoslovakia and Yugoslavia),
— ideological vacuum resulted from the collapse of the communist ideology (and of the idea of the "Soviet Nation" in the special case of the USSR) being fulfilled by new ideas like all kinds of territorial and ethnic identities, religion (or more exactly by religious rituals — this doesn't apply for Poland where secularisation and anti-clericalism started to grow), and a kind of "religion of money" (feverish primitive business, widespread corruption, criminality), etc.,
— weakening of the central authorities as a result of the general political crisis and/or of the fighting for power of influential political groups or personalities which encouraged or pushed regional and local authori-

ties to take more power or even, like in the case of the Soviet Union, to declare independence or autonomy,
— transformation of the economic system and changing economic situation resulting in a new economic situation of individual regions: some of them are beneficiaries of the changes (some urban centres without structural deficiencies, some oil, gold etc. producing areas, etc), some backward regions have become more backward, some once prosperous regions are faced with severe social, economic and ecologic problems (mostly regions dominated by heavy, mining, military, etc. industries) which strengthen inter-regional tensions and the tensions between central authorities and regional communities or authorities; in the case of Russia it can be added dramatically growing transportation costs which enforce regions to be economically more "closed" and to loosen personal contacts with other regions (it is especially true for relations between Russian Far East and Siberia with Russia's European part),
— a kind of imitation of the West and an attempt to adopt its political and administrative system with its supposed important role of regions.

As it was mentioned before, despite some similarities, differences in the regional question between Eastern European countries are considerable. Therefore a more detailed insight into some countries of the area seems to be necessary. The main attention will be given to the Polish case.

## 3.2. Poland

### 3.2.1. General remarks

The regional question in the post-war Poland has been insignificant: regional identities have been negligible and regional movements, with few exceptions, inexistent. Such a situation is due to the geography (flat territory, no natural barriers to migration of the population) and the history. The historical factor, however, deserves a comment, because the history created both favourable and unfavourable conditions for emergence of regional differences, identities and movements.

The present territory of Poland is composed by parts having very different past. It can be roughly divided into two big parts: the "old territory" — 2/3 of the national territory, which belonged to Poland in the inter-war time, and the "new territory" — included to Poland after the World War II (according to the decision of the winning powers of the war as a recompensation for the territory included to the USSR). Both parts are populated now almost exclusively by ethnic Poles (national minorities account for about 2–3% of the population) — in the "old" part they are the indigenous population, in the "new" one they are mostly migrants and repatriants from the territory included to the USSR, from the rest of the present territory of Poland and from abroad. So, the population of the "new" territory is a mixture of all regional elements of Poland with a rather weak sense of identity with regions it lives in.

The "old" territory, in turn, can be divided, at least, in three large historical parts: those which in the time of inexistence of the Polish state (late XVIII century — end of the World War I) belonged to three states — Germany (or Prussia), Russia and Austria. Each of them can also be divided into smaller pieces.

It is especially important for the German/Prussian part. It consisted of two regions: Upper Silesia which dropped out from Poland many centuries ago (in middle ages) and Wielkopolska (the Poznań region) included to Prussia in the late XVIII century. Although the two regions were populated mostly by a similar population — Polish speaking Roman Catholics, there was a significant difference in their ethnic identity: while the Polish identity in Wielkopolska was very strong (the region was included to Prussia when the Polish national identity had been formed), the ethnic identity of the indigenous population of Silesia was rather weak and hesitating between Polish and German identities with constant progress made by the German identity (not without direct influence by the Prussian/German authorities).

Also the Russian part was composed by two parts: it was so-called "Kingdom of Poland" (later on renamed into "Vistula Country") — a region with a limited administrative autonomy (under full control of Russia) and the territory belonging directly to the Russian Empire. Now only a small part of the latter belongs to Poland.

The bulk of the territory belonging to Austria was the region named Galicia which in 1860s obtained a far-reaching autonomy and was dominated mostly by Poles although Poles accounted for about one half of the population (the remaining significant ethnic groups were Ukrainians and Jews). (Now the western part of former Galicia belongs to Poland, and the eastern part — to Ukraine). This region in the second half of the

XIX and in the beginning of the XX century was the main centre of the political, cultural, scientific and even military life of the Polish nation — therefore it used to be called "Polish Piedmont". The rest of the territory belonging to Austria was a small region of Cieszyn Silesia. (Now its northern part belongs to Poland, and its southern part — to the Czech Republic).

More than one hundred years of separation and different experiences considerably differentiated the three parts of Poland in many respects. Nevertheless, those differences didn't cause emergence of significant regional identities and regionalistic movements, probably because the differences were attributed to the negatively assessed period of the "national slavery" and to "hostile enemies of the nation", so they couldn't be a source of pride and reference point for regional identities. The other way round, in the inter-war Poland the main desire of the authorities and of the prevailing part of the Polish population was to "wash away" traces of the past and unify and homogenize the national territory.

This process continued after the World War II and was supported by demographic, social, economic and political factors related to the socialist system and consequences of the war. As a result, the Polish population became extraordinarily homogenous from the ethnic point of view. It is reflected, e.g. in the linguistic situation: overwhelming majority of the population speaks only standard Polish without any traces of regional differences and the dialects (otherwise, with few exceptions, only slightly differentiated) are used only by older people in the countryside and the sphere of its use is very reduced. This situation is also attributable to the gentry origins of the Polish national identity and culture with its characteristic disdain for peasantry and its culture and language. (It is interesting to note that the Polish standard language wasn't based on any regional dialect — it was formed in XVI–XVII century as a kind of supraterritorial social dialect, namely as a dialect of the gentry of the Commonwealth of the Two Nations, i.e. the pre-partitioning Poland).

Despite this homogeneity, some regional identities persist or are regenerating and some regionalisms are coming to the fore. Now two or three regionalisms of big regions and two regionalisms of "medium-sized" regions seem to be distinguishable. The two big regions are Upper Silesia and Wielkopolska, the third, doubtful, region being Galicia. The two medium-sized regions are Podhale (Tatra mountains and surroundings) and Kaszuby (in the Gdańsk province).

## 3.2.2. Upper Silesia

It is the only Polish region with distinct regional identity and a meaningful regionalistic movement. The regional identity is based on some characteristics of the region. Taking into account the typology of regions presented in section 2 of this paper, Upper Silesia can be described as follows: *Upper Silesia = ER + EthCLR + HR (HR4 + HR5)*. In other words, it is an economic, ethno-cultural and linguistic, and historical region being result of changing national borders, which once have administrative autonomy. (Eastern part of Upper Silesia had a special status in the inter-war Poland). The region has no clear borders, its supposed territory belongs to several voivodships (provinces) and doesn't occupy any of them entirely, although it is usually identified with Katowice voivodship.

Upper Silesia is a region with a clear economic specificity. It has been traditionally dominated by heavy industries: coal mining, metallurgy, energy production etc. The region has been characterized by the highest in Poland wages, in the time of market shortages — by the best supply, and other privileges which resulted in considerable inflow of population, and, at the same, by serious ecological problems. Now, the region in on the threshold of a deep restructuring implying, i.a. considerable reductions in employment in loss-making and environment polluting mining industry, steel works etc., deterioration of the relative wages (in comparison with the national average) which, in fact, is already taking place, etc. This situation starts to create frustration, feeling of injustice and exploitation by the rest of the country.

It is also a region with some ethnol-cultural and linguistic specificity. It is composed by two big groups of population: immigrants from the rest of Poland (and Poles from abroad) representing slightly more than 50%, and the local indigenous Silesian population. The latter, in turn, consists of people of various ethnic identity: Polish, German and indefinite. The ethnic identity of this group is very unstable and has little to do with objective criteria like language, religion or folklore: they all speak Polish (the German speaking population is insignificant), mostly Roman Catholics, their folklore is deeply rooted in the Polish folk culture, etc. To some extent the division of Silesians into Poles and Germans is artificial. Recently, a tendency among the indigenous population is getting importance to neglect the division into Poles and Germans and to accentuate Silesian identity of the local population as opposed to the immigrants.

The local population differs from the immigrants by some psychological and sociological characteristics (organisation of the family life and the like) and by some linguistic characteristics, namely by a stronger position of the local dialect of Polish (used also by the urban population which is unimaginable in the rest of Poland) and by a large number of German words in this dialect.

Upper Silesia is a region with a complicated history: it was a part of Poland in the Middle Ages, then a part of the Czech Kingdom, of Austria and of Prussia/Germany. After the World War I, as a result of three uprising of the local Polish population, the eastern part of Upper Silesia was included to Poland, and the western part remained in Germany. The latter was included to Poland after the World War II. The Polish part of Upper Silesia in the inter-war period had autonomy its parliament and special regulations in many fields.

The history and the present situation have created two kinds of Silesian identity: a regional-territorial identity of the whole inhabitants of the region, and a regional-ethnic identity of the indigenous population, the latter being stronger and more dynamic. This "regional-ethnic" Silesian regional identity has given rise to an organised regional movement. Using the previous typology, this movement can be assessed as medium in its intensity (MI) and elitarian in its character (EM). Regionalistic organisations play a significant role in the political scene of the region despite a rather moderate support of the population.

As regards demands of the Silesian regionalism, they are, first of all, economic demands (ED) (protection of the living standards and work places, improvement of the ecological situation, etc.) which unify the whole population, then (re)establishing of the Upper Silesian autonomy (PD) (a demand which has, so far, gained little support), and a cultural demand (CD) of recognition and revaluation of the Silesian "cultural values".

So, the full "formula" for the Silesian region and regionalism would be as follows:

$$Silesian\ region = ER + EthCLR + HR\ (HR4 + HR5)$$
$$Silesian\ regionalism = MI + EM + ED + PD + CD$$

### 3.2.3. Wielkopolska

In all respects the Wielkopolska's regionalism is weaker than that of Silesia. Specificity of this region (located in the western part of central Poland, around Poznań) is mainly its economy. It has been traditionally one of the richest regions of Poland with well developed agriculture, diversified industry and commercial tradition. Now it is a region which successfully adapts itself to the economic system. In opinion, at least of a part of its population, the economic successes of the region are due to the skills, hard work, high culture, entrepreneurial spirit, etc. of inhabitants of the region.

The region is also a product of the History. It was the first historical centre of the Polish state and played a crucial role in the medieval Poland; later on it was one of constitutive self-governed provinces of the Crown of Poland; after the partitions of Poland in late 18th century it was included to Prussia and returned to Poland after the successful uprising in 1918. Wielkopolska's regionalism makes reference to the pre-partition tradition of Wielkopolska, although the influence of the 19-th century Prussian/German domination isn't negligible.

Existence of Wielkopolska's regionalism can be seen in a number of institutions, like Union of Wielkopolska's People (Unia Wielkopolan), Union of Wielkopolska's Communes, etc. Aims of this regionalism are difficult to define, as there is no ethnic, cultural, linguistic or religious differences to be protected or promoted vis-a-vis the rest of the country, nor clear economic interest to be defended (as a matter of fact the liberal economic policy pursued by the govenment is favourable for the region). In such a situation, the only reasonable aim of the Wielkopolska's regionalism is a kind of self-confirmation. One can not exclude, however, possibility of economic demands if the economic policy would or the economic situation of the region deteriorate.

So the Wielkopolska's region and regionalism can be described as follows:

*Wielkopolska region = ER + HR (H4 + H5)*
*Wielkopolska regionalism = WI + EM + RD*

### 3.2.4. Galicia

Existence of Galician identity and regionalism are controversial because their intensity and diffusion are extremely limited. This regionalism, however, deserves attention. It is the only (the first?) regionalism in Poland which makes direct reference to the time of non-existence of the Polish state. Specificity of the region is easily discernible is some social phenomena like political behaviours of the population (greater political activity, especially in local government; political preferences, etc), in demographic characteristics etc. Galician identity and regionalism, however, are based on other factors, namely on the "Galicianness" — the memory and glorification of the Galician autonomy of the late 19-th and early 20-th century, with its real or imaginary virtues. One of stimulus for the Galician regionalism is existence of the Silesian and Wielkopolska regionalisms. Galician regionalism is highly elitarian, almost exclusively limited to academic intellectuals and artists (mostly from Cracow), and by many of them "the Galician idea" is not taken for serious. It is also expressed in a "decorative way", as the word "Galician" or "Galicia" is recently appearing quite frequently in names of institutions or goods. Unlike Silesia or Wielkopolska there is no organisation of Galicians. The main aim of the Galician regionalism is "self-recognition" and promotion of knowledge on Galicia's role in the Polish and international history.

Galician region and regionalisms have the following synthetic characteristics:

$$Galician\ region\ =\ HR\ (H4\ +\ H5)$$
$$Galician\ regionalism\ =\ WI\ +\ EM\ +\ RD$$

### 3.2.5. Podhale and Kaszuby

These are two small regions in the extreme south (Podhale) and in the extreme north (Kaszuby) of Poland. Both have very distinct and easily recognizable ethnol-cultural and linguistic specificity and regional movements and organisations with long traditions. What differs the two regions from the rest of Poland is their geography (high mountains or the sea), their folklores and linguistic specificity: namely a stronger social position and prestige of their dialects and a considerable distance between those dialects and standard Polish. It is especially true for Kaszubian dialects which are for "ordinary" Poles less understandable than some "regular" languages like Slovak or Ukrainian. There exists also a literature in Kaszubian dialects, mainly poetry and short stories, and there are attempts to create one Kaszubian standard language. It is interesting to note, that the present upheaval of regionalistic sentiments in big regions (Silesia, Wielkopolska, Galicia) seems to have no impact on those two small regions.

## 3.3. Ukraine

Until its declaration of independence in 1991 (confirmed by the all-Ukrainian referendum of 1st of December 1991) Ukraine could be considered as a case of region and regionalism within the Soviet Union. Constitutive elements of this region were its ethnol-cultural and linguistic specificity, administrative unity and its historical background. The ethnol-cultural and linguistic specificity consisted first of all in the ethnic composition of the population — overwhelmingly Ukrainian (which didn't exclude supra-ethnic territorial identification with Ukraine of non-Ukrainians), and in the use of the Ukrainian language (closely related to Russian and Polish) — either in both private and public life, or only in private life. Despite complicated fates of individual parts of Ukraine, the History provided significant symbols of Ukrainian identity: they were, first of all the medieval Kievian state and some episodes in the modern history of existence of an independent Ukrainian state. The last such episode was the People's Republic of Ukraine in 1918–1920. Despite its short existence, its symbolic significance was innegligible: it inspired many Ukrainians in Ukraine and in the diaspora to preserve Ukrainian identity and strive for independence. The Ukrainian identity of the vast majority of population was combined with a all-Soviet or great-Russian identity making the Ukrainian identity really a regional identity. The situation changed considerably in the late 1980s when the all-Soviet (or great-Russian) identity diminished. Ukraine was also an administrative territorial unit as member of the federal Soviet state, with its government, parliament and other institution. This circumstance turned out to be of crucial significance in transforming, at least nominally, Ukraine from a region into a nation-state.

Ukraine presents a variety of regions and the regional question is becoming one of the most important. The main determinants of the regional question are ethnol-cultural and linguistic differences among regions and the economic factor, sometimes strengthened by the geographical factor. The principal source of the ethnol-cultural and linguistic differentiation is the History that can be reduced to the time of inclusion of individual territories to the Russian Empire (or the Soviet Union).

From the ethnic point of view, the population of Ukraine is composed by two groups: Ukrainians (about 3/4) and Russians (1/5). This division doesn't present the real complexity of the situation, because, on the one hand, the division between Ukrainians and Russians is very unclear and, on the other hand, there are considerable differences in the intensity of ethnic identity both among Ukrainians and among Russians. Roughly speaking, territorial differences of the ethnic composition are as follows: the extreme western regions (included to the USSR after the World War II, except Transcarpathia which was also included in that time but which represents a special case) are populated overwhelmingly by population of strong Ukrainian identity (sometimes with elements of chauvinism); central-western regions (included to Russia by the end of 18-th century) are dominated by a population of rather moderate or weak Ukrainian identity (often with a strong sense of ethnol-cultural affinity with Russians); eastern regions (included to Russia in mid-17th century) and the Black Sea Coast (except Crimea) are populated mostly by Russian speaking Ukrainians and Russians, who are usually deeply rooted in Ukraine and feel considerable sense of identity with this country; and finally Crimea whose present population are mostly recent Russian settlers of strong Russian identity (with elements of anti-Ukrainism).

When analyzing the regional question in Ukraine, some regions of this country deserves special attention. These are: Crimea, Donbass, Transcarpathia and (eastern) Galicia.

Crimea was originally populated by Tatars and was included to Russia at the beginning of 19th century when Russian settlement began; Tatars were deported from the peninsula after the Second World War; Crimea was included to the Ukrainian SSR in 1954. Now Crimea is an autonomous region in Ukraine. This region is populated in 3/4 by Russians, Ukrainians are in minority and Ukrainian language absent in the public life (attempts to introduce it in schools as obligatory subject have failed because of the opposition of local Russians; there is only one Ukrainian-language newspaper). Crimea has played a very important military role in Russia and the USSR and is still playing it for the new Russia. The transfer of Crimea to Ukraine in 1954 is not recognized by a considerable part of the society and politicians in Russia which encourages separatist tendencies in the region (demands for inclusion to Russia or for independence). Situation in Crimea is of great importance for Ukraine as it can play a catalytic role for centrifugal tendencies in other regions, mainly in the mostly Russian-speaking eastern and southern regions.

Donbass is a region in eastern Ukraine constituted by two main characteristics: economy and ethnol-cultural and linguistic situation. It is the major industrial region of Ukraine, its main energy producer, an enormous concentration of heavy industries, environmental and social problems. The region's economy has had tight linkages with other parts of the (former) USSR which are now to a large extent broken. The region is populated mostly by Russians and Russian-speaking Ukrainians which make it culturally and linguistically orientated towards Russia. As the whole country, Donbass is undergoing a severe economic crisis, which together with other problems is causing protests of the working class of the region. (When this paper was written — mid-June 1993, a big strike of about 1.5 million workers is under way). The public opinion of the region attributes this crisis to broken economic (as well as political) ties with Russia and to incompetent central authorities in Kiev. Therefore the now emerging workers' movement in Donbass demands closer relationships with Russia, and an economic-administrative autonomy for Donbass (or for all Russian-speaking regions of eastern Ukraine), as well as a number of demands that would dramatically change the situation in Ukraine (e.g. dismission of the president of the republic). Satisfying of these and other popular in Donbass demands, like the right for double Ukrainian-Russian citizenship and recognition of Russian as one of official languages of Ukraine or of the region (this role is played by Russian de facto, but not de iure), could be interpreted as a threat for Ukrainian independence and territorial integrity by people of other regions, so it can cause deterioration of the inter-regional relations and acceleration of centrifugal tendencies.

Transcarpathia is another region of centrifugal tendencies. It is a region with clear geographic, ethnol-cultural and linguistic, administrative and historical personality. It is separated from the rest of Ukrainian territory by the chain of Carpathian Mountains, alongside which for many centuries national borders went. For many centuries it belonged to Hungary (or Austro-Hungary), in the inter-war time to Czechoslovakia and since 1939 again to Hungary and in 1945 was included to the Ukrainian SSR. In the inter-war period Transcarpathia (called "Eastern Slovakia") had autonomy, and in 1939 was even one-day independent state with its parliament and government which went in exile after annexation by Hungary. This historical background is a reference point for regional identity. Another source of regional identity of Transcarpathia is its ethnol-cultural and linguistic specificity. It is populated mostly by Carpatho-Ruthenians, a people who, according to one opinion (until recently the official opinion) is an ethnic group of Ukrainians and its language is a Ukrainian dialect, and according to another opinion, that seems to prevail among Carpatho-Ruthenians themselves, it is a separate nation with its own language. Transcarpathia is also populated by considerable minorities: Hungarian, Rumanian and Slovak. Unlike most Ukrainians who are Orthodoxes, Carpatho-Ruthenians are predominantly Uniates (Greek-Catholics). All those factors are source of strong regionalism and demand for autonomy as well as of orientation towards Central Europe. The desire for autonomy was confirmed by the referendum of 1st of December of 1993 when the vast majority of Transcarpathian voted at the same time for independence of Ukraine and for autonomy of Transcarpathia. Now the transcapathian regionalism seems to be the strongest regional movement in Central Europe.

Ukrainian Galicia (three "oblasts" in western Ukraine: Lvov, Ternopol and Ivano-Frankovsk) is a very specific region. It differs in many respects from the rest of the country: ethnol-cultural, linguistic, religious and historical, but the Galician regionalism is very weak. This situation is due to the strong Ukrainian identity of its population, which suppresses the regional identity. The strong Ukrainian identity of Galicia is another product of the History: this identity was a reaction to the strong Polish identity and national movement in 19th century Galicia and in the inter-war Poland to which the whole Galicia belonged. The Ukrainian identity was also supported by an influential institution, namely by the Uniate Church in Galicia. Another specificity of the region is the strong position of Ukrainian language both in the private and in the public sphere, both in the rural and urban population. Galicia is traditionally a region diffusing the idea of Ukrainian identity and independence, Ukrainian language, knowledge of Ukrainian history, etc. to the rest of Ukraine. It is an example if a centripetal region.

It is to expect that the regional question of Ukraine will develop and will gain importance with possible consequences going beyond Ukrainian borders.

## 3.4. Belarus

Byelorussia (or Belarus), a nominally independent nation-state, is an example of an ethnic and territorial community searching for its identity and hesitating between a regional identity (as a part of Russia) and a separate national identity. Specificity of the Byelorussians when compared with the (rest of) Russians consists in some ethnol-cultural and linguistic factors, namely in the sense of being (slightly) different than the (rest of) Russians and in the Byelorussian language, which, however, easily can be treated and is often treated as a dialect of Russian.

Byelorussian specificity was created by the History, namely by the fact that the present territory of Byelorussia for four hundred years (end of 14th – end of 18th century) belonged to a country other than Moscow-dominated Russia. This country was the Great Duchy of Lithuania, which together with the Crown (of Poland) formed the Commonwealth of the Two Nations. As a matter of fact, proponents of the Byelorussian national idea consider the Great Duchy of Lithuania a predecessor of Byelorussia which is reflected, among other things, in national symbolic of the contemporary Byelorussian state. Byelorussian nationalism emerged at the end of 19th century but never reached such intensity or diffusion like in neighbouring nations and Byelorussians remained a "double-souled people". Of special importance for development of the Byelorussian ethnicity was the inter-war period. In that time the territory of present Byelorussia was divided between Poland (the western part) and the Soviet Union (where an administrative unit called "Byelorussian SSR" was established). In the Soviet part of Byelorussia, after the initial period of promotion of the Byelorussian culture, language and identity, a process of russification began accelerated by massive repressions and physical exterminations of the Byelorussian intellectual elite (and not only of it). In this situation conscious Byelorussian activists, Byelorussian culture and language had more chances to survive in Poland. It is reflected now in the ethnol-cultural and linguistic differentiation of the territory of Byelorussia: western regions with quite strong position of the Byelorussian national identity and living Byelorussian language and eastern regions populated by people of Russian identity or Russian-speaking Byelorussians.

Unlike in Ukraine, in Byelorussia there are no regions with centrifugal tendencies or with special regional identity. The situation can change, however. The source of such tendencies may be in the currently pursued action of revitalisation of the Byelorussian language (declared the only "national language" of Byelorussia) and attempts to substitute it for Russian as the official language which causes protests of a part of the Russian-speaking population. A serious conflict is, however, unlikely.

So, the Byelorussian case can serve as an example of indefinition of regional and national identities and as an illustration of transformation of a regional identity into a national identity.

## 3.5. Russia

The Russian case is so complex that only some general tendencies and problems will be mentioned here. Russian regions represent a rich variety of types: there are "one-dimensioned" regions (e.g. only administrative or only economic ones, etc) and "multi-dimensioned" regions; regions with different political status; regions with weaker and stronger sense of identity; ethnically Russian and non-Russian regions; ethnically homogeneous and diversified regions; regions in different economic conditions; regions representing weaker or stronger centrifugal tendencies, etc.

From the point of view of the impact of the regional question on the general situation in Russia, four issues seem to be of special interest. They are: 1)relations between the central and regional authorities, 2)relations between two types of regions-members of the Russian Federation, 3)interdependence between the economic and the regional question, 4)interdependence between the ethnic and the regional question.

Since the beginning of "perestroika" a process of decentralisation of political and economic power is taking place in the USSR and Russia. Given the previous overcentralisation of power and the changing economic and political system, such decentralisation is inevitable and needed to establish an economically and politically more efficient system of distribution of power between the central and regional (local) authorities.

Thus, the search for a new central-regional equilibrium isn't per se disintegration of Russia. This process, however, may cause and is causing some by-products that can disturb the political and economic transformations in Russia. On one hand there is a danger of excessive and chaotic decentralisation that can bring about quite counter-productive results for the economic efficiency and political viability of the system. On the other hand, even the rational transfer of power towards regions may agitate defenders of the "yedinaya i nedelimaya" ("one and indivisible" Russia) to stop the process and to reestablish the Moscow domination not only over the regions of Russia, but also over the post-Soviet republics and even the Central European countries.

Now the Russian Federations consists of almost one hundred (about 90) units — "subjects (i.e. members) of the federation". These units are about 20 republics (formally "sovereign", some of them call themselves "independent") occupying majority of the territory of Russia, and provinces ("oblasts") as well as two "capital cities" — Moscow and Petersburg. There are some differences in the legal status (and the range of power) between the republics and other members of the federation, although the differences are still diminishing. (The recognition of the provinces and cities as "members of the federation is an element in this process). The republics require retention of their special status and oppose further egalisation with provinces arguing that the republics are forms of statehood of the ethnic communities. As a matter of fact in most republics of Siberia and the north of Russia, the local indigenous population represents only a small percentage of the population (usually it is highly assimilated) and doesn't play a meaning role in the political or economic life of their republics and thus the differences between some republics and provinces are negligible. Therefore representatives of the provinces consider privileges of the republics unjustified and require equalisation of the status. In Moscow and Petersburg there exist even movements for obtaining the republican status by these cities. When analyzing the structure of the Russian Federation, one should mention three special cases, namely three republics: Chechenia, Tatarstan and Bashkortostan. The first has declared independence and doesn't participate in the political life (institutions of power) of Russia, the second has declared itself "an independent state associated with Russia" (although the Russian constitution doesn't know such a status) and participate in the political life of Russia when it considers necessary or advantageous, the third tries to follow the neighbouring Tatarstan. So, the process of decentralisation of Russia has many things in common with the Western European integration: in both cases there is the question of uniformity of diversity of status of members.

Serious corrections into the above described picture can be and are being introduced by the economic factor. The economic factor acts in several directions. The first one is to strengthen the economic position of some regions (individual republics or provinces or geographical regions) encouraging them to demand more power and more control over their wealth and profits. It is the case, for instance, of the Republic of Saha-Yakutia in Siberia — a major producer of gold and diamonds, and the oil-producing region of Tiumen, etc. The second direction of action of the economic factor is the forced regional self-reliance resulted from strictly pragmatic reasons: high transportation costs, instability of economic links. The third direction is the growing orientation of some peripheral regions of Russia — first of all the Far East and the Kaliningrad enclave — towards the economic co-operation with the neighbouring countries: Japan, China and South Korea in the case of the Far East, Western Europe (Germany), Scandinavia and Poland in the case of Kaliningrad. (One can also mention the tendency for co-operation with Scandinavia in Karelia and other north-western regions). The fourth direction of action of the economic factor is quite opposite to the former three, namely it tempers some exaggerated ambitions for political independence and economic self-reliance.

As regards the ethnol-regional situation, it should be stressed that the vast majority of the population of Russia (about 80%) are ethnic Russians and that Russians, with negligible exceptions, are culturally and linguistically extremely homogenous on the whole territory and, thus, emergence of a regionalism based on differences among Russians can be hardly expected. The only meaningful exception is the Kaliningrad enclave (populated after 1995) where signs of searching for its own regional identity can be observed. The ethnic homogeneity of Russians doesn't exclude possibility of centrifugal tendencies based on economic interests or stimulated by personal ambitions or political conflicts.

The remaining 20% of the population of Russia are composed by about 100 ethnic groups of different degree of sense of ethnic identity and cultural and linguistic assimilation. Most of those ethnic groups have no "statehood", some have "too large" republics in which they are in minority and without influence, some ethnic groups must "share" their republic with other non-Russian groups, some others live mostly outside their republic, while a few groups live mostly in their republic where they are in majority. From the point of view of possibility of centrifugal tendencies, regions of Russia can be located between two extremes: on the one extreme there is "the hard of Russia" composed by the ethnically Russian regions of the European part; on the opposite extreme there are regions populated predominantly by non-Russians of non-Christian (mostly Moslem) cultural background with traditions of conflicts with Russia: such regions are mostly northern Caucasus (the best example is Chechenia), Tatarstan (in the central part of European Russia) and Tuva in Siberia (in the inter-war period a nominally independent republic, populated mostly by Buddhist Tuvinians, a group related to Mongolians). In between there are ethnically Russian regions of Siberia and the Far East and regions populated by non-Russians of Christian (orthodox) background in both the European and Asian part.

As can be seen from the above discussion, the future of Russia will largely depend on the developments in its regional question, which, in turn, will be result of a complex interplay of the economic situation of whole country, economic interests of individual regions, personal ambitions and skills of central and regional politicians and political groups, and the desire of ethnic communities for protection and expression of their identity.

## 3.6. Other countries

Focusing on the bigger countries of Central-Eastern Europe doesn't mean lack of the regional question in other countries. The other way round, in some small countries the regional question is much serious than in some of the above four. The most complicated situation is in Moldavia which is divided into three separate parts with their own authorities and military forces: Moldavia proper claiming for control over the whole territory of former Soviet Moldavia, Dnestr Republic (populated mostly by Russians and Ukrainians) and Gagausia (populated by a russificated once Turkish-speaking Orthodoxes). Ethnic Moldavians themselves are hesitating between a regional identity (as a part of Rumania) and a separate national identity, which influences their attitude towards the idea of unification with Rumania. (It seems that the all-Rumanian identity of Moldavians is disappearing). Not much less complicated is the situation in the Baltic republics where considerable minorities accusing central governments for discrimination, in some regions are in majority (e.g. Russians in Narva and other north-eastern parts of Estonia, in Riga and in the south and east of Latvia, Poles in surroundings of Vilna in Lithuania). So, the ethnic tensions there can turn into inter-regional ones. Big concentrations of ethnic minorities are also in Slovakia (Hungarians in the south and Ruthenians/Ukrainians in the north-east), Rumania (mainly Hungarians in the central and western regions) and Bulgaria (Turks and Moslems in Kardjali in the south, and in the north-east). Even in the ethnically quite homogeneous Czech Republic there is a regional movement in Moravia and minorities represent considerable share of population in some regions. Former Yugoslavia is undoubtedly the most dramatic case of the regional-ethnic question. Its analysis would require, however, a special treatment. It can be said that the Yugoslav case isn't typical for Central and Eastern Europe: in the whole post-war period Yugoslavia featured more characteristics of a Third World country than of an Eastern European country.

# 4. Final remarks

In this paper the analysis of examples of the regional question was concentrated on Central-Eastern European countries which are transforming their political and economic systems, and, doing this, are sometimes "discovering" ethnic minorities, regional movements and territorial differentiations. It doesn't mean that the regional and ethnic question in Western Europe is much more simple or resolved. It is enough to mention the cases of Northern Ireland, Bask Country and Corsica and less dramatic cases of Catalonia, Belgium, the North Italian regionalism etc. It seems that both halves of the continent are facing the question of finding new ways of expression of several types and levels of identities: local, regional, national, European, ethnic, religious, etc. and at the same time have to find ways of economic and political co-operation among regions and nations. This question is and will be resolved in a learning-by-doing process and there are no easy suggestions how to do it. Some conclusions resulting from the above discussion, however, should be taken into consideration: regional and ethnic identities are natural forms of human collective identities, created by the History or Geography and so, suppressing them as such would cause human sufferings and conflicts; representatives of regional and ethnic movements must take into account the right of people not only to express a regional but also a national identity; a powerful determinant of regional and ethnic movements is the economy — a well working economy and small inter-regional differences in living conditions is the best way of solving the regional and ethnic problems.

Warsaw, June 1993

**A.U. Khomra**
**Ukrainian Academy of Science**
**Kiev**

# ETHNICAL STRUCTURE
# OF MIGRATION BALANCE
# OF UKRAINE'S POPULATION:
# REGIONAL ASPECT

## Introductory remarks

Sovereign Ukraine has inherited a territorial and administrative division from a republic which was a part of a larger state formation — the Soviet Union. Naturally, this division was more in function of interests of the Soviet Union as a whole than of Ukraine. Threfore a radical transformation of the administrative and territorial system of Ukraine is now one of the most important tasks. Its full realisation, however, should take place in a more distant time, after overcoming the present economic crisis. Nevertheless, we have to begin preparing scientific foundations for this transformation. So, an important role in the formation the new administrative-territorial order (based on units called "zemli" — lands) should be played by the regional ethno-demographic research, in the first place in the fields of migration relations.

This paper tries to contribute to this research. Its aim is to present changes in the ethnic structure of the population of Ukraine and of its regions in the post-war period as a result of migration and assimilation processes.

# 1. Methodology of the study

The study is based on census data of 1959, 1970, 1979 and 1989 which included information about ethnicity of the population (every citizen had to declare his/her ethnic belonging and he/she could declare belonging to any ethnic group) as well as current population statistics (births and deaths) which also included information about ethnicity of the population (the ethnicity was registered in identity cards or, in the case of births, in mother's identity card). The data for the ethnic structure of interregional migrations were obtained from the census and current statistics data by using the balance method, i.e. by comparing the total number and the ethnic composition of a given region's population in two or more time points.

Unfortunately, the existing data do not allow to distinguish between the effects of migration and the effects of assimilation on changes in the ethnic composition of individual regions and the country as a whole.

# 2. General tendencies

For 30 years which passed since the time of the first postwar census, the number of Russians in Ukraine as a result of migration and assimilation increased by 2230.3 thousand people. The number of Ukrainians as a result of the same factors decreased by 1297.8 ths people, the number of Jews decreased by 202.5 ths, Poles — by 157 ths, Moldavians — by 13.3 ths people. In the countryside the balance of migration and assimilation of all ethnic groups enumerated in population accounts was negative for the analyzed years (the three last intercensus periods). Due to migrations, assimilation and administrative-territorial transformations, the number of Ukrainians in rural areas decreased by 7507 ths people, Russians — by 219.5 ths, Poles — by 138 ths, Moldavians — on 39 ths people. In urban areas the migration (with assimilation and administrative-territorial transformations) caused the decrease of the number of Jews (by 181.2 ths people) and Poles (by 19 ths people).

With regard to the dynamics, the migration inflow (with assimilation) of Russians represents a decreasing tendency: in 1970–1978 its annual average value decreased in comparison with 1959–1969 by 1.56 times, in 1979–1988 in comparison with 1970–1978 by 2.73 times[1].

A decreasing tendency also occurred in the outflow (and assimilation) of Ukrainians and Poles (table 1). But while in the case of Russians the cause of the decreased inflow (and assimilation) was the decreased inflow (and assimilation) in urban areas, the cause of the decreased outflow (and assimilation) of Ukrainians and Poles was the decreased outflow from rural settlements.

Table 1

**Average annual balance of migration, assimilation and administrative-territorial transformation of some ethnic groups of Ukraine in 1959–1988, ths people**

| ethnic group | settlements | | | | | | | | |
|---|---|---|---|---|---|---|---|---|---|
| | total | | | urban | | | rural | | |
| | 1959–1969 | 1970–1978 | 1979–1988 | 1959–1969 | 1970–1978 | 1979–1988 | 1959–1969 | 1970–1978 | 1979–1988 |
| Ukrainian | −58.7 | −51.4 | −24.9 | 260.0 | 201.1 | 179.8 | −318.7 | −252.5 | −204.7 |
| Russian | 123.2 | 78.8 | 28.9 | 132.3 | 85.9 | 35.4 | −9.1 | −7.1 | −6.5 |
| Byelorussian | 2.8 | −1.8 | 0.9 | 3.9 | −0.1 | 1.5 | −1.1 | −1.7 | −0.6 |
| Jewish | −4.1 | −10.1 | −7.1 | −2.4 | −9.6 | −7.1 | −1.7 | −0.5 | 0.0 |
| Polish | −9.0 | −4.2 | −2.9 | −0.9 | −0.2 | −0.8 | −8.1 | −4.0 | −2.1 |
| Moldavian | −1.2 | 0.3 | −0.5 | 0.9 | 1.0 | 0.7 | −2.1 | −0.7 | −1.2 |
| others | 0.1 | 0.6 | 9.2 | 8.1 | 3.8 | 8.5 | −8.0 | −3.2 | 0.7 |

The highest positive relative migration balance in 1979–1988 was recorded in the item "other ethnic groups" wich was due mainly to the immigrations of Crimean Tatars. The relative balance of migration (and assimilation) of Russians decreased in 1979–1988 in relation to 1959–1969 by 5.74 times (in relation to 1970–1978 — by 2.73 times). The intensity of the outflow (and assimilation) of Ukrainians was also characterized by the decreasing tendency, but the pace of decrease was lower: in 1979–1988 the

---

[1] According to assessments by M.N.Rutkevich — approximately one half of the 870 ths increment of the number of Russians in Ukraine in the years of the last intercensus period was a result of the excess of inflow over outflow /Руткевич М.Н. *О двух аспектах межнациональных отношений* // Социологические исследования. 1991, No 3., pp. 9–15/ These assessments are, in our opinion, significantly (more than by one third) overestimated. This overestimation will be even greater if we take into account the assimilation in our calculation.

negative balance of migration and assimilation of Ukrainians decreased
in relation to 1959–1969 by 2.6 times (in relation to 1970–1978 — by 1.93
times). The intensity of outflow of Jews, which sharply increased in the
70s, in the last intercensus period it continued to remain on a steady high
level (table 2).

**Table 2**

**Relative balance of migration, assimilation
and administrative-territorial transformations
of some ethnic groups of Ukraine in 1959–1988, ‰**

| ethnic group | settlements | | | | | | | | |
|---|---|---|---|---|---|---|---|---|---|
| | total | | | urban | | | rural | | |
| | 1959–<br>–1969 | 1970–<br>–1978 | 1979–<br>–1988 | 1959–<br>–1969 | 1970–<br>–1978 | 1979–<br>–1988 | 1959–<br>–1969 | 1970–<br>–1978 | 1979–<br>–1988 |
| Ukrainian | −1.74 | −1.29 | −0.67 | 18.61 | 10.20 | 8.58 | −16.14 | −12.53 | −12.80 |
| Russian | 15.20 | 7.24 | 2.65 | 19.69 | 9.22 | 3.73 | −6.53 | −4.51 | −4.58 |
| Byelorussian | 8.27 | −4.07 | 2.12 | 15.40 | −0.17 | 4.33 | −13.25 | −17.47 | −6.32 |
| Jewish | −5.08 | −12.89 | −12.62 | −3.12 | −12.46 | −12.65 | −76.76 | −43.69 | −9.81 |
| Polish | −27.36 | −13.55 | −12.30 | −5.41 | −0.99 | −5.50 | −48.96 | 31.46 | −24.93 |
| Moldavian | −4.70 | 0.98 | −14.86 | 15.16 | 0.11 | 7.06 | −11.22 | −3.07 | −5.47 |
| others | 0.07 | 0.52 | 81.02 | 17.61 | 6.14 | 13.37 | −16.74 | −5.96 | 1.13 |

The very high relative values of the negative balance of migration
(together with assimilation and administrative-territorial transformations)
of Poles were caused probably by the intensive process of assimilation.
Somewhat lower, but still quite high (more than 2 times as high as the
intensity of the outflow of Russians, Byelorussians and Moldavians) values of the intensity the outflow of Ukrainians from the countryside were
caused by their migration. With regard to the dynamics, after quite a significant lowering of the intensity of the outflow of Russians, Ukrainians
and Moldavians in 1970–1978, later on this intensity remained stable and
even started to grow. In urban settlements, as a result of migrations, assimilation and administrative-territorial transformations in 1979–1988, the
most intensive was the increase of the number of Ukrainians, although in
1959–1969 the value of this indicator for Russians was (slightly — only by
1.08 point — but still) above that of Ukrainians. While for Russians the
decrease of the values of this indicator was very sharp, for Ukrainians in
the last intercensus period it was considerably stopped (table 2).

# 3. Regional tendencies

The number of Ukrainians decreased in the result of migration and assimilation during the years between the first postwar census of the population and the last one in most provinces (oblasts) of Ukraine. That reduction was especially sensible in the Vinnitsa (by 430.9 ths people), Zhitomir (338.6), Khmelnitsky (291.2), Chernihiv (263.9) and Sumy (211.3 ths people) provinces. The negative balance of migration and assimilation of Ukrainians was considerable during the years of that period in Donbas (the Lugansk and Donetsk provinces), the Central Dniepr Regions (the Cherkassy, Kirovograd and Poltava prowinces) and the East Volyno-Podollya (Rivne and Ternopil provinces). The positive balance of migrations and assimilation of Ukrainians in the Kiev, Kharkiv and Odessa provinces was caused by the inflow of Ukrainians in the provincial centres — big cities. The inflow (with the assimilation) of Ukrainians to Kiev was especially intensive. The number of Ukrainians there, due to these factors, increased by 790.3 ths people. The provinces towards which the main waves of migration of Ukrainians were directed were the Dniepropietrovsk, Crimea, Zaporizhya and Kherson provinces. As a rule, the assimilation was taking the opposite direction in these regions. In all provinces with the highest reduction of the number of Ukrainians as a result of migration and assimilation, there was a tendency to slowing the pace of this reduction.

The negative balance of migration and assimilation of Ukrainians was observed in 1979–1988 in 17 provinces of Ukraine. This process was especially intensive in the Zhitomir, Vinnitsa, Chernihiv, Khmelnitsy and Rivne provinces, where the negative relative balance of migration and assimilation exceeded 4‰ . The Ternopil, Sumy, Volyn, Kiev-countryside (without the town of Kiev), Kirovograd, Transcarpathia and Cherkassy provinces represented a group of provinces, where the values of the balance of migration and assimilation of Ukrainians was 2–4‰. Quite considerable was also the intensity of the outflow and assimilation of Ukrainians in the Lugansk and Ivano-Frankivsk provinces. In the majority of provinces the outflow and assimilation of Ukrainians caused a reduction of the total number of their inhabitants. Generally, the values of the relative negative balance of migration and assimilation of Ukrainians were higher than the values of the relative negative balance of migration of the whole population.

The positive balance of migration and assimilation of Ukrainians was characteristic for the provinces whose provincial capitals were big cities (Zaporizhya, Dnipropetrovsk, Kharkiv, Odessa, Donetsk, Lvov) as well as for those where a massive organised agricultural resettlement was directed (Crimean, Nikolaev provinces). The most intensive process of migration and assimilation of Ukrainians took place in Kiev, where the value of that balance reached 14.5‰. It is worth noting, that this value considerably (by 27.2%) exceeded the value of the relative balance of migration of the total population of Kiev. The value of the relative balance of migration and assimilation of Ukrainians exceeded the relative balance of migration of the total population also in the Odessa and Lvov provinces.

In the years of the last intercensus period (1979–1988) the outflow and assimilation of Russians were observed mainly in the provinces of the Western Podillya and Volyn (the Rivne, Ternopil, Lvov, Volyn) and of the Donbas (Donetsk, Lugansk). That process was quite intensive in the Vinnitsa province where the negative relative balance of migration and assimilation of Russians was 1.6‰. A higher value of this index was only in the Rivne (3.5‰), Ternopil (1.9‰) and Lvov provinces. In all provinces where the balance of migration and assimilation of Russians was negative, there took place a more intensive migration outflow of the whole population (except the Donetsk province).

The main areas of inflow (with the assimilation) of Russians were the Southern and the Eastern provinces where the provincial capitals were, as a rule, big cities (Crimean, Dnipropetrovsk, Odessa, Kharkiv, Kiev (city), Zaporizhya, Nikolaev provinces). The share of this group of provinces in the total increase of the number of Russians resulting form migration and assimilation in all provinces where this increase took place, was 84.2%.

Relatively high positive balance of migration and assimilation of Byelorussians was observed in the provinces with the highest values of the positive balance of migration and assimilation of Russians. The outflow (with assimilation) of Byelorussians took place in the Rivne, Kiev-countryside (mainly to the Kiev-city), Lugansk and Donetsk provinces. The very high value of the relative balance of migration and assimilation of Byelorussians in the Rivne province (19.9‰) testifies to the domination of the assimilation in this process.

The decrease of the numbers of Moldavians as a result of migration and assimilation was typical for the Odessa and Chernivitsi provinces; the increase of their numbers as a result of these factors, by far not comparable with the outflow (and assimilation) from the above mentioned provinces, occurred in the Nikolaev and Kirovograd provinces. The numbers of Poles due to migration and assimilation decreased practically in all provinces of their compact inhabitance. This process was extremely intensive in the Ternopil, Chernivtsi, Zhitomir, Odessa, Kiev, Khmelnitsy, Vinnitsa and Lvov provinces.

**Table 3**

**Relative balance of migration and assimilation
of Ukrainians and Russians in the provinces of Ukraine
in 1959–1988, ‰**

| Provinces | ukrainian | | | russian | | |
|---|---|---|---|---|---|---|
| | 1959–<br>–1969 | 1970–<br>–1978 | 1979–<br>–1988 | 1959–<br>–1969 | 1970–<br>–1978 | 1979–<br>–1988 |
| Kiev (city) | 29.7 | 23.8 | 14.5 | 28.1 | 19.3 | 6.6 |
| Crimea | 23.5 | 1.7 | 5.1 | 23.3 | 13.1 | 5.3 |
| Zaporizya | 3.5 | 1.8 | 1.7 | 18.9 | 10.2 | 3.2 |
| Dnipropetrovsk | 4.7 | 1.5 | 1.5 | 26.3 | 10.9 | 4.4 |
| Kharkiov | −0.3 | 1.5 | 1.5 | 12.2 | 10.6 | 3.6 |
| Odessa | 4.1 | 0.8 | 1.3 | 18.7 | 8.6 | 5.5 |
| Donetsk | −2.6 | −3.4 | 0.6 | 9.4 | 6.3 | −0.8 |
| Lvov | 1.3 | 0.3 | 0.3 | 1.4 | −8.8 | −1.9 |
| Nikolaev | −1.2 | 1.2 | 0.3 | 17.9 | 12.6 | 7.0 |
| Poltava | −3.4 | −1.0 | −0.1 | 25.5 | 15.2 | 4.3 |
| Chernivitsi | −0.8 | 1.2 | −0.3 | −3.9 | 3.7 | 3.5 |
| Kherson | 5.5 | 4.3 | −0.8 | 23.9 | 13.2 | 1.8 |
| Ivano–Frankovsk | −1.0 | −1.4 | −1.4 | 8.0 | −13.3 | 7.6 |
| Lugansk | −5.7 | −7.0 | −1.4 | 6.4 | 0.5 | −0.5 |
| Cherkassy | −5.8 | −2.9 | −2.2 | 15.6 | 10.7 | 7.5 |
| Transcarpathia | −2.4 | −1.2 | −2.4 | 3.7 | 5.5 | 6.6 |
| Kirovograd | −4.3 | −5.0 | −2.5 | 4.0 | 4.2 | 4.6 |
| Volyn | 4.8 | −4.2 | −3.0 | 4.7 | −0.1 | −0.8 |
| Kiev–country side | −3.6 | −0.6 | −2.8 | 36.3 | 19.9 | 3.8 |
| Sumy | −7.7 | −5.3 | −3.0 | −3.8 | −1.9 | −0.3 |
| Ternopol | −3.4 | −3.5 | −3.1 | −12.0 | −13.3 | −1.9 |
| Rivne | −4.1 | −3.1 | −4.1 | 2.9 | 6.6 | −3.5 |
| Khmelnitsky | −8.2 | −7.7 | −4.3 | 0.9 | 0.7 | 6.0 |
| Chernihiv | −6.6 | −6.6 | −5.4 | 6.7 | 9.9 | 2.4 |
| Vinnitsa | −8.5 | −7.6 | −6.5 | 1.7 | −0.6 | −1.6 |
| Zhitomir | −10.0 | −8.2 | −6.6 | 2.9 | 2.5 | 0.7 |

The outflow of Jews, mainly abroad, took place in all provinces. This process was the most intensive in the Central and Western provinces including the province that suffered more than others from the accident at Chornobyl power station. So, the value of the negative relative balance of migration of Jews in the Chernivtsi province was equal 21.5‰, in Kiev–countryside province — 19.2, in Kiev-city — 15.2, in Zitomir province — 14.9, Chernihiv province — 14.3, in Cherkassy province — 14.1, in Vinnitsa province — 13.8‰. The intencity of the outflow of Jews from the provinces of the Dniepr region, Donbas and the South was considerable lower; it was below 8‰ for this area as a whole.

In the majority of provinces with the outflow and assimilation of Ukrainians in the years of the last intercensus period, there was a tendency in the analyzed post-war period to reducing the outflow and assimilation of Ukrainians.

The same tendency to decrease of the relative balance of migration and assimilation of Ukrainians took also place in the provinces where this balance was positive. It was especially true for Kiew-city.

The all-Ukrainian tendency to decrease of the intensity of inflow and assimilation of Russian took place in majority of provinces with the positive balance of migration and assimilation of Russians. A clear tendency to decrease of the relative balance of migration and assimilation of Russians was observed in the Kherson, Kiev-countryside, Dnipropetrovsk, Poltava, Zaporizhya, Crimea, Zhitomir, Odessa, Kharkiv, Mikolaev and Cherkassy provinces as well as in Kiev-city.

The intensity of the outflow (with assimilation) of Jews remained on the high level over the whole analyzed period in all provinces of Ukraine. In such provinces like the Kherson, Kharkiv, Poltava, Dnipropetrovsk, Donetsk, Kiev (coutryside), Lugansk, Zhitomir, this intensity was characterized by a increasing tedency. The same tendency was observed in the Odessa province and in Kiev-city, where in 1959–1969 the balance of migration and assimilation of Jews was positive.

The tendency to decrease of the value of the negative balance of migration and assimilation of Poles in most provinces was quite clear. The intensity of outflow and assimilation of Poles especially sharply decreased in areas of their compact inhabitance (Vinnitsa, Lvov, Khmelnitsky, Ternopil, Kiev and Zhitomir provinces).

Taking into account the values of the balances of migration and assimilation of the main ethnic groups in 1959–1988, we divided provinces of Ukraine into seven groups:

a) provinces with a positive balance of migration and assimilation of Ukrainians and Russians, with higher values of this balance for

Ukrainians — it is Kiev-city only (where a significant negative balance of migration and assimilation of Jews took place),

b) provinces with a positive balance of migration and assimilation of Ukrainians and Russians, with higher values of this balance for Russians — Crimea, Dnipropetrovsk, Zaporizhya, Kharkiv, Kherson, Odessa (where a significant negative balance of migration and assimilation of Jews and Moldavians took place),

c) provinces with a positive balance of migration and assimilation of Russians — Mikolaev province only,

d) provinces with a positive balance of migration and assimilation of Russians and a negative balance of migration and assimilation of Ukrainians — Donetsk, Lugansk, Poltava, Cherkassy, Kiev-countryside,

e) provinces with a negative balance of migration and assimilation of Ukrainians — Vinnitsa, Chernihiv, Sumy, Kirovograd, Volyn, Rivne, Ternopil, Transcarpathia, Ivano-Frankivsk,

f) provinces with a negative balance of migration and assimilation of Ukrainians and Poles, with higher values of this balance for Ukrainians — Zhitomir, Khmelnitsky, Lvov,

g) provinces with insignificant values of the balance of migration and assimilation of the main ethnic groups — Chernivtsi province only.

Studying the regional aspects of migrations of the main ethnic groups allows not only to get a more detailed information about the process of migration in Ukraine as a whole, but also to introduce substantial corrections in its assessment from the point of view of building the statehood of Ukraine. The ethnic policy of Ukraine in the present time can not be other than an ethnic-regional one.

From Ukrainian translated by *Roman Szul*

André Fischer
Université Paris I,
Panthéon — Sorbonne

# L'EMERGENCE CONTEMPORAINE DE LA REGION DANS LA PLANIFICATION TERRITORIALE EN FRANCE

## 1. De la notion de planification

Compte tenu de l'ampleur des besoins économiques et sociaux, du caractère toujours limité des ressources et des moyens disponibles, des conflits d'intérêts qui opposent les divers acteurs (secteur public — secteur, privé, individus — entreprises — collectivités...), laisser se développer les seules évolutions spontanées ne peut que conduire à une multiplication des incohérences, des risques et des conflits. Pour diminuer les risques et pour réduire le champ des incertitudes, il faut contrôler les évolutions économiques et sociales, prévoir les développements et anticiper sur le futur. Il faut donc faire des choix. C'est là précisément l'objet de la planification.

Toute planification repose sur un double ensemble de décisions: d'une part, elle implique que soient définis des objectifs, dégagés des moyens financiers, déterminés des échéanciers de réalisation; d'autre part, elle suppose que des choix soient faits en matière de priorités d'intervention (dans le temps), d'arbitrages entre les actions à entreprendre (entre les secteurs), de techniques d'anticipation à plus ou moins long terme à mettre en oeuvre.

Admettre que la planification consiste avant tout à anticiper les évolutions à venir, pour les organiser et les contrôler, c'est reconnaître que les moyens et les compétences dont disposent les différents acteurs et les différents niveaux de l'échelle géographique sont d'une importance fondamentale pour la mise en oeuvre d'une planification économique et sociale. Or, la relation entre la capacité décisionnelle et la dimension spatiale dépend pour l'essentiel des structures territoriales dans lesquelles s'inscrivent la concentration ou la décentralisation spatiales des pouvoirs (politiques, administratifs, économiques). En d'autres termes, la planification, surtout si elle vise à permettre une bonne maîtrise de l'espace, génère une double exigence en ce qui concerne les structures territoriales: une exigence de pertinence par rapport aux structures politiques; une exigence d'adéquation par rapport aux tendances lourdes des évolutions économiques et sociales.

## 2. Planification territoriale et régions

C'est en 1946, pour les besoins de la Reconstruction, qu'apparaît le Plan. Jusque dans les années quatre-vingt, la planification française conservera grosso modo les mêmes caractéristiques dominantes: une planification économique nationale et sectorielle, une planification dans laquelle la dimension territoriale est largement ignorée ou minorée en dépit de la création des régions, une planification de type technocratique dont les procédures hiérarchiques verticales expriment avant tout l'hégémonie parisienne.

Peu à peu, avec la prise de conscience des déséquilibres régionaux puis la prise en compte des nécessités de la décentralisation et de l'aménagement du territoire, s'impose la nécessité de développer une planification territoriale et en particulier régionale, afin que les initiatives locales puissent s'exprimer, que les potentialités locales puissent être mises en oeuvre, que des relations horizontales entre divers acteurs puissent accompagner les seules relations sectorielles verticales et amortir quelque peu les conflits de compétence qui tendent à se multiplier entre les différents niveaux de la hiérarchie territoriale;

Apparemment, les choses vont vite: les régions de programme sont déterminées en 1956; la procédure des plans régionaux est définie en 1958; les régions de programme se transforment en 21 circonscriptions d'action régionale en 1960; les tranches opératoires du Plan (perspectives régionalisées du développement économique et des opérations de développement à réaliser) apparaissent en 1962; la première régionalisation du budget de l'État se fait en 1964; une véritable régionalisation du Plan est réalisée au cours des années 1972–1975 pour le VI ème Plan.

En réalité, bien des problèmes majeurs de la planification territoriales ne sont pas résolus, problèmes d'autant plus délicats que, au cours de ces années, le phénomène de région reste étroitement lié à l'idée de développement économique. Dans leurs potentiels démographique et économiques comme dans leurs capacités d'investissements et de décisions, les structures traditionnelles du territoire français (plus de 36 000 communes — 95 départements) sont parfaitement inadaptées par rapport aux exigences de la planification. La nécessité d'introduire un nouvel échelon dans la structure de l'État — Nation s'est vite imposée, sans que soit pour autant clairement répondu à une double question-clef: quel type de région? Et pour quoi faire? Pourtant, la question d'un découpage régionale de la France n'est pas nouvelle, ni non plus l'interrogation sur les fonctions qui devraient être attribuées à la région: entre 1851 et 1947, 29 projets privés prévoyant un découpage de 7 à 47 „régions" sont discutés: les projets parlementaires soumis à Chambre entre 1871 et 1952 sont au nombre de 15 et font varier le découpage de 18 à 34 „régions"; en 1945–1946, la structure territoriale liée aux Commissaires de la République compte 20 régions: en 1947, Michel Debre propose de découper la France en 47 „régions" tandis que le projet Medecin-Billieres rendu public en 1955 en propose 10 (pour sa part, J.F. Gravier a souhaité en 1949 que 19 „régions" soient créées en France pour lutter contre le „désert français")! Et pendant toutes ces années, les choix fondamentaux aux plans structurel et fonctionnel ne sont pas faits: la région doit-elle résulter d'une désagrégation vers le bas avec transfert de compétence de l'État central ou bien d'un regroupement vers le haut d'unités territoriales plus petites, avec un regroupement spatial de compétence? Faut-il limiter la compétence du niveau régional à la seule gestion du quotidien ou bien accorder à la région une réelle capacité de décision et d'anticipation pour ce qui concerne l'organisation de sont développement? Bien entendu, ce sont là des questions éminemment politiques, des questions sur lesquelles s'affrontent les tenants du pouvoir centralisé et parisien et les partisans d'une plus grande autonomie régionale (un affrontement qui, en termes de politique régionale, va opposer les tenants de l'action technocratique aux partisans de la structure démocratique).

Bien plus, la question essentielle de la pertinence des structures territoriales n'est pas vraiment discutée. Pourtant, l'espace administratif-institutionnel, correspondant à un ressort de compétences ayant des limites fixes à l'intérieur desquelles s'accumulent des stocks (populations, ressources, richesses...), est inévitablement plus ou moins inadapté aux nécessités de l'entreprise dont l'espace est mobile et structuré par des réseaux de flux de type informationnel, commercial ou productif. Par ailleurs, l'inertie des limites administratives peut, en provoquant l'obsolescence des structures spatiales, constituer un sérieux handicap pour la planification territoriale: les limites des régions françaises n'ont pas changé de façon significative depuis 1960 alors que la France a connu depuis lors la crise mondiale de l'énergie, la crise économique généralisée, la remise en cause du système de production fordiste et l'émergence du système de production flexible, la course aux technologies nouvelles, la fin du rôle des grandes entreprises dans la création d'emplois, l'émergence d'un nouveau modèle de développement régional fondé sur la dynamique endogène...!

La planification territoriale en France a d'abord et surtout été appliquée au niveau régionale, au point que nous parlerons ici de „planification régionale „; elle ne concerne vraiment les communes qu'après les lois de décentralisation administrative de 1982–1983; elle s'exprime de façon spécifique au niveau départemental à partir de 1992 seulement (première demande exprimée par la DATAR pour que soit élaboré un schéma départemental de développement, celui de l'Aisne). Cette planification régionale peut être définie comme „l'organisation de la dimension spatiale (géographique) des phénomènes économiques et sociaux"; elle ne concerne donc pas seulement la localisation des infrastructures, des équipements publics et des activités. Au fil des années, cette planification régionale s'est exprimée sous des formes diverses: modèles de fonctionnement d'une région, schémas de développement, plans régionaux, programmes de création d'équipement ou d'implantation d'activités, projet global de développement économique et social.

La planification territoriale, quelle que soit appliquée à la région ou à d'autres niveaux géographiques, à certaines implications et soulève quelques problèmes. Le rappel des unes et des autres est utile pour comprendre les difficultés et l'évolution très progressive de la planification régionale en France. Au niveau du territoire, la possibilité de développer une planification est étroitement dépendante des moyens financiers, des moyens en hommes et surtout des compétences spécifiques attribués à la collectivité; en d'autres termes, la capacité d'une collectivité de décider-concevoir-élaborer-contrôler-programmer dépend étroitement de la marge d'autonomie que lui concède l'État central ainsi que des moyens et des compétences qu'il lui transfère. C'est précisément ce côté politique des choses qui explique les tâtonnements de la planification régionale ainsi que les différences essentielles qui opposent les réformes de 1982–1983 à celle de 1972. Par ailleurs, la planification régionale, si elle veut résulter d'une véritable concertation entre les acteurs, suppose que soit réalisée une triple articulation: avec les collectivités locales dont les objectifs ne peut être ignorés, avec les régions voisines au moins pour les grandes infrastructures et les grands équipements. Cette concertation est bien sûr la condition sine qua non d'une planification cohérente à toutes les échelles.

## 3. Vers la planification décentralisée

Les régions de programme définies en 1958 sont transformées, avec les mêmes limites, en circonscriptions d'action régionale en 1960. Or, ce n'est qu'en 1965 que sont définies les huit métropoles d'équilibre censées constituer les moteurs principaux du développement régional (la politique des villes moyennes et les contrats de villes moyennes apparaissant en 1971–1973 et la politique des petites villes et des contrats de pays en 1975). Cela signifie que dans les premières années, la planification régionale en France n'est pas liée à la polarisation métropolitaine, ni même à l'idée de réseaux urbains hiérarchisés, ce qui ne deviendra le credo fondamental que dans la seconde moitié de la décennie soixante-dix. La planification 'territoriale" n'est encore qu'une planification économique plus ou moins régionalisée et toujours pilotée par le pouvoir central.

Cette opération est confirmée par le contenu des premiers plans régionaux (celui de Bretagne est publié en 1956, celui de Lorraine en 1957). Sur la base des perspectives démographiques des unités régionales et d'une quantification des évolutions économiques, les grandeurs nationales sont simplement désagrégées en un certain nombre de „programmes régionaux d'investissements" permettant de mettre en place une programmation des équipements collectifs; l'échelon régional, n'ayant qu'une réalité administrative, n'intervient que très peu dans ce processus et seulement sous forme d'avis; dans cette phase, deux préoccupations de l'État restent dominantes: assurer la réalisation de la planification nationale, d'une part, permettre une correction progressive des disparités régionales, d'autre part.

En principe, les premiers changements véritables interviennent avec le VIème Plan (1972–1975), c'est à dire avec la première véritable régionalisation du Plan. A partir de ce moment, l'échelon régional s'exprime vis à vis de la planification nationale par l'intermédiaire des Rapports Régionaux d'Orientation (données de base en matière de développement régional et d'aménagement urbain), des Esquisses Régionales (financement des équipements collectifs et détermination des enveloppes financières attribuées aux régions), des Programmes Régionaux de Développement Économique, trois catégories de documents désormais élaborés avant la détermination des options du Plan.

En réalité, la planification régionale n'est pas encore fondamentalement améliorée; d'une part, parce que le rapport des forces et la répartition des compétences entre l'État et la Région ne sont toujours pas clairs; d'autre part, parce que l'échelon régional n'a encore acquis ni les structures internes ni les compétences lui permettant d'exprimer un projet et des perspectives quelque peu autonomes.

En matière de capacité décisionnelle et de potentiel de planification, la situation de l'échelon régional au cours des années soixante se caractérise par la toute puissance du représentant local de l'État, la faiblesse des pouvoirs accordés aux représentations locales, l'influence diverse et grandissante des structures extérieures dépendant du pouvoir central. La totalité exécutif est entre les mains du Préfet de Région, secondé par la Conférence Administrative Régionale (réunissant les Préfets des départements ainsi que les directeurs régionaux des services extérieurs de l'État) et par la Mission Économique Régionale (groupe de spécialistes et d'experts remplissant la fonction de bureau d'études). Les émanations de la population et des activités économiques, et en particulier la Commission de développement Économique Régional (CODER), n'ont qu'un pouvoir consultatif, la possibilité de formuler des avis et des propositions soumis au Préfet de Région. En revanche, une part croissante des travaux de planification territoriale est réalisée, surtout après 1963 date de la création de la Délégation à l'Aménagement du Territoire et à l'Action Régionale (DATAR), par des services et organismes parachutés dans les régions par la DATAR, différents Ministères ou divers services centraux de l'État (les OREAM pour les schémas d'aménagement des aires métropolitaines — les Missions Interministérielles d'Aménagement — les Agences d'Urbanisme et les Groupes de Programmation — les agence régionales de la Société Centrale d'Équipement du Territoire — des sociétés d'économie mixte pour la mise en valeur et le développement des régions... etc.). Un véritable travail d'élaboration d'une planification régionale, prenant en compte les perspectives à moyen et long termes, se réalise alors en France..; mais pour l'essentiel, ce travail échappe à la Région pour ce qui est de sa conception, de son élaboration et de son contrôle.

La planification implique l'anticipation, c'est à dire une information telle qu'elle permette de réaliser des projections — des prévisions — une prospective des évolutions futures. C'est ici que l'on rencontre l'un des handicaps majeurs de la planification régionale en France: les insuffisances chroniques de l'information statistique régionale. En dépit de la création des Observatoires Économiques Régionaux en 1967, il a fallu attendre plus de dix ans pour que l'échelon régional dispose de comptes régionaux permettant d'établir des plans sur des bases informationnelles sérieuses. En fait, la centralisation du système statistique français est telle que l'information régionale n'a pas été en mesure de dépasser les indicateurs traditionnels de la comptabilité nationale; ceci revient à dire que les plans régionaux et les modèles statistiques de l'époque ont plus exprimé la situation nationale que la réalité socio-économique des régions. Ce handicap sera lourdement ressenti dans les années quatre-vingt, lorsque la mise en route de la décentralisation administrative permettra l'émergence d'une nouvelle planification régionale fondée sur la maîtrise et la dynamique endogènes des régions.

A ce stade de l'évolution, une question essentielle doit être posée: les réformes régionales de 1972 et de 1982 ont-elles modifié la problématique et la pratique de la planification régionale? Dans une large mesure, il faut répondre par la négative pour ce qui concerne la réforme de 1972

qui ne modifie pas grand chose en matière de relations entre l'exécutif
et le législatif dans la région et encore moins pour ce qui concerne les
compétences reconnues à l'échelon régional. La loi du 5 juillet 1972
porte création et organisation des régions et créé dans chacune d'elles
un Établissement Public Régional (EPR). Le choix de cette formule
juridique est très significatif: d'une part, elle permet d'éviter que la
gestion de la région soit liée au principe de la représentation élective,
comme pour les collectivités locales; d'autre part, elle permet de limiter
les compétences de la région parce que l'EPR ne peut avoir que des
compétences limitées et spécialisées. Le maintien de la dépendance vis
à vis du pouvoir central demeure total, d'autant plus que la réalité du
pouvoir exécutif reste entre les mains du Préfet de Région qui est en
même temps l'exécutif régional et le représentant local de l'État dans la
circonscription. L'EPR comporte un Conseil Régional, qui peut délibérer
(sénateurs-députés-représentants des collectivités locales) et un Comité
Économique et Social, qui n'a qu'une fonction consultative (représentants
des agents économiques, administratifs, sociaux); il doit contribuer au
développement régional par des études, un rôle de coordination des
investissements des collectivités, une participation au financement des
équipements collectifs. La région n'est donc alors qu'une structure de
gestion immédiate au pouvoirs limités, incapable de générer et de mettre
en oeuvre un projet socio-économique spécifique pour le futur.

Les changements radicaux interviennent avec la Réforme Régionale
de 1982 et les lois de décentralisation administrative de 1982–1983.
La région devient alors une collectivité territoriale jouissant de droits
et de compétences comparables à ceux des collectivités traditionnelles
(départements et communes). La région est gérée par un président et
un conseil régional élus au suffrage universel; elle a donc récupéré
tout à la fois la capacité de décision, une certaine aura de démocratie
et un surcroît, au moins théorique, d'autonomie. Surtout, la loi du
2 mars 1982 attribue à la région une compétence très générale en
matière d'aménagement mais aussi le soin d'élaborer et d'approuver
le „plan régional” qui détermine à moyen terme les objectifs du
développement économique, social et culturel de la région. Cette
vocation est confirmée par les lois de décentralisation administrative qui
transfèrent à l'échelon régional les compétences essentielles en matière
de planification, d'aménagement et de développement économique,
pour ce qui concerne les travaux de réflexion, de coordination et de

programmation. Par ailleurs, la région a désormais compétence pour intervenir directement dans les activités économiques, en particulier aux bénéfices des petites et moyennes entreprises. La région est ainsi devenu un niveau fondamental de l'élaboration de la planification territoriale, qui est désormais décentralisée et qui va se développer sur des bases de plus en plus contractuelles.

La loi du 29 juillet 1982, portant réforme de la planification, donne aux régions la possibilité d'élaborer de véritables projets régionaux et d'élaborer leur propre plan, ce dernier étant conçu comme un outil de programmation pluriannuelle devant s'appuyer sur une réflexion à moyen terme. En outre, l loi de 1982 donne aux régions la possibilité d'intervenir dans la définition et l'orientation du Plan national (la préparation du IX ème Plan, pour les années 1984–1988, a précisément commencé par l'élaboration des plans régionaux). Enfin, la loi de 1982 modifiée en profondeur les relations juridiques et financières entre l'État central et les régions en instituant le Contrat de Plan État / Région (la formule des procédures contractuelles n'est pas nouvelle en France où l'État avait déjà conclu des contrats de localisation avec les grandes entreprises, des contrats de programme avec des entreprises publiques, des contrats de pays avec des syndicats intercommunaux... Mais aucune n'aura l'importance et le succès des contrats de plan État/Région). Instituant une égalité juridique entre les contractants et un co-financement des investissements retenus (pour les contrats de plan correspondant au IX ème Plan. Le financement assuré par l'État a représenté au total 1,5 fois celui assuré par les régions), le contrat de plan peut être effectivement considéré comme un instrument majeur de la décentralisation. Le champ sectoriel couvert par le contrat de plan ne cesse de s'élargir et donne de plus en plus la priorité au développement économique et à la sauvegarde de l'emploi; mais il concerne aussi l'urbanisme, la technologie, l'environnement, le tourisme...; en fait, l'intervention des contrats de plan n'est limitée que par les programmes prioritaires de l'État (autoroutes, universités, grands aéroports...) et par les impératifs de la coordination au sein du Plan national.

Toutes les régions ont adopté et renouvelé la procédure du contrat de plan signé avec l'État; elles y trouvent sans doute le moyen de concrétiser au mieux leurs souhaits d'autonomie mais aussi leur volonté de mettre en oeuvre le modèle de développement fondé sur la dynamique endogène. Au plan pratique, on peut formuler au moins deux critiques à

l'encontre de ces contrats de plan: d'une part, leur durée d'exécution est
de cinq ans, ce qui signifie que la synchronisation avec le Plan national
n'est pas possible puisque celui-ci est prévu pour une durée de quatre
ans (le Xème Plan s'achève en 1992 alors que les contrats de plan de
troisième génération se terminent en 1993); d'autre part, la diversification
des interventions régionales est telle que le contrat de plan tend à se
transformer en une accumulation de mini-contrats et de mini-programmes
qui multiplient les négociations avec les administrations concernées et
rendent la coordination des interventions et la cohérence des objectifs
bien problématiques.

## 4. Région — planification — dimension communautaire

La planification territoriale au niveau de la région n'est, évidemment,
pas restée à l'écart des problèmes soulevés par l'existence de la
Communauté Européenne et par l'hypothèse de la création d'une
politique régionale commune. Au-delà de l'hétérogénéité géographique
qui caractérise l'espace français, on peut dire que la dimension
européenne a susciter l'émergence de trois problème particuliers au
regard de la planification territoriale en France: très soucieuse de son
indépendance et de sa souveraineté nationales, la France, longtemps
réticente à l'égard de toute supranationalité, a eu tendance à considérer
que la question régionale constituait une affaire strictement inférieure
dans laquelle la CEE n'avait pas à intervenir car ce serait alors une
ingérence politiquement inacceptable; en France comme dans les pays
voisins, l'essor des mobilités spatiales et sectorielles renforce les tendances
à la décentralisation des pouvoirs et génère un déclin relatif de la
puissance de l'État central, aux bénéfices soit des régions soit de
l'Europe: la Communauté a elle-même longuement hésité entre la volonté
d'accompagner l'action régionale des États membres (par des systèmes
d'aides et de subventions) et le désir de créer une politique régionale
communautaire spécifique (à l'origine d'institutions particulières).

Au regard de la planification régionale en France, deux grandes
périodes doivent être distinguées pour ce qui concerne l'influence de
la CEE: jusqu'en 1984–1985, l'État est l'intermédiaire obligé et le
seul interlocuteur reconnu des institutions communautaires, les régions

n'ont de relations avec Bruxelles (subventions aux programmes de développement) que dans la mesure où elles s'inscrivent dans le système exclusif des relations bilatérales État — Commission; depuis 1984–1985 (réforme du FEDER et multiplication des programmes intégrés de développement), les relations directes des régions avec les instances communautaires se multiplient rapidement (avec la DG XVI en particulier) et l'aide financière directe de Bruxelles aux programmes et aux plans régionaux s'accentue, au moins jusqu'à la fin de la décennie quatre-vingt. Faut-il vraiment s'étonner que ce soit la Bretagne, objet des préoccupation majeurs de l'État, qui ait bénéficié de la plus grande part des financements communautaires au cours des quinze premières années?

L'évolution des relations régions françaises-Communauté est jalonnée par quelques dates et évènements-clefs. La première intervention européenne dans le développement régional est celle de la CECA, mise en plan en 1951; elle intervient aux profits des régions touchées par les crises du charbon et de la sidérurgie (Nord-Pas-de Calais, Lorraine, Bassin du Creusot, Bassin de Saint-Étienne, Bassin d'Alès, Zone de Decazeville-Carmaux), par des aides financières destinées à la conversion, par des subventions destinées à la réadaptation des travailleurs, par des primes accordées pour lutter contre le chômage; c'est l'État qui détermine le caractère éligible des régions aux aides CECA et en aucune façon un quelconque plan de développement de celles-ci; finalement, la CECA n'aura réussi ni à assurer le repli du charbon, ni à limiter les effets de la crise sidérurgique, ni même à promouvoir une large requalification de la main-d'oeuvre des industries traditionnelles en crise. Avec la création de la Banque Européenne d'Investissement (BEI en 1958), on se rapproche quelque peu de la préoccupation planificatrice puisque cette banque doit en priorité contribuer au développement à long terme de la Communauté. Dans les régions, toujours par l'intermédiaire de l'État, elle intervient surtout par des prêts destinés à la réalisation de travaux d'infrastructures, ses apports étant seulement complémentaires et toujours inférieurs à 50% du coût total du projet.

Contrairement à ce qui se passe pour l'agriculture ou les transports, le Traité de Rome ne prévoit pas de façon explicite une politique régionale et ne donne aucun mandat particulier aux institutions communautaires pour créer une politique commune en matière de développement régional. Le Traité, dans son article 130, se contente de mentionner la lutte contre les disparités régionales parmi les objectifs fondamentaux de la

Communauté et invite les États membres à „tenir compte des aspects régionaux des politiques économiques et sectorielles globales". Le Traité assigne à la CEE une fonction de coordination des politiques régionales des États membres, afin que ces politiques n'accroissent pas les disparités et ne faussent pas les conditions de concurrence; la Commission a le pouvoir de contrôler les aides régionales accordées par les États, ces derniers étant tenus de l'informer des projets d'aide et des programmes de développement.

La décision, prise en 1971, de reconnaître l'existence de régions qui doivent être prioritaires pour l'attribution des aides CEE au développement marque à coup sûr une étape essentielle. Ces région correspondent aux espaces agricoles défavorisés (une partie de l'Ouest français), aux vieilles régions industrielles en crise (les vieux bassins où intervenait déjà la CECA), aux régions frontalières (l'ensemble Sarre-Lorraine-Luxembourg, l'ensemble Alsace-Suisse-pays de Bade). Peu après le premier élargissement de la CEE (1972), la Commission propose de plafonner ses subventions régionales à 20% du montant de l'investissement prévu, ce qui signifie que les subventions communautaires seront liées à la soumission de projets et de programmes par les État membres; en d'autres termes, vu des régions, les travaux de planification doivent obtenir une double reconnaissance: celle de l'État et celle de la CEE, d'où bien des lenteurs et bien des conflits.

En 1973 est publié le Rapport THOMSON (Rapport sur les problèmes régionaux de la Communauté élargie), premier document proposant une analyse exhaustive des situations régionales à partir d'une large palette d'indicateurs (densité de population, ventilation sectorielle des actifs, PIB par habitant, taux de chômage, taux migratoires...). Ce rapport permet à la CEE de définir les régions de priorité absolue pour l'attribution des aides (la France n'en compte aucune; elles se localisent surtout en Irlande, Grèce, Mezzogiorno), les régions à aider (en France, en majorité des zones de moyennes montagnes en cours de désertification et de déprise économique), les régions que la politique régionale communautaire devra soutenir. Le même rapport est également à la base de la création, en 1975, du Comité de Politique Régionale (organisme consultatif chargé de suivre le développement des régions) et surtout du Fonds Européen de Développement régional (FEDER) qui constitue l'instrument financier fondamental de la politique régionale commune. En principe donc, il existe désormais au niveau communautaire un organisme financier spécifique susceptible de conforter les efforts de planification territoriale des régions, en leur apportant un soutien financier particulier. La réalité est quelque peu différente. Le choix des actions à financer par le FEDER appartient exclusivement à l'Etat — membre qui, seul reçoit les fonds débloqués par le FEDER (l'État a donc tendance à considérer que ces fonds ne sont que des remboursements des prêts consentis aux régions par le Trésor), à quoi s'ajoutent l'excessive longueur des procédures administratives, la trop forte dispersion des crédits, les effets négatifs de la règle de complémentarité, la faiblesse des crédits affectés aux actions de développement régional (par comparaison avec les crédits affectés au Fonds Européen d'Orientation et de Garantie Agricole, le FEOGA). En somme, les fonds du FEDER sont trop budgétisés et insuffisamment régionalisés; c'est, au moins en partie, ce qui explique l'importance attachée par les régions à la réforme de cette institution. L'échec du programme Grand Sud-Ouest, présenté en 1979 par l'État français et bénéficiant des crédits du FEDER, est très expressif de cette inadaptation des systèmes centralisés aux besoins de la planification régionale: conçu pour accélérer le développement des trois régions Aquitaine-Midi Pyrénées-Languedoc-Roussillon, dans la perspective de l'entrée prochaine du concurrent ibérique, ce programme, pourtant annoncé à grands coups d'effets médiatiques, doit être suspendu dès 1981, faute de cohérence, de bases structurelles solides et de véritable adhésion de la part des régions concernées.

La période qui s'ouvre en 1984–1985 est décisive pour les régions et pour leurs efforts de planification à moyen terme: elle voit, d'une part, se réaliser la réforme du FEDER, d'autre part, émerger les interventions pluriannuelles intégrées. La réforme du FEDER, accompagnant les effets de la décentralisation administrative, permet enfin aux régions et aux collectivités locales de développer des relations directes avec les institutions communautaires, donc de faire participer celles-ci à l'élaboration de leurs plans de développement, et pas seulement de leur demander un soutien financier. Dans une large mesure, et avant même la ratification de l'Acte Unique de 1986, on peut considérer que c'est de cette période que date la véritable reconnaissance de la région par les instances communautaires. L'année 1984 est celle de la mise en place des opérations Intégrées de Développement (O.I.D.) qui visent à intégrer la Communauté, les autorités nationales, les autorités locales et les organismes financiers à finalités structurelle (FEDER, FEOGA-

Orientation, Fonds Social) dans le cadre de programmes définis pour des zones géographiques subissant une crise grave ou souffrant d'importants retards. Des OID seront ainsi proposées par la France pour la région du Nord, la partie septentrionale du bassin sidérurgique lorrain, le Tarn-Aveyron, une partie de l'Ariège. Dans le cadre de la CEE, l'Europe méditerranéenne se distingue par d'importants retards en matière de développement, retards qui n'épargnent pas la France méridionale. C'est pourquoi apparaissent en 1985 les Programmes Intégrés Méditerranéens (PIM) qui présentent une double caractéristique essentielle au regard de la planification régionale: ils sont fondés sur le principe du financement conjoint (entre Communauté, État et Région) et sur la pratique de l'élaboration commune entre la CEE et les régions bénéficiaires. Ces PIM, mis en place pour une période de sept ans (1985–1992) dans les cinq régions de la France méridionale, ont largement bénéficié, pour leur mise au point, de la pratique de la planification contractuelle qui a permis de dégager très vite les espaces et les secteurs nécessitant un soutien. Il faut, enfin, mentionner l'apparition, en 1986, des Programmes Nationaux d'Intérêt Communautaire (PNIC) qui vient l'amélioration des infrastructures, l'aide aux entreprises, la mise en valeur des potentiels endogènes, dans des zones déterminées et sur des bases pluriannuelles (exemples: le „pôle européen" de Longwy-Aubange-Pétange, le PNIC de Lorraine, le PNIC de l'Ouest aveyronnais...).

Un bilan de l'évolution des relations entre les régions françaises et les instances communautaires fait apparaître l'existence de deux grandes phases pour ce qui concerne la planification territoriale: jusqu'aux débuts de la décennie quatre-vingt, la politique régionale et la planification régionale sont des chasses gardées exclusives de l'État central, la région française n'a aucune existence concrète ou spécifique à Bruxelles; depuis 1984–1985, donc depuis l'essor en France de la planification contractuelle et décentralisée, le poids et l'intervention des instances communautaires ne cessent de croître au niveau des régions qui sont devenues de véritables interlocuteurs pour les institutions de Bruxelles (plusieurs régions françaises ont aujourd'hui une représentation permanente auprès des Communautés).

# 5. Pour conclure

Depuis la généralisation du système de production fordiste et l'essor des firmes multinationales, la régulation économique tend à se faire à l'échelle mondiale alors que la régulation sociale relève toujours du niveau national voire des groupements régionaux d'États. On peut aujourd'hui se poser la question de savoir si on assiste pas à un changement profond en matière pouvoir de régulation? Le triomphe du système de production flexible, l'émergence du modèle de développement endogène par le bas, l'autonomie croissante des régions et le rôle toujours plus grand dévolue aux petites et moyennes entreprises, ne font-ils pas de la région un niveau de régulation, tant économique que sociale, de jour en jour plus important?

## Orientation bibliographique

Bailly A.S. et alii, 1987, *Comprendre et maîtriser l'espace ou la science régionale et l'aménagement du territoire*. Montpellier. GIP-Reclus.

Commissariat Général au Plan, 1985, *Evaluation de la planification décentralisée*. Paris. Doc. Française.

Drevet J.F., 1988, *1992–2000: les régions françaises entre l'Europe et le déclin*. Paris. Souffles.

De Lanversin J. et alii, 1989, *La région et l'aménagement du territoire dans la décentralisation*. Paris. Economica. 4ème éd.

Fischer A., 1991, *La politique régionale des communautés européennes*. Paris. Note de Recherche du CRIA no 2.

Labasse J., 1991, *l'Europe des régions*. Paris. Flammarion.

Marette M., 1987, *La politique régionale européenne en France*. Paris. DATAR-Doc. Française.

Piatier A., 1990, *Les régions de l'Europe: comment et pourquoi envisager une autre approche*. Poitiers. Revue d'Économie Régionale et Urbaine. no 1 pages 137–165.

Pontier J. M., 1988, *La région*. Paris. Dalloz.

S.S. Artobolevskiy
Russian Academy of Science
Moscow

# REGIONAL PROBLEMS IN RUSSIA AND RESPONCES OF STATE

From the middle of the 80-s one can see that all regional problems in Russia (social-economic, national-political etc.) became more painful and create advanced interest from the population as well as from politicians. This is most remarkable during the last two years after the disintegration of the USSR and the beginning of the acute economic crisis. At present even the existence of Russia as a indivisible state is under threat: Chechnya and Tatarstan have already declared their independence. And other former autonomic republics ask for more independence up to the possibility of leaving Russia. In reality this means already a transfer to confederation as the federation doesn't afford a possibility of leaving the country. We can see that in many republics struggling for independence the share of the "title" population is rather small. It varies from 6% in Yamalo-Nenetsk okrug to 75,1% in Daghestan: 10% in Karelia, 21,9% on Bashkiria, 31% in Altai republic, 32,5% in Mordovia, 33,4% in Yakutia, 48,5% in Tatarstan (data of 1989 Census).

But disaggragation of the country goes on not only according to national boundaries. In the limits of Russian mononational space separate regions ("oblasti") require more and more sovereignty (as the plan of creating of Vologda republic).

Russia/USSR never had regional policy (as it is understood in the West). Now even the old economic regional policy, realized by ministries, has disappeared.

The traditional regional policy was directed to the opening up of new territories and resources (less attention was paid to putting in order of existing potential). This policy war realized by separate industry ministries and it solved social problems only as it was necessary for the economical activities in their (ministries) main areas. Through central authorities vast means were specially redistributed, but mainly according to the interests of separate ministries i.e. monopolies. The interests of the society and the whole economy were not considered. The withdrawal in recent years from the industry type of management lead to the change of the regional distribution of state means.

The central government give to some areas/regions large grants, financial and other privileges (for example in the field of rates or foreign trade). They are given not only according to the level of crisis in areas/regions but because of the political pressure, "pre-election" considerations, the danger of strike and so on.

The principles of regional privileges distribution are not published anywhere, there are no laws in this field. It is quite natural that subject approach prevails. Offended areas/regions begin to compete for their privileges, and that leads to disintegration of the country. It is natural that the national factor is important when the help is distributed. But it is difficult to explain why national republics occupying the same position received help so different (up to ten–twenty times). As one can see from the map 1 the regional distribution of state help is very uneven, but unfortunately it goes not according to the geography of crisis. Many regions in equal socio-economic position received help differs (in some cases) by order. North Caucasus or East regions is good illustration of this.

Devolution is declared as the new regional policy. Under the new title still exists the old idea of regional self-accounting: regional authorities become the owners of local economy, and the life of the population depends on the income of the latter. The further non-controlled devolution, especially in the field of economy, will lead to disintegration of the common market and the creation of regional monopolies. It's fully ignored that it is more practical to carry on different functions on the definite territorial level: the utilisation of ordinary wastes on the local level and of radioactive wastes on the country level. Instead we see the attempts to overbalance the power between the centre and the regions accompanied by the active rhetoric of oppression, center dictate, state disintegration.

But another myth is more dangerous. Devolution is in no way the regional policy (as some leaders declare) and it often makes more difficult the realisation of the latter. The regional policy can be realized only by the Centre, which deliberately puts separate regions/areas in equal state (giving the help to one regions and limiting the development of others). In the course of devolution when the main rights are given over to all territorial units of the same level, only the most prosperous gain the benefits (if they are possible). As a result the spacial social-economic disproportions become greater instead of being smaller.

The devolution can not be regarded as a part of the policy of the development of crisis regions/areas on the base of the "bottom" (local) resources. And in this case new rights, means and so on must be received not by all the areas/territorial units of the country but only by "selected" (the most crises ones).

Regional policy cannot be created when the state is not only the controller organ but the economy owner. Normal privatisation (limited not only by the transfer of everything into private hands) is necessary. When the state owns and regulates at the same time the economy the regional interests makes a sacrifice to the economic efficiency. The state must regulate, first of all, the social and political life of the country and carry on the strategy of economy development. And this cannot be fulfilled without the regional policy.

The absence of official regional policy with institutional and legal base will have as a result the further disintegration of the state, even in the mononational space. The main obstacle for its creation is the opposition of authorities (especially central ones). The existence of declared principles of regional policy diminishes the possibilities of the subject approach which is often of interest for concrete persons. The opposition from the side of population of the most prospering regions is also possible. Only these regions can be "exporters" of help in the realm of the regional policy. But the progressing disintegration of the country will be price paid for the absence of regional policy. It's necessary to realize that the spatial redistribution of mean between "rich" and "poor" regions is reasonable price for the unity of the country (and more than modest). But in order that the population acquires and supports the regional policy a large pro-

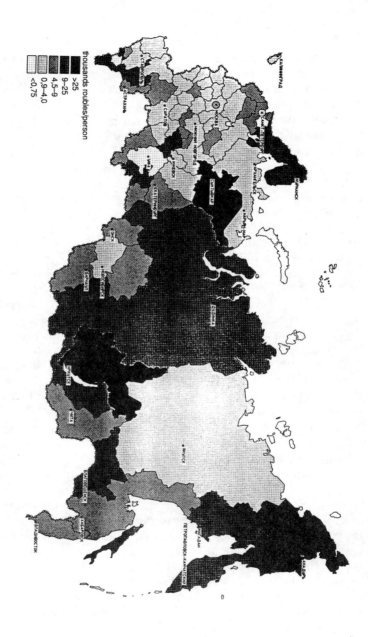

The map is prepared by Society "Analitic" the telephone number of which is indicated.

**Map 1.** Assignation of federal means to regions (grants, loans, preferencies). Per head of population, 1992.

gramme of its propaganda is absolutely necessary. The regional policy has to become part of common political life and culture.

The experience of the West in this field could be very useful in the course of the development of the native regional policy as well as in its propaganda activity. It would be beneficial if western specialists (scientists, civil servants from national government and the EC) participate in this activity.

# Literature

Artobolevskiy S., 1991, *The regional policy in the USSR in the period of perestroika*, Revue Belgede Geographie, v. 15.

Artobolevskiy S., Treivish A., 1992, *Regional development and state policy in Eastern and Western Europe*. EPRC Research Papers, N 12., Glasgow.

Dmitrieva O.G., 1990, *Regional policy and regional structure in the USSR*, Leningrad, „In Russian".

Khorev B.S., 1989, *Regional policy in the USSR*, Moscow, „In Russian".

*Geography and problems of regional development*, Moscow, 1989, „In Russian".

Jeanine Cohen
Laboratoire Stratégies territoriales
et Dynamique des Espaces
Paris

# ENTREPRISES ET REGIONS DE FRANCE DANS LES TRANSFORMATIONS DE L'EMPLOI LIEES AUX PHENOMENES D'INTERNATIONALISATION

## Introduction

En France, depuis au moins deux décennies, on a pu faire le constat de la transformation rapide de l'emploi et de sa localisation et mettre en évidence le rôle essentiel de la production et de son organisation dans ce processus[1].

Les aspects de cette organisation qui jouent un rôle déterminant dans la localisation des emplois sont ses caractéristiques fonctionnelles (la

---

[1] du côté des géographes français, voir notamment:
— Browaeys (Xavier) et Chatelain (Paul), 1984, *Les France du travail*, Paris, PUF, 267 p.
— Saint-Julien (Thérèse), 1983, *Industrie et système urbain*, Paris, Economica.
ainsi que les travaux de l'équipe CNRS-Université de Paris-I de STRATES (Laboratoire de Géographie humaine), surtout:

fabrication et la promotion commerciale pouvant être géographiquement séparées l'une de l'autre, par exemple), et ses caractéristiques financières. En effet, les grands groupes d'entreprises ont des buts et des moyens que ne peuvent avoir les „PME" (petites et moyennes entreprises), et par ailleurs, au sein même de la catégorie des groupes d'entreprises, les finalités et l'attitude vis-à-vis du territoire seront différentes selon qu'il s'agit de capitaux nationaux publics ou privés ou de capitaux étrangers.

Cette question est directement liée aux déséquilibres de développement entre les régions. Dans les années 60, les gouvernements de la France avaient voulu résoudre ce problème par la régionalisation de programme. Mais celle-ci restait décidée centralement. Désormais, depuis les lois de décentralisation administrative de 1982–84, pour combattre les suppressions massives d'emplois dues à l'intégration des marchés, à l'aiguisement de la concurrence, à la concentration financière et aux redéploiements (surtout des plus grandes entreprises), on donne des pouvoirs économiques aux échelons locaux et régionaux pour qu'ils puissent défendre et entretenir leurs propres potentiels d'emplois.

Au début de la décennie 90, où en est-on en France ? En regard des politiques de régionalisation mises en place, que l'on rappellera brièvement, on exposera les transformations observées dans la localisation régionale des emplois des divers types d'entreprises, en vue de discuter de l'efficience de ces politiques et de souligner certains aspects nouveaux des dynamiques spatiales des emplois.

— Barat (Isabelle), Beckouche (Pierre), Cohen (Jeanine), Pluet (Nicolas) et Scheibling (Jacques), 1984, *L'emploi industriel en France, croissance et crise, dimensions régionale et urbaine des stratégies des capitaux*, Montreuil, ISERES, 288p.
— Beckouche (Pierre), Carroué (Laurent), Cohen (Jeanine), Damette (Félix) et Scheibling (Jacques), 1987, *La crise de l'industrie française. Etude géographique, régions et villes*, Paris, CNRS-UP1 UA 142 „STRATES", Rapport pour le CNRS-ATP „Histoire industrielle de la France", 604 p.
et:
— Cohen (Jeanine), 1989, Paris et la province: vingt ans de mutation du système productif français, in *Ile-de-France, un nouveau territoire*, Montpellier-Paris, RECLUS-La Documentation française, pp. 9–25.
— Cohen (Jeanine), 1990, *S'engager moins pour organiser mieux?* Le paradoxe des stratégies territoriales d'entreprises, in STRATES no 5 pp. 49–57.
Des quantités de travaux ont été également consacrés à ces questions par des auteurs d'autres disciplines. On citera notamment:
— Taddei (Dominique) et Coriat (Benjamin), 1993, *Made in France*, Paris, Le Livre de Poche-Librairie Générale française, 471 p. (coll. biblio-essais).
— Veltz (Pierre) et Savy (Michel), 1991, *Tendances de l'économie; questions pour le territoire*, Paris, DATAR, (ronéoté).

# 1. La région:
## déséquilibres, remèdes proposés et réalités

Pour une administration équilibrée et juste du territoire national, les Révolutionnaires de 1789 avaient doté la France d'un découpage en 90 départements qui restaient „proches du Peuple", et la question régionale ne s'est véritablement posée avec acuité qu'après la seconde guerre mondiale, lorsqu'on a estimé que pour ses grands programmes d'ensemble, l'Etat avait besoin de beaucoup moins que 90 interlocuteurs. Le bref historique que l'on se propose de présenter ici couvrira donc la période 1950–1990.

Deux périodes de régionalisation peuvent être distinguées:

1. 1950–1970: la question régionale est posée à cause des congestions induites par la polarisation des activités économiques et ses nuisances. Ce chapître de l'histoire et de la géographie françaises est bien connu grâce au livre de Jean-François Gravier, „Paris et le désert français" (1947) ainsi qu'aux travaux des économistes François Perroux ou Jacques Boudeville sur la polarisation et des géographes Gabriel Dessus et Jacques Weulersse, puis Jean Hautreux, Lecourt et Michel Rochefort[2]. Les idées d'aménagement proposées visent à la redistribution de la croissance par une „géographie volontaire". On procède en 1955 au découpage de régions de programme qui constitueront des circonscriptions d'action adéquates pour régionaliser les politiques de l'Etat puis, vers 1963, à la désignation des quelques villes aptes à jouer le rôle de „métropoles d'équilibre". Mais après quelques années de mise en place de ces nouvelles structures, le référendum qui visait à donner aux circonscriptions d'action régionale le statut de collectivités territoriales échoua (1969), de sorte que les régions ne furent considérées que comme des „établissements publics" (en 1972). Simultanément, les résultats des recensements (1968, 1975) et enquêtes statistiques montraient que les dynamiques des entreprises se portaient moins sur les métropoles d'équilibre que sur des entités

---

[2]— Perroux (François), 1955, *La notion de pôle de croissance*, in Economie appliquée no 1–2.
— Boudeville (Jacques), 1961, *Les espaces économiques*, Paris, PUF (coll. Que sais-je? no 950).
— Boudeville (Jacques), 1972, *Aménagement du territoire et polarisation*, Paris, Génin.
— George (Pierre), 1964, *La géographie active*, Paris, PUF.
— Hautreux (Jean), Rochefort (Michel) et Lecourt, 1963, *Le niveau supérieur de l'armature urbaine française, Paris*, Rapport pour le Ministère de l'Equipement.

spatiales plus modestes, en foi de quoi les politiques d'aménagement furent infléchies en direction des villes moyennes, puis des „pays".

2. En 1982–1984 on a repris la question régionale dans une volonté de régler les problèmes en suspens et d'organiser par une législation d'ensemble une véritable dévolution de pouvoirs aux autorités territoriales des différents niveaux. Cette volonté s'inscrivait dans une période d'appel à l'initiative locale et régionale pour compenser les désengagements des plus grandes entreprises et l'impuissance des autorités centrales à organiser quelque redistribution que ce fût dans un contexte de fin de la croissance. A cette fin, dans la „décentralisation administrative" ainsi mise en place, les collectivités territoriales et notamment les régions sont dotées de pouvoirs nouveaux, dont économiques[3].

## 2. 1945–1990: dynamiques régionales et locales de l'emploi

Cette période a d'abord été marquée par la croissance exceptionnellement longue des „trente glorieuses" (1945–1975), qui correspondent à la succession d'une période de reconstruction des bases industrielles nationales (1945–1950), et d'une période de déploiement spontané des entreprises essentiellement parisiennes, déploiement renforcé par les „décentralisations industrielles" mises en oeuvre par les politiques d'action régionale (sur ces phénomènes, la bibliographie est abondante; on pourra se référer à celle que l'auteur a présentée dans la revue STRATES no 2, 1987). Dans leur croissance, les entreprises pouvaient envisager une extension de leur activité par l'installation de la fonction de fabrication dans les régions rurales et sous-industrialisées à forts excédents de main d'oeuvre. Le manque de qualification ouvrière pouvait être pallié par le recours à une organisation adéquate du travail (ce fut en l'occurrence le modèle fordien de production de masse, avec une forte segmentation des tâches). Mais les logiques de croissance ne se sont pas arrêtées au territoire national, et le „déploiement" a débouché sur un

---

[3] Voir:
- Billaudot (Françoise), Besson-Guillaumot (Michèle), 1984, *Environnement, Urbanisme, Cadre de vie, le Droit et l'Administration*, addendum au 1er octobre 1984, Paris, Editions Montchrestien.
- Merlin (Pierre), Choay (Françoise), dir., 1988, *Dictionnaire de l'urbanisme et de l'aménagement*, Paris, PUF.

„redéploiement" international visant aussi bien la conquête de nouveaux marchés que la réduction des coûts de main d'oeuvre.

Face à ce relatif désengagement des grands groupes industriels vis-à-vis du territoire national, un mouvement de création de petites et moyennes entreprises, relayé par toute une batterie d'aides de l'Etat et des collectivités territoriales, s'est développé, de 1975 au début des années 1980. Dès 1985 toutefois, il apparaissait que ces petites et moyennes entreprises se débattaient face à une conjoncture durablement difficile pour elles, et perdaient dans l'ensemble plus d'emplois qu'elles n'en créaient. Malgré tout, les disparitions n'étaient pas équivalentes aux créations et, en appui aux transformations des grandes entreprises, il en est résulté une modernisation et une fonctionnalisation évidentes: nouvelle organisation de la production en réseaux, importance de la logistique et des services (ainsi que de l'organisation sociale).

De 1985 à 1990, cette modernisation a semblé permettre un début de relance, mais à partir de 1990 le „cycle infernal" amélioration de la productivité-réductions d'effectifs-réduction de la consommation s'est remis en marche sans qu'on en voie jusqu'ici la fin.

## 3.  Le rôle des capitaux: le jeu public/privé et le branchement international

L'évolution récente (1985–1990) des effectifs est très différente selon l'origine des capitaux des entreprises auxquelles ils se rattachent (tableau 1).

Si l'on tient compte des privatisations qui ont été opérées entre les deux dates (par le gouvernement de Jacques CHIRAC) et qui expliquent le caractère positif du bilan des effectifs des groupes privés français en même temps qu'une partie des pertes des groupes publics, puisque des emplois ont ainsi été transférés des seconds vers les premiers, on voit que, prises dans leur ensemble, les entreprises françaises ont perdu de nombreux emplois (605 000 en moins de cinq ans, soit −7% de l'effectif 1985). Faute de données plus récentes, on ne sait pas encore précisément ce qu'il est advenu des emplois transférés au secteur privé, mais on peut s'interroger car, dans la fin des années 70 et le début des années 80, l'idée des nationalisations avait fini par être acceptée par l'opinion publique au vu de l'effet négatif sur l'emploi des strictes logiques de rentabilité

Tableau 1

**France, emplois: évolution des effectifs entre mars 1985 et décembre 1989
selon l'origine des capitaux des entreprises**

| capitaux: | (milliers) | (%) |
|---|---|---|
| toutes entreprises | −440 | − 5 |
| groupes publics | −319 | −19 |
| groupes privés français | + 76 | + 4 |
| groupes étrangers | +164 | +42 |
| PME | −362 | − 8 |

Source: ESE

financière. Et pourtant, à l'époque, les PME semblaient capables de compenser en partie ces pertes, alors que désormais on s'aperçoit qu'elles sont soumises à très rude épreuve, puisqu'entre 1985 et 1990 leurs pertes (8%) sont supérieures à la moyenne de 7% pour les entreprises françaises.

Or, dans le même temps, les capitaux étrangers ont apporté 164 000 emplois supplémentaires, soient +42% de leur effectif de 1985. Celui-ci, il est vrai, ne représentait alors que 4,6% du total des emplois de la France, mais il est donc monté à 6,9% en décembre 1989.

Plusieurs questions se posent. Il serait d'abord intéressant de savoir si les régions ont joué un rôle particulier dans ce nouveau dynamisme. On s'efforcera ensuite de comprendre quelles transformations des structures d'emploi sont induites par ces modifications d'influence respective des différents types de capitaux, et enfin, d'entrevoir les conséquences qui sont en train d'en découler.

## 4. Le changement dans les régions

Les cartes par types de capitaux des régions créatrices nettes d'emplois montrent très logiquement que ces régions sont plus nombreuses pour les emplois dépendant des groupes étrangers que pour ceux dépendant des groupes privés français, des PME même les plus petites (voir ci-dessous le paragraphe les concernant) et a fortiori des groupes publics français (cartes 2 à 5).

Pour ces derniers, trois régions seulement échappent à la régression générale entre 1985 et 1990. Ce sont la Corse, l'Auvergne et le Centre.

La Corse dispose à l'origine de si peu d'emplois que l'on peut à peine parler d'un début de rattrapage, qui commence classiquement par l'équipement énergétique (EDF).

L'Auvergne fait à peine plus que sauvegarder ses emplois du secteur public industriel (non-ferreux, armement, tabac..), ce qui suffit dans le contexte de reflux général à la distinguer.

Le Centre est donc le seul à présenter une augmentation significative de l'emploi du secteur public d'entreprise, et il en est redevable à la SNCF et à l'EDF: TGV et énergie nucléaire symbolisent bien la modernisation des équipements du pays dans ces années.

Sans les privatisations, le secteur public d'entreprise aurait de toutes façons perdu des emplois, mais son bilan négatif a été alourdi par ces transferts. Ce sont les groupes privés français qui en bénéficient. En valeur absolue, l'emploi de ces groupes progresse surtout dans l'Ile-de-France, en Lorraine, en Bretagne, en Provence-Alpes-Côte d'Azur, puis en Rhône-Alpes, en Aquitaine, Midi-Pyrénées, Languedoc-Roussillon, Pays de la Loire et enfin en Bourgogne et Poitou-Charentes. En outre, le bilan de quatre autres régions (Centre, Basse-Normandie, Limousin et Corse) est légèrement positif.

Dans certains cas, comme la Lorraine, le facteur essentiel de l'évolution positive a été les privatisations (notamment dans la sidérurgie...), mais dans la plupart des autres c'est une prise en charge de plus en plus poussée par les entreprises du mode de vie des populations (commerces de grande surfaces, transports, banques), qui rejaillit souvent sur le Bâtiment, et qui peut inclure — dans le cas de la Bretagne par exemple — une industrialisation de l'Agriculture (industries agro-alimentaires). La région Rhône-Alpes combine ces deux facteurs et l'Ile-de-France y ajoute un développement „technopolitain" fondé essentiellement sur les services de haut niveau.

Si les PME sont durement frappées par les réductions d'effectifs, on trouve encore trace dans quelques régions du mouvement de gonflement des plus petites d'entre elles qui connut son plus grand développement dans la fin des années 70 et au tout début des années 80. On doit ici donner une explication méthodologique: les données sur lesquelles on s'appuie pour évaluer la dynamique spatiale des emplois sont issues de l'enquête „Structure des Emplois" du Ministère du Travail, gérée par l'INSEE.

Le seuil en-deçà duquel les établissements sont exemptés de répondre à cette enquête est de 20 salariés. La tranche inférieure que nous avons constituée est donc de 20 à 99 salariés[4]. C'est la seule pour laquelle la dynamique 1985–1989 est créatrice nette d'emplois dans quelques régions: la majeure partie de „l'arc nord-ouest" traditionnellement prolifique sur le plan démographique mais assez peu qualifié et de la „diagonale aride" souvent observés par les géographes français, alors que des régions où ce mouvement était particulièrement actif dans la période antérieure enregistrent maintenant des reflux. Pour les PME plus importantes, le bilan de ces années est partout négatif, à la seule exception d'un petit supplément n'excédant guère le millier d'emplois en Basse-Normandie.

C'est l'emploi des groupes étrangers qui progresse de la façon la plus significative. Seules deux régions, l'Aquitaine et surtout la Champagne-Ardennes, le voient quelque peu régresser; toutes les autres sont en croissance. Ce sont les trois régions aux effectifs les plus importants qui ont les plus fortes augmentations, mais si l'Ile-de-France et „la Rhône-Alpes" font ainsi la preuve de leur constante vitalité, le Nord en revanche s'est livré là à un rattrapage qui lui permet de revenir au quatrième rang, qui est son rang général, alors qu'en 1985 il s'était retrouvé distancé, au dixième rang, derrière les régions du Bassin Parisien et du Midi. L'Alsace elle aussi connaît un rattrapage récent, tandis que la Picardie continue à progresser particulièrement pour ce type de capitaux puisqu'elle reste au .. troisième rang des régions françaises pour la présence étrangère en nombre d'emplois, alors qu'elle n'est qu'au douzième rang pour les groupes privés français et au treizième pour les groupes publics.

En constatant que les régions suivantes les plus irriguées par ce flux nouveau sont situées autour de l'Ile-de-France (Centre, Haute-Normandie) et notamment entre cette dernière et Rhône-Alpes (Bourgogne), on est tentée d'en conclure que les capitaux étrangers ne veulent plus se contenter de localisations de rééquilibrage, même s'ils acceptent fréquemment de s'installer dans les franges des grandes régions urbaines plutôt que dans leurs centres.

Ce faisant, ces entreprises tendent de plus en plus à se comporter comme le font traditionnellement les firmes françaises, c'est-à-dire non plus comme des acteurs économiques qui cherchent à prendre pied sur

---

[4]L'évaluation des mouvements concernant les plus petites entreprises n'est pas aisée, en raison même de la conjonction de leur faible visibilité et de leur forte mortalité. On pourra se reporter aux travaux de Denis Carré et du LAREA (CNRS-Université de Paris-X Nanterre).

un territoire déjà occupé en acceptant de „jouer les utilités", mais tout simplement comme des entreprises utilisant les opportunités existantes en matière de bassins de main d'oeuvre, de fournisseurs, de clients et d'équipements d'infrastructure -ce qui, bien entendu, est tout-à-fait compréhensible, mais ne contribue plus à compenser les dépressions qui se creusent au large des polarisations majeures. Dans l'état actuel, il serait toutefois injuste de mettre davantage l'accent sur la crainte d'une concurrence néfaste pour les firmes françaises que sur la reconnaissance des apports étrangers dans le Nord, en Alsace ou en Picardie.

Doit-on voir les différents éventails d'activités apportés par des firmes étrangères dans les différentes régions comme résultant en partie des choix des responsables de celles-ci depuis qu'ils disposent de pouvoirs plus importants dans ce domaine, ou plutôt comme résultant des possibles, compte-tenu des approches et des besoins des entreprises d'une part, et des profils de qualification de la population active d'autre part ? Sans doute ces deux éléments se combinent, mais dans des proportions variables. Par exemple, les implantations en Alsace sont fortement déterminées par les besoins des firmes allemandes, alors qu'une même dominante industrielle semble davantage traduire la possibilité pour la grande région lyonnaise-grenobloise, „Rhône-Alpes", de se poser en marché métropolitain du travail et de la consommation. Ce haut niveau de qualification apparaît particulièrement dans le grand Paris, où les apports étrangers les plus massifs concernent aussi bien l'industrie de haute technologie au sein de laquelle la recherche est la plus vive (industrie pharmaceutique, par exemple..) que la finance et les activités de reproduction sociale.

## 5. Les transformations des structures de l'emploi

En 1985, les groupes publics avaient davantage de cadres, de techniciens et d'ouvriers qualifiés que la moyenne française générale (tous types de capitaux confondus), et ceci correspondait à une spécialisation sur les fonctions d'administration-gestion, de conception et de transport, la part de la fabrication restant elle aussi au-dessus de la moyenne (voir tableau 2 en annexe). En 1989, la part ouvrière qualifiée et celle de la fabrication s'alignent sur la moyenne, et les groupes publics ne gardent plus que leurs autres spécificités (directionnelles et d'infrastrucures), qui en revanche s'affirment. Dans ces groupes publics, la part des ouvriers non qualifiés et des fonctions commerciale et de service restent très en-dessous de la moyenne toutes entreprises.

Les groupes privés français qui étaient, eux, caractérisés par une forte présence d'ouvriers non qualifiés et de la fabrication, ainsi que secondairement d'emplois de la fonction commerciale, affirment surtout cette dernière en 1989 tandis que le caractère manufacturier peu qualifié s'estompe et se rapproche de la moyenne.

Aux mêmes caractéristiques de départ que les groupes privés français, les groupes étrangers ajoutaient une présence plus importante de techniciens et même forte de cadres. La bi-polarisation demeure, en qualifications (embauches de contingents remarquables d'ingénieurs-cadres / et secondairement d'ouvriers non qualifiés) comme en fonctions (le commercial d'un côté / la fabrication de l'autre côté); à peine note t-on un léger étoffement de la fonction de service.

Par comparaison avec les groupes, les PME se spécialisent davantage sur les employés (dans toutes les tailles de PME), ainsi que sur les ouvriers non qualifiés (dans les entreprises moyennes de 100 à 499 salariés) et qualifiés (dans les petites de 20 à 99 salariés). Ces spécialisations sont encore visibles à l'orée de 1990 et correspondent toujours à une vocation très marquée pour la fonction de service.

La prise en considération de l'implantation régionale de ces emplois montre toujours une primatie parisienne qui constitue véritablement une constante très forte dans les dynamiques nationales. Seule la région Ile-de-France a un taux de cadres (22%) supérieur à la moyenne française (12%), que les régions suivantes n'atteignent pas (Provence-Alpes-Côte d'Azur et Midi-Pyrénées: 11%, Rhône-Alpes: 10%). Si la Provence-A-CA, avec 27%, a un taux d'emplois d'administration-gestion qui dépasse les 26% moyens, elle reste très loin des 40% franciliens ! Paris garde donc une bonne part des responsabilités dirigeantes sur l'ensemble du territoire français. L'Ile-de-France présente également les plus forts taux d'emplois de conception (6% des emplois franciliens sont consacrés à cette fonction) et de la fonction commerciale (12%), mais ils sont moins éloignés des moyennes nationales (4% et 9%) que ceux de l'administration-gestion et le partage des responsabilités territoriales est plus effectif. Midi-Pyrénées et Rhône-Alpes se distinguent pour la conception, voire l'Aquitaine et la Provence-A-CA; la Provence encore, le Languedoc-Roussillon, l'Aquitaine, Rhône-Alpes et l'Alsace réservent une part importante de leurs emplois à la fonction commerciale.

A travers la fonctionnalisation géographique actuelle, quelques grandes villes ou régions urbaines se révèlent capables de jouer le rôle de pôles secondaires dotés d'une spécialisation, malgré le caractère parfois fort ou durable de certaines crises et de certains effacements.

La dynamique actuelle d'internationalisation du capital des entreprises est-elle susceptible de modifier les structures d'emploi des régions ? Rien n'est moins sûr, car il semble plutôt que les deux types d'implantations étrangères que l'on retrouve le plus souvent continuent à correspondre à la typologie duale des marchés régionaux du travail que l'on vient d'évoquer et qui rappelle le classement déjà proposé par Michel Delapierre et Chardes-Albert Michalet en 1976[5]. Les „relais", qui s'intègrent désormais très fortement dans des réseaux d'entreprises, utilisent les hautes qualifications des candidats locaux au recrutement ou l'importance des marchés de clientèle de l'Ile-de-France, de Rhône-Alpes, de Midi-Pyrénées et de quelques autres régions urbaines et/ou ensoleillées; les „ateliers" continuent d'apporter un nombre non négligeable d'emplois de fabrication, y compris des emplois ne nécessitant guère de formation professionnelle préalable, dans la plupart des autres régions (Bassin Parisien, Est, Pays de la Loire..). Il conviendrait en fait d'y ajouter un troisième type, présent dans quelques régions frontalières (le Nord, la Champagne-Ardennes, la Franche-Comté) et intervenant dans la fonction de transport-magasinage-manutention.

Mais trois points sont toutefois à souligner:

— Même quand ils emploient une proportion également élevée d'ingénieurs-cadres et techniciens, ce qui est fréquent, les groupes étrangers se consacrent beaucoup moins que les groupes publics français à la conception (recherche et recherche-développement), et beaucoup plus à la fonction commerciale (tissage et maintenance des réseaux de clients). L'utilisation et la valorisation des innovations résultant de leurs activités doivent donc être organisées par ailleurs, de façon volontaire, puisqu'elles ne font pas, en tant que telles, l'objet de ces activités.

— Le soulagement relatif de voir des capitaux étrangers apporter des emplois de fabrication quand les capitaux français en suppriment

[5]— Delapierre (Michel) et Michalet (Charles-Albert), 1976, *Les implantations étrangères en France, stratégies et structures*, Paris, Calmann-Lévy, 279 p.

massivement devrait certainement être tempéré d'une réflexion critique: la logique de ces suppressions d'emplois découle largement de la concurrence entre les uns et les autres, et les entreprises étrangères sont elles aussi susceptibles de procéder à des coupes douloureuses, en se laissant par exemple tenter par le „dumping social" d'autres pays ou régions d'accueil.

— Enfin, les évolutions d'ensemble que l'on constate sont le produit d'un jeu complexe où interviennent de multiples facteurs. La plupart d'entre eux font partie de l'héritage français: les faibles densités et les retards d'industrialisation de nombreuses régions de „l'hexagone", la tradition „colbertiste" d'intervention de l'Etat dans l'économie et l'existence d'un important secteur public, vecteur de la modernisation du pays, le rôle politique de la France conduisant à la constitution d'un „complexe militaro-industriel", les traditions centralisatrices qui ont pu faire obstacle au développement des coopérations intra-régionales,..etc. Toutefois, en venant s'inscrire dans ce jeu complexe, l'internationalisation en a influé le cours, et on peut probablement lui imputer largement non seulement la chute des emplois de fabrication, mais également l'élévation continue de la qualification, même si ces grandes tendances affectent finalement davantage d'autres entreprises que les étrangères.

## Conclusions

Dans la mesure où ce sont leurs difficultés durables de reconversion et leur situation devenue parfois hautement critique qui ont amené certaines régions, souvent anciennement industrialisées, à rechercher un maximum d'investissements étrangers, ce serait un jeu quelque peu stérile que de vouloir discuter de l'opportunité de ces investissements ou de leurs risques dans les termes qui auraient pu être de mise si l'alternative avait existé. Celà n'oblige pas à en faire un nouveau „credo", et, pour les investissements étrangers comme pour toute autre action territoriale, une maîtrise avisée vaut certainement mieux qu'un émerveillement irréfléchi.

En tous cas, s'il est indéniable que des acteurs régionaux font preuve d'initiative et s'attellent avec courage à leurs problèmes de développement, ce que l'on pouvait d'ailleurs déjà constater en mainte région avant la „décentralisation administrative" officielle, il faut malheureusement constater que maintenant qu'ils disposent de plus de pouvoir en matière économique, ils se retrouvent en butte à des difficultés accrues. Alourdissement des coûts financiers, rétraction des marchés, fragilisation des plus petites entreprises par les difficultés de toutes... mettent constamment en danger ces initiatives.

Par ailleurs, si la mobilisation d'énergies relativement „libres" est indispensable, celà ne peut se poursuivre favorablement qu'à condition de déboucher sur une sorte de nouveau „contrat", compromis qui se dégagera comme favorable au plus grand nombre et offrant de nouvelles opportunités, autant que possible durables. On ne peut se dissimuler qu'en multipliant les niveaux de pouvoirs, on prend le risque de voir se multiplier les „féodalités" qui peut-être seront à l'origine de nouveaux cloisonnements, sans toujours les voir oeuvrer efficacement au développement régional. Mais l'attentisme est cause lui aussi de très grands inconvénients, et, en matière de prospective socio-économique, les hypothèses les plus pessimistes n'ont pas toujours les probabilités les plus fortes

En France, si l'on peut en juger par les résultats de nos analyses sur la période 1985–89, les évolutions d'ensemble ont été dans le sens d'une plus grande qualification et de la suppression de très nombreux emplois, le plus souvent de fabrication, sans que la production en soit réduite d'autant, très loin de là ! si l'on ne peut nier la modernisation et la fonctionalisation qui ont accompagné cette mutation, on ne peut davantage ignorer le problème très préoccupant du chômage. S'il semble aujourd'hui loin d'être jugulé (puisqu'au contraire il semble s'approfondir), les initiatives des régions (comme toutes les autres) sont a priori préférables à l'absence d'initiatives...

En tout état de cause, la constitution par l'Etat des régions qui ont ici servi à mener la réflexion ne fait pas de ces entités administratives fixes les cadres „naturels" du développement assuré d'une dynamique régionale, et en particulier l'ensemble du Bassin Parisien et même d'autres régions voisines restent très largement sous l'influence du grand centre qu'est Paris. Mais les „régions" ainsi définies semblent avoir pu servir dans la période récente 1985–1989 à certaines reprises d'initiative et à certains déblocages. A terme, on peut même présager qu'elles joueront un rôle de repère largement reconnu, comme c'est par exemple le cas de nos „départements" bicentenaires.

# Annexes

**Tableau 2**

**France, structure des emplois des entreprises
en mars 1985 et décembre 1989
(„1990") selon l'origine des capitaux**
*(hors Administration et petits établissements de moins de 20 salariés)*

### a. structures par sexes et qualifications

| (milliers) | | %:Femmes | Cd* | T* | E* | OQ* | OSM* |
|---|---|---|---|---|---|---|---|
| France entière: | | | | | | | |
| 1985 | 8 513 | 35 | 10 | 20 | 22 | 31 | 17 |
| 1990 | 8 073 | 36 | 12 | 21 | 22 | 31 | 14 |
| groupes publics: | | | | | | | |
| 1985 | 1 645 | 22 | 12 | 27 | 17 | 33 | 11 |
| 1990 | 1 327 | 24 | 15 | 30 | 16 | 30 | 08 |
| gr.privés français: | | | | | | | |
| 1985 | 1 977 | 32 | 9 | 17 | 21 | 32 | 21 |
| 1990 | 2 053 | 33 | 11 | 18 | 23 | 31 | 16 |
| groupes étrangers: | | | | | | | |
| 1985 | 0 391 | 32 | 15 | 22 | 16 | 30 | 18 |
| 1990 | 0 555 | 35 | 16 | 23 | 15 | 29 | 16 |
| PME > 999 salariés: | | | | | | | |
| 1985 | 0 209 | 55 | 12 | 22 | 16 | 30 | 18 |
| 1990 | 0 141 | 55 | 13 | 22 | 36 | 18 | 11 |
| PME 500–999 salariés: | | | | | | | |
| 1985 | 0 296 | 45 | 10 | 19 | 33 | 22 | 16 |
| 1990 | 0 206 | 49 | 13 | 23 | 33 | 18 | 14 |
| PME 100–499 salariés: | | | | | | | |
| 1985 | 1 543 | 45 | 9 | 18 | 25 | 28 | 20 |
| 1990 | 1 389 | 44 | 11 | 19 | 25 | 28 | 18 |
| PME 20–99 salariés: | | | | | | | |
| 1985 | 2 452 | 38 | 10 | 17 | 24 | 33 | 16 |
| 1990 | 2 392 | 38 | 10 | 18 | 23 | 34 | 14 |

Source ESE

* Cd=cadres; T=techniciens et professions intermédiaires;
E=employés; OQ=ouvriers qualifiés; OSM=ouvriers spécialisés et manoeuvres.

**b. structures par fonctions:**

| (milliers) | | %: Adm* | Com* | Cpt* | Ser* | MMT* | Fab* |
|---|---|---|---|---|---|---|---|
| France entière: | | | | | | | |
| 1985 | 8 513 | 25 | 8 | 4 | 11 | 10 | 41 |
| 1990 | 8 073 | 26 | 9 | 4 | 12 | 10 | 39 |
| | | | | | | | |
| groupes publics: | | | | | | | |
| 1985 | 1 645 | 30 | 3 | 8 | 3 | 13 | 43 |
| 1990 | 1 327 | 33 | 4 | 8 | 3 | 13 | 38 |
| gr.privés français: | | | | | | | |
| 1985 | 1 977 | 20 | 11 | 4 | 7 | 11 | 46 |
| 1990 | 2 053 | 23 | 13 | 4 | 8 | 10 | 41 |
| groupes étrangers: | | | | | | | |
| 1985 | 0 391 | 24 | 14 | 4 | 3 | 9 | 46 |
| 1990 | 0 555 | 24 | 15 | 4 | 6 | 8 | 44 |
| PME ¿ 999 salariés: | | | | | | | |
| 1985 | 0 209 | 50 | 5 | 3 | 19 | 3 | 19 |
| 1990 | 0 141 | 44 | 2 | 6 | 25 | 3 | 2O |
| PME 500–999 salariés: | | | | | | | |
| 1985 | 0 296 | 38 | 3 | 3 | 19 | 5 | 31 |
| 1990 | 0 206 | 35 | 4 | 4 | 28 | 5 | 24 |
| PME 100–499 salariés: | | | | | | | |
| 1985 | 1 543 | 24 | 8 | 2 | 18 | 8 | 40 |
| 1990 | 1 389 | 25 | 8 | 3 | 18 | 8 | 38 |
| PME 20–99 salariés: | | | | | | | |
| 1985 | 2 452 | 23 | 9 | 2 | 15 | 10 | 39 |
| 1990 | 2 392 | 23 | 10 | 2 | 16 | 10 | 38 |

Source ESE.

*Adm=administration-gestion; Com=fonction commerciale;
Cpt=conception; Ser=fonction de service;
MMT=magasinage-manutention-transport; Fab=fabrication.

**Tableau 3**

**Structures d'emploi des entreprises en mars 1985 et décembre 1989 („1990")**
**selon les régions**

*(hors Administration et petits établissements de moins de 20 salariés)*

**a. structures de sexes et qualifications:**

| (milliers) | | %:Femmes | Cd* | T* | E* | OQ* | OSM* |
|---|---|---|---|---|---|---|---|
| **France entière:** | | | | | | | |
| 1985 | 8 513 | 35 | 10 | 20 | 22 | 31 | 17 |
| 1990 | 8 073 | 36 | 12 | 21 | 22 | 31 | 14 |
| **Ile-de-France:** | | | | | | | |
| 1985 | 2 212 | 38 | 18 | 24 | 26 | 21 | 10 |
| 1990 | 2 115 | 39 | 22 | 25 | 25 | 19 | 8 |
| **Champagne-Ardennes:** | | | | | | | |
| 1985 | 211 | 34 | 6 | 16 | 18 | 36 | 23 |
| 1990 | 189 | 34 | 7 | 17 | 18 | 37 | 22 |
| **Picardie:** | | | | | | | |
| 1985 | 259 | 34 | 6 | 15 | 18 | 36 | 25 |
| 1990 | 243 | 34 | 7 | 16 | 18 | 37 | 22 |
| **Haute-Normandie:** | | | | | | | |
| 1985 | 284 | 32 | 7 | 17 | 18 | 36 | 22 |
| 1990 | 265 | 34 | 8 | 19 | 19 | 36 | 19 |
| **Centre:** | | | | | | | |
| 1985 | 356 | 39 | 7 | 17 | 20 | 34 | 22 |
| 1990 | 349 | 38 | 8 | 18 | 19 | 35 | 2O |
| **Basse-Normandie:** | | | | | | | |
| 1985 | 176 | 35 | 6 | 17 | 19 | 36 | 22 |
| 1990 | 176 | 36 | 6 | 18 | 19 | 37 | 19 |
| **Bourgogne:** | | | | | | | |
| 1985 | 226 | 35 | 6 | 17 | 19 | 36 | 21 |
| 1990 | 219 | 35 | 7 | 18 | 20 | 37 | 19 |
| **Nord:** | | | | | | | |
| 1985 | 593 | 30 | 6 | 17 | 19 | 37 | 21 |
| 1990 | 528 | 33 | 8 | 17 | 21 | 36 | 19 |
| **Lorraine:** | | | | | | | |
| 1985 | 375 | 29 | 6 | 17 | 18 | 40 | 18 |
| 1990 | 324 | 31 | 7 | 19 | 19 | 39 | 17 |
| **Alsace:** | | | | | | | |
| 1985 | 295 | 34 | 8 | 17 | 21 | 34 | 20 |
| 1990 | 279 | 34 | 9 | 18 | 21 | 36 | 16 |
| **Franche-Comté:** | | | | | | | |
| 1985 | 171 | 33 | 6 | 16 | 16 | 36 | 26 |

| | | | | | | | |
|---|---|---|---|---|---|---|---|
| 1990 | 159 | 33 | 6 | 17 | 16 | 40 | 20 |
| Pays de la Loire: | | | | | | | |
| 1985 | 427 | 37 | 7 | 17 | 19 | 35 | 21 |
| 1990 | 420 | 36 | 8 | 18 | 19 | 36 | 19 |
| Bretagne: | | | | | | | |
| 1985 | 283 | 38 | 7 | 17 | 22 | 34 | 19 |
| 1990 | 280 | 38 | 8 | 18 | 21 | 35 | 18 |
| Poitou-Charentes: | | | | | | | |
| 1985 | 174 | 36 | 7 | 16 | 21 | 35 | 20 |
| 1990 | 169 | 36 | 7 | 17 | 21 | 36 | 18 |
| Aquitaine: | | | | | | | |
| 1985 | 296 | 36 | 8 | 19 | 23 | 33 | 16 |
| 1990 | 288 | 36 | 9 | 20 | 24 | 34 | 14 |
| Midi-Pyrénées: | | | | | | | |
| 1985 | 248 | 36 | 9 | 21 | 23 | 33 | 14 |
| 1990 | 253 | 37 | 11 | 23 | 23 | 31 | 12 |
| Limousin: | | | | | | | |
| 1985 | 82 | 38 | 7 | 17 | 22 | 37 | 18 |
| 1990 | 79 | 37 | 7 | 18 | 21 | 37 | 16 |
| Rhône-Alpes: | | | | | | | |
| 1985 | 822 | 34 | 9 | 20 | 20 | 32 | 18 |
| 1990 | 803 | 35 | 10 | 21 | 20 | 33 | 15 |
| Auvergne: | | | | | | | |
| 1985 | 155 | 34 | 6 | 19 | 20 | 33 | 21 |
| 1990 | 155 | 34 | 7 | 20 | 20 | 35 | 17 |
| Languedoc-Roussillon: | | | | | | | |
| 1985 | 164 | 36 | 8 | 20 | 27 | 31 | 13 |
| 1990 | 165 | 38 | 9 | 21 | 29 | 29 | 12 |
| Provence-Alpes-Côte d"Azur: | | | | | | | |
| 1985 | 414 | 34 | 9 | 21 | 28 | 29 | 12 |
| 1990 | 426 | 36 | 11 | 22 | 29 | 27 | 10 |
| Corse: | | | | | | | |
| 1985 | 10 | 32 | 7 | 20 | 32 | 26 | 15 |
| 1990 | 14 | 32 | 7 | 21 | 34 | 28 | 10 |

Source ESE.

\* Cd=cadres;T=techniciens et professions intermédiaires;
E=employés; OQ=ouvriers qualifiés; OSM=ouvriers spécialisés et
manoeuvres.

**b. structures par fonctions:**

| (milliers) | | %: Adm* | Com* | Cpt* | Ser* | MMT* | Fab* |
|---|---|---|---|---|---|---|---|
| France entière: | | | | | | | |
| 1985 | 8 513 | 25 | 8 | 4 | 11 | 10 | 41 |
| 1990 | 8 073 | 26 | 9 | 4 | 12 | 10 | 39 |
| Ile-de-France: | | | | | | | |
| 1985 | 2 212 | 38 | 11 | 6 | 12 | 8 | 25 |
| 1990 | 2 115 | 40 | 12 | 6 | 12 | 7 | 22 |
| Champagne-Ardennes: | | | | | | | |
| 1985 | 211 | 18 | 8 | 2 | 8 | 12 | 52 |
| 1990 | 189 | 18 | 7 | 3 | 10 | 11 | 51 |
| Picardie: | | | | | | | |
| 1985 | 259 | 18 | 6 | 2 | 8 | 12 | 54 |
| 1990 | 243 | 18 | 7 | 3 | 9 | 12 | 52 |
| Haute-Normandie: | | | | | | | |
| 1985 | 284 | 19 | 5 | 3 | 8 | 12 | 52 |
| 1990 | 265 | 19 | 7 | 4 | 10 | 11 | 49 |
| Centre: | | | | | | | |
| 1985 | 356 | 21 | 7 | 3 | 10 | 11 | 49 |
| 1990 | 349 | 21 | 7 | 3 | 10 | 11 | 47 |
| Basse-Normandie: | | | | | | | |
| 1985 | 176 | 19 | 6 | 3 | 10 | 11 | 52 |
| 1990 | 176 | 19 | 6 | 4 | 12 | 10 | 49 |
| Bourgogne: | | | | | | | |
| 1985 | 226 | 19 | 7 | 3 | 9 | 11 | 51 |
| 1990 | 219 | 19 | 8 | 3 | 11 | 11 | 48 |
| Nord: | | | | | | | |
| 1985 | 593 | 20 | 6 | 3 | 9 | 12 | 51 |
| 1990 | 528 | 21 | 8 | 3 | 12 | 11 | 45 |
| Lorraine | | | | | | | |
| 1985 | 375 | 17 | 6 | 3 | 10 | 11 | 53 |
| 1990 | 324 | 18 | 7 | 3 | 11 | 11 | 50 |
| Alsace: | | | | | | | |
| 1985 | 295 | 20 | 8 | 3 | 11 | 10 | 48 |
| 1990 | 279 | 20 | 9 | 3 | 11 | 10 | 46 |
| Franche-Comté: | | | | | | | |
| 1985 | 171 | 16 | 6 | 4 | 8 | 10 | 57 |
| 1990 | 159 | 16 | 6 | 5 | 9 | 10 | 55 |
| Pays de la Loire: | | | | | | | |
| 1985 | 427 | 21 | 6 | 3 | 9 | 10 | 50 |
| 1990 | 420 | 21 | 7 | 3 | 10 | 10 | 49 |

| | | | | | | | |
|---|---|---|---|---|---|---|---|
| **Bretagne:** | | | | | | | |
| 1985 | 283 | 22 | 8 | 3 | 11 | 12 | 44 |
| 1990 | 280 | 21 | 8 | 3 | 12 | 12 | 44 |
| **Poitou-Charentes:** | | | | | | | |
| 1985 | 174 | 23 | 7 | 2 | 9 | 10 | 48 |
| 1990 | 169 | 23 | 8 | 3 | 9 | 10 | 47 |
| **Aquitaine:** | | | | | | | |
| 1985 | 296 | 22 | 9 | 3 | 12 | 11 | 42 |
| 1990 | 288 | 22 | 10 | 4 | 13 | 10 | 40 |
| **Midi-Pyrénées:** | | | | | | | |
| 1985 | 248 | 23 | 8 | 5 | 13 | 9 | 42 |
| 1990 | 253 | 24 | 8 | 5 | 15 | 9 | 39 |
| **Limousin:** | | | | | | | |
| 1985 | 82 | 21 | 6 | 3 | 10 | 11 | 49 |
| 1990 | 79 | 20 | 7 | 3 | 11 | 11 | 48 |
| **Rhône-Alpes:** | | | | | | | |
| 1985 | 822 | 22 | 7 | 4 | 10 | 10 | 46 |
| 1990 | 803 | 23 | 9 | 5 | 11 | 10 | 43 |
| **Auvergne:** | | | | | | | |
| 1985 | 155 | 20 | 6 | 4 | 10 | 10 | 49 |
| 1990 | 155 | 20 | 8 | 4 | 12 | 10 | 47 |
| **Languedoc-Roussillon:** | | | | | | | |
| 1985 | 164 | 24 | 9 | 2 | 17 | 11 | 37 |
| 1990 | 165 | 23 | 11 | 3 | 18 | 11 | 33 |
| **Provence-Alpes-Côte d"Azur:** | | | | | | | |
| 1985 | 414 | 25 | 10 | 4 | 16 | 12 | 33 |
| 1990 | 426 | 27 | 12 | 4 | 17 | 11 | 30 |
| **Corse:** | | | | | | | |
| 1985 | 10 | 27 | 18 | 1 | 17 | 11 | 33 |
| 1990 | 14 | 26 | 11 | 1 | 19 | 10 | 32. |

Source ESE.

*Adm=administration-gestion; Com=fonction commerciale;
Cpt=conception; Ser=fonction de service;
MMT=magasinage-manutention-transport; Fab=fabrication.

**Carte 1.** *Régions de programme*

bilans des emplois
entre mars 1985 et
décembre 1989:

\> 0

\< 0

Source: ESE (hors Administration et établissements de moins de 20 salariés).

**Carte 2.** *Evolution 1985–1990 des effects des GROUPES PUBLICS*

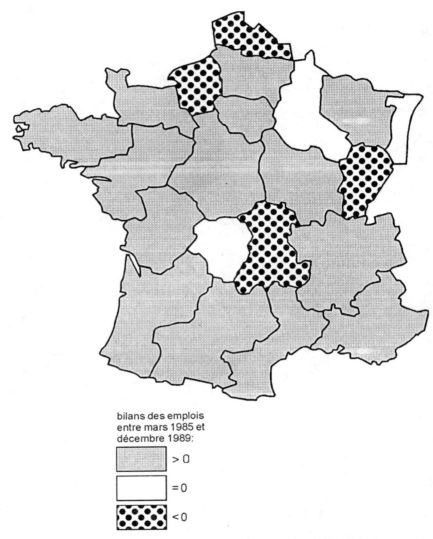

bilans des emplois
entre mars 1985 et
décembre 1989:

> 0

= 0

< 0

Source: ESE (hors Administration et établissements de moins de 20 salariés).

**Carte 3.** *Evolution 1985–1990 des effectifs des GROUPES PRIVES FRANCAIS*

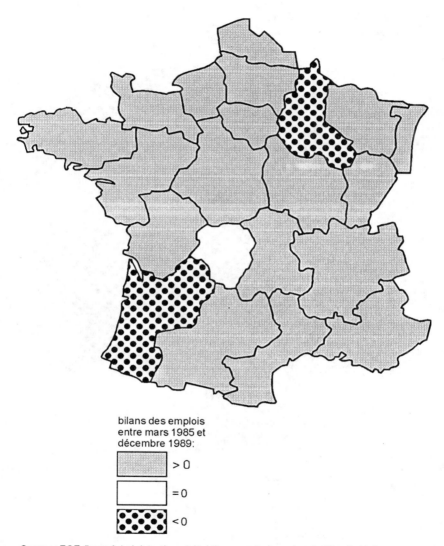

bilans des emplois
entre mars 1985 et
décembre 1989:

> 0

= 0

< 0

Source: ESE (hors Administration et établissements de moins de 20 salariés).

**Carte 4.** *Evolution 1985–1990 des effectifs des GROUPES ETRANGERS*

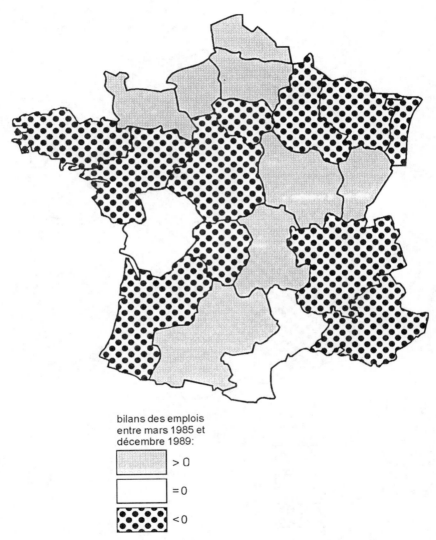

bilans des emplois
entre mars 1985 et
décembre 1989:

> 0

= 0

< 0

Source: ESE (hors Administration et établissements de moins de 20 salariés).

**Carte 5.** *Evolution 1985–1990 des effectifs des PME de 20 à 99 salariés*

Jan Groenendijk
Institute for Human Geography
University of Amsterdam

# THE PERSISTENT STATE PROMOTING AGRICULTURAL INTEREST AT REGIONAL AND EUROPEAN LEVEL

Is the State retreating in favour of regions within or across its borders (Murphy 1993) and of the supra-national level? True enough, states bind themselves in treaty organisations and incurr loss of autonomy that way. The European Community has taken over part of the rule making authority of its Member States. Below state level, internationalisation of the economy allows regions to compete internationally for business. For support in the EC regions may even pass their own state capital and present their case in Brussels.

In the following the position is taken that although, to a marginal degree, power has been handed over to other levels, still the political system in essence remains a state-centered system, and that there are strong forces in society to keep it that way. In particular the argument is developed, that the state system is not only a matter of territorial strategies and national loyalties. The strength of states is maintained as well by communities of interest that develop along sectoral lines. As main building blocks of the state they keep using the state as their main stronghold in promoting their case.

Here we present the case of agriculture, a major domain of EC policy. Two recent problems are studied for the development of policy at regional, state and supra state level. The first problem is checking the surplus of agricultural production, the second the problem of intensification of agriculture beyond the carrying capacity of the environment.

# 1. Retreat of the state?

The inter-state system and the state are thought to be on retreat (Taylor 1993). State-centered thinking should loose its monopoly (Murphy 1993). What forces are destroying the state? Taylor discernes destroyers undermining the system from within and from without. The first ones are the "formal political actors". In Europe this is the European Community that will not become a federal state but a "triple layering of political power", a new spatiality replacing the current system of Member States. Regional and Community level will complement state level. From without the system is destroyed by new social movements such as the peace movement, human rights, feminist and environmental movement. There can be no doubt that these forces are in operation. Rather it seems wise to look to state policies to find out what states do to counter threats and to look beyond new movements to societal relations for relevance and vitality of the state. Harvey (1989) has pointed to internationalisation of the economy that gives metropolitan areas chances for direct competition. New levels of government have been created to manage developments on that level. But one of the oldest (London) is no longer there, and Barlow (1991) shows that states are effectively checking the public power of metropolitan regions. Neither does it seem right to consider the European Community as "taking over" from the states. Milward (1992) presents the formative years of the EC from a different perspective as the "Rescue of the Nation-State". New movements are not simply a threat to the state. Political parties as part of the (inter) state system take ideas of these movements when they consider them useful for their strategy. Johnston (1989) in discussing the prospects for environmental policy sees no reason to dissociate this perspective from the inter-state system.

There is every reason to be critical of state-policy as solution to the worlds problems. Taylor (1993, 89) is of course right in hoping for "a new spatiality in which decentralisation is used to try and reconcile economic growth with human needs". In this paper we will use a rational vision on the future of agricultural land-use in Europe to question the ability of current political systems to deal with decisions that should be on the agenda. But in doing that we try to test state power in policy making on the subject, which leaves us with no illusions.

In bringing the inter-state system to a test, both vertical depth and horizontal linkages (Krasner 1989) of social practices are relevant. Applying this to agriculture in the Dutch setting, the depth is illustrated by identification of farmers with their nation-state via their pillarized organisations as part of the Dutch social system. Breadth of linkages for farmers is binding them more to their own state than to the EC. Tax system, land-use and environmental regulation, penetration in local government system, school system and subsidies for infrastructure (not in the least the agricultural), the corporatist system to influence state operation are among the linkages that condition succes of agriculture for the Dutch farmers. Many of these conditions were developed when the Common Agricultural Policy (CAP) was in operation. In other states conditions are far from the same.

From an institutional perspective, agriculture, like other sectors of the economic and social system, is organised in a "policy community" to further its interest. In The Netherlands a Board of Agriculture for the trade as a whole and Production Boards for several products are statutory trade organisations in which private and public partners cooperate to strenghten their domain. These sectoral communities have been developed at state level during an era of broadening state activity. Naturally social activity initiates from professionals at this level for the state territory and reproduces state relations. From there, other levels may be approached when they are more appropriate to deal with a particular situation. Organisations of the state counter threats in the way that is best for them. The Ministry of Agriculture uses the EC mechanism (the quota system) to keep the Dutch share of the market (see next section). The Ministry of Spatial Planning and the Environment develops a regional concept for dealing with the problem of "bio-industry" to show that the planning system can be used for this purpose and to break through agricultural blockade of environmental measures (see last section).

## 2. Agricultural surplus and the steps to be taken

There can be no doubt that European agriculture is badly in want of a solution for its surplus production. Outside the Common Agricultural Policy (CAP) circle of the EC it can be heard, that surplus production is the one evil to fight and that all other aims in reforming the CAP (such as sustaining the environment, maintaining the landscape, survival of the rural community) are no more than a pretext to keep a claim on the EC budget (The Economist 1992). The future for agriculture is bleak indeed. But it is of more interest to know whether a truly "Common" CAP will be able to allocate appropriate reductions in shares of production over regions of the EC or that market forces will prevail.

While we look further into EC policy making and the persistent (or even reviving) role of the State level in the next paragraph, here we try to formulate what type of decisions are needed to deal with severe reductions and alternative land use in a rational way. To this end we make use of a report of the Netherlands Scientific Council for Government Policy (NSCGP 1992). The report "Ground for choices" starts from the idea, that further growth of productivity per hectare and per worker is inevitable. So there will be a huge surplus of land and of rural working population. This poses questions as to which land can best be taken out of production and how to allocate the production of several agricultural products over the total amount of land. Apart from information on the technical potential of rural areas, this requires criteria or policy objectives to direct these choices.

Using data on the production potential of Europe's rural areas for different crops and types of agricultural use, the NSCGP developed four distinct scenarios: A) free market and free trade; B) regional development; C) nature and landscape; D) environmental protection. Each scenario assumes the use of "best technical means".

The main finding (apart from the more or less appalling surplus of land according to the objective chosen) is that the potential of areas allows for different systems of agricultural production (milk, cereals etc.) to shift around Europe, in relation to the chief objective chosen. In this way, scenario B (bringing as much work as possible to the people on the land) means bringing relatively labour-intensive milk production to the Mediterranean areas. Therefore, the centre of gravity shifts considerably over Europe according to the objective chosen.

The Council's research makes it perfectly clear that there are far ranging choices to be made. On the basis of this research, the EC will be able to develop a new CAP that will have none of the adverse effects of current policy.

There are, however, two conditions to be fulfilled. Prior to the choices and as a condition of any further change of land-use, the price of land will have to come down and brought in accordance with the surplus position which this input commodity without market distortion (by subsidies and quotas) has. The severe capital loss of dropping landprice will have to be catered for somewhere. Only then will it be possible for alternative uses of land to become viable in the land market. Secondly, the EC — and its Agricultural Council in particular — will have to develop powers to reallocate agricultural production areas between regions and, by implication, between states.

The NSCGP's finding was that agricultural potential allows for several alternative arrangements of rural production areas does not make this easier. It means, that there is apparently no inherent technical argument to convince politicians that any one allocational pattern is optimal. Were this the case, then a model of Pareto optimality could work. Every Member State could then be made to believe that (as is required in Article 1 of the Treaty of Rome) production should be situated where optimal conditions prevail. All states then would profit from reallocation. According to the Council's report, keeping too much arable land would create massive inefficiency. So Europe at large would profit (at least in its budget) from concentrating productivity on less land and less people. So far, Member States could probably agree. But as the centre of gravity of the various agricultural businesses could be located in more than one area, an allocation decision has to be made. This is a zero-sum conflict: a gain by one state will mean a loss to another. And there will be heavy losses, especially in land values. Where agricultural use is no longer supported under some quota system, land value will drop enormously. The recent CAP reform discussions show that Member States will not accept a reversal of the status quo, but on the contrary will want to hold on to their share of production. This seems to be a continuation of the type of discussions which Member State profits most that dominated the Agricultural Council year after year, instead of concentrating on improvements for the Community as a whole (Meester, 1986, Buckwell et al 1982). This characterises the Community more as an international treaty organisation than as a federated state in statu nascendi. An analysis of the present decision-making structure in this paper will leave little hope that the EC is ready for a "community" type of decision-making.

The NSCGP's main contribution seems to be the lesson that the EC cannot escape from presenting its objectives more clearly and taking more appropriate steps to avoid major trouble in the near future. To get to a position where agriculture retreats to a much smaller share of rural land-use, a completely different structure of decision-making will have to be developed in the EC. The European Councils of Ministers for which Finance, Nature, Environment, Recreation will have to be placed on an equal footing with the now heavily developed agricultural policy community of the EC. Although Phillips (1990) showed, that the Financial Council already in the 1980s already had a heavier hand in agricultural matters compared with the decades before, the recent CAP reform shows that the agricultural sector was allowed to proceed without much intervention from other sectors. On top of that, Member States have to allow for reallocation of agricultural production among them.

Will these requirements be met? This type of political decision-making does exist in democratic states that reached stability and were democratically legitimised long after they were first established. But in the uncertain post-Maastricht era one would not believe that the EC will reach that stage in the near future. First a true Parliament would have to be in place to create legitimacy for the far ranging choices to be made.

If the structure of decision-making is not yet sufficient and other requirements for policy making are not met at the moment, is Europe moving in a direction where there will be solutions to zero-sum conflicts? To find out how the structure has functioned recently, we shall examine in more detail the process leading to the MacSharry reform (Commission of the European Communities 1991a, 1991b, Council of the European Communities 1992).

# 3. CAP reform; tendencies of re-nationalisation.

The principal switch from price support to income support opened the way for differentiation between Member States. Implementation of sophisticated compensation schemes had to be tailored to national peculiarities. National organisations of farmers played a key role in this excercise.

On the whole, the new measures address the surplus problem only in an indirect way. Several other goals have been defined: assuring the position of the (small) family farm, improving the environmental standard for land-use and a balanced development for the countryside. Income support in contrast to price support could be used to redirect support to the small, extensively operated family farm. By implication, support would be redirected to areas, where what are known as "inefficient farms" prevail. Much of the decision-making procedures can be characterised as a struggle of pressure groups and Member States representing the interest of "efficient farmers".

The Comite des Organisations Professionnelles Agricoles de la CE (COPA 1991) reacted with counter proposals that were in fact a prolongation of the existing system to curtail amounts of production. As a Committee representing the farmers' organisations of the EC countries, the interests of efficient farmers predominated. Their aim was to ensure that if it were impossible to prevent price support being replaced by direct income support, then large farms should benefit from it too. A special appendix to their proposals provided a narrow definition for the small farm excluding part-time farming from compensating payment: a small farm is a full-time exploitation that lacks the appropriate size (so that steps have to be taken to make it a viable farm). Apparently, after the enlargement of the EC, many small farmers in the Southern countries make it for the COPA more difficult to formulate its policy. The May 1991 reaction has remained the only statement during the CAP reform discussions. The conflict of interests among members did not allow any further statement to be made.

In this way the role of COPA was undermined. The main benefits from negotiations were to be had through concessions to farmers of a particular Member State.

Moreover, the structure for decision making on proposals of the European Commission by the Council of Ministers has remained under close scrutiny of Member States' bureaucrats.

The Council does not immediately consider the proposals. First, for every agricultural product a working group made up of specialist civil servants from the Member States analyses the proposal thoroughly, of course mainly to find out what it means for the respective national economies.

The next stage is the Comite Special Agraire (CSA, again formed of national civil servants) which convenes every week in Brussels to discuss what proposals are ripe for decision making in the Council during its monthly gathering. During this process, the EP plays a role by deciding whether or not the proposal has reached a stage at which they can give their advice to the Council. If not, the proposal will be sent back to a working group. It follows, that after preparation on a true European level by DG VI (an administration loyal to the Community) there is a long route through Member State administrators where national interests are predominant. On the way, avenues for compromise in the Council are being prepared.

Over the years the position of the actors in this arena has changed. In the years of expanding agriculture to self-suffiency in the Europe of the 6, DG VI and COPA could arrange matters among themselves (Phillips 1990). During the 1970s, the Council more and more had to make compromises. Debate on Andriessen's Green Paper (1985) resulted mainly in a financial discussion. After that, the Agricultural Council was placed under the influence of the Council of Finance ministers. Prominent Member States in the Council had crucial influence on decisions. In that way COPA lost influence because national farmers organisations had to approach their own ministers, making their electoral influence felt.

This structure for making decisions in the agricultural domain shows the famous Eurocrats losing control and initiative moving to the Member States' agro-economic specialists as soon as a proposal leaves the Commission.

The main reason that the MacSharry proposals laid down in the Reflections Paper survived at all, is the fact that reactions were so divided among Member States. The only consensus was that something had to be done. In fact, it is now realised, that the CAP has been a wonderous compromise between contrasting interests. No wonder that any principle change again brings forward these contrasts. A major division of interests is that between Member States in agricultural deficit (net importers: Germany, Italy) and those in surplus (net exporters: such as The Netherlands and Denmark).

Income support is not new. France was originally in favour of the MacSharry plan because it might make grain competitive in the world market and also bring some relief for small farmers in its southern regions. Exporting countries were interested in a GATT solution, but their modern agriculture would have to pay heavily for the redistribution to small farms elsewhere in the Community. For Ireland, the MacSharry plan, which focused on cheaper grain (making it competitive for raising cattle) woul imperil its grass based agriculture. Efficient farming versus smallholdings reflects as well a North-South devide.

The compromise the Council reached in May 1992 clearly revealed the priorities for Member States. The main proposal of drastic price cut for cereals practically survived.

But very systematically two objectives of the proposals (the redistribution to small farms and the extensification of agricultural land-use) were curtailed. Compensation for set-aside is not restricted to a maximum. Milk price and quota stay practically as they are; this means that premiums reserved for small and extensive farms do not show up either. Redistribution of quota to southern Member States would be an issue only in later years, when it has been clearly shown that the new Member States are applying the quota system properly.

Little remains of general instruments to improve the environment. What is left then are the "Accompanying instruments" that are planned and applied within national frameworks. So within Member States it is possible, under EC scrutiny, to draw up regulations for specific areas, where activities that improve the environment will be compensated for, co-financed by the EC. Water protection, several extensification measures, organic farming, opening up of areas for recreation and even training, will all be entitled to receive compensation co-financed by the EC. The same national framewworks apply for afforestation and pre-retirement.

The conclusion must be, that the idea of location-allocation planning on EC level is out of the question as that will inevitably of a redistributive nature. Member States hold strongly to existing quota and reference numbers.

The member States that have agriculture as a major part of their economies will not easily give up. As yet, there is no new decision-making system at hand that is suitable to take Europe's rural areas beyond the uncertain stage where they find themselves now.

There are even signs of re-nationalisation. MacSharry — and the Commission with him — were eager to reach an agreement on the principle of income support taking the place of price support. Too many bribes were given out to the Agricultural Departments of Member States. While COPA lost influence, national farmers' pressure groups won the prizes.

The next steps to be taken by the Commission are the bilateral agreements with Member States to create national (or regional) programmes for the environment and early retirement of farmers. The main schemes to take land out of agricultural production are to be decided on a bilateral basis. On the whole it is clear, that while price support is bound to be in terms of general measures, this is not the case with "social agriculture" and even less with environmental measures (cf Baden-Wurtemberg programmes of this year, Groenendijk 1992).

The MacSharry plan — especially in its original form — tried to counter the process of growing duality between large prosperous farms and marginal ones. The Departments of Agriculture of Member States along with the farmers' unions have been fighting hard and successfully to curtail the MacSharry plan on this point.

## 4. Agricultural interest and regional concept.

The aim to keep its share in agricultural production places the Ministry of Agriculture, Nature and Fishery for the task to deal with environmental impact of intensive forms of agriculture in The Netherlands. Intensification of agriculture resulted in more serious problems of manure and harmful emissions and depositions than anywhere in the EC. Nor is there a strategy in the EC that offers an easy solution to this problem, other than desintensification. Industrial processing paid by a levy on all farms of a certain category has been waved by the Commission.

Within the Dutch Administration the Ministry of Agriculture is in an uncomfortable dependency relation with the Ministry of Physical Planning and Environment. The manure problem before long has been kept from the agenda, but had to be dealt with one day. The strength of the agricultural policy community (Groenendijk 1991) has been such, that intensification was allowed to proceed. The Planning Ministry as an outsider to this policy community was unable to proceed with its environmental agenda in matters of agriculture. The capacity for the organisation of policy in the own interest of the agricultural policy community is not to be equalled (Frouws 1988). The modernisation proces of dutch agriculture during the twentieth century, consisting of educating farmers up to university level, of creating of a marketing infrastructure, of land reclamation and of land consolidation, has mobilised a strong policy community firmly committed to recurrent innovations in their trade. It took the form of corporatist organisation culminating in its position at state level. Although their numbers dwindled during emancipation, members of this community hold on to every seat in boards and councils that furthers their interest. On all three levels of government, physical planning of rural areas has therefore to make room for new ways of agricultural production that change the landscape completely. Compromises on ministerial level to keep old landscapes and "natural" elements, may be de facto cancelled in a rural municipality. A fortiori, generic measures of the Directorate for the Environment were hardly implemented at municipal level.

Conflict between values of environment and economy are of course not limited to agriculture. In the Netherlands the conflict between new items of economic policy, the "mainports" for European competition, and the environment was all to obvious. In compensation, the idea was launched by the Ministry of Physical Planning and Environment that had to cater for both spatial conditions for economic competition and for improving the environment, that regional measures should complement the spectre of environmental instruments. In this way, the Directorate for the Environment would be postively committed to instruments of physical planning in the other — rival — part of the Ministry. To this end, Area Oriented Policy has been developed as a third type of Environmental Policy next to "Theme-oriented" and "Target group" oriented policy. Area oriented policy integrates measures for a particular area, where environmental problems tend to cumulate due to characteristics of functions in that area. It is termed ROM policy (Dutch acronym for Physical planning and Environmental Policy) because integration with Physical planning is the main strategy to address these locally concentrated environmental problems.

At first sight, this strategy should be in the domain of local or regional government that seems to be in the best position to formulate and implement policy for local and regional use. However, by not only developing this new, third type of Environmental Policy, but at the same time selecting the areas where it will be applied, the Ministry set the priorities as central policy. Designation therefore has much of a national distribution rationale behind it. Moreover, as financing has to come mainly from central state funding, dependency is clearly present.

The ROM strategy aims at the following:
— to develop integrated views on the environmental quality desired in the area and the measures that will realise that quality.

— to quicken implementation of environmental policy by bundling resources of the (economic) actors and authorities involved.
— to make use of specific regional possibilities
— to involve environmental management directly into plan making and
not only set constraints.
— to create a policy community that carries the plans by allowing every
one involved to participate

The strategic integration of several plans (mostly on the level of the
Province) leads to an "Operational Plan" made up by a "project team". As
conflict of interests in such a team may not lead to consensus, a "direction
team" with representatives of State, Province and a few municipalities may
take over. The national Cabinet will decide in case of a draw.

Area oriented policy is oriented at the same time towards immediate
implementation. This means, that actors that participate in investments
(the producers) in that area have a prominent position. Policy coordination between public and private partners is the main aim. According to
Scharpf (1978) succes of policy coordination depends on (a) interdependence of actors and (b) on the possibility to gain by yielding to coordination. Not every municipality will gain by solutions, and in the case that
many economic actors are involved, not everyone of them will gain; in
this last instance, a corporatist structure will be the solution to smoothen
the decision process.

In the case of the Guelder Valley a Valley Commission has been
created with a long list of participating authorities, institutions and organisations. Two Provinces, Associations of farmers, water boards, sewer-
age boards, a small local government representation, trade and industry,
Union of Countryside Women Organisations, banks, environmental pressure groups and the Guelder Agrarian Youth Organisation took part in
deliberations and decision making on the Operational Plan. Apart from
two seats for environmental pressure groups all participants belong to the
agricultural policy community. Even then it has proved very difficult to get
all of them united around this Plan, that has known an indefinetaly number of versions. Although agricultural production has been safeguarded
as far as possible, farmers have to retreat from the full and uncondion-
ally exploitation of a large stretch of rural areas adjoining valuable nature
and landscape areas (Veluwe and Utrechtse Heuvelrug). Growth has been
curtailed and nature zones will reconnect large natural landscapes. The
solution for agriculture is sought in concentration in the centre of this

area. Large scale farms, able to invest in environmental measures are to take over production there. Elsewhere less contaminating forms of agriculture will be allowed, but it is clear that the small farmers there will loose out. A main stumbling block is still the money that will be given to farmers for a move to the new concentration area. A second barrier will be the decision making on all the new physical plans to be made by the muncipalities to detail the Operational Plan for their own rural territory. There, in the Councils will again be opposition from farmers, although a process to commit all municipalities to the Operational Plan has been concluded in April of this year. The financing depends partly by the possibility to change land use to other purposes, able to pay off the farmers. There even has been a plan to allow big residential estates in this area to provide the money. This already has been denied by local councils, that have not been able to cater for local housing need.

In conclusion, the long, weary process towards consensus in the Guelder Valley seems not to be completely in vain. Ideas of change have been mobilised. But the fact that participants were nearly restricted to the agricultural policy community is clearly reflected in the Operational Plan

Although officially aiming at an "integrated view" and "everyone involved" participating, the whole process is clearly biased by a focus on the survival of agricultural production in the region. The project group has taken up its job in direct relation to central government policy. The regional concept for this area was preeminent. The Guelder Valley (although situated between Randstad and the "Half way zone" of cities) is indicated as "open space", hence its functions are agriculture, nature, open air recreation etc. To guarantee implementation of a plan to clear the area of contaminating types of agricultural production, cooperation has been mobilised exclusively in agriculture and agribusiness. The compromise found and adopted as solution is that small farms will be replaced by large farms, able to invest in measures that preclude emissions etc. Manure processing would be dealt with collectively. To keep the amount of production, agriculture will be rearranged in large scale enterprises, through heavy investment in these farms and the surrounding infrastructure.

The idea that this "open space" is in fact part of an "urban field" that has high potential for development (Hoekveld 1990) is kept from the agenda that is in the hands of agricultural interest. The regional organisation that materialised from the ROM initiative produced reification of the chosen regional concept of "open space" in the functional delimitation of areas for large scale agriculture, nature and recreation. Alternative economic development in conjunction with the "urban field" (which in fact is taking place as the area is under urban pressure) is kept from the decision making process.

## 5. Conclusion

The question whether the state is retreating has been taken up from institutional perspective. In the cases we presented, it rather seems that the state is taking back some of what it had handed over earlier. The institutionalisation at European level that was well developed in agriculture lost some of its effect as well. National institutions resumed their main function as pressure groups.

Is it possible to generalize this finding to other sectors of European policy making? Of course, that question cannot be answered here. At least it can be stated, that judging from its share in the European budget, agriculture has been, and still is, a major sector of policy. Secondly, an institutional approach seems the right way to evaluate European development beyond pure speculation.

With respect to the regional level it can be said, that often decentralisation looses pace because sectoral organisations at state level compete successfully for power. Territorial decentralisation has often to compete with functional decentralisation. This detracts influence from regions.

## References

Barlow, I.M., 1991, *Metropolitan Government*. London, Routledge.

Buckwell, A.E., Harvey, D.R., Thomson, K.J., 1982, *The costs of the Common Agricultural Policy*, Croom Helm, London.

Commission of the European Communities, 1991a, *The development and future of the CAP; reflections paper of the commission*. Communication of the commission to the Council. COM (91) 100. Brussels: The Commission.

Commission of the European Communities, 1991b, *The development and future of the CAP; follow-up of the Reflections Paper — Proposals of the Commission*. COM (91) 258. Brussels: The Commission.

COPA, 1991, *COPA proposals on the future of the Common Agricultural Policy.* Brussels, COPA.

Council of the European Communities, 1992, Communication to the press. 6539/92.

Economist, The, 1992, *Grotesque; a survey of agriculture.* Issue 12 december.

Frouws, J., 1988, *State and society with respect to agriculture and the rural environment in the Netherlands.* [In:] J.Frouws and W.T. de Groot (eds.) *Environment and agriculture and agriculture in the Netherlands.* Leiden, Centrum voor Milieukunde mededelingen nr.47

Groenendijk, J.G., 1991, *Deciding and implementing limits to agricultural land-use; an interorganisational perspective on the solution to environmental problems in The Netherlands.* [In:] Oort, G.M.R.A. van, L.M. van den Berg, J.G.Groenendijk and A.H.H.M. Kempers (eds) *Limits to rural land use.* Wageningen, Pudoc.

Groenendijk, J.G. (ed.), 1992, *Landbouwpolitiek in alle staten; hervorming van het Gemeenschappelijk Landbouw Beleid onder MacSharry.* Verslag doctoraal excursie Politieke Geografie september 1992. Amsterdam, Instituut voor Sociale Geografie.

Harvey, D., 1989, *From managerialism to entrepreneurialism: the transformation in urban governance in late capitalism.* [In:] "Geografiska Annaler" 71 B pp 3–17.

Hoekveld, G.A., 1990, *De Gelderse Vallei; een regionaal-geografische benadering.* Utrecht, Fac. Ruimtelijke Wetenschappen.

Johnston, R.J., 1989, *Environmental Problems: Nature, Economy and State.* London and New York, Belhaven Press.

Krasner, S.D., 1989, *Sovereignty: An Institutional Perspective.* [In:] J.A. Caporaso, *The Elusive State,* Newbury Park, Sage.

Meester, G., 1986, *De groene zorgen van Europa; drie studies over het EG landbouwbeleid.* Diss. Wageningen.

Milward, A.S., 1992, *The European Rescue of the Nation State.* London, Routledge.

Murphy, A.B., 1993, *Emerging Regional Linkages within the European Community: Challenging the Dominance of the State.* [In:] Tijdschrift voor Economische en Sociale Geografie, vol 84,2 pp. 103–118.

Netherlands Scientific Council for Government Policy, 1992, *Ground for choices; four perspectifs for the rural areas in the European Community.* Den Haag: SDU.

Phillips, P.W.B., 1990, *Wheat, Europe and the GATT; a political economy analysis.* London: Pinter.

Scharpf, F.W., 1978, *Interorganisational policy studies.* [In:] K. Hanf and F.W. Scharpf, *Interorganisational policy making,* pp. 345–370. London: Sage.

Taylor, P.J., 1993, *Contra Political Geography.* [In:] Tijdschrift voor Economische en Sociale Geografie, vol 84 2, pp 82–90.

Jean-François Langlais
Université Laval
Québec

# DE LA REGION EN MOUVEMENT AU MOUVEMENT COOPERATIF; LE CAS DU MOUVEMENT DES CAISSES POPULAIRES DESJARDINS

## 1. Entrée en matière

Les trois types de régions telles que les présente Antoni Kukliński se définissent comme suit:

— Les régions *innovatrices*, qui intègrent efficacement l'esprit innovateur et d'entrepreneurship nécessaires à la création de technologies, de produits, de nouveaux modes d'organisation et de gestion. L'occurrence de ce type de région dans chaque période historique donnée est plutôt rare. (caractère avant-gardiste)

— Les régions *adaptatives*, qui ont pour caractéristique de composer avec le changement, en vue d'utiliser adéquatement les mécanismes de diffusion et d'innovation pour optimiser les ressources économiques, politiques et sociales mises à leur disposition, assurant un équilibre

économique propice à la production d'un développement durable, sur une longue période. (caractère réactionnaire)
— Les régions *de type «Scansen»*, dont les mécanismes de restructuration sont dysfonctionnels; on y observe une paralysie des systèmes qui entraîne de graves retards technologiques, économiques, sociaux et politiques.

L'examen théorique des caractéristiques respectives des trois types de régions, présentées dans ce modèle, nous permet de constater qu'il est possible d'établir une analogie entre celui-ci et la grille d'analyse de Talcott Parsons. En d'autres termes, les caractéristiques propres à chaque type de région peuvent être considérées dans l'optique des quatre dimensions systémiques élaborées par Parsons, soit l'adaptation, la latence (*latency*), l'intégration, et la poursuite de buts (*goal attainment*). Ces quatre dimensions interagissent en temps normal dans un état d'équilibre dynamique et dans un rapport de complémentarité. En outre, elles doivent nécessairement être présentes toutes les quatre pour assurer l'existence d'un système, grâce à la coordination de ses activités internes et externes. Considérant chaque type de région comme „l'idéal théorique" d'une réalité existante, il nous est possible de les traiter individuellement en tant que systèmes (dans l'acception parsonnienne du terme) normalement constitués, en vue de mettre en évidence les aspects importants de chacun de ces types. Dans cette perspective le trait marquant de la région innovatrice semble être la dimension de la poursuite de buts, qui tiendrait alors lieu d'instance structurante, sous laquelle s'organiseraient les autres fonctions. Dans le cas de la région dite «adaptative», la dimension la plus importante serait celle de l'adaptation, étant caractérisée par la recherche des facilités de fonctionnement du milieu environnant et l'adaptation en fonction de ce contexte. Quant aux régions de type «Scansen», l'instance qui semble leur faire défaut est celle de l'intégration, qui assure normalement le contrôle et la coordination des activités et fixe les finalités internes du système.

Nous verrons plus loin que, dans cette logique, la coopération intervient à titre d'organe de régulation, pouvant entre autres raffermir les mécanismes d'intégration, chargés d'assurer la cohésion interne du système et d'en organiser les ressources en vue de permettre l'effectivité de la poursuite de buts. D'une façon plus générale, la coopération peut être envisagée comme un instrument de développement qui prend ses racines dans un milieu, apparaissant en réaction à un problème donné sous la pression des forces en présence dans ce milieu, et dont l'objectif (*Goal Attainment*) concorde avec celui des individus ou des groupes composant ce milieu.

## 2. La coopération

A partir de la problématique de „région" énoncée par Kukliński, le développement régional devant être endogène, autonome et différencié, comment se situe le mouvement coopératif et quel rôle doit-il adopter ? La nature des coopératives telle que la définit Laidlaw en fait:

> „*Un groupe de personnes, grand ou petit, engagé dans une action commune fondée sur la démocratie et l'effort propre afin de se livrer à des activités économiques ou de services utiles et bénéfiques pour tous ceux qui y sont associés.*"[1]

Tout en faisant de cette définition une référence souple et adaptable aux formes multiples que peuvent adopter les coopératives dans un milieu donné, Laidlaw considère que certaines caractéristiques constitutives de leur *essence* doivent nécessairement être présentes pour les qualifier ainsi. Ces caractéristiques sont:

— La propriété et l'autorité démocratique;

— La notion associationniste, mise en rapport avec le rôle accordé au sociétariat qui règle l'activité de la coopérative. Cette condition représente le présupposé de l'existence de la coopérative, établissant le statut des utilisateurs des services comme „membres" plutôt que comme clients.

— Les méthodes, qui bien qu'elles soient fréquemment similaires à celles des entreprises capitalistes dans leur aspect commercial et leurs objectifs de rentabilité, ont pour finalité ultime une satisfaction toujours plus grande des besoins des utilisateurs et non l'accumulation de richesses devant profiter à un nombre restreint d'individus.

Dans cette perspective, la taille de la coopérative n'apparaît pas comme un élément déterminant pour la distinguer, quoiqu'un plus grand nombre de sociétaires pose différemment le problème de l'exercice de la gestion démocratique.

Les principes de l'exercice coopératif, si on se réfère à l'énoncé qu'en a fait Colombain en 1976 sont: 1) la solidarité et l'engagement mutuel;

---

[1]*Les coopératives en l'an 2000*, A.F. Laidlaw, p. 28.

2) l'égalité et l'exercice de la démocratie; 3) la gestion de service; 4) l'équité et la proportionnalité; 5) le développement et l'éducation. Prenant en considération ces lignes directrices, nous constatons immédiatement l'adéquation entre les besoins en développement de la „région" et la pertinence de la coopération en tant qu'instrument de ce développement.

Bien sûr, la coopérative peut, à l'intérieur de ces limites, prendre différentes formes, en accord avec les exigences du milieu dans lequel elle opère et des activités qui légitiment leur existence.

D'un point de vue théorique, Laidlaw relève également l'occurrence de crises cycliques que rencontrent les coopératives, les identifiant au nombre de trois: crises de crédibilité, de gestionnaires et d'idéologie. La première crise correspond au moment du démarrage de la coopérative, et s'explique par la difficulté qu'elle éprouve à obtenir une reconnaissance de son existence et de son bien-fondé par les populations auxquelles s'adressent ses activités et par les instances politiques et les élites en place, qui tendent à douter de la viabilité de telles entreprises. La seconde crise concerne les gestionnaires de la coopérative, qui trop souvent sont des gens de bonne volonté, mais ne disposant pas des compétences et des qualifications nécessaires pour administrer une entreprise commerciale. Ce problème s'est traduit dans bien des cas par des échecs financiers sérieux ou la disparition pure et simple de coopératives. La troisième et dernière crise qu'identifie Laidlaw est une crise qu'il qualifie d'„idéologique". En regard des transformations que subit le monde à l'heure actuelle, il nous est possible d'exprimer des doutes quant à la façon dont le mouvement coopératif doit s'adapter aux nouvelles réalités et s'insérer dans les mécanismes de fonctionnement en place. Plusieurs auteurs ont revendiqué le droit aux coopératives d'être en quelque sorte les clefs de voûte d'un projet de société nouveau, fondé sur les principes généraux de la coopération. A ce propos, Claude Beauchamp précise le détail des enjeux d'une telle problématique en distinguant deux formes de coopération, soit le mouvement coopératif et l'institution coopérative. Le mouvement coopératif est envisagé dans cette perspective comme un mouvement social à caractère réformiste, dont le discours et les pratiques tendent vers l'établissement d'une forme d'organisation économique et sociale entièrement nouvelle. L'institution coopérative quand à elle serait une forme d'organisation économique aspirant à s'intégrer de façon fonctionnelle dans le système déjà en place, proposant à ses utilisateurs

„l'alternative coopérative", mais ne prétendant en rien altérer ce système par ses activités.

Nous verrons plus loin dans quelle mesure le Mouvement des caisses populaires Desjardins s'inscrit dans ces définitions de l'essence, des principes et des crises qui caractérisent l'existence coopérative. En réduisant la dimension de ce champ d'observation, nous allons maintenant tenter d'esquisser un portrait d'ensemble de la coopération au Québec.

Celle-ci s'est développée, principalement depuis le début du siècle, en relation avec le nationalisme canadien-français et la religion catholique. Très présente au Québec au moment de l'émergence de la coopération, la religion était déjà le support d'une doctrine sociale pouvant aisément être conciliée avec le discours coopératif naissant. En effet, la plupart des formes de soutien économique ou matériel accordées aux individus et aux familles étaient prodiguées par l'Eglise ou par les congrégations religieuses. Souvent associée à la religion, la coopération sera également liée au nationalisme, en raison des conditions dans lesquelles elle fera son apparition. En effet, la coopération au Québec, comme dans la plupart des cas, est issue d'un malaise, d'un stress structurel (*structural strain*) comme le qualifie Smelser, en raison duquel on considère qu'elle s'inscrit dans un mouvement de réaction d'une collectivité aux conditions d'existence dans lesquelles sont confinés ses membres. La naissance du coopératisme apparaît dans le cas présent comme un mode d'action qui découle d'une idéologie à caractère nationaliste, comme un moment de prise en charge d'une communauté par elle-même.

Cette pression résulte en grande partie de l'émergence et de l'expansion du contrôle du capitalisme de monopole sur les marchés québécois. D'abord contrôlés par les financiers Canadiens anglais, qui se voyaient avantageusement positionnés par rapport aux marchés britanniques, les pôles de ce capitalisme de monopole se sont progressivement déplacé vers les Etats-Unis. Mais la dépendance des Canadiens français envers cette forme de contrôle persiste. Cette concentration des capitaux aux mains des financiers anglophones et l'absence de ressources financières à la disposition des petits entrepreneurs laisse ceux-ci aux prises avec une concurrence inégale au profit de la grande entreprise. L'agriculteur ne dispose pas, pour sa part, des moyens lui permettant d'acquérir de meilleurs outils de production et se trouve captif d'un marché largement dominé par des intermédiaires dont la mainmise n'est contrebalancée ni par des syndicats, ni par des coopératives.

Voyons plus en détail le contexte dans lequel s'établit cette dynamique. En 1901, le Québec compte 80% de francophones, 15,9% de citoyens d'origine britannique et environ 10,000 amérindiens. Les plus fortes concentrations urbaines se retrouvent à Québec et à Montréal (60,6%), alors que près des deux tiers de la population vit en milieu rural. La société québécoise est à cette époque considérée comme rurale, bien qu'une forte poussée d'industrialisation absorbe dans les villes une grande partie des surplus démographiques de la campagne. Par ailleurs, le Québec accuse à ce moment un sérieux retard sur le plan social, l'industrialisation et la concentration des capitaux ayant laissé les populations urbaines dans un état de pauvreté à l'encontre duquel aucune mesure sociale étatique n'avait été mise en place.

Les instances politiques prônent pour leur part un „libéralisme" en lequel elles fondent l'espoir de voir éclore et fructifier les investissements qui permettront l'implantation d'une industrie florissante, dont les effets assureront la prospérité des habitants. En outre, les politiciens canadiens-français ne détiennent qu'une faible voix au chapitre des enjeux politiques de l'ensemble du pays, les Canadiens anglais bénéficiant d'un poids démographique supérieur leur conférant une représentation plus importante sur la scène politique nationale.

Au Québec, le clergé catholique, quant à lui, entretient une vision „conservatrice" de la société, dans laquelle dominent des valeurs traditionalistes, prônant la résignation plutôt que la promotion d'initiatives et d'idées nouvelles. Les élites intellectuelles détenant une certaine visibilité sont à cette époque assimilées au clergé, soit qu'elles en fassent elles-mêmes partie ou qu'elles y soient étroitement associées intellectuellement.

En élargissant du secteur coopératif à la société dans son ensemble, nous tenterons maintenant d'exposer brièvement, dans une rétrospective à caractère historique, les débuts de la coopération dans le développement de la société québécoise.

Après une période de prospérité au XVIIIè siècle, les conditions de vie au Québec se dégradèrent considérablement au cours du siècle suivant, tant en milieu urbain qu'en milieu rural. C'est dans ce contexte qu'on assiste à l'éclosion de nombreux mouvements sociaux à caractère associationnistes, dont certaines initiatives coopératives. Parmi ces dernières, plusieurs prenaient leur source idéologique à la doctrine socialiste, mais sans l'appui du clergé, qui tenait cette doctrine pour suspecte, elles ne purent acquérir la reconnaissance institutionnelle nécessaire pour assurer leur survie. Un autre facteur qui jouait à leur désavantage est leur caractère urbain et ouvrier, alors que la pierre angulaire du développement et de la préservation de l'identité canadienne-française de l'époque était la terre, la survie de la culture et de la langue lui étant fortement associées.

Les premières coopératives qui connurent un succès véritable firent leur apparition sous des formes inspirées des modèles européens déjà existants (comme les caisses Raiffeisen), empreints des valeurs du catholicisme social européen, et obtenant de ce fait l'approbation de l'Eglise au Québec. En 1907, le clergé met sur pied l'Action Sociale Catholique, institution dont les activités sont principalement axées sur l'éducation populaire et qui accordera par la suite son soutien au développement des coopératives. C'est à ce moment que le mouvement coopératif québécois prendra véritablement son essor.

Le fondateur des caisses populaires auxquelles il a donné son nom, Alphonse Desjardins, s'intéressait déjà depuis plusieurs années aux conditions d'existence dans lesquelles vivaient les Canadiens français lorsqu'il obtint le poste de sténographe français à la Chambre des communes à Ottawa. Cette position lui offre un point de vue privilégié, d'où il constate dans toute son ampleur le problème que pose le manque d'organisation économique et sociale des classes populaires et l'impossibilité pour elles d'avoir accès au crédit à des conditions acceptables. En effet, les banques, pour la plupart sous le contrôle de capitaux britanniques, offraient à cette époque des services financiers d'abord aux commerces et aux industries, et ensuite aux clients pouvant offrir des garanties. Les représentants des classes laborieuses, tels que les agriculteurs, les artisans, les ouvriers et les petits commerçants n'avaient d'autre choix que de se tourner vers des prêteurs d'argent privés qui leur fixaient souvent des taux d'intérêts usuraires. Desjardins, qui s'intéresse d'abord au mutualisme, puis à la coopération, effectue des recherches, se documente, établit des correspondances avec plusieurs coopérateurs européens, pour finalement élaborer un modèle de caisse populaire applicable au contexte de la Province de Québec de l'époque. Son projet coopératif peut être envisagé dans la perspective plus large d'un projet de société, visant à développer le sens de l'épargne, cette épargne qui, accumulée dans une communauté, pourrait ensuite servir à répondre aux besoins en crédit des membres de la même communauté, et ce par l'intermédiaire d'une coopérative demeurant la propriété de ses utilisateurs.

On reconnaît, à travers ce principe, les bases d'une action répondant aux critères primordiaux énoncés par Antoni Kukliński quant aux nécessités du développement des régions, c'est-à-dire un processus endogène, autonome et différencié.

En premier lieu, chaque caisse populaire est fondée, sur une base locale, à la demande de ses citoyens, ceux-ci en devenant les propriétaires-usagers et élisant parmi eux les administrateurs de la caisse, répondant ainsi à la nécessité d'un développement endogène. En second lieu, observant le principe de l'autonomie, chaque caisse, étant démocratique et décentralisée, est responsable des orientations qu'elle donne à ses activités par le biais des décisions prises par ses membres.En troisième lieu, ce sont les sociétaires qui décident des orientations de la caisse et qui déterminent les activités et les services à offrir en fonction de leurs besoins. Puisque la composition du sociétariat tend à refléter celle de la population issue d'une région donnée, les orientations spécifiques de chaque caisse se traduiront par un développement différencié selon les régions. On constate que les impératifs du développement régional, (tels qu'ils sont envisagés par Kukliński) sont rencontrés dans ce mode d'action. Ainsi, le projet initial de Desjardins vise à donner aux masses populaires les moyens d'organiser leurs efforts pour parvenir à une meilleure situation socio-économique. Près d'un siècle plus tard, examinons maintenant ce qu'est devenu ce projet et son évolution dans le temps.

## 3. Le Mouvement Desjardins

A l'heure actuelle, le Mouvement des caisses Desjardins compte 5 millions de membres, ce qui correspond à environ 2 Québécois sur 3, et détient un actif de 52 milliards de dollars. Ces sociétaires sont issus de toutes les couches de la population et utilisent les services d'un réseau de 1327 caisses populaires et d'économie, plus 152 caisses populaires hors Québec. Ces caisses sont regroupées en 11 fédérations, plus 3 fédérations hors Québec, soit en Ontario, au Manitoba et en Acadie. Un palier confédératif chapeaute toute cette organisation, avec mandat d'établir les orientations générales et de coordonner les activités du Mouvement. A ces structures s'ajoute une caisse centrale qui gère de façon centralisée les liquidités du réseau. Trois sociétés de portefeuille sont détenues par le Mouvement. La première, la Société financière des caisses Desjardins offre des services d'assurances générales, d'assurance-vie, de fiducie, de crédit industriel et de vente de valeurs mobilières. La seconde est formée de sociétés d'investissement, qui ont la charge d'acquérir une participation dans diverses sociétés par actions par l'entremise de sociétés filiales. Enfin, la Société de services regroupe diverses branches s'occupant de sécurité, de cartes de crédit, de traitement de paie informatique, etc...

Dans cette organisation d'une complexité croissante, la caisse populaire demeure la base des processus décisionnels. L'agencement interne des instances qui la composent, soit la commission de crédit, le conseil de surveillance et le conseil d'administration est demeuré le même au fil du temps, bien qu'il ait connu quelques modifications reflétant les réalités nouvelles dans lesquelles opèrent les caisses. La commission de crédit a pour mandat principal d'évaluer les demandes de crédit faites par les membres, le conseil de surveillance voit pour sa part au bon fonctionnement administratif et au respect des règlements légaux dans l'exercice financier de la caisse, alors que le conseil d'administration préside aux grandes orientations et à l'établissement des politiques de fonctionnement de la caisse.

Une description détaillée du rôle du Mouvement Desjardins en tant que moteur de développement économique et social pour la „*région québécoise*" devrait tenir compte des différences propres à chaque région et de l'apport respectif de chaque caisse en relation avec ces disparités.

Dans ses grandes lignes, ce développement s'est accompli à l'intérieur des transformations d'un „double rapport" comprenant d'une part la centralisation administrative et d'autre part, la décentralisation décisionnelle, cette dialectique étant observable lors de chaque période de l'histoire du Mouvement Desjardins. En plus de l'évolution de ces enjeux relevant de la dynamique interne du Mouvement, nous verrons également, à travers cette histoire, les modifications de ses rapports avec les différents contextes socio-économiques au sein desquels le Mouvement a évolué.

La première caisse populaire est fondée par Alphonse Desjardins à Lévis le 6 décembre 1900. Le cadre d'action qu'il fixera pour les activités des caisses est la paroisse, qui était considérée à cette époque comme l'unité idéale de référence spatiale et sociale, à l'intérieur de laquelle tous les membres de la communauté étaient connus les uns des autres. Dans cet espace social limité, les instances politiques, administratives, religieuses, économiques et sociales formaient en quelque sorte un noyau autour duquel gravitaient les autres paroissiens. Les dirigeants de la caisse étaient ainsi au fait de la situation économique et sociale des autres membres de la communauté, ce qui leur permettait, entre autres, d'évaluer leurs qualités morales avant de consentir à ce que la caisse leur accorde un prêt.

En plus de s'appuyer sur la paroisse, la caisse populaire telle que l'avait conçue Desjardins devait s'appuyer sur la famille, tous ses membres pouvant en faire partie. C'est dans cette foulée que les femmes ont vu leur rôle dans l'unité familiale se transposer dans les activités de la caisse, assumant là aussi un rôle de soutien. C'est ainsi qu'on retrouve, dès la fondation des premières caisses, des femmes occupant le poste de gérantes sans pouvoir en arborer le titre, la loi ne leur concédant pas, à cette époque, le droit à cette reconnaissance.

A ce moment, les valeurs sociales véhiculées par l'Eglise s'expriment assez bien à travers les politiques de crédit des caisses populaires et l'encouragement à l'épargne. Le recours au crédit n'est alors permis que pour un usage productif et l'épargne était considérée notamment comme une façon de favoriser la tempérance.

En plus d'être le véhicule de valeurs sociales, la caisse populaire favorisait la cohésion sociale par ses activités. En effet, par l'intermédiaire de la caisse, les actions des représentants des diverses classes sociales dans la paroisse tendaient à se concerter en vue de l'amélioration générale des conditions de vie de l'ensemble de la communauté. Puisque les autorités sociales locales, à commencer par les curés, étaient invitées à participer à la fondation et à l'administration des caisses, cette pratique contribuait à établir un rapport de complémentarité, et non d'opposition, avec les représentants des classes moins bien nanties. En effet, on constate dès les premières fondations de caisses une forte participation des élites locales et du clergé.

La croissance du nombre des caisses connaîtra une progression plutôt lente dans les débuts, les premières années pouvant être considérées comme expérimentales. Desjardins s'occupait alors de fonder lui-même des caisses dans les paroisses où il était invité. Au démarrage plutôt lent des premières années succédera un engouement de plus en plus grand, de sorte qu'il devra s'entourer de collaborateurs qui lui prêteront leur concours pour s'occuper de la fondation des caisses. A son décès, en

1920, 140 caisses étaient en activité sur les 187 qui avaient été fondées. Les fermetures de caisses étaient attribuables en grande partie à la fragilité des bases sociales sur lesquelles elles s'étaient établies. Reprenant la typologie des crises élaborée par Laidlaw, on peut considérer que la première crise, celle de la crédibilité, sera assez aisément surmontée, surtout grâce à l'implication des membres du clergé, qui par leur participation à la propagande, à la fondation et à l'administration des caisses, rassuraient les populations quant au sérieux de l'entreprise.

La première crise économique que devront affronter les caisses survient en 1921 et se poursuivra tout au cours de cette décennie, ébranlant les bases encore fragiles du projet de Desjardins. Plusieurs caisses connaissent des difficultés financières; certaines sont même dans l'obligation de cesser leurs activités ou de les suspendre pour des périodes allant parfois jusqu'à plusieurs années. A la suite de ces circonstances, l'Eglise exprimera des réserves dans son soutien aux caisses, manifestant des craintes quant à leur stabilité économique. Sous l'effet combiné des difficultés de gestion dues à la formation insuffisante des administrateurs, du manque de crédibilité auprès de la population, et des pressions attribuables à la conjoncture économique de crise, le développement des caisses connaît une période de latence, qu'on peut rattacher, toujours en référence aux crises de Laidlaw, aux premier et second type, soit de crédibilité et de gestionnaires.

Suivra de 1925 à 1929 une période de forte croissance économique qui accélérera le processus d'industrialisation au Québec, entraînant du même coup une accélération de l'urbanisation et une présence toujours plus massive des capitaux étrangers dans l'économie du Québec. Cette période est également caractérisée par une forte spéculation financière, qui contribuera à édifier le climat d'instabilité économique qui donnera lieu peu après à une seconde crise économique encore plus importante.

Cette seconde crise, provoquée par le Krach boursier de 1929, suscite un éveil de la part des élites politiques et du clergé et une prise de conscience de l'importance des caisses populaires face aux défis que posait le développement du Québec. Confrontées à un marasme économique qui se prolongera pendant plusieurs années, les caisses populaires apparaîtront, aux lendemains de la crise, comme un instrument providentiel pour le salut économique des Québécois. A compter de ce moment, le processus de fondation de nouvelles caisses reprit et atteignit son apogée vers 1937–1938. Parallèlement à ces facteurs d'influence extérieurs qui se sont exercé sur les caisses et en ont affecté la progression et la diffusion, un mouvement de structuration interne a graduellement transformé la morphologie du réseau Desjardins.

Les caisses populaires, tout à fait indépendantes les unes des autres jusqu'en 1920, commencèrent alors à coordonner leurs activités dans un cadre structuré, avec la formation d'une première union régionale à Trois-Rivières. Cette nouvelle instance assurait les fonctions de coordination, de contrôle, de diffusion et de sécurité des activités des caisses. L'Union Régionale officiait sous la direction d'un conseil d'administration formé de dirigeants délégués par les caisses populaires membres de cette union. Un tel projet n'avait toutefois pas suscité l'enthousiasme de tous les dirigeants de caisses, certains d'entre-eux percevant cette nouvelle entité comme une menace à l'autonomie de leur caisse, entre autres en raison de la formation d'un service d'inspection chargé d'assurer la surveillance de leurs activités.

Les Unions régionales adoptèrent tout naturellement comme critère de délimitation géographique le diocèse, prolongeant ainsi le mode de répartition paroissial adopté par les caisses. D'autres unions régionales furent fondées, se dotant de caisses régionales pour concentrer leurs liquidités et ainsi renforcer leurs assises économiques. A ce deuxième palier s'en ajoutera par la suite un troisième, complétant la structure du Mouvement telle qu'elle existe aujourd'hui.

En 1932, une fédération provinciale est créée à Lévis, avec pour mandats principaux l'inspection et la propagande des caisses populaires en collaboration avec les unions régionales. Cette initiative résulte au départ d'une exigence du gouvernement du Québec, qui refusait autrement d'accorder des subsides aux caisses pour favoriser de nouvelles fondations et étendre le réseau· déjà établi. La création de ce nouveau palier administratif rencontra des objections de la part des opposants à la centralisation mais permit aux caisses d'assurer de façon autonome leur inspection, sans ingérence du gouvernement. Il n'en demeure pas moins que le gouvernement voulait transiger avec une seule instance centrale considérée comme le seul interlocuteur responsable pour le réseau entier.

Ce processus de hiérarchisation structurelle est allé de pair avec une série de modifications des statuts juridiques reconnus aux caisses et à ces instances. D'abord régies par la loi des syndicats coopératifs de 1906, les caisses possédaient en outre leurs propres statuts et règlements, maintes fois amendés par la suite, notamment en ce qui a trait à l'inspection, aux règles de fonctionnement et d'administration et aux conditions d'admission des membres.

Le sociétariat était composé à l'origine principalement d'agriculteurs, l'implantation des caisses étant beaucoup plus poussée dans le monde rural qu'en milieu urbain. Cet équilibre se renverse toutefois progressivement de sorte que la diversité des occupations des membres augmente peu à peu avec l'augmentation du nombre de caisses urbaines.

La diversification et la multiplication des institutions de services qui ont donné lieu à l'organisation du Mouvement Desjardins que nous connaissons maintenant s'est effectuée progressivement, sous l'effet de besoins ressentis par l'une ou l'autre composante du Mouvement.

Au cours de l'évolution du Mouvement, plusieurs générations de dirigeants se sont succédé aux postes de direction. Certains anciens dirigeants, rencontrés dans le cadre d'un projet de recherche visant à constituer un fonds d'histoire orale sur la base de témoignages rapportant leur vie et leur carrière au sein du Mouvement, ont rendu compte de ces changements. Ils reconnaissent généralement trois moments importants dans l'histoire des gestionnaires. En premier lieu, les fondateurs, qui durent travailler souvent à contre-courant des idées reçues de leurs époques pour faire valoir les qualités de leur projet. Pourvus de moyens restreints, d'appuis politiques et économiques difficilement acquis, leur rôle en est principalement un d'information et de propagande. La seconde génération est celle des bâtisseurs, qui reprenant l'héritage laissé derrière eux par les fondateurs, le firent fructifier et multiplièrent les efforts pour assurer au Mouvement une expansion et une consolidation des éléments déjà en place. Quand à la dernière génération, celle qui assure en ce moment même la direction des opérations du Mouvement, aucun nom n'a encore pu leur être donné. La plupart des anciens dirigeants rencontrés conçoivent leur rôle comme tout aussi important que les précédents, consistant à guider sur sa lancée le Mouvement déjà pleinement développé et à ajuster et adapter les services et activités qu'il offre à ses membres aux changements de leurs besoins et en fonction du contexte socio-économique dans lequel ils évoluent.

## 4. Des régions à la coopération

En regard des critères élaborés par Laidlaw concernant les principes coopératifs et l'essence de la coopération, le Mouvement Desjardins rencontre de façon satisfaisante le titre de «coopérative». Si on se replace dans le processus de son évolution, il semble être parvenu au stade de la crise «idéologique», qui correspond selon Laidlaw à une remise en question des modalités de son fonctionnement reliée à une incertitude quant aux finalités de son action. L'existence d'une telle crise serait attribuable à l'ambivalence des rapports qu'entretiennent les coopératives avec le milieu dans lequel elles opèrent. En effet, bien qu'elles entretiennent un statut distinct dans l'espace économique qu'elles partagent avec diverses autres formes d'organisations financières, les coopératives, devant la nécessité d'assurer leur survie et leur rentabilité économique, doivent emprunter diverses pratiques et idées en usage chez les entreprises capitalistes concurrentes. Il en résulte une culture d'entreprise hybride, dont les systèmes normatifs et les référents culturels sont plus difficiles à identifier, tant pour les usagers des services que pour les individus qui y oeuvrent et qui les administrent.

Cette expérience de coopération, sans être envisagée comme un modèle à reproduire, possède certaines caractéristiques „exportables" qui pourraient probablement enrichir la démarche des banques coopératives polonaises et s'appliquer à la résolution de certains de leurs problèmes spécifiques.

De nombreux problèmes tendent à faire surface au coeur des remous causés par la vague de mondialisation qui déferle sur le monde à l'heure actuelle. Cette mondialisation se présente aux régions sous de multiples facettes — économique, culturelle, politique, sociale, etc — qui modifient la dynamique interne du fonctionnement des régions de même que les conditions du milieu dans lequel elles évoluent. Ces transformations requièrent de nouvelles façons de penser le développement régional, la conception de nouveaux instruments de recherche permettant la compréhension des changements en cours et éventuellement la mise au point de solutions aux problèmes en émergence. Dans ce contexte, la coopération apparaît comme un outil de développement privilégié pour les régions, comme le cas du Mouvement des caisses populaires Desjardins, par les caractéristiques de son évolution, nous a permis de le démontrer.

# Bibliographie

Beauchamp C., 1991, *Défis et enjeux de la coopération québécoise*. Communication présentée au Colloque Rerum Novarum. Université Laval.

Bellefleur M., Levasseur R. et Rousseau Y., 1993, „*La libéralisation du crédit dans le mouvement des caisses Desjardins*". *La culture inventée. Les stratégies culturelles aux 19e et 20e siècles*. Québec, Institut québécois de recherche sur la culture, pp. 211–229.

Boily Y. Martel D. et Morin A., 1991, *Projet d'appui aux banques coopératives polonaises. Plan d'opération*. Lévis, Société de développement international Desjardins.

*Desjardins 1992. Brochure institutionnelle.* Confédération des caisses populaires et d'économie Desjardins, Vice-présidence Coordination stratégique et financière.

Boily Y. et Morin A., 1990, *Projet d'appui aux banques coopératives polonaises. Etude de faisabilité*. Lévis, Société de développement international Desjardins.

Desroche H., 1961, *Coopération et socialisme. Eléments sociographiques du secteur coopératif polonais. Extrait de: Archives Internationales de Sociologie de la Coopération, no III (juillet–décembre 1960)*. Paris, Bureau d'Etudes Coopératives Communautaires, 50 p. (Coll. „Centre de Recherches Coopératives E.P.H.E.", fasc. 9).

Desroche H. (éd.), 1963, *Planification et volontariat dans les développements coopératifs. Quinzaine d'études (15–27 janvier 1962) organisée par le Collège Coopératif — Paris, sous la direction de Henri Desroche*. Paris, Mouton et Co, 422 p. (Coll. „Recherches Coopératives", T. III).

Desroche H., 1992, *Le projet coopératif à l'Ouest, à l'Est et au Sud: situations mutantes*, Coopératives et Développement, vol. 22, no 2 (1990–1991), pp. 13–31.

*En Perspective. Bulletin économique.* Confédération des caisses populaires et d'économie Desjardins, Direction Etudes économiques et stratégiques, vol. 2, no 3 (mars 1992), 12 p.

*Evolution des structures juridiques et financières de Desjardins, 1900–1989*. Lévis, Confédération des caisses populaires et d'économie Desjardins du Québec, 1989.

Fisera J., 1964, *Syndicalismes ouvriers et planifications socialistes*. Extrait de: Archives Internationales de Sociologie de la Coopération. (janvier–juin 1964). Paris, Bureau d'Etudes Coopératives Communautaires, 50 p. (Coll. „Centre de Recherches Coopératives E.P.H.E.", fasc. 21).

Gorzelak G. et Kukliński A. (éd.), 1992, *Dilemmas of regional policies in Eastern and Central Europe*. Warszawa, University of Warsaw, European Institute for Regional and Local Development, 512 p. (Coll. „Regional and Local Studies", no 8).

Kowalak T., 1976, „*La coopérative d'épargne et de crédit en Pologne" et „Les fonctions économiques et sociales de la coopération d'épargne et de crédit en Pologne contemporaine". Les institutions coopératives d'épargne et de crédit dans le développement économique et social*. Actes de la rencontre internationale de Montréal, octobre 1975. Lévis, La Fédération de Québec des Caisses populaires Desjardins, pp. 105–112, 288–296.

Levasseur R. et Rousseau Y., 1992, *L'évolution des bases sociales du Mouvement des Caisses Desjardins. Le sociétariat de la Fédération régionale du Centre du Québec*, Revue d'histoire de l'Amérique française, vol. 45, no 3, pp. 343–374.

Levasseur R., 1992, *Vers une histoire sociale du mouvement des caisses populaires Desjardins en Mauricie: de 1909 à nos jours*, Coopératives et Développement, vol. 22, no 2 (1990–1991), pp. 167–178.

Levesque D., 1991, *L'expérience coopérative québécoise: émergence, essor, diffusion du mouvement coopératif québécois*, Coopératives et Développement, vol. 21, no 1 (1989–1990), pp. 183–223.

Levesque B., 1991, *Les coopératives au Québec: deux projets pour une société distincte. Communication présentée à la Chaire inter-universitaire de coopération*. Université Catholique de Louvain.

Mink G., 1993, *Pologne. Crise politique et «national-moralisme». L'Etat du monde 1993*. Annuaire économique et géopolitique mondial. Paris, Editions La Découverte/Boréal, pp. 211–215.

Poulin P. *Histoire du Mouvement Desjardins*. T.2 [...] 1921–1944. A paraître.

Poulin P., 1990, *Histoire du Mouvement Desjardins. T.I: Desjardins et la naissance descaisses populaires, 1900–1920*. Montréal, Québec/Amérique, 373 p. (Coll. „Desjardins").

Rudin R., 1989, „*Class and cooperatives: The struggle for control within the caisses populaires of Québec, 1900–45*. Canadian Papers in Business History. Victoria, British Columbia, The Public History Group, vol. I, pp. 153–188.

Soule V., 1993, *Europe centrale. Hongrie, Pologne, Tchéco-Slovaquie. L'Etat du monde 1993*. Annuaire économique et géopolitique mondial. Paris, Editions La Découverte/Boréal, pp. 496–499.

Stanek O. (éd.), 1993, *Le vertige de la liberté. Essais sur la Pologne postcommuniste*. Rimouski, Université du Québec à Rimouski, Groupe de recherche interdisciplinaire en développement de l'Est du Québec, 220 p. (Coll. „Actes et instruments de la recherche en développement régional", no 10).

Vienney C., 1961, *Vers une analyse économique du secteur coopératif. Extrait de: Archives Internationales de Sociologie de la Coopération, no III (janvier–juin 1960)*. Paris, Bureau d'Etudes Coopératives Communautaires, 204 p. (Coll. „Centre de Recherches Coopératives E.P.H.E.", fasc. 5).

Yves Hurtubise
Université Laval
Québec

# DES COMMUNAUTES ACTIVES: LA CONTRIBUTION DE L'ORGANISATION COMMUNAUTAIRE

Avec un taux de chômage de plus de 12% et un nombre d'assistés sociaux qui voisine les 900,000 personnes,le Québec vit des années difficiles. Les crises successives qui secouent notre société (comme toutes les sociétés occidentales d'ailleurs) appellent une certaine modestie, sinon une modestie certaine, dans la formulation de solutions aux problèmes sociaux. L'échange que nous poursuivons entre partenaires européens et nord-américains doit être pensé dans les termes d'un partage de réflexions sur des problèmes similaires dans des contextes différents.

En me situant dans une perspective multidisciplinaire, je voudrais présenter quelques idées sur l'intervention sociale et son rapport avec le développement des régions en illustrant le tout à l'aide d'extraits d'une enquête récente. On voudra bien y voir, non pas un modèle à reproduire, mais une expérience à interroger.

Avant d'entrer dans le vif du sujet, trois remarques préliminaires permettront de situer ce propos. La première se rapporte à la définition du concept de „région" dont il m'apparait qu'il faille prévilégier le vécu qu'il représente plutôt que l'univers technocratique auquel il sert de référent. La seconde remarque est à l'effet que la question régionale n'a de sens qu'en fonction des besoins et désirs (aspirations) des gens qui y habitent; en ce sens, elle est bien davantage qu'une unité territoriale à partir de laquelle le système de production peut s'arrimer. La question régionale est aussi une question politique (c'est là la troisième remarque) au sens où elle dévoile le projet de société sous-jacent à sa formulation.

# 1. Le service social et l'organisation communautaire

Dans le monde anglo-saxon, le service social prend une coloration particulière; il ne vise pas que les «oeuvres» ou le «support économique des plus démunis»; il se définit comme une profession dont l'objet est la relation personne-milieu.

Une des composantes de cette profession est l'organisation communautaire dont l'objet particulier est l'analyse et l'intervention sur les problèmes sociaux collectifs. Ce mode d'intervention a été développé chez nous, au début des années soixante, au moment où nos gouvernements lançaient une audacieuse opération de planification rurale désignée sous le nom de BAEQ (Bureau d'Aménagement de l'Est du Québec). Une des particularités de cette opération était d'associée la population des villes et des villages au processus de planification même. Les résultats de cette opération sont intéressants du point de vue qui nous préoccupe ici:

— expérimentation d'un modèle d'intervention communautaire qui allait avoir des répercussions importantes sur la profession du service social,
— développement de formes modernes de formation civique,
— développement d'une conscience régionale,
— développement d'un leadership régional.

Les modèles d'organisation communautaire sont mieux connus aujourd'hui: l'action sociale rend compte des pratiques de revendications sociales, la planification sociale rend compte des efforts pour rendre les services publics plus efficaces, les développement local, celui des pratiques endogènes de développement.

Les rôles d'un organisateur communautaire sont diversifiés. Ils sont fonction du cadre de travail de l'intervenant (agit-il dans un groupe

autonome ou dans une institution?). Ils sont fonction également, et surtout, des problématiques abordées. Dans tous les cas, il semble se dégager cinq rôles pour lesquels l'intervenant est formé par nos universités:
— la mobilisation des forces vives d'un milieu,
— la médiation entre ces mêmes forces,
— la formation des citoyens à l'action collective,
— la liaison entre les associations et les institutions,
— le rôle de personne ressource qui cherche, décode et transmet l'information utile à l'action.

## 2. L'organisation communautaire en CLSC

Le CLSC (Centre local de services communautaires) est une organisation définie sur une base territoriale dont le mandat est de fournir des services de santé et des services sociaux de base par une approche multidisciplinaire. Près de cent cinquante centres ont à leur emploi près de 350 intervenants communautaires. La population est associée à ces centres par une représentation aux conseils d'administration. A l'origine, elle était également impliquée dans l'élaboration des programmes d'intervention.

A l'occasion d'une recherche récente concernant l'évolution de l'organisation communautaire en CLSC, nous avons pu faire un certain nombre de constats utiles à la réflexion poursuivie par le présent colloque.

## 3. Le contexte général d'une nouvelle dynamique sociale

Dans le contexte des années 80–90 à la différence des années 60–70, les mesures protectrices de l'Etat ne sont plus vues comme des mesures de redistribution sociale, mais plutôt comme un fardeau financier porté par les classes moyennes pour soutenir certaines couches de la population en voie d'exclusion du marché du travail et de marginalisation sociale.

Le marché du travail se divise de plus en plus en deux sphères:
— à une extrémité, une sphère performante, intégrée dans une économie mondialisée, bien rémunérée et dont les travailleurs sont mieux protégés: c'est la place dévolue aux grandes entreprises couvrant

des secteurs en progression comme celui de l'informatique, celui des communications, certains secteurs de l'Etat;

— à l'autre extrémité, une sphère dite non performante, constituée par des activités non liées à la haute technologie, souvent précaires et faiblement rémunérées, services de proximité s'adressant aux personnes et aux communautés, services de nature plus locale.

Cette ré-organisation du marché du travail accentuerait le retour du développement inégal entre régions et le clivage entre groupes de travailleurs car les grandes entreprises ne créent plus d'emplois en nombre suffisant; le secteur public a perdu sa fonction intégratrice; le travail précaire augmente de façon constante par rapport au travail régulier; les quartiers populaires des villes s'enfoncent dans la détérioration et certaines régions dans le sous-développement[1]. C'est dans cet espace que se déploient les efforts des communautés locales, du mouvement populaire et communautaire, de l'organisation communautaire et des CLSC.

## 4. Les caractéristiques de cette nouvelle dynamique sociale.

Quelle analyse nous suggère l'évolution du mouvement populaire et communautaire à l'intérieur de ce nouveau paysage socio-économique? D'abord, que nous assistons progressivement à *un déplacement du lieu des enjeux*. Dans les années 60–70, l'enjeu de la mobilisation allait vers l'Etat dans la double construction d'un Etat-nation (sous la poussée d'un mouvement pluri-classiste d'affirmation nationale) et d'un Etat social (l'Etat-providence) sous la poussée d'importantes demandes sociales. Dans les années 70–80, la mobilisation s'est morcelée en autant de groupes qu'il y avait d'intérêts catégoriels. Tandis qu'aujourd'hui, les référents étatiques et les espaces nationaux semblent en perte de vitesse au bénéfice de l'espace local comme cadre de vie, comme unité d'action, et de l'espace régional comme cadre de référence ou d'appartenance (Gagnon et Klein, 1991). La société fragmentée par la crise se reconstruit aujourd'hui plus qu'hier par le bas, par les communautés locales, par les régions: ۷

*Dans cet univers déboussolé, l'économie-territoire apparaît comme une alternative de développement plus contrôlable que*

---

[1] Tendance qui se généralise et qu'on retrouve dans la plupart des pays d'Europe et aux Etats-Unis. Voir B. Droz et A. Rowley (1992).

*l'économie-monde. C'est sur le terrain local que les mutations sont les moins difficiles à maîtriser et les partenariats les plus faciles à susciter.* (Dommergues, 1988: 26)

**Ensuite, le développement local comme stratégie qui renouvelle l'action collective des groupes communautaires et des CLSC**[2] n'est pas, ou est de moins en moins, le lot exclusif des régions d'économie-ressource (comme le JAL dans le Bas du Fleuve, ou le village de Guyenne en Abitibi). Le développement local a pris racine dans des économies de régions intermédiaires et de centres urbains de taille moyenne; il n'est plus le lot des seuls vieux quartiers populaires dans un grand centre urbain comme Montréal. Il est sorti de sa concentration géographique au sein de la pauvreté rurale des régions excentriques et de la pauvreté urbaine des quartiers populaires des centre-villes.

Enfin, le développement local s'inscrit dans des **démarches de partenariat interinstitutionnel** où la «coopération conflictuelle» est de mise (Laville, 1989: 309–339). Ici trois remarques s'imposent. D'abord, le partenariat est partie intégrante d'une approche de développement local. On ne voit pas très bien comment on pourrait faire du développement local sans de larges alliances. Ensuite, le partenariat ne se confond pas avec une forme quelconque de «corporatisme» car il s'agit de pratiques peu planifiées, très souvent dues aux efforts revendicatifs des communautés locales en direction de l'Etat plutôt que l'inverse, et de pratiques qui n'excluent pas le conflit entre les différentes forces existantes au sein des communautés concernées. Enfin, ces pratiques ne tentent pas de faire converger de façon obligée les intérêts de tous dans un même projet social mais bien plutôt d'assurer la survie de micro-territoires menacés (Hamel et Klein, 1991: 235).

Cette nouvelle dynamique pose des défis de type nouveau comme la gestion rigoureuse d'entreprises, des efforts d'auto-financement, la création de réseaux économiques d'information, de promotion de services.

---

[2]Voir à ce propos l'aval donné par la Fédération des CLSC au développement local dans l'article de J. Beauregard dans le *CLSC Express* de juin–juillet 1990, vol. 3, no 5, p. 5 et intitulé „Les CLSC s'engagent dans la lutte à la pauvreté". Ce bulletin est une publication officielle de la FCLSC. Il y est expressément affirmé que „La Fédération des CLSC du Québec suggère la tenue, au cours de l'année qui vient, d'un forum majeur, panquébois, **portant sur le développement local dans toutes ses dimensions** et souhaite s'associer à des partenaires socio-économiques québécois de même niveau pour s'assurer de sa réalisation... A l'instar du Conseil des affaires sociales, les CLSC reconnaissent que l'emploi... est un instrument essentiel pour prévenir la pauvreté...".

Bref, les communautés locales et le secteur communautaire, que ce soit par le développement local ou par la participation à des régies régionales ou autrement, sont objectivement inscrits dans une nouvelle dynamique sociale où ils tentent à leur manière de **résoudre la crise des formes traditionnelles d'engagement de l'Etat.** Sous la pression directe et indirecte venant des communautés locales, des régions et des mouvements, **l'Etat s'est en effet vu obligé de concéder certaines tâches de gestion du social et du socio-économique (urbanisme et logement, formation professionnelle et employabilité, développement local, santé et services sociaux).** Ce qui n'efface pas pour autant le leadership étatique dans la détermination du cadre général de gestion de ce social. D'où l'idée que ce social se bâtisse autour d'une démarche de partenariat.

Les organisations populaires et communautaires et l'organisation communautaire des CLSC sont donc à l'intersection de la relation Etat-société civile, de la relation communautés locales-développement et de la relation entre l'«économique» (la micro-économie à tout le moins) et le «social». Nous pouvons y ajouter: dans le cadre d'un nouveau contrat social en voie de se constituer au niveau des entreprises (entre le patronat et les syndicats), au niveau des régions (entre les municipalités et l'Etat central), au niveau des quartiers et des régions (entre les citoyens, leur communauté locale et l'Etat), au niveau de l'environnement (entre les communautés locales, l'Etat et les entreprises). Bref, à l'intersection du «local» et du «global».

Cet effacement conjoncturel de l'action sociale et cette montée du développement local et du partenariat s'inscrivent dans l'ensemble des mutations en cours dans les mouvements sociaux, anciens et nouveaux, contribuant ainsi à les faire sortir de la fragmentation créée par la crise et les faire participer à la construction de nouveaux compromis sociaux (Lipietz, 1989: 15–66). Les jeux ne sont pas faits et ce processus est encore relativement jeune et fragile. Comment s'explique cette évolution inattendue, cette construction lente de nouveaux compromis sociaux?

Disons d'abord qu'il y a eu l'initiative d'acteurs sociaux qui ont su modifier leur position défensive, notamment de nouvelles générations d'intervenants qui ont su développer une capacité d'intervention. Celle-ci n'était ni prévue, ni peut-être prévisible. Ensuite, certains ont commencé à remettre en question l'approche traditionnelle héritée des années 70, décennie identifiée aux dix «glorieuses» de la mobilisation et du changement social, sorte de décennie-référence, de décennie qui définit le changement social. Or, après-coup et avec une certaine distance, on se rend bien compte que les années 70 ont vu se transformer une action revendicative efficace en une stratégie d'action collective très défensive et très souvent perdante pendant les années 80, car elle était centrée trop exclusivement sur la demande sociale étatique. Troisièmement, il faut enregistrer une modification substantielle de l'attitude d'une partie des classes dirigeantes tant au plan économique que politique. Avec la fin des années 70, les institutions liées à l'Etat et les classes dirigeantes ont commencé à perdre de leur assurance dans la résolution des problèmes sociaux. Les années 80–90 sont une période d'incertitudes et de recherche de nouvelles avenues, une période d'élaboration de nouveaux compromis entre groupes sociaux face à la gravité d'une crise économique, sociale, écologique.... Période où tout n'est pas tracé d'avance, période où les institutions ont une attitude plus contradictoire, et par là plus ouverte à des formes nouvelles de relations avec les autres composantes de la société.

Notre enquête confirme une diminution de l'intensité des formes d'action communautaire de type «action sociale» et confirme également le développement relativement stabilisé d'un travail communautaire de type «planning social» (implantation de services pour des clientèles-cibles). D'où la conclusion que certains peuvent avoir tiré à l'effet que les CLSC sont de moins en moins des acteurs de changement social.

En revanche, nous avons pu observer et voir se manifester l'émergence de pratiques nouvelles de lutte contre la pauvreté qui redonnent de la vigueur à des communautés locales et viennent renforcer le caractère socio-communautaire de plusieurs CLSC. Dans le chapitre précédent, nous avons parlé de la montée de la stratégie de «développement local»[3] en dehors de ces milieux «naturels» d'éclosion, les milieux ruraux. En effet, une étude rapide de la vingtaine de corporations de développement communautaire (CDC) et de corporations de développement économique communautaire (CDEC) existantes depuis quelques années, a permis de confirmer l'implication directe, à des degrés divers, d'organisateurs communautaires de CLSC dans la majorité de celles-ci, et la mise en

---

[3]Pour une caractérisation de l'«action sociale», du «planning social» et du «développement local», voir Laval Doucet et Louis Favreau, 1991, p. 5–34.

oeuvre d'une stratégie de développement local dans des milieux fortement urbanisés[4].

En deuxième lieu, la montée d'un partenariat public/communautaire, voire public/privé/communautaire — partenariat pris ici dans son sens le plus large d'addition des forces vives d'un milieu — qui est très souvent dû à l'initiative des CLSC et de leurs organisateurs communautaires. Ce phénomène a pris beaucoup d'ampleur ces dernières années, ce que confirme l'étude récente de Panet-Raymond et Bourque (1991).

En troisième lieu, le soutien au démarrage de groupes d'entraide communautaire, mais de type nouveau, groupes considérés d'abord et avant tout comme des lieux de rencontre et d'échange et seulement occasionnellement comme des lieux de secours et de dépannage. Mieux, les groupes d'entraide et les réseaux primaires peuvent, aujourd'hui plus qu'hier, être considérés comme „des lieux privilégiés de micro-politisation" en plus de représenter „un cadre propice à l'identification de leaders qui pourront être mis à contribution pour la réalisation d'actions plus larges ou plus difficiles" (Turcotte, 1992).

## 5. Conclusion

Le colloque a ouvert des pistes de réflexion intéressantes sur beaucoup de questions liées au développement des régions. L'intervention sociale planifiée est un type d'intervention qui peut apporter des résultats tangibles en terme de développement d'une identité, de moyens de résister à la paupérisation et à l'exclusion sociale. Nous espérons que les présentes réflexions sauront être utiles pour le développement d'une vitalité démocratique.

---

[4]Voir à ce propos Louis Favreau et William Ninacs (1992), „Le développement économique local communautaire au Québec", *Coopératives et développement*, vol. 23, no 2, p. 115–123.

# Bibliographie

Dommergues, P. (sous la dir.), 1988, *La société de partenariat (économie-territoire et revitalisation régionale aux Etats-Unis et en France)*. Afnor-Anthropos, Paris.

Droz, B. et A. Rowley, 1992, *Histoire générale du XXe siècle*. Tome 4, Seuil/Histoire, p. 231–251.

Favreau, Louis et Yves Hurtubise «CLSC et communautés locales: la contribution de l'organisation communautaire», Laboratoire de recherche de l'Ecole de service social, Université Laval, Québec.

Gagnon Christiane et Juan-Luis Klein, 1991, „Le partenariat dans le développement local: tendances actuelles et perspectives de changement social", *Cahiers de géographie du Québec*, vol. 35, no 95, p. 239–255.

Hamel, Pierre et Juan-Luis Klein, 1991, „Partenariat et territoire: vers une nouvelle géographicité du social?" *Cahiers de géographie du Québec*, vol. 35, no 95, sept. 91, p. 233–236.

Laville, Jean-Louis, 1989, „Economie et solidarité: trois axes de développement et de recherche" in LEVESQUE, B., A.

JoyalL et O. Chouinard, *L'autre économie, une économie alternative*. PUQ, Sillery, p. 309–339.

Lipietz, Alain, 1989, *Choisir l'audace*. Ed. La Découverte, Paris.

Panet-Raymond, Jean et Denis Bourque, 1991, *Partenariat ou paternariat? (la collaboration entre établissements publics et organismes communautaires oeuvrant auprès des personnes âgées à domicile)*. Ecole de service social, Université de Montréal, 175 p. plus annexes.

Bogdan Kacprzyński
European Institute
for Regional and Local Development
Warsaw

# THE EUROPEAN REGIONAL DEVELOPMENT SCHEME AND THE POST-SOCIALIST TRANSITION PROCESS

The leading idea of the work that has been conducted since long ago in the European Commission was elaboration of certain principles which could constitute a reference system for the conduct of direct policies of spatial development. Such a reference system should account for the perspectives of development of Europe, for its future policies in other domains and for its internal organisation.

The European scheme of regional development (called SEAT in short) was elaborated within the framework of activities conducted by the European Conference of Ministers responsible for Spatial Development (this body being called CEMAT for short) of the Council of Europe. The scheme was presented during 8th session of the CEMAT in 1988 in Lausanne by Mr. Nicolas Momper, the secretary of the institution responsible for spatial development in the Grand Duchy of Luxemburg (Schéma..., 1991). According to the opinion of Ms. Catherine Lalumière, Secretary General of the Council of Europe, this scheme is conform to the activities of the Council of Europe, aiming at establishment of an equilibrated and stable development that would observe the human rights and the principle of social justice (Schéma..., 1991, p.6).

SEAT is constituted by a set of goals of spatial development of countries and regions belonging to the EC, considered to be the goals of European importance, such as, for instance, growth poles, zones of transboundary integration and transport infrastructure of highest priority. Simultaneously, it is a reference system for all the public and private decision makers, and in particular for the regional and local governments and authorities, which are vested with taking of location decisions. It is thought that such a scheme should constitute an aid in making of adequate decisions of long-term, strategic character.

SEAT should, by virtue of assumption, be adapted to the current internal situation of the countries belonging to the EC and to the situation of the external environment of the EC, which is composed of all the other European countries and the most economically important non-European countries.

There is a requirement in SEAT stipulating that the countries and regions for which this scheme is valid provide information on location of spatial development elements of European importance and that they feel responsible for introduction into the spatial development, within the areas subject to their authority, of the elements of spatial development having country-wide and regional significance, all this within the framework of general recommendations of the Council of Europe.

The political and economic changes which take place in the countries of Central and Eastern Europe form a new situation in Europe, making it possible to perceive and consider Europe as a whole. Conditions are being established for a new stage of deep transformations encompassing the area of the whole continent, which, in turn, requires preparation of an adequate organisational framework, of adequate policies, of consideration of location and spatial dimensions of problems solved, and even perhaps of creation of a new SEAT which could be acceptable for all the countries and regions.

It should be remembered that the post-socialist transition process which has been taking place for the last few years in Central and Eastern Europe has already partly changed the internal situation of the EC (e.g. the effects of the additional burden on the economy resulting from the cost of restructuration of the former German Democratic Republic), has certainly changed the external situation of the EC in the territories of some of the post-socialist countries, and has first of all changed in a radical manner the perspective of further development of the whole of Europe. This change of the status and of the development perspectives of Europe will have to be accompanied by a change in the scheme of regional development within the EC and of the principles of spatial development in the remaining countries of Europe.

Simultaneously, the lack of consequence in the conduct of post-socialist transition process in some countries of Central and Eastern Europe, as well as lack of true willingness on the side of the EC of introducing the post-socialist countries to the Community entails certain difficulties in forecasting the directions of changes in the economic situation in Europe, and consequently also the difficulties in forecasting of the direction of changes concerning SEAT, as well as the countries in which it would be observed and the degree to which it would be observed.

# 1. The general principles of managing regional development on the scale of a continent

Spatial development is always an extremely complex process. Even in an idealized abstract situation it must be treated as a polyoptimisation process. In Paretian perspective optimal solutions have as a rule the form of sets of equally "good" solutions, so that the preferred action is not defined unambiguously.

Finding of solutions to polyoptimisation problems in complex systems, such as the ones related to spatial development on the scale of a continent, is, as mentioned before, extremely difficult, and it requires undertaking of a number of activities, like decomposition into smaller systems, division with respect to the cost of reaching and implementing solutions (decisions, undertakings) and with respect to time of their validity, these activities making altogether finding of solutions much easier and diminishing the scope of undeterminacy of these solutions.

The consequence of the above is the necessity of forming hierarchical structures of management. Due to the same reasons the significance of coordination of local solutions, obtained after the spatial, temporal and substantial decompositions have been performed, is as high as the very finding of them. It turns also out that, for instance, the post-socialist transition process in the countries of Central and Eastern Europe is taking place in a part of the previously mentioned hierarchical system, which lacks to some extent — or entirely — some links that are meant to coordinate local solutions. This causes that, by assumption, an effective coordination of local solutions in the area of spatial development cannot be carried out.

Taking into account the necessity of performing spatial decomposition the problem of spatial development of the European territory can be considered as the problem of development of a territory within which such units are distinguished as:

1) regions
2) countries  } i.e. various levels of spatial decomposition
3) blocks of countries

and the "central" institution is defined which is responsible for the development of the territory on the level of blocks of countries and of the whole of the continent.

Thereby a system which possesses a hierarchical structure is formed having levels corresponding to (see figure 1):
a) regions,
b) countries,
c) blocks of countries,
d) whole of the continent.

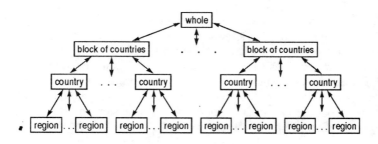

**Fig. 1**

The system referred to contains also horizontal connections between the neighbouring subsystems (regions, countries, blocks of countries), where neighbourhood is understood in terms of:

— geography (these horizontal connections will be referred to as geographical connections), and
— systemic relations, i.e. the resulting connections are implemented through economic cooperation, migrations, trade, cultural and scientific exchange (all these kinds of connections will be generally referred to as trade connections).

In any system of governing (of control) it is necessary to define authority, competency (capacity of making decisions) and the manner of execution of power (i.e. the type of decisions which can be legally taken) for each subsystem, at every level of the hierarchical structure of power (Kacprzyński, 1991).

It is usually thought that lower levels take decisions requiring involvement of a lesser power (e.g. economic power as expressed through the magnitude of allowed outlays), per unit of time, while higher levels take decisions requiring greater scopes of means. In practice, there are more of smaller decisions to be taken than of the greater ones, and smaller decisions are usually related to attainment of tactical goals, while greater decisions are related to attainment of strategic goals.

Such a type of decomposition of the set of tasks connected with the development of a territory makes finding of solutions as well as coordination much easier, but is not always conform to the actual breakdowns of authority among the levels of management structure. Still, giving up of the possibility of segregating tasks and assigning them to decision makers related to appropriate levels of the hierarchical structure of governing the spatial development would significantly hamper or even make impossible organisationally rational functioning, leading as a rule to conflict situations, resulting from the impossibility of compromising excess power and rational use of information. Negative experience of the Polish postsocialist transition process (e.g. conflicts between the voivodship and the communal authorities) provide one more confirmation of the necessity of such classification of tasks.

In a correct situation the responsibility for the decisions made should be proportional to the value of decisions made. The value of decisions is understood here in terms of value of resources engaged in realisation of undertakings encompassed by a given decision.

Decisions made in the domain of development of a territory may concern location of:

— productive and service activities,
— expanding infrastructure,
— new elements of the settlement network,
and may also concern resolution of disputes connected with conflict situations among the users of a given territory, and in particular the disputes related to:
— protection of human environment,
— protection of cultural heritage, of landscapes, of natural resources etc.

It should be noted that horizontal trade relations within the hierarchical structure of power may have quite a significant influence upon the scope of power of regions, countries and blocks of countries (through revenues and taxes, when power scope is measured through outlays allowed, as mentioned before). The power scope can also be changed due to execution of appropriate policies on a higher level, which may determine a special pattern of distribution of means from the budget of this higher level (the level of a country, of a block of countries or of the center itself).

It should be also noted that horizontal geographical connections change much slower than the trade relations, excepting, of course, such situations as war or martial law. Along with economic growth and with introduction of new technologies the significance of trade connections grows quicker than significance of geographical connections, which means that the spatial factor plays presently a decreasing role, due, in particular, to rapidly dwindling transport and communication costs.

The increase of intensity of horizontal connections within the power structure considered here and the increase of power of some levels, resulting from this, causes, in turn, the necessity of amplifying power wielded by the higher levels of the system of hierarchical governing of spatial development in order to preserve the capacity of coordination of decisions in this system. This amplification of power of higher levels is performed, in particular, through enabling higher levels to apply the policy of preferences and subsidies from the central budget with respect to certain subsystems of the lower level (regions and countries).

Simultaneously, it is noticed that intensification of horizontal connections (geographic and trade ones) due to local changes of power of particular links (regions, for instance) located on a given level of the power structure, makes the division of competences among the higher levels of the structure much more difficult. Consequently, certain links of the structure (e.g. regions) may in practical terms be incapacitated, while other ones may be granted a broad autonomy and the possibility of free implementation of any of own plans.

Temporal variability of intensity of horizontal connections would require introduction of a changeable division of competences among the levels of structure responsible for spatial development. This postulate is partly being implemented in practice, but always with a certain delay with respect to the needs of effective coordination, which entails a periodical intensification of conflict situations that cannot be resolved due to lack of adequate competences.

Summing up we can say that every subsystem (region, country, block of countries, "the center") of the hierarchical system of governing the spatial development ought to be described with the following triple (see figure 2):

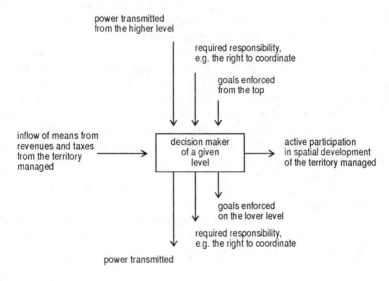

**Fig. 2**

— it disposes of a definite actual economic power (capacity of making respective decisions),
— it is responsible for the decisions made,
— it has definite goals of activity (problems which should be solved by application of the power wielded).

A part of the goals of activity may be enforced together with corresponding power scope, and thereafter coordinated by a higher level of the hierarchical power structure.

It is often so that a subsystem resolves only a part of problems related to the territory which is managed by it (see the selection of goals, mentioned before), and uses for this purpose only a part of the power scope at its disposition, while the unresolved part of problems, together with a portion of power is transmitted to the subsystems located beneath it in the power structure, retaining, of course, the right to coordinate their solutions.

Thereby each subsystem has the scope of power composed of own power resulting from the economic activity of a given area and of the power transmitted by the higher level. Each subsystem can give up, out of own will, a part of the power wielded transmitting this part to the lower level subsystems, while retaining the right to coordinate the solutions adopted by these lower level subsystems.

Each subsystem is solving its own problems, as well as the problems accepted from or enforced by the respective higher level, and it can transmit some of these problems to be solved on the lower level, transmitting simultaneously, as mentioned before, a part of own power. This means that independence of subsystems consists in the freedom of associating goals of activity and problems which it wants to solve by itself with the scope of power which it wants to devote to this purpose.

The subsystems located on lower levels have, as a rule, to accept the problems transmitted to them from the top for solution, and have also to accept the fact of coordination of their solutions by the higher level, irrespective of the scope of additional power transmitted together with these problems (e.g. in the form of budgetary means). This requirement is not an expression of an excessive centralism, but the result of the assumption making it possible to decompose problems (tasks).

## 2. Coordination of spatial development in Europe

In Europe of 1980s there existed a clear structure of power responsible for the development of space, characterised by the fact that the level of the "whole" was lacking, and the level of blocks (EC and CMEA —

Comecon) did not encompass with its reach all the countries of Europe (see figure 3).

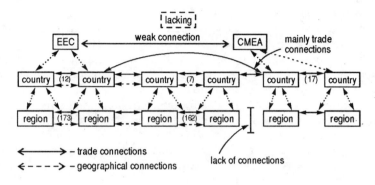

**Fig. 3**

It is worth emphasizing that there existed in the framework of this overall structure the strong horizontal connections within the EC and separately within the CMEA, as well as weaker, but still significant connections of countries remaining outside of the two main blocks with the countries within these blocks (a case to be cited here is Finland).

The horizontal connections on the level of blocks of countries had the nature of treaties, like a disarmament treaty or a treaty on protection of environmental resources.

The European communities have established their central economic power below the threshold of 1.2% of the GDP of the member countries. The goals of the EC block in terms of regional development were:
— equilibrated socio-economic development of the societies of particular regions,
— improvement of the living standard,
— responsible management of the use of natural resources and protection of human environment,
— rational use of the territory (Schéma..., 1991).

Since particular countries and regions of the structure coordinated by the EC have various scopes of own power (this scope depending upon local economic activity, intensity of geographical and trade connections, as well as the level of economic development), clear principles were elaborated of

transmitting parts of power by the higher levels to the lower ones, together
with the corresponding packages of tasks to be solved in parallel with
the relations resulting from the country-wide power structure (Schéma...,
1991, pp. 62–67).

One can observe a tendency towards achievement of a certain equilibrium between the problems which have to be solved by a given subsystem
and the net power that can be devoted to these problems. This equilibrium is the expression of the drive towards achievement of the generally
balanced development within the framework of the EC.

The equilibrium mentioned above does not mean that strong horizontal connection of a given subsystem with other subsystems and high own
revenues resulting from this imply weak vertical connections. There may
namely appear strong vertical connections in the domain of transmission
of problems to be solved and a deeply reaching coordination of solutions
adopted by subsystems with simultaneously existing weak connections in
the domain of power transmitted (the "top" orders something to be done,
while not giving adequate means for this purpose).

It can be assumed that until 1989 the ground rules forming the process
of spatial development in Europe have been as follows:
1) the set of resolutions and recommendations of the Parliamentary
   Assembly of the Council of Europe concerning regional development
   and representing the views of the Council of Europe in this domain
   (Schéma..., 1991),
2) the plans of spatial development which had been previously in force
   in the former countries of the CMEA,
3) the principles of spatial development in force in the countries not
   belonging to the two blocks (especially interesting in Switzerland in
   view of internal structure of power in this country).

The characteristic feature of this European structure (see figure 3)
was, as said, only symbolic presence of the highest level (corresponding to a center, to the whole continent), lack of horizontal geographical
connections between the part of the overall structure coordinated by the
Comecon and rest (the iron curtain effect), and finally also lack of coordination performed at the level of blocks with respect to European countries
which do not belong neither to the EC nor to the CMEA.

In 1989 the CMEA block was liquidated. German Democratic Republic became the element of the structure dependent of the EC, several
countries of the Comecon block started the post-socialist process of tran-

sition, horizontal connections on the levels of countries and regions within the substructure previously subject to the CMEA became looser or broke down entirely, while horizontal trade connections between, on the one hand, the post-socialist countries currently passing through the transition process, and the countries belonging to the EC and the independent countries, on the other hand, became tighter (see figure 4). An additional gap appeared at the level of blocks, making coordination of actions in the domain of rational development of European space virutally impossible or at least very difficult indeed.

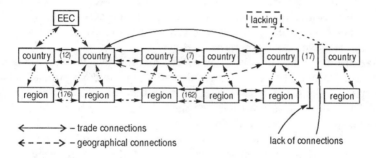

**Fig. 4**

It can presently be assumed that the current ground rules shaping spatial development in Europe are:

A) the European scheme of regional development, representing the views of the Council of Europe in this domain (with no essential changes in comparison with the previous years),

B) the remainders of the regional development plans previously in force in countries belonging to the Comecon (if new principles were not explicitly formulated then, due to inertia of the present authorities, the previous ground rules are still being kept to without greater changes), though there is no block-level coordination among particular countries and regions within countries (Szlachta, 1993),

C) new regulations which were introduced after 1989 (not too many of them, and the partial and stage-wise only, concerning, for instance, regions affected by ecological catastrophes, regions affected by catastrophic levels of unemployment, border regions, or the transport network), see (Rybicki, 1993).

Presently, due to rapid changes of the structure of trade connections, of power structure and of the scope of power itself, appropriate shifts must take place on all the levels of hierarchical structure with respect to the structure of authorities responsible for regional development, together with appropriate changes in the very principles of development of space.

A proposition can be forwarded that we are witnessing presently a process of uncontrolled rapid convergence of the first two principles of spatial development, and that of these two schemes the dominating one will be the scheme elaborated within the EC, as better adapted to the principles of market economy and of democratic state, although it remains a great unknown how will this dominating scheme account for the effects of changes taking place in Central and Eastern Europe, whose ultimate outcome is as yet not determined.

We are undoubtedly observing a deep quantitative change taking place under the influence of controls resulting from respective policies in some countries of the former CMEA. This deep quantitative change is accompanied by the qualitative one, this fact giving the right to speak of the true transition process (Kacprzyński, 1991).

The quantitative change consists in the decrease of power of central authorities and in transmission of a part of this power, together with respective responsibility, down to the level of regions and even lower, to the local substructures. Coordination of regional and local solutions, though, has not been brought to attainment of the necessary efficiency, which makes it impossible to conduct, for instance, restructuring economy in the regions of ecological catastrophe, or finding of solution to the question of restructuring agriculture, or provision of water of adequate quality, or finally finding of solutions to the very important question of dramatic unemployment levels (Rybicki, 1993).

The qualitative change consists in liquidation of the centrally directed planned economy and replacement of this rejected model by the one of market economy.

The analysis of evolution of the structure of capital and labour productivity, conducted for 138 branches of the so called socialized economy in Poland indicated the appearance of large structural changes after 1989 and then the return towards the structure as of 1989, which would mean that the transition process in this domain stopped at an instant of time. It can

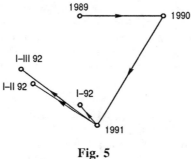

Fig. 5

be estimated that this fact took place in 1991 (see figure 5), Kacprzyński (1993a).

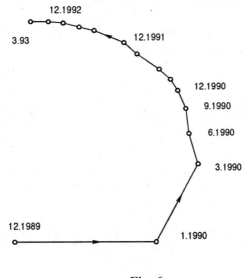

Fig. 6

The analysis of evolution of the spatial structure of unemployment indicates that rapid changes in this structure terminated in the middle of 1990, and that the changes which occurred later on had the nature of seasonal moevements, with the continuing increase of the percentage share of unemployed labour force. This abrupt termination of changes in spatial unemployment structure allows also to formulate the proposition postulating that the post-socialist transition process in Poland may have stopped or even terminated altogether already in the middle of the year 1990 (figure 6), Kacprzyński (1993b).

Taking these two indications jointly one can conclude that the post-socialist transition process stopped or ended in Poland in the period between the middle of 1990 and the middle of 1991, when actual appearance of the capitalist system without capital occurred, charged with all the deficiencies of the situation of hardly accessible investment credits and lack of turnover capital, these two making it impossible to quickly overcome the economic crisis.

# 3. The European transition process

Let us call the whole constituted by the recently quoted points A), B) and C) the European transition process in the domain of spatial development, since this is undoubtedly the greatest of possible changes of qualitative and quantitative nature that took place without triggering off another world war.

The direction and the speed of changes of principles governing regional development in Europe will depend upon the direction of the post-socialist transition process, and, after it would have been terminated, upon the speed of further evolution in the countries of Central and Eastern Europe and upon the reaction of the European "background" composed by the stable, well developed European countries, to these changes. This reaction of the "European background" in the years 1992 and 1993 has been so intense (restrictions with respect to immigrants, economic restrictions with respect to the post-socialist countries) that one is justified in proposing that a European transition process has started for which the post-socialist transition process was the triggering factor (Kacprzyński, 1993c).

The direction of changes in the principles of development of European space will get decided upon in the instant of termination of the post-socialist transition process in Europe, and the speed of changes will depend upon the local speeds of evolution in the socio-economic systems after the post-socialist transition process would have been finished in particular countries, which, however, is not only dependent upon the internal siutation in particular countries, but on the situation in the respective block of countries, this situation making it possible — or not — to eliminate the disproportions of economic power of particular regions.

Economic situation within the block of 12 countries of the EC is being shaped within the broader arena defined by the world sales markets. This situation is quite difficult (there is even talk of the economic crisis in the EC) and it requires undertaking of an additional investment effort aiming at maintenance of the previous competitive capacities of the countries belonging to the EC. This means, in practice, slowing down of the process of integration of the post-socialist countries with the EC, and thereby also slowing down of the process of taking over the European scheme of regional development as the valid one for a part of countries belonging previously to the CMEA block.

In 1989 hopes were incited that each of the post-socialist countries would quickly make up for the delay in development and would be able to face the challenge of Europe of highly developed countries. It quickly turned out to be just to the contrary — the very idea of catching up was a challenge for this Europe and the thus understood Europe has not been at all interested in rapid equalisation of the differences in the development.

The internal situation in the post-socialist countries in which the transition process is going on did not allow giving of a unique answer to the question of the direction of future changes in these countries (Kukliński, 1992). The spectrum of possible and probable options is wide and the wavering policies of the EC are one of the factors of further widening of this spectrum. One thing is certain. In the hierarchical structure of governance over the territorial development the level of the Comecon disappeared together with the horizontal and oblique connections on the two lower levels, these connections having been forced from the top, but regions and countries remained, and their number is even growing. A new internal hierarchical structure must now be established, making it possible to solve greater, supraregional problems (mainly liquidation of conflict situations). In Poland, for instance, an additional level of authority is being planned presently, namely "poviats" (counties), assuming, simultaneously, a decrease of the number of voivodships (provinces, departments). This change will certainly serve the short-term purposes of political nature (getting rid of the rests of the old power apparatus), but it may also limit the excess power of local self-governments, expressed mainly in their opposition to new investment projects meant to satisfy the needs of greater areas, and force these self-governing bodies to use lesser power, true, but in a way much more constructive than during the recent three years.

# 4. The post-socialist transition process and the development of space

The post-socialist transition process in Poland in the domain of development of space consists, as mentioned before, in particular, in the division of power once held by the central authorities of the country among regions (voivodships) and local self-governing bodies (communes), and in the adaptation of the responsibility of persons taking decisions to the scope of (economic) power they hold. This is a new situation. Such a situation could not exist before without a conflict with the doctrine stipulating that the whole power must be wielded from the center, which, however, is not responsible for the decisions taken. All the other levels of the hierarchy should receive from the top that which is necessary for the fulfilment of the plan and then to execute the plan in such a way as not to leave aside any reserves that could be the source of their informal power. As is known, however, such reserves did in practice arise (like, for instance, labour force reserves, land reserves that could be used for investment projects, or the accompanying ivestment projects).

The European developed countries are presently forced by the world leaders of economic growth (USA, Japan) to provoke the appropriate transition processes within their own confines in order to make possible a radical improvement of their competitiveness on the world sales markets.

It cannot be predicted now what will be the relation between the European transition process connected with the consequences of the year 1989 and the European transition process which has to be undertaken in order to respond to the challenge of the world economic leaders. The best solution would be to associate these two processes into one and to form the general European principles of economic and social order at the end of 20th century. In the EC, however, under the pressure of growing unemployment, the option of rapid finalisation of the first transition process may take the upper hand (e.g. in the form of stiffening of the principles of cooperation with the post-socialist countries), connected with intensive realisation of the second (by sharpening of competition with the post-socialist countries on the commodity, labour and capital markets). This would mean, in fact, establishment of another "Berlin wall", though placed a bit more to the East (if not along the Oder-Neisse line then along Bug river) and spanning a much longer distnce. This option seems very probable at present (June 1993), especially in view of the internal economic crisis within the EC, caused by the integration of the German Democratic Republic into the Federal Republic of Germany and by the announcement of the new economic policy of the United States.

The post-socialist countries may, but not necessarily, apply a realistic, moderate policy of challenging the Europe of the developed countries, which would mean enforcing upon own populations the acceptance for:

— a significant effort connected with preparation of conditions making it possible to get integrated with the EC on partnership principles,

— the fact that developed countries would probably like to locate within the areas of the post-socialist countries production of declining industries, thereby setting free within own territory the possibilities for production of innovation (within the framework of the previously mentioned second European transition process),

— outmigration of highly skilled blue collar labour force and inmigration of managerial staff,

— import of products which are not too modern, thereby freeing the market of the EC from the excessive stock of hard-to-sell products, and simultaneously very quickly raising the requirements with respect to local production.

The societies of the post-socialist countries may also follow the populist slogans of some of their leaders, and the boundary with western Europe may become a dividing line to an even greater extent than at present. These countries may happen to decide not to link their economic policies with the world trends (world trends of introduction of innovations) through the intermediary of the EC, but to look for the models of Iranian or Balkan type or to let in the investors from the most developed countries of the world (USA, Japan, Far East countries). In the latter cases there would not exist the necessity of unification of the principles of spatial development policies according to the European scheme, for horizontal connections of geographical and trade types would not be getting intensified.

The regional development policy is always secondary with respect to economic policy, but it may also be inspiring, especially when in a given country there is in reality no economic policy, while the society is adequately developed and knows what to expect within its environment from the self-governing bodies and from the authorities of higher levels. This would mean that the European scheme of development of space could be adopted as a source of inspiration in view of its attractiveness irrespective of trade and geographical connections, though without the coordination with the activities conducted according to the contents of the scheme in the countries of the EC. This is possible, but little probable, in view of the economic crisis ravaging the post-socialist countries. Some activities resulting from the scheme referred here to do not namely have a direct (improving) influence on the gross domestic product value, and therefore also on the speed of overcoming of the crisis, while they require spending of significant means from the budget (like in the case of protection and cleanup of waters of Baltic Sea).

## 5. The future of the European Regional Development Scheme

When analysing the contents of 30 resolutions and recommendations of the Committee of Ministers of the Council of Europe from the period 1967–1990, and of 65 resolutions and recommendations of the Parliamentary Assembly of the Council of Europe from the period 1961–1991, as well as of 96 resolutions and recommendations of the standing Conference of local and regional authorities of Europe from the period 1957–1990, one observes that the same principles, organisational forms, proposed means and methods of solving the problems considered may be applied without particular reservations for the scheme of regional development encompassing the whole of Europe.

The fundamental difficulty, however, is constituted by the excessive disproportions of the state of development of the space, causing different reactions of the regions to the same input having the form of recommendations, indications or even subsidies, as well as by the lack of mechanisms which are necessary for the conduct of relatively uniform policies over the whole territory. One should not forget, neither, of the cumulated conflicts connected with the effects of multiannual negligence in the domains of environmental protection, of the development of the settlement system, of the technical infrastructure as well as organisation of industrial and agricultural production.

In connection with the above the fundamental question appears, namely whether the disproportions mentioned should be liquidated, whether efforts should be made in the direction of adaptation to the scheme elaborated for the situation devoid of such disproportions and negligences, that is — of gaining the necessary means and then only of swift liquidation of these phenomena, still considered as grave deficiencies. This would mean maintenance, at least for some period of time, of the areas ridden with conflicts and negligences, excluded from the operation of the scheme of development of the territories, with simultaneous development of the spatial objects which may quickly bring in stable growth. This, therefore, would in turn mean establishment of a two-tier scale of disproportions: developed countries — developed regions of post-socialist countries on the one hand, and: developed regions of the post-socialist countries — backward regions of these countries, on the other hand.

In the circumstances of the closed economic system adoption of the two-tier disproportion setting is a reasonable solution both from the tactical and the strategic points of view, since it makes possible gaining of means which may then be subject to appropriate redistribution carried out in order to alleviate the intra-national disproportions. International situation does not indicate the possibility of treating the post-socialist countries as an open economic system, for there are no real sources of economic assistance that could support these countries in their efforts aiming at filling of the existing lacunae (e.g. in housing construction).

In practice this would reduce to formation within the post-socialist countries of a polycentric network of the centers of growth being a continuous extension of the western European network, with omission of the backward and conflict-prone areas. In further course of activities the network (the node-and-belt system) could exert influence upon the previously mentioned enclaves surrounded by it, contributing to their gradual liquidation.

The solution in the form of the node-and-belt system has the advantage of being, in a definite approximation, a "transparent" system for the external environment (e.g. obstacles in the form of inadequate infrastructure are being omitted by channeling the activities along the network).

In Polish conditions such a system can hardly be realized technically in view of the collisions with, for instance, the network of surface water bodies constituting the main source of water supply, the dominating direction of winds transporting air pollution, the remnants of former partition of Poland among Russia, Prussia and Austria, the spatial distribution of areas of ecological disasters, of the highest unemployment and the greatest housing shortage. It should be remembered that, simultaneously, this is the simplest manner of connecting the actions on the European scale (along the branches of the network) and the actions of local nature (perpendicularly to the network).

The starting point for the discussion on the polycentric node-and-belt system in the post-socialist countries involved directly in the European scheme of regional development may be constituted by figure 12 presented in the report of ARL and DATAR (Perspectiven..., 1992), see also figure 7 here.

The structure there presented requires, of course, completion considered necessary from the point of view of interested countries and regions within these countries, as well as from the point of view of the greater area constituted by the whole part of Europe not belonging to the EC.

The node-and-belt system can be treated as an expanded system based upon the one formed by the network of transport infrastructure together with its nodes constituted by the developed centers of the settlement network.

The second possibility is to confine oneself to the practice of stimulation of the regional development, tried out in the history of the EC to date. Szlachta and Zawadzki (1993) adopt in their report just such a variant of regional policy in the process of association with the EC. This variant in certainly more advantageous for the post-socialist countries, since with the present criteria it will encompass with its reach the aid from the EC for the whole territories of the post-socialist countries being associated. The unknowns which still remain are: what will be the instant of actual occurrence and whether at that instant the present criteria of regional policy of the Community will continue to be valid (the criteria of granting assistance to backward regions).

A slowdown in the proces of European integration may also activate the idea of establishment of the second EC, on the basis, for instance, of the Visegrad grouping (Kukliński, 1992). This solution is little probable, but it finds a certain objective justification. M.Foucher (1992), in

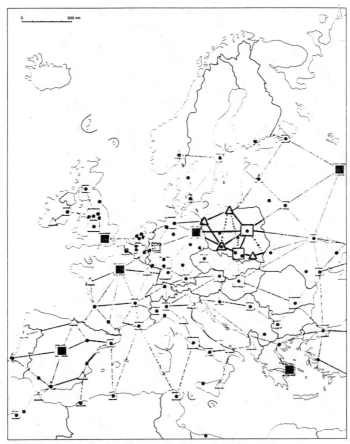

**Source:** *Perspectiven...,* 1992, p. A–28

**Legend:** • City > 500,000 Inhabitants,

◉ Large monocentric agglomeration > 2,000,000 Inhabitants,

▣ Large polycentric agglomeration > 2,000,000 Inhabitants and Conurbations,

△ Development centres of European importance,

— Continental main lines of European importance,

···· Continental main lines of national importance,

**Fig. 7**

particular, considers in this context the setting including such countries as Poland, Bohemia, Hungary and Slovenia.

A full stop to the process of European integration would require consideration of the possibility of resuscitation of the idea of a second CMEA with the present independent states which emerged on place of the countries forming the Comecon in the past. It is held that the transition process in the majority of these countries is either being slowed down by the considerations of political nature (Slovakia, Rumania, Bulgaria), or has in fact not yet been started (countries resulting from the collapse of the former USSR). The economic crisis will, however, force the necessity of undertaking appropriate regional policy, in order to make these countries adequately attractive for the developed countries. It would be bad if such actions were undertaken without any coordination whatsoever on the supraregional and supranational levels.

## Conclusions

The adequate development of the space of European continent requires existence of a power structure making possible coordination of activities with this respect over the whole continent. This results, for instance, from the physical nature of some of the components of human environment (e.g. the mechanism of propagation of air pollutants). Until now such a structure has not existed, although at some period little was needed in order to actually implement this kind of structure (what was lacking was the level above the EC and the CMEA and the non-associated countries).

In the present situation we observe a step backward with this respect, as expressed by the disappearance of the Comecon as the coordinating level, while the EC does not consider it purposeful from its point of view to expand the reach of the coordinating activity of the Community in the domain of territorial development even so as to include just a few of post-socialist countries (Poland, Hungary, Bohemia and Slovakia). It is said to be too costly and too risky for the EC.

It is not possible now to carry out an impartial evaluation whether from the perspective of the EC such a movement would be justified. On the other hand, nothing seems to indicate that the post-socialist countries are themselves on the road towards creation of a supranational structure of coordination of activities in this domain.

What is probable only is the achievement of bilateral agreements, and even that for the limited, local questions, and of multilateral agreements concerning selected projects of infrastructure (motorways, high speed trains,...). The separatistic tendencies in the domain of of spatial economic development may turn out to be in accordance with the separatistic tendencies in the domain of general economic activity, which will altogether slow down significantly the process of economic growth of each of the post-socialist countries.

We can ask the question: how much the common coordination of European space may cost and what will be the advantages accruing for its participants? The cost will most likely be as high as is the cost of assistance extended to the weaker regions of the EC (in particular — Greece, Portugal, Ireland and Spain), increased in proportion to the area covered by the coordinating mechanism. What, then, will be the advantages for the financing, well economically developed countries? Most likely — not lesser than they presently get from the subsidizing of the economically weaker regions of the EC.

For the post-socialist countries, given their current levels of national income per capita, coordination within the framework of the bigger EC may only mean advantage. For the countries of the EC such coordination within the framework of the bigger EC means the repetition of the old questions:

— whether to finance the development along the East-West axis or along the North-South axis (Amoroso..., 1993)?

— whether to assist financially the developed regions in order to promote them as local engines of growth or to decrease the overall development disproportions?

As is known, the spatial reach of geographical connections is much smaller than the reach of trade connections and that is why there are no reasons for linking the European problems of the North-South axis with the problems of the East-West axis. What is observed, on the other hand, is the distinct difference in the possibilities of economic cooperation of the present EC with the countries of Central and Eastern Europe in comparison with the countries located to the South of the Mediterranean, to the advantage of the East-West axis.

With regard to liquidation of the disproportions of the development levels we propose the possibility of considering this question in two stages: first in relation to the previously mentioned distinct node-and-belt system, and only then with respect to the whole areas of particular regions.

The European scheme of regional development is changeable and should be adapted to the shifting situation. It would be good if the situation and the scheme were both changing in the direction considered objectively to be positive. The prerequisites of the policies in the domain of spatial development, declared and implemented until now by the European Commission, can certainly be considered as oriented in just such a positive direction.

# References

Amoroso B., Gomez y Paloma S., Infante D., Perrone N., 1993, *Marginalisation, Specialisation and Cooperation in the Baltic and Mediterranean Region*. Frederico Caffe Centre for Southern European and Mediterranean Studies, Roskilde University (draft).

Cooke P., 1992, *Regional Innovation. Networks: An Evaluation of Six European Cases*. Spetses European Workshop: "Policies and Institutions for the Development of Cities and Regions in the Single European Market", September 24–26.

*Europe 2000. Les pérspectives de développement du territoire communautaire*, 1991 (The perspectives of development of the territory of community; in French). Communication de la Commission au Conseil et au Parlement Européen. Bruxelles, Luxembourg.

Foucher M., 1993, *Une interaction inédite: la France et l'Europe centrale et orientale* (An uncovered interaction: France and the central and eastern Europe; in French). [In:] *Le continent retrouvé*. M. Foucher and J.-Y. Potel, eds. Datar, Éditions de l'Aube, Paris.

Kacprzyński B., 1991, *Polski kryzys, proces przejścia, restrukturalizacja* (Polish crisis, process of transition, restructuration; in Polish). EIRRiL UW, University of Warsaw, Warszawa.

Kacprzyński B., 1993a, *Polska nauka, technologia, restrukturalizacja '93* (Polish science, technology, restructuration '93; in Polish). EIRRiL UW, UNiversity of Warsaw, Warszawa.

Kacprzyński B., 1993b, *Czy postsocjalistyczny proces przejścia w Polsce już się zakończył?* (Has the post-socialist transition process in Poland already ended?; in Polish). EIRRiL UW, University of Warsaw, Warszawa (typescript).

Kacprzyński B., 1993c, *Jeden czy dwa europejskie procesy przejścia?* (One or two European transition processes?; in Polish). EIRRiL UW, University of Warsaw, Warszawa (typescript).

Kacprzyński B., 1992, *Évolution socio-politique dans les pays d'Europe Centrale et de l'Est: repercussions et transformations spatiales et économiques européennes* (The socio-political evolution in the countries of Central and Eastern Europe: European economic and spatial repercussions and transformations; in French). [In:] *Les défis pour la societé européenne à l'aube de l'aménagement du territoire dans une optique de développement durable.* Aménagement du territoire Européen, no. 54, Conseil de l'Europe.

*Perspektiven einer europäischen Raumordnung*, 1992, (Perspectives of a European spatial order; in German). ARL-DATAR, Hannover–Paris.

Rybicki M., 1993, *Kierunki polityki regionalnej w latach 1992–1994* (Directions of regional policy in the years 1992–1994; in Polish). Gospodarka Narodowa, 2 (38).

*Schéma Européen d'Aménagement du Territoire*, 1991 (The European Regional Development Scheme; in French). Conseil de l'Europe, Strasbourg.

Szlachta J., Zawadzki S.M., 1993, *Polityka regionalna w warunkach stowarzyszenia ze Wspólnotami Europejskimi* (Regional policy in conditions of association with the European Communities; in Polish). Gospodarka Narodowa, 2 (38).

Janusz T. Hryniewicz
European Institute
for Regional and Local Development
Warsaw

# REGIONALISATION OF POLAND UNDER CURRENT SOCIAL AND POLITICAL CONDITIONS

## 1. Location of regions in the state political and administrative structure

This paper will discuss proposals concerning the systemic aspects of regionalisation of Poland.

By political status of the region I will understand its situation in the system of state administration, that is the extent of the region's relative independence of or subordination to central authorities. The administrative structure, on the other hand, will mean all of the links and interdependence between the state and the self-government organs.

So far, in the analyses of the problems under discussion the terms region and voivodship have been used interchangeably. This will also be the case in this paper.

The authors of the proposals aimed to solve the regional issue published so far have focused on two problems: a concrete territorial shape of the future regions and their situation in the administrative and political system of the state.

The first intellectual current, extremely colourful and expressive, is most strongly represented by the various resolutions of regional councils saying that a given voivodship, town, is more predestined than any other to become a capital of the future region, e.g. Siedlce or Gorzów (Biuletyny 4/1991 and 2/1991). Further fragments of this paper will be devoted to discussion in more detail of potential conflicts which may result from this.

Generally speaking, any hitherto attempts at situating the region in the country's administrative and political structure may be confined to four proposals mentioned below, which are based on the analyses made by M.Kulesza.

The first one is called an administrative voivodship by the above-mentioned author. Voivodship organs form part of the government administration and are headed by a voivode who also represents the government in political matters. The voivodship has a local council being an organ of the territorial self-government.

The functional voivodship is encountered when certain specific public tasks are distinguished; they are carried out at the voivodship level, e.g. water management, economic activity, roads etc. For implementation of these tasks a separate institution may be set up (independent of the State Treasury), to be headed by a voivode controlled by the board of supervisors. There are no equivalents of this type of solutions in Poland...

A self-governing voivodship is the voivodship which is granted — like the present-day commune — a civil and legal, as well as economic independence. This voivodship is ruled by the voivodship council, while a voivode is the head of the organ responsible for bringing its resolutions into force.

An autonomous voivodship (region) arises when the voivodship authorities are granted legislative powers. This voivodship is governed by a regional government, its political background being the local (voivodship) council (Kulesza, Biuletyn 11/1991).

Poland's economy, or at least its part determining the functioning of industrial civilisation, is linked up by various types of dependence. This has led to emergence of relatively stable groupings having common economic and political interests. Uniformity of sectoral interests is strengthened by a great role of state ownership in the economy; this status quo is unlikely to be altered by large-scale commercialisation of enterprises, that is by transforming them into the State Treasury companies.

Thus, a specific economico-political system has been formed consisting of sectoral solidarity of the enterprises which are able to easily transfer their total economic potential to political capital, which in turn is used to exert pressure on state authorities to enforce decisions advantageous for the given sector but socially disadvantageous, such as reductions, subsidies, exemptions from tax etc.

This system is composed of private and state-owned enterprises, though the latter play a much greater role.

The stability of the system is reinforced by a centralised trade union structure and semi-formal agreements between employers and managers. This reinforcement stems from the fact that the managers of state-owned enterprises and of State Treasury companies, being afraid of confrontation with a centralized trade union movement which is capable of mobilisation on a sectoral scale, have been making attempts to create counterbalance by means of a lesser or greater solidarity of their own group.

Trade unionists and managers alike are interested in the stability of the system because being its member frees one from the market uncertainty and makes it easier to exert joint pressure on state authorities (and both groups are interested in the success of this pressure).

There is no doubt that the economic restructuring and pro-market reforms are opposed by various sectoral economico-political relationships.

In that case, central organs of economic administration are a proper partner for these groupings. Local authorities might be such a partner only in case when sectoral economico-political relationships were destroyed or when the given sector would not go beyond the region. Both cases does not seem likely to happen.

Another problem is the counteracting of entropy by introducing various social classes into the economic and political system.

The activity aimed to achieve this purpose will have to be based on redistribution of means on the scale of regions, sectors or social classes. This involves such phenomena as social services and funds for the requalifying of the employees of the collapsing industrial sectors, towns or even entire regions; a separate problem are the costs of the restructuring of Polish agriculture.

It is very likely that the costs of these undertakings could not be covered by coordination of common economic policy between the interested autonomous regions. The problem is similar as regards the restoration of the natural environment in some regions of the country, e.g. the Sudety Mountains, Baltic sea coast, Mazurian district etc.

This indicates the possibility of emergence of the various types of conflicts between classes, groups and sectors, as well as local conflicts which will overlap and thus may threaten the realisation of public goals and stability of democratic institutions in Poland at present and in the near future.

From the point of view of concrete solutions, this means that the principal economic decisions should be concentrated at the level of central state and economic authorities.

What decisions may be involved here?

Apart from such decisions as taxes, rates of exchange etc., obviously connected with central authorities, they include: privatisation initiative, negotiations with trade unions, social security, supervision of large state enterpises and State Treasury companies, as well as creation of emergency funds (e.g. for restructuring).

This relative concentration of economic power realized by means of sectoral and trade union groups of interest must go hand in hand with appropriate political background. Concentration of political and economic capital under administrative and industrial system simply enforces a centralisation of state power.

The state which is encumbered, among other tasks, with supervision of industrial conflicts, cannot have a smaller extent of control and potential mobilisation of means than analogous possibilities of the groups of interest. The above remarks lead to the conclusion that a far-reaching deconcentration of decision making and decentralisation of state authority is highly inadvisable in Poland at the present stage of advance of industrial civilisation.

What is then the type of the region which may be regarded as a model under current Polish conditions?

The analyses presented herein show that the most optimal would be proposals of an administrative region with elements of self-government which should be gradually strengthened along with the political transformation. In the future, one might examine the advisability of a differentiated location of regions in the country's administrative and political structure.

## 2. Conflicts occurring during regionalisation and their expected intensity

Let us present some remarks on conflicts bound up with delimitation of boundaries of the future regions; let us also try to evaluate on the basis of various premises their anticipated intensity and relative political power of their participants. Let us assume that the regionalisation will be based on the division of the country into 10–12 regions.

Potential conflicts over this division will largely appear in those towns which were capitals of the voivodships but which will not be local metropolitan areas. Conflicts are also likely to appear due to location of smaller towns not in those regions in which they would prefer to be. However, this type of conflicts will be much less important, that is why it will not be discussed here.

The present voivodship towns may be divided into two groups from the point of view of their attitude towards the regional reform. The first group encompasses relatively small towns, which have no chances to aspire to the role of the capital of a new region, for example Ciechanów or Ostrołęka. The second group includes larger towns which might become regional capitals if there were 15 to 20 of them.

As the example of Ciechanów shows, voivodships established around towns of the first group have not won the acceptance of the inhabitants of the urban communes forming their part.

Thus, for example, the mayors of towns of Ciechanów voivodship interviewed by Gazeta all — including the president of Ciechanów — said they would not regret Ciechanów voivodship. The inhabitants of this voivodship established a "committee for saving a voivodship," which, however, admitted at its first meeting that it will not defend the voivodship at all costs, but that it will try not to let the Ciechanów region lose any advantages because of the changes proposed (Gazeta 1992). It seems that a similar public feeling can be found in other towns of this group.

Some scarce observations show that people who regret most such voivodships as Ciechanów are the leaders of peasants' parties operating in the given voivodship. However, the problem of liquidation of such voivodships does not seem to give rise to more serious conflicts.

The second group of towns poses a more complicated problem. The hitherto information shows that in many towns "threatened" with a new reform measures are undertaken to give it such a shape as to ensure local urban aspirations.

Thus, the representatives of 11 voivodships who held a meeting in Koszalin in February 1991 stated that a new administrative division must be preceded by a wide discussion during which the "attitude of 37 threatened voivodships" should be considered with particular care.

The next meeting was held in Toruń in March 1991 and its participants stated, among other things, that "a number of new voivodships and their capitals proved correct in terms of organisation, as well as in economic, social and cultural terms and they must not be hastily liquidated" (Biuletyn no.2/1991).

The hitherto activity mirrored in various elaborations, memoranda, resolutions and appeals shows that most active supporters of the status of regional capital are leaders from such towns as Opole, Gorzów, Siedlce and Częstochowa.

The arguments are fairly similar in all cases. There is a frontier crossing in one place, or a factory in some other place, or a big river, or moral rights in yet another place...

However, the most impressive is the argument of the inhabitants of Częstochowa who claim that it would be extremely clumsy and disadvantageous not to make Częstochowa, a town of the cult of the Virgin Mary, the capital of the region.

In fact, only in Opole the battle for the "region" has been supported by a political party. The local Democratic Union has backed up the attempts at the establishment of the Opole region; they were also supported by one of the organisations representing the German minority (Biuletyn no. 2/1991).

In all the remaining cases the core of the groups engaged in the "battle for the region" seems to consist of voivodship officials or — sometimes — activists of voivodship councils. The weak commitment of the political parties stems not only from their weak position; there are much more important reasons for this.

One of the most important reasons is the conviction that it is not the way to acquire popularity beyond town directly "affected" by the administrative reform. This conviction seems to be rightful in the light of the above-mentioned investigations on the popularity of a regional issue among public opinion. Besides, such commitment might threaten with "internal breakdown" of some voivodship organisations of political parties because commune-oriented preferences in the voivodship do not always coincide with those of the activists from the voivodship capital.

For evaluation of the phenomena under investigation extremely useful might be the results of research on the attitudes of the communes towards regionalisation of the country. In 1991, a research team appointed by Prime Minister Bielecki asked local self-governments what town should be the capital of the region in which their commune might be found and should be found.

It appeared that the leaders of the local self-government would wish to have their communes in large regions with the largest Polish towns as their capitals. The overwhelming majority of the answers shows that communes naturally gravitate towards such towns as: Warsaw, Poznań, Gdańsk, Cracow, Katowice, Lublin, Wrocław, Szczecin, Łódź and Olsztyn (Miazga 1992).

The information presented herein shows quite clearly that the action undertaken to defend the above-mentioned voivodships and transformation of them into regions could not count on a solidary support from the communes forming their part.

It is quite likely that the battle — if any — will be waged by activists from voivodship towns linked up with the organs of the hitherto voivodship administration and having support (if any) from the local press. Apart from few exceptions, these actions will not be able to count on support from the voivodship party organisations.

It may be expected that the "battle for the region" will not be strongly supported by public opinion due to fairly poor interest in this problematique, which is indicated by the above-mentioned investigations.

In a nutshell, regionalisation at the present moment does not seem to cause the rise of large-scale social conflicts.

The considerations presented herein lead to a very interesting conclusion concerning the perception of regional reform by public opinion. Assumming that we are speaking about the division into 10–12 regions, social support for location of the regional capitals will be greater than in the case of any other solution.

If other solutions are chosen, the inhabitants of the "additional voivodship towns" will rest satisfied, but dissatisfaction will grow in the communes in which the inhabitants would prefer a large town as the capital of their region.

# References

Adamowicz P., 1991, *Konstytucyjne podstawy regionu autonomicznego* (Constitutional foundations of an autonomous region), Biuletyn no. 3/1991.

Articles in the Bulletins published by the Team for Elaboration of Conceptions of Changes in Territorial Organisation of the State at the Council of Ministers; if not signed, the numbers of the Bulletins were given in the text.

Bauman Z., 1987, *Legislators and Interpreters. On Modernity, Post-modernity and Intellectuals*, New York.

Błasiak W., 1990, *Śląska zbiorowość terytorialna i jej kultura w latach 1945–56* (Silesian territorial community and its culture in the years 1945–56), [in:] M. Błaszczak-Wacławik, W. Błasiak, T. Nawrocki, *Górny Śląsk — szczególny przypadek kulturowy* (Upper Silesia: a Specific Cultural Case), Jan Szumacher, Kielce, p. 136.

Dahrendorf R., 1959, *Class and Class Conflict in Industrial Society*, Stanford, pp. 157–206.

Esterbauer P., 1991, *Federalizm i regionalizm w Europie Środkowej* (Federalism and regionalism in Central Europe), Biuletyn no. 9/1991.

Gazeta na Mazowszu of 1st December, 1992.

Gazeta Wyborcza of 22nd October, 1992.

Gorzelak G., 1992, *Dilemmas of Polish regional policies during transition*, [in:] *Dilemmas of Regional Policies in Eastern and Central Europe*, ed. by G. Gorzelak and A. Kukliński, Warszawa.

Hryniewicz J., 1990, *Struktura społeczna i społeczne nierówności* (Social Structure and Social Inequalities), [in:] *Społeczności lokalne u progu przemian ustrojowych* (Local Communities on the Threshold of Systemic Change), ed. by J. Hryniewicz, IGPUW, Warszawa, pp. 48–50.

Jałowiecki B., *Kwestia regionalna* (The regional question), Wspólnota no. 109–110.

Jałowiecki B., *The regional question*, [in:] *Dilemmas...*, op.cit.

Jałowiecki B., 1989, *Rozwój lokalny*, Część I (Local Development. Part I), IGPUW, Warszawa.

Jawłowska A., 1991, *Tu i teraz w perspektywie kultury postmodernistycznej* (Here and now in the perspective of postmodernist culture), Kultura i Społeczeństwo no. 1/1991.

Kuźniar R., 1991, *Współpraca transgraniczna w rejonie wschodnich Karpat* (Cooperation on the border in the region of the East Carpathians), Biuletyn no. 5/1991.

Kukliński A., *Restructuring of Polish regions as a problem of European cooperation (remarks for discussion)*, [in:] *Dilemmas of Regional...*, op.cit.

Kulesza M., 1991, *Reforma ustroju terytorialnego państwa* (The reform of the state territorial system), Biuletyn no. 11/1991.

Łabno-Jabłońska A., 1992, *Regiony w rozwiązaniach konstytucyjnych* (Regions in constitutional solutions), Sejmik Samorządowy, Katowice, no. 14/1992.

Mielech M., 1991, *Hiszpańska ścieżka do państwa regionalnego*, Biuletyn no. 6/1991.

Mażewski L., 1991, *Republika prezydencko-parlamentarna, regiony i samorząd terytorialny*, Biuletyn no. 12/1991.

Mażewski L., 1991, Wspólnota no. 36/1990 and 19/1991.

Miazga M., 1992, *Ośrodki regionalne w opiniach samorządów*, Wspólnota no. 109–110/1992.

Nawrocki T., *Społeczne uwarunkowania restrukturyzacji Górnego Śląska*, [in:] *Restrukturyzacja regionów...*, op.cit.

*Opinie na temat regionalizacji kraju*, 1991, Biuletyn no. 8.

Pietrzyk I., 1991, *Polityka regionalna wspólnot europejskich*, [in:] *Regiony w Europie: Polityka EWG. Zgromadzenie regionów i jego członkowie*, ed.: B. Gruchman, Poznań.

Ratajczak L., Nowaczewski F., Doliński J., 1991, *Ekologia w Wielkopolsce*, Biuletyn no. 3/1991.

*Rocznik Statystyczny*, 1992.

Szczepański M.S., 1991, *Kulturowe uwarunkowania restrukturyzacji Górnego Śląska*, [in:] *Restrukturyzacja regionów jako problem współpracy europejskiej*, eds.: B. Jałowiecki, A. Kukliński, Warsaw.

*Uchwała Międzyregionalnej Komisji Koordynacyjnej Unii Demokratycznej dla województw: ciechanowskiego, ostrołęckiego i łomżyńskiego*, Gazeta na Mazowszu, 6.12.1992.

Wojtasiewicz L., 1991, *Restrukturyzacja gospodarki Wielkopolski w ramach gospodarki europejskiej*, [in:] *Restrukturyzacja gospodarki regionalnej i lokalnej*.

Grzegorz Gorzelak
European Institute
for Regional and Local Development
Warsaw

# THE REGIONAL PATTERNS
# OF POLISH TRANSFORMATION*

## I. The National Economy

### 1. General course of Polish reforms

### 1.1. Basic features of Polish economic reforms

The economic reform which was introduced in Poland on January 1, 1990 followed the pattern of a *shock therapy*. The results of this policy have been mixed.

Firstly, L. Balcerowicz (then the deputy-Prime Minister, responsible for economy in two consecutive governments) and his team underestimated the attachment of Polish industry (especially of managers of big state enterprises) to old mechanisms and patterns of economic behaviour. During first two years of the reform these enterprises have adopted a *survival strategy* which, in principle, aimed at simple surviving difficult conditions and applying to central authorities for assistance.

---

*This paper is based on my report prepared for the European Policies Research Center University of Strathclyde.

Secondly, the liberal doctrine was pushed too far. As some critics expressed it, L.Balcerowicz seemed to believe that *the market will create the market*. In fact, no *policies* have been formulated and implemented. This led to uncontrolled changes in several sectors of Polish economy, often not necessary and hampering the general course of reforms.

Thirdly, inflation was higher than assumed. It resulted in very high interest rates (up to over 30% monthly in the beginning of 1990) and also in implementation of very strict monetary policies which, in turn, lead to deep decline of consumption, drastic drop of real wages (mostly in the so-called budgetary sphere) and, in general, deepened overall economic recession.

## 1.2. The breakthrough

During 1992, almost all of a sudden, Poland assumed the role of a leader in economic transformation among European post-socialist countries. Poland was the first post-socialist country to show signs of economic recovery. 1992 was the first year which did not bring further decline of overall economic output. According to the most recent estimated, the GDP has even slightly increased. In this respect Poland appeared to be unique among all other post-socialist countries (see figure 1).

Table 1 presents dynamics of main economic categories during the transformation period.

Economic and legal conditions created for foreign investors have been evaluated as most favourable, in comparison with other post-socialist countries. If the facts that Poland presents the largest potential market, that it has been able to create institutional fundament for foreign and domestic capital and its labour force demonstrates relatively high skills are taken into account are considered, it becomes clear why foreign capital looks at Poland with growing interest. In the period 1990–1992 foreign capital invested or declared to be invested in Poland amounted in consecutive years to 374 mln, 694 mln and over 1,200 mln USD, respectively. Table 2 presents the distribution of this inflow according to the country of origin.

This acceleration was the result of several factors: stabilising of general political and economic situation, changing attitudes of foreign investors towards Central European countries as such and — last but not least

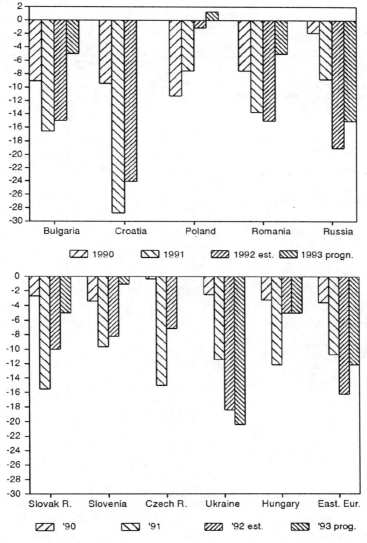

**Fig. 1** GDP in the post-socialist countries, 1990–1992 (the previous year=100).
Source: "Rzeczpospolita" 25 March 1993.

**Table 1**

**Dynamics of basic categories, 1989–1992**

| Categories | previous year = 100 | | | |
|---|---|---|---|---|
| | 1989 | 1990 | 1991 | 1992 |
| Gross Domestic Product | 100.2 | 88.4 | 92.4 | 100.5––102.0[a] |
| Industrial production | 97.9 | 77.9 | 82.9 | 104.2[a] |
| Agricultural production | 100.9 | 99.7 | 106.8 | 88.0[a] |
| Fixed capital formation | 97.6 | 89.9 | 95.9 | 100.0[a] |
| Consumption | 104.9 | 84.6 | 98.6 | · |
| Exports | 100.2 | 113.7 | 97.6 | · |
| Imports | 101.5 | 82.1 | 137.8 | · |
| Foreign investment | · | · | 185.0[b] | 135.0[b] |
| Working population— total | 99.0 | 93.8 | 96.3 | · |
| (yearly average)     — public | · | 86.6 | 85.5 | · |
| — private | · | 102.3 | 107.0 | · |
| Inflation | 332.0 | 586.0 | 170.3 | 143.0[b] |

[a] estimate, basing on 11 months of 1992 related to 11 months of 1991;

[b] rough estimate — no precise data available; ·: no data

— introduction of more favourable rules and conditions for foreign investors. According to the present law there are very few restrictions for establishing a company with foreign capital in Poland (no restrictions on the amount of capital to be invested), all profits may be repatriated and tax reliefs are possible in several cases. Comparison of Poland, Czech and Slovak Republics and Hungary indicates that all these four countries of-

**Table 2**

**Inflow of foreign capital
to Poland by country of origin,
1991–1993 (mln USD)**

| countries | capital invested |
|---|---|
| USA | 873 |
| Italy | 215 |
| Austria | 135 |
| France | 132 |
| Germany | 126 |
| The Netherlands | 85 |
| Sweden | 60 |
| Gretat Britain | 44 |
| Switzerland | 40 |
| Finland | 8 |

Source: J.Bołdok, *Dżentelmeni nie mówią o pieniądzach*
(Gentlemen do not talk about money),
"Polityka" No. 28(1888), 10 July 1993

fer similar conditions for foreign investors, markedly better thatn other post-socialist countries.

Polish economy has shifted its exports from the former European COMECON and, to some degree from other (mainly Third World) countries, to the EC countries. In general, it was not entirely the Polish choice, however. The former "eastern" markets closed down almost suddenly in 1990, due to different reasons. In the case of the former Soviet Union it was the economic collapse of this economic system. In the case of more advanced Eastern and Central European economies it was the result of their opening to the West and their choice to import products technologically more advanced (in 1992 Czecho-Slovakia participated in 4–5% and Hungary in less that 1% of Polish foreign trade). As widely known, losing the eastern markets created severe economic difficulties, especially for branches oriented to these particular directions (e.g. military complex, heavy industry, textiles).

Foreign debt — amounting to some 48 billion USD — is still a heavy burden for Polish economy. Even in spite of debt reduction (agreement with the Paris Club) in 1991 its relation to total exports equalled to 3.8, i.e. it was much higher than commonly accepted "safety limit". Further negotiations are being carried out with both clubs (of London and Paris) and it is probable that Polish debt will be still more reduced.

Economic restructuring — though not as fast as assumed — has proceeded throughout the entire period. Two "sides" of this process should be, however, distinguished:

— collapse of several enterprises in all economic sectors, which has not always reflected their real economic situation and growth potential, but often has been the result of external conditions (mainly collapse of traditional markets and "debt trap");

— growth of old firms and establishing new economic units, mostly in progressive economic sectors.

Table 3 presents changes in main sectoral structures during 1989–1991 (data for 1992 not available yet).

**Table 3**

**Creation of GDP, by sectors,
1989–1991**

| Sectors | Share in creation of GDP[a] | | |
|---|---|---|---|
| | 1989 | 1990 | 1991 |
| industry | 41.0 | 43.6 36.2 | 39.2 |
| construction | 9.6 | 9.5 9.3 | 10.9 |
| agriculture | 12.2 | 7.3 13.8 | 8.4 |
| other | 37.2 | 39.6 40.7 | 48.5 |

[a] 1989 and upper figure for 1990: constant prices 1985; lower figure for 1990 and 1991: constant prices 1990.
Source: Rocznik Statystyczny (Statistical Yearbook) 1992

Industrial branches have presented different performance during the transition period. In general, most of them have undergone deep decline in 1990 and 1991. In 1992 this situation has changed dramatically. Traditional branches of heavy industry have still been in deep decline, while consumer-oriented branches showed substantial growth. It can be foreseen that these tendencies will persist also in the future.

Privatisation has continued during the entire period of transition (see tables 4 and 5).

**Table 4**

**Working in the public sphere as % of total number of working in the national economy**

| Sector | shares (in %) | | | differences (% points) | | |
|---|---|---|---|---|---|---|
| | 1989 | 1990 | 1991 | 1990–1989 | 1991–1990 | 1991–1989 |
| total | 52.4 | 50.0 | 44.5 | −4.2 | −5.6 | −9.7 |
| industry | 71.3 | 69.2 | 64.2 | −2.1 | −5.0 | −7.1 |
| construction | 62.8 | 58.0 | 40.5 | −4.8 | −17.5 | −22.3 |
| agriculture | 12.4 | 10.9 | 8.0 | −1.5 | −2.9 | −4.4 |
| domestic trade | 27.5 | 17.9 | 11.7 | −9.5 | −6.3 | −15.8 |

**Table 5**

**Dynamics of the number of working, by sectors and ownership, 1989–1991**

| Sectors | total | public | private | total | public | private | total | public | private |
|---|---|---|---|---|---|---|---|---|---|
| | 1990, 1989=100 | | | 1991, 1990=100 | | | 1991, 1989=100 | | |
| total | 93.8 | 86.6 | 102.3 | 96.3 | 85.5 | 107.0 | 90.3 | 74.1 | 109.5 |
| industry | 88.6 | 85.9 | 95.2 | 91.3 | 84.8 | 106.1 | 80.9 | 72.9 | 100.9 |
| construction | 88.8 | 81.9 | 100.3 | 96.8 | 67.6 | 137.0 | 85.9 | 55.4 | 137.4 |
| agriculture | 96.8 | 85.3 | 98.4 | 96.6 | 70.8 | 99.8 | 93.5 | 60.4 | 98.2 |
| domestic trade | 100.7 | 65.7 | 113.9 | 116.0 | 75.5 | 124.9 | 116.8 | 46.9 | 142.3 |

Table 4 clearly indicates that the changes in the ownership structures were mainly due to the decline of the public sphere and — in some sectors — to the growth of the private one. Domestic trade and construction noted the fastest growth of employment in the private sphere, while in industry this employment was stable and in agriculture even declined (though in a slower pace than in the public sphere).

Being the first country to enter on the transformation path, Poland was also the first to pay economic and social costs incurred by this process. Pauperisation and unemployment have hit wide strata of population which resulted in worsening of both level and structure of consumption. Unemployment is the most common and the most painful manifestation of these costs.

The number of working has been constantly dropping since 1989. This is shown in table 6.

**Table 6**

**Number of working, 1990–1992 (31 December)**

| Years | Total 1000s (=100%) | Type of ownership | | | |
|-------|------|-------|------|-------|------|
| | | public | | private | |
| | | 1000s | % | 1000s | % |
| 1990 | 16,474.3 | 8,243.4 | 50.0 | 8,230.6 | 50.0 |
| 1991 | 15,861.2 | 7,052.1 | 44.5 | 8,809.1 | 55.5 |

Source: Rocznik Statystyczny (Statistical Yearbook) 1992, table 2.

The sectoral structure of employment has also changed. It is illustrated in table 7.

**Table 7**

**Sectoral structure of working
1990–1992 (yearly averages)**

| Years | Total working 100s (=100%) | Economic sector | | | | | |
|-------|------|-------|------|-------|------|-------|------|
| | | industry | | construction | | agriculture | |
| | | 1000s | % | 1000s | % | 1000s | % |
| 1990 | 16,511.4 | 4,620 | 28.0 | 1,243 | 7.5 | 4,425 | 26.8 |
| 1991 | 15,601.4 | 4,250 | 27.2 | 1,116 | 7.2 | 4,265 | 27.3 |

Source: Rocznik Statystyczny (Statistical Yearbook) 1992, table I.

On December 31, 1992 there were 2,509,342 registered unemployed, which equals to 13.6% of economically active population and to 21.1% of active outside private agriculture[1]. The rate of growth of this last indicator

---

[1] The rate of unemployment is defined as the relation of unemployed to the economically active population.

was faster than of the total unemployment rate which tells that the non-agricultural labour market shrinks faster.

# II. The Regional Patterns

## 1. Basic features

### 1.1. Demography

The regional distribution of population is stable. The population in Poland is spread more or less evenly across its territory with one but important exception for the Upper Silesia Region. The Katowice voivodship (2.0% of the country's area) is inhabited by 10% of the total population of Poland. The biggest town in Poland, Warszawa, has 1.7 mln inhabitants, the second biggest, Łódź, 1 million. The urban system follows the rank-size rule. By comparison with other countries, the population of Poland is characterised by a high degree of ethnic homogeneity although there are certain differences in the demographic structure of some regions.

The decrease of migrations, started along with the emergence of the overall economic crisis at the beginning of the 1980s, continued during the second half of the decade. The average yearly number of migrants equals to some half a million, a bit more than a half of all migrations in the 1970s. This persisting decrease of domestic migrations reflects the decrease of real incomes and shortage of new housing. It leads to petrification of the regional structure of job opportunities. It is a kind of a vicious circle: no "working" labour market may be created without sufficient supply of new housing and propensity to migrate which leads to slower economic growth even in the regions which could develop faster and which could accommodate new labour force from areas of heavy unemployment.

The overall increase of the number of population during two years (1991, 1992) amounted to 0.57%. The following voivodships noted during this period an increase higher than 1%: Bielsko-Biała, Krosno, Legnica, Leszno, Nowy Sącz (1.46% — the highest in the country), Rzeszów, Słupsk, Suwałki, Tarnów. These regions fall in two groups: South-Eastern part of Poland, with high share of rural population and Northern and

Western part of the country, with younger population. Both these two factors are responsible for traditionally high natural increase due to high rate of births.

There have been two regions which lost population. These were Łódź and Wałbrzych — the two regions of especially heavy restructuring problems. Warszawa kept its population stable, which is a clear confirmation of the phenomena mentioned above. This region could have accommodated new in-comers and could have offered them jobs. This was not possible due to housing shortages.

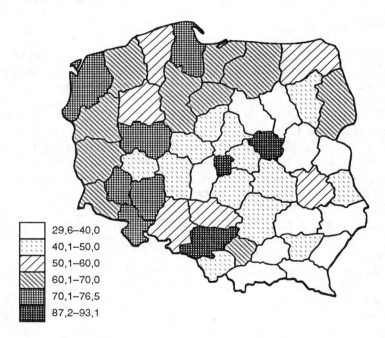

| | |
|---|---|
| | 29,6–40,0 |
| | 40,1–50,0 |
| | 50,1–60,0 |
| | 60,1–70,0 |
| | 70,1–76,5 |
| | 87,2–93,1 |

**Fig. 2** Share of urban population, 1991

Regional differences in the urban/rural ratio have been stable (see figure 2). The mostly urbanised regions in 1991 were the following: Łódź — 93.1%, Warszawa — 88.8%, Katowice — 87.2%, Szczecin — 76.5%, Gdańsk — 76.2%, Wrocław — 74.2%, Wałbrzych — 74.0%, Poznań — 71.3%, and the least urbanised: Biała Podlaska — 36.5%, Nowy Sącz —

36.1%, Tarnów — 36.0%, Krosno — 35.3%, Ostrołęka — 34.7%, Siedlce — 32.1%, Zamość — 29.6, i.e. the regions of eastern and southern parts of Poland.

The age structure of Polish population is much less regionally differentiated (figures 3, 4). The Western and Northern regions are demographically "younger" — i.e. the shares of the pre-productive age-groups are high and the shares of the post-productive age-groups low. In the rural, eastern and southern regions, the age structure of population is the most polarised: high birth rates make the shares of the pre-productive age groups high, but also the shares of the post-productive age groups are the highest in the country. As a result, the urbanised regions have the highest shares of the productive age-groups (Katowice — 60.9%, Warszawa — 60.7%, Łódź — 60.0%, Szczecin — 59.8%, Wrocław — 59.6%, Kraków — 59.3%, Opole — 59.3%, Legnica — 59.0% and, on the other pole,

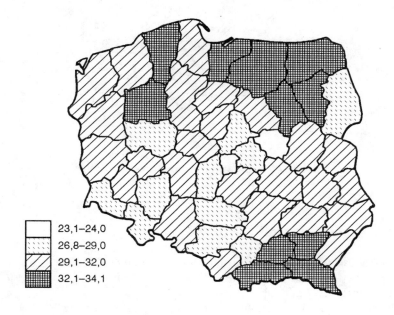

23,1–24,0
26,8–29,0
29,1–32,0
32,1–34,1

**Fig. 3** Share of population in pre-productive age

Ostrołęka — 54.4%, Nowy Sącz — 54.1%, Chełm — 54.0%, Przemyśl
— 53.9%, Zamość — 53.3%, Siedlce — 53.3%, Łomża — 53.2%, Biała
Podlaska — 52.9%).

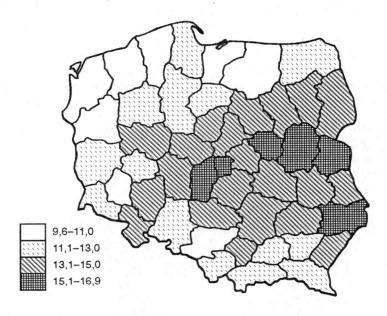

9,6–11,0
11,1–13,0
13,1–15,0
15,1–16,9

**Fig. 4** Share of population in post-productive age

## 1.2. The labour market

Changes on the labour market have become one of the most strongly
pronounced effect of Polish transformation. These changes have also been
reflected on the regional labour markets.

All Polish regions lost some jobs during 1989–1991. In the Northern
and Western voivodships this loss amounted to some 15% of the number
of working in 1989. This was mainly due to the collapse of state farms
— for example, the loss of jobs in public agricultural sector amounted in

these regions from 32% to 50% (and state agriculture employed in these regions some 25–30% of the overall labour force active in agriculture).

The shift from public to private sphere took place mostly in the regions with big urban centres: Warszawa, Poznań, Łódź, Wrocław, Kraków, Szczecin. These were the regions in which both the decrease of the number of working on the public sphere and increase in the private sphere were the greatest. In rural, backward regions both spheres lost employment.

This shift did not, however, follow a clear regional pattern, according to which the regions losing most of jobs in the public sphere would gain the most in the private one. The correlation coefficient between dynamics of the number of working in both sphere during the period 1989–1991 was equal to only 0.42, i.e. it was not too high.

There is no general pattern of the regional dynamics of private employment in industry, though big urban centres demonstrate higher dynamics than rural areas. On the other hand, in such sectors as construction, and especially trade, the growth of the private sphere was exceptionally high in highly urbanised regions.

The private sphere was unable to create as many new jobs and have been shed within the public sphere. Growth of unemployment was the direct effect of these (dis)proportions.

Figure 5 presents the regional differentiation of the unemployment rate in 49 administrative regions (voivodships).

In several localities he situation on the labour market is even more dramatic than it can be seen in the "averaged" picture. There are areas where number of unemployed exceeds even by 50% the number of those who have work. Several localities have been left almost without any economic base, since a dominating factory or state agricultural farm had collapsed. Especially dramatic situation occurs in remote, underdeveloped rural ares where job opportunities are virtually non-existing.

The spatial pattern of unemployment is the outcome of the reaction of particular regional economic structures to changing economic conditions. In Poland there have been several regional patterns of such reactions[2]:

1. North-eastern part of Poland is mostly endangered by structural unemployment. The non-agricultural sectors are poorly developed and employment opportunities besides agriculture are scarce. Agriculture itself is rather weak, poorly equipped with fixed capital and run by el-

---

[2] According to: *Bezrobocie w układzie przestrzennym: czynniki i zagrożenia* (Spatial Distribution of Unemployment: Factors and Threats), CPO, Warszawa, March 1992, pp. 16–26.

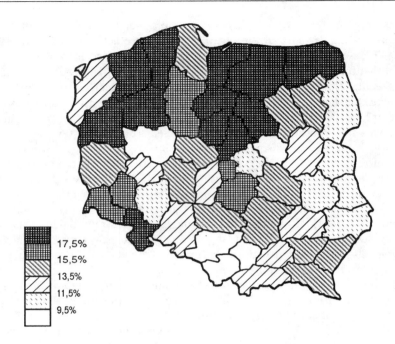

**Fig. 5** Unemployment rates in 49 voivodships, December 31, 1992.
Source: Regional differentiation of unemployment in 1993, CPO,
Warszawa, February 1993, fig. 1.

derly farmers with low skills and little incentive. Tourist services cannot
develop properly due to general decrease of incomes and low demand
for such services. The region does not create promising opportunities for potential foreign investors due to its remoteness and overall
economic, social and cultural backwardness. Links with the eastern
markets are poor and do not create hopes for revitalising local economy.

2. South-eastern part of Poland is the concentration of "company-towns"
   hosting declining branches, such as metallurgic, military, transportation industries which are in a difficult economic situation. The collapse
   of the former Soviet market to which this region directed great share
   of its industrial production has been one of the most important factors

of present economic difficulties. This region has also been the concentration of the "bi-professionals" who combined their work in industry with running a small agricultural farm. They were first to be dismissed from their industrial occupation, but the remaining source of maintenance — farm — is usually too small to provide sufficient incomes. The urban structure is relatively well developed but would undergo accelerated deterioration along with worsening of the economic situation of the state industrial enterprises which used to construct and support the communal facilities. There are no other promising directions of development: agriculture is (traditionally) heavily overpopulated and tourist services underdeveloped. Trade with new eastern markets could be the direction of regional specialisation in the future.

3. Northern and western Polish regions have a specific agricultural structure: the share of state and cooperative farms is the highest and reaches in some regions over 50% of agricultural land. These big farms collapse and are put for privatisation, which is slow due to lack of wanting to buy land. Though unemployment created as the result of restructuring of this economic sector is not big by absolute numbers it can strongly influence some local labour markets deprived of other employment opportunities.

4. Typical old industrial regions constitute another type of Polish problem employment regions. These are, at present, Łódź and Wałbrzych regions. In the future Upper Silesia (which will be discussed separately) main join this group. In the case of Łódź it is textile industry and in the Wałbrzych region coal mining and textile industries which have constituted the economic base in the past and almost have collapsed. Traditional Soviet market for textiles has virtually closed down and coal has been almost totally extracted from the Wałbrzych pits (none of them has been closed yet). Devising promising development strategy is difficult due the mono-functional qualification structure of the local workforce, polluted environment, worn-down infrastructure and — in the Wałbrzych region — exploited natural resources. In some parts of the Wałbrzych region tourism seems to be the most promising direction of local development.

5. Upper Silesia of which Katowice voivodship constitutes the main part and the major economic unit, traditionally providing more than 20% of the national industrial production, is on the edge of massive restructuring and dramatic increase of unemployment. Coal-mining, the

most important branch in the regional economy, will undergo deep structural changes. Production of coal dropped by more than 30%, while employment in this branch has not changed substantially. Heavy and chemical industries, being at the moment in decline, are the other dominating sectors of Upper Silesia and will produce unemployment in the nearest future. The economic profile of Upper Silesia can no longer be maintained and possibilities of building new industrial structures even on the ruins of the old are vague. Environment is too heavily damaged, labour force too mono-functional, infrastructure too obsolete. In the meantime, the rate of unemployment in the katowice and Bielsko-Biała voivodships is one of the lowest in Poland, which — as explained above — should not be the case in the future.

Łódź and Upper Silesia could become two **political bombs** hidden under Polish economic reforms. Should these bombs explode, the course of the reforms would be challenged and very difficult to defend.

6. At the moment, the lowest rate of unemployment exists in the following regions (besides Katowice and Bielsko-Biała already mentioned): Warszawa, Poznań, Kraków and Wrocław, i.e. in the regions having big cities with diversified economic structures. This reflects greater employment opportunities, created also by private and foreign enterprises flourishing in these regions. Economic situation of these regions seems promising, with a possible exception of Kraków, in which the future of huge steel-mill, Nowa Huta (employing over 20,000 persons), is not certain.

7. In smaller territorial units the spatial differences of the unemployment rate are, obviously, much higher. On June 30, 1992 the highest rate among the 353 "employment districts" (see the next section) equals to 33.5 (in the Suwałki voivodship, north-east of Poland) and there are many cases with unemployment rate exceeding 25. On the other hand there are several spatial units with unemployment lower than 5%. Between municipalities (there are some 2,500 of them in Poland) these differences would be even higher.

## 1.3. Industry

Traditionally, big Polish urban centres are also the industrial centres. New processes have not changed this general pattern, though some modifications have been introduced. Figure 6 presents the distribution of industrial employment throughout the Polish regions.

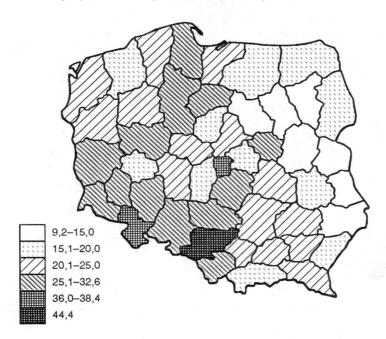

9,2–15,0
15,1–20,0
20,1–25,0
25,1–32,6
36,0–38,4
44,4

**Fig. 6** Share of working in industry in the total number of working, 1991

Regional differences in **labour productivity** (see figure 7) can be considered as the most meaningful indicator of the changes in regional economic structures. This indicator, however, is sensitive to several processes and phenomena. The two most important ones are the regional structures themselves and their dynamics and the dynamics of price relations. The joint effect of both these processes may be said to reflect the regions' economic potential and their reaction to changing economic environment.

Table 8 presents the changes of voivodships' positions on the lists of labour productivity in industry. First and last in 1991 eight voivodships are shown and the changes of their places in comparison to the arrangement for 1990 is indicated.

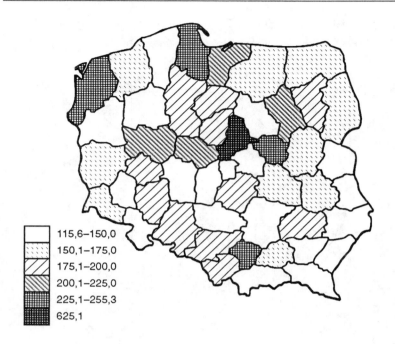

115,6–150,0
150,1–175,0
175,1–200,0
200,1–225,0
225,1–255,3
625,1

**Fig. 7** Labour productivity in industry, 1991

Though table 8 provides a fragmentary picture, several observations can be made.

Firstly, it shows the regions with the highest productivity in industry: Płock (oil refinery), Warszawa, Gdańsk, Kraków, Szczecin (diversified industry) and of the lowest, among which we find the two regions demanding heavy restructuring: Łódź and Wałbrzych. Correlation between labour productivity in industry in the public sector and the regional GDP is significantly positive, though not very high (0.47). The case of Łódź is especially instructive from the point of view of internal consistency of low productivity in both public and private spheres.

Secondly, the table demonstrates how instable the situation in industry is. Several voivodships have changed their position dramatically (some such cases are not presented in table 8 — for example Skierniewice voivodship noted the highest productivity in private industry in 1990, but in 1991

Table 8

**Arrangements of voivodships according to labour productivity
in industry in 1991 and change of places
in comparison with 1990**

| total | | | public | | | private | | |
|---|---|---|---|---|---|---|---|---|
| No | voivodship | change | No | voivodship | change | No | voivodship | change |
| 1 | Płock | 0 | 1 | Płock | 0 | 1 | Łomża | +2 |
| 2 | Warszawa | +1 | 2 | Warszawa | 0 | 2 | Toruń | 0 |
| 3 | Gdańsk | +5 | 3 | Kraków | 0 | 3 | Ostrołęka | +26 |
| 4 | Kraków | −0 | 4 | Gdańsk | +4 | 4 | Szczecin | 0 |
| 5 | Szczecin | +0 | 5 | Ostrołęka | +6 | 5 | Elbląg | +12 |
| 6 | Ostrołęka | +12 | 6 | Szczecin | −2 | 6 | Koszalin | −1 |
| 7 | Konin | +3 | 7 | Konin | +6 | 7 | Leszno | +8 |
| 8 | Elbląg | +13 | 8 | Włocławek | +1 | 8 | Gdańsk | +5 |
| 42 | Nowy Sącz | +5 | 42 | Łódź | +3 | 42 | Kalisz | +5 |
| 43 | Legnica | −41 | 43 | Legnica | −38 | 43 | Zamość | −1 |
| 44 | Chełm | −21 | 44 | Chełm | −23 | 44 | Łódź | −12 |
| 45 | Wałbrzych | −1 | 45 | Wałbrzych | +1 | 45 | Częstochowa | +1 |
| 46 | Łódź | −1 | 46 | Piła | −10 | 46 | Rzeszów | −3 |
| 47 | Biała Podlaska | +1 | 47 | Kalisz | −8 | 47 | Krosno | −2 |
| 48 | Kalisz | −6 | 48 | Kielce | −6 | 48 | Przemyśl | −2 |
| 49 | Kielce | −9 | 49 | Biała Podlaska | −2 | 49 | Tarnobrzeg | 0 |

it occupied only 22 position). Changes in the relations of prices, collapse of one big enterprise or putting into motion a new establishment (especially in a less industrialised region) may change the relative position of a region from the very best to the very worst.

Thirdly, the table demonstrates the differences between the regional patterns of labour productivity in private and public industry (the correlation coefficient between these two variables for 1991 was equal to zero). It is impossible to evaluate what impact on that have had the informalities, tax offenses etc., so common in the private business in Poland these days. On the other hand one cannot rule out the possibility that the private sector in Poland begins to establish new patterns regional of efficiency and productivity. Final answers will be available much later.

## 1.4. Foreign capital

The regional patterns of foreign investment in Poland are very clear. Two types of regions are highly preferred by investors: big urban centres with good international (air) transport and telecommunication facilities, which — at the same time — may offer good living conditions and the whole western part of the country. International capital locates itself in the urban centres — the German capital concentrates in the West Eastern part of the country, in general, has been omitted by foreign capital.

Comparisons of Poland with Czecho-Slovakia and Hungary indicate that the regional concentration of foreign capital in Warsaw is much smaller than in the other two capitals. Up to 1991 Warsaw has attracted only 32.6% of all firms with foreign capital present in Poland (Prague — 49% and Budapest — 56%); the same shares for capital engaged were equal: Warsaw — 39.4%, Prague — 45.4%, Budapest — 57.5%.

This regional pattern of foreign capital's activity in Poland is due to the overall structure of Polish settlement system. In Poland there are several relatively big urban centres able to compete with the capital in many respects — also in these which are considered by foreign investors when they chose a location for their business. Detailed picture of activities of foreign capital in Poland (and also in Hungary and former Czecho-Slovakia) is given in the paper by W.Dziemianowicz published in this volume.

## 1.5. Privatisation

As in other processes of transformation, the regional differentiation is great. Figure 8 presents the regional patterns of privatising state enterprises in a "capital way", i.e. by selling prosperous firms to private owners.

As in several other process, the fastest pace of capital privatisation occurs in highly industrialised regions. In several eastern regions of Poland there were no such cases, while in the Katowice voivodship 27 companies were privatised in this way and in the Warsaw region 24.

The deepest changes in the ownerships structure, represented by the differences of share of employment in the public sphere, took place in the most urbanised and highly developed regions. On the other pole of

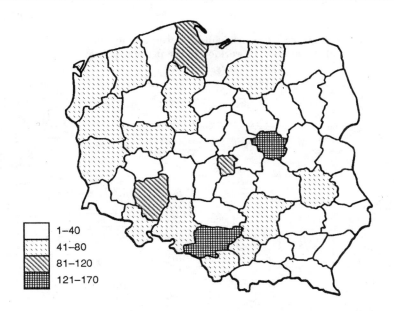

1–40
41–80
81–120
121–170

**Fig. 8** Regional distribution of privatisation processes, end of 1992.
Source: "Rzeczpospolita", 25 March 1993.

this arrangement are the rural, peripheral voivodships in which this share dropped by some 5–6 percentage points.

The growth of the number of working in the private economy was differentiated among particular sectors. Its regional/sectoral patterns are demonstrated in table 9.

There is no general pattern of the regional dynamics of private employment in industry, though big urban centres demonstrate higher dynamics than rural areas. On the other hand, in such sectors as construction, and especially trade, the growth of the private sphere was exceptionally high in highly urbanised voivodships.

The private sphere was unable to create as many new jobs and have been shed within the public sphere. Growth of **unemployment** was the direct effect of these (dis)proportions. General description of unemploy-

**Table 9**

**Arrangements of voivodships according to dynamics
of the number of working in the private sphere
by sectors, 1989–1991**

| industry | | | construction | | | domestic trade | | |
|---|---|---|---|---|---|---|---|---|
| No | voivodship | 1991 1989=100 | No | voivodship | 1991 1989=100 | No | voivodship | 1991 1989=100 |
| 1 | Bydgoszcz | 143.8 | 1 | Szczecin | 187.4 | 1 | Łódź | 204.2 |
| 2 | Krosno | 132.6 | 2 | Opole | 181.1 | 2 | Warszawa | 185.5 |
| 3 | Toruń | 120.1 | 3 | Katowice | 176.2 | 3 | Kraków | 184.4 |
| 4 | Poznań | 188.7 | 4 | Bielsko-Biała | 175.2 | 4 | Szczecin | 176.4 |
| 5 | Piła | 117.8 | 5 | Kraków | 158.3 | 5 | Poznań | 171.2 |
| 6 | Elbląg | 117.3 | 6 | Legnica | 157.1 | 6 | Gdańsk | 170.7 |
| 7 | Gdańsk | 114.7 | 7 | Kalisz | 155.1 | 7 | Legnica | 167.6 |
| 8 | Katowice | 113.9 | 8 | Częstochowa | 154.7 | 8 | Lublin | 166.9 |
| 42 | Rzeszów | 86.9 | 42 | Przemyśl | 103.6 | 42 | Kalisz | 110.5 |
| 43 | Siedlce | 86.2 | 43 | Zamość | 102.9 | 43 | Białystok | 110.4 |
| 44 | Jelenia Góra | 84.6 | 44 | Olsztyn | 102.4 | 44 | Zamość | 105.3 |
| 45 | Łomża | 84.1 | 45 | Siedlce | 100.0 | 45 | Chełm | 103.1 |
| 46 | Częstochowa | 83.5 | 46 | Suwałki | 97.8 | 46 | Suwałki | 102.9 |
| 47 | Piotrków | 81.1 | 47 | Łomża | 90.0 | 47 | Biała Podlaska | 101.1 |
| 48 | Przemyśl | 80.4 | 48 | Wałbrzych | 89.9 | 48 | Łomża | 100.0 |
| 49 | Zamość | 69.6 | 49 | Koszalin | 84.3 | 49 | Ciechanów | 99.1 |

ment in Poland has been presented in section I.7 of this report. In this chapter its regional differentiation is presented and explained.

## 1.6. The regional GDP

There are no official statistics of the regional product in Poland (GDP in regional break-downs). Only rough estimates of this economic category are available[3].

The regional differentiation of GDP per inhabitant in 1991 (estimate) and the share of agriculture are is presented on figures 9 and 10, respectively.

---

[3] Prepared by the Centre for Economic and Statistical Studies of the Central Statistical Office and the Polish Academy of Sciences, March 1993 (draft). This estimates provide regional structures of GDP creation by sectors and industrial branches for 1990 and 1991.

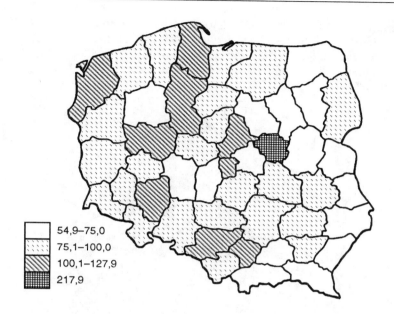

**Fig. 9** Regional GDP per inhabitant in 1991, factor costs, national average = 100.
Source: estimates of the Centre for Economic and Statistical Studies of the Central Statistical Office and the Polish Academy of Sciences, March 1993

No major differences between these regional structures in 1990 and 1991 occurred. However, there has been an interesting pattern of changes in the regional structures of GDP creation. In the majority of regions heavily depending upon the fuel/energy production this sector has gained some percentage points during 1991. This could be interpreted in different ways: as a result of collapse of other activities outside the dominating sector (which would lead to petrification of such regional economies) or a prove of delayed restructuring of this sector in Poland. However, the possible impact of faster than average growth of prices for fuels and energy cannot be ruled out. This situation occurred in the following regions (for Poland these shares equalled to 7.3% in 1990 and 8.4% in 1991): Jelenia Góra: 13.8 and 15.9; Katowice: 24.8 and 27.8; Konin: 16.6 and 22.7; Krosno: 12.9 and 13.7; Piotrków: 21.4 and 29.0; Płock: 36.9 and 38.5; Wałbrzych: 10.7 and 13.6.

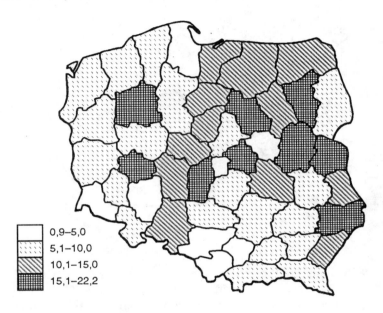

**Fig. 10** Share of agriculture in regional GDP creation, factor costs, 1991. Source: estimates of the Centre for Economic and Statistical Studies of the Central Statistical Office and the Polish Academy of Sciences, March 1993

In general, the regions in which agriculture used to dominate the regional economy, the share of this sector decreased considerably (for example from 23.9 to 19.6% in Biała Podlaska; from 23.9 to 20.8% in Zamość; from 25.3 to 22.% in Ciechanów). There have been, however, regions which noted smaller decrease of the share of agriculture that in the entire Polish economy (from 7.5 to 6.3%); this happened, for example, in the "best" agricultural region of Poland, Leszno (drop form 22.6 to 21.9%).

No other clear patterns of regional changes in the structure of GDP creation could be observed for these two years. In some cases the industries which had usually dominated the (obsolete) regional structures have lost in importance (textiles in Łódź and Wałbrzych, for example), in some other signs of increased regional specialisation can be noted.

Definitely, just two years is a too short period for observing any marked changes of regional economic structures expressed by a synthetic measure of regional GDP, especially in a fast-changing and unstable economic situation. A more clear picture will be available after more distinct restructuring takes place in Polish regions.

## 2. Interrelations and regional structural change

Just two years is a too short period for drawing conclusions about the regional patterns of Polish transformation. However, the available data prove one thing without any doubt: **the change is dramatic and leads to great instability of regional differentiations within the country.** However, some more general observations can be made even on the basis of this limited data base and time span.

The first observation is the following: **there has been great inconsistency of changes during the years 1990 and 1991.** Several correlation coefficients between the variables representing the changes in these particular years are very low which means that the regional pattern of change in 1990 was different from the pattern in 1991. This is especially true in the variables representing the differences of shares of working in the public sphere, though in some cases the differences of shares of particular sectors demonstrate the same irregularities. This is a clear proof for observations already made, according to which the structural changes in Polish economy were mainly the outcome of negative processes, like decrease of production and employment, and not of positive signs of economic growth. These decrements took place sometimes at random and particular sectors suffered at different moments. In result, the structural changes which occurred in consecutive years have followed different regional patterns.

The second observation refers to the position of particular groups and types of regions in the transformation process. The general picture is clear: **the regions which have traditionally been mostly urbanised and mostly industrialised and which have been well equipped with infrastructure**

**appeared to be the less vulnerable to the costs and negative sides of transformation.** They were able to proceed with privatisation in the fastest pace, to attract new (also foreign) investment, to defend their position on the (changing) economic map of the country[4]. In result, the traditional industrial-urban-infrastructural complex, which has shaped the regional structure of Poland[5] has not vanished and even has been reinforced.

The third observation applies to some regional cases, of which Katowice and Łódź could be the most interesting examples. To some extent surprisingly these regions locate quite well in arrangements describing the structural changes, especially in the ownerships structures and inflow of foreign capital. This positive picture should not, however, overshadow the real dramatic problems with industrial restructuring which should take place there and the environmental hazards, especially in Upper Silesia.

## 3. Conclusions: regional potential for transformation[6]

Summing up earlier remarks on economic, social and technological aspects of regional development of Poland, we may present the regional diversification of Polish transformation along the following major dimensions of spatial differentiation, shaping the regions' ability to adapt to new economic conditions:

1. **Diversification of economic structure**. This dimension includes also the level and differentiation of skills of the workforce, the modernity of the fixed assets. In brief, the more diversified economic structure, the more qualified population and higher level of technological advancement.

---

[4] The same result was found for the period of the previous Polish crisis 1976–1985, when the "strongest" regions were stricken by the crisis in the hardest way, but were the first to emerge from it and rebuilt former structures. See my book: *Rozwój regionalny Polski w warunkach kryzysu i reformy* (Regional Development of Poland under Crisis and Reform), series "Rozwój regionalny — rozwój lokalny — samorząd terytorialny" vol. 14, IGP UW, Warszawa 1989.

[5] See: *Analiza porównawcza regionalnych procesów rozwoju w wybranych krajach* (Comparative Analysis of Regional Processes of Development in Chosen Countries) "Biuletyn KPZK PAN" no 113, PWN, Warszawa 1981 (co-author: B. Wyżnikiewicz) in which this complex has been found in 1974 in Poland, Spain and Japan, as opposed to its lack in France, Czechoslovakia and former GDR.

[6] This section is based on Chapter 6 of the *Polish Scenario — A Summary*, prepared by G.Gorzelak and B.Jałowiecki within the EC-sponsored project "Eastern and Central Europe 2000", Warszawa, December 1992.

2. **Overall level of socio-economic development.** This dimension "operates" on two levels: it discriminates rural areas (less developed) from towns and eastern part of the country (less developed) from the western part. It also captures the "regional spirit" of entrepreneurship and the scale of job opportunities.
3. **Distance to sources of capital and innovation.** Several factors are of importance here: proximity to an international airport, proximity to the western border (i.e. to the German capital), proximity to a big urban centre. "The capital" is not restricted to "foreign capital" only, but also to domestic sources of finance, though the role of inflow of capital from abroad (and of new technologies) is of crucial importance for overall development of Polish economy.

**Table 10**

**Types of regions from the point of view
of their transformation potential**

| types of regions | regions | socio-economic structure | level of development | proximity to capital |
|---|---|---|---|---|
| **Type 1:** strong, leaders of transformation | Warsaw, Poznań, Wrocław, Kraków, Gdańsk | diversified | high | good |
| **Type 2:** well prepared for transformation | Bydgoszcz, Toruń, Szczecin, Gorzów, Zielona Góra, Kalisz, Opole, Bielsko-Biała, Lublin, Leszno, Elbląg | diversified | medium | good |
| **Type 3:** restructuring needed, possible | Jelenia Góra, Legnica, Piła, Koszalin, Słupsk, Olsztyn, Tarnobrzeg, Tarnów, Kielce Częstochowa, Białystok, Rzeszów, Płock | diversified, with company-towns | medium-low | bad |
| **Type 4:** deep restructuring necessary, difficult | Katowice, Łódź, Wałbrzych | monofunctional (industrial) | high | good/medium |
| **Type 5:** presenting some potential for development | Suwałki, Ciechanów, Ostrołęka, Łomża, Biała-Podlaska, Chełm, Zamość, Przemyśl, Krosno | monofunctional (agricultural) | low | bad |
| **Type 6:** neutral, some sectors need restructuring | Konin, Piotrków, Sieradz, Włocławek, Skierniewice, Radom, Nowy Sącz, Siedlce | diversified, | medium | medium |

There are, of course, several other dimensions shaping the regional ability to transformation, like the agricultural structure, the density of "company towns" with collapsing industry, vulnerability to decline of eastern markets, ethnic tensions, etc. However, when looking into the chances

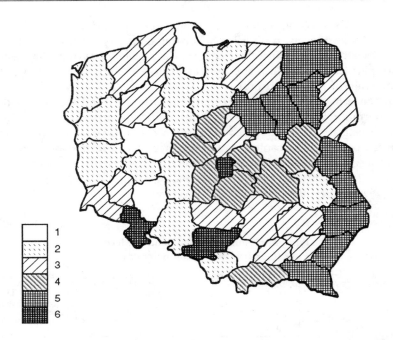

**Fig. 11** The regional potential for transformation (based on table 10)

of particular regions for their emergence form (often accidental) economic difficulties and their potential role in transforming Polish economy, the above three dimensions seem to be 2of primary importance.

Superimposition of these three dimensions produces a typology of Polish regions. It is presented in table 10 and figure 11.

Position of few voivodships in the above table may be disputable. For example, three voivodships: Szczecin, Bielsko-Biała and Bydgoszcz may claim their belonging to group 1, which would be justified by fast rate of privatisation, high involvement of foreign capital, proximity to international airports etc. However, these voivodships do not contain big urban centres with high scientific and cultural potential. Perhaps assigning some regions to group 2 (like Elbląg, Leszno) could be considered as premature. One should also keep in mind that the potential of several regions is at the moment dominated by current difficulties. For example the region of Łódź may overcome its structural crisis caused by collapse of textile industry and join even the regions of type 1. Similar remarks can be also made for several other individual cases. These reservations should not, however, overshadow the fact that Polish economic space is differentiated according to the three major factors which constituted the typology and that the spatial patterns, as presented in table 10, do reflect regions' potentialities for transformation.

This regional pattern of regions' ability to cope with the challenges of transformation is a tentative proposal and it should be — and will be — tested by more detailed analyses and investigations.

# III. Policy Response[7]

## 1. Weaknesses of national regional policies

It has to be admitted that regional policy has been very weak during the period of Polish crisis and reform, i.e. during the decade of the 1980s. The regional processes have been the outcome of the phenomena occurring in the sectors and branches of the national economy and the regional/spatial dimensions used to be of secondary importance of any economic decisions taken throughout this period.

The above statement applies also to the most recent policies. The neo-liberal doctrine adopted by the non-communist government does not provide much room for state intervention or for state financed programmes and projects. "The Market" is to solve the current problems of the economy and is even supposed to create market. This means that regional development of the country and development of particular regions are left to "natural market forces".

There are governmental agencies responsible for formulating and implementing "regional" or "spatial" policies. The Department of Physical and Long-Term Planning of the Central Planning Office is supposed to formulate perspective economic and physical plans for Poland and to establish foundations for the state regional policy. The Ministry for Physical Planning and Construction is responsible for urban planning and physical

---

[7]In the following section I used some parts of my report *The country paper — Poland*, prepared for the LEDA Programme, January 1992.

planning on the local level as well as for new regulations concerning land use, ownership of land, building standards, etc.

Neither of these bodies have formulated progressive, offensive regional/spatial, whole-national policy. The CPO puts forward proposals for regional state policy which are based on defensive assumptions, oriented towards reacting to processes and phenomena that already emerged (like unemployment) instead of forecasting the processes that will take place and provide adequate regional/spatial framework for them. Thus the existing assumptions of regional policies are not directed towards facilitating reforming the national economy but are rooted in past doctrines of supporting the places facing current difficulties and problems.

New developments have not changed this — rather gloomy — picture. An integrated development policy has not been formulated and the regional aspects of any social or economic policy (as weak as they are) are still almost non-existing. This applies also to the spatial aspects of the employment/unemployment policies conducted by the Ministry of Labour and Social Policy, which — all of a sudden — emerged as the governmental agency with the strongest inputs into regional policies. It deals with severe cases of structural unemployment, which leads this ministry to become involved in regional/local intervention. It has to be said, however, that this is — obviously — only one element of regional development and regional policy. Moreover, the doctrine adopted by this ministry is — perhaps necessarily — one-sided. It is oriented towards *"assisting the poor and the weak"* and any assistance for *"the good and the strong"* (which becomes a more and more pronounced doctrine of some modern regional policies) is not present in activities of this particular ministry.

Employment policy[8] is the only one which uses special areas on which some economic instruments are used. On 24 August 1992 the Council of Ministers approved a new list of 245 municipalities especially endangered by structural unemployment. These municipalities occupy 12.4% of the country's area and are inhabited by some 10% of the total population of Poland.

The idea of identifying regions with high structural unemployment is not new and has been introduced already in 1990. The municipalities

---

[8]In this section I refer to my paper *Unemployment & Employment Policies in Poland*, prepared for the workshop on Employment, Assistance and Employment Policies in Central and Eastern European countries, Budapest, September 21, 1992.

endangered by structural unemployment enjoy the following measures and incentives ("Rzeczpospolita", 25 August 1992):

1. Accelerated amortisation rates of fixed assets bought after 1 January 1991. The enterprises are allowed to calculate amortisation according to the highest rates, which should create resources for new investment and new job creation.
2. Infrastructural grants from the state budget which will come to the local budget and would allow for infrastructure development, in this way creating new jobs.
3. Income tax reliefs for private businesses which run vocational training and re-training and a right to exceed the limit of employment without paying higher taxes.
4. Firms which employ graduates of vocational, secondary and university-level schools who have been directed by the Employment Offices are exempted from the compulsory payments for the Work Fund and from income and salary taxes for a period of 12 months.
5. A right for business with foreign capital higher than 2 mln Ecu to apply to the Ministry of Finance for income tax reliefs. The enterprises introducing new technologies and declaring exports of at least of 20% of their production will have preferences. Up to now only 5 such firms have been granted the reductions.
6. Grants from the Work Fund for active forms of coping with unemployment.

Until now there is no comprehensive evaluation of the efficiency of these measures and incentives. The measures and incentives applied on the local level in order to alleviate unemployment function, to some extent, "in a mist".

There are also few other instruments of regional policy in Poland, related to the environment protection. These are:

1. Fees for water used for other purposes then production of energy.
2. There are special (restrictive) norms of air pollution for some areas — natural reserves, national parks, health resorts etc.

No evaluation of these instruments was available to the author.

There have been attempts to cope with specific, "problem" regions. In two cases the Governmental Representatives have been nominated for regional restructuring: one (within the structure of the Ministry of Labour and Social Policy) for the Wałbrzych region and another (in February 1993) for the Łódź region. A plan of regional restructuring has been formulated which included statements on the magnitude and time-table of closing coal-pits and social allowances for the released employees. This plan is based on state funds. Full evaluation of the results of the first case is not available to the author.

## 2. For new approaches to regional policies in Poland

Since I have discussed these problems elsewhere[9], I shall limit myself only to very general remarks.

The following problems seem to be of crucial importance for the future regional development of Poland and should become the skeleton of active regional policy in the coming years:

1. Restructuring of selected regional and local systems in the framework of restructuring of the national economy. The role of particular regions has to be identified, state, regional and local programmes of restructuring should be formulated, goals, barriers, mechanisms and means of national, regional and local policies formulated and implemented.

2. Regional diversification of the social and economic potential of Poland vis a vis international cooperation. Particular Polish regions present very differentiated potential for foreign cooperation. If internationalisation of the Polish economy is really to take place, some regions, already best prepared for this process, should be supported in their efforts to develop infrastructure and facilities necessary for becoming the potential location for international investment.

3. The role of Poland in the trans-European network of telecommunications and transport. The state should be responsible, at least in the transitionary period, for constructing basic transportation and communication infrastructure enabling the integration of national economy into the European and global economy. The trans-European networks crossing Poland should become the first premise for formulating national policy in this respect.

4. Environmental protection is one of the most important problems of Poland and has to incorporated into regional/spatial policies, also from the point of view of international cooperation. The policy should indicate the solution of the dilemma: more production at the expense

---

[9] See G. Gorzelak, *Dilemmas of regional policies in Poland*, [in:] G. Gorzelak, A. Kukliński (eds.), *Dilemmas of Regional Policies in Central and Eastern Europe*, EUROREG, vol. 8, 1993

of environment (continuation of traditional trends), or less production and turning to environment protection. This dilemma would be solved differently in particular regions, but general guidelines from the national policies should be provided.

5. Changes in the territorial organisation of the country as one of the components of restructuring. The current territorial division of Poland has to be changed if the Polish administrative units of the regional level are to become more powerful units of regional development and international cooperation. Only the local, municipal level should be left unchanged. This reform implies new division of competence and power between the state, regions and municipalities and has to be incorporated in the framework of the future regional policies conducted by each of these three levels.

It has to be stressed that there is an urgent need of creating integrated approach to sectoral and regional aspects of the national economy. Traditionally, both systems (sectoral and territorial) used to be considered and "planned" separately, what left regional policies weak and effective, constantly losing to preferences of most powerful economic sectors and branches.

In the process of formulating new regional policies West-European experience should be of crucial importance. Especially, a critical review of European theories and practical experience in restructuring and regional development should be taken into account. Europe presents a great sample of differentiated examples how to solve the regional problems facing Poland and these experiences should be thoroughly examined and adapted to Polish conditions. Providing Polish regionalists with information on this sphere should be considered as one of the most effective ways of foreign aid, considerably improving efficiency of other means of this aid (direct funding, investment, credits etc.).

These issues have been assessed only in "an intellectual" way by scientists and practitioners[10] — and not yet by official institutions. Poland still awaits the rebirth of active approach to its regional problems.

---

[10]See for example A. Pyszkowski, *Polish regional policies: diagnosis — problems — options*, in: G. Gorzelak, A. Kukliński (eds.) *Dilemmas of Regional Policies in Eastern and Central Europe*, EUROREG, vol. 8, Warszawa 1992.

Wojciech Dziemianowicz
European Institute
for Regional and Local Development
Warsaw

# FOREIGN CAPITAL IN CZECHO-SLOVAKIA, POLAND AND HUNGARY, 1989–1992

## 1. Introduction

Present activity of firms with foreign capital is not an unprecedented phenomenon in the economic reality of Czecho-Slovakia, Hungary and Poland. It is, however, only now, in the new political and economic situation, when the countries considered started to make important efforts aiming at attracting foreign investors, that the problem gives rise to a lot of emotions. This is expressed through frequent press publications and pronouncements of numerous politicians related to the issue of foreign investments.

This report present a systematisation of knowledge, indication of barriers and motives of inflow of foreign investment capital into the Vysegrad Triangle[1].

---

[1] This study has been performed before the breakdown of Czecho-Slovakia into two inmdependent republics. Nowadays one should rather speak about the Visegrad Rectangle.

Information on regulations and conditions created for foreign capital in the three countries and direct foreign investment there was collected in the central statistical offices in Budapest, Prague and Warsaw, in research institutes as well as from institutions in all these three cities dealing with foreign investment. Indirect sources have been used, too. It was not possible, alas, to gather all the necessary information because, in particular, of confidentiality or high costs of acquisition.

Statistical data presented here may differ and do in fact differ from those functioning in some other reports. These differences are explained below on the example of Poland.

There are three kinds of statistics in Poland, concerning the numbers and characteristics of enterprises which are of interest for us (Szromik, 1992):

1. On companies which have been granted license to undertake activity in Poland.
2. On companies which were registered in the Central Statistical Office (GUS) through the issue of the company's registry number.
3. On companies which reported to GUS on their activity. These latter numbers reflect the numbers of actually functioning companies.

I did try to present the data belonging to the third group. In several cases, though, this turned out to be impossible, of which the Readers will be informed.

An additional problem was formed by establishment of a common denominator of the phenomena described. Some values could be obtained after conversion of (Czecho-Slovak) crowns, (Hungarian) forints and (Polish) zlotys into US dollars, according to average exchange rates. Until July 4th, 1991, the data on companies with foreign capital were gathered in Poland by the Agency for Foreign Investments (AIZ), and this function was afterwards transferred to the organ issuing licenses for activity in Poland to foreign investors, namely to the Ministry of Privatisation (MPW). Since that time the sums invested in Poland are converted into zlotys according to daily exchange rates. This would not have a greater importance if not for high inflation and frequently changing rates of foreign currencies.

# 2. Foreign investment in Czecho-Slovakia

## 2.1. Legal conditions

The first legal regulation concerning foreign investments was established in Czecho-Slovakia in 1985. It was not allowed at that time that a foreign investor have a majority share in a company. This was changed in 1988 by the law on enterprises with a foreign share (173/1988).

Table 1 presents a selection of legal regulations concerning enterprises with foreign capital share.

As can be seen, legal regulations encourage to making of investments mainly through automatic tax vacations and limitless transfer of profits. The regulation introducing a limitation on employment of foreigners aims at alleviation of unemployment. In spite of the increase of minimum capital necessary for establishment of a company this value remains still quite low, for it amounts to approximately 34,000 US dollars.

## 2.2. The number of enterprises with foreign capital and the value of foreign capital invested

Until 1989 the activity of foreign capital in Czecho-Slovakia was insignificant. This situation was caused by the law, mentioned in the preceding section, forbidding the foreigners to take over the majority shares in the companies. As the legal regulations have been improved by the government, and the advantageous climate around foreign investments was being established, the number of foreign firms and the value of capital involved increased significantly.

There were only 55 companies with foreign capital, functioning at the end of 1989, and until 1990 the foreign investment value in Czecho-Slovakia totalled approximately 400,000 crowns (the least value among the countries of Vysegrad Triangle).

Presently, we are witnessing a vigourous growth of foreign investments in Czecho-Slovakia, with particularly rapid rate of increase of the number of enterprises with foreign capital share.

**Table 1**

## Legal conditions of investing foreign capital
## in Czecho-Slovakia

| 1.01.1989 | Changes |
|---|---|
| 1. License for the start of activity is issued by the Minister of Finance or Minister of Foreign Trade | Presently companies do not need a license to be established. Court registration suffices. License is required only for investments in enterprises from the privatisation pool. |
| 2. Enterprises with 100% of foreign capital cannot be established. | Since 1.05.1990 such firms can be established. |
| 3. In order to obtain license it was necessary, in particular, to pay the security of 100,000 crowns. | No limitations. |
| 4. Economic activity can be undertaken in any domain excepting national defense and economic security of the state. | No changes. |
| 5. Minister of Finance may grant 2 years of tax vacations. | Presently, foreign investors can obtain tax vacations for 2 years, and the new investors, whose contribution amounts to at least 1 million crowns (cash + other assets) are automatically granted 1 year of tax vacations. |
| 6. Enterprises with foreign share pay the following income tax: 20% when income does not exceed 200,000 crowns, 20% out of the first 200,000 crowns and, out of the surplus: 40% when the share of foreign capital in the company is higher than 35%, 55% when the share of foreign capital in the company is lower than 35%. | Since January 1st, 1990: 20% when income does not exceed 200,000 crowns 20% out of the first 200,000 crowns and, out of the surplus: 40% when the share of foreign capital exceeds 30%, 55% when the share of foreign capital is lower than 30%. |
| 7. Transfer of profits — up to entire dividend from exports and up to 20% from other dividends. | Since January 1st, 1991 — possibility of transferring the whole of dividend, after crowns have been converted in a bank into foreign currency. |
| 8. Possibility of employing foreigners: without limitations. | Since January 1st, 1992, the limit of 5% on employment of foreigners is in force. |

Source: Joint ventures, "Życie Gospodarcze", 21.04.1991; Investment Guide for Foreign Entrepreneurs in the Czech and Slovak Republic, Federal Agency for Foreign Investment, Prague, 1991; Frydman, Rapaczyński, Earle (1992).

Table 2

**The number of enterprises with foreign capital
in Czecho-Slovakia**

| Status as of: | Number of enterprises: |
|---|---|
| 31.12.1989 | 55 |
| 30.10.1990 | 776 |
| 01.06.1991 | 2899 |
| 01.10.1991 | 5921 |
| 01.12.1992 | 11362 |

Source: Federalni Statisticky Urad (FSU) — Federal Statistical Office.

Table 3

**The value of foreign capital**

| Status as of: | Value in million USD |
|---|---|
| 31.05.1990 | 0.4 |
| 28.02.1991 | 159.2 |
| 31.12.1991 | 466.8 |
| 30.09.1992 | 1725.3 |

Source: Piskova (1992), own calculations on the basis of data provided in Dubska (1992) and Privatisation Newsletter of Czechoslovakia (1991).

## 2.3. Origins of foreign capital

German capital turns out to be the most active in Czecho-Slovakia. Germans did invest the most here and participated in the greatest number of enterprises. This situation is, in the opinion of this author, due to the fact that Germans, who border with both Poland and Czecho-Slovakia, opted for the latter as the main area of their economic expansion (not overlooking other countries of the Vysegrad Triangle, of course).

American investments are characterised by quite significant investment volumes, but a limited number of companies, which is also confirmed in Hungary and in Poland. This results from the fact that it is corporations with large capital which locate their investments in these countries, while

**Table 4**

**The number of enterprises with foreign capital share**

| Country | Numbers as of 01.06.1991 |
|---|---|
| 1. Germany | 865 |
| 2. Austria | 825 |
| 3. Switzerland | 179 |
| 4. Italy | 134 |
| 5. USA | 132 |
| 6. The Netherlands | 92 |
| 7. United Kingdom | 88 |
| 8. Sweden | 82 |
| 9. France | 72 |
| 10. Hungary | 66 |
| TOTAL | 2899 |

Source: Drabek (1992).

**Table 5**

**Capital invested according to countries of origin**

| Country | 30.06.1992 |
|---|---|
|  | Out of 100% |
| 1. Germany | 52.1% |
| 2. USA | 11.9% |
| 3. France | 11.8% |
| 4. Austria | 7.6% |
| 5. Belgium | 7.0% |
| 6. remaining countries | 9.7% |

Source: Econom 39/1992

small American investors prefer to locate their capital nearer to the States, for instance in Mexico.

Quite a contrary situation exists in the group of Austrian investments, i.e. a large number of companies, but with low volume of capital each. The cause of this situation is, it seems, a better assessment of Hungary as the place for locating capital, at least because of previous uncertainty as to the fate of the federation of Czech and Slovak Republics.

It is not since yesterday that people speak of Germans wishing to subordinate economically Poland, Hungary, and especially Czecho-Slovakia. One might say that a fight for the influence zones and for the best starting position to investments within the area of the former Soviet Union is going on. The best example of this is provided by the recently intensified activity of French capital, which at the beginning was insignificant, and now is at the top of the list. This hypothesis is confirmed by the most recent statistical data: 25.4% of capital which came to Czecho-Slovakia between January 1st and June 30th, 1992, was French, 22.9% — German, and 15.2% — American.

Among the largest investors we find German firms of Volkswagen, Siemens and Mercedes. In terms of money the greatest investment until now was made by American company Dow Chemicals Co. (11.5 billion crowns). Other American firms, classified among the largest investors are: Philip Morris, US West, Procter and Gamble. Similarly, such French firms as Rhone Poulenc, Nestle/BSN and Air France, are among twelve largest investors.

## 2.4. Spatial distribution of foreign capital

Spatial distribution of enterprises with foreign capital share over the territory of Czecho-Slovakia features certain regularity. Thus, joint venture companies are more or less evenly distributed over the whole country, while the firms with 100% share of foreign capital are mostly located in the Czech Republic. If we compare the spatial distribution of enterprises with 100% share of foreign capital and the value of capital invested, we can see that these firms locate quite significant capital in their undertakings. In Slovakia a greater number of such enterprises is concentrated only in Bratislava, this fact being caused by more difficult conditions encountered by foreign investors in this republic (worse economic effects than in Czech Republic, concentration of energy-intensive resource-oriented industries and of the enterprises which have been until quite recently producing almost exclusively for exports to the Soviet Union, and finally — location of enterprises of military industries, see Dominiczak, 1991).

Majority of German capital is concentrated in three regions: in Central Bohemia (most of it), in Prague and in Bratislava. It also seems interesting to note that at the beginning of 1992 German capital constituted 92.1% of foreign capital invested in Central Bohemia, 44.1% in Prague and 66.1% in Bratislava (Dubska, 1992).

## 2.5. Enterprises with foreign capital according to sectors of economy

Until the end of 1992 the greatest volumes of foreign capital were invested in the sphere of production of transport equipment (39.5%). Consecutive ranks were occupied by: food processing industry (10.1%), service (8.0%) and construction (7.4%).

**Table 6**

**The number of enterprises with foreign capital in particular sectors of Czecho-Slovak economy in 1991**

| Sectors | Number of enterprises as of 1.10.1991 |
|---|---|
| Manufacturing | 560 |
| Construction | 339 |
| Transport and communication | 115 |
| Forestry and agriculture | 28 |
| Trade | 2202 |
| Service | 2282 |
| Other activities | 395 |
| Total | 5921 |

Source: Huskova (1992)

## 2.6. The structure of the enterprises with foreign capital according to the initial capital value

The firms with foreign capital, which existed at the time of the present study within the territory of Czecho-Slovakia had for the most part only a limited financial value of the foreign capital share. This seems natural, on the one hand, but a low number of greater investments also indicates precautions taken by the investors.

Table 7

**The number of enterprises with foreign share
according to the magnitude of initial capital**

| The value of initial capital | Number of enterprises as of 31.05.1991 |
|---|---|
| up to 100,000 crowns | 1178 |
| 0.1–1.0 million crowns | 1279 |
| 1–10 million crowns | 350 |
| 10–100 million crowns | 74 |
| 100–1000 million crowns | 14 |
| more than 1000 million crowns | 6 |

Source: Drabek (1992)

# 3. Foreign investment in Poland

## 3.1. Legal conditions

Since January 1st, 1989, a new law on economic activity conducted with participation of foreign economic agents became valid (Dziennik Ustaw no.41, position 325, of December 28th, 1988 [1]). This law was thereafter modified by introduction of changes contained in the law given in Dziennik Ustaw no.74, position 442, of 1989 [2]. These laws constituted the legal basis for the activity of foreign investors until July 4th, 1991, when the law of June 14th, 1991, in force until today, became valid (Dziennik Ustaw no.60, position 253, [3]).

The law denoted [1] regulates the conditions of functioning of newly established foreign investments and also conditions of functioning of foreign enterprises of petty industries (called further on FEPI), which had before been functioning on the basis of the law of July 6th, 1982 (Dziennik Ustaw no.13 of 1985). In accordance with the law [1] the FEPI may function on the basis of new regulations, i.e. [1], or of the old ones, i.e. [3].

Companies, which were established on the basis of the law of April 23rd, 1986, concerning companies with a share of foreign economic agents (Dziennik Ustaw no.17, position 88, of 1986), became joint venture companies in the meaning of law [1].

In comparison with the previous law from 1989, the present law gives the possibility of unlimited transfer of profits, and although it annulates the three year tax vacations, it also defines a lot of cases in which an investor may obtain tax exemption on income tax. This regulation, though, gives only a theoretical possibility of getting tax exemption. Information obtained by this author from the Ministry of Privatisation indicates that between the middle of 1991 and the end of 1992 just a couple of such exemptions were granted.

## 3.2. The number of enterprises with foreign capital and the value of the foreign capital invested

Foreign capital has been flowing to Poland since 1977. The number of enterprises, as well as the value of money invested was, however, insignificant initially in comparison with the period 1989–1992.

In the first years of existence of foreign investments in Poland they could function as foreign enterprises on the territory of our country. This was not the most convenient form of cooperation, and, additionally, the political climate together with legal barriers existing then were not advantageous for undertaking of economic activity.

It was only after the regulations were changed (possibility of functioning in the form of joint venture companies) and the economic reforms were started that the dynamics of foreign investments intensified.

**Table 8**

### Regulations concerning enterprises with foreign capital

| Law of 23.12.1988 and changes from 1989, as well as other regulations concerning firms with foreign capital | Law of 14.06.1991 (valid until today) and other regulations concerning firms with foreign capital |
|---|---|
| 1. Licenses for starting of activity are issued by the President of the Agency for Foreign Investments | Licenses are issued by the Minister for Privatisation |
| 2. License is not granted if conduct of economic activity would not be purposeful because of:<br>— threat to economic interest of the state,<br>— requirements of the environmental protection,<br>— security and defense of the state or protection of the state secret | The same, but without the point concerning environmental protection |
| 3. Licenses are granted if economic activity is going to ensure, in particular:<br>— implementation of advanced technological and organisational solutions in national economy,<br>— supply of goods and services for exports,<br>— improvement of internal market supplies in terms of modern goods and services of high quality,<br>— protection of natural environment. | Lack of respective regulation |
| 4. Following kinds of activity require obtaining of a concession:<br>a) exploitation of and search for mineral resources<br>b) processing and trade with noble metals and precious stones<br>c) production of and trade in explosives, arms and ammunition<br>d) activity related to production of alcoholic beverages<br>e) production of tobacco products<br>f) running of pharmacies and other | The author did not get information on the kinds of activities subject to granting of concessions<br>Establishment of a company requires having a license if its activity encompasses at least one of the following domains:<br>a) management of airports and harbours<br>b) estate agencies<br>c) defense industry not included in concessions<br>d) wholesale trade in imported consumption goods<br>e) legal counselling |
| 5. Limitations on foreign capital share:<br>— share of foreign capital cannot be lower than 20% of the initial capital of a company;<br>— minimum value of foreign capital share in a company is 50,000 US dollars. | No limitations |
| 6. Tax reliefs:<br>— automatic tax vacations (on income tax) for 3 years, with possibility of prolongation for the subsequent 3 years | A company may obtain income tax exemption if:<br>a)input of foreign economic agents to the initial capital exceeds the equivalent of 2 million ECU,<br>b)economic activity of the company will, in particular<br>— be conducted in regions with especially high structural unemployment risk, or<br>— ensure implementation of new technological solutions in national economy, or<br>— enable export sales of at least 20% of total sales |
| 7. Transfer of profits — 15% after Polish zlotys have been converted to foreign currency | No limitations, after Polish zlotys are converted to foreign currency |
| 8. Possibility of employing foreigners — without limitations | No changes |

Source: Joint ventures, "Życie Gospodarcze", 21.04.1991; Frąckowiak, Kieres, Krzes, Malecki (1990); Ustawa z dnia 14.06.1991 o spółkach z udziałem zagranicznym (Law of 14.06.1991 on companies with foreign share), Dziennik Ustaw RP, no. 60.

**Table 9**

**The numbers of joint ventures and of foreign enterprises
of petty industries**

| Poland as a whole | 1989 | 1990 | 1991 | 30.09.1992 |
|---|---|---|---|---|
| Joint ventures | 429 | 1645 | 4796 | 8860 |
| FEPI | 841 | 862 | 787 | 714 |

Source: Zmiany strukturalne grup podmiotów gospodarczych w trzech kwartałach 1992,
GUS, Warszawa, 1992.

**Table 10**

**Value of foreign capital in Poland in million US dollars**

| 1989 | 1990 | 05.10.1991 | 1992 |
|---|---|---|---|
| 152.1 | 370.8 | 694.0 | 1300 |

Source: Szromik (1992) and data from the Agency for Foreign Investments

## 3.3. Origins of foreign capital

Germany has always been ranking first among the countries investing their capital in Poland. German capital is characterized by a high number of joint venture companies, but not the highest value of capital per one undertaking. This distribution of capital among companies was to a great extent caused by the fact that numerous German investors coming to Poland are of Polish extraction, and the capital they dispose of is not very important. In numerous cases Polish-German companies can be referred to as Polish, since the German side is represented by a German citizen of Polish origin, living in Germany for a relatively short period.

Second rank in terms of total capital invested and of the number of enterprises is taken by United States. In the recent period, in Poland as well as in Czecho-Slovakia and in Hungary, one also observes intensified activity of French capital (see table 11).

Table 13 lists some firms, whose capital involved in Poland is known. At the same time there were other great corporations which had oper-

Table 11

**The numbers of enterprises with foreign capital in Poland**

| Country of origin | 1985 | 1991 |
|---|---|---|
| Germany | 154 | 1658 |
| USA | 89 | 504 |
| Sweden | 84 | 389 |
| Austria | 64 | 375 |
| The Netherlands | * | 344 |
| France | 57 | 297 |
| United Kingdom | 73 | 283 |
| Italy | * | 264 |
| Total | * | 5444 |

Source: Skalmowski (1988), and Podmioty gospodarcze ... op.cit.

Table 12

**Capital declared according to countries in million USD**

| Countries | 1989 | 1990 | 1991 |
|---|---|---|---|
| Germany | 45.200 | 105.425 | 161.4 |
| USA | 15.143 | 33.863 | 75.9 |
| France | 3.188 | 15.710 | 67.7 |
| Sweden | 17.326 | 31.928 | 55.3 |
| Netherlands | 22.236 | 32.937 | 48.9 |
| Utd.Kingdom | 12.520 | 22.455 | 41.6 |
| Austria | 6.435 | 22.993 | 41.1 |
| Italy | 7.639 | 22.429 | 35.3 |
| Totals | 152.102 | 370.880 | 694.0 |

Source: Szromik (1992), and the data from the Agency for Foreign Investments.

ations in Poland or were negotiating their entry to Polish market. The respective examples are: Johnson & Johnson (USA), Procter & Gamble (USA), RJ Reynolds Tobacco (USA/Switzerland), Marriott (USA), ICI (United Kingdom), ICL (United Kingdom), Siemens (Germany), Adidas (Germany), IKEA (Sweden).

Table 13

**Major investments made by foreign capital in Poland
(as of mid-1992, in million US dollars)**

| Name of the firm | Country | Capital involved |
|---|---|---|
| Fiat | Italy | 180 |
| International Paper | USA | 120 |
| Volvo | Sweden | 80 |
| General Motors | USA | 75 |
| ABB | Sweden | 70 |
| Thompson C.E. | France | 35 |
| Peugeot | France | 32 |
| Pepsico | USA | 25 |
| Henkel KG | Germany | 20 |
| Ringnes | Norway | 20 |
| Kvaerner | Norway | 17.5 |
| Philips | The Netherlands | 17 |
| Gerber | International | 11.3 |
| ABB Part Ltd. | International | 10.4 |
| Levi Strauss | USA | 9.5 |

Source: Dobrzański (1992).

Until quite recently a lack of presence of great corporations could be felt in Poland. As can be seen, this problem has already been resolved, though the capital invested by these firms is still insignificant.

## 3.4. Spatial distribution of foreign capital

Foreign firms were established as early as in 1977 in six provinces of Poland, i.e. in Warsaw, Siedlce, Bielsko-Biała, Kraków, Częstochowa and Wałbrzych voivodships (Skalmowski, 1988). With time, more and more firms with foreign capital were installing themselves in large voivodship centers. This process continues until today.

The greatest numbers of enterprises with foreign capital are located in Warsaw and, generally speaking, in the voivodships of Western and North-western Poland. Among these voivodships we should especially mention Łódź, Gdańsk, Szczecin, Poznań, Wrocław, Katowice and Kraków regions.

In comparison with 1990 there has been a visible growth of the numbers of joint venture companies in some voivodships of eastern Poland, e.g. in Lublin and in Kielce voivodships. There is, however, still a group of voivodships in which the number of economic undertakings with a share of foreign investments is minimal. These voivodships are: Ostrołęka, Łomża, Tarnobrzeg, Zamość, Przemyśl and Krosno.

In 1990 the greatest value of foreign capital was — in terms of declarations pronounced — invested in Warsaw voivodship (mainly in Warsaw itself), then in these voivodships, in which large ports are located — Gdańsk and Szczecin, and in such voivodships as Poznań, Zielona Góra, Wrocław, Katowice and Kraków.

## 3.5. Enterprises with foreign capital according to sectors of economy

Industry and trade turn out to be the most popular sectors of economy with respect to foreign investments. Domination of investments in industry could already be noticed in 1990. The number of joint venture companies in trade in the third quarter of 1992 has been quite close to that of industrial enterprises. Thus, it could be said that trade is the most rapidly developing sector of our economy in terms of foreign investments.

In the "remaining branches of material production" the growth of numbers of enterprises with foreign capital share displays high dynamics as well, although there are much less of these firms. The lowest growth dynamics (within the sphere of material production) of numbers of joint venture companies occurs in forestry and agriculture.

In comparison with other countries of the Vysegrad Triangle, there is in Poland a relatively low number of enterprises with a share of foreign capital which function in the sector of service.

The distribution of numbers of joint venture companies among particular sectors of national economy is presented in table 14.

**Table 14**

Enterprises with a share of foreign capital
according to sectors of national economy

| Sectors | 1990 | 1991 | 30.09.1992 |
|---|---|---|---|
| Industry | 853 | 2099 | 3152 |
| Construction | 71 | 319 | 661 |
| Agriculture and forestry | 52 | 70 | 109 |
| Transport and communication | 72 | 221 | 341 |
| Trade | 198 | 1158 | 2959 |
| Other branches of material production | 258 | 413 | 580 |
| Municipal economy | 6 | 14 | 36 |
| Housing economy and non-material municipal service | 1 | 2 | 8 |
| Research and technology development | 8 | 6 | 11 |
| Education and upbringing | 1 | 13 | 34 |
| Culture and arts | 15 | 27 | 53 |
| Sports, tourism and recreation | 33 | 105 | 177 |
| Other branches of non-material service | 67 | 280 | 610 |
| Remaining activities | 10 | 69 | 129 |

Source: Podmioty gospodarcze ... op.cit., and Zmiany strukturalne... op.cit.

## 3.6. The structure of enterprises with foreign capital according to the share of this capital in the company stock

Three most important capital share brackets can be distinguished in the description of this structure. The highest number (23.4%) of companies belong to the segment defined by the share of foreign capital in the company between 91 and 100%, then there is a bit less of companies (17.3%) in which the share of foreign capital lies between 0 and 10%, and yet a bit less (14.9%) of companies in which the share of foreign capital is between 41 and 50%. The numbers of companies in other share-defined segments are much smaller and relatively evenly distributed (see table 15).

The fact that foreign investors prefer the companies with their maximum or else minimum shares indicates certain apprehensions related to investing. When analyzing the data from tables 15 and 16 we can notice that foreigners are investing very cautiously and are most often entering such alliances in which their share of capital allows them to have the possibility of managing the firm.

**Table 15**

**The structure of the set of joint venture companies
in Poland according to the share of foreign capital in 1991**

| | Share of foreign capital in % | | | | | | | | | |
|---|---|---|---|---|---|---|---|---|---|---|
| | up to 10% | 11 – 20 | 21 – 30 | 31 – 40 | 41 – 50 | 51 – 60 | 61 – 70 | 71 – 80 | 81 – 90 | 91 – 100 |
| Number of companies = 100% | 17.3 | 6.0 | 5.5 | 6.5 | 14.9 | 8.0 | 5.6 | 6.4 | 6.4 | 23.4 |

Source: Podmioty gospodarcze ..., op.cit.

**Table 16**

**The structure of foreign capital in joint venture companies
in Poland according to the shares of foreign capital
in these companies in 1991**

| | Share of foreign capital in % | | | | | | | | | |
|---|---|---|---|---|---|---|---|---|---|---|
| | up to 10% | 11 – 20 | 21 – 30 | 31 – 40 | 41 – 50 | 51 – 60 | 61 – 70 | 71 – 80 | 81 – 90 | 91 – 100 |
| Total capital value = 100% | 2.0 | 3.7 | 5.8 | 7.5 | 24.7 | 12.6 | 7.9 | 5.4 | 5.6 | 24.8 |

Source: Podmioty gospodarcze ... op.cit.

# 4. Foreign investment in Hungary

## 4.1. Legal conditions

In Hungary, similarly as in Poland, a new law was introduced on January 1st, 1989, concerning functioning of enterprises with foreign capital share (Law no. XXIV of 1988). In accordance with the authors of the book "The Privatisation Process in Central Europe", Frydman, Rapaczyński and Earle (1992), this law is still in force, and only some regulations from it have been changed by additional legal regulations, like, for instance, new tax rates defined by the law no. LXXXVI of 1991.

## 4.2. The number of enterprises with foreign capital and the value of foreign capital invested

The number of foreign investors is in Hungary the highest among all the countries of the former socialist block. The first foreign investments started to appear in Hungary in 1972, but a more intensive inflow of foreign capital has been observed only since 1989.

In the recent period the dynamics of growth of the number of joint ventures slowed down, but this has not had a negative influence on the overall volume of foreign capital invested. This may mean the beginning of the situation, for which each of the countries of Vysegrad Triangle waited, i.e. the growth of the average volume of foreign capital invested in one undertaking.

## 4.3. Origins of foreign capital

The greatest part of the foreign investments established in Vysegrad Triangle is concentrated in Hungary. At the end of 1992 the greatest share of volume of foreign capital invested in Hungary was due to Americans. Similarly as in Czecho-Slovakia and in Poland, German entrepreneurs are also very active in this country. In their investments, though, one can hardly notice any regularity in terms of investment volumes. Small firms are active, for instance, in tourism, mainly along the coasts of Balaton

**Table 17**

**Laws regulating functioning of enterprises
with a share of foreign capital**

| As of January 1st, 1989 | Changes |
|---|---|
| 1. If a foreign partner has the majority share in a company then Ministry of Finance or Ministry of Foreign Trade must be asked to agree to founding of this company | No changes |
| 2. Licenses are not granted if a company wishes to undertake activity in the sphere of defense or security of the state | No changes |
| 3. Automatic tax vacations for the period of three years | Tax vacations annulled, but tax reliefs may reach even 100% (see point 4.) |
| 4. Companies with a share of foreign capital are entitled to the following tax reliefs: 20% relief if the share of foreign capital is at least 20% or 5 million forints, 60% relief for 5 years and 40% for the subsequent 5 years, if more than half of income comes from hotel goods and services, initial capital of the company is higher than 25 million forints, and the foreign share is at least 30%, up to 100% over 5 years and 60% over the following 6 years if the company takes up activity especially important for the interests of the country, e.g. production of car subassemblies, food, agriculture, machine parts, pharmaceuticals, computers, construction of hotels and improvement of telecommunication. | Law no. LXXXVI introduces tax reliefs for Hungarian firms (of which foreign investors can also take advantage), and for the firms with a share of foreign capital as well: 60% over the first 5 years and 40% over the following 5 years if the initial capital is bigger than 50 million forints and at least 30% of capital is contributed by the foreign partner and at least half of income comes from the following kinds of activity: construction and running of hotels, production of computer hardware, production of car subassemblies, production of packings. |
| 5. Transfer of profits — no limitations, in the form of the whole dividend accruing, after forints have been converted to foreign currency. | No changes |
| 6. Employment of foreigners — no limitations. | No changes |

Sources: Nyiri (1990); Joint ventures, "Gazeta Wyborcza", 21.04.1991; Frydman, Rapaczyński, Earle (1992).

Table 18

**The number of joint venture companies in Hungary**

| 1980 | 1984 | 1987 | 1990 | 1991 | 30.09.1992 |
|------|------|------|------|------|------------|
| 4 | 32 | 130 | 1350 | 5693 | 12,110 |

Source: Csaki (1992); data from Kozponti Statisztikai Hivatal (KSH). (The counterpart of the Polish Central Statistical Office.)

Table 19

**The value of foreign capital invested in Hungary
as of the end of respective year**

| Year | Capital invested in million USD |
|------|----------------------------------|
| 1972–1988 | 250 |
| 1989 | 550 |
| 1990 | 1450 |
| 1991 | 2850 |
| 1992 | 4500 |

Source: Csaki (1992); statistical data from KSH; Kraj jak towar, "Gazeta Wyborcza", 10.02.1993.

lake, while medium firms are often active in the sphere of trade. Large German companies are also present in Hungary, as exemplified by the car making corporations, and by Siemens or BASF.

The greatest number of small enterprises cooperate with Austrians. Austrian investors, irrespective of the fact that they continue to establish numerous small companies (like in Czecho-Slovakia and in Poland), do also locate in Hungary greater capital volumes than in the other countries of Vysegrad Triangle.

## 4.4. Spatial distribution of foreign capital

Almost all of the administrative regions (komitats) had already then quite important numbers of companies with foreign capital share on their territories. The greatest number of enterprises with foreign capital and the greatest foreign capital value could be observed in Budapest and in Pecs.

**Table 20**

**Capital invested in Hungary coming from particular countries**

| Country | Million USD as of 30.09.1992 | Million USD estimated |
|---|---|---|
| 1. USA | 900 | 1118 |
| 2. Germany | 500 | 621 |
| 3. Austria | 400 | 497 |
| 4. United Kingdom | 250 | 310 |
| 5. France | 250 | 310 |
| 6. Other countries | 1000 | 1242 |
| Totals | 3300 | 4100 |

Source: Frydman, Rapaczyński, Earle (1992)

**Table 21**

**The numbers of joint ventures**

| Country | As of 30.09.1992 | New ones, established between 01.01. and 30.09. |
|---|---|---|
| 1. Germany | 1117 | 655 |
| 2. Austria | 960 | 435 |
| 3. USA | 264 | 204 |
| 4. Switzerland | 230 | 114 |
| 5. Italy | 176 | 171 |
| 6. Utd.Kingdom | 149 | 82 |
| 7. Sweden | 147 | 46 |

Source: Statistical data from KSH.

The regions where a relatively low number of joint venture companies functioned were Nograd, Heves, Jasz-Nagykun-Szolnok.

Following the two regions mentioned — Budapest and Pecs — leading with respect to the value of foreign capital invested, other regions with high value of foreign investments were Fejer and Borsod-Abauj-Zemplen.

The least value of foreign capital was invested in Tolna and Heves komitats.

## 4.5. Enterprises with foreign capital according to sectors of economy

In terms of sectors of economy the greatest number of firms with foreign capital were established in trade, then in industry and in service. Foreign investors seem to be less interested in such sectors as agriculture and forestry or transport and communication.

**Table 22**

**Enterprises with foreign capital share
according to sectors of national economy in 1991**

| Sector | Number |
|--------|--------|
| Industry | 2171 |
| Construction | 811 |
| Agriculture and forestry | 142 |
| Transport and communication | 198 |
| Trade | 4203 |
| Other branches of material production | 242 |
| Non-material service | 1350 |
| Total | 9117 |

Source: "Foreign Joint Ventures in Hungary, 1991"

## 4.6. The structure of enterprises with foreign capital according to the share of this capital in the company stock

Foreign investors are most often associating themselves in Hungary with domestic firms by contributing between 31 and 50% of total capital of the company. This phenomenon is, it seems, caused by the fact that such a share is the minimum required to take advantage from tax reliefs.

**Table 23**

**The structure of the set of joint venture companies
according to the share of foreign capital**

| Share of foreign capital | Number of companies | | |
|---|---|---|---|
| | 1989 | 1990 | 30.06.1991 |
| up to 20% | 195 | 793 | 1301 |
| 21–30 | 176 | 798 | 1150 |
| 31–50 | 817 | 327 | 4556 |
| 51–80 | 118 | 433 | 739 |
| 81–99 | 17 | 146 | 261 |
| 100 | 27 | 244 | 759 |

Source: "Foreign Joint Ventures in Hungary, 1991"

**Table 24**

**The structure of foreign capital in joint venture companies
according to the shares of this capital***

| Share of foreign capital | Value of foreign capital in million USD | | |
|---|---|---|---|
| | 1989 | 1990 | 30.06.1991 |
| up to 20% | 16.4 | 58.5 | 12.9 |
| 21–30 | 43.6 | 126.2 | 50.0 |
| 31–50 | 390.0 | 753.8 | 175.7 |
| 51–80 | 81.0 | 356.9 | 72.9 |
| 81–99 | 3.64 | 7.7 | 5.7 |
| 100% | 7.3 | 90.8 | 54.3 |

* Data expressed in forints were converted into US dollars according to annual averages of exchange rates: 55 forints per 1 USD in 1989, 65 forints in 1990 and 70 forints in 1991.

Source: "Foreign Joint Ventures in Hungary, 1991"

# 5. Foreign capital in Czecho-Slovakia, Hungary and Poland — a comparison

The present chapter constitutes an attempt at comparing the legal conditions and the current state of foreign investments in Vysegrad Triangle.

## 5.1. Legal conditions

Table 25 shows the outline of legal conditions, which have formed the framework of activity of foreign investors in particular countries until mid-1992. The present author has, alas, no information as to the possible changes that could have taken place at the end of 1992.

**Table 25**

**Legal conditions in the countries of Vysegrad Triangle state as of middle of 1992**

| Legal aspect | Czecho-Slovakia | Poland | Hungary |
|---|---|---|---|
| 1. Limitations on shares | No limitations | No limitations | No limitations |
| 2. Inaccessible spheres of economy | Defence, economic security of the state | Defence economic security of the state | Defence or security of the country |
| 3. Tax vacations | Automatic — 1 year, when the input of a foreigner is higher than 1 million crowns | Possibility of exemption from income tax by Ministry of Privatisation under definite conditions | The sum of tax reliefs may attain 100% |
| 4. Tax exemptions and reliefs | Strictly defined, automatic | Strictly defined, but granted by Ministry of Privatisation | Strictly defined, automatic |
| 5. Transfer of profits | No limitations | No limitations | No limitations |
| 6. Employment of foreigners | Up to 5% of employees | No limitations | No limitations |

Legal regulations, to which foreign investors are subject in particular countries of Vysegrad Triangle are in several points very much alike (see, for instance, the case of share limitations, economic spheres inaccessible to foreign investors, transfer of profits etc.).

Automatic tax vacations are presently offered to foreign investors only in Czecho-Slovakia. Although there is no such regulation in Hungary, tax reliefs may be obtained, reaching altogether even 100%, provided definite conditions are fulfilled. Hungarian law, besides encouraging larger investments, directs foreign undertakings towards certain economic spheres through fiscal incentives. In Poland and in Czecho-Slovakia the main role is played by the volume of capital invested by a foreigner and the share in a company. In addition, there is a negative side to the regulation in force in Poland consisting in the fact that there is no guarantee for a foreign investor of tax relief or exemption, even if appropriate conditions envisaged in the law are fulfilled.

## 5.2. Foreign investment

On September 30, 1992 there were in Hungary and in Poland respectively 12,110 and 9,574 firms with a share of foreign capital. In Czecho-Slovakia, on December 1st, 1992, there were 11,362 of them. Foreign investors appeared at the earliest in Hungary, but until the end of 1988 the greatest number of foreign firms existed in Poland (the so called Polish emigre enterprises), though the volume of capital invested in them was rather limited. The highest dynamics of growth of the numbers of firms with foreign capital is presently observed in Czecho-Slovakia, although there were only some 800 such firms at the end of 1990. With regard to the volume of foreign capital invested the first place is taken by Hungary — 4.5 billion USD (31.12.1992), followed by Czecho-Slovakia — 1.7 billion USD (30.09.1992) and finally Poland — 1.3 billion USD (31.12.1992).

The countries which have invested through their entrepreneurs the most in Vysegrad Triangle were Germany and United States. Other countries, from which important capital investment inputs came, were Austria (especially in Hungary), France and United Kingdom. German capital is involved in the greatest number of joint venture companies. There are also numerous joint ventures in which capital from Austria (first of all in Czecho-Slovakia and Hungary), United States, Italy, Switzerland and Sweden (particularly in Poland) is involved.

In terms of sectors of economy the greatest number of companies with foreign capital functioned within Vysegrad Triangle in trade, service and industry. In 1991 in Czecho-Slovakia there were approximately equal numbers of joint venture companies in trade and service (2,202 and 2,282, respectively), while the number of firms with foreign capital active in industry was very low, in comparison with Hungary and Poland — only 560. In Poland the leading sector with that respect was industry — 2,099 joint venture companies, followed by trade — 1,158 companies. In Hungary the leading sector was trade — 4,203 companies with a share of foreign capital, followed by industry and service (2,171 and 1,350, respectively).

The lowest numbers of joint venture companies active in the sphere of material production in the countries of Vysegrad Triangle existed in agriculture and forestry.

The majority of companies with foreign capital dispose of small capital and employ a limited number of persons. The "large" firms are still rare.

A comparative view of foreign investments is shown in table 26.

## 5.3. Spatial distribution of enterprises with a share of foreign capital in the countries of Vysegrad Triangle

The highest numbers of enterprises with a share of foreign capital existed in 1991 in the capitals of the respective countries.

The spatial distribution of these enterprises in Hungary is very homogeneous. There were only two administrative regions (komitats) — Nograd and Heves — where there were distinctly less of joint venture companies. In Czecho-Slovakia the regions which constituted the location of bigger numbers of these companies, besides Prague, of course, were Southern Moravia and Bratislava. In Poland the voivodships in which the numbers of joint venture companies were the highest are: Warsaw, Poznań, Gdańsk, Łódź, Kraków, Katowice, Wrocław, Szczecin and Zielona Góra. The eastern and south-eastern parts of Poland enjoyed much less interest from the side of foreign investors.

The highest volume of foreign capital within the administrative division of the countries of Vysegrad Triangle is invested in Budapest. Quite significant foreign capital was also invested in Warsaw voivodship, in Prague and

Table 26

Foreign investments in Vysegrad Triangle

| Aspect | Czecho-Slovakia | Poland | Hungary |
|---|---|---|---|
| 1. Number of enterprises with a share of foreign capital | 01.12.1992<br><br>11,362 | 30.09.1992<br><br>9,574 | 30.09.1992<br><br>12,110 |
| 2. Total value of foreign capital in million USD | 30.09.1992<br><br>1,725 | 31.12.1992<br><br>1,300 | 31.12.1992<br><br>, 4,500 |
| 3. Countries of origin of most "active" entrepreneurs | Germany<br>USA<br>Austria<br>France<br>Belgium<br>Switzerland<br>Italy | Germany<br>USA<br>France<br>Sweden<br>Netherlands<br>Austria<br>Utd. Kingdom | USA<br>Germany<br>Austria<br>Utd. Kingdom<br>France<br>Switzerland<br>Italy |
| 4. Presence of large corporations | Yes | Yes | Yes |
| 5. Sectors of economy preferred by foreign investors | Service<br>Trade<br>Industry | Industry<br>Trade<br>Service | Trade<br>Industry<br>Service |

in Central Bohemia, in komitats of Pest, Gyor-Moson-Sopron, Komarom-Esztergom and Borsod-Abauj-Zemplen.

In Czecho-Slovakia one can notice a very distinct division between two federal republics. At the end of 1991 80% of enterprises with a share of foreign capital were located within the Czech republic. Similarly, the volume of capital was very unevenly distributed, namely 74.3% of total capital was located in Czech Republic, while only 25.7% — in Slovak Republic. The data for the three quarters of 1992 indicate that the differ-

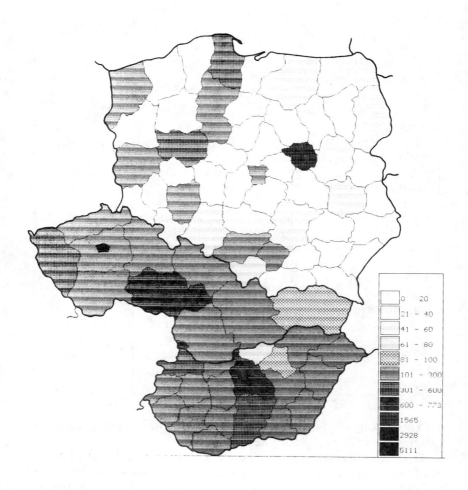

**Fig. 1** *Numbers of enterprises with foreign capital in 1991*

VALUE OF FOREIGN CAPITAL IN 1991 IN MILLION USD

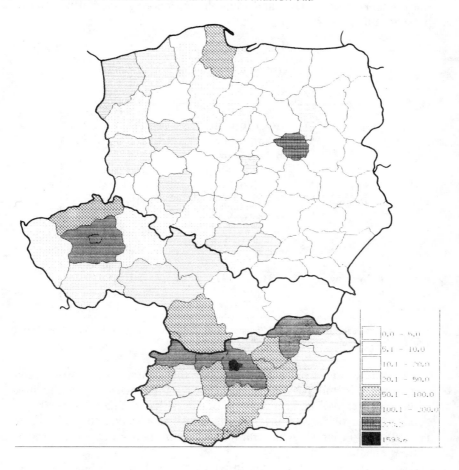

**Fig. 2** *Value of foreign capital in 1991 in million USD*

ences shown are getting even deeper: 92.3% of the total foreign capital invested in Czecho-Slovakia in this period was located in Bohemia, and only 7.7% — in Slovakia.

A comparison among Budapest, Prague and Warsaw with respect to the number of enterprises and the volume of foreign capital involved is presented in table 27.

**Table 27**

**Capitals as centers of location of foreign capital**

| Capitals | Number of firms with foreign capital in a given country=100% | Total foreign capital in a given country=100% |
|---|---|---|
| Budapest | 31.12.1991 56.0% | 31.12.1991 57.5% |
| Prague | 5.10.1991 49.0% | 31.12.1991 45.4% (without firms with 100% foreign share) |
| Warsaw | 31.12.1991 32.6% | 5.10.1991 39.4% (declared capital) |

Source: "Foreign Joint Ventures in Hungary, 1991"; Dubska (1992); Huskova (1992); Zmiany strukturalne..., op.cit.; Dobrzański (1992).

As can be seen from table 27, among the capitals of the three states considered it is Budapest that concentrates to the highest degree the firms with foreign capital and the volume of capital itself. The relatively lower concentration of foreign investments in Warsaw is due to existence in Poland of other large agglomerations, where investors locate their undertakings equally willingly.

There are only few regions in which this indicator attains high values. Such regions are: Central Bohemia, Borsod-Abuj-Zemplen and Komarom. There are some regions, like Ostrołęka or Chełm voivodships in Poland, where there are low numbers of firms with foreign capital, and one of them disposes of a significant capital, which makes the average capital per firm reach relatively high values.

The existing division of Czecho-Slovakia with respect to foreign investments is caused, in particular, by the disadvantageous economic structure of Slovakia. Within the area of Slovakia the majority of plants of the energy-intensive resource industries are located, along with the plants which until quite recently have been producing almost exclusively for exports to the Soviet Union. Factories of the military sector are also located here (Dominiczak, Dominiewski, Roman, Wasilewski, 1992). Investors are additionally driven away by worse economic results of Slovakia.

One can observe in Poland a division into the western and southern part, on the one hand (significant urban centers, developed industry, proximity of western border), and the eastern and south-eastern part, on the other hand (worse infrastructure and the agricultural character of these areas).

In Hungary, the existing structure of relatively small and more or less equal towns (excepting, of course, Budapest), forms the basis for the similar "urban" conditions for location of investments. It is the effect of roughly even distribution of enterprises with foreign capital in the majority of Hungarian regions.

# Bibliography

*Abstracts of Hungarian economic literature*. Institute for World Economics of the Hungarian Academy of Sciences, no. 2, Budapest 1992.

Adamczyk F., Masewicz W., Gieorgica J.P., 1992, *Rynek pracy w Polsce 1990–1992* (Labour market in Poland 1990–1992; in Polish), Warszawa.

Brabeck R., 1992, *Qualitatsvergleich der Stadorte Ungarn, CSFR und Polen aus der Sicht von Experten* (Comparison of quality of locations in Hungary, Czecho-Slovakia and Poland from the point of view of experts; in German). Unternehmensberatung, Muenchen.

Csaki G., 1992, *East-West corporate joint ventures: promises and disappointments*. Institute for World Economics of the Hungarian Academy of Sciences, Working Paper no.3, Budapest.

Dobrzański J., 1992, *Inwestycje zagraniczne w Polsce* (Foreign investments in Poland; in Polish). Dział Prawno-Ekonomiczny PAIZ, Warszawa.

Dominiczak M., Dominiewski A., Roman W., Wasilewski M., 1991, *Przekształcenia własnosciowe w Czecho-Słowacji* (Ownership transformations in Czecho-Slovakia; in Polish). Zycie Gospodarcze, no.32.

Drabek Z., 1992, *Foreign Investment in Czechoslovakia: Proposals for Fine-Tuning Measures of Policy Reform*. Charles University, Working Paper no.4, Prague.

Dubska D., 1992, *K regionalnimu rozdeleni joint ventures v cs. ekonomice* (On regional distribution of joint ventures in Czecho-Slovak economy; in Czech). Narodni Hospodarstvi, 10/1992, 11/1992.

*East-West Joint Ventures and Investment News*, no.8, July 1991; no.1, March 1992..

Fallenbuchl Z., 1990, *Bezpośrednie inwestycje zagraniczne* (Direct foreign investments; in Polish). Życie Gospodarcze, 16 December 1990.

Fazekas K., 1992, *Dilemmas of Hungarian regional policies during the transition*, (in:) G. Gorzelak, A. Kukliński (eds.) *Dilemmas of regional policies in Eastern and Central Europe*, EUROREG, vol. 8, Warszawa.

*Foreign Joint Ventures in Hungary*, 1991. Central Statistical Office, Division of National Accounts. Budapest.

Frąckowiak J., Kieres L., Krzes S., Malecki C.A., 1990, *Ustawa z dnia 23.XII.1988r. o działalnosci gospodarczej z udziałem podmiotów zagranicznych (Dz.U. nr41, poz.325 z 28.XII.1988) z komentarzem* (The law of December 23rd, 1988, on economic activity with a share of foreign agents (Dz.U. no.41, position 325 of 28.XII.1988) with comments; in Polish). Wroclaw.

Frydman R., Rapaczynski A., Early J.S., 1993, *The privatisation process in Central Europe*. London.

Ginsburg H.J., 1992, *Provinzielle Konkurrenz* (Provincial competition; in German). Wirtschafts Woche, no.43.

Glismann H.H., Schrader K., 1992, *Zur ordnungspolitischen Situation in der Landem Osteuropas* (On the situation with respect to political stability in the countries of Eastern Europe; in German). Die Weltwirtschaft, Heft 2, 1992.

Gorzelak G., Jałowiecki B., 1991, *Możliwosci lokalizacji przemyslow zaawansowanej technologii w Polsce* (Potentialities for location of high-tech industries in Poland; in Polish), [in:] *Nauka jako stymulator rozwoju przemysłów wysokiej technologii w Polsce* (Science as a stimulator of development of high-tech industries in Poland; in Polish). Prace Instytutu Technologii Elektronowej CEMI, issue 1–3, Warszawa.

Gorzelak G., Jałowiecki B., 1992, *The optimistic scenario of the development of Poland until 2005*, EUROREG, Warszawa.

Huskova A., 1992, *Foreign capital in the CSFR*. Prague Economic Papers, no.3.

*Investment Guide for Foreign Entrepreneurs in the Czech and Slovak Federal Republic, Basic conditions for foreign investment in the Czecho-Slovak economy*. Federal Agency for Foreign Investment. Prague, July 1991.

Kania J.M., 1992, *Jak to widzą Amerykanie* (How do Americans see this; in Polish). Gazeta Wyborcza, no. 145, 22.VI.1992.

Kleer J., 1992, *Jak nas widzą* (How are we seen; in Polish). Polityka.

Korosi I., 1990, *Situation, problems and prospects of joint ventures in Hungary: An overview of past experience in the light of domestic research and literature*. Trends in World Economy, no.64. Budapest.

*Kraj jak towar* (Country like a commodity; in Polish). Gazeta Wyborcza, no.34, 1993.

Malecki L., 1992, *Charakterystyka ogólna joint ventures na Węgrzech* (General characteristics of joint ventures in Hungary; in Polish). Biznes jest wszędzie — miesiecznik dla menadżerów. September 1992.

Martin P., *Prospects for Joint Ventures in Czechoslovakia.* RFE/RL Research Report.

Mync A., 1992, *Aktywność kapitału zagranicznego w Polsce* (Activity of foreign capital in Poland; in Polish). [In:] *Gmina, przedsiebiorczosc, promocja* (Community, entrepreneurship, promotion; in Polish). Europejski Instytut Rozwoju Regionalnego i Lokalnego. Warszawa.

*Najlepsi na wschodzie* (The best ones in the East; in Polish). Gazeta Wyborcza, 6 November 1992.

Nyiri K., 1990, *Some comments on direct investments and joint venture legislation and practices in Hungary.* Institute for World Economics of the Hungarian Academy of Sciences. Budapest.

Piskova H., 1992, *Letos vedou americke firmy* (American firms are on the lead now; in Czech).

*Podmioty gospodarcze z udziałem kapitału zagranicznego w latach 1990 i 1991* (Economic agents with foreign capital in the years 1990 and 1991; in Polish). GUS, Warszawa, 1992.

*Polska — Czechosłowacja — Węgry* (Poland — Czechoslovakia — Hungary; in Polish) 1992/4. GUS, Warszawa, December 1992.

*Polska na tle krajów Trójkata Wyszegradzkiego oraz pozostałych krajów Europy Środkowej i Wschodniej* (Poland against the background of the countries of Vysegrad Triangle and other countries of Central and Eastern Europe; in Polish). CUP, Warszawa, October 1992.

Pomianowski W., 1992, *Pesymistyczny optymizm* (Pessimistic optimism; in Polish). Życie Warszawy, 21/22 November 1992.

*Regional development studies.* Commission of the European Communities, no.2, 1992.

*Reporting system for FDI in Hungary.* Central Statistical Office. Budapest.

Skalmowski W., 1988, *Rozprzestrzenianie sie przedsiębiorstw zagranicznych w Polsce w latach 1977–1986* (Expansion of foreign enterprises in Poland in the years 1977–1986; in Polish). [In:] B. Jałowiecki (ed.) *Percepcja, scenariusze i przedsiebiorczość (Perception, scenarios and entrepreneurship; in Polish).* Warszawa.

Sojka M., Havel J., Mertlik P., 1992, *Czech Republic economic scenario.* Institute of Sociology, Czechoslovak Academy of Sciences, Prague, November 1992.

Starkowski M., *Wejdą, nie wejdą...* (Will they come, will they not...; in Polish). Spotkania, 12–18 November 1992.

*Sytuacja gospodarcza Polski w 1991 roku na tle innych krajów* (Economic situation of Poland in 1991 against the background of other countries; in Polish). GUS, Warszawa, April 1992.

Szromik A., 1992, *Kapitał niemiecki w Polsce. Warunki podejmowania wspólnych przedsięwzięć gospodarczych* (German capital in Poland. Conditions for undertaking of joint economic ventures; in Polish). Friedrich Ebert Foundation, Polityka ekonomiczna i społeczna, issue 14, Warszawa.

*Ustawa o spółkach z udziałem zagranicznym z dnia 14 czerwca 1991 r.* (The law on companies with a foreign share of June 14th, 1991; in Polish). Warszawa.

*Wszystko o joint ventures* (Everything on joint ventures; in Polish). Agencja do Spraw Inwestycji Zagranicznych, Warszawa, March 1990.

Webber R.A., 1990, *Zasady zarządzania organizacjami* (The priciples of management of organisations; Polish translation). PWE, Warszawa.

Ząbkowicz A., 1991, *Węgierska lekcja* (Hungarian lesson; in Polish). Życie Gospodarcze, no.6, 10 February 1991.

*Zmiany strukturalne grup podmiotów gospodarczych w trzech kwartałach 1992* (Structural changes of groups of economic agents during three quarters of 1992; in Polish). GUS, Warszawa, October 1992.

Żukowska B., 1991, *Solo w tercecie?* (Solo in a trio?; in Polish). Życie Gospodarcze, no.41, 13 October 1991.